THE ESSENTIAL
CROSSWORD SOLVER

The easy way to find that
elusive word

THE ESSENTIAL CROSSWORD SOLVER

The easy way to find that
elusive word

Abbeydale Press

THE ESSENTIAL CROSSWORD SOLVER

This edition published in 2005
by Abbeydale Press
An imprint of Bookmart Limited
Blaby Road, Wigston
Leicester LE18 4SE
England

ISBN 1-86147-157-2

Production by Omnipress, Eastbourne

Printed in Great Britain

CONTENTS

ABBREVIATIONS

1

a	ante, acre, area
A	ampere
b	born
c	circa, cent
c.	century
C	Celsius, centigrade
d	old pence
d.	died
E	east, Ecstacy
f	feminine, franc
F	Fahrenheit, French
g	gram
G	German
h	hour
J	joule
k	kilo, knit
K	kelvin
L	large, Latin, left
l	litre
m	male, masculine, metre, mile, minute, million
m.	married
M	motorway
n	neuter, noun
N	north
p	page, pence, penny, purl
q	query, question
Q	Quarterly (in titles)
r	rupee
r.	recto (on the right-hand page)
R	Royal, right, river
s	second, shilling, singular, son

S	saint, south
v	verb, verse, verso (on the left-hand page), versus
V	Volunteers
V	volt
W	watt, Welsh, west

2

A1	first class
AA	Alcoholics Anonymous, Automobile Association
a/c	account current
AD	*anno Domini*
AI	artificial insemination
a.m.	*ante meridiem* (before noon)
av.	average
AV	Authorized Version
AZ	Arizona
BA	Bachelor of Arts, British Academy, British Airways, Buenos Aires
BC	before Christ, British Columbia
BD	Bachelor of Divinity
b.e.	bill of exchange
bk	book
b.l.	bill of lading
b.p.	boiling point, blood pressure
Bp.	Bishop
BR	British Rail
BT	British Telecom
CA	California, chartered accountant
cc	cubic centimetre
CC	Chamber of Commerce, County Council, County Councillor, Cricket Club
CD	compact disc, Civil Defence
CE	Church of England
cf.	confer, 'compare'
Ch.	Church

ch.	chapter
CI	Channel Islands
cl.	class, clause
cm	centimetre
CO	Colorado
c/o	care of
Co.	company, county
CO	commanding officer, conscientious objector
CP	Communist Party
Cr.	credit
CT	Connecticut
cu.	cubic
CV	curriculum vitae
DA	District Attorney
Da.	Danish
dB	decibel
DC	de capo, Detective Constable, District of Columbia
DD	direct debit
DE	Delaware
DG	*Dei gratia* (by the grace of God)
DI	Detective Inspector
DM	Deutschmark, Deutsche Mark
do.	ditto (the same)
Dr	doctor
dr.	drive
Du.	Dutch
ea.	each
EC	European Community
ed.	edition, editor
e.g.	*exampli gratia* (for example)
Ep.	Epistle
eq.	equal
ER	*Elizabetha Regina* (Queen Elizabeth)
ex.	example
FA	Football Association
FC	Football Club

FD	*fidei defensor* (Defender of the Faith)
ff	fortissimo
FL	Florida
fl.	*floruit* (flourished)
FO	Foreign Office
f.p.	freezing point
Fr.	French
ft	feet, foot
GA	Georgia
GB	Great Britain
GC	George Cross
Gr.	Greece, Greek
gt.	great
HC	House of Commons
HE	high explosive, His Eminence, His/Her Excellency
hf.	half
HF	high frequency
HH	His/Her Highness
HI	Hawaii
HM	Head Master/Mistress, His/Her Majesty
HO	Home Office
h.p.	high pressure, horsepower
HP	hire purchase
HQ	headquarters
hr.	hour
ht.	height
HV	high voltage
Hz	hertz
IA	Iowa
id	*idem* (the same)
ID	identification
i.e.	*id est* (that is)
IL	Illinois
IN	Indiana
in.	inch
IQ	intelligence quotient

Ir.	Irish
IR	Inland Revenue
Is.	island
It.	Italian, Italy
JC	Jesus Christ, Julius Caesar
JP	Justice of the Peace
Jr.	junior
kc	kilocycle
KC	King's Counsel
kg	kilogram
km	kilometre
KO	knockout
KS	Kansas
Kt.	Knight
kV	kilovolt
kW	kilowatt
KY	Kentucky
LA	Louisiana
lb	*libra* (pound)
l.c.	lower case (small letters)
Ld.	lord
l.f.	low frequency
l.h.	left hand
LP	long-playing record
Lt.	Lieutenant
LW	long wave
MA	Massachusetts, Master of Arts
MC	Master of Ceremonies, Military Cross
MD	Managing Director, Maryland
ME	Maine, myalgic encephalomyelitis, Middle English
mf	mezzo forte
mg	milligram
MI	Michigan
mm	millimetre
MN	Merchant Navy, Minnesota
MO	Medical Officer, Missouri

MP	Member of Parliament, Metropolitan Police, Military Police
MS	manuscript, Mississippi, multiple sclerosis
Mt.	Mount
MT	Montana
n/a	not applicable
NB	New Brunswick, *nota bene* (note well)
NC	North Carolina
ND	North Dakota
NE	Nebraska, New England, North East
NF	National Front
No.	number
n.p.	new paragraph, new pence
n.q.	no quotations
NT	National Trust, New Testament
NV	Nevada
NW	north-west
NY	New York
NZ	New Zealand
ob.	*obiit* (died)
OB	Old Boy, outside broadcast,
OE	Old English (Anglo-Saxon)
OH	Ohio
OK	Oklahoma
OM	Order of Merit
op.	*opus*
OR	Oregon
O.S.	Old Saxon, ordinary seaman, Ordnance Survey, outsize
OT	occupational therapy, Old Testament
OU	Open University, Oxford University
oz	ounce
p.a.	per annum
PA	Pennsylvania
p.c.	per cent, postcard
PC	personal computer, police constable, Privy Counsellor

pd.	paid
PE	physical education
pf.	perfect
PG	parental guidance, paying guest
pl.	place, plural
p.m.	*post meridiem*
PM	post-mortem, Prime Minister
PO	petty officer, postal order, post office
pp.	pages
pp	pianissimo
p.p.	*per procurationem* (by proxy)
pr.	pair, present, price
Pr.	Provencal
PR	Public Relations, Puerto Rico
Ps.	Psalm
PS	post-script
pt.	part, pint, point
PT	physical training
QC	Queen's Counsel
qr.	quarter, quire
qt.	quantity, quart
q.v.	*quod vide* (which see)
RA	Royal Academy, Royal Artillery
RC	Red Cross, Roman Catholic
Rd	road
RE	religious education
r.h.	relative humidity, right hand
RI	religious instruction, Rhode Island, Royal Institution
RM	Royal Mail, Royal Marines
RN	Royal Navy
RU	Rugby Union
RV	Revised Version
SA	Salvation Army, South Africa, South America
sb.	substantive
sc.	*scilicet* (understand or supply)
s.c.	small capitals

SC	South Carolina
SD	South Dakota
SE	south-east
SF	San Francisco, science fiction
SM	Sergeant Major
sp.	species, spelling
Sp.	Spain, Spanish
sq.	square
s.s.	same size
SS	steamship
st.	stone
St	saint
St.	street
s.v.	*sub voce* (under the word)
Sw.	Sweden, Swedish
SW	South Wales, south-west
TA	Territorial Army
TB	tubercle bacillus (tuberculosis)
TM	trademark, transcendental meditation
TN	Tennessee
tr.	transfer, translate
TT	teetotal, tuberculin tested
TU	trade union
TV	television
TX	Texas
u.c.	upper case (capital letters)
UK	United Kingdom
UT	Utah
VA	Virginia
vb.	verb
VC	Vice-Chancellor, Victoria Cross
VD	venereal disease
VE	Victory in Europe
v.g.	very good
VP	Vice-President
VS	veterinary surgeon, vital statistics
VT	Vermont

v.w.	weak verb
WA	Washington State
WC	water closet
wd.	word
WI	Wisconsin
wk.	week
Wm.	William
WO	Warrant Officer
WP	word processor
WV	West Virginia
WY	Wyoming
XL	extra large
Xn	Christian
yd	yard
yr	year

3

AAA	Amateur Athletics Association
ABA	Amateur Boxing Association
ABC	alphabet
abl.	ablative
abr.	abridged
abs.	absolute
acc.	accusative
add.	addenda
adj.	adjective
Adj.	adjutant
Adm.	Admiral
adv.	adverb
Adv.	Advance
Afr.	Africa, African
Alb.	Albania, Albanian
alt.	alternative, altitude
amp	ampere
anc.	ancient
ANC	African National Congress

AOB	any other business
app.	apparently, appendix
Apr.	April
APR	annual percentage rate
arr.	arrival, arrive(s)
ASA	Advertising Standards Authority
ATC	Air Traffic Control, Air Training Corps
ATS	Auxiliary Territorial Service
aug.	augmentative
Aug.	August
aux.	auxiliary
ave	avenue
BAA	British Airports Authority
BAC	British Aerospace Corportion
B&B	bed and breakfast
BBC	British Broadcasting Corporation
Bde	brigade
B.Ed.	Bachelor of Education
bef.	before
b.h.p.	brake horsepower
BMA	British Medical Association
bor.	borough
B.o.T.	Board of Trade
bro.	brother
BSI	British Standards Institution
BST	British Summer Time
B.t.u.	British Thermal Unit
CAD	computer-aided design
cal.	calendar
cap.	capital
cat.	catalogue
Cdr.	Commander
CET	Central European Time
Chr.	Christian
CIA	Central Intelligence Agency
c.i.f.	cost, insurance and freight
COD	cash on delivery

Col.	Colonel
col.	colony, column
Con.	Consul
cos	cosine
cpd.	compound
cwt	hundredweight
dat.	dative
Dec.	December
def.	definite, definition
deg.	degree
der.	derivative
dil.	dilute
dim.	diminutive
Dip.	Diploma
dis.	discipline, discontinue
div.	divide, dividend
DIY	do-it-yourself
DOA	dead on arrival
DOB	date of birth
D.o.T.	Department of Transport
doz.	dozen
D.Sc.	Doctor of Science
DSS	Department of Social Security
D.Th.	Doctor of Theology
DTI	Department of Trade and Industry
EEC	European Economic Community (Common Market)
emf	electromotive force
enc.	enclosed, enclosure
ENT	ear, nose and throat
EOC	Equal Opportunities Commission
esp.	especially
Esq.	Esquire
etc.	et cetera
exc.	excellent, except
FBI	Federal Bureau of Investigation
FCA	Fellow of the Institute of Chartered Accountants

Feb.	February
fig.	figure
f.o.b.	free on board
F.O.C.	free of charge
FPA	Family Planning Association
Fri.	Friday
FRS	Fellow of the Royal Society
fur.	furlong
fwd	forward
gal.	gallon
GBH	grievous bodily harm
GCE	General Certificate of Education
GCF	greatest common factor
GCM	greatest common measure
GDR	German Democratic Republic
gen.	general, generally
GHQ	general headquarters
Gib.	Gibraltar
GLC	Greater London Council
GMT	Greenwich Mean Time
GNP	gross national product
GPO	General Post Office
GTC	Girls' Training Corps
gym	gymnasium
HCF	highest common factor
Heb.	Hebrew
HGV	heavy goods vehicle
HIV	human immunodeficiency virus
H.N.C.	Higher National Certificate
H.N.D.	Higher National Diploma
hrs.	hours
IBA	Independent Broadcasting Authority
ICI	Imperial Chemical Industries
ign.	*ignotus* (unknown)
imp.	imperative, impersonal
inc.	incorporated
ind.	industrial, industry

inf.	infinitive
ins.	insurance
int.	interior, interjection
IOM	Isle of Man
IOW	Isle of Wight
IRA	Irish Republican Army
ITV	Independent Television
IWA	Inland Waterways Association
Jan.	January
Jap.	Japanese
jun.	junior
KGB	Komitet Gosudarstvennoi Bezopasnosti (Committee of State Security)
KKK	Ku Klux Klan
K.L.I.	King's Light Infantry
Lab	Labour
lat.	latitude
lbw	leg before wicket
LCC	London County Council
LCD	liquid crystal display, lowest common denominator
LCJ	Lord Chief Justice
LEA	Local Education Authority
Let.	letter, letters
Lib.	Liberal
lit.	literal, literally, literature, literary
loq.	*loquitor* (speaks)
LPG	liquefied petroleum gas
LPO	London Philharmonic Orchestra
LPS	Lord Privy Seal
l.s.d.	librae, solidi, denarii (pounds, shillings, pence)
LSD	lysergic acid diethylamide
LTA	Lawn Tennis Association
Ltd	limited
mag.	magazine
Maj.	Major
man.	manual

Mar.	March
max.	maximum
MBE	Member of the Order of the British Empire
MEP	Member of the European Parliament
mfg.	manufacturing
mfr.	manufacture
min.	minimum
MLR	minimum lending rate
Mme	Madame
mod.	modern
MOD	Ministry of Defence
Mon.	Monday
MOT	Ministry of Transport
mpg	miles per gallon
mph	miles per hour
M.Sc.	Master of Science
MSS	manuscripts
NCO	non-commissioned officer
NCP	National Car Parks
NCV	no commercial value
neg.	negative
NGA	National Graphical Association
n.h.p.	nominal horsepower
NHS	National Health Service
nom.	nominative
nos.	numbers
Nov.	November
NSB	National Savings Bank
NSW	New South Wales
OAP	old age pensioner
OBE	Officer of the Order of the British Empire
obj.	object
obl.	oblique
obs.	observed, obsolete
Oct.	October
OED	Oxford English Dictionary
ONC	Ordinary National Certificate

OND	Ordinary National Diploma
o.n.o.	or near offer
Ont.	Ontario
opp.	opposite, opposed (to)
ops.	operations
org.	organic
OTC	Officers' Training Corps
Pan.	Panama
par.	paragraph, parallel, parish
pa.t.	past tense
pers.	person, personal
phr.	phrase
Pol.	Polish
pop.	popular, population
POW	prisoner of war
pro	professional
PRO	Public Relations Officer
PTA	Parent–Teacher Association
Pte.	Private
PTO	please turn over
PVC	polyvinyl chloride
RAC	Royal Armoured Corps, Royal Automobile Club
RAF	Royal Air Force
rec.	record
ref.	reference
reg.	regular
Reg.	Register
rel.	related to, relative, religion
rep.	report, representative, republic
rev.	reverse, revised, revolution
RHA	Royal Horse Artillery
RHS	Royal Horticultural Society
RIP	*requiescat in pace* (rest in peace)
RMA	Royal Military Academy
RMC	Royal Military College
rpm	revolutions per minute
RSA	Royal Society of Arts

RSM	Regimental Sergeant Major
sae	stamped addressed envelope
SAS	Special Air Service
Sat.	Saturday
sch.	school
SDP	Social Democratic Party
sec.	second, secretary
Sen.	senior
SEN	State Enrolled Nurse
seq.	*sequens* (the following)
Sgt.	Sergeant
Soc.	Society
SNP	Scottish National Party
SOS	distress signal
SRN	State Registered Nurse
STC	Senior Training Corps
STD	subscriber trunk dialling
Sun.	Sunday
tan	tangent
TNT	trinitrotoluene
trs.	transpose
TUC	Trades Union Congress
typ.	typography
UFO	unidentified flying object
UHF	ultra-high frequency
UHT	ultra heat treated
ult.	ultimo, ultimately
USA	United States of America
usu.	usually
VAT	value added tax
VDU	visual display unit
Ven.	Venerable
vet	veterinary surgeon
VHF	very high frequency
VIP	very important person

viz.	*videlicet* (namely)
VLF	very low frequency
vol.	volume
Wed.	Wednesday
WPC	woman police constable
WWF	World Wildlife Fund for Nature
YHA	Youth Hostels Association
yrs	years

4

abbr.	abbreviation
ABTA	Association of British Travel Agents
advt.	advertisement
AIDS	acquired immune deficiency syndrome
Amer.	American
anon.	anonymous
asap	as soon as possible
asst.	assistant
astr.	astronomy
attn.	attention
AWOL	absent without leave
B.Com	Bachelor of Commerce
B.Eng.	Bachelor of Engineering
B.Mus.	Bachelor of Music
biol.	biology
Brit.	Britain, British
bros.	brothers
B.th.u.	British Thermal Unit
Camb.	Cambridge
Capt.	Captain
Cdre.	Commodore
cent.	central, century
cert.	certificate, certified, certify
Cllr.	Councillor

C. of E.	Church of England
C. of S.	Church of Scotland
coll.	college
comb.	combine
comp.	comparative, comparison, compound, composition
cong.	congress
conj.	conjunction
Conn.	Connecticut
Cons	Conservative
cons.	consonant
cont.	containing, continued
Corp.	corporation
corr.	correspondence, correction, corruption
dept.	department
D.Mus.	Doctor of Music
dial.	dialect
diss.	dissertation
ecol.	ecology
econ.	economics, economy
Edin.	Edinburgh
educ.	education
elec.	electrical, electricity
ency.	encyclopedia
EPNS	electroplated nickel silver
et al.	*et alii* (and others)
exam	examination
F.I.F.A.	International Football Federation
freq.	frequent, frequently
geog.	geographical, geography
geol.	geology
geom.	geometry
Govt.	government
gram.	grammar, grammatical
hist.	history, historical
HMSO	His/Her Majesty's Stationery Office
Hons.	Honours

hort.	horticulture
ibid.	*ibidem* (in the same book or passage)
incl.	included, including, inclusive
infl.	influenced
inst.	instant, institute, institution
irreg.	irregular, irregularly
ital.	italic
Lit.D.	Doctor of Literature
masc.	masculine
MASH	mobile army surgical hospital
Mass.	Massachusetts
Matt.	Matthew
mech.	mechanical, mechanics, mechanism
memo	memorandum
misc.	miscellaneous, miscellany
Miss.	Mississippi
Mlle	Mademoiselle
myst.	mystery
myth.	mythological, mythology
NATO	North Atlantic Treaty Organization
path.	pathology
PAYE	pay as you earn
PDSA	People's Dispensary for Sick Animals
phon.	phonetics, phonetically
phys.	physical, physician, physics
pict.	pictorial, picture
Port.	Portuguese
poss.	possessive
pref.	preface, preference
pres.	present
prob.	problem, problematical
Prof.	Professor
quot.	quotation
RADA	Royal Academy of Dramatic Art
RAMC	Royal Army Medical Corps
recd.	received
refl.	reflection, reflexive

regt.	regiment
repr.	representative, representing, reprint
Revd	Reverend
rhet.	rhetoric
RIBA	Royal Institute of British Architects
RICS	Royal Institution of Chartered Surveyors
RNIB	Royal National Institute for the Blind
RNLI	Royal National Lifeboat Institution
RSPB	Royal Society for the Protection of Birds
RSVP	*repondez s'il vous plait* (please reply)
Russ.	Russian
SAYE	save as you earn
Scot.	Scotland, Scottish
Senr.	senior
Sept.	September
sing.	singular
spec.	specifically, specimen
sp.gr.	specific gravity
subj.	subject
suff.	suffix
supt.	superintendent
surg.	surgeon, surgery, surgical
tech.	technical, technically
TGWU	Transport and General Workers' Union
Thos.	Thomas
trig.	trigonometry
trop.	tropical
Turk.	Turkey, Turkish
UEFA	Union of European Football Associations
Univ.	University
unkn.	unknown
USSR	Union of Soviet Socialist Republics
WAAC	Women's Army Auxiliary Corps
W/Cdr.	Wing Commander
WRAC	Women's Royal Army Corps
WRAF	Women's Royal Air Force
WRNS	Women's Royal Naval Service

YMCA	Young Men's Christian Association
YWCA	Young Women's Christian Association
zool.	zoology

5

ad lib	*ad libitum* (as much as desired)
agric.	agriculture
ARIBA	Associate of the Royal Institute of British Architects
ARICS	Associate of the Royal Institution of Chartered Surveyors
ASCII	American Standard Code for Information Interchange
Aslef	Associated Society of Locomotive Engineers and Firemen
assoc.	associate, association
BAFTA	British Academy of Film and Television Arts
Bart's	St Bartholomew's Hospital
B.Litt.	Bachelor of Letters
B.Phil.	Bachelor of Philosophy
C and G	City and Guilds
CD-ROM	compact disc read-only memory
chron.	chronicle, chronologically, chronology,
cog.	cognate
COHSE	Confederation of Health Service Employees
compl.	complement
Compl.	Complete
conch.	conchology
concr.	concrete, concretely
const.	construction
contr.	contract, contrary
D.Litt.	Doctor of Letters
demon.	demonstrative
derog.	derogatory
descr.	description, descriptive
diagn.	diagnosis, diagnostic

D.Phil.	Doctor of Philosophy
entom.	entomology
episc.	episcopal
EPROM	erasable programmable read-only memory
equiv.	equivalent
ERNIE	Electronic Random Number Indicator Equipment
erron.	erroneously
et seq.	*et sequens* (and what follows)
exerc.	exercise
exper.	experiment, experimental
Found.	Foundation
FRIBA	Fellow of the Royal Institute of British Architects
FRICS	Fellow of the Royal Institution of Chartered Surveyors
genit.	genitive
gloss.	glossary
Hants.	Hampshire
Herts.	Hertfordshire
horol.	horology
illit.	illiterate
immed.	immediately
incog.	incognito
indef.	indefinite
infin.	infinitive
instr.	instrument, instrumental
intro	introduction
irreg.	irregular, irregularly
knowl.	knowledge
Lancs.	Lancashire
Lieut.	Lieutenant
Lincs.	Lincolnshire
LRCVS	Licentiate of the Royal College of Veterinary Surgeons
Lt. Col.	Lieutenant Colonel
Lt. Com.	Lieutenant Commander
Lt. Gen.	Lieutenant General

Lt. Gov.	Lieutenant Governor
Mlles	Mesdemoiselles
MRCVS	Member of the Royal College of Veterinary Surgeons
NAAFI	Navy, Army and Air Force Institutes
NALGO	National and Local Government Officers' Association
NSPCC	National Society for the Prevention of Cruelty to Children
occas.	occasional, occasionally
Oxfam	Oxford Committee for Famine Relief
pharm.	pharmaceutical, pharmacy
photo	photograph, photography
phren.	phrenology
polit.	political, politics
Pract.	Practice
propr.	proprietary
psych.	psychic
R and D	research and development
RoSPA	Royal Society for the Prevention of Accidents
RSPCA	Royal Society for the Prevention of Cruelty to Animals
Rt. Hon.	Right Honourable
Salop.	Shropshire
Scand.	Scandinavia, Scandinavian
SHAPE	Supreme Headquarters, Allied Powers, Europe
SOGAT	Society of Graphical and Allied Trades
stand.	standard
struct.	structure, structural
subst.	substantively
suppl.	supplement
theat.	theatre, theatrical
theol.	theology
Thurs.	Thursday
trans.	translated, translation
Treas.	Treasury, treasurer
typog.	typography

UNHCR	United Nations High Commission for Refugees
Westm.	Westminster
Wilts.	Wiltshire
Yorks.	Yorkshire

6

applic.	application, applicable
approx.	approximately
astrol.	astrology
attrib.	attributive
Cantab.	of Cambridge
colloq.	colloquial, colloquially
compan.	companion
constr.	construction
dissim.	dissimilar, dissimilated
eccles.	ecclesiastical
ellipt.	elliptical, elliptically
ethnol.	ethnology
euphem.	euphemism, euphemistically
exclam.	exclamation
explor.	exploration
Gk. hist.	Greek history
histol.	histology
househ.	household
housek.	housekeeping
incept.	inceptive
indecl.	indeclinable
Lit. Hum.	*Literae Humaniores* (study of classics)
Messrs	plural of Mr
metaph.	metaphorical, metaphysics
metath.	metathesis
meteor.	meteorology
obstet.	obstetric
Ofsted	Office for Standards in Education
ornith.	ornithology
per pro.	*per procurationem* (by proxy)

philol.	philology
philos.	philosophy
phonol.	phonology
photog.	photography, photographical
prelim.	preliminary
pro tem	*pro tempore* (for the time being)
sociol.	sociology
struct.	structure, structural
subord.	subordinate
subsec.	subsection
subseq.	subsequently
superl.	superlative
teleph.	telephone, telephony
transf.	transferred
treatm.	treatment
UNESCO	United Nations Educational, Scientific and Cultural Organization
UNICEF	United Nations International Children's Emergency Fund

7

anthrop.	anthropology
Austral.	Australian
biochem.	biochemistry
Cantaur.	of Canterbury
collect.	collective, collectively
contrib.	contribution
distrib.	distributive
embryol.	embryology
immunol.	immunology
managem.	management
mineral.	mineralogy
mod. cons.	modern conveniences
nat. hist.	natural history
palaeog.	palaeography
physiol.	physiology

pol. econ.	political economy
pronunc.	pronunciation
psychol.	psychology
rel. pron.	relative pronoun
Rom. hist.	Roman history
Shakesp.	Shakespeare
technol.	technological, technology,
theoret.	theoretical
vertebr.	vertebrate(s)

8

aeronaut.	aeronautics
archaeol.	archaeology
criminol.	criminology
Interpol	International Criminal Police Commission
interrog.	interrogation, interrogative, interrogatively
Lieut. Col.	Lieutenant Colonel
Lieut. Gen.	Lieutenant General
Lieut. Gov.	Lieutenant Governor
ophthalm.	ophthalmology
palaeont.	palaeontology
reminisc.	reminiscence, reminiscent,
subord. cl.	subordinate clause
zoogeogr.	zoogeography

ACTORS
Film, Theatre and TV

SURNAME	CHRISTIAN NAMES	PLACE OF BIRTH
3		
COX	Robert	UK
FOX	James	UK
FOX	Michael J.	Canada
FOY	Eddie	US
FRY	Stephen	UK
HAY	Will	UK
LAW	Jude	UK
LEE	Brandon	US
LEE	Bruce	US
LEE	Christopher	UK
LEE	Spike	US
RAY	Aldo	US
REY	Fernando	Spain
RIX	Sir Brian	UK
SIM	Alastair	Scotland
4		
ALDA	Alan	US
BIRD	Theophilus	UK
BOND	Edward	UK
BURR	Raymond	Canada
CAAN	James	US
CAGE	Nicolas	US
CHAN	Jackie	Hong Kong
COBB	Lee J.	US
COOK	Peter	UK

SURNAME	CHRISTIAN NAMES	PLACE OF BIRTH
DEAN	James	US
DEPP	Johnny	US
DERN	Bruce	US
FALK	Peter	US
FORD	Glenn	Canada
FORD	Harrison	US
GANZ	Bruno	Switzerland
GERE	Richard	US
HART	William S.	US
HILL	Benny	UK
HOPE	Bob	UK
HURT	John	UK
HURT	William	US
IDLE	Eric	UK
KAYE	Danny	US
KEAN	Edmund	UK
KNOX	Teddy	UK
LADD	Alan	US
LOWE	Rob	US
MARX	Chico	US
MARX	Groucho	US
MARX	Gummo	US
MARX	Harpo	US
MARX	Zeppo	US
MORE	Kenneth	UK
NUNN	Trevor	UK
PECK	Gregory	US
PENN	Sean	US
PITT	Brad	US
RAFT	George	US
ROSI	Francesco	Italy
RUSH	Geoffrey	Australia
SHAW	Robert	UK
SHER	Sir Antony	South Africa

SURNAME	CHRISTIAN NAMES	PLACE OF BIRTH
TATI	Jacques	France
THAW	John	UK
TODD	Richard	Ireland
TORN	Rip	US
TREE	Sir Herbert Beerbohm	UK
WEBB	Clifton	US
WEBB	Jack	US
WISE	Ernie	UK
ZANE	Billy	US

5

ALLEN	Chesney	UK
ALLEN	Woody	US
ARKIN	Alan	US
ARMIN	Robert	UK
ARNAZ	Desi	Cuba
ASKEY	Arthur	UK
BACON	Kevin	US
BADEL	Alan	UK
BARON	André	France
BARON	Michel	France
BATES	Alan	UK
BENNY	Jack	US
BETTY	William Henry West	UK
BOLES	John	US
BOYER	Charles	France
BROOK	Peter	UK
BURNS	George	US
BUSEY	Gary	US
CAINE	Sir Michael	UK
CANDY	John	Canada
CAREY	Drew	US
CLIFT	Montgomery	US
COSBY	Bill	US

SURNAME	CHRISTIAN NAMES	PLACE OF BIRTH
CROWE	Russell	New Zealand
DAFOE	Willem	US
DAMON	Matt	US
DAVIS	Sammy, Jr.	US
EBSEN	Buddy	US
EKHOF	Konrad	Germany
ELTON	Ben	UK
FINCH	Peter	UK
FLYNN	Errol	Tasmania
FONDA	Henry	US
FONDA	Peter	US
GABIN	Jean	France
GABLE	Clark	US
GARCIA	Andy	Cuba
GRANT	Cary	UK
GRANT	Hugh	UK
GRANT	Lee	US
GRANT	Richard E.	Swaziland
HAIGH	Kenneth	UK
HANKS	Tom	US
HARDY	Oliver	US
HAUER	Rutger	Netherlands
HENRY	Lenny	UK
HOGAN	Paul	Australia
IRONS	Jeremy	UK
JAMES	Sid	South Africa
JONES	James Earl	US
JONES	Tommy Lee	US
KELLY	Gene	US
KLINE	Kevin	US
KORDA	Sir Alexander	Hungary
LEWIS	Jerry	US
LORRE	Peter	Hungary

ACTORS

SURNAME	CHRISTIAN NAMES	PLACE OF BIRTH
LUCAS	George	US
MAGEE	Patrick	UK
MARCH	Fredric	US
MILLS	Sir John	UK
MOORE	Dudley	UK
MOORE	Sir Roger	UK
NEILL	Sam	N. Ireland
NIMMO	Derek	UK
NIMOY	Leonard	US
NIVEN	David	UK
NOLTE	Nick	US
OATES	Warren	US
O'NEAL	Ryan	US
PALIN	Michael	UK
PARKS	Larry	US
PASCO	Richard	UK
PESCI	Joe	US
POLUS		Greece
POWER	Tyrone	US
PRICE	Vincent	US
PRYCE	Jonathan	UK
PRYOR	Richard	US
QUAID	Dennis	US
QUAID	Randy	US
QUINN	Anthony	Mexico
RAINS	Claude	UK
REEVE	Christopher	US
SEGAL	George	US
SHEEN	Charlie	US
SHEEN	Martin	US
SMITH	Will	US
STACK	Robert	US
STAMP	Terence	UK
STONE	Oliver	US
SWANN	Donald	Wales

SURNAME	CHRISTIAN NAMES	PLACE OF BIRTH
TOPOL	Chaim	Israel
TRACY	Spencer	US
URICH	Robert	US
WAYNE	John	US
YOUNG	Gig	US
YOUNG	Robert	US

6

ABBOTT	Bud	US
ADRIAN	Max	N. Ireland
AINLEY	Henry	UK
ALIZON		France
AMECHE	Don	US
ARNESS	James	US
ARTAUD	Antonin	France
BEATTY	Warren	US
BERMAN	Shelley	US
BOCAGE		France
BOGART	Humphrey	US
BRANDO	Marlon, Jr.	US
BROOKS	Mel	US
BURTON	Richard	Wales
CAGNEY	James	US
CANTOR	Eddie	US
CARREY	Jim	Canada
CARSON	Jack	Canada
CASSON	Sir Lewis	UK
CHANEY	Lon	US
CLEESE	John	UK
COBURN	James	US
CONRAD	William	US
COOPER	Gary	US
COTTEN	Joseph	US
COWARD	Sir Noel	UK

SURNAME	CHRISTIAN NAMES	PLACE OF BIRTH
CRAVEN	Wes	US
CROSBY	Bing	US
CRUISE	Tom	US
CURTIS	Tony	US
CUSACK	John	US
DALTON	Timothy	Wales
DANSON	Ted	US
DE NIRO	Robert	US
DENNIS	Sandy	US
DE SICA	Vittorio	Italy
DEVINE	Andy	US
DE VITO	Danny	US
DILLON	Matt	US
DOOHAN	James	Canada
DUVALL	Robert	US
FIELDS	W. C. (William Claude)	US
FINLAY	Frank	UK
FINNEY	Albert	UK
FLEURY		France
FRASER	Brendan	US
GAMBON	Michael	Ireland
GIBSON	Mel	US
GLOVER	Danny	US
GORING	Marius	UK
GRAVES	Peter	US
GREENE	Lorne	Canada
GREENE	Richard	UK
GUITRY	Sacha	France
HANNAH	John	Scotland
HARMON	Mark	US
HARRIS	Richard	Ireland
HARVEY	Laurence	Lithuania
HEFLIN	Van	US
HERMAN	Pee-Wee	US
HESTON	Charlton	US

SURNAME	CHRISTIAN NAMES	PLACE OF BIRTH
HOLDEN	William	US
HOPPER	Dennis	US
HOWARD	Leslie	UK
HOWARD	Trevor	UK
HOWERD	Frankie	UK
HUDSON	Rock	US
IRVING	Sir Henry	UK
JACOBI	Sir Derek	UK
JOLSON	Al	US
JOUVET	Louis	France
KEATON	Buster	US
KEATON	Michael	US
KEITEL	Harvey	US
KEMBLE	John Philip	UK
LANDEN	Dinsdale	UK
LAUREL	Stan	UK
LEMMON	Jack	US
LESSOR	Anton	UK
LUGOSI	Bela	Hungary
MACRAE	Gordon	US
MAJORS	Lee	US
MARTIN	Dean	US
MARTIN	Jesse L.	US
MARTIN	Steve	US
MARVIN	Lee	US
MASSEY	Daniel	UK
MASSEY	Raymond	Canada
MCKERN	Leo	Australia
MODINE	Matthew	US
MORLEY	Robert	UK
MURPHY	Eddie	US
MURRAY	BILL	US
NEESON	Liam	N. Ireland
NEWMAN	Paul	US
NORRIS	Chuck	US

SURNAME	CHRISTIAN NAMES	PLACE OF BIRTH
O'BRIAN	Hugh	US
OLDMAN	Gary	UK
ORBACH	Jerry	US
O'TOOLE	Peter	Ireland
PACINO	Al	US
PARKER	Alan	UK
PORTER	Eric	UK
POWELL	Dick	US
QUAYLE	Sir Anthony	UK
REAGAN	Ronald	US
REEVES	Keanu	Lebanon
ROGERS	Roy	US
ROGERS	Will	US
ROONEY	Mickey	US
ROURKE	Mickey	US
ROWLEY	Thomas	UK
SADLER	William	US
SEAGAL	Steven	US
SHARIF	Omar	Egypt
SHUTER	Ned	UK
SLATER	Christian	US
SNIPES	Wesley	US
SPADER	James	US
SWAYZE	Patrick	US
TAYLOR	Robert	US
TAYLOR	Rod	Australia
TEARLE	Sir Godfrey Seymour	UK
TURPIN	Ben	US
VAUGHN	Robert	US
VOIGHT	Jon	US
WAGNER	Robert	US
WALKEN	Christopher	US
WARDEN	Jack	US
WARREN	William	UK
WAYANS	Damon	US

SURNAME	CHRISTIAN NAMES	PLACE OF BIRTH
WELLES	Orson	US
WILDER	Gene	US
WILLIS	Bruce	Germany
WOLFIT	Sir Donald	UK

7

AFFLECK	Ben	US
ANTOINE	Andre	France
ASTAIRE	Fred	US
AYKROYD	Dan	Canada
BALDWIN	Alec	US
BEAUVAL		France
BELLAMY	Ralph	US
BELUSHI	James	US
BELUSHI	John	US
BENNETT	Hywel	Wales
BLAKELY	Colin	Ireland
BLOCKER	Dan	US
BOGARDE	Sir Dirk	UK
BRANAGH	Kenneth	N. Ireland
BRENNAN	Walter	US
BRESSON	Robert	France
BRIDGES	Beau	US
BRIDGES	Lloyd	US
BRONSON	Charles	US
BROSNAN	Pierce	Ireland
BRYNNER	Yul	Russia
BURBAGE	Richard	UK
BUTTONS	Red	US
CALHOUN	Rory	US
CALVERT	Louis	UK
CAMERON	Rod	Canada
CARLYLE	Robert	Scotland
CHAPLIN	Sir Charles	UK

SURNAME	CHRISTIAN NAMES	PLACE OF BIRTH
CLOONEY	George	US
CONNERY	Sir Sean	Scotland
CONNORS	Chuck	US
CORBETT	Harry H.	Burma
COSTNER	Kevin	US
CRYSTAL	Billy	US
CUSHING	Peter	UK
DE MILLE	Cecil B.	US
DENNEHY	Brian	US
DOGGETT	Thomas	UK
DONAHUE	Troy	US
DONLEVY	Brian	Ireland
DOTRICE	Roy	UK
DOUGLAS	Kirk	US
DOUGLAS	Michael	US
DURANTE	Jimmy	US
EDWARDS	Blake	US
ELLIOTT	Denholm	UK
ESTEVEZ	Emilio	US
FELDMAN	Marty	UK
FELLINI	Federico	Italy
FIENNES	Ralph	UK
FREEMAN	Morgan	US
GARRICK	David	UK
GASSMAN	Vittorio	Italy
GAZZARA	Ben	US
GIELGUD	Sir John	UK
GLEASON	Jackie	US
GOODMAN	John	US
GOSSETT	Louis, Jr.	US
GRANGER	Stewart	UK
HACKMAN	Gene	US
HANCOCK	Tony	UK
HAWKINS	Jack	UK
HAWTREY	Sir Charles	UK

SURNAME	CHRISTIAN NAMES	PLACE OF BIRTH
HOFFMAN	Dustin	US
HOPKINS	Sir Anthony	Wales
HORDERN	Sir Michael	UK
HOSKINS	Bob	UK
IFFLAND	August Wilhelm	Germany
JOHNSON	Van	US
JURGENS	Curt	Germany
KARLOFF	Boris	UK
KENNEDY	George	US
KENNEDY	Graham	Australia
KINNEAR	Roy	UK
KLUGMAN	Jack	US
KUBRICK	Stanley	US
LACKAYE	Wilton	US
LANGDON	Harry	US
LAROQUE		France
MARCEAU	Marcel	France
MATTHAU	Walter	US
MCMANUS	Mark	Scotland
MCQUEEN	Steve	US
MICHELL	Keith	Australia
MILLAND	Ray	Wales
MITCHUM	Robert	US
MONTAND	Yves	Italy
MORANIS	Rick	Canada
NEWHART	Bob	US
O'CONNOR	Kevin	US
OLIVIER	Sir Laurence	UK
O'ROURKE	Kevin	US
OXBERRY	William	UK
PALANCE	Jack	US
PEPPARD	George	US
PERKINS	Anthony	US
PIDGEON	Walter	Canada
PLUMMER	Christopher	Canada

SURNAME	CHRISTIAN NAMES	PLACE OF BIRTH
POITIER	Sidney	US
PRESLEY	Elvis	US
QUILLEY	Denis	UK
REDFORD	Robert	US
ROBARDS	Jason	US
ROBBINS	Tim	US
ROBESON	Paul	US
RUSSELL	Kurt	US
SALVINI	Tommaso	Italy
SANDERS	George	Russia
SAVALAS	Telly	US
SELLECK	Tom	US
SELLERS	Peter	UK
SHATNER	William	Canada
SILVERS	Phil	US
SIMPSON	O. J.	US
SINATRA	Frank	US
SKELTON	Red	US
STEIGER	Rod	US
STEWART	James	US
TRAVERS	Bill	UK
USTINOV	Sir Peter	UK
VAN DYKE	Dick	US
WHITMAN	Stuart	US
WINKLER	Henry	US
WINTERS	Jonathon	US

8

ALDRIDGE	Ira Frederick	US
ANDREINI	Francesco	Italy
ANDREINI	Giovann Battista	Italy
ATKINSON	Rowan	UK
AZNAVOUR	Charles	France
BANDERAS	Antonio	Spain

SURNAME	CHRISTIAN NAMES	PLACE OF BIRTH
BASEHART	Richard	US
BENEDICT	William	US
BERENGER	Tom	US
BERRYMAN	Michael	US
BORGNINE	Ernest	US
BRASSEUR	Pierre	France
BUCHANAN	Jack	Scotland
CONNOLLY	Billy	Scotland
COSTELLO	Lou	US
CRAWFORD	Broderick	US
CRAWFORD	Michael	UK
CUMMINGS	Robert	US
DEBUREAU	Jean-Gaspard	France
DEVRIENT	Ludwig	Germany
DICAPRIO	Leonardo	US
DREYFUSS	Richard	US
DRISCOLL	Bobby	US
EASTWOOD	Clint	US
ESTCOURT	Richard	UK
FLANAGAN	Bud	UK
FLORENCE	William Jermyn	US
FORSYTHE	John	US
GARFIELD	John	US
GOLDBLUM	Jeff	US
GRIFFITH	Andy	US
GUINNESS	Sir Alec	UK
HARRISON	Rex	UK
HOLLOWAY	Stanley	UK
KINGSLEY	Ben	UK
KNOPFLER	Mark	Scotland
KYNASTON	Ned	UK
LAUGHTON	Charles	UK
LOCKWOOD	Gary	US
LUNDGREN	Dolph	Sweden
MACREADY	George	US

SURNAME	CHRISTIAN NAMES	PLACE OF BIRTH
MACREADY	William Charles	UK
MCCALLUM	David	Scotland
MCDOWELL	Malcolm	UK
MCGREGOR	Ewan	Scotland
MCKELLEN	Ian	UK
MILLIGAN	Spike	India
MITCHELL	Warren	UK
RATHBONE	Basil	South Africa
REDGRAVE	Corin	UK
REDGRAVE	Sir Michael	UK
REYNOLDS	Burt	US
ROBINSON	Edward G.	Romania
SCHEIDER	Roy	US
SCOFIELD	Paul	UK
SEINFELD	Jerry	US
STALLONE	Sylvester	US
THOMPSON	Jack	Australia
TINGWELL	Charles	Australia
TOGNAZZI	Ugo	Italy
TRAVOLTA	John	US
VAN CLEEF	Lee	US
VAN DAMME	Jean-Claude	Belgium
VON SYDOW	Max	Sweden
WHITMORE	James	US
WILLIAMS	Kenneth	UK
WILLIAMS	Michael	UK
WILLIAMS	Robin	US
WOODWARD	Edward	UK

SURNAME	CHRISTIAN NAMES	PLACE OF BIRTH

9

SURNAME	CHRISTIAN NAMES	PLACE OF BIRTH
BARKWORTH	Peter	UK
BARRYMORE	John	US
BARRYMORE	Lionel	US
BARRYMORE	Maurice	India
BETTERTON	Thomas	UK
BRODERICK	Matthew	US
CHEVALIER	Maurice	France
COURTENAY	Tom	UK
DAVENPORT	Nigel	UK
DEPARDIEU	Gerard	France
DEVEREAUX	Ed	Australia
DU MAURIER	Sir Gerald	UK
FAIRBANKS	Douglas, Jr.	US
FISHBURNE	Lawrence	US
GROSSMITH	George	UK
GRUNDGENS	Gustav	Germany
HAWTHORNE	Sir Nigel	UK
HUMPHRIES	Barry	Australia
LANCASTER	Burt	US
MACMURRAY	Fred	US
MALKOVICH	John	US
MORECOMBE	Eric	UK
NICHOLSON	Jack	US
PLEASENCE	Donald	UK
VALENTINO	Rudolf	Italy
ZIMBALIST	Efrem, Jr.	US

10

SURNAME	CHRISTIAN NAMES	PLACE OF BIRTH
BASSERMANN	Albert	Germany
CARTWRIGHT	William	UK
GUTTENBURG	Steve	US
HASSELHOFF	David	US

SURNAME	CHRISTIAN NAMES	PLACE OF BIRTH
MONTGOMERY	George	US
MONTGOMERY	Robert	US
RICHARDSON	Ian	UK
RICHARDSON	Sir Ralph	UK
ROSSELLINI	Roberto	Italy
SUTHERLAND	Donald	US
SUTHERLAND	Kiefer	UK
WASHINGTON	Denzel	US

11

CHAMBERLAIN	Richard	US
GREENSTREET	Sydney	UK
MASTROIANNI	Marcello	Italy
WEISSMULLER	Johnny	Romania

12

ATTENBOROUGH	Sir Richard	UK
STANISLAVSKY	Konstantin	Russia

13

KRISTOFFERSON	Kris	US

14

SCHWARZENEGGER	Arnold	Austria

ACTRESSES
Film, Theatre and TV

SURNAME	CHRISTIAN NAMES	PLACE OF BIRTH

3

SURNAME	CHRISTIAN NAMES	PLACE OF BIRTH
BOW	Clara	US
DAY	Doris	US
LEE	Gypsy Rose	US
LOY	Myrna	US

4

SURNAME	CHRISTIAN NAMES	PLACE OF BIRTH
ARNE	Susanna Maria	UK
BALL	Lucille	US
CHER		US
CRUZ	Penelope	Spain
DALY	Tyne	US
DERN	Laura	US
DIAZ	Cameron	US
DOWN	Lesley-Anne	UK
DUKE	Patty	US
DUSE	Eleonora	Italy
EDEN	Barbara	US
FENN	Sherilyn	US
GISH	Dorothy	US
GISH	Lillian	US
GWYN	Nell	UK
HALE	Barbara	US
HAWN	Goldie	US
HUNT	Helen	US
KERR	Deborah	Scotland
LADD	Cheryl	US
LADD	Diane	US
LAKE	Veronica	US

SURNAME	CHRISTIAN NAMES	PLACE OF BIRTH
LONG	Shelley	US
MAYO	Virginia	US
PAGE	Geraldine	US
PIAF	Edith	France
REED	Donna	US
REID	Beryl	UK
RIGG	Dame Diana	UK
ROHM	Elisabth	Germany
RYAN	Meg	US
WARD	Rachel	UK
WEST	Mae	US
WOOD	Natalie	US
YORK	Susannah	UK

5

ALLEN	Gracie	US
ALLEY	Kirstie	US
ARDEN	Eve	US
BAKER	Carroll	US
BARRY	Elizabeth	UK
BATES	Kathy	UK
BLACK	Karen	US
BLAIR	Linda	US
BLOOM	Claire	UK
BRICE	Fanny	US
BROWN	Pamela	UK
BRYAN	Dora	UK
CAREY	Joyce	UK
CLIVE	Kitty	UK
CLOSE	Glenn	US
DAVIS	Bette	US
DAVIS	Geena	US
DENCH	Dame Judi	UK
DEREK	Bo	US

SURNAME	CHRISTIAN NAMES	PLACE OF BIRTH
DUNST	Kirsten	US
EVANS	Dame Edith	UK
EVANS	Linda	US
FIELD	Sally	US
FONDA	Bridget	US
FONDA	Jane	US
GABOR	Eva	Hungary
GABOR	Zsa Zsa	Hungary
GARBO	Greta	Sweden
HAYES	Helen	US
HENIE	Sonja	Norway
HICKS	Catherine	US
JOHNS	Glynis	South Africa
JONES	Grace	Jamaica
KELLY	Grace	US
LANGE	Jessica	US
LEIGH	Janet	US
LEIGH	Jennifer Jason	US
LEIGH	Vivien	India
LEWIS	Juliette	US
LOCKE	Sondra	US
LOPEZ	Jennifer	US
LORDS	Traci	US
LOREN	Sophia	Italy
MILES	Sarah	UK
MILES	Vera	US
MILLS	Hayley	UK
MOORE	Demi	US
MOORE	Mary Tyler	US
NOVAK	Kim	US
O'HARA	Catherine	Canada
O'HARA	Maureen	Ireland
O'NEAL	Jennifer	Brazil
O'NEAL	Tatum	US
PAIGE	Elaine	UK

SURNAME	CHRISTIAN NAMES	PLACE OF BIRTH
PLUMB	Gwen	Australia
RYDER	Winona	US
SAINT	Eva Marie	US
SMITH	Maggie	UK
STONE	Sharon	US
TANDY	Jessica	UK
TERRY	Dame Ellen Alice	UK
TILLY	Meg	US
TUTIN	Dorothy	UK
TYLER	Liv	US
WEISZ	Rachel	UK
WELCH	Raquel	US
WIEST	Dianne	US
WYATT	Jane	US
WYMAN	Jane	US
YOUNG	Loretta	US

6

SURNAME	CHRISTIAN NAMES	PLACE OF BIRTH
AITKEN	Maria	UK
ARNAUD	Yvonne Germaine	France
ATKINS	Eileen	UK
BACALL	Lauren	US
BARDOT	Brigitte	France
BARKIN	Ellen	US
BARRIE	Barbara	US
BAXTER	Anne	US
BENING	Annette	US
BERGEN	Candice	US
BERGER	Senta	Austria
BIRKIN	Jane	UK
COOPER	Dame Gladys	UK
CURTIS	Jamie Lee	US
DENNIS	Sandy	Nebraska
DRAPER	Ruth	US

SURNAME	CHRISTIAN NAMES	PLACE OF BIRTH
DRIVER	Minnie	UK
EKBERG	Anita	Sweden
FARROW	Mia	US
FELDON	Barbara	US
FIELDS	Dame Gracie	UK
FISHER	Carrie	US
FOSTER	Jodie	US
GARSON	Greer	UK
GAYNOR	Janet	US
GAYNOR	Mitzi	US
GRABLE	Betty	US
HANNAH	Daryl	US
HARLOW	Jean	US
HILLER	Dame Wendy	UK
HUNTER	Holly	US
HURLEY	Elizabeth	UK
KARINA	Anna	Denmark
KEATON	Diane	US
KELLER	Marthe	Switzerland
KENDAL	Felicity	UK
KIDMAN	Nicole	US
KINSKI	Natassja	Germany
KOONEN	Alisa Georgievna	Russia
LAMOUR	Dorothy	US
LAURIE	Piper	US
LILLIE	Beatrice Gladys	Canada
LIPMAN	Maureen	UK
LONDON	Julie	US
LYNLEY	Carol	US
MARTIN	Mary	US
MERMAN	Ethel	US
MIDLER	Bette	US
MONROE	Marilyn	US
MOREAU	Jeanne	France
OBERON	Merle	India

SURNAME	CHRISTIAN NAMES	PLACE OF BIRTH
ORMOND	Julia	UK
PALMER	Lilli	Germany
PARKER	Sarah Jessica	US
PARTON	Dolly	US
POWELL	Jane	US
POWERS	Stefanie	US
REMICK	Lee	US
RITTER	Thelma	US
RIVERS	Joan	US
ROBSON	Dame Flora	UK
ROGERS	Ginger	US
SOMMER	Elke	Germany
SPACEK	Sissy	US
ST JOHN	Jill	US
STREEP	Meryl	US
SUZMAN	Janet	South Africa
TAYLOR	Dame Elizabeth	UK
TEMPLE	Shirley	US
TOMLIN	Lily	US
TURNER	Kathleen	US
TURNER	Lana	US
TWIGGY		UK
WAGNER	Lindsay	US
WEAVER	Sigourney	US
WELCHE	Rachel	France
WINGER	Debra	US
WYNTER	Dana	UK

7

SURNAME	CHRISTIAN NAMES	PLACE OF BIRTH
ACHURCH	Janet	UK
ALLGOOD	Sara	Ireland
ANDRESS	Ursula	Switzerland
ANDREWS	Dame Julie	UK
ANISTON	Jennifer	US

SURNAME	CHRISTIAN NAMES	PLACE OF BIRTH
BELLAMY	George Anne	UK
BENNETT	Jill	UK
BERGMAN	Ingrid	Sweden
BERGNER	Elisabeth	Austria
BINOCHE	Juliette	France
BISSETT	Jacqueline	UK
BULLOCK	Sandra	US
BURNETT	Carol	US
BURSTYN	Ellen	US
CARRERA	Barbara	Nicaragua
CASARES	Maria	France
CELESTE	Celine	France
CHAPLIN	Geraldine	US
CILENTO	Diane	Australia
CLOONEY	Rosemary	US
COLBERT	Claudette	France
COLLIER	Constance	UK
COLLINS	Joan	UK
DENEUVE	Catherine	France
DOTRICE	Michel	UK
DUKAKIS	Olympia	US
DUNAWAY	Faye	US
ECKLAND	Britt	Sweden
ELECTRA	Carmen	US
FAWCETT	Farrah	US
GARDNER	Ava	US
GARLAND	Judy	US
GINGOLD	Hermione	UK
GRAYSON	Kathryn	US
HANCOCK	Sheila	UK
HAYWARD	Susan	US
HEPBURN	Audrey	Belgium
HEPBURN	Katharine	US
HERSHEY	Barbara	US
HOUSTON	Whitney	US

SURNAME	CHRISTIAN NAMES	PLACE OF BIRTH
JACKSON	Glenda	UK
JACQUES	Hattie	UK
JOHNSON	Dame Celia	UK
KENDALL	Kate	UK
KRISTEL	Sylvia	US
LANGTRY	Lillie	UK
LEDOYER	Virginnie	France
LOMBARD	Carole	US
MACGRAW	Ali	US
MADONNA		US
MCKENNA	Siobhan	Ireland
MIRANDA	Carmen	Portugal
O'CONNOR	Frances	UK
PALTROW	Gwyneth	US
ROBERTS	Julia	US
ROBERTS	Rachel	Wales
ROBERTS	Tanya	US
RUSSELL	Jane	US
RUSSELL	Rosalind	US
RUSSELL	Theresa	US
SCACCHI	Greta	Italy
SEYMOUR	Jane	UK
SHEARER	Moira	Scotland
SHEARER	Norma	Canada
SHIELDS	Brooke	US
SIDDONS	Sarah	UK
SIMMONS	Jean	UK
SINATRA	Nancy	US
STRITCH	Elaine	US
SWANSON	Gloria	US
TEMPEST	Dame Marie	UK
ULLMANN	Liv	Tokyo
WINDSOR	Barbra	UK
WINFREY	Oprah	US
WINSLET	Kate	UK

SURNAME	CHRISTIAN NAMES	PLACE OF BIRTH
WINTERS	Shelley	US
WITHERS	Googie	UK
WYNYARD	Diana	UK

8

ABINGTON	Frances	UK
ANDERSON	Dame Judith	Australia
ANDERSON	Gillian	US
ANDERSON	Pamela	US
ANDREINI	Isabella	Italy
ASHCROFT	Dame Peggy	UK
BADDELEY	Hermione	UK
BANCROFT	Anne	US
BANKHEAD	Tallulah	US
BASINGER	Kim	US
BLACKMAN	Honor	UK
BLONDELL	Claire	US
CALDWELL	Zoe	Australia
CAMPBELL	Mrs Patrick	UK
CHANNING	Carol	US
CHARISSE	Cyd	US
CHRISTIE	Julie	India
CRAWFORD	Joan	US
DE LA TOUR	Frances	UK
DE MORNAY	Rebecca	US
DEWHURST	Colleen	Canada
DIETRICH	Marlene	Germany
FLETCHER	Louise	US
FONTAINE	Jane	Tokyo
GOLDBERG	Whoopi	US
GRENFELL	Joyce	UK
GRIFFITH	Melanie	US
HAMILTON	Linda	US

ACTRESSES

SURNAME	CHRISTIAN NAMES	PLACE OF BIRTH
HAYWORTH	Rita	US
HOLLIDAY	Judy	US
KIRKLAND	Sally	US
LANSBURY	Angela	UK
LAWRENCE	Gertrude	UK
LEIGHTON	Margaret	UK
LOCKLEAR	Heather	US
LOCKWOOD	Margaret	India
MACLAINE	Shirley	US
MCGOVERN	Elizabeth	US
MERCOURI	Melina	Greece
MINNELLI	Liza	US
NAZIMOVA	Alla	Russia
PFEIFFER	Michelle	US
PICKFORD	Mary	Canada
PRENTISS	Paula	US
RAMPLING	Charlotte	UK
REDGRAVE	Amanda	UK
REDGRAVE	Lynn	UK
REDGRAVE	Vanessa	UK
REYNOLDS	Debbie	US
RINGWALD	Molly	US
SARANDON	Susan	US
SHEPHERD	Cybill	US
SHERIDAN	Ann	US
SIGNORET	Simone	Germany
STANWYCK	Barbara	US
THOMPSON	Emma	UK
THORNTON	Sigrid	Australia
WHITELAW	Billie	UK
WILLIAMS	Esther	US
WOODWARD	Joanne	US

SURNAME	CHRISTIAN NAMES	PLACE OF BIRTH

9

SURNAME	CHRISTIAN NAMES	PLACE OF BIRTH
ALEXANDER	Jane	US
APPLEGATE	Christina	US
BARRYMORE	Drew	US
BARRYMORE	Ethel	US
BERNHARDT	Sarah	France
CARDINALE	Claudia	Tunisia
CLAYBURGH	Jill	US
CRACKNELL	Ruth	Australia
DICKINSON	Angie	US
FAIRCHILD	Morgan	US
FEUILLERE	Edwige	France
GRAMATICA	Irma	Italy
GRIFFITHS	Rachael	Australia
KELLERMAN	Sally	US
LAPOTAIRE	Jane	UK
MACDONALD	Jeanette	US
MACDOWELL	Andie	US
MANSFIELD	Jayne	US
MERKERSON	S. Epatha	US
MONCRIEFF	Gladys	Australia
MOOREHEAD	Agnes	US
PLOWRIGHT	Dame Joan Anne	UK
SCHNEIDER	Maria	France
SCHNEIDER	Romy	Austria
STREISAND	Barbra	US
THORNDIKE	Dame Sybil	UK
ZELLWEGER	Renee	US
ZETA-JONES	Catherine	Wales

10

SURNAME	CHRISTIAN NAMES	PLACE OF BIRTH
BOUCICAULT	Nina	UK
MACPHERSON	Ellie	Australia

SURNAME	CHRISTIAN NAMES	PLACE OF BIRTH
MONTGOMERY	Elizabeth	US
RICHARDSON	Joely	UK
RUTHERFORD	Dame Margaret	UK
STEPHENSON	Dr Pamela	New Zealand
WOFFINGTON	Peg	Ireland

11

BRACEGIRDLE	Anne	UK
BRAITHWAITE	Dame Lilian	UK
COURTNEIDGE	Dame Cicely	UK
DE HAVILLAND	Olivia	Japan
SCOTT THOMAS	Kristin	US
SILVERSTONE	Alicia	US

12

BONHAM-CARTER	Helena	UK
LOLLOBRIGIDA	Gina	Italy

AIR FORCE RANKS
British and American

UNITED STATES AIR FORCE

5 Major

6 Airman

7 Captain; Colonel; General

11 Airman Basic

12 Major-General

13 Staff Sergeant

15 First Lieutenant

16 Airman First Class
Brigadier-General
Second Lieutenant

17 Lieutenant-Colonel
Lieutenant-General
Technical Sergeant

19 Chief Master Sergeant

20 General of the Air Force
Senior Master Sergeant
Sergeant Senior Airman

32 Chief Master Sergeant
of the Air Force

ROYAL AIR FORCE

8 Corporal
Sergeant

10 Air Marshal

12 Air Commodore
Group Captain
Pilot Officer

13 Flying Officer
Wing Commander

14 Air Vice-Marshal
Flight Sergeant
Squadron Leader
Warrant Officer

15 Air Chief Marshal

16 Flight Lieutenant

25 Marshal of the Royal
Air Force

ALCOHOLIC BEVERAGES
including wines, aperitifs, beers,
cocktails, spirits and liqueurs

3
ALE
FIX
GIN
KIR
NOG
RUM

4
ARAK
CAVA
FINO
FIZZ
FLIP
GAVI
GROG
HOCK
MARC
MEAD
MILD
OUZO
PORT
RAKI
ROSE
SAKE
SAKI
SEKT
SOUR

BYRRH
CHOUM
CIDER
CREPY
FITOU
GLOGG
JULEP
KVASS
LAGER
LOIRE
MACON
MEDOC
MOSEL
NEGUS
PERRY
PUNCH
RHONE
RIOJA
SHOTZ
SOAVE
STOUT
TOKAY
TAVEL
TODDY
VIDAL
VODKA

5
AIREN
ANISE
ANRAM
BLANC

6
ALSACE
BANDOL
BAROLO
BARSAC

6

BEADLE
BEAUNE
BISHOP
BITTER
BOUKHA
BRANDY
CAHORS
CASSIS
CHICHA
CHINON
CLARET
COGNAC
EGG-NOG
FRANGY
GIMLET
GRAPPA
GRAVES
KIRSCH
KUMMEL
LAMBIC
MALAGA
MALBEC
MELISS
MERLOT
MESCAL
METAXA
MUSCAT
PASTIS
PERNOD
POSSET
PULQUE
QETSCH
SAUMUR
SHANDY
SHERRY
SHIRAZ (SYRA)
STREGA

TOKAY
VOLNAY
WHISKY

7

ALCAMAS
ALIGOTE
ALLASCH
AQUAVIT
AMARONE
BACARDI
BAILEYS
BANYULS
BARBERA
BOUKHRA
BOURBON
BRAGGOT
CAMPARI
CHABLIS
CHIANTI
CLAIRET
COTE D'OR
CREMANT
CURACAO
ESCUBAC
FALERNO
GAILLAC
ICEWINE
MADEIRA
MARGAUX
MARSALA
MARTINI
MOSELLE
ORVIETO
POMMARD
RATAFIA
RETSINA
SAMBUCA

7

SANGRIA
SCHNAPS
SIDECAR
TEQUILA
VOUVRAY
WALDORF
WHISKEY

PAUILLAC
PERSICOT
PINK LADY
PINOTAGE
RIESLING
ROSE WINE
SANCERRE
SANTENAY
SCHNAPPS
SEMILLON
VALENCAY
VERMOUTH
VIN JAUNE
VIOGHIER
WHIZ BANG

8

ABSINTHE
ADVOCAAT
ANISETTE
APPLE CAR
ARMAGNAC
BACO NOIR
BORDEAUX
BROUILLY
BURGUNDY
CALVADOS
DAIQUIRI
DRAMBUIE
DUBONNET
FALERNUM
FRASCATI
GIGONDAS
GIN AND IT
GIN SLING
GRENACHE
GUINNESS
HIGHBALL
HYDROMEL
MERCUREY
MERITAGE
MONTAGNY
MONTILLA
MUSCADET
NEBBIOLO
NIGHTCAP

9

ALEXANDER
APPLEJACK
ARQUEBUSE
BEE'S KNEES
BOURGUEIL
BUCK JONES
BUCKS FIZZ
CHAMPAGNE
CLAIRETTE
COINTREAU
COMMODORE
COTE-ROTIE
FRAMBOISE
GUIGNOLET
HERMITAGE
LAMBRUSCO
MANHATTAN
MEURSAULT
MINT JULEP
MIRABELLE
MONTLOUIS

9
MOONLIGHT
MOONSHINE
MULLED ALE
PINOT GRIS (GRIGIO)
PINOT NOIR
SAUTERNES
SAUVIGNON
SLIVOVITZ
TREBBIANO
TRIPLE SEC
ZINFANDEL (RED)
ZINFANDEL (WHITE)
WHITE LADY

10
ANGEL'S KISS
ARCHBISHOP
BARBARESCO
BARLEY BEER
BARLEY WINE
BEAUJOLAIS
BLACK MARIA
BLOODY MARY
BROU DE NOIX
BULL'S BLOOD
CHARDONNAY
CHARTREUSE
HORSE'S NECK
KOSHER WINE
MANZANILLA
MARASCHINO
MERRY WIDOW
MONTRACHET
MULLED WINE
PETIT SIRAH
PINA COLADA
PINOT BLANC
RICHEBOURG

RIVESALTES
RUM COLLINS
RYE WHISKEY
SANGIOVESE
TOM COLLINS
VINHO VERDE

11
AGUARDIENTE
ALOXE-CORTON
AMONTILLADO
BEACHCOMBER
BENEDICTINE
BLACK VELVET
CHENIN BLANC
FALLEN ANGEL
MONBAZILLAC
PETITE SIRAH
POUILLY-FUME
SAINT JULIEN
TEMPRANILLO
TRAPPISTINE
VIN DE PAILLE
WASSAIL BOWL

12
BLACK RUSSIAN
CHERRY BRANDY
CHURCHWARDEN
COSMOPOLITAN
COTES-DU-RHONE
CREME DE CACAO
ELEPHANT'S EAR
FINE AND DANDY
GRAND MARNIER
OLD-FASHIONED
ROMANEE-CONTI
SAINT-EMILION
SAINT ESTEPHE

12
VALPOLICELLA
VOSNE-ROMANEE
WHITE GIN SOUR
WHITE RUSSIAN

13
CABERNET FRANC
CHAMPAGNE BUCK
CHATEAU D'YQUEM
CHATEAU LAFITE
CHATEAU LATOUR
CORPSE REVIVER
CREME DE MENTHE
ENTRE-DEUX-MERS
KNICKERBOCKER
LIEBFRAUMILCH
MAIDEN'S PRAYER
PLANTER'S PUNCH
POUILLY-FUISSE
PRAIRIE OYSTER
QUALITATSWEIN

14
CHATEAU MARGAUX
COTES-DU-VENTOUX
GEWURZTRAMINER
LACRIMA CHRISTI
SAUVIGNON BLANC
TEQUILA SUNRISE

15
COTES-DE-PROVENCE
COTES-DU-VIVARAIS
CROZES-HERMITAGE
HAUT POITOU WINES
MOREY-SAINT-DENIS
SOUTHERN COMFORT

16
BETWEEN THE SHEETS
CHAMBOLLE-MUSIGNY
CHATEAU HAUT-BRION

16 GEVREY-CHAMBERTIN
HARVEY WALLBANGER
SAVIGNY-LES-BEAUNE

17 AMARETTO DI SARANNO
CABERNET SAUVIGNON
CORTON-CHARLEMAGNE
COTES-DU-ROUSSILLON
NUITS-SAINT-GEORGES

18 BLANQUETTE DE LIMOUX

19 CHASSAGNE-MONTRACHET

21 MONTEPULCIANO D'ABRUZZO

23 CHATEAU MOUTON ROTHSCHILD

ANIMALS
including Gender and Young

ANIMAL	MALE	FEMALE	YOUNG
2			
ox	bull	cow	calf, stot
3			
ape	–	–	pup
ass	dicky, jack jackass	jenny she-ass	colt (m) filly (f), foal
bat	–	–	pup
cat	tomcat	queen	kitten
cow	bull	cow	calf
dog	dog	bitch	pup
elk	bull	cow	calf
fox	reynard	vixen	kit, cub, pup
gnu	bull	cow	calf
hog	boar	gilt, sow	farrow, shoat piglet
pig	barrow, boar	gilt, sow	piglet, farrow shoat

ANIMAL	MALE	FEMALE	YOUNG
rat	buck	doe	pup, pinkie, kitten
yak	bull	cow, dri, nak	calf

4

ANIMAL	MALE	FEMALE	YOUNG
bear	boar	sow, ursa	cub
boar	boar	sow	calf, farrow, piglet
clam	–	–	chiton, littleneck
deer	buck, hart stag	doe, hind roe, teg	calf, kid, fawn
frog	–	–	froglet, polliwog tadpole
goat	buck, billy	doe, nanny	kid, billy
hare	buck, jack	doe, jill, puss	leveret
ibex	bull, evecka	cow	calf
lion	lion	lioness	cub, lionet, shelp
lynx	male	female	kitten
mink	boar	sow	cub, kit
mole	–	–	pup
mule	jack	hinney	foal
seal	bull	cow	pup

ANIMAL	MALE	FEMALE	YOUNG
toad	–	–	tadpole
wolf	dog he-wolf	bitch she-wolf	cub, pup, whelp

5

ANIMAL	MALE	FEMALE	YOUNG
bison	bull	cow	calf
camel	bull, stallion	cow, mare	calf, colt, foal
eland	buck, bull	cow, doe	calf
horse	sire, stallion stud	dam, mare	foal colt (m), filly (f)
hyena	dog	bitch	cub, pup
hyrax	buck	doe	bunny
koala	–	–	joey
lemur	–	–	infant
llama	–	–	cria
moose	bull	cow	calf
mouse	buck	doe	kitten, pinkie, pup
otter	–	–	pup, whelp
panda	boar	sow	cub

ANIMAL	MALE	FEMALE	YOUNG
sheep	ram, tup	ewe	cosset, hog, lamb lambling, teg
skunk	boar	–	kit, kitten
snake	–	–	snakelet
stoat	buck, dog hob, jack	bitch, doe jill	kit
tapir	–	–	calf
tiger	tiger	tigress	cub, whelp
viper	–	–	snakelet
zebra	stallion	mare	colt, foal

6

alpaca	stallion	mare	cria
baboon	–	–	infant
badger	boar	sow	cub, kit
beaver	–	–	kitten, pup
bobcat			cub, kitten
cattle	bull	cow	calf, stirk bullock (m) heifer (f)
cougar	–	–	cub, kitten

ANIMAL	MALE	FEMALE	YOUNG
coyote	dog	bitch, gyp	pup, whelp
donkey	jack, jackass	jennet, jenny	colt, foal
ferret	dog, hob buck, jack	doe, jill, bitch	kit
gerbil	buck	doe	pup
impala	buck	doe	calf
marten	–	–	kit
monkey	–	–	infant, suckling
oyster	–	–	brood, spat
possum	jack	jill	joey
quokka	–	–	joey
rabbit	buck	doe	bunny, kit, kitten leveret, nestling
turtle	–	–	hatchling
vicuna	–	–	cria
walrus	bull	cow	pup
weasel	buck, dog	bitch, doe, jill	kit
wombat	jack	jill	joey

ANIMAL	MALE	FEMALE	YOUNG
7			
buffalo	bull	cow	calf
chamois	buck	doe	calf
cheetah	–	–	cub
dolphin	bull	cow	calf, pup
giraffe	bull	cow, doe	calf
gorilla	–	–	infant
hamster	buck	doe	pup
lamprey	–	–	–
leopard	leopard	leopardess	cub
lobster	–	–	–
manatee	bull	cow	calf
meerkat	–	–	pup
muskrat	–	–	kit
opossum	jack	jill	joey
polecat	hob	jill	kit
raccoon	boar	sow	cub, kit
red deer	stag	hind	calf

ANIMAL	MALE	FEMALE	YOUNG
wallaby	jack	jill	joey

8

aardvark	–	–	pup
anteater	–	–	pup
antelope	buck	doe	calf
bacteria	–	–	–
dinosaur	bull	cow	hatchling, juvenile
elephant	bull	cow, koomkie	calf
hedgehog	boar	sow	piglet, pup
kangaroo	boomer buck, jack	doe, flyer jill, roo	joey
porpoise	bull	cow	calf
reindeer	bull	cow	calf
squirrel	buck	doe	kit, kitten nestling, pup
tortoise	–	–	–

9

alligator	bull	cow	hatchling

ANIMAL	MALE	FEMALE	YOUNG
armadillo	–	–	pup
crocodile	bull	cow	crocklet
greyhound	dog	bitch	pup, puppy whelp
guinea pig	boar, buck	doe, sow	pup
jellyfish	–	–	ephyna
orangutan	–	–	–
polar bear	boar	sow	cub
porcupine	boar	sow	cub
woodchuck	he-chuck	she-chuck	cub, kit

10

chimpanzee	–	–	infant
prairie dog	boar	sow	pup
rhinoceros	bull	cow	calf

ANIMALS
Group Names

ANIMAL	GROUP NAME

4

ants	army, colony, swarm
apes	shrewdness
bass	shoal
bees	grist, hive, swarm
cats	clowder, clutter, pounce, cluster
cows	kine
cubs	litter
curs	cowardice
deer	herd, leash, mob
dogs	kennel, litter, pack
elks	gang, herd
emus	mob
fish	catch, drought, haul, run, school, shoal
gnus	implausibility
hens	brood
hogs	drift, passel, parcel
jays	party, scold
owls	parliament
oxen	drove, herd, team, yoke
pigs	herd, litter, sounder
pups	litter
rats	colony, pack, plague, swarm
teal	spring

5

asses	herd, pace
bears	sleuth, sloth
birds	congregation, dissimulation, flight, flock, volary

ANIMAL	GROUP NAME
boars	sounder, singular
bucks	brace, clash
clams	bed, flaccidity
colts	rag, rake
coots	covert
crows	murder
doves	bevy, cote, dole, dule, flight, paddling, piteousness
ducks	paddling, raft, team
flies	cloud, swarm
foxes	earth, lead, leash, skulk
frogs	army, colony, knot
geese	gaggle, skein {in flight}, team, wedge
gnats	cloud, horde, swarm
goats	drove, herd, tribe, trip
hares	down, husk, mute
hawks	cast, kettle {when riding a thermal)
larks	ascension, bevy, exaltation
lions	pride, sawt, troop
mares	stud
moles	company, labour, movement
mules	barren, pack, rake, span
peeps	litter
quail	bevy, covey
rooks	building, clamour, parliament
rooks, crows	storytelling
seals	bob, colony, crash, harem, herd, pod, team
sheep	down, drift, drove, flock, fold, herd, hurtle, trip
snipe	walk, wisp
swans	bevy, herd, wedge {when flying in a 'V' formation}
swine	drift, herd, sounder
toads	knot
trout	hover

ANIMAL	GROUP NAME

6

cattle	drift, drove, herd, mob, team
chicks	clutch, chattering
cobras	quiver
coyote	band
cranes	herd, sedge, siege
eagles	convocation
horses	herd, haras, stable, team, troop
hounds	cry, mute, pack
otters	bevy, family, romp
ponies	string
ravens	unkindness
sharks	shiver
snakes	den, nest, pit
storks	muster, mustering
swifts	flock
tigers	ambush
vipers	generation, nest
whales	gam, herd, pod, school
wolves	pack, rout
zebras	crossing, herd

7

badgers	cete, colony
beavers	colony
buffalo	gang, herd
curlews	herd
donkeys	drove, herd, pace
ferrets	business, cast, fesnying
finches	charm
herring	shoal
kittens	litter, kindle
lapwing	deceit
lizards	lounge
locusts	plague

ANIMAL	GROUP NAME
magpies	tiding
martens	richesse
monkeys	cartload, tribe, troop, troup
parrots	company
pigeons	flight, flock, kit
piglets	farrow
plovers	congregation, wing
rabbits	bury, colony, down, drove, husk, leash, trace, trip, nest {young}
turkeys	raft, rafter
turtles	bale

8

ANIMAL	GROUP NAME
antelope	herd
bacteria	culture
bitterns	sedge, siege
buzzards	wake
chickens	brood, clutch, peep
dolphins	pod
dotterel	trip
goldfish	glint, troubling
gorillas	band
leopards	leap, leep, lepe
mallards	sord
peacocks	muster, ostentation
penguins	colony, crèche {nursery group}, huddles, muster, parcel, rookery
polecats	chine
raccoons	gaze
roebucks	bevy
sparrows	host
swallows	flight
walruses	herd, pod
wild cats	destruction, gam, herd, pod, school

ANIMALS

ANIMAL	GROUP NAME
wildfowl	plump

9

ANIMAL	GROUP NAME
bobolinks	chain
housecats	clowder, cluster, dowt, nuisance
jellyfish	smack
kangaroos	herd, mob, troop
pheasants {on the ground}	head, nide, nye
pheasants {when flushed}	bouquet
pilchards	shoal
porpoises	herd, pod, school
squirrels	dray, scurry
starlings	murmuration
woodcocks	fall

10

ANIMAL	GROUP NAME
crocodiles	float
greyhounds	leash
partridges	covey
rhinoceros	crash

11

ANIMAL	GROUP NAME
goldfinches	charm
jackrabbits	husk
turtledoves	dule, pitying
woodpeckers	descent

12

ANIMAL	GROUP NAME
caterpillars	army
nightingales	watch
rattlesnakes	rhumba

13

ANIMAL	GROUP NAME
elephant seals	pod

ARCHBISHOPS OF CANTERBURY

(AD 597–Present)

3 ODA, the Severe, St (942)

4 KEMP, John (1452)
LANG, Cosmo Gordon (1928)
LAUD, William (1633)
POLE, Reginald (1556)
RICH, St Edmund (1234)
TAIT, Archibald Campbell (1868)
WAKE, William (1716)

5 ABBOT, George (1611)
CAREY, George Leonard (1991)
DEANE, Henry (1501)
ISLIP, Simon (1349)
JUXON, William (1660)
MOORE, John (1783)

6 ANSELM, St (1093)
ATHELM (914)
BENSON, Edward White (1883)
COGGAN, Frederick Donald (1974)
FISHER, Geoffrey Francis (1945)
HOWLEY, William (1828)
HUTTON, Matthew (1757)
JUSTUS, St (624)
LYFING (1013)
MORTON, John (1486)
PARKER, Matthew (1559)
PECHAM, John (1279)
POTTER, John (1737)
RAMSEY, Arthur Michael (1961)

6 RUNCIE, Robert Alexander Kennedy (1980)
SECKER, Thomas (1758)
SUMNER, John Bird (1848)
SUTTON, Charles Manners (1805)
TEMPLE, Frederick (1896)
TEMPLE, William (1942)
WALDEN, Roger (1398)
WALTER, Hubert (1193)
WARHAM, William (1503)

7 A'BECKET, Thomas (1162)
AELFRIC (995)
ARUNDEL, Thomas (1396 and 1399)
CRANMER, Thomas (1533)
DUNSTAN, St (960)
EADSIGE (1038)
GRINDAL, Edmund (1576)
HERRING, Thomas (1747)
LANGHAM, Simon (1366)
LANGTON, Stephen (1207)
LE GRANT, Richard (1229)
LONGLEY, Charles Thomas (1862)
MEOPHAM, Simon (1328)
NOTHELM, St (735)
SHELDON, Gilbert (1663)
SIGERIC, the Serious (990)
STIGAND (1052)
SUDBURY, Simon (1375)
TATWINE, St (731)
TENISON, Thomas (1695)
WULFRED (805)

8 AELFHEAH, St Alphege (1005)
AELFSIGE (959)
BANCROFT, Richard (1604)
BERTHELM (959)
CEOLNOTH (833)

8 CHICHELE, Henry (1414)
CUTHBERT (740)
DAVIDSON, Randall Thomas (1903)
D'ESCURES, Ralph (1114)
HONORIUS, St (627)
JAENBERT, St (765)
LANFRANC (1070)
MELLITUS, St (619)
PLEGMUND (890)
REYNOLDS, Walter (1313)
SANCROFT, William (1678)
STAFFORD, John (1443)
THEODORE, St (668)
WHITGIFT, John (1583)
WILLIAMS, Rowan (2002)
WULFHELM (923)

9 AETHELGAR (988)
AETHELRED (870)
AUGUSTINE, St (597)
BERHTWALD, St (693)
BOURCHIER, Thomas (1454)
BREGOWINE, St (761)
COURTENAY, William (1381)
DE CORBEIL, William (1123)
DEUSDEDIT, St (655)
ETHELHARD (793)
FEOLOGELD (832)
KILWARDBY, Robert (1273)
TILLOTSON, John (1691)

10 AETHELNOTH (1020)
CORNWALLIS, Frederick (1768)
LAURENTIUS, St (604)
WHITTLESEY, William (1368)
WINCHELSEY, Robert (1294)

11 BRADWARDINE, Thomas (1349)
DE STRATFORD, John (1333)
FITZ-JOCELIN, Reginald (1191)

13 THEOBALD OF BEC (1139)

14 RICHARD OF DOVER (1174)

15 BALDWIN OF EXETER (1184)
BONIFACE OF SAVOY (1245)

16 ROBERT OF JUMIEGES (1051)

ARCHITECTS

3 OUD, Jacobus Johannes Pieter

4 ADAM, Robert
CRET, Paul Philippe
GOFF, Bruce
KAHN, Albert
KAHN, Louis I.
KENT, William
LOOS, Adolf
NASH, John
POST, George Browne
ROOT, John Wellborn
SERT, Jose Luis
SHAW, Norman
TAUT, Bruno
WOOD, John of Bath
WREN, Sir Christopher

5 AALTO, Alvar
BARRY, Sir Charles
CAMPI, Giulio
DANCE, George
DUDOK, Willem M.
EAMES, Charles and Ray
EIFFEL, Gustave
GAUDI, Antoni
GIBBS, James
HORTA, Victor
JONES, Inigo
LE VAU, Louis
McKIM, Charles Follen
MILLS, Robert

5
MOORE, Charles
NERVI, Pier Luigi
PONTI, Gio
PUGIN, A.W.N.
ROSSI, Giovanni Antonio di
SCOTT, Sir George Gilbert
SOANE, Sir John
STONE, Edward Durell
WYATT, James

6
ARCHER, Thomas
BREUER, Marcel
CASSON, Sir Hugh
FULLER, Richard Buckminster
GREENE, Charles Sumner
GREENE, Henry Arthur
JENNEY, William Le Baron
LASDUN, Sir Denys
LEDOUX, Claude-Nicolas
LESCOT, Pierre
MORGAN, Julia
MORRIS, William
NEUTRA, Richard
OLBRICH, Joseph Maria
PAXTON, Sir Joseph
PERRET, Auguste
SCARPA, Carlo
SPENCE, Sir Basil
TATLIN, Vladimir Evgrafovich
VOYSEY, Charles Francis Annesley
WAGNER, Otto
WRIGHT, Frank Lloyd

7
ALBERTI, Leon Battista
ASPLUND, Erik Gunnar
BEHRENS, Peter
BERNINI, Gianlorenzo

7

DELORME, Philibert
BOULLEE, Etienne-Louis
BURNHAM, Daniel Hudson
FONTANA, Domenico
GARNIER, Jean-Louis-Charles
GARNIER, Tony
GILBERT, Cass
GROPIUS, Walter
GUARINI, Guarino
GUIMARD, Hector
HERRERA, Francisco de, The Younger
HERRERA, Juan de
HOLABIRD, William
HOLLAND, Henry
LATROBE, Benjamin H.
LUTYENS, Sir Edwin Landseer
DA VINCI, Leonardo
MADERNO, Carlo
MANSART, François
MANSART, Jules
MAYBECK, Bernard
NEUMANN, Balthasar
PIETILA, Reima
PLECNIK, Jose
RUDOLPH, Paul

8

BULFINCH, Charles
BUNSHAFT, Gordon
CAMPBELL, Colen
CHAMBERS, Sir William
DOESBURG, Theo van
HOFFMANN, Josef
MELNIKOV, Konstantin
NIEMEYER, Oscar
PALLADIO, Andrea
PIRANESI, Giovanni Battista
RIETVELD, Gerrit

8 SAARINEN, Eero
SAARINEN, Eliel
SANT'ELIA, Antonio
SOUFFLOT, Jacques Germain
STIRLING, Sir James
SULLIVAN, Louis Henry
VANBRUGH, Sir John
YAMASAKI, Minoru

9 BELLUSCHI, Pietro
BORROMINI, Francesco
COCKERELL, Charles Robert
HAWKSMOOR, Nicholas
LABROUSTE, Henri
SCHINDLER, R.M.
VITRUVIUS

10 BUONARROTI, Michelangelo
BURLINGTON, Richard Boyle, Earl of
MACKINTOSH, Charles Rennie
MENDELSOHN, Erich
RICHARDSON, Henry Hobson
WATERHOUSE, Alfred

11 ABERCROMBIE, Sir Patrick
BUTTERFIELD, William
LE CORBUSIER, Charles Edouard Jeanneret

12 BRUNELLESCHI, Filippo
MICHELANGELO, Buonarroti

14 MIES VAN DER ROHE, Ludwig

15 HARDOUIN-MANSART, Jules

16 FISCHER VON ERLACH, Johann Bernhard

ARTISTS & PAINTERS

SURNAME	CHRISTIAN NAMES	PLACE OF BIRTH

3

SURNAME	CHRISTIAN NAMES	PLACE OF BIRTH
ARP	Jean	Germany
AST	Balthasar van der	Holland
DIX	Otto	Germany
DOU	Gerrit	Holland
FRY	Roger	UK
RAY	Man	US

4

SURNAME	CHRISTIAN NAMES	PLACE OF BIRTH
BONE	Sir Muirhead	UK
BOYD	Arthur	Australia
CANO	Alonso	Spain
COLE	Thomas	UK
CUYP	Aelbert Jacobsz	Holland
DADD	Richard	UK
DALI	Salvador	Spain
DORE	Gustave	France
DUFY	Raoul	France
DYCK	Sir Anthony van	Belgium
ETTY	William	UK
EYCK	Jan van	Belgium
FEKE	Robert	US
GOES	Hugo van der	Holland
GOGH	Vincent van	Holland
GOYA	Francisco de	Spain
GRIS	Juan	Spain
GROS	Antoine Jean	France
HALS	Frans	Holland
HART	Pro	Australia
HEDA	Willem Claesz	Holland

SURNAME	CHRISTIAN NAMES	PLACE OF BIRTH
HEEM	Jan Davidsz. de	Holland
KLEE	Paul	Switzerland
MARC	Franz	Germany
MIRO	Joan	Spain
OPIE	John	UK
PUGH	Clifton	Australia
SHAW	Joshua	UK
TROY	Jean-Francois de	France
WEST	Benjamin	US

5

APPEL	Karel	Holland
BACON	Francis	Ireland
BAKST	Leon	Russia
BALLA	Giacomo	Italy
BARRY	James	Ireland
BEUYS	Joseph	Germany
BLAKE	Peter	UK
BLAKE	William	UK
BOSCH	Hieronymus	Holland
BOUTS	Dierick	Holland
BROWN	Ford Madox	France
BURRA	Edward	UK
CARON	Antoine	France
CARRA	Carlo	Italy
CHASE	William Merritt	US
COROT	Jean-Baptise Camille	France
CRANE	Walter	UK
CROME	John	UK
DEGAS	Edgar	France
DAGLY	Gerhard	Belgium
DANBY	Francis	Ireland
DAVID	Gerard	Holland
DAVID	Jacques Louis	France

SURNAME	CHRISTIAN NAMES	PLACE OF BIRTH
DAVIS	Stuart	US
DEGAS	Edgar	France
DENIS	Maurice	France
DOSSI	Dosso	Italy
DURER	Albrecht	Germany
ENSOR	James	Belgium
ERNST	Max	Germany
FRITH	William Powell	UK
FREUD	Lucian	Germany
GADDI	Taddeo	Italy
GORKY	Arshile	Armenia
GOYEN	Jan Josephszoon van	Holland
GRANT	Duncan James	Scotland
GROSZ	George	Germany
HOMER	Winslow	US
HOOCH	Pieter de	Holland
JOHNS	Jasper	US
KEENE	Charles Samuel	UK
KITAJ	Ron B.	US
KLIMT	Gustav	Austria
KUPKA	Frantisek	Czech.
LEGER	Fernand	France
LIPPI	Fra Filippo	Italy
LOTTO	Lorenzo	Italy
LOWRY	Laurence Stephen	UK
MACKE	August	Germany
MANET	Edouard	France
MONET	Claude	France
MUNCH	Edvard	Norway
NOLAN	Sidney, Sir	Australia
NOLDE	Emil	Germany
OUDRY	Jean-Baptiste	France
PATEL	Pierre	France
PIERO	della Francesca	Italy
PIPER	John	UK

SURNAME	CHRISTIAN NAMES	PLACE OF BIRTH
REDON	Odilon	France
RICCI	Sebastiano	Italy
RILEY	Dame Bridget Louise	UK
RODIN	Auguste	France
SHAHN	Ben	Lithuania
SMITH	Sir Matthew	UK
STAEL	Nicholas de	Russia
STEEN	Jan	Holland
TOBEY	Mark	US
WATTS	George Frederick	UK
WYETH	Andrew	US

6

ALBERS	Josef	Germany
ASTRUC	Zacharie	France
BENTON	Thomas Hart	US
BOUDIN	Eugene	France
BRAQUE	Georges	France
BRATBY	John	UK
BUFFET	Bernard	France
CALLOT	Jacques	France
CAMPIN	Robert	Holland
CLOUET	Jean	France
COOPER	Samuel	UK
COPLEY	John Singleton	US
COSWAY	Richard	UK
COTMAN	John Sell	UK
DERAIN	Andre	France
DE WINT	Peter	UK
DOBELL	Sir William	Australia
DOBSON	William	UK
DONGEN	Kees van	Holland
EAKINS	Thomas	US
FLORIS	Cornelis	Belgium

SURNAME	CHRISTIAN NAMES	PLACE OF BIRTH
FLORIS	Frans	Belgium
FUSELI	Henry	Switzerland
GELDER	Aert de	Holland
GERARD	Francois	Italy
GEROME	Jean-Leon	France
GIRTIN	Thomas	UK
GREUZE	Jean-Baptiste	France
GUARDI	Francesco	Italy
HOLLAR	Wenceslaus	Czech.
HOPPER	Edward	US
HUDSON	Thomas	UK
INGRES	Jean-Auguste-Dominique	France
ISABEY	Eugene-Gabriel	France
KIEFER	Anselm	Germany
KNIGHT	Dame Laura	UK
LA HYRE	Laurent de	France
LA TOUR	Maurice-Quentin de	France
LE BRUN	Charles	France
LEGROS	Alphonse	France
LE NAIN	Antoine	France
LE NAIN	Louis	France
LE NAIN	Mathieu	France
LEYDEN	Lucas van	Holland
LONGHI	Pietro	Italy
LURCAT	Jean	France
MARINI	Marino	Italy
MARTIN	John	UK
MASSYS	Quentin	Belgium
MILLET	Jean-Francois	France
MOREAU	Gustave	France
MORONI	Giovanni Battista	Italy
OLIVER	Isaac	France
OROZCO	Jose Clemente	Mexico
OSTADE	Adrien van	Holland
PALMER	Samuel	UK

SURNAME	CHRISTIAN NAMES	PLACE OF BIRTH
PIETTE	Ludovic	Brittany
RAMSAY	Allan	Scotland
RENOIR	Pierre-August	France
RIBERA	Jose de	Spain
RIGAUD	Hyacinthe	France
RIVERA	Diego	Mexico
RUBENS	Sir Peter Paul	Belgium
SEURAT	Georges	France
SIGNAC	Paul	France
SISLEY	Alfred	France
STUBBS	George	UK
TANGUY	Yves	France
TISSOT	James	France
TITIAN	Tiziano Vecellio	Italy
TUCKER	Albert	Australian
TURNER	Joseph Mallord William	UK
WARHOL	Andy	US
WEYDEN	Rogier van der	Belgium
WRIGHT	Joseph	UK

7

AERTSEN	Pieter	Holland
ALLSTON	Washington	US
AUDUBON	John James	West Indies
BABUREN	Dirck van	Holland
BAROCCI	Federico	Italy
BASSANO	Jacopo	Italy
BAZILLE	Frederic	France
BELLINI	Giovanni	Italy
BEYEREN	Abraham van	Holland
BONNARD	Pierre	France
BOUCHER	Francois	France
BROUWER	Adriaen	Belgium
BRUEGEL	Pieter the Elder	Belgium

SURNAME	CHRISTIAN NAMES	PLACE OF BIRTH
CABANEL	Alexandre	France
CASSATT	Mary	US
CENNINI	Cennino	Italy
CEZANNE	Paul	France
CHAGALL	Marc	Belarus
CHARDIN	Jean-Baptiste-Simeon	France
CHIRICO	Giorgio de	Greece
CIMABUE	Giovanni	Italy
CORNELL	Joseph	US
COURBET	Gustave	France
COUTURE	Thomas	France
CRANACH	Lucas (the Elder)	German
CROPSEY	Jasper	US
DAUMIER	Honore	France
DA VINCI	Leonardo	Italy
DELVAUX	Paul	Belgium
EL GRECO	Domenikos Theotokopoulos	Crete
FOUQUET	Jean	France
GAUGUIN	Eugene-Henri-Paul	France
GILBERT	Sir John	UK
GOZZOLI	Benozzo	Italy
HASSALL	John	UK
HERRERA	Francisco the Younger	Spain
HOBBEMA	Meindert	Holland
HOCKNEY	David	UK
HOGARTH	William	UK
HOKUSAI	Katsushika	Japan
HOLBEIN	Hans, the Younger	Germany
HOPPNER	John	UK
JOHNSON	Cornelius	UK
KNELLER	Sir Godfrey	Belgium
LA FOSSE	Charles de	France
LANCRET	Nicolas	France
LIMOSIN	Stefan	France
LINDSAY	Norman	Australia

SURNAME	CHRISTIAN NAMES	PLACE OF BIRTH
LORRAIN	Claude	France
MACLISE	Daniel	Ireland
MARTINI	Simone	Italy
MATISSE	Henri	France
MAUREAU	Alphonse	France
MEMLING/		
MEMLINC	Hans	Germany
MILLAIS	Sir John Everett	UK
MORANDI	Giorgio	Italy
MORISOT	Berthe	France
MORLAND	George	UK
MURILLO	Bartolome Esteban	Spain
O'KEEFFE	Georgia	US
ORCAGNA	Andrea	Italy
PASMORE	Victor	UK
PATINIR	Joachim	Belgium
PEVSNER	Antoine	Russia
PICABIA	Francis	France
PICASSO	Pablo	Spain
POLLOCK	Jackson	US
POUSSIN	Nicolas	France
PRUD'HON	Pierre Paul	France
RACKHAM	Arthur	UK
RAEBURN	Sir Henry	Scotland
RAPHAEL	(Raffaello Sanzio)	Italy
REDOUTE	Pierre-Joseph	Belgium
ROBERTS	Tom	UK
ROUAULT	Georges	France
RUBLEV	Andrei	Russia
SARGENT	John Singer	US
SCHIELE	Egon	Austria
SEGHERS	Hercules Pieterzoon	Holland
SHEPARD	Ernest Howard	US
SICKERT	Walter Richard	UK
SNYDERS	Frans	Belgium

SURNAME	CHRISTIAN NAMES	PLACE OF BIRTH
SOUTINE	Chaim	Lithuania
SPENCER	Sir Stanley	UK
TANNING	Dorothea	US
TENIERS	David, the Younger	Belgium
TENNIEL	Sir John	UK
TIBALDI	Pellegrino	Italy
TIEPOLO	Giovanni Battista	Italy
TREVINO	Jesse	Mexico
UCCELLO	Paolo	Italy
UTAMARO	Kitagawa	Japan
UTRILLO	Maurice	France
VERMEER	Jan	Holland
WATTEAU	Jean-Antoine	France
ZOFFANY	Johann	German
ZUCCARO	Federico	Italy
ZUCCARO	Taddeo	Italy

8

SURNAME	CHRISTIAN NAMES	PLACE OF BIRTH
ANGELICO	Fra	Italy
ANNIGONI	Pietro	Italy
AUERBACH	Frank	Germany
AVERCAMP	Hendrik	Holland
BECKMANN	Max	Germany
BOCCIONI	Umberto	Italy
BRONZINO	Agnolo	Italy
BRUEGHEL	Jan	Belgium
BRUEGHEL	Pieter, the Elder	Belgium
CARRACCI	Annibale	Italy
CASTAGNO	Andrea del	Italy
CHRISTUS	Petrus	Holland
CRIVELLI	Carlo	Italy
DAUBIGNY	Charles-Francois	France
DELAUNAY	Robert	France
DRYSDALE	Sir Russell	UK

SURNAME	CHRISTIAN NAMES	PLACE OF BIRTH
DUBUFFET	Jean	France
FABRIANO	Gentile da	Italy
GIORDANO	Luca	Italy
GOSSAERT	Jan	Belgium
GUERCINO	Giovanni	Italy
HAMILTON	Richard	UK
HIGHMORE	Joseph	UK
HILLIARD	Nicholas	UK
JONGKIND	Johan-Barthold	Holland
JORDAENS	Jacob	Belgium
KIRCHNER	Ernst Ludwig	Germany
LANDSEER	Charles	UK
LANDSEER	Sir Edwin	UK
LAWRENCE	Sir Thomas	UK
LORRAINE	Claude	France
MAGRITTE	Rene	Belgium
MALEVICH	Kazimir	Ukraine
MANTEGNA	Andrea	Italy
MEEGEREN	Han van	Holland
MONDRIAN	Piet	Holland
MULREADY	William	Ireland
MUNNINGS	Sir Alfred	UK
PERCEVAL	John	Australia
PIRANESI	Giovanni Battista	Italy
PISSARRO	Camille	West Indies
PONTORMO	Jacopo da	Italy
REYNOLDS	Sir Joshua	UK
ROSSETTI	Dante Gabriel	UK
ROUSSEAU	Henri	France
ROUSSEAU	Theodore	France
RUISDAEL	Jacob van	Holland
SASSETTA	Stefano di Giovanni	Italy
SEVERINI	Gino	Italy
STREETON	Sir Arthur	Australia
TERBORCH	Gerard	Holland

SURNAME	CHRISTIAN NAMES	PLACE OF BIRTH
VASARELY	Victor	Hungary
VERONESE	Paolo	Italy
VLAMINCK	Maurice de	France
VUILLARD	Edouard	France
WHISTLER	James Abbott McNeill	US
WHISTLER	Rex	UK
ZURBARAN	Francisco de	Spain

9

ALTDORFER	Albrecht	Germany
BONINGTON	Richard Parkes	UK
BURGKMAIR	Hans the Elder	Germany
CANALETTO	Antonio	Italy
CARPACCIO	Vittore	Italy
CAVALLINI	Pietro	Italy
CONSTABLE	John	UK
CORNELIUS	Peter von	Germany
CORREGGIO	Antonio Allegri	Italy
DE KOONING	Willem	Holland
DELACROIX	Eugene	France
DELAROCHE	Paul	France
DE MESSINA	Antonello	Italy
DESPORTES	Alexandre-Francois	France
ELSHEIMER	Adam	Germany
FABRITIUS	Carel	Holland
FEININGER	Lyonel	US
FRAGONARD	Jean-Honore	France
FRIEDRICH	Caspar David	Germany
GERICAULT	Theodore	France
GONCALVES	Nuno	Portugal
GREENAWAY	Kate	UK
GRUNEWALD	Matthias	Germany
HIROSHIGE	Ando Tokitaro	Japan
HONTHORST	Gerard van	Holland

SURNAME	CHRISTIAN NAMES	PLACE OF BIRTH
JAWLENSKY	Alexej von	Russia
KANDINSKY	Wassily	Russia
KAUFFMANN	Angelica	Switzerland
KOKOSCHKA	Oskar	Austria
LISSITZKY	El	Russia
NAMATJIRA	Albert	Australia
NICHOLSON	Ben	UK
PARTRIDGE	Nehemiah	US
PISANELLO	Antonio Pisano	Italy
REMBRANDT	Rembrandt Harmenszoon van Rijn	Holland
SIQUEIROS	David Alfaro	Mexico
THORNHILL	Sir James	UK
VELAZQUEZ	Diego Rodriguez de Silva	Spain
WOUWERMAN	Philips	Holland

10

ALMA-TADEMA	Sir Lawrence	Holland
ALTICHIERO	de Zevio	Italy
ARCHIPENKO	Alexander	Ukraine
ARCIMBOLDO	Giuseppe	Italy
BERRUGUETE	Alonso	Spain
BERRUGUETE	Pedro	Spain
BOTTICELLI	Sandro	Italy
BOUGUEREAU	Adolphe-William	France
BROEDERLAM	Melchior	Holland
BURNE-JONES	Sir Edward Coley	UK
CARAVAGGIO	Michelangelo Merisi da	Italy
CHAMPAIGNE	Philippe de	Belgium
CRUIKSHANK	George	UK
GIACOMETTI	Alberto	Switzerland
GUILLAUMIN	Jean-Baptiste Armand	France
LORENZETTI	Ambrogio	Italy
MEISSONIER	Jean-Louis-Ernest	France

SURNAME	CHRISTIAN NAMES	PLACE OF BIRTH
MODIGLIANI	Amedeo	Italy
MOHOLY-NAGY	Laszlo	Hungary
MOTHERWELL	Robert	US
POLLAIUOLO	Antonio	Italy
POLLAIUOLO	Piero	Italy
SCHWITTERS	Kurt	Germany
SIGNORELLI	Luca	Italy
SUTHERLAND	Graham Vivian	UK
TINTORETTO	Jacopo Robusti	Italy
VAN DE VELDE	Henri	Belgium
VERROCCHIO	Andrea del	Italy
WASSENHOVE	Joos van	Holland
WATERHOUSE	John William	Italy
WINSTANLEY	William	UK
ZUCCARELLI	Francesco	Italy

11

BARTOLOMMEO	Fra	Italy
BRACQUEMOND	Marie	France
CAILLEBOTTE	Gustave	France
CHODOWIECKI	Daniel Nikolaus	Poland
DOMENICHINO	Domenico Zampieri	Italy
LARGILLIERE	Nicolas de	France
TERBRUGGHEN	Hendrick	Holland

12

BALDUNG GRIEN	Hans	Germany
FANTIN-LATOUR	Henri	France
GAINSBOROUGH	Thomas	UK
GIULIO ROMANO	Giulio Pippi	Italy
LICHTENSTEIN	Roy	US

SURNAME	CHRISTIAN NAMES	PLACE OF BIRTH
MICHELANGELO	Buonarroti	Italy
PALMA VECCHIO	Jacopo	Italy
PARMIGIANINO	Francesco Mazzola	Italy
PINTURICCHIO	Bernadino di Betto	Italy
RAUSCHENBERG	Robert	Italy
WINTERHALTER	Franz Xavier	Germany

13

LORENZO MONACO		Italy
PIERO DI COSIMO		Italy

15

TOULOUSE-LAUTREC	Henri de	France

16

MASTER OF FLEMALLE (Robert Campin)		Belgium
PUVIS DE CHAVANNES	Pierre	France

17

GENTILE DA FABRIANO		Italy
DOMENICO VENEZIANO		Italy

18

PIERO DELLA FRANCESCA		Italy

AUTHORS
Before AD 1000

4
BEDE, the Venerable
BION
CATO, Dionysius
LI PO
LIVY (Titus Livius)
OVID
TU FU

5
AESOP
ANTAR
BHASA
LUCAN
NEPOS, Cornelius
PLATO
PLINY
VARRO, Marcus

6
ALCUIN
ALFRED the Great
CAESAR, Julius
CELSUS, Aulus
CICERO, Marcus
ENNIUS, Quintus
GALLUS, Gaius
LUCIAN
PINDAR
SAPPHO
VIRGIL
   (Publius Vergilius
   Maro)

7
AELFRIC
AKAHITO, Yamabe no
ALCAEUS
ANEIRIN or ANEURIN
CAEDMON
COLUMBA, St
CORINNA
GELLIUS, Aulus
MARTIAL (Marcus
   Valerius Martialis)
PLAUTUS, Titus Maccius
TACITUS
TERENCE
TULLIUS

8
ANACREON
APULEIUS
AURELIUS, Marcus
AUSONIUS, Decimus
   Magnus
BOETHIUS, Anicius
   Manlius
BONIFACE, St
   (WYNFRITH)
CATULLUS, Gaius
   Valerius
CLAUDIAN
   (Claudianus)
COLUMBAN, St
CRATINUS
DIOGENES, Laertuis

8 FLODOARD of Rheims
MENANDER
PHAEDRUS
PLUTARCH
TALIESIN
THEOGNIS
TYRTAEUS
WULFSTAN, St
WYNFRITH
XENOPHON

9 AESCHYLUS
ATHENAEUS
AUGUSTINE of Hippo
DIONYSIUS of
   Halicarnassus
EURIPIDES
LUCRETIUS
MARTIALIS, Marcus
   Valerius
SOPHOCLES
SUETONIUS (Gaius
   Suetonius
   Tranquillus)
TUDUR ALED

10
APOLLONIUS
COLUMBANUS, St
PROPERTIUS, Sextus
THEOCRITUS
THUCYDIDES

11
BACCHYLIDES
BHARTRIHARI
CALLIMACHUS

12
ARISTOPHANES

15
SIMONIDES OF CEOS

16 LIVIUS ANDRONICUS

17 APOLLONIUS
   RHODIUS
CALPURNIUS
   SICULUS, Titus

18 CLAUDIUS
   CLAUDIANUS
   (Claudian)

AUTHORS
AD 1000–1500

3 MAP, Walter

4 FOLZ, Hans
MARC, Ausias
RUIZ, Juan
TODI, Jacopone da
WACE, Robert

5 BRANT, Sebastian
DANTE
GOWER, John
LILLO, George
TASSO, Bernardo

6 CAXTON, William
DANIEL, Arnaut
DE MENA, Juan
DUNBAR, William
LA SALE (OR SALLE),
    Antoine de
LATINI, Brunetto
MALORY, Sir Thomas
VILLON, Francois

7 ABUL-ALA, Ahmed
BARBOUR, John
CHAUCER, Geoffrey
DE PISAN, Christine
ECKHART, Johannes
    (MEISTER)

GUILHEM, Duke of
    Aquitaine
LAYAMON
LYDGATE, John
WALTHER von der
    Vogelweide
WOLFRAM von
    Eschenbach

8 ABU NUWAS
BERTRAND, de Born
BOAIARDO, Matteo
CHARTIER, Alain
CHRETIEN
FIRDAUSI (a.k.a.
    Abu Ol'Qasem
    Mansur)
LANGLAND, William
PETRARCH, Francesco
SORDELLO
TULSIDAS

9 BOCCACCIO, Giovanni
DESCHAMPS, Eustache
GACE BRULE
GOTTFRIED von
    Strassburg
LAMPRECHT, Pfaffe
LANGHORNE, John
SACCHETTI, Franco
STURLUSON, Snorri

10 ABD-UL-LATIF
BLIND HARRY
CAVALCANTI, Guido
COLIN MUSET
DE SAN PEDRO, Diego
GAWAIN POET, The
MANDEVILLE, Sir John
TANNHAUSER

11 OMAR KHAYYAM

12 DAFYDD NANMOR
RUDOLF VON EMS

13 GERALD OF WALES

14 CONON DE BETHUNE
DAFYDD AP GWILYM
DANTE ALIGHIERI
GUIRAUT RIQUIER

15 GUITTONE D'AREZZO
JOHN OF SALISBURY
THOMAS THE RHYMER

16 CHRETIEN DE TROYES
CHRISTINA DE PISAN
QUESNES DE BETHUNE

18 GIRALDUS
CAMBRENSIS

19 CYNDDELW
BRYDYDD MAWR
WILLIAM OF
MALMESBURY

AUTHORS
1500–1800

3 DAY, John
DAY, Thomas
GAY, John

4 BAGE, Robert
BAIF, Jean de
BALE, John
BEER, Johann
BEHN, Aphra
CRUZ, Ramon de la
CRUZ, Sor Juana Ines de la
DUCK, Stephen
FORD, John
FOXE, John
GAMA, Jose Basilio da
GRAY, Thomas
LOBO, Francisco
LYLY, John
POPE, Alexander
ROWE, Nicholas
SADE, Marquis de
TATE, Nahum
VEGA, Lope de
VERE, Edward de (Earl of Oxford)
WYSS, Johann

5 AMORY, Thomas
BANKS, John

BASHO (pen name of Matsuo Munefusa)
BERNI, Francesco
BLAIR, Robert
BLAKE, William
BOHME, Jakob
BOYLE, John (5th Earl of Cork)
BROME, Richard
BROWN, Thomas
BURKE, Edmund
BURNS, Robert
CAREW, Thomas
CHUTE, Anthony
DALIN, Olof von
DEFOE, Daniel
DONNE, John
GARTH, Sir Samuel
GOZZI, Carlo (Count)
LEWIS, M(atthew) G(regory)
LLWDD, Morgan
NASHE, Thomas
OTWAY, Thomas
PAINE, Tom
PEELE, George
PEPYS, Samuel
SACHS, Hans
SMART, Christopher
STAEL, Madame de
SWIFT, Jonathan

5 TASSO, Torquato
UDALL, Nicholas
WYATT, Sir Thomas

6 AXULAR, Pedro de
BARNES, Barnabe
BOCAGE, Manoel
BRETON, Nicholas
BROOKE, Henry
BROWNE, William
BUNYAN, John
BURNEY, Fanny (or
    Frances)
BURTON, Robert
COTTON, Charles
COWLEY, Abraham
COWPER, William
CRABBE, George
CRETIN, Guillaume
DANIEL, Samuel
DEKKER, Thomas
DENHAM, Sir John
DENNIS, John
DIAPER, William
DRYDEN, John
D'URFEY, Thomas
EVELYN, John
FAVART, Charles
GODWIN, Francis
GODWIN, William
GOETHE, Johann
    Wolfgang von
GREENE, Robert
GREVIN, Jacques
LACLOS, Pierre
LAGUNA, Andres
LE SAGE, Alain Rene

MANLEY, Mary
MILTON, John
RACINE, Jean
RAMSAY, Allan
SAVAGE, Richard
SIDNEY, Sir Philip
STEELE, Richard
STERNE, Laurence
WALLER, Edmund
WALTON, Izaak

7 ALFIERI, Vittorio
ARETINO, Pietro
ARIOSTO, Ludovico
BAILLIE, Grizel, Lady
BARCLAY, Alexander
BOILEAU, Nicholas
BOSWELL, James
BUDGELL, Eustace
CAMOENS (or
    CAMOES), Luis de
CAMPION, Thomas
CHAPMAN, George
CHETTLE, Henry
CLELAND, John
COLLINS, William
CRASHAW, Richard
DAMPIER, William
DA PONTE, Lorenzo
    (pen name of
    Emanuele
    Conegliano)
DELILLE, Jacques
DELONEY, Thomas
DIDEROT, Denis
DODSLEY, Robert
DRAYTON, Michael

7 EGERTON, Sarah
ERASMUS, Desiderius
FENELON, Francois
FLEMING, Paul
GARNIER, Robert
GELLERT, Christian
GESSNER, Salomon
GIRALDI, Giambattista
GOLDONI, Carlo
GONZAGA, Tomas
LA HARPE, Jean de
LESSING, Gotthold
MARLOWE, Christopher
MARSTON, John
MARVELL, Andrew
MOLIERE (pen name of
  Jean Poquelin)
MONTAGU, Lady Mary
  Wortley
PURCHAS, Samuel
QUARLES, Francis
RIBEIRO, Bernardin
RONSARD, Pierre de
SHIRLEY, James
SKELTON, John
SPENSER, Edmund
THOMSON, James
VAUGHAN, Henry
WALPOLE, Horace (Earl
  of Orford)
WEBSTER, John

8 BAGGESEN, Jens
BALBUENA, Bernardo de
BANDELLO, Matteo
BEAUMONT, Francis
BECKFORD, William

BRADFORD, William
BUCHANAN, George
CALDERON de la
  Barca, Pedro
CONGREVE, William
DANCOURT, Florent
D'AUBIGNE, Theodore
DAVENANT, Sir William
DRUMMOND, William
ETHEREGE, Sir George
FALCONER, William
FANSHAWE, Sir
  Richard
FARQUHAR, George
FIELDING, Henry
FIELDING, Sarah
FLETCHER, Giles
FLETCHER, John
FLETCHER, Phineas
FRANKLIN, Benjamin
GREVILLE, Sir Fulke
GRYPHIUS, Andreas
LOVELACE, Richard
MARIVAUX, Pierre de
PERRAULT, Charles
RABELAIS, Francois
ROUSSEAU, Jean
  Jacques
SCHILLER, Johann
  Christoph Friedrich von
SHADWELL, Thomas
SHERIDAN, Richard
  Brinsley
SMOLLETT, Tobias
TOURNEUR, Cyril
TRAHERNE, Thomas
VANBRUGH, Sir John

8
VILLIERS, George (Duke of Buckingham)
VOLTAIRE (pen name of Francois Marie Arouet)

9
BELLENDEN (or Ballantyne), John
CENTLIVRE, Susannah
CERVANTES, Miguel de
CHUDLEIGH, Lady Mary
CHURCHILL, Charles
CLEVELAND, John
CORNEILLE, Pierre
COVERDALE, Miles
CREBILLON, Claude
CREBILLON, Prosper
DECHEPARE, Bernard
DELLA CASA, Giovanni
DESMARETS, Jean
EDGEWORTH, Maria
FERGUSSON, Robert
FRISCHLIN, Phillipp
GASCOIGNE, George
GOLDSMITH, Oliver
GRINGOIRE, Pierre
LA BRUYERE, Jean de
LA FAYETTE, Marie, Comtesse de
LOMONOSOV, Mikhail
MASSINGER, Philip
MIDDLETON, Thomas
MONTAIGNE, Michel de
RADCLIFFE, Ann
ROCHESTER, John Wilmot, Lord

SACKVILLE, Thomas
SOUTHWELL, Robert

10
BRADSTREET, Anne
CASTILLEJO, Cristobal de
CHATTERTON, Thomas
CHURCHYARD, Thomas
DELLA VALLE, Federico
DESMASURES, Louis
DESTOUCHES, Philippe
FONTENELLE, Bernard
LA FONTAINE, Jean de
LUIS DE LEON, Fray
RICHARDSON, Samuel

11
MACHIAVELLI, Niccolo
MONTESQUIEU, Charles, Baron de
MUNCHHAUSEN, Karl, Baron von
SHAKESPEARE, William

12
BEAUMARCHAIS, Pierre
BICKERSTAFF, Isaac
BRACKENRIDGE, Hugh Henry

14
VELES DE GUEVARA, Luis

15
DIAZ DEL CASTILLO, Bernal
LA ROCHEFOUCAULD, Francois (Duc de)
TRISTAN L'HERMITE

16 CYRANO DE
  BERGERAC, Savinien
GONZALEZ DE
  ESLAVA, Fernan
QUEVEDO, Y
  VILLEGAS, Francisco

17 CERVANTES SAAVEDRA,
  Miguel de
DE ZAYAS Y
  SOTOMAYOR, Maria

19 MARGARET OF
  ANGOULEME

AUTHORS
1800–1900

3 POE, Edgar Allan

4 BAHR, Hermann
BANG, Hermann
   Joachim
BAUM, L(yman) Frank
DALY, Thomas Augustin
DANA, Richard Henry
DYER, Sir Edward
EGAN, Pierce
FORD, Richard
GALT, John
LAMB, Charles
LANG, Andrew
LEAR, Edward
LOTI, Pierre
SAKI (pen name of
   H. H. Munro)
SALA, George
SAND, George (pen
   name of Amantine
   Dupin)
WOOD, Mrs Henry
   (Ellen Price)
ZOLA, Emile

5 BELLO, Andres
BLUNT, Wilfrid
BOITO, Arrigo
BROWN, William Wells

BYRON, George
   Gordon (Lord Byron)
CAINE, Hall
CAMPO, Estanislao del
CLARE, John
CRAIK, Dinah
CRANE, Stephen
DAVIS, Rebecca
   Harding
DINIS, Julio (pen name
   of Joaquin Coelho)
DOYLE, Arthur Conan
DUMAS, Alexandre
EEDEN, Frederick van
ELIOT, George (pen
   name of Marian Evans)
EVANS, Augusta
FREUD, Sigmund
GAUNT, Mary
GLEIG, George Robert
GOGOL, Nikolai
GORKY, Maxim (pen
   name of Aleksei
   Peshkov)
GOSSE, Sir Edmund
GRIMM, Jacob
GRIMM, Wilhelm
LEVER, Charles
LOVER, Samuel
MACHA, Karel
MOORE, George

5 MUNRO, Hector Hugh
(pen name Saki)
OUIDA (pen name of
Marie de la Ramee)
PATER, Walter
READE, Charles
RILKE, Rainer Maria
ROLFE, Frederick (pen
name Baron Corvo)
SCOTT, Sir Walter
SMITH, Sydney
SYNGE, John Millington
TWAIN, Mark
(pen name of Samuel
Clemens)
VERNE, Jules
VIGNY, Alfred,
Comte de
WILDE, Oscar
YEATS, W(illiam) B(utler)

6 ARNOLD, Matthew
AUSTEN, Jane
AUSTIN, Alfred
BALZAC, Honoræ de
BARHAM (Ingoldsby),
Richard
BARNES, William
BARRIE, J. M. (Sir
James)
BARTON, Bernard
BENSON, Arthur
Christopher
BESANT, Sir Walter
BIERCE, Ambrose
BORROW, George
BRAZIL, Angela

BRONTE, Anne (pen
name Acton Bell)
BRONTE, Charlotte
(pen name Currer Bell)
BRONTE, Emily (pen
name of Ellis Bell)
BURTON, Sir Richard
BUTLER, Samuel
CAVAFY, Constantine
(pen name of
Konstantinos Kavafis)
CLOUGH, Arthur Hugh
CONRAD, Joseph
(pen name of Jozef
Korzeniowski)
COOPER, James
Fenimore
DARLEY, George
DAUDET, Alphonse
DAUDET, Leon
DE VERE, Aubrey
DOBELL, Sydney
DOWSON, Ernest
FARRAR, Frederic
William (Dean)
FIKRET, Tevfik
FRANCE, Anatole
(pen name of Anatole
Thibault)
GEIBEL, Emanuel von
GEIJER, Erik
GIRAUD, Albert
GIUSTI, Giuseppe
GOODGE, W(illiam)
T(homas)
GORDON, Adam
GORTER, Herman

6
GRAVES, Robert
LANDOR, Walter
Savage
LAWSON, Henry
LE FANU, Sheridan
LESKOV, Nicolai
LONDON, Jack
MILLER, Hugh
MORRIS, William
MUSSET, Alfred de
NERUDA, Jan
NERVAL, Gerard de
(pen name of Gerard
Labrunie)
PINERO, Sir Arthur Wing
PROUST, Marcel
QUINET, Edgar
REUTER, Fritz
ROGERS, Samuel
RUSKIN, John
SARDOU, Victorien
STOKER, Bram

7
AHLGREN, Ernst
(pen name of Victoria
Benedictson)
AKSAKOV, Sergei
Timofeyevich
BEDDOES, Thomas
BELASCO, David
BENNETT, (Enoch)
Arnold
BERGSON, Henri
BRACKEN, Thomas
BRADLEY, Edward (pen
name Cuthbert Bede)
BRIDGES, Robert

BUCHNER, Georg
BURNETT, Frances
Hodgson
CARLYLE, Thomas
CARROLL, Lewis
(pen name of Charles
Dodgson)
CHEKHOV, Anton
CHENIER, Andre
COBBETT, William
COLLINS, (William)
Wilkie
CORELLI, Marie
(pen name of Mary
Mackay)
DICKENS, Charles
(John Huffam)
DOUGHTY, Charles
EMERSON, Ralph Waldo
FERRIER, Susan
FEYDEAU, Georges
FIBIGER, Mathilde
FLECKER, James Elroy
FREYTAG, Gustav
FRODING, Gustaf
GARSHIN, Vsevolod
GASKELL, Elizabeth
GAUTIER, Theophile
GEZELLE, Guido
GIACOSA, Giuseppe
GILBERT, Sir W(illiam)
S(chwenck)
GISSING, George
Robert
GOZZANO, Guido
MARRYAT, Frederick
MERIMEE, Prosper

7 PATMORE, Coventry
PUSHKIN, Alexander
RIMBAUD, Arthur
ROSTAND, Edmond
SHELLEY, Mary
SOUTHEY, Robert
SURTEES, R(obert) S(mith)
THOREAU, Henry
TOLSTOY, Leo, Count
WHITMAN, Walt

8 A BECKETT, Gilbert
ANNENSKY, Innocenty
ATTERBOM, Per
AUERBACH, Berthold
(pen name of Moses
Auerbacher)
BANVILLE, Thæodore de
BERANGER, Pierre
BERTRAND, Louis
BJORNSON, Bjornstjerne
BROWNING, Elizabeth
(Barrett)
BROWNING, Robert
BUCHANAN, Robert
CARLETON, William
CHATRIAN, Alexandre
CLARETIE, Jules
(pen name of Arsene
Arnaud)
CONSTANT, Benjamin
COUVREUR, Jessie
CRAWFORD, F(rancis)
Marion
DAVIDSON, John
DE AMICIS, Edmondo
DISRAELI, Benjamin

DISRAELI, Isaac
DONNELLY, Ignatius
DOUGLASS, Frederick
DRACHMAN, Holger
ERCKMANN, Emile
ESQUIROS, Henri
FITZBALL, Edward
FLAUBERT, Gustave
GABORIAU, Emile
GONCOURT, Jules de
LAFORGUE, Jules
LAGERLOF, Selma
LEOPARDI, Giacomo
LOCKHART, John
MACAULAY, Thomas
Babington (Lord)
MALLARME, Stephane
MELVILLE, Herman
MEREDITH, George
OLIPIIANT, Margaret
PALGRAVE, Francis
ROSSETTI, Christina
SAAVEDRA, Angel de
STENDIIAL (pen name
of Marie Henri Beyle)
TENNYSON, Alfred, Lord
TRESSELL, Robert
TROLLOPE, Anthony
TURGENEV, Ivan
VERLAINE, Paul
WEDEKIND, Frank

9 AARESTRUP, Emil
AINSWORTH, William
Harrison
BLACKMORE, Richard
Doddridge

9
COLERIDGE, Hartley
COLERIDGE, Samuel
Taylor
D'ANNUNZIO, Gabriele
DE QUINCEY, Thomas
DICKINSON, Emily
DU MAURIER, George
FINDLATER, Jane
FINDLATER, Mary
FOGAZZARO, Antonio
GROSSMITH, George
GUERRAZZI, Francesco
LAMARTINE, Alphonse
LERMONTOV, Mikhail
MARTINEAU, Harriet
NIETZSCHE, Friedrich
SCHREINER, Olive
STEVENSON, Robert
Louis
SWINBURNE, Algernon
THACKERAY, William

10
BALLANTYNE, Robert
Michael
BARATYNSKI, Evgeny
BAUDELAIRE, Charles
BOLDREWOOD, Rolf
(pen name of Thomas
Browne)
BOUCICAULT, Dion
CONSCIENCE, Hendrik
FITZGERALD, Edward
LONGFELLOW, Henry
Wadsworth
MAUPASSANT, Guy de
SAINT-BEUVE, Charles
Augustin

STRINDBERG, August
WORDSWORTH,
Dorothy
WORDSWORTH,
William

11
CARMEN SYLVA
(pen name of Queen
Elisabeth of Romania)
DOSTOYEVSKY, Fyodor
EICHENDORFF, Joseph
ETCHAHOUNIA, Pierre
GRILLPARZER, Franz

12
BULWER-LYTTON,
Edward (Lord Lytton)
ECA DE QUEIROZ, Jose
Maria de
GIL Y CARRASCO,
Enrique
SCHOPENHAUER, Arthur

13
ALAIN-FOURNIER (pen
name of Henri-Alban
Fournier)
CHATEAUBRIAND,
Francois (Vicomte de)

14
LECONTE DE LISLE,
Charles
SULLY-PRUDHOMME
(pen name for Rene
Prudhomme)

15
EBNER-ESCHENBACH,
Marie
GARCIA GUTIERREZ,
Antonio

AUTHORS
1900–2005

2 MO, Timothy

3 ABE, Kobo
AUB, Max
ECO, Umberto
FRY, Christopher
KEE, Robert
KUO, Mo-jo
LEE, (Nelle) Harper
LEE, Laurie
NIN, Anais
PYM, Barbara
TEY, Josephine

4 AMIS, Kingsley
AMIS, Martin
ARLT, Roberto
BECK, Beatrix
BELL, Julian
BELY, Andrey
BOLL, Heinrich
BOLT, Robert
BOND, Edward
BOYD, William
BOYE, Karin
BUCK, Pearl
BUZO, Alexander
CARR, J(ames) L(loyd)
CARY, (Arthur) Joyce Lunel
CELA, Camilo
CHAR, Rene

DAHL, Roald
DANE, Clemence
(pen name of
Winifred Ashton)
DARK, Eleanor
DELL, Ethel Mary
DERY, Tery
EDEN, Dorothy
FAIZ, Faiz Ahmed
FINE, Anne
FORD, Ford Madox
(pen name of Ford
Hermann Hueffer)
GALE, Zona
GHIL, Rene
GIDE, Andre
GOLD, Michael
GOLL, Yvan
GRAU, Jacinto
GRAY, Alisdair
GRAY, Simon
GREY, Zane
GUNN, Thom(son)
HALL, Willis
HARE, David
HART, Moss
HILL, Susan
HOEL, Sigurd
HOLT, Victoria (pen
name of Eleanor
Hibbert)

4
JUNG, Carl Gustav
KATZ, Steve
KAYE, M(ary) M(argaret)
KING, Stephen
LEVI, Carlo
LEVI, Primo
LOOS, Anita
MANN, Thomas
NASH, Ogden
OBEY, Andre
OKRI, Ben
OWEN, Wilfred
RHYS, Jean (pen name
  of Gwen Williams)
ROTH, Philip
SETH, Vikram
SHAW, George Bernard
SNOW, C(harles) P(ercy)
VINE, Barbara (pen name
  of Ruth Rendell)
WAIN, John
WEST, Dame Rebecca

5
ABBAS, Ahmad
ABELL, Kjeld
ABISH, Walter
ADAMS, Douglas
ADAMS, Richard
AIKEN, Joan
ALBEE, Edward
ALLEN, Woody
  (pen name of Allen
  Konigsberg)
AMADO, Jorge
ANAND, Mulk Raj
ANDAY, Melih Cedvat
ARDEN, John

AYALA, Francisco
BAKER, Elliott
BANKS, Lynne Reid
BANKS, Iain
BATES, H(erbert) E(rnest)
BEHAN, Brendan
BENDA, Julien
BERRY, Wendell
BERTO, Guiseppe
BLOOM, Ursula
BLUME, Judy
BOOTH, Martin
BRAGG, Melvyn
BRAND, Max (pen
  name of Frederich
  Schiller Faust)
BROCH, Hermann
BROWN, Dan
BROWN, George
  Mackay
BUBER, Martin
BUNIN, Ivan
BYATT, A(ntonia) S(usan)
CAMUS, Albert
CAPEK, Karel
CAREY, Peter
CAUTE, David
CELAN, Paul (pen name
  of Paul Ancel)
COHAN, George
  M(ichael)
COLUM, Padraic
CRANE, Hart
DABIT, Eugene
DAVIE, Donald
DAVIS, Owen
DAZAI, Osamu

5

DESSI, Guiseppe
DISCH, Thomas
DIXON, Thomas
DOYLE, Roddy
DUFFY, Carol Ann
EDGAR, David
EKMAN, Kerstin
ELIOT, T(homas) S(tearns)
ELLIS, Alice Thomas
ESSON, Louis
EWART, Gavin
FEDIN, Konstantine
FRAME, Ronald
FRANK, Anne
FRAYN, Michael
FROST, Robert
GADDA, Carlo Emilio
GATTI, Armand
GATTO, Alfonso
GAVIN, Catherine
GENET, Jean
GHOSE, Zulfikar
GIONO, Jean
GLOAG, Julian
GRACQ, Julien
GRASS, Gunther
GRIEG, Nordahl
HALAS, Frantisek
HALEY, Alex
HAVEL, Vaclav
HENRY, O. (pen name of
   William Porter)
HESSE, Hermann
HEYER, Georgette
HIMES, Chester
HINES, Barry
HOYLE, Fred

JACOB, Naomi
JAMES, P(hyllis) D(orothy)
JOHNS, W(illiam) E(arl)
JOYCE, James
KAFKA, Franz
KEANE, Molly
KRIGE, Uys
LASKI, Marghanita
LAVIN, Mary
LEWIS, C(live) S(taples)
LEWIS, (Percy) Wyndham
LODGE, David
LOFTS, Norah
LOWRY, Malcolm
MAMET, David
MARSH, Ngaio
MILNE, A(lan)
   A(lexander)
MURRY, John Middleton
NOWRY, Laurence
NOYES, Alfred
PEAKE, Mervyn
PLATH, Sylvia
POUND, Ezra
POWYS, John Cowper
QUEEN, Ellery (pen
   name of Frederic
   Dannay
RABAN, Jonathan
RAMOS, Graciliano
RAVEN, Simon
REYES, Alfonso
SETON, Anya
SHUTE, Nevil
SMITH, Dodie
SMITH, Stevie (pen name
   of Florence Smith)

5
SMITH, Zadie
SPARK, Muriel
STARK, Dame Freya
STEIN, Gertrude
SWIFT, Graham
UTLEY, Alison
VIDAL, Gore
WAUGH, Alec
WAUGH, Auberon
WAUGH, Evelyn
WELLS, H(erbert)
  G(eorge)
WHITE, Antonia (pen
  name of Eirene Botting)
WHITE, Edmund
WHITE, Patrick
WHITE, T(erence)
  H(anbury)
WOLFE, Thomas Clayton
WOLFE, Tom
WOOLF, Virginia
YATES, Dornford (pen
  name of Cecil Mercer)
YOUNG, Andrew
YOUNG, Francis Brett

6
ABBOTT, George Francis
ACHEBE, Chinua
  (originally Albert)
ADCOCK, Fleur
AI QING
ALDISS, Brian
AMBLER, Eric
AMICIS, Edmondo de
AMORIM, Enrique
ARANHA, Jose Pereira
  da Graca

ARCHER, Jeffrey
ARENAS, Reinaldo
ARTAUD, Antonin
ASIMOV, Isaac
ASTLEY, Thea
ATWOOD, Margaret
AUDEN, W(ystan)
  H(ugh)
AZUELA, Mariano
BAGLEY, Desmond
BAILEY, Paul
BARKER, Howard
BARNES, Julian
BAWDEN, Nina
BEAGLE, Peter
BELLOC, Hilaire
BELLOW, Saul
BENSON, E(dward)
  F(rederic)
BERGER, John
BIALIK, Chaim
BINCHY, Maeve
BINYON, Laurence
BLIXEN, Karen (pen
  name Isak Dinesen)
BLYTON, Enid
BORGES, Jorge
BOULLE, Pierre
BRAINE, John
BRECHT, Bertolt
BRETON, Andre
BROOKE, Rupert
BROPHY, Brigid
BUCHAN, John
CAPOTE, Truman
CARTER, Angela
CARTER, Martin

6 CELINE, Louis-
Ferdinand
CHURCH, Richard
CLARKE, Arthur
C(harles)
CLEARY, Jon
COOPER, Jilly
COUZYN, Jeni
COWARD, Noel
CROFTS, Freeman Wills
CRONIN, A(rchibald)
J(oseph)
DALLEY, John
DAVICO, Oskar
DAVIES, Rhys
DAVIES, (William)
Robertson
DAVIES, W(illiam)
H(enry)
DESANI, Govindas
DOBLIN, Alfred
DUGGAN, Alfred
ELYTIS, Odysseus
EMPSON, Sir William
FALLON, Peter
FARGUE, Leon-Paul
FARNOL, John Jeffery
FAUSET, Jessie
FERMOR, Patrick Leigh
FIDLER, Kathleen
FINLAY, Ian Hamilton
FISHER, Roy
FOWLES, John
FRASER, George
MacDonald
FRISCH, Max
FUGARD, Athol

FULLER, Roy
GAMBOA, Federico
GARDAM, Jane
GARNER, Alan
GELBER, Jack
GIBBON, Lewis Grassic
GIBRAN, Khalil
GIJSEN, Marnix (pen
name of Jan-Albert
Goris)
GODDEN, Rumer
GOUDGE, Elizabeth
GRAHAM, W(illiam)
S(ydney)
GRAVES, Robert
GREENE, (Henry)
Graham
GURNEY, Ivor
GUZMAN, Martin
HADDON, Mark
HAILEY, Arthur
HASAYN, Taha
HEANEY, Seamus
HELLER, Joseph
HILTON, James
HOLTBY, Winifred
HOWARD, Elizabeth
Jane
HUGHES, Richard
HUXLEY, Aldous
HUXLEY, Elspeth
KAISER, Georg
KELMAN, James
KUNERT, Gunter
LA COUR, Paul
L'AMOUR, Louis
LARKIN, Philip

6 LAWLER, Ray
LEAVIS, F(rank)
  R(aymond)
LEAVIS, Q(ueenie)
  D(orothy)
LE GUIN, Ursula
LIVELY, Penelope
LOWELL, Robert
LUDLUM, Robert
MACHEN, Arthur
MAILER, Norman
MALOUF, David
MAO DUN
MASSIE, Allan
MAUPIN, Armistead
MERCER, David
MILLER, Arthur
MILLER, Henry
MOTION, Andrew
NERUDA, Pablo
  (originally known as
  Neftali Ricardo Reyes
  Basoalto)
O'BRIEN, Edna
O'BRIEN, Flann (pen
  name of Brian O'Nolan)
O'BRIEN, Kate
O'CASEY, Sean
O'NEILL, Eugene
ORWELL, George
PARKER, Dorothy
PATTEN, Brian
PINTER, Harold
PLATER, Alan
POTTER, Beatrix
POTTER, Dennis
POWELL, Anthony

RITSOS, Iannis
RIVERA, Jose
RUNYON, Damon
SABATO, Ernesto
SAPPER (pen name of
  Herman McNeile)
SARTRE, Jean-Paul
SAYERS, Dorothy L(eigh)
SENDAK, Maurice
SEWELL, Anna
SHARPE, Tom
SINGER, Isaac Bashevis
STOREY, David
TAGORE, Rabindranath
THOMAS, Edward
THOMAS, Leslie
THOMAS, R(onald)
  S(tuart)
TREASE, Geoffrey
TREVOR, William
UPDIKE, John
VALERY, Paul
WELDON, Fay
WESKER, Arnold
WESLEY, Mary (pen
  name of Aline Farmer)
WILDER, Thornton
WILSON, Sir Angus
WILSON, Colin
WILSON, Edmund
WRIGHT, Judith

7 AAKJAER, Jeppe
ACKROYD, Peter
ADDISON, Joseph
ALBERTI, Rafael
ALEGRIA, Ciro

7 ALLENDE, Isabel
ALVAREZ, A(lfred)
ANOUILH, Jean
ARGHEZI, Tudor
(pen name of Ion
Theodorescu)
ARRABAL, Fernando
ARREOLA, Juan Jose
ASHFORD, Daisy
AWOONOR, Kofi
BACOVIA, George
BAGNOLD, Enid
BAILLON, Andræ
BALDWIN, James
BALLARD, J(ames)
G(raham)
BANERJI, Bibhuti
BARRIOS, Edourdo
BARSTOW, Stan
BECKETT, Samuel
BEDFORD, Sybille
BELLIDO, Jose Maria
BENNETT, Alan
BENTLEY, Edmund
Clerihew
BERGMAN, Hjalmar
BERKOFF, Steven
BERMANT, Chaim
BERNARD, Jean-Jacques
BESTALL, Alfred
BICHSEL, Peter
BLUNDEN, Edmund
BRADDON, Russell
BRENTON, Howard
BRODKEY, Harold
BRODSKY, Joseph
BROGGER, Suzanne

BUCKLEY, William
BUNTING, Basil
BURGESS, Anthony
(pen name of John
Wilson)
CALVINO, Italo
CAMPANA, Dino
CANETTI, Elias
CANNING, Victor
CAUSLEY, Charles
CERNUDA, Luis
CHATWIN, Bruce
CHEEVER, John
CHOCANO, Jose Santos
COCTEAU, Jean
COETZEE, J(ohn)
M(ichael)
COLETTE, Sidonie-
Gabrielle
COMFORT, Alex
COOKSON, Catherine
CREASEY, John
DARWISH, Mahmud
DEAMER, Dulcie
DE CAMP, L(yon)
Sprague
DEEPING, (George)
Warwick
DELANEY, Shelagh
DELEDDA, Grazia
DELIBES, Miguel
DELILLO, Don
DESNICA, Vladen
DE VRIES, Peter
DIAMOND, Itek
DICKENS, Monica
DI PRIMA, Diane

7 DODERER, Heimoto, von
DOUGLAS, Lord Alfred
DOUGLAS, (George)
Norman
DRABBLE, Margaret
DUHAMEL, Georges
DUNSANY, Lord
(Edward Plunkett)
DURRELL, Gerald
DURRELL, Lawrence
EDWARDS, Hugh
FADEYEV, Aleksandr
FAGUNWA, Daniel
FIRBANK, Ronald
FLEMING, Ian
FLEMING, Peter
FOLLETT, Ken
FORSTER, E(dward)
M(organ)
FORSTER, Margaret
FORSYTH, Frederick
FRANCIS, Dick
FUENTES, Carlos
GALLICO, Paul
GARBORG, Arne
GARDNER, Erle Stanley
GARDNER, John
Champlin
GARDNER, John
Edmund
GARLAND, Alex
GARNETT, David
GARNETT, Richard
GIBBONS, Stella
GLASSCO, John
GOLDING, William
GRAHAME, Kenneth

GRIGSON, Geoffrey
HAMMETT, Dashiell
HAMPTON, Christopher
HARTLEY, L(eslie) P(oles)
HELLMAN, Lillian
HERBERT, A(lan) P(atrick)
HIGGINS, Jack
(pen name of Harry
Patterson)
HOUSMAN, A(lfred)
E(dward)
HOUSMAN, Laurence
HOWATCH, Susan
IONESCU, Eugene
JACKSON, Shirley
JAMESON, Storm
JANSSON, Tove
JIMENEZ, Juan Ramon
JOHNSON, Pamela
Hansford
KATAYEV, Valentin
KEILLOR, Garrison
KEROUAC, Jack
KILLENS, John
KUTTNER, Henry
LARDNER, Ring
LAXNESS, Halldor
LEACOCK, Stephen
LE CARRE, John (pen
name of David
Cornwell)
LESSING, Doris
LINDSAY, Jack
MACBETH, George
MACLEAN, Alistair
MAHFOUZ, Naguib
MALAMUD, Bernard

7 MALRAUX, Andre
MAUGHAM, William
Somerset
MAURIAC, Francois
MCCLURE, Michael
MCGOUGH, Roger
MCLUHAN, Marshall
MISHIMA, Yukio
MITFORD, Nancy
MORAVIA, Alberto
MORETTI, Marino
MURDOCH, Iris
NABOKOV, Vladimir
NAIPAUL, V(idiadhar)
S(urajprasad)
OSBORNE, John
PANDURO, Leif
PILCHER, Rosamunde
PYNCHON, Thomas
QUENEAU, Raymond
RANSOME, Arthur
RENAULT, Mary
(pen name of Mary
Challans)
RENDELL, Ruth
RICHLER, Mordecai
ROBBINS, Harold
ROLLAND, Romain
ROWLING, J(oanne)
K(athleen)
RUSHDIE, Salman
RUSSELL, Bertrand
(Lord)
RUSSELL, Willy
SASSOON, Siegfried
SIMENON, Georges
SIMPSON, N(orman)

F(rederick)
SITWELL, Dame Edith
SITWELL, Sir Osbert
SITWELL, Sir Sacheverell
SOYINKA, Wole
SPENDER, Sir Stephen
THEROUX, Paul
THURBER, James
THWAITE, Anthony
TOLKIEN, J(ohn)
R(onald) R(euel)
TRAVERS, Ben
TREMAIN, Rose
USTINOV, Peter
WALCOTT, Derek
WHARTON, Edith
WHITING, John
WYNDHAM, John
YESENIN, Sergey

8 ABRAHAMS, Peter
ANDERSEN, Hans
Christian
ANDERSON, Maxwell
ARGUEDAS, Alcides
ARNICHES, Carlos
BACHMANN, Ingeborg
BANDEIRA, Manuel
BANVILLE, John
BAUMBACH, Jonathan
BECKMANN, Gunnell
BEERBOHM, Max (Sir
Henry Maximilian)
BENCHLEY, Robert
BENJAMIN, Walter
BERNHARD, Thomas
BERRYMAN, John

8

BETJEMAN, Sir John
BETOCCHI, Carlo
BJORNVIG, Thorkild
BRADBURY, Malcolm
BRADBURY, Ray
BRADFORD, Barbara
  Taylor
BRITTAIN, Vera
BROOKNER, Anita
BULGAKOV, Mikhail
CAMPBELL, Roy
CARTLAND, Barbara
CHANDLER, Raymond
CHILDERS, (Robert)
  Erskine
CHRISTIE, Agatha
COLEGATE, Isabel
CONNOLLY, Cyril
CORNFORD, Frances
  Crofts
CROMPTON, Richmal
CUMMINGS, E(dward)
  E(stlin)
DABYDEEN, David
DAGLARCA, Fazil
DAHLGREN, Karl
DAY-LEWIS, Cecil
DEIGHTON, Len
DE LA MARE, Walter
DICKMANN, Max
DING LING (pen name
  of Jiang Bingzhi)
DONLEAVY, J(ames)
  P(atrick)
FAULKNER, William
FORESTER, C(ecil) S(cott)
GALLEGOS, Romulo

GARFIELD, Leon
GELLHORN, Martha
GILLIATT, Penelope
GINSBERG, Allen
GORDIMER, Nadine
HAAVIKKO, Paavo
HAGIWARA, Sakutaro
HAMILTON, Patrick
HAN SUYIN
HARRISON, Tony
HOCHHUTH, Rolf
ISHIGURO, Kazuo
JACOBSON, Howard
JHABVALA, Ruth
KAVANAGH, Patrick
  Joseph
KENEALLY, Thomas
KINSELLA, Thomas
KOESTLER, Arthur
KUREISHI, Hanif
LANDOLFO, Tomasso
LAWRENCE, D(avid)
  H(erbert)
LE CLEZIO, Jean-Marie
LINDGREN, Astrid
MACNEICE, Louis
MICHENER, James
MITCHELL, Margaret
MORPURGO, Michael
MORTIMER, John
MORTIMER, Penelope
O'DONNELL, Peadar
ONDAATJE, Michael
PARGETER, Edith
RATTIGAN, Terence
REDGROVE, Peter
RICHARDS, Frank

8

RIFBJERG, Klaus
SALINGER, J(erome)
  D(avid)
SANDBURG, Carl
SHERRIFF, R(obert)
  C(edric)
SILLITOE, Alan
STOPPARD, Tom (pen
  name of Thomas
  Straussler)
STRACHEY, Lytton
SUTCLIFF, Rosemary
THESIGER, Wilfred
THIRKELL, Angela
TRILLING, Lionel
UNSWORTH, Barry
URQUHART, Fred
VAUTHIER, Jean
VONNEGUT, Kurt
WHEATLEY, Denis
WILLIAMS, Tennessee
WILLIAMS, William
  Carlos
ZAMYATIN, Yevgeny

9

ANDERSSON, Dan
AUDIBERTI, Jacques
AUROBINDO, Sri
  (Aurobindo Ghose)
AYCKBOURN, Alan
BARTHELME, Donald
BENGTSSON, Frans
BLACKWOOD, Algernon
BLEASDALE, Alan
BODENHEIM, Maxwell
BRENT-DYER, Elinor
BRICKHILL, Paul

BRIGHOUSE, Harold
BURROUGHS, Edgar
  Rice
BURROUGHS, William
CASTLEDEN, Rodney
CHARTERIS, Leslie
CHURCHILL, Winston
  (Sir Winston Spencer)
DE FILIPPO, Eduardo
DELAFIELD E. M. (pen
  name of Edmee
  Monica Dashwood)
DE LA ROCHE, Mazo
DICKINSON, Peter
DIKTONIUS, Elmer
DITLEVSEN, Tove
DOOLITTLE, Hilda
DOS PASSOS, John
DU MAURIER, Daphne
DURBRIDGE, Francis
EMBIRIKOS, Andreas
FIERSTEIN, Harvey
  Forbes
FUTABATEI, Shimei
GERHARDIE, William
GIRAUDOUX, Jean
GLANVILLE, Brian
GOROSTIZA, Jose
GUIRALDES, Ricardo
HASHIMOTO, Osamu
HAUPTMANN, Gerhart
HEMINGWAY, Ernest
HIGHSMITH, Patricia
HOUSEHOLD, Geoffrey
ISHERWOOD,
  Christopher
KAYE-SMITH, Sheila

9

KINOSHITA, Junji
KLITGAARD, Mogens
KOLLONTAI, Alexandra
LAMPEDUSA, Giuseppe
LATTIMORE, Richard
LINKLATER, Eric
LISPECTOR, Clarice
LOVECRAFT, H(oward)
  P(hillips)
LUNDKVIST, Artur
MACKENZIE, Sir
  Compton
MANSFIELD, Katherine
MASEFIELD, John
MIDDLETON,
  Christopher
MONSARRAT, Nicholas
MUDROOROO
PASTERNAK, Boris
PRATCHETT, Terry
PRIESTLEY, J(ohn)
  B(oynton)
PRITCHETT, Sir V(ictor)
  S(awdon)
ROA BASTOS, Augusto
ROSENTHAL, Jack
SANTAYANA, George
SHOLOKHOV, Mikhail
WINTERSON, Jeanette
WODEHOUSE,
  Sir P(elham) G(renville)
YOURCENAR,
  Marguerite

Rahman
BARBA JACOB, Porfiro
  (pen name of Miguel
  Benitez)
BILLETDOUX, Francois
BUCKERIDGE, Anthony
CHESTERTON, G(ilbert)
  K(eith)
COLLIANDER, Tito
DE BEAUVOIR, Simone
DEBELYANOV, Dimcho
DRINKWATER, John
DURRENMATT, Friedrich
FITZGERALD, F(rancis)
  Scott
FITZGERALD, Penelope
GALCZYNSKI, Konstanty
GALSWORTHY, John
GOMBROWICZ, Witold
GUNNARSSON, Gunnar
HO CHING-CHI
KARAGATSIS, Michaelis
KHLEBNIKOV, Velimir
LACRETELLE, Jacques de
MACDIARMID, Hugh
MAYAKOVSKY, Vladimir
MONTGOMERY, L(ucy)
  M(aud)
NANLOWESKA
PIRANDELLO, Luigi
VAN DER POST,
  Sir Laurens
WATERHOUSE, Keith

10

ACHTERBERG, Gerrit
ALEIXANDRE, Vicente
AL-SHARQAWI, Abd al

11

ABERCROMBIE, Lascelles
APOLLINAIRE,
  Guillaume

11 ARTZYBASHEV, Mikhail
BAYLEBRIDGE, William
BIOY CASARES, Adolfo
BONTEMPELLI,
  Massimo
BRANTENBERG, Gerd
CASTELLANOS, Rosario
CHRISTENSEN, Inger
CROMMELYNCK,
  Fernand
DELDERFIELD, R(onald)
  F(rederick)
DOUGLAS-HOME,
  William
GARCIA LORCA,
  Federico
GIARDINELLI, Mempo
HAMMERSTEIN, Oscar
MAC LIAMMOIR,
  Michael
MAETERLINCK, Count
  Maurice
MONTHERLANT,
  Henri de
PALAZZESCHI, Aldo
SERRAILLIER, Ian
VARGAS LLOSA, Mario
YEVTUSHENKO,
  Yevegeny

12 ANDRZEJEWSKI, Jerzy
BIALOSZEWSKI, Miron
CARRASQUILLA, Tomas
CECCHI D'AMICO, Suso
FEUCHTWANGER,
  Lion

HAMMOND INNES,
  Ralph
MARTIN-SANTOS, Luis
QUILLER-COUCH, Sir
  Arthur ('Q')
ROBBE-GRILLET, Alain
SAINT-EXUPERY,
  Antoine de
SOLZHENITSYN,
  Aleksandr

13 AGUILERA MALTA,
  Demetrio
GARCIA MARQUEZ,
  Gabriel
SACKVILLE-WEST, Vita

14 ABD AL-MALIK NURI
BJELKE-PETERSEN,
  Marie
CARRERA ANDRADE,
  Jorge
COMPTON-BURNETT,
  Dame Ivy
GOMEZ DE LA SERNA,
  Ramon

15 GRANVILLE-BARKER,
  Harley

16 CABRAL DE MELO
  NETO, Joao
FERREIRA DE CASTRO,
  Jose Maria

20 ABDULLHAK HAMID
  TARHAN

BALLET TERMS

3 PAS

4 BRAS
DEMI
JETE
PLIE
POSE
SAUT
TOUR
TUTU
VOLE

5 ARQUE
BARRE
BATTU
BEATS
BRISE
COLLE
COUPE
DECOR
ELEVE
FONDU
LIGNE
PASSE
PIQUE
PIVOT
PORTE
ROSIN
SAUTE
SERRE
TOMBE

6 ADAGIO
APLOMB
A TERRE
ATTACK
BAISSE
BALLON
CAMBRE
CHAINE
CHANGE
CHASSE
CROISE
DE COTE
DEGAGE
DETIRE
DEVANT
ECARTE
EFFACE
ELANCE
EN FACE
ENTREE
EPAULE
ETENDU
ETOILE
FAILLI
GLISSE
GRANDE
JARRET
MONTER
PENCHE
POINTE
RELEVE

6
RETIRE
VOYAGE

7
ALLONGE
ARRONDI
ATTAQUE
BALANCE
DANSEUR
DEBOITE
ECHAPPE
EMBOITE
ETENDRE
FOUETTE
JARRETE
LEOTARD
MAILLOT
MARQUER
OUVERTE
PAS SEUL
POISSON
RAMASSE
RETOMBE
SISSONE
SOUTENU
TAQUETE

8
ASSEMBLE
ATTITUDE
BACK BEND
BALLONNE
BALLOTTE
BATTERIE
CABRIOLE
CAGNEAUX
CORYPHEE
DAMSEUSE
DEBOULES

DEMI-PLIE
DERRIERE
DETOURNE
ENCHAPPE
GLISSADE
PAS BRISE
PISTOLET
RENVERSE
SERPETTE
SPOTTING
STULCHIK
TONNELET

9
ARABESQUE
BALLABILE
BALLERINA
BELLERINO
BATTEMENT
COU DE PIED
DEVELOPPE
ELEVATION
ENTRECHAT
ENVELOPPE
EQUILIBRE
GRAND-PLIE
HORTENSIA
JUPONNAGE
LIMBERING
MARCHEUSE
PAS DE CHAT
PAS DE DEUX
PIROUETTE
RACCOURCI
REVERENCE
REVOLTADE
VARIATION
A LA SECONDE

10 BATTEMENTS
ENLEVEMENT
EPAULEMENT
PAS BALLONE
PORT DE BRAS
SOUBRESAUT
TAQUETERIE

11 CONTRETEMPS
PAS DE BASQUE
ROND DE JAMBE

12 CHOREOGRAPHY
ENCHAINEMENT
GARGOUILLADE
PAS DE BOURREE

13 CHOREOGRAPHER
CORPS DE BALLET
SUR LES POINTES

14 CLOSED POSITION
DIVERTISSEMENT
GRAND BATTEMENT
MAITRE DE BALLET
PRIMA BALLERINA

15 AUTOUR DE LA SALLE

17 REGISSEUR-GENERALE

BATTLES

3
DIU, 1509
ULM, 1805

4
ALMA, 1854
GAZA, 312 BC
JENA, 1806
KIEV, 1941
LAON, 1814
NEVA, 1240
NOVI, 1799
SUEZ, 1956
ZAMA, 202 BC
ZELA, 47 BC

5
ANUAL, 1922
ARRAS, 1917
BADON, 515
CHIOS, 201 BC
CRECY, 1346
DARAS, 528
ELASA, 161 BC
GANJA, 1826
GIJON, 1937
IPSUS, 301 BC
KOLIN, 1757
KURSK, 1943
LAGOS, 1693
LARGS, 1263
LEWES, 1264
MARNE, 1914
MUNDA, 45 BC

MURET, 1213
MYLAE, 260 BC
NEZIB, 1839
NIDDA, 1246
PYDNA, 168 BC
SEDAN, 1870
SOMME, 1916
TOURS, 732
WAIRU (massacre), 1843
YPRES, 1914
ZENTA, 1679

6
ACTIUM, 31 BC
ARCIS-SUR-AUBE, 1814
AROGEE, 1868
ASSAYE, 1803
BARNET, 1471
CAMLAN, 537
CANNAE, 216 BC
CANNAE, 1018
CHESME, 1770
CRACOW, 1914
CUENCA, 1099
DOGALI, 1887
DUNBAR, 1650
DYRHAM, 577
EDESSA, 260
JARNAC, 1569
KADESH (or Qadesh),
   c.1294 BC
KATHIO, 1747

6 LUTZEN, 1632
LUTZEN, 1813
MODENA, 43 BC
MOHACZ, 1687
MUKDEN, 1905
MUTINA, 43 BC
NASEBY, 1645
NICAEA, 1097
NOTIUM, 407 BC
NOVARA, 1821
PANIUM, 198 BC
PEIPUS, 1242
PUEBLA, 1862
QARQAR, 854 BC
RAMLEH, 1177
RIVOLI, 1797
ROCOUX, 1746
ROCROI, 1643
SHILOH, 1862
TERTRY, 687
TOBRUK, 1942
TOWTON, 1461
VERDUN, 1916
WAGRAM, 1809
ZURICH, 1799

7 ALMANZA, 1707
ANTIOCH, 218
AUGHRIM, 1691
BAUTZEN, 1813
BLENEAU, 1652
BREMULE, 1119
BRITAIN, 1940
BULL RUN, 1862
CAMBRAI, 1917
CAMLANN, 537
CARRHAE, 53 BC

CASEROS, 1852
CHALCIS, 429 BC
CHALONS, 451
CORONEA, 447 BC
CORONEL, 1914
CORUNNA, 1809
COUTRAS, 1587
COWPENS, 1781
DRESDEN, 1813
EVESHAM, 1265
FALKIRK, 1298
FALKIRK, 1746
FLEURUS, 1690
FLEURUS, 1794
FLODDEN, 1513
GHAGHRA, 1529
GLENCOE (massacre),
   1692
GUJARAT, 1849
HAMADAN, 1630
JUTLAND, 1916
KANVAHA, 1527
KREFELD, 1758
LEPANTO, 1571
LEUCTRA, 371 BC
LEUTHEN, 1757
MAKALLE, 1935
MARENGO, 1800
MEGIDDO, 1469 BC
NEWBURN, 1640
OSTROWO, 1812
PANIPAT 1556
PANIPAT 1761
RAVENNA, 539
READING, 871
SALAMIS, 480 BC
SENTIUM, 295 BC

7
TAGINAE, 552
TALIKOT, 1565
THAPSUS, 46 BC
THE NILE, 1798
TIVEDEN, 1520
TOLBIAC, 496
TRENTON, 1776
UPPSALA, 1520
WINWAED, 655
ZALLAKA, 1088

8
ANTIETAM, 1862
AQUILEIA, 340
AYACUCHO, 1824
BLENHEIM, 1704
BOSWORTH, 1485
BOUVINES, 1214
CERESOLE, 1544
CLONTARF, 1014
CULLODEN, 1746
EDINGTON, 878
ESSAMAKO, 1824
FARISKUR, 1250
FONTENOY, 1745
FORMIGNY, 1450
FRANKLIN, 1864
FRETEVAL, 1194
GOLLHEIM, 1298
HASTINGS, 1066
INKERMAN, 1854
JOTAPATA, 67
KALANJAR, 1553
KATZBACH, 1813
KULIKOVO, 1380
LAUFFELD, 1747
LECHFELD, 955
LIEGNITZ, 1241

MANTINEA, 362 BC
MANTINEA, 418 BC
MIRABEAU, 1202
MITYLENE, 427 BC
MOLLWITZ, 1741
MONMOUTH, 1778
MUNYCHIA, 403 BC
NAVARINO, 1827
PALO ALTO, 1846
PHILIPPI, 42 BC
POITIERS, 1356
ROSSBACH, 1757
SAN MATEO, 1814
SAPIENZA, 1354
SARATOGA, 1777
ST ALBANS (first battle), 1455
ST ALBANS (second battle), 1461
SYRACUSE, 415–413 BC
TALAVERA, 1809
TEMESVAR, 1849
THE BOYNE, 1690
THE BULGE, 1944
THE MASTS, 655
THE SPURS, 1513
TRIFANUM, 338 BC
WATERLOO, 1815
WIESLOCH, 1622
WURSCHEN, 1813
ZORNDORF, 1758

9
ALEXINATZ, 1876
BALACLAVA, 1854
CHACABUCO, 1817
DETTINGEN, 1743
DRAGASANI, 1821

9

DUNSINANE, 1054
FRIEDLAND, 1807
GALLIPOLI, 1915
HOCHKIRCH, 1758
HYDERABAD, 1843
ITUZAINGO, 1827
LANDESHUT, 1760
MANILA BAY, 1898
MANZIKERT, 1071
MARJDABIK, 1516
MARRAKESH, 1668
MASERFELD, 641
MERSEBURG, 933
MILLESIMO, 1796
NAUPACTUS, 429 BC
NIHARVAND, 642
OUDENARDE, 1708
PICHINCHA, 1822
PRINCETON, 1777
SALAMANCA, 1812
SEDGEMOOR, 1685
SOLFERINO, 1859
ST QUENTIN, 1557
THE SAINTS, 1782
THE THAMES, 1813
TRAFALGAR, 1805
VARAVILLE, 1058
VICKSBURG, 1862
VIMY RIDGE, 1917
WORCESTER, 1651

10

ABOUKIR BAY, 1799
ADAM'S GRAVE, 591
ADRIANOPLE, 323
ADRIANOPLE, 378
AUSTERLITZ, 1805
BALL'S BLUFF, 1861

BATON ROUGE, 1810
BEACHY HEAD, 1690
BENNINGTON, 1777
BUNKER HILL, 1775
CALLINICUM, 531
CARCHEMISH, 605 BC
CERRO GORDO, 1847
CHIPPENHAM, 878
COLD HARBOR, 1864
CORUPEDIUM, 281 BC
FALL OF VEIL, 396 BC
GETTYSBURG, 1863
GOLDEN HILL, 1770
GOOSE GREEN, 1982
HAFRSFJORD, 900
HELLESPONT, 323 BC
KHYBER PASS, 1738
KUNERSDORF, 1759
LAKE GEORGE, 1755
LA ROTHIERE, 1814
LONG ISLAND, 1776
NEERWINDEN, 1693
NEW ORLEANS, 1815
OSTROLENKA, 1831
PLATTSBURG, 1814
QUATRE BRAS, 1815
RAWALPINDI, 1849
SACK OF TROY, c. 1184 BC
SEBASTOPOL, 1855
SEKIGAHARA, 1600
STALINGRAD, 1942
STEENKERKE, 1692
STIKLESTAD, 1030
TANNENBERG, 1914
TEWKESBURY, 1471
TINCHEBRAI, 1106
TIPPECANOE, 1811

11
BANNOCKBURN, 1314
BREITENFELD, 1631
CHICKAMAUGA, 1863
GROSS-BEEREN, 1813
MARSTON MOOR, 1644
MOUNT GILBOA,
1013 BC
NECTANSMERE, 685
PEARL HARBOR, 1941
PORT STANLEY, 1982
PRESTONPANS, 1745
RORKE'S DRIFT, 1879
SACK OF DELHI, 1737
SAN JUAN HILL, 1898
SANTIAGO BAY, 1898
SHERIFFMUIR, 1715
SZALANKEMEN, 1691
THE GRANICUS,
334 BC
THE PYRAMIDS, 1798
THERMOPYLAE, 480 BC
THERMOPYLAE, 191 BC
TICONDEROGA, 1758
VINEGAR HILL, 1798
WHITE PLAINS, 1776
WOUNDED KNEE, 1890

12
FALL OF MASADA, 74
FALL OF SHILOH,
1050 BC
FLODDEN FIELD, 1513
HARPER'S FERRY, 1859
RONCESVALLES, 778
SACK OF LONDON, 61
SOUTHWOLD BAY, 1672
THE FRONTIERS, 1914
THE TROCADERO,
1823

13
BOROUGHBRIDGE,
1322
BOSWORTH FIELD, 1485
CAPE ST VINCENT, 1797
CHESAPEAKE BAY, 1781
CYNOSCEPHALAE,
197 BC
FALL OF ANTIOCH, 1098
HATFIELD CHASE, 632
HILL OF SAMARIA,
724–722 BC
JAMESTOWN FORD,
1781
LAKE TRASIMENE,
217 BC
MALCOLM'S CROSS,
1093
NEVILLE'S CROSS, 1346
PASSCHENDAELE, 1917
POINT PLEASANT, 1774
SIEGE OF ATHENS,
414–404 BC
SIEGE OF ZAMORA,
939
SPANISH ARMADA,
1588
WATLING STREET, 61

14
BRIDGE OF DESSAU
1626
FALL OF CARTHAGE
146 BC
FREDERICKSBURG,
1862
HOHENFRIEDBERG,
1745
MACASSAR STRAIT,
1942

14 PEASANTS' REVOLT,
1381
STAMFORD BRIDGE,
1066
STIRLING BRIDGE,
1297
THE BISMARCK SEA,
1943

15 FALL OF JERUSALEM,
1187
KENESAW MOUNTAIN,
1864
RESACA DE LA PALMA,
1846
TEUTOBERG FOREST,
AD 9
THE CAUDINE FORKS,
321 BC
TSUSHIMA STRAITS,
1905

16 LAS NAVAS DE
TOLOSA, 1212
SACK OF COLCHESTER,
61
THE LITTLE BIG HORN,
1876
THE MILVIAN BRIDGE,
312
THE PHILIPPINE SEA,
1944
THE WHITE
MOUNTAIN, 1620

17 CAMPUS
VOGLADENSIS, 507
LA FERE-
CHAMPENOISE, 1814

18 THE FALKLAND
ISLANDS, 1914
THE PLAINS OF
ABRAHAM, 1759

20 FALL OF
CONSTANTINOPLE,
1453

BIBLICAL CHARACTERS

3
ASA
EVE
JOB
LOT

4
ABEL
ADAM
AHIO
AMOS
BAAL
CAIN
ESAU
GAAL
JOAB
JOHN
LUKE
MARK
MARY
NOAH
PAUL
RUTH
SAUL
TEMA
UZZI
ZUPH

5
AARON
CARMI
DAVID
ENOCH
HANAN

HEROD
HOSEA
ISHMA
ISAAC
JACOB
JAMES
JESUS
JONAH
JUDAH
JUDAS
MOSES
PETER
SARAH
SIMON
TITUS
URBANUS
ZABAD
ZADOK

6
ANDREW
BALAAM
CEPHAS
DANIEL
ELIJAH
ELISHA
ESTHER
GABBAI
GIDEON
HANNAH
HULDAH
ISAIAH

6 ISRAEL
JOSEPH
JOSHUA
MARTHA
MIRIAM
NATHAN
PHILIP
PILATE
RACHEL
SALOME
SAMSON
SAMUEL
THOMAS
VASHTI
YAHWEH
ZURIEL

7 ABRAHAM
ABSALOM
ANANIAS
BERNICE
DEBORAH
DELILAH
EPHRAIM
EZEKIEL
GABRIEL
GOLIATH
ISHMAEL
JEZEBEL
LAZARUS
MATTHEW
MICHAEL
OTHNIEL
PHARAOH
REBEKAH
SOLOMON
STEPHEN

7 TIMOTHY
ZABDIEL

8 BARRABAS
BARNABAS
BEREKIAH
BENJAMIN
CAIAPHAS
HABAKKUK
HEZEKIAH
JEREMIAH
JOCHEBED
JONATHAN
MATTHIAS
NEHEMIAH
SAPPHIRA

9 BATHSHEBA
CORNELIUS
NATHANAEL
NICODEMUS
QUIRINIUS
SHELEMIAH
ZEPHANIAH

10 AHITHOPHEL
BELSHAZZAR
METHUSELAH

11 BARTHOLOMEW

13 MARY MAGDALENE

14 JOHN THE BAPTIST
NEBUCHADNEZZAR

BIBLE – BOOKS OF THE
(N) = New Testament / (O) = Old Testament

4
AMOS (O)
EZRA (O)
JOEL (O)
JOHN (N)
JUDE (N)
LUKE (N)
MARK (N)
RUTH (O)

5
HOSEA (O)
JAMES (N)
JONAH (O)
KINGS (O)
MICAH (O)
NAHUM (O)
PETER (N)
TITUS (N)

6
DANIEL (O)
ESTHER (O)
EXODUS (O)
HAGGAI (O)
ISAIAH (O)
JOSHUA (O)
JUDGES (O)
PSALMS (O)
ROMANS (N)
SAMUEL (O)

7
EZEKIEL (O)
GENESIS (O)
HEBREWS (N)
MALACHI (O)

MATTHEW (N)
NUMBERS (O)
OBADIAH (O)
TIMOTHY (N)

8
HABBAKUK (O)
JEREMIAH (O)
NEHEMIAH (O)
PHILEMON (N)
PROVERBS (O)

9
EPHESIANS (N)
GALATIANS (N)
LEVITICUS (O)
ZECHARIAH (O)
ZEPHANIAH (O)

10
CHRONICLES (O)
COLOSSIANS (N)
REVELATION (N)

11
CORINTHIANS (N)
DEUTERONOMY (O)
PHILIPPIANS (N)

12
ECCLESIASTES (O)
LAMENTATIONS (O)

13
SONG OF SOLOMON (O)
THESSALONIANS (N)

17
ACTS OF THE
APOSTLES (N)

BIRDS
Orders of class

10 GRUIFORMES
PICIFORMES
RHEIFORMES

11 APODIFORMES
COLIIFORMES
GALLIFORMES
GAVIIFORMES

12 ANSERIFORMES
CUCULIFORMES
STRIGIFORMES
TINAMIFORMES

13 COLUMBIFORMES
CORACIIFORMES
CICONIIFORMES
FALCONIFORMES
PASSERIFORMES
TROGONIFORMES

14 APTERYGIFORMES
CASUARIIFORMES
PELECANIFORMES
PSITTACIFORMES

15 CHARADRIIFORMES
SPHENISCIFORMES

16 CAPRIMULGIFORMES
PODICIPEDIFORMES
STRUTHIONIFORMES

17 PROCELLARIIFORMES

NOTE: THE SUFFIX '-FORMES' IS THE ENDING FOR ALL
ORDERS OF BIRDS AND SOME OTHER ANIMAL GROUPS.
THE SUFFIX '-IDAE' IS THE FAMILY INDICATOR.

BIRDS
Species

3 ANI
AUK
EMU
JAY
   Blue, Eurasian
OWL
   Barn, Horned, Little,
   Long-eared, Snowy,
   Tawny
TIT
   Blue, Crested, Great,
   Long-tailed, Marsh,
   Penduline, Willow
TUI

4 CHAT
COLY
COOT
CROW
   Carrion, Hooded
DODO
DOVE
DUCK
GULL
   Common, Herring
HAWK
IBIS
KAGU
KITE
KNOT
LARK

LOON
RUFF
RHEA
SHAG
SKUA
SWAN
   Bewick's, Mute,
   Trumpeted, Whooper
TEAL
TERN
   Arctic, Common, Little,
   Roseate, Sandwich
WREN

5 ASITY
BOOBY
CRAKE
CRANE
EAGLE
   American Bald,
   Booted, Harpy, Snake
EGRET
EIDER
FINCH
   Gold, Society, Zebra
GREBE
GOOSE
   Barnacle, Brent, Canada
HERON
JUNCO
MACAW

5
MYNAH
NODDY
OUZEL
PIPIT
PITTA
PRION
QUAIL
RAVEN
ROBIN
SCAUP
SERIN
SNIPE
SWIFT
STORK

6
AVOCET
AUKLET
 Crested, Parakeet,
 Rhinoceros
BARBET
 Crested, Fire-tuffed,
 Moustached
BULBUL
CANARY
CHOUGH
CONDOR
 Andean
CORVID
CUCKOO
CURLEW
DANPHE
DARTER
DIPPER
DRONGO
DUNLIN
FALCON
 Peregrine

FULMAR
GANNET
GROUSE
GODWIT
HOOPOE
JABIRU
JACANA
KAKAPO
LINNET
MAGPIE
MARTIN
 Crag, Fairy, House,
 Purple, Sand
MERLIN
MOTMOT
ORIOLE
OSPREY
PARROT
PARULA
PEEWIT
PETREL
PIGEON
 African green, Feral,
 Rock dove, Wood
PLOVER
 Golden, Ringed
PUFFIN
 Atlantic, Horned, Tufted
SHRIKE
 Great Grey, Red-backed
SISKIN
TAKAHE
THRUSH
 Ashy ground, Hermit,
 Mistle Siberian
 ground, Song, Wood
TOUCAN

6 TOWHEE
TROGON
TURACO
TURKEY
WHIDAH
WIGEON

7 ANTBIRD
ANHINGA
BABBLER
BITTERN
BUNTING
BUSTARD
BUZZARD
CATBIRD
COWBIRD
FIGBIRD
FLICKER
GADWALL
GRACKLE
HARRIER
HOATZIN
JACAMAR
JACKDAW
KESTREL
LAPWING
LIMPKIN
MALLARD
MANAKIN
MARABOU
MINIVET
MOORHEN
OSTRICH
PEACOCK
PELICAN
PENGUIN
   Chinstrap, Little,

Rockhopper, Yelloweyed
QUETZAL
REDPOLL
REDWING
SKIMMER
SKYLARK
SPARROW
SWALLOW
TANAGER
VULTURE
WARBLER
   Barred, Cetti's, Dartford,
   Golden-winged,
   Icterine, Reed
WAXBILL
WAXWING
WRYBILL
WRYNECK

8 ACCENTOR
AVADAVAT
BATELEUR
BEE-EATER
BELLBIRD
BLACKCAP
BLUEBIRD
BOATBILL
BOBOLINK
BOBWHITE
CARACARA
CARDINAL
CHICKDEE
CURASSOW
DABCHICK
DOTTEREL
FLAMINGO
GARGANEY

8
GROSBEAK
HAWFINCH
HORNBILL
KILLDEER
LOVEBIRD
LYREBIRD
MANNIKIN
NIGHTJAR
NUTHATCH
OVENBIRD
PHEASANT
REDSTART
STARLING
UMBRELLABIRD
WHIMBREL
WOODCOCK

9
ALBATROSS
BLACKBIRD
BOWERBIRD
BRAMBLING
CASSOWARY
CHAFFINCH
CORMORANT
CORNCRAKE
CROSSBILL
DOWITCHER
FROGMOUTH
GALLINULE
GYRFALCON
KITTIWAKE
PARDOLOTE
PARTRIDGE
PHALAROPE
PTARMIGAN
SANDPIPER
SAPSUCKER

SCRUBFOWL
SPOONBILL
TURNSTONE
   Ruddy, Black

10 BLUETHROAT
BUDGERIGAR
BUFFLEHEAD
CANVASBACK
DEMOISELLE
FLYCATCHER
HAMMERHEAD
KINGFISHER
KOOKABURRA
MEADOWLARK
NIGHTHERON
ROADRUNNER
SHEARWATER
WOODPECKER
   Black, Great Spotted,
   Green, Lesser Spotted,
   Pileated

11 CRESTED LARK
HUMMINGBIRD
MOCKINGBIRD
NIGHTINGALE
SPARROWHAWK

12 GROUNDROLLER

13 OYSTERCATCHER
CROCODILE BIRD

14 BIRD OF PARADISE

15 LAUGHING JACKASS

BOATS
including aircraft carriers, dinghies, ships, submersibles and yachts

3 ARK
COG
GIG
HOY
TUG

4 ARGO
BARK (alt. spelling)
BOAT
BRIG
DHOW
HULK
JUNK
PRAM (alt. spelling)
PROA
PUNT
RAFT
SAIC
TROW
YAWL

5 BARGE
CANOE
COBLE
CRAFT
DANDY
FERRY
FUNNY
KAYAK
KETCH
LINER

MOTOR
POWER
PRAAM (alt. spelling)
PRAHU
SKIFF
SLOOP
SMACK
TRAMP
U-BOAT
UMIAK
XEBEC
YACHT

6 ARGOSY
BARQUE (alt. spelling)
BIREME
CAIQUE
CARVEL
CUTTER
DINGHY
DOGGER
DUGOUT
GALLEY
HOOKER
HOPPER
LAUNCH
LORCHA
LUGGER
PACKET
ROWING
SAMPAN

6
SEALER
SLAVER
TANKER
TARTAN
TENDER
VESSEL
WHALER
WHERRY

7
BUMBOAT
CARAVEL
CARRACK
CLIPPER
COASTER
COLLIER
CORACLE
CORSAIR
CRUISER
CURRACH
DREDGER
DRIFTER
DROMOND
FELUCCA
FRIGATE
GABBARD
GALLEON
GALLIOT
GONDOLA
GUNBOAT
JANGADA
LIGHTER
PINNACE
POLACCA
ROWBOAT
SAILING
SCULLER
SHALLOP

STEAMER
TRAWLER
TRIREME
WARSHIP

8
BILANDER
BUDGEROW
CORVETTE
FIRESHIP
FLAGSHIP
LIFEBOAT
LONGBOAT
MAILSHIP
MAN-OF-WAR
SCHOONER
SHOWBOAT
TRIMARAN

9
BUCENTAUR
CARGO BOAT
CATAMARAN
DESTROYER
FREIGHTER
HOUSEBOAT
JOLLY BOAT
MINELAYER
MOTORBOAT
MUD-HOPPER
OUTRIGGER
POWERBOAT
SLAVE SHIP
SPEEDBOAT
STEAMBOAT
SUBMARINE
TROOPSHIP

10 BANANA BOAT
BARKENTINE
   (alt. spelling)
BATHYSCAPE
   (alt. spelling)
BATHYSCAPH
   (alt. spelling)
BATTLESHIP
BRIGANTINE
DAHABEEYAH
PADDLEBOAT
PIRATE SHIP
PRISON SHIP
QUADRIREME
ROWING BOAT
TEA CLIPPER
TRAIN FERRY
VIKING SHIP
WINDJAMMER

11 BARQUANTINE
   (alt. spelling)
BARQUENTINE
   (alt. spelling)
BATHYSCAPHE
   (alt. spelling)
DREADNOUGHT
FISHING BOAT
MERCHANTMAN
MINESWEEPER
PENTECONTER
PILOT VESSEL
QUINQUEREME
SAILING SHIP
TORPEDO BOAT

12 CABIN CRUISER

ESCORT VESSEL
FISHING SMACK
HOSPITAL SHIP
MERCHANT SHIP
PATROL VESSEL
PLEASURE BOAT
SAILING BARGE
STERNWHEELER

13 BATTLECRUISER
PADDLESTEAMER
PASSENGER SHIP
TRANSPORT SHIP

14 FLOATING PALACE
OCEAN GREYHOUND

15 AIRCRAFT CARRIER

BOYS' NAMES

2

AL
CY
ED

3

ABE
ALF
BEN
BOB
DAI
DAN
DEL
DES
DON
ELI
ERN
GIL
GUS
GUY
HAL
HUW
IAN
IKE
JAY
JED
JEM
JIM
JOB
JOE
JON
KEN
KIT

LEE
LEN
LEO
LEW
LOU
MAT
MAX
MEL
NAT
NED
NYE
PAT
PIP
RAB
RAY
REG
REX
ROB
ROD
SAM
SEB
SID
STU
SYD
TED
TIM
TOM
VIC
VIN
WAL
ZAK

4	
ABEL	DOUG
ADAM	DREW
ALAN	DUKE
ALEC	EARL
ALED	EDDY
ALEX	EDEN
ALGY	EMIL
ALUN	ERIC
ALVA	ERLE
AMOS	ESAU
ANDY	EUAN
AXEL	EVAN
BART	EWAN
BEAU	EZRA
BERT	FRED
BILL	GARY
BING	GENE
BOYD	GLEN
BRAD	GLYN
BRAM	GREG
BRET	GWYN
CARL	HANK
CARY	HANS
CHAD	HERB
CHAS	HUGH
CLEM	HUGO
CODY	IAGO
COLE	IAIN
CORY	IFOR
DALE	IGOR
DANE	IVAN
DAVE	JACK
DAVY	JAKE
DEAN	JEFF
DICK	JESS
DION	JOCK
DIRK	JOEL

4 JOEY

JOHN

JOSE

JOSH

JUAN

JUDD

JUDE

KANE

KARL

KEIR

KENT

KING

KIRK

KRIS

KURT

KYLE

LEON

LEVI

LIAM

LUIS

LUKE

LYLE

MARC

MARK

MATT

MERV

MICK

MIKE

MILO

MORT

MUIR

NEIL

NICK

NOAH

NOEL

NORM

OLAF

OMAR

OTHO

OTIS

OTTO

OWEN

PAUL

PETE

PHIL

RAFE

RENE

RHYS

RORY

ROSS

RUDI

RYAN

RYUI

SAUL

SEAN

SETH

SHEA

SHEM

STAN

STEW

THEO

TOBY

TODD

TREV

TROY

VERE

WALT

WARD

YVES

ZACK

ZANE

5 AARON

ABNER

5

ABRAM	BLASE
ADOLF	BOBBY
AIDAN	BONAR
AIDEN	BORIS
ALAIN	BRENT
ALBAN	BRETT
ALBIN	BRIAN
ALDEN	BRICE
ALDIS	BRUCE
ALDUS	BRUNO
ALFIE	BRYAN
ALGIE	BRYCE
ALLAN	BYRON
ALVAR	CAIUS
ALVIS	CALEB
ALWYN	CALUM
AMYAS	CAROL
ANDRE	CECIL
ANGEL	CHASE
ANGUS	CHRIS
ANSON	CHUCK
ANTON	CLARK
ARCHY	CLAUD
ARRAN	CLIFF
ARRON	CLINT
ARTIE	CLIVE
ATHOL	CLYDE
BARRY	COLIN
BASIL	CONAN
BENJY	CONOR
BENNY	COSMO
BERNY	CRAIG
BERTY	CYRIL
BILLY	CYRUS
BJORN	DAMON
BLAIR	DANNY
BLAKE	DARCY

5

DARYL	GAVIN
DAVID	GEOFF
DENIS	GERRY
DENYS	GILES
DEREK	GLENN
DERYK	GLYNN
DEVIN	GRANT
DICKY	GREGG
DIEGO	HARDY
DIGBY	HARRY
DONNY	HAYDN
DUANE	HEATH
DYLAN	HENRI
EAMON	HENRY
EARLE	HIRAM
EDDIE	HUMPH
EDGAR	HYMAN
EDWIN	HYMIE
EDWYN	HYWEL
ELIAS	INIGO
ELIOT	IRVIN
ELLIS	IRWIN
ELMER	ISAAC
ELVIS	IZAAC
EMILE	JABEZ
EMLYN	JACKY
EMRYS	JACOB
ENOCH	JADEN
ERROL	JAMES
ETHAN	JAMIE
FELIX	JARED
FLOYD	JASON
FRANK	JEMMY
FRANZ	JERRY
FRITZ	JESSE
GARRY	JESUS
GARTH	JIMMY

5

JONAH	NEVIL
JUDAH	NIALL
JUDAS	NICKY
JULES	NIGEL
KAREL	NIKKI
KAROL	NORRY
KEITH	OLLIE
KELLY	ORSON
KEVIN	OSCAR
LANCE	OWAIN
LARRY	PABLO
LAURI	PADDY
LEIGH	PAOLO
LEROY	PEDRO
LEWIS	PERCE
LLOYD	PERCY
LOGAN	PERRY
LORNE	PETER
LOUIE	PIERS
LOUIS	QUINN
LUCAS	RALPH
LUIGI	RAMON
MADOC	RANDY
MANNY	RAOUL
MARCO	RICKI
MARIO	RICKY
MARTY	RIKKI
MASON	ROALD
MICAH	ROBIN
MICKY	RODDY
MILES	ROGER
MONTY	ROLLO
MORAY	ROLPH
MOSES	RONAN
MYLES	RUFUS
NEDDY	SACHA
NEILL	SAMMY

5
SANDY
SCOTT
SELBY
SERGE
SHANE
SHAUN
SHAWN
SIMON
STEVE
TEDDY
TERRI
TERRY
TIMMY
TITUS
TOMMY
TYLER
URIAH
VINCE
VITUS
WALDO
WALLY
WAYNE
WILLY
WOODY
XANTI

6
ADOLPH
ADRIAN
AENEAS
ALBERT
ALDOUS
ALDRED
ALEXIS
ALFRED
ANDREW
ANGELO
ANSELM

ANTONY
ARCHIE
ARMAND
ARNAUD
ARNOLD
ARTHUR
ASHLEY
AUBREY
AUGUST
AUSTIN
AYLMER
BARNEY
BARRIE
BENITO
BERNIE
BERTIE
BILLIE
BLAINE
BLAISE
BOBBIE
BROOKE
CAESAR
CALLUM
CALVIN
CARLOS
CARSON
CASPAR
CEDRIC
CLAUDE
CONNOR
CONRAD
CURTIS
DAFYDD
DAMIAN
DAMIEN
DANIEL
DARREL

6

DARREN	FREDDY
DARRYL	GARETH
DECLAN	GARNET
DENNIS	GASPER
DENZIL	GEORGE
DERMOT	GERALD
DERYCK	GERARD
DEXTER	GIDEON
DICKIE	GODWIN
DONALD	GORDON
DORIAN	GRAEME
DOUGAL	GRAHAM
DUDLEY	GREGOR
DUGGIE	GUNTER
DUNCAN	GUSSIE
DUSTIN	GUSTAF
DWAYNE	GUSTAV
DWIGHT	GWYLIM
EAMONN	HAMISH
EDMOND	HAMLET
EDMUND	HAMLYN
EDUARD	HARLEY
EDWARD	HAROLD
EGBERT	HARVEY
ELDRED	HAYDEN
ELIJAH	HAYDON
ELLIOT	HECTOR
ERNEST	HEDLEY
ESMOND	HERMAN
EUGENE	HIKARU
EVELYN	HILARY
FABIAN	HILTON
FERGUS	HOBART
FINLAY	HOLMAN
FRANCO	HORACE
FRASER	HOWARD
FRAZER	HOWELL

6

HUBERT	LUTHER
HUGHIE	LYNDON
HUNTER	MADDOX
IRVINE	MAGNUS
IRVING	MARCEL
ISAIAH	MARCUS
ISRAEL	MARIUS
JACKIE	MARTIN
JARROD	MARTYN
JARVIS	MARVIN
JASPER	MARVYN
JAYDEN	MELVIN
JEREMY	MELVYN
JEROME	MERLIN
JETHRO	MERVIN
JOHNNY	MERVYN
JOLYON	MICKEY
JORDAN	MIGUEL
JOSEPH	MORRIS
JOSHUA	MOSTYN
JOSIAH	MURRAY
JOSIAS	NATHAN
JULIAN	NEDDIE
JULIUS	NELSON
JUSTIN	NINIAN
KEIRAN	NORMAN
KEIRON	NORRIE
KENTON	NORRIS
LANDON	NORTON
LAURIE	NOWELL
LAWRIE	OLIVER
LESLIE	OSBERT
LESTER	OSMOND
LIONEL	OSMUND
LUCIAN	OSWALD
LUCIEN	PASCAL
LUDWIG	PASCOE

6 PELHAM
PHILIP
PIERRE
PRINCE
RAFAEL
RAMSAY
RAMSEY
RANDAL
RAYNER
RAYNOR
REGGIE
REUBEN
RICHIE
ROBBIE
ROBERT
RODGER
RODNEY
ROLAND
RONALD
RONNIE
ROWLEY
RUDOLF
RUPERT
SAMSON
SAMUEL
SEFTON
SELWYN
SERGEI
SERGIO
SHAMUS
SHELLY
SIDNEY
SIMEON
STEVEN
STEVIE
STUART
SYDNEY

TEDDIE
THOMAS
TOBIAS
TRAVIS
TREVOR
TYRONE
VAUGHN
VERNON
VICTOR
VIVIAN
VIVIEN
WALLIS
WALTER
WARREN
WESLEY
WILBUR
WILLIE
WILLIS
WILMER
XAVIER
YEHUDI

7 ABRAHAM
ABSALOM
AINSLEY
ALFONSO
AMBROSE
ANDREAS
ANEIRIN
ANEURIN
ANTHONY
ANTONIO
ARTEMUS
BALDWIN
BARNABY
BARNARD
BERTRAM

7

BRADLEY	GILBERT
BRANDON	GODFREY
CAMERON	GRAHAME
CHARLES	GREGORY
CHARLEY	GUNTHER
CHARLIE	GUSTAVE
CHESTER	HADRIAN
CLAYTON	HARTLEY
CLEMENT	HERBERT
CLINTON	HERMANN
CORDELL	HILLARY
CRISPIN	HORATIO
CYPRIAN	HUMBERT
DARRELL	HUSSEIN
DENHOLM	ISIDORE
DERRICK	JACKSON
DOMINIC	JEFFERY
DONOVAN	JEFFREY
DOUGLAS	JOCELYN
EDOUARD	JOHNNIE
ELLIOTT	KENNETH
EMANUEL	KENTARO
EPHRAIM	LACHLAN
EUSTACE	LAMBERT
EVERARD	LAZARUS
EZEKIEL	LEONARD
FITZROY	LEOPOLD
FLORIAN	LINDSAY
FRANCIS	LINFORD
FRANKIE	LUDOVIC
FREDDIE	MALACHI
FREDRIC	MALCOLM
GABRIEL	MANFRED
GEORGIE	MATTHEW
GERRARD	MAURICE
GERVAIS	MAXWELL
GERVASE	MICHAEL

7

MOHAMAD
MONTAGU
MURDOCH
NEVILLE
NICOLAS
OBADIAH
ORLANDO
OSBORNE
PATRICK
PHILLIP
PHINEAS
QUENTIN
QUINTIN
RANDALL
RAPHAEL
RAYMOND
RAYMUND
REDVERS
REYNARD
RICARDO
RICHARD
RODOLPH
RODRIGO
ROWLAND
ROYSTON
RUDOLPH
RUSSELL
SERGIUS
SEYMORE
SHELDON
SIGMUND
SOLOMON
SPENCER
STANLEY
STEPHEN
STEWART
SWITHIN

TERENCE
TIMOTHY
TORQUIL
TRAVERS
TRISTAN
ULYSSES
VAUGHAN
VINCENT
WALLACE
WARWICK
WILFRED
WILLIAM
WINSTON
WOODROW
WYNDHAM
WYNFORD
YANNICK
ZACHARY
ZEBEDEE
ZEESHAN

8

ADOLPHUS
ALASDAIR
ALASTAIR
ALGERNON
ALISTAIR
ALOYSIUS
ALPHONSE
ALPHONSO
AUGUSTUS
BARNABAS
BENEDICK
BENEDICT
BENJAMIN
BERTRAND
BEVERLEY
BONIFACE

8

CAMPBELL	MARSHALL
CLARENCE	MATTHIAS
CLAUDIUS	MELVILLE
CLIFFORD	MEREDITH
COURTNEY	MITCHELL
CRISPIAN	MONTAGUE
DIARMUID	MORDECAI
DOMINICK	MORTIMER
EBENEZER	NICHOLAS
EMILIANO	OCTAVIUS
EMMANUEL	PERCEVAL
ETHELRED	PERCIVAL
FARQUHAR	PHILEMON
FERNANDO	RANDOLPH
FLETCHER	REGINALD
FRANKLIN	RODERICK
FREDERIC	SALVADOR
GARFIELD	SEPTIMUS
GEOFFREY	SHERIDAN
GUSTAVUS	SILVANUS
HARRISON	SINCLAIR
HERCULES	STAFFORD
HEREWARD	STIRLING
HEZEKIAH	SYLVANUS
HUMPHREY	TERRENCE
IGNATIUS	THADDEUS
JEREMIAH	THEOBALD
JERMAINE	THEODORE
JOHANNES	TRISTRAM
JONATHAN	VLADIMIR
JONATHON	WINTHROP
KINGSLEY	
LANCELOT	**9** ALEJANDRO
LAURENCE	ALEXANDER
LAWRENCE	ALPHONSUS
LEIGHTON	ARCHIBALD
LLEWELYN	ATHELSTAN

9
AUGUSTINE
BALTHASAR
BRODERICK
CHRISTIAN
CORNELIUS
COURTENAY
DIONYSIUS
ETHELBERT
FERDINAND
FRANCESCO
FRANCISCO
FREDERICK
GERONTIUS
GRANVILLE
GRENVILLE
GUILLAUME
JEFFERSON
MARCELLUS
MARMADUKE
NATHANIEL
NICODEMUS
PEREGRINE
SEBASTIAN
SIEGFRIED
SIGISMUND
SILVESTER
STANISLAS
SYLVESTER
VALENTINE
ZACHARIAS
ZECHARIAH

10
CARACTACUS
CARMICHAEL
HILDEBRAND
MAXIMILIAN
MONTGOMERY

STANISLAUS
WASHINGTON
WILLOUGHBY

11
BARTHOLOMEW
CHRISTOPHER
CONSTANTINE
NATHANESHAN
SACHEVERELL

CAR MANUFACTURERS

2
AC
AV
MG

3
ARO
BMW
BSA
DKW
FAW
FSO
GAZ
GEO
GMC
KIA
NSU
TVR
ZAZ

4
AUDI
BAIC
BOND
CLAN
ELVA
FIAT
FORD
JEEP
LADA
MINI
NAZA
OPEL
SAAB

SEAT
TATA

5
ACURA
ASUNA
BUICK
DODGE
EAGLE
EDSEL
GEELY
HONDA
HONQI
HUALI
HUAPU
ISUZU
LEXUS
LOTUS
MAZDA
NOBLE
PANOZ
PIPER
QVALE
RILEY
ROVER
SCION
SIMCA
SKODA
SMART
STUTZ
VOLGA
VOLVO

6 ABARTH
ALBION
ALLARD
ARKLEY
ASHLEY
AUSTIN
BARNES
CHAIKA
CHERRY
DAEWOO
DATSUN
DELLOW
DE SOTO
HOLDEN
HUDSON
HUMBER
INOKOM
JAGUAR
JENSEN
JINBEI
JOWETT
LANCIA
LISTER
LOCOST
MARCOS
MARUTI
MERCER
MERKUR
MORGAN
MORRIS
NISSAN
PRINCE
PROTON
SATURN
SINGER
SUBARU
SUZUKI

TALBOT
TOYOTA
TURNER

7 ADAMSON
AUTOVAZ
BENTLEY
BRISTOL
BUGATTI
CHANGHE
CITROEN
DAIMLER
FERRARI
GILBERN
GINETTA
HAOQING
HILLMAN
HUMMERS
HYUNDAI
LAGONDA
MCLAREN
LASALLE
LINCOLN
MAXWELL
MAYBACH
MERCURY
PANTHER
PEUGEOT
PONTIAC
PORSCHE
PERODUA
RELIANT
RENAULT
SUNBEAM
SWALLOW
TORNADO
TRIDENT

7 TRIUMPH
WARWICK

8 BERKELEY
CADILLAC
CATERHAM
CHRYSLER
CROSSLEY
DAIHATSU
DE LOREAN
DE TOMASO
DONGFENG
INFINITI
MAHINDRA
MASERATI
METROCAB
PASSPORT
PLYMOUTH
PSA GROUP
ROCHDALE
STANDARD
STERLING
TICKFORD
VAUXHALL
WANDERER
WOLSELEY

9 ALFA ROMEO
AUTO UNION
CHEVROLET
HINDUSTAN
LAND ROVER
RED BANNER
SSANGYONG
WESTFIELD

10 ASIA MOTORS

FAIRTHORPE
FRAZER NASH
LANCHESTER
LEA-FRANCIS
MACNEILLIE
MITSUBISHI
OLDSMOBILE
RANGE ROVER
ROLLS-ROYCE
TALBOT-LAGO
VANDEN PLAS
VOLKSWAGEN

11 AUTOBIANCHI
ASTON MARTIN
CONTINENTAL
LAMBORGHINI

12 AUSTIN-HEALEY
BRILLIANAUTO
GORDON-KEEBLE
MERCEDES-BENZ

13 ARROL-JOHNSTON
GENERAL MOTORS

14 AMERICAN MOTORS
BRITISH SALMSON
JAMES AND BROWNE
WILLYS-OVERLAND

15 DAIMLER-CHRYSLER
GREATWALL MOTORS

17 ARMSTRONG SIDDELEY

18 SHANGHAI
AUTOMOTIVE

CHEESES
and their country of produce

CHEESE	COUNTRY

3

BRA	Italy

4

BRIE	France
CURD	All
EDAM	Netherlands
FETA	sheep, Greece
ORLA	Ireland
SAGA	Denmark
TUPI	Spain

5

AUTUN	France
BANON	France
BRICK	USA
CABOC	Scotland
COLBY	USA
COMTE	France
CREAM	All
DANBO	Denmark
DERBY	England
ESROM	Denmark
FETTA	Greece
GOUDA	Netherlands
HERVE	Belgium
LEIGH	England
MEIRA	Iraq
QUARK	Germany
ROULE	France
SAMSO	Denmark

CHEESE	COUNTRY

5

SARDO	Argentina
SELVA	Spain
SERAT	Afghanistan
TOMME	France

6

ASIAGO	Italy
BANDEL	India
BREBIS	sheep, France
CACHAT	France
CANTAL	France
CHEVRE	goat, France
DUNLOP	Scotland
ETORKI	France
HALUMI	Greece
HRAMSA	Scotland
LEIDEN	Netherlands
PANEER	India
POSTEL	Belgium
RIDDER	Netherlands
RONCAL	Spain
SBRINZ	Switzerland
SIRENE	Bulgaria
SMOKED	Bavaria, Austria
SURATI	India
TILSIT	Germany
VENACO	Corsica

7

ABERTAM	Czech Republic
ALVERCA	Portugal
BABYBEL	France
BONDARD	France
BOURSIN	France

CHEESE	COUNTRY

7

BROCCIO	Corsica
BROCCIU	Corsica
BROUSSE	France
BRUCCIU	Corsica
CABECOU	France
CHAUMES	France
CHEDDAR	England
COTTAGE	Originated North America
DANABLU	Denmark
DAUPHIN	France
DEMI-SEL	France
DRY JACK	USA
GEITOST	Norway
GJETOST	Norway
GRUYERE	Switzerland
HAVARTI	Denmark
HIPI ITI	New Zealand
LANGRES	France
LEVROUX	France
LIMBURG	Belgium
LIVAROT	France
MACQUEE	France
MONT-D'OR	France
MORBIER	France
MUNSTER	Germany
RABACAL	Portugal
RICOTTA	Italy
SCHLOSS	Austria
STILTON	England
VENDOME	France

8

AIREDALE	England
ARDRAHAN	Ireland

CHEESE	COUNTRY

8

AUVERGNE	France
AYRSHIRE	Scotland
BEAUFORT	France
BEL PAESE	Italy
BIERKASE	Germany
BLUE VEIN	England
CHAOURCE	France
CHESHIRE	England
EDELPILZ	Germany
EPOISSES	France
GARROTXA	Spain
HALLOUMI	Cyprus
MANCHEGO	Spain
MENONITA	Spain
MONDSEER	Austria
PARMESAN	Italy
PECORINO	Italy
REMOUDOU	Belgium
SCAMORZE	Italy
TALEGGIO	Italy
TESTOURI	Egypt
VALENCAY	France
VIGNOTTE	France
ZAMORANO	Spain

9

APPENZELL	Switzerland
AVAXTSKYR	Iceland
CAITHNESS	Scotland
CAMBOZOLA	Germany
CAMEMBERT	France
CHABICHOU	France
EMMENTHAL	Switzerland

CHEESE	COUNTRY

9

GAMMELOST	Norway
KADCHGALL	Afghanistan
KIK ORANGI	New Zealand
KUGELKASE	Austria
LEICESTER	England
LIMBURGER	Belgium
MAREDSOUS	Belgium
MAROILLES	France
MIMOLETTE	France
NEUCHATEL	France
NOKKELOST	Norway
OSZCZYPEK	Poland
PAVE D'AUGE	France
PORT SALUT	France
REBLOCHON	France
RICHELIEU	Canada
ROQUEFORT	France
SAGE DERBY	England

10

BEER CHEESE	Germany
BRAUDOSTUR	Iceland
BRIN D'AMOUR	Corsica
CAERPHILLY	Wales
DANISH BLUE	Denmark
DOLCELLATE	Italy
DUROBLANDO	Mexico
GLOUCESTER	England
GORGONZOLA	Italy
JARLESBERG	Norway
LANCASHIRE	England
LEERDAMMER	Netherlands
MASCARPONE	Italy
MOZZARELLA	Italy

CHEESE	COUNTRY

10

NEUFCHATEL	Switzerland
PASSENDALE	Belgium
RED WINDSOR	England
REGGIANITO	Argentina
SAINGORLON	France
STRACCHINO	Italy

11

BEYAZ PEYNIR	Turkey
CARRE DE L'EST	France
COEUR DE BRAY	France
COULOMMIERS	France
KATSHKAWALJ	Bulgaria
PETIT-SUISSE	France
PODHALANSKI	Poland
PONT L'EVEQUE	France
QUESO FRESCO	Mexico
SAINT-PAULIN	France
SCHABZIEGER	Switzerland
WEISSLACKER	Germany
WENSLEYDALE	England

12

BLEU DE BRESSE	France
CACIOCAVALLO	Italy
L'AVEYRONNAIS	France
RED LEICESTER	England
SOUMAINTRAIN	France

13

BLEU D'AUVERGNE	France
DARALAGJAZSKY	Russia
GORNYALTAJSKI	Russia
LA VACHE QUI RIT	France

CHEESE	COUNTRY

13

SAINT-NECTAIRE	France
SELLES-SUR-CHER	France

14

ARMENIAN STRING	Armenia
BRILLAT-SAVARIN	France
FEUILLE DE DREUX	France
LAGUIOLE-AUBRAC	France
MICHALAC PEYNIR	Turkey
PLATEAU DE HERVE	Belgium
SAINT-FLORENTIN	France
SAINT-MARCELLIN	France
TRAPPISTENKASE	Germany

15

BOUTON-DE-CULOTTE	France
DESSERTNYJ BELYJ	Russia

16

DOUBLE GLOUCESTER	England
DOPPELRHAMSTUFEL	Germany

17

RIGOTTE DE PELUSSIN	France

18

CHEVROTIN DES ARAVIS	France
CROTTIN DE CHAVIGNOL	France

19

POULIGNY-SAINT-PIERRE	France

CITIES OF THE WORLD
Capital cities are marked with an asterisk (*)

3	FEZ	ADANA
	UFA	AMMAN*
		BASRA
4	AGRA	BELEM
	BAKU	BENXI
	BERN*	BURSA
	BONN	BUSAN
	CALI	CAIRO*
	CEBU	DAEGU
	GAZA	DAKAR*
	KANO	DAVAO
	KIEV*	DELHI*
	LEON	DHAKA
	LIMA*	DUBAI
	LODZ	ESSEN
	LYON	GENOA
	NAHA	HANOI*
	OMSK	HOFEI
	ORAN	IZMIR
	OSLO	JILIN
	PERM	JINAN
	RIGA*	KABUL*
	ROME*	KAZAN
	RUHR	KOCHI
	SANA*	LAGOS
	WUXI	LA PAZ
	XI'AN	LEEDS
	ZIBO	LILLE
		MECCA
5	ABUJA	MEDAN
	ACCRA*	MIAMI

5

MILAN
MINSK*
MOSUL
NAMPO
NASIK
NATAL
OSAKA
PARIS*
PATNA
PERTH
POONA
PORTO
PUSAN
QUITO*
RABAT*
ROUEN
SANAA
SEOUL*
SOFIA*
SURAT
TAMPA
TOKYO*
TUNIS*
TURIN
ULSAN
WUHAN

6

ALBANY
ALEPPO
ANKARA*
ANSHAN
ATHENS*
AUSTIN
BAMAKO*
BAOTOU
BEIRUT*
BERGEN

BERLIN*
BHILAI
BHOPAL
BILBAO
BOGOTA*
BOMBAY
BOSTON
CANTON
DAIREN
DALIAN
DALLAS
DAMMAM
DARWIN
DATONG
DAYTON
DENVER
DODOMA*
DOUALA
DUBLIN*
DURBAN
FRESNO
FUSHUN
FUZHOU
GDANSK
HANDAN
HARARE*
HARBIN
HAVANA*
HIMEJI
HOBART
IBADAN
INDORE
JEDDAH
JAIPUR
KANPUR
KHULNA
LAHORE

6 LISBON*
LONDON*
LUANDA*
LUSAKA*
MACEIO
MADRAS
MADRID*
MANAUS
MANILA*
MAPUTO*
MEDINA
MEERUT
MESHED
MOSCOW*
MULTAN
MUNICH
MUSCAT*
NAGOYA
NAGPUR
NANTES
NAPLES
NIAMEY
NINGBO
ODESSA
OTTAWA*
PRAGUE*
PUEBLA
QUEBEC
RAJKOT
RANCHI
RECIFE
RIYADH*
SAMARA
SANTOS
SENDAI
SHIRAZ
SKOPJE*

SUZHOU
SYDNEY
TABRIZ
TAEJON
TAINAN
TAIPEI*
TEHRAN*
TIRANA*
TOLUCA
URUMQI
VENICE
VIENNA*
WARSAW*
XUZHOU
ZAGREB
ZURICH

7 ABIDJAN
ALGIERS*
ASTANA*
ANTWERP
ASANSOL
ATLANTA
BAGHDAD*
BANDUNG
BANGKOK*
BEIJING*
BELFAST
BENARES
BUFFALO
CALGARY
CARACAS*
CHENGTU
CHICAGO
CHUNGLI
COLOGNE
COLOMBO*

7

CONAKRY*
CORDOBA
DETROIT
DHANBAD
DONETSK
DRESDEN
DUNEDIN
FUKUOKA
GLASGOW
GOIANIA
GUIYANG
GWALIOR
GWANGJU
HAMBURG
HANOVER
HOUSTON
HUAINAN
HUHEHOT
IRKUTSK
ISFAHAN
JAKARTA*
JODHPUR
KADDUNA
KAMPALA*
KARACHI
KHARKOV
KUNMING
LANZHOU
LUCKNOW
LUOYANG
MADURAI
MANAGUA*
MARACAY
MEMPHIS
MOMBASA
NAIROBI*
NANKING

NANNING
NEW YORK
OKAYAMA
ORLANDO
PALERMO
PHOENIX
QIQIHAR
RALEIGH
RANGOON*
ROSARIO
SAN JOSE*
SAN JUAN*
SAO LUIS
SAPPORO
SARATOV
SEATTLE
SEVILLA
SHANTOU
ST LOUIS
TAIYUAN
TALLINN*
TBILISI*
TIJUANA
TORONTO
TORREON
TRIESTE
TRIPOLI*
VILNIUS*
VITORIA
YAOUNDE*
YEREVAN

8

ADELAIDE
AMRITSAR
ASUNCION
AUCKLAND
BELGRADE*

8

BRASILIA*
BRIGHTON (AND HOVE)
BRISBANE
BRUSSELS*
BUDAPEST*
CALCUTTA
CAMPINAS
CANBERRA*
CAPE TOWN
CHANGSHA
COLUMBUS
CURITIBA
DAMASCUS*
DORTMUND
EDMONTON
FREETOWN*
HAIPHONG
HANGCHOU
HARTFORD
HELSINKI*
HONG KONG
ISTANBUL
JABALPUR
KATMANDU*
KATOWICE
KHARTOUM*
KINSHASA*
KISHINEV*
KUMAMOTO
LAS VEGAS
LILONGWE*
LUDHIANA
MANNHEIM
MEDELLIN
MONTREAL
NANCHANG
NURNBERG

PESHAWAR
PORTLAND
PRETORIA*
RICHMOND
ROCHESTER
SALVADOR
SAN DIEGO
SANTIAGO*
SAO PAULO
SEMARANG
SHANGHAI
SHENYANG
SHENZHEN
SHIZUOKA
SHOLAPUR
SRINAGAR
SURABAYA
TAICHUNG
TANGSHAN
TASHKENT*
TIENTSIN
TOULOUSE
TSINGTAO
VADODARA
VALENCIA
VICTORIA*
WINNIPEG

9

AHMADABAD
ALLAHABAD
AMSTERDAM*
ASHKHABAD*
BANGALORE
BARCELONA
BENIN CITY
BUCHAREST*
CARTAGENA

CHANGCHUN
CHARLOTTE
CHUNGKING
CLEVELAND
FORTALEZA
FRANKFURT
GAZIANTEP
GUAYAQUIL
HAMAMATSU
HIROSHIMA
HYDERABAD
ISLAMABAD*
JERUSALEM*
JOINVILLE
KAOHSIUNG
KATHMANDU*
LIVERPOOL
MARACAIBO
MARRAKECH
MARSEILLE
MBUJI-MAYI
MELBOURNE
MILWAUKEE
MOGADISHU*
MONTERREY
NASHVILLE
PALEMBANG
PHNOM PENH*
PYONGYANG*
ROTTERDAM
SANTA CRUZ*
SHEFFIELD
SINGAPORE*
STOCKHOLM*
STUTTGART
ULAN BATOR*
VANCOUVER

VOLGOGRAD
ZHENGZHOU

10 ADDIS ABABA*
ALEXANDRIA
AURANGABAD
BIRMINGHAM (UK)
BIRMINGHAM (USA)
BRATISLAVA*
CASABLANCA
CHANDIGARH
CHITTAGONG
CINCINNATI
COIMBATORE
COPENHAGEN*
DUSSELDORF
FAISALABAD
GREENSBORO
GREENVILLE
GUJRANWALA
JAMSHEDPUR
JOAO PESSOA
KANSAS CITY
KITAKYUSHU
KUWAIT CITY*
LOS ANGELES
LUBUMBASHI
LUXEMBOURG*
MANCHESTER
MEXICO CITY*
MONTEVIDEO*
NEW ORLEANS
PANAMA CITY*
PITTSBURGH
PROVIDENCE
RAWALPINDI
SACRAMENTO

10
SAN ANTONIO
VIJAYAWADA
WASHINGTON*
WELLINGTON*

11
BRAZZAVILLE*
BUCARAMANGA
BUENOS AIRES*
CHELYABINSK
DAR ES SALAAM
GRAND RAPIDS
GUADALAJARA
JOHOR BAHARU
KRASNOYARSK
KUALA LUMPUR*
MINNEAPOLIS
NOVOSIBIRSK
OUAGADOUGOU*
PORTO ALEGRE
PORT MORESBY
SAN SALVADOR*
TEL AVIV YAFO
VLADIVOSTOK

12
ANTANANARIVO*
BARQUISIMETO
BARRANQUILLA
CHRISTCHURCH
CIUDAD JUAREZ
INDIANAPOLIS
JACKSONVILLE
JOHANNESBURG
OKLAHOMA CITY
PHILADELPHIA
PORT-AU-PRINCE*
PORT HARCOURT
RIO DE JANEIRO

ROSTOV-NA-DONU
SALT LAKE CITY
SAN FRANCISCO
SAN PEDRO SULA
SAN SEBASTIAN
SANTO DOMINGO*
SHIJIAZHUANG
ST PETERSBURG
UJUNG PANDANG

13
BELO HORIZONTE
GUATEMALA CITY*
HO CHI MINH CITY
PORT ELIZABETH
SAN LUIS POTOSI
TANJUNGKARANG
VIRGINIA BEACH
YEKATERINBURG

14
DNEPROPETROVSK
NIZNIJ NOVGOROD
SANTIAGO DE CUBA
VISHAKHAPATNAM

17
NEWCASTLE UPON
TYNE

COMPOSERS
1500–1800

3 FUX, Johann

4 AHLE, Johann
ARNE, Thomas
BACH, Carl Philipp
Emanuel
BACH, Johann (or John)
Christian
BACH, Johann
Christoph
BACH, Johann Michael
BACH, Johann
Sebastian
BULL, John
BYRD, William

5 ANDRE, Johann
BIBER, Heinrich
CAREY, Henry
GLUCK, Christoph
HAYDN, Franz Joseph
LAWES, Henry
LAWES, William
LOCKE, Matthew
LULLI, Giambattista
LULLY, Jean-Baptiste
(orig. Giambattista
Lulli)
MEHUL, Etienne-Nicolas
SACHS, Hans
VINCI, Leonardo de

WEBER, Carl Maria von
ZUMPE, Herman

6 ALBERT, Domenico
ALBERT, Heinrich
ALCOCK, John
AUBERT, Jacques
BENNET, John
CLARKE, Jeremiah
GREENE, Maurice
GRETRY, Andre
HANDEL, George
Frideric (orig. Georg
Friedrich)
LASSUS, Roland de
(Orlando di Lasso)
LINLEY, Thomas
MORLEY, Thomas
MOZART, Wolfgang
Amadeus
RAMEAU, Jean-Philippe
SCHUTZ, Heinrich
TALLIS, Thomas
WESLEY, Samuel
WILBYE, John

7 ALLEGRI, Gregorio
ARIOSTI, Attilio
ATTWOOD, Thomas
BARTLET, John
BERTONI, Ferdinando

7 DOWLAND, John
FARNABY, Giles
FARRANT, Richard
FAYRFAX, Robert
GIBBONS, Christopher
GIBBONS, Orlando
JENKINS, John
PURCELL, Henry
REINKEN, Jan
SALIERI, Antonio
STANLEY, John
STOLZEL, Gottfried
STORACE, Stephen
STRAUSS, Christoph
TARTINI, Giuseppe
TOMKINS, Thomas
TORELLI, Giuseppe
VIVALDI, Antonio

8 AGAZZARI, Agostino
AGOSTINI, Paolo
AGRICOLA, Johann
AGRICOLA, Martin
ALBINONI, Tommaso
CIMAROSA, Domenico
COUPERIN, Francois
GABRIELI, Andrea
GABRIELI, Giovanni
GESUALDO, Carlo
STOLTZER, Thomas
TAVERNER, John
TELEMANN, Georg
   Michael
TELEMANN, Georg
   Philipp

9 BUXTEHUDE, Diederik
CAVENDISH, Michael
PACHELBEL, Johann
PACHELBEL, Wilhelm
SCARLATTI, Alessandro
SWEELINCK, Jan
WAGENSEIL, Georg
   Christoph

10 ALESSANDRI, Felice
BOCCHERINI, Luigi
KIRNBERGER, Johann
MONTEVERDI, Claudio
PALESTRINA, Giovanni
   Pierluigi da
PRAETORIUS,
   Hieronymus
PRAETORIUS, Michael
SAMMARTINI,
   Giovanni Battista
SAMMARTINI,
   Giuseppe

11 CHARPENTIER, Marc-
   Antoine
FRESCOBALDI,
   Girolamo

13 ROUGET DE LISLE,
   Claude-Joseph

COMPOSERS
1800–1900

3 ABT, Franz

4 ADAM, Adolphe
BIZET, Georges
GADE, Niels
INDY, Vincent d' (or
D'INDY)
LALO, Victor
RAFF, Joseph Joachim
WOLF, Hugo

5 ALKAN, Charles (pen
name of Charles
Morhange)
AUBER, Daniel
BALFE, Michael
BOITO, Arrigo
BRUCH, Max
D'INDY, Vincent
DUKAS, Paul
ELGAR, Edward
FAURE, Gabriel
FIELD, John
HOLST, Gustav
LISZT, Franz
PARRY, (Charles) Hubert
REGER, Max
SATIE, Erik
SOUSA, John Philip
SPOHR, Ludwig
SUPPE, Franz von

VERDI, Giuseppe
WIDOR, Charles

6 ALBERT, Eugen
AUDRAN, Edmond
BARNBY, Joseph
BISHOP, Sir Henry
BLOCKX, Jan
BRAHMS, Johannes
CHOPIN, Frederic (or
Fryderyk)
CZERNY, Karl
DELIUS, Frederick
DVORAK, Antonin
FOSTER, Stephen
FRANCK, Cesar
GERMAN, Sir Edward
HEROLD, Louis
VIERNE, Louis
WAGNER, Richard

7 ARENSKY, Anton
BARNETT, John
BELLINI, Vincenzo
BENNETT, Sir William
Sterndale
BERLIOZ, Hector
BERWALD, Franz
DEBUSSY, Claude
DELIBES, Clement Leo
JANACEK, Leos

7
NIELSEN, Carl
PUCCINI, Giacomo
ROSSINI, Gioachino
SMETANA, Bedrich
STRAUSS, Johann
STRAUSS, Josef

8
BENEDICT, Sir Julius
CHABRIER, Alexis
  Emmanuel
CHAUSSON, Ernest
CLEMENTI, Muzio
DIABELLI, Anton
GLAZUNOV, Alexander
GRANADOS, Enrique
LORTZING, Gustav
MASSENET, Jules
MESSAGER, Andre
PAGANINI, Niccolo
REINECKE, Carl
SCHUBERT, Franz
SCHUMANN, Robert
SCRIABIN, Alexander
SPONTINI, Gaspare
STANFORD, Sir Charles
SULLIVAN, Arthur

9
BALAKIREV, Mily
BEETHOVEN, Ludwig
  van
BERGGREEN, Andreas
BOIELDIEU, Francois
CHERUBINI, Maria
  Luigi
CORNELIUS, Peter
DONIZETTI, Gaetano
MARSCHNER, Heinrich

MEYERBEER, Giacomo
OFFENBACH, Jacques
SOMERVELL, Sir Arthur

10
ALEXANDROV, Anatol
MIASKOVSKY, Nikolai
RUBINSTEIN, Anton
SAINT-SAENS, Charles
  Camille
STENHAMMAR, Karl
WALDTEUFEL, Emile

11
DARGOMIJSKY,
  Alexander
HUMPERDINCK,
  Engelbert
LEONCAVALLO,
  Ruggiero
MENDELSSOHN, Felix
MOUSSORGSKY,
  Modest
RHEINBERGER, Joseph
TCHAIKOVSKY, Peter
  Ilyich

14
ARRIETA Y CORERA,
  Emilio R
RIMSKY-KORSAKOV,
  Nicolas

15
COLERIDGE-TAYLOR,
  Samuel

COMPOSERS
1900–2005

3
BAX, Arnold
MAW, Nicholas
ORR, Robin

4
ADES, Thomas
AHLE, Johann
BECK, Conrad
BERG, Alban
BURT, Francis
BUSH, Alan
CAGE, John
CARY, Tristram
COLE, Bruce
HOLD, Trevor
IVES, Charles
JOHN, Elton
NONO, Luigi
ORFF, Carl
PART, Arvo
WEIR, Judith
WOOD, Hugh

5
ADAMS, John
ALWYN, William
AURIC, Georges
BAIRD, Tadeusz
BERIO, Luciano
BLAKE, David
BLISS, Sir Arthur
BLOCH, Ernest
BRIAN, Havergal

COWIE, Edward
DUPRE, Marcel
ELLIS, David
FALLA, Manuel de
FINZI, Gerald
GLASS, Philip
GOEHR, Alexander
HARTY, Sir Herbert
  Hamilton
HENZE, Hans Werner
LLOYD, George
NYMAN, Michael
OGDON, John
PARRY, Sir (Charles)
  Hubert
PAYNE, Anthony
PONCE, Manuel
RANDS, Bernard
RAVEL, Maurice
REICH, Steve
ROUTH, Francis
SAWER, David
SMYTH, Dame Ethel
STYNE, Jule
TUBIN, Eduard
WEILL, Kurt
WHITE, John

6
ALFVEN, Hugo
ARNOLD, Sir Malcolm
BARBER, Samuel

6

BARLOW, David
BARTOK, Bela
BERLIN, Irving
BIALAS, Gunter
BLYTON, Carey
BOULEZ, Pierre
BRIDGE, Frank
BROMAN, Sten
BURGON, Geoffrey
BUSONI, Ferruccio
CANNON, Philip
CARDEW, Cornelius
CARTER, Elliott
COATES, Albert
COATES, Eric
CROSSE, Gordon
DAVIES, Sir Peter
  Maxwell
FORBES, Sebastian
GLIERE, Reinhold
GURNEY, Ivor
HADLEY, Patrick
HANSON, Howard
HARRIS, Roy
HARVEY, Jonathan
HEDGES, Anthony
KODALY, Zoltan
LAWSON, Gordon
LEFANU, Nicola
LENNON, John
LIGETI, Gyorgy
MARTIN, Frank
MCCABE, John
MOERAN, Ernest
MORGAN, David
NEWSON, George
OLDHAM, Arthur

PARKER, Jim
PISTON, Walter
PURSER, John
RIDOUT, Alan
RUBBRA, Edmund
SAXTON, Robert
SEARLE, Humphrey
TURINA, Joaquin
VARESE, Edgard
WALTON, Sir William
WEBERN, Anton von

7

ADDISON, John
ANTHEIL, George
BABBITT, Milton
BANTOCK, Sir Granville
BEDFORD, David
BENNETT, Richard
  Rodney
BERNERS, Lord (Gerald
  Tyrwhitt-Wilson)
BRITTEN, Benjamin
CHAPPLE, Brian
COPLAND, Aaron
DIAMOND, David
DODGSON, Stephen
DURUFLE, Maurice
FRANKEL, Benjamin
FRICKER, Peter Racine
GERHARD, Roberto
GORECKI, Henryk
HOWELLS, Herbert
IRELAND, John
JOHNSON, Robert
  Sherlaw
JOSEPHS, Wilfred
KNUSSEN, Oliver

7 LAMBERT, Constant
LEGRAND, Michel
LOESSER, Frank
LUTYENS, Elisabeth
MANCINI, Henry
MARTINU, Bohuslav
MATHIAS, William
MENOTTI, Gian Carlo
MILHAUD, Darius
POULENC, Francis
RODGERS, Richard
ROUSSEL, Albert
SIMPSON, Robert
SMALLEY, Roger
SOUSTER, Tim
STRAUSS, Richard
TAVENER, Sir John
THOMSON, Virgil
TIPPETT, Sir Michael
TURNAGE, Mark-
　Anthony
WARLOCK, Peter
WELLESZ, Egon
WHETTAM, Graham
XENAKIS, Iannis

8 AKIMENKO, Feodor
BENJAMIN, Arthur
BENJAMIN, George
BERKELEY, Sir Lennox
BERKELEY, Michael
BOUGHTON, Rutland
CONNOLLY, Justin
DOHNANYI, Erno
FINNISSY, Michael
GERSHWIN, George
GRAINGER, Percy

HAMILTON, Iain
HOLLOWAY, Robin
HONEGGER, Arthur
KORNGOLD, Erich
LEIGHTON, Kenneth
MESSIAEN, Olivier
MUSGRAVE, Thea
PANUFNIK, Sir Andrzej
PFITZNER, Hans
RESPIGHI, Ottorino
ROXBURGH, Edwin
SESSIONS, Roger
SHRAPNEL, Hugh
SIBELIUS, Jean

9 ATTERBERG, Kurt
BACHARACH, Burt
BERNSTEIN, Leonard
BOURGEOIS, Derek
CASTLEDEN, Rodney
DANKWORTH, John
DICKINSON, Peter
DUTILLEUX, Henri
HESELTINE, Philip (pen
　name Peter Warlock)
HINDEMITH, Paul
HODDINOTT, Alun
MACMILLAN, James
MCCARTNEY, Paul
PATTERSON, Paul
PROKOFIEV, Sergei
STANDFORD, Patric
STEVENSON, Ronald
TAKEMITSU, Toru

ANDRIESSEN, Louis
BAINBRIDGE, Simon

10 BIRTWISTLE, Harrison
HEADINGTON,
 Christopher
KABALEVSKY, Dmitri
PADEREWSKI, Ignacy
RAWSTHORNE, Alan
SCHOENBERG, Arnold
STRAVINSKY, Igor
TCHEREPNIN,
 Alexander
VILLA-LOBOS, Heitor
WOOLFENDEN, Guy

11 CHARPENTIER, Gustave
FERNEYHOUGH, Brian
LLOYD WEBBER,
 Andrew
LUTOSLAWSKI, Witold
MITROPOULOS,
 Dimitri
RACHMANINOV,
 Sergei
STOCKHAUSEN,
 Karlheinz
SZYMANOWSKI, Karol
WOLF-FERRARI,
 Ermanno

12 DALLAPICCOLA, Luigi
KHACHATURIAN,
 Aram
SHOSTAKOVICH,
 Dmitri

15 VAUGHAN WILLIAMS,
 Ralph

COUNTIES
Administrative counties of
England, Northern Ireland, Scotland and Wales

Administrative England

4 KENT

5 DEVON
ESSEX

6 DORSET
DURHAM
SURREY

7 BRISTOL
CUMBRIA
NORFOLK
RUTLAND
SUFFOLK

8 CHESHIRE
SOMERSET

9 BERKSHIRE
HAMPSHIRE
WILTSHIRE

10 DERBYSHIRE
EAST SUSSEX
LANCASHIRE
MERSEYSIDE
SHROPSHIRE
WEST SUSSEX

11 ISLE OF WIGHT
OXFORDSHIRE
TYNE AND WEAR

12 BEDFORDSHIRE
LINCOLNSHIRE
WARWICKSHIRE
WEST MIDLANDS

13 GREATER LONDON
HEREFORDSHIRE
HERTFORDSHIRE
STAFFORDSHIRE
WEST YORKSHIRE

14 CAMBRIDGESHIRE
LEICESTERSHIRE
NORTHUMBERLAND
NORTH YORKSHIRE
SOUTH YORKSHIRE
WORCESTERSHIRE

15 BUCKINGHAMSHIRE
GLOUCESTERSHIRE
NOTTINGHAMSHIRE

16 NORTHAMPTONSHIRE

17 GREATER MANCHESTER
CORNWALL AND
SCILLY

21 EAST RIDING OF
YORKSHIRE

Administrative Scotland

4 FIFE

5 ANGUS
MORAY

6 ORKNEY

7 FALKIRK

8 HIGHLAND
SHETLAND
STIRLING

10 DUNDEE CITY
INVERCLYDE
MIDLOTHIAN

11 EAST LOTHIAN
WEST LOTHIAN

12 ABERDEEN CITY
EAST AYRSHIRE
RENFREWSHIRE
WESTERN ISLES

13 ABERDEENSHIRE
ARGYLL AND BUTE
CITY OF GLASGOW
NORTH AYRSHIRE
SOUTH AYRSHIRE

15 CITY OF EDINBURGH
PERTH AND KINROSS
SCOTTISH BORDERS

16 CLACKMANNANSHIRE
EAST RENFREWSHIRE
NORTH LANARKSHIRE
SOUTH LANARKSHIRE

18 EAST
DUNBARTONSHIRE
WEST
DUNBARTONSHIRE

19 DUMFRIES AND
GALLOWAY

Administrative Wales

5 POWYS

7 CARDIFF
GWYNEDD
NEWPORT
SWANSEA
TORFAEN
WREXHAM

8 ANGLESEY
BRIDGEND

10 CAERPHILLY
FLINTSHIRE

12 BLAENAU GWENT
DENBIGHSHIRE

13 CARDIGANSHIRE
MERTHYR TYDFIL
MONMOUTHSHIRE

13 PEMBROKESHIRE

15 CARMARTHENSHIRE
VALE OF
GLAMORGAN

16 RHONDDA, CYNON
TAFF

18 ABERCONWY AND
COLWYN
NEATH AND PORT
TALBOT

**Administrative
Northern Ireland**

4 DOWN

6 ANTRIM
ARMAGH
TYRONE

9 FERMANAGH

11 LONDONDERRY
(DERRY)

193

COUNTRIES
and their capitals

COUNTRY	CAPITAL

4

CHAD	N'djamena
CUBA	Havana
FIJI	Suva
IRAN	Tehran
IRAQ	Baghdad
LAOS	Vientiane
MALI	Bamako
OMAN	Muscat
PERU	Lima
TOGO	Lome

5

BENIN	Porto-Novo
CHILE	Santiago
EGYPT	Cairo
GABON	Libreville
GHANA	Accra
HAITI	Port-au-Prince
ITALY	Rome
INDIA	New Delhi
JAPAN	Tokyo
KENYA	Nairobi
LIBYA	Tripoli
MALTA	Valletta
NAURU	Yaren District
NEPAL	Kathmandu
NIGER	Niamey
PALAU	Koror

COUNTRY	CAPITAL

5

QATAR	Doha
SAMOA	Apia
SPAIN	Madrid
SUDAN	Khartoum
SYRIA	Damascus
TONGA	Nuku'alofa
YEMEN	Sana

6

ANGOLA	Luanda
BELIZE	Belmopan
BHUTAN	Thimphu
BRAZIL	Brasilia
BRUNEI	Bandar Seri Begawan
CANADA	Ottawa
CYPRUS	Nicosia
FRANCE	Paris
GAMBIA (The)	Banjul
GREECE	Athens
GUINEA	Conakry
GUYANA	Georgetown
ISRAEL	Jerusalem
JORDAN	Amman
KUWAIT	Kuwait City
LATVIA	Riga
MALAWI	Lilongwe
MEXICO	Mexico City
MONACO	Monaco City
NORWAY	Oslo
PANAMA	Panama City
POLAND	Warsaw
RUSSIA	Moscow
RWANDA	Kigali

COUNTRY	CAPITAL

6

SWEDEN	Stockholm
TAIWAN	Taipei
TURKEY	Ankara
TUVALU	Funafuti
UGANDA	Kampala
ZAMBIA	Lusaka

7

ALBANIA	Tirana
ALGERIA	Algiers
ANDORRA	Andorra La Vella
ARMENIA	Yerevan
AUSTRIA	Vienna
BAHAMAS (The)	Nassau
BAHRAIN	Manama
BELARUS	Minsk
BELGIUM	Brussels
BOLIVIA	La Paz (administrative)
	Sucre (judicial)
BURUNDI	Bujumbura
COMOROS	Moroni
CROATIA	Zagreb
DENMARK	Copenhagen
ECUADOR	Quito
ERITREA	Asmara
ESTONIA	Tallinn
FINLAND	Helsinki
GEORGIA	Tbilisi
GERMANY	Berlin
GRENADA	St George's
HUNGARY	Budapest
ICELAND	Reykjavik
IRELAND	Dublin
JAMAICA	Kingston

COUNTRY	CAPITAL

7

LEBANON	Beirut
LESOTHO	Maseru
LIBERIA	Monrovia
MOLDOVA	Chisinau
MOROCCO	Rabat
MYANMAR (Burma)	Rangoon
NAMIBIA	Windhoek
NIGERIA	Abuja
ROMANIA	Bucharest
SENEGAL	Dakar
SOMALIA	Mogadishu
TUNISIA	Tunis
UKRAINE	Kiev
URUGUAY	Montevideo
VANUATU	Port Vila
VIETNAM	Hanoi

8

BARBADOS	Bridgetown
BOTSWANA	Gaborone
BULGARIA	Sofia
CAMBODIA	Phnom Penn
CAMEROON	Yaounde
COLOMBIA	Bogota
DJIBOUTI	Djibouti
DOMINICA	Roseau
ETHIOPIA	Addis Ababa
HONDURAS	Tegucigalpa
KIRIBATI	Tarawa
MALAYSIA	Kuala Lumpur
MALDIVES	Male
MONGOLIA	Ulaanbaatar
PAKISTAN	Islamabad
PARAGUAY	Asuncion

COUNTRY	CAPITAL

8

PORTUGAL	Lisbon
SLOVAKIA	Bratislava
SLOVENIA	Ljubljana
SRI LANKA	Sri Jayawardenapura
SURINAME	Paramaribo
TANZANIA	Dodoma (Dar es Salaam)
THAILAND	Bangkok
ZIMBABWE	Harare

9

ARGENTINA	Buenos Aires
AUSTRALIA	Canberra
CAPE VERDE	Praia
COSTA RICA	San Jose
EAST TIMOR	Dili
GUATEMALA	Guatemala City
GREENLAND	Nuuk (but part of Denmark)
INDONESIA	Jakarta
LITHUANIA	Vilnius
MACEDONIA	Skopje
MAURITIUS	Port Louis
NICARAGUA	Managua
SAN MARINO	San Marino
SINGAPORE	Singapore City
SWAZILAND	Mbabane
VENEZUELA	Caracas

10

AZERBAIJAN	Baku
BANGLADESH	Dhaka
EL SALVADOR	San Salvador
KAZAKHSTAN	Astana
KOREA, NORTH	Pyongyang
KOREA, SOUTH	Seoul
KYRGYZSTAN	Bishkek

COUNTRY	CAPITAL

10

LUXEMBOURG	Luxembourg
MADAGASCAR	Antananarivo
MAURITANIA	Nouakchott
MOZAMBIQUE	Maputo
NEW ZEALAND	Wellington
SAINT LUCIA	Castries
SEYCHELLES	Victoria
TAJIKISTAN	Dushanbe Taibei
UZBEKISTAN	Tashkent

11

AFGHANISTAN	Kabul
BURKINA FASO	Ouagadougou
COTE D'IVOIRE	Yamoussoukro (official) Abidjan (de facto)
NETHERLANDS	Amsterdam
PHILIPPINES	Manila
SAUDI ARABIA	Riyadh
SIERRA LEONE	Freetown
SOUTH AFRICA	Pretoria (administrative) Cape Town (legislative) Bloemfontein (judiciary)
SWITZERLAND	Bern
VATICAN CITY	Vatican City

12

GUINEA-BISSAU	Bissau
TURKMENISTAN	Ashkhabad

13

CZECH REPUBLIC	Prague
LIECHTENSTEIN	Vaduz
UNITED KINGDOM	London
WESTERN SAHARA	None (under de facto control of Morocco)

COUNTRY	CAPITAL

14

PAPUA NEW GUINEA	Port Moresby
SOLOMAN ISLANDS	Honiara

15

CONGO, Republic of (Formerly The Congo)	Brazzaville
MARSHALL ISLANDS	Majuro

16

EQUATORIAL GUINEA	Malabo

17

ANTIGUA and BARBUDA	Saint John's
DOMINICAN REPUBLIC	Santo Domingo
TRINIDAD and TOBAGO	Port of Spain

18

SAINT KITTS and NEVIS	Basseterre
SAO TOME and PRINCIPE	Sao Tome
UNITED ARAB EMIRATES	Abu Dhabi

19

SERBIA and MONTENEGRO (Former Yugoslavia)	Belgrade

20

BOSNIA and HERZEGOVINA	Savajevo

21

UNITED STATES of AMERICA	Washington D.C.

COUNTRY	CAPITAL

22

| CENTRAL AFRICAN REPUBLIC | Bangui |

27

| FEDERATED STATES of MICRONESIA | Palikir |

28

| CONGO, Democratic Republic of the (Formerly Zaire) | Kinshasa |
| SAINT VINCENT and the GRENADINES | Kingstown |

CRICKET GROUNDS
UK

GROUND	COUNTY/LOCATION
5	
LORD'S	London
7	
HORSHAM	Sussex
NEVILLE	Tunbridge Wells, Kent
NEW ROAD	Worcester, Worcestershire
THE OVAL	London/ Surrey
8	
MOTE PARK	Maidstone, Kent
RICHMOND	Middlesex
SAFFRONS	Eastbourne, Sussex
ST HELENS	Swansea, Glamorgan
9	
EATON ROAD	Hove, Sussex
EDGBASTON	Birmingham, Warwickshire
GRACE ROAD	Leicester, Leicestershire
NEVIL ROAD	Bristol, Gloucestershire
RIVERSIDE	Chester-le-Street, Durham
SOUTHGATE	Middlesex
10	
HEADINGLEY	Leeds, Yorkshire
ST LAWRENCE	Canterbury, Kent
11	
OLD TRAFFORD	Manchester, Lancashire

GROUND	COUNTY/LOCATION

11

SHENLEY PARK	Middlesex
STANLEY PARK	Blackpool, Lancashire
TRENT BRIDGE	Nottingham, Nottinghamshire
WANTAGE ROAD	Northampton, Northamptonshire

12

| AIGBURTH ROAD | Liverpool, Lancashire |

13

ARUNDEL CASTLE	Arundel, Sussex
CENTRAL AVENUE	Worksop, Nottinghamshire
SOPHIA GARDENS	Cardiff, Glamorgan
ST JAMES' STREET	Taunton, Somerset

14

| NORTHLANDS ROAD | Southampton, Hampshire |
| WHITGIFT SCHOOL | Croydon, Surrey |

16

| NEW WRITTLE STREET | Chelmsford, Essex |
| RACECOURSE GROUND | Derby, Derbyshire |

CURRENCIES
and the countries that use them

CURRENCY	COUNTRY
3	
KIP	Laos
LAT	Latvia
LEK	Albania
LEU	Romania, Moldova
LEV (New)	Bulgaria
SOM	Kyrgyzstan, Uzbekistan
WON	North Korea, South Korea
YEN	Japan
4	
BAHT	Thailand
BIRR	Ethiopia
CEDI (New)	Ghana
DONG (New)	Vietnam
DRAM	Armenia
EURO	Austria, Belgium, France, Finland, Germany, Greece, Ireland, Italy, Luxembourg, Monaco, Netherlands, Portugal, Spain
KINA	Papua New Guinea
KUNA	Croatia
KYAT	Myanmar (Burma)
LARI	Georgia
LIRA	Italy (–2002), Turkey (–2004, New Lira 2005–)
LIRA (Maltese)	Malta

CURRENCY	COUNTRY

4

LOTI	Lesoth
PESO	Argentina, Chile, Colombia, Cuba, Dominican Republic, Guinea-Bissau (–April 1997), Mexico, Philippines, Uruguay (–1975), 1975–1993 New Peso), Sudan (–1992), Syria
PESO (Uruguano)	Uruguay (1993–)
PULA	Botswana
PUNT	Ireland (–1998)
RAND	South Africa
REAL	Brazil
RIAL	Iran, Oman
RIAL (Yemeni)	Yemen
RIEL (New)	Cambodia
TAKA	Bangladesh
TALA	Samoa
VATU	Vanuatu
YUAN	China

5

COLON	Costa Rica, El Salvador
DENAR	Macedonia
DINAR	Algeria, Bahrain, Iraq, Jordan, Kuwait, Libya, Serbia and Montenegro, Sudan (1992–), Tunisia
DOBRA	Sao Tome & Principe
FRANC	Belgium (–1998), Benin, Burkina Faso, Burundi,Cameroon, Central African Republic, Chad, Comoros, Congo, Cote d'Ivoire, Djibouti, Equatorial Guinea,

CURRENCY	COUNTRY

5

FRANC (cont.)	France (–1998), Gabon, Guinea, Guinea Bissau (1997–), Luxembourg (–1998),Madagascar, Mali, Niger, Rwanda, Senegal, Switzerland, Togo
KRONA	Sweden
KRONE	Denmark, Norway
KROON	Estonia
LEONE	Sierra Leone
LITAS	Lithuania
MANAT	Azerbaijan, Turkmenistan
NAIRA	Nigeria
NAKFA	Eritrea
POUND	Cyprus, Egypt, Lebanon, Sudan (–1992), Syria, UK
RIYAL	Qatar, Saudi Arabia, Yemen
RUPEE	India, Mauritius, Nepal, Pakistan, Seychelles, Sri Lanka
SUCRE	Ecuador
TENGE	Kazakhstan
TOLAR	Slovenia
ZLOTY	Poland

6

BALBOA	Panama
DALASI	Gambia
DIRHAM	Morocco, United Arab, Emirates
DOLLAR	Anguilla, Antigua & Barbuda, Australia, Bahamas, Barbados, Belize, Brunei, Canada, Cayman Islands, Dominica, Fiji, Grenada, Guyana, Hong Kong, Jamaica, Liberia, Namibia, New Zealand, Singapore, Soloman Islands,

CURRENCY	COUNTRY

6

DOLLAR (cont.)	St Lucia, St Kitts and Nevis, St Vincent and the Grenadines, Suriname, Taiwan (New dollar), Trinidad and Tobago, United States of America, Zimbabwe
ESCUDO	Portugal (–1998)
FORINT	Hungary
GOURDE	Haiti
HRYVNA	Ukraine
KORUNA	Czech Republic, Slovakia
KRONUR	Iceland
KWACHA	Malawi, Zambia
KWANZA	Angola
MARKKA	Finland (–1998), Bosnia-Herzegovina
PA'ANGA	Tonga
PESETA	Spain (–1998)
ROUBLE	Belarus (2000–), Russia, Tajikistan (–Nov. 2000)
RUPIAH	Indonesia
SHEKEL (New)	Israel
SOMONI	Tajikistan (Nov. 2000–)

7

AFGHANI	Afghanistan
AUSTRAL	Argentina (–1991)
CORDOBA (Gold)	Nicaragua
DRACHMA	Greece (–1998)
GUARANI	Paraguay
GUILDER	Netherlands (–1998)
LEMPIRA	Honduras
METICAL	Mozambique
OUGUIJA	Mauritania
QUETZAL	Guatemala

CURRENCY	COUNTRY

7

| RINGGIT | Malaysia |
| RUFIYAA | Maldives |

8

| NGULTRUM | Bhutan |
| SHILLING | Kenya, Somalia, Tanzania, Uganda |

9

BOLIVIANO	Bolivia
LILANGENI	Swaziland
SCHILLING	Austria (–1998)

11

| DEUTSCHMARK | Germany (–2002) |

DANCES
of the world

3
BOP
FAN
HOP
JIG
TAP
WAR

4
BALL
BUYO
CLOG
HORA
JAZZ
JIVE
JOTA
KOLO
LINE
MOSH
POLE
RAVE
REEL
SA SA
SKIP

5
BELLY
BEBOP
BREAK
CONGA
DISCO
GIGUE
HALAY
IRISH

LATIN
LIMBO
MAMBO
POLKA
RUMBA
SABRE
SALSA
SAMBA
SWORD
SYRTO
TANGO
TWIST
WALTZ

6
BALLET
BALLOS (Greece)
BOLERO
BRANLE
CANCAN
CIRCLE
FLORAL
HEJSZA
KATHAK
LE ROCK
MINUET
MODERN
MORRIS
ODISSI
PAVANE
SQUARE
VALETA

6
VELETA
WATUSI
ZERVOS

7
BHANGRA
BOURREE
CHOCHEK
COUNTRY
FOXTROT
GAVOTTE
LAMBADA
MAYPOLE
MAZURKA
SIGANOS
STA TRIA
SYRTAKI
TSAMIKO

8
BALLROOM
CACHUCHA
CAKEWALK
CASCARDA
COURANTE
DIRLANDA
FANDANGO
FLAMENCO
GALLIARD
HAND JIVE
HAWAIIAN
HORNPIPE
MACARINA
MANIPURI
MERENGUE
PRAVO OVO

9
BARNDANCE
CHA-CHA-CHA
CLASSICAL

DROPULLIT
FARANDOLE
FREYLEKHS
HANTER DRO
HASSAPIKO
JITTERBUG
KATHAKALI
KUCHIPUDI
LONGSWORD
PASO DOBLE
POLONAISE
QUADRILLE
QUICK-STEP
SARABANDE
ZEYBEKIKO

10
AGIR GOVENK
CHARLESTON
GAY GORDONS
GRAND MARCH
HOKEY-COKEY
KARSILAMAS
KETRI-KETRI
LOCOMOTION
MASQUERADE
MEXICAN HAT
PASSAMEZZO
RAGS SHARGI (Belly)
STILT DANCE
STRATHSPEY
STRIPTEASE
TSIFTETELI
TURKEY TROT

11
APPALACHIAN
ANTIKRYSTOS
BLACK BOTTOM
KALAMATIANO

11
LAMBETH WALK
RAPPER SWORD
ROCK AND ROLL
ZORBA'S DANCE

12
CHICKEN DANCE
CONTEMPORARY
DANCE OF DEATH
DANSE MACABRE
ZONARADHIKOS

13
BHARATA NATYAN
EIGHTSOME REEL
HIGHLAND FLING
LATIN AMERICAN

14
CUMBERLAND REEL
HASSAPOSERVIKO

15
MILITARY TWOSTEP

16
SILYVRIANO SYRTOS

17
APTALIKO ZEYBEKIKO

18
PRAVO TRADIJSKO HORO

20
DANCE OF THE SEVEN VEILS
DASHING WHITE SERGEANT

21
SCOTTISH HIGHLAND SWORD

DESERTS

4
GILA
GOBI
THAR
YUMA

5
KAVIR
MONTE
NAFUD
NAMIB
NEGEV
OLMOS
ORDOS
SINAI
STURT

6
ARUNTA
CHALBI
GIBSON
LIBYAN
MOJAVE
NUBIAN
OGADEN
SAHARA
SYRIAN
TANAMI
UST-URT

7
ALASHAN
ARABIAN
ATACAMA
IRANIAN

KARA-KUM
MORROPE
PAINTED
RANGIPO
SECHURA
SIMPSON
SONORAN

8
COLORADO
ISMAILIA
KALAHARI
KYZYL-KUM
MUYUNKUM
VIZCAINO
XINJIANG

9
ALTIPLANO
BLACK ROCK
DASHT-E-LUT
DZUNGARIA
TURKESTAN

10
AUSTRALIAN
BET-PAK-DALA
CHIHUAHUAN
DRAA VALLEY
GREAT BASIN
GREAT SANDY
PATAGONIAN
RUB AL'KHALI
TAKLA MAKAN

11 DASHT-E-KAVIR
DASHT-E-MARGO
DEATH VALLEY
DIDI GÁLGALU
GREAT INDIAN

12 STEWART STONY
TAR-CHOLISTAN

13 GREAT SALT LAKE
GREAT VICTORIA
THAR CHOLISTAN

14 BOLSON DE MAPIMI

15 COLORADO PLATEAU

16 TURFAN DEPRESSION

CHARLES DICKENS
Novels and short stories

9 HARD TIMES
THE CHIMES

10 BLEAK HOUSE
HUNTED DOWN

11 OLIVER TWIST

12 BARNABY RUDGE
DOMBEY AND SON
LITTLE DORRIT
NOBODY'S STORY
THE HOLLY-TREE

13 MUGBY JUNCTION
NO THROUGHFARE

14 A CHRISTMAS TREE
DOCTOR MARIGOLD
HOLIDAY ROMANCE
THE CHILD'S STORY
THE LAMPLIGHTER

15 A CHRISTMAS CAROL
OUR MUTUAL FRIEND
SOMBODY'S LUGGAGE
THE BATTLE OF LIFE
THE HAUNTED HOUSE

16 A TALE OF TWO CITIES
DAVID COPPERFIELD

GOING INTO SOCIETY
MARTIN CHUZZLEWIT
NICHOLAS NICKLELBY

17 GREAT EXPECTATIONS
THE PICKWICK PAPERS
THE TRIAL FOR MURDER
TOM TIDDLER'S GROUND

18 MRS LIRRIPER'S LEGACY
THE SCHOOLBOY'S STORY
A MESSAGE FROM THE
SEA

19 THE OLD CURIOSITY SHOP

20 MASTER HUMPHREY'S
CLOCK
MRS LIRRIPER'S LODGINGS

21 THE CRICKET ON THE
HEARTH
THE POOR RELATION'S
STORY
SUNDAY UNDER THREE
HEADS

22 THE MYSTERY OF EDWIN
DROOD
THE SEVEN POOR
TRAVELLERS

DINOSAURS
and other prehistoric animals

8
AVIMIMUS
BARYONYX
COELURUS
EOHIPPUS
EORAPTOR
RUTIODON
SMILODON

9
IGUANODON
MAIASAURA
MUSSAURUS
OVIRAPTOR
RHABDODON
SAICHANIA
TRACHODON

10
ALLOSAURUS
ALTISPINAX
AMMOSAURUS
ANATOTITAN
BAROSAURUS
DIPLODOCUS
DRYOSAURUS
EDMONTONIA
EUPARKERIA
GALLIMIMUS
GASOSAURUS
MESOHIPPUS
NODOSAURUS
ORODROMEUS
ORTHOMERUS

PLIOHIPPUS
PTERANODON
STEGOCERAS
UTAHRAPTOR

11
ABELISAURUS
AFROVENATOR
ALAMOSAURUS
ANATOSAURUS
ANCHISAURUS
ANSERIMIMUS
APATOSAURUS
APHANERAMMA
CARNOTAURUS
CAUDIPTERYX
CETIOSAURUS
COELOPHYSIS
DACENTRURUS
DATOUSAURUS
DEINONYCHUS
HADROSAURUS
KRITOSAURUS
MANDASUCHUS
MERYCHIPPUS
MICRORAPTOR
MONOCLONIUS
POLACANTHUS
PTERODACTYL
RIOJASAURUS
SALTASAURUS
SAUROLOPHUS

11
SEGNOSAURUS
SHUNOSAURUS
SPINOSAURUS
STEGOSAURUS
TARBOSAURUS
TRICERATOPS

12
AMARGASAURUS
ANKYLOSAURUS
BAGACERATOPS
BARAPASAURUS
BRONTOSAURUS
CAMARASAURUS
CAMPTOSAURUS
CENTROSAURUS
CERATOSAURUS
CHASMOSAURUS
DEINOCHEIRUS
DRYPTOSAURUS
HYLAEOSAURUS
KENTROSAURUS
LAMBEOSAURUS
MEGALOSAURUS
ORNITHOMIMUS
OURANOSAURUS
PARKSOSAURUS
PELOROSAURUS
PLATEOSAURUS
SCHOLOSAURUS
SEISMOSAURUS
TICINOSUCHUS
VELOCIRAPTOR

13
ACHELOUSAURUS
AEGYPTOSAURUS
ALBERTOSAURUS
ALECTROSAURUS

ALVAREZSAURUS
ANCHICERATOPS
ARCHAEOPTERYX
BRACHIOSAURUS
COMPSOGNATHUS
CORYTHOSAURUS
DESMATOSUCHUS
DICRAEOSAURUS
DILOPHOSAURUS
DROMAEOSAURUS
EDMONTOSAURUS
ERYTHROSUCHUS
HERRERASAURUS
HYPSELOSAURUS
HYPSILOPHODON
LESOTHOSAURUS
LUFENGOSAURUS
ORNITHOLESTES
PANOPLOSAURUS
PENTACERATOPS
PROTOCERATOPS
PTERODACTYLUS
SCELIDOSAURUS
SCLEROMOCHLUS
STRUTHIOMIMUS
STYRACOSAURUS
TENONTOSAURUS
TYRANNOSAURUS
ZEPHYROSAURUS

14
ANTARCTOSAURUS
BALUCHITHERIUM
CETIOSAURISCUS
CHASMATOSAURUS
DASPLETOSAURUS
DROMICEIOMIMUS
EUOPLOCEPHALUS

14
GIGANOTOSAURUS
GILMOREOSAURUS
HUAYANGOSAURUS
LEAELLYNASAURA
MAMENCHISAURUS
MASSOSPONDYLUS
PSITTACOSAURUS
THESCELOSAURUS

15
ARGENTINOSAURUS
CRYOLOPHOSAURUS
PARASAUROLOPHUS
PROCHENEOSAURUS
SAURORNITHOIDES
SHANTUNGOSAURUS

16
ACROCANTHOSAURUS
ATLASCOPCOSAURUS
MUTTABURRASAURUS
PACHYRHINOSAURUS
PROCOMPSOGNATHUS
YANGCHUANOSAURUS

17
HETERODONTOSAURUS

18
ARCHAEORNITHOMIMUS
PACHYCEPHALOSAURUS

19
CARCHARODONTOSAURUS

ENGINEERS, INVENTORS and SCIENTISTS
Before 1800

3
GED, William
KAY, John
LEE, William

4
CORT, Henry
DAVY, Sir Humphry
HELE, Petrus
NOCK, Henry
TULL, Jethro
WATT, James

5
BACON, Roger
BAUME, Antoine
BOYLE, Robert
BRAHE, Tycho
BRAND, Hennig
DARBY, Abraham
FITCH, John
PAPIN, Denis
ROMER, Olaus
SAINT, Thomas

6
CAWLEY, Thomas
EUCLID
FERMAT, Pierre de
FULTON, Robert
HALLEY, Edmond
HARVEY, William
JENNER, Edward
KEPLER, Johannes
KOTTER, Joseph

MOUTON, Gabriel
NAPIER, John
NEWTON, Sir Isaac
PASCAL, Blaise
SAVERY, Thomas
VOLTA, Alessandro
WISTAR, Caspar

7
CELSIUS, Anders
ELHUYAR, Fausto de
ELHUYAR, Joan Jose de
GALILEO (Galileo Galilei)
HUYGENS, Christiaan
JANSSEN, Zacharias
LEBLANC, Nicolas
LEIBNIZ, Gottfried
LEIBNIZ, Wilhelm von
PTOLEMY
REAUMUR, Rene de
SCHEELE, Karl
T'SAI LUN
WHITNEY, Eli

8
BRINDLEY, James
BUSHNELL, David
FRANKLIN, Benjamin
GUERICKE, Otto von
HARRISON, John
HERSCHEL, Sir William
HUNTSMAN, Benjamin

8
KLAPROTH, Martin
NEWCOMEN, Thomas
VESALIUS, Andreas
WEDGWOOD, Thomas

9
ARISTOTLE
ARKWRIGHT, Sir Richard
CAVENDISH, Henry
CRONSTEDT, Axel
DESCARTES, Rene
GASCOIGNE, William
GUTENBERG, Johannes
LAVOISIER, Antoine
LENORMAND, Louis
PRIESTLEY, Joseph
VAUQUELIN, Nicolas Louis

10
ARCHIMEDES
CARTWRIGHT, Edmund
COPERNICUS, Nicolas
DIOPHANTUS
FAHRENHEIT, Gabriel
HARGREAVES, James
HEROPHILUS
HIPPARCHUS
LIPPERSHEY, Hans
MAUPERTUIS, Pierre de
PYTHAGORAS
RUTHERFORD, Daniel
SENEFELDER, Aloys
TORRICELLI, Evangelista

11
MONTGOLFIER, Jacques
MONTGOLFIER, Joseph

12
ERATOSTHENES

ENGINEERS, INVENTORS and SCIENTISTS
1800–1900

3 HOE, Richard

4 BELL, Alexander
    Graham
BELL, Henry
BENZ, Karl
COLT, Samuel
DAFT, Leo
DAVY, Sir Humphry
FORD, Henry
HILL, James
HOWE, Elias
HUNT, Walter
IVES, Frederick
KOCH, Robert
MOHL, Hugo von
NOCK, Henry
OTIS, Elisha
SNOW, John
SWAN, Sir Joseph
VAIL, Andrew
YALE, Linus

5 BAIRD, James
BAKER, Sir Benjamin
BEVAN, Edward
BOLLE, Leon
BRAUN, Karl
CARRE, Ferdinand
CLARK, Patrick
COOKE, Sir William
CROSS, Charles

CURIE, Marie
CURIE, Pierre
DEERE, John
ELLET, Charles
FREUD, Sigmund
GALLE, Johann
GATES, John
GREEN, Charles
HENRY, Joseph
JOULE, James
KELLY, William
LEBON, Philippe
LOGAN, James
MARSH, Sylvester
MAXIM, Sir Hiram
MCKAY, Donald
MOORE, Thomas
MORSE, Samuel
NOBEL, Alfred
PAGET, Sir James
PROUT, William
RITTY, James
SEELY, H. W.
SMITH, Gideon
SMITH, Hamilton
SOULE, Samuel
STILL, Andrew
TERRY, Eli
ZEISS, Carl

6 ASPDIN, Joseph
BAILEY, Leonard

6

BALARD, Antoine
BORDEN, Gail
BOYDEN, Seth
BRUNEL, Isambard
  Kingdom
BUNSEN, Robert
CAYLEY, Arthur
CAYLEY, Sir George
DALTON, John
DARWIN, Charles
DREYSE, Johann
DUNLOP, John Boyd
EIFFEL, Gustave
EDISON, Thomas
FOWLER, Sir John
FRASCH, Hermann
GALTON, Sir Francis
GORRIE, John
HALLEY, John
HANSOM, Joseph
HARVEY, Charles T.
HORNER, W. C. van
HUGHES, David
HUSSEY, Obed
JUDSON, Whitcomb
KELLER, Gottlob
LIEBIG, Justus, Baron
  von
LISTER, Joseph
LOWELL, Percival
MAUSER, Peter
MCADAM, John
MENDEL, Gregor
MORTON, William
MOUTON, Gabriel
NIEPCE, Joseph
NOBILI, Leopoldo

PARKES, Alexander
PERKIN, Sir William
PITMAN, Sir Isaac
PLANCK, Max
PUTNAM, Silas
RAMSAY, Sir William
RENNIE, John
ROGERS, Henry
SEGUIN, Marc
SELDEN, George B.
SHOLES, Christopher
SLATER, Samuel
SPERRY, Elmer
TALBOT, William Fox
TAYLOR, Augustus
WALKER, John
WALTON, Frederick
WINSOR, Frederick
WISTAR, Caspar
ZACHOS, John

7

BABBAGE, Charles
BEHRING, Emil von
BILHARZ, Theodore
BISSELL, Melville
BRAILLE, Louis
CROOKES, Sir William
DAIMLER, Gottlieb
DANIELL, John
DEVILLE, Henri
DE VRIES, Hugo
EASTMAN, George
FARADAY, Michael
GATLING, Richard J.
GLIDDEN, Carlos
GUINARD, P. L.
GUTHRIE, Samuel

7

HOFMANN, August
    Wilhelm, von
JANSSON, Zacharias
LAMARCK, Jean
LAVERAN, Charles
LESSEPS, Ferdinand de
MAELZEL, Johann
MOISSAN, Henri
NASMYTH, James
NEILSON, James
OERSTED, Hans
PARSONS, Sir Charles
PASTEUR, Louis
PFEFFER, Wilhelm
POULSEN, Valdemar
RONALDS, Francis
SCHWANN, Theodor
SIEMENS, Friedrich
STEVENS, John
TELFORD, Thomas
THOMSON, Sir Joseph
THOMSON, Sir William
WHEELER, Schuyler

8

AVOGADRO, Amedeo
BEAUFORT, Sir Francis
BEAUMONT, William
BESSEMER, Sir Henry
BOWDITCH, Nathaniel
BREWSTER, Sir David
BUSHNELL, David
CAMPBELL, John
CROMPTON, Samuel
DAGUERRE, Louis
FOUCAULT, Leon
GILLETTE, King Camp
GOODYEAR, Charles

HADFIELD, Sir Robert
HECKFORD, Henry
HORROCKS, William
JACQUARD, Joseph
KITAZATO, Shibasaburo
MAUDSLAY, Henry
MCNAUGHT, William
MICHELIN, Andre
MICHELIN, Edouard
NEILSSON, James
ROBINSON, William
ROENTGEN, Wilhelm
SILLIMAN, Benjamin
STURGEON, William
SULLIVAN, Louis
WATERMAN, Lewis
WELSBACH, Carl von
WILLIAMS, Daniel

9

ACKERMANN, Rudolph
ARFVEDSON, A.
ARMSTRONG, William
BECQUEREL, Antoine
BERZELIUS, Jons
BURROUGHS, William
DAVENPORT, James
FAIRBANKS, Thaddeus
FOX TALBOT, William
    Henry
GESTETNER, David
HELMHOLTZ, Hermann
LECLANCHE, Georges
MACMILLAN,
    Kirkpatrick
MCCORMICK, Cyrus
PRIESTLEY, Joseph
REMINGTON, William

9
SCHLEIDEN, Matthias
SCHONBEIN, Christian
STROMEYER, Friedrich
VAUQUELIN, Louis
WILKINSON, John

10
MENDELEYEV, Dmitri
SAUERBRONN, Karl von
STEPHENSON, George
STROHMEYER, Friedrich
SULZBERGER, Jacob
THIMMONIER, Barthelemy
TREVITHICK, Richard
WHEATSTONE, Sir Charles

12
WESTINGHOUSE, George

13
MUSSCHENBROEK, Pieter van

ENGINEERS, INVENTORS and SCIENTISTS
1900–2005

4
BOHR, Niels
BUSH, Vannevar
FORD, Henry
FUNK, Casimir
HOLT, Benjamin
JUNG, Carl Gustav
KATO, Satori
LAND, Edwin
UREY, Harold

5
AIKEN, Howard
BACON, Francis
BAIRD, John Logie
BOOTH, Hubert Cecil
BOSCH, Karl
BRAUN, Heinrich
CRICK, Francis
FERMI, Enrico
GATES, Bill
GIBBS, Josiah
GOULD, R. Gordon
HOYLE, Sir Fred
IBUKA, Masaru
KERST, Donald
KILBY, Jack
KOLFF, Willem
KOWAL, Charles
MAGEE, Carlton
NOYCE, Robert
RAMON, Gaston
REARD, Louis

REBER, Grote
SMITH, Hamilton
SODDY, Frederick

6
AMMANS, Othmar
BENDIX, Vincent
DOMAGK, Gerhard
ECKERT, J. Presper
ENDERS, John
FLOREY, Howard
FOKKER, Anthony
GEIGER, Hans
JORPES, Erik
KEYNES, John Maynard
LEVENE, Phoebus
LITTLE, Arthur
LORENZ, Konrad
MAIMAN, Theodore
MCLEOD, John James
NERNST, Walther
PINCUS, Gregory G.
SCHICK, Jacob
TAYLOR, William
TERMAN, Lewis
WALTON, Ernest
WANKEL, Felix
WATSON, James
WRIGHT, Orville
WRIGHT, Wilbur

7
BARDEEN, John

224

7
BARNARD, Christiaan
BROGLIE, Louis duc de
BULLARD, Sir Edward
CARLSON, Chester
DEBAKEY, Michael
FEYNMAN, Richard,
FLEMING, Sir Alexander
GODDARD, Robert
HOFFMAN, Karl
KUHNOLD, Rudolf
MAUCHLY, John W.
MOSELEY, Henry
NORMANN, William
OCHSNER, Alton
PEARSON, D.
PERTHES, Georg
RUSSELL, Henry
SANDAGE, Allan
SHAPLEY, Harlow
STEVENS, Edwin
SWINTON, Sir Ernest
WHITTLE, Sir Frank

8
ANDERSON, Carl
BENEDICT, Edouard
BIRDSEYE, Clarence
BRATTAIN, Walter
BROWNING, John
CHADWICK, Sir James
CHALMERS, William
EINSTEIN, Albert
FUREHAUF, August
GOLDMARK, Peter
HEIMLICH, Henry
LAWRENCE, Ernest
MATTHEWS, Thomas
PLUNKETT, Roy

SHOCKLEY, William
SIKORSKY, Igor
SULLIVAN, Eugene
TOMBAUGH, Clyde
VAN ALLEN, James
VON BRAUN, Wernher
ZWORYKIN, Vladimir

9
ABPLANALP, Robert
BAEKELAND, Leo
CAROTHERS, Wallace
COCKCROFT, Sir John
COCKERELL, Sir
   Christopher
PONIATOFF, Alexander
SCHWINGER, Julian
WHINFIELD, John

10
HEISENBERG, Werner
HOUNSFIELD, Sir
   Godfrey
RUTHERFORD, Ernest
WATSON-WATT, Sir
   Robert

11
HERTZSPRUNG, Ejnar
SCHRODINGER, Erwin

13
BRANDENBURGER,
   Jacques

14
ANSCHUTZ-KAMPFE,
   Hermann

EXPLORERS

3 CAO, Diogo
PET, William

4 BACK, Sir George
CANO, Diogo
COOK, James
COSA, Juan de la
DIAZ, Bartolomeu
DIAZ, Dinis
EYRE, Edward
GAMA, Vasco da
GRAY, Robert
HALL, James
KING, Philip Parker
LANE, Ralph
NIZA, Fray Marcos de
PARK, Mungo
POLO, Marco
ROSS, Sir John
SOTO, Hernando de
VACA, Alvar Cabeza de

5 ABREU, Antonio de
BAKER, Sir Samuel
BARTH, Heinrich
BATES, Henry
BOONE, Daniel
BURKE, Robert
BYLOT, Robert
CABOT, John
CABOT, Sebastian

COLON, Cristobal
(Christopher Columbus)
DAVIS, John
DRAKE, Francis
FITCH, Ralph
FUCHS, Sir Vivian
GLENN, John
GOMES, Diogo
GOMES, Estevao
HENRY the Navigator,
Prince
LAING, Alexander
LEACH, John
MAIRE, Jacob Le
NEYRA, Albaro de
Menadana de
OJEDA, Alonso de
NECHO
PARRY, Sir William
Edward
PEARY, Robert
PINTO, Fernao Mendes
('Mendax')
QUAST, Matthijs
RETES, Ortiz de
SALLE, Rene-Robert de la
SARIS, John
SCOTT, Robert Falcon
(Captain)
SHARP, Bartholomew
SMITH, Jedediah

5 SMITH, William
SOLIS, Juan de
SPEKE, John Hanning
STURT, Charles
VRIES, Maarten
WILLS, William

6 ALDRIN, Edwin ('Buzz')
ASHLEY, William
BAFFIN, William
BALBOA, Vasco Nunez
de
BARROW, Sir John
BERING, Vitus
BIANCO, Andrea
BISCOE, John
BURTON, Sir Richard
CABRAL, Gonzalo
CABRAL Pedro Alvares
CORTES, Hernan
COSMAS,
Indicopleustes
DA GAMA, Vasco
GAMBOA, Pedro
Sarmiento de
GUZMAN, Nuno de
HARTOG, Dirk
HEARNE, Samuel
HUDSON, Henry
LANDER, John
LANDER, Richard
MALLET, Paul
MALLET, Pierre
MARSAL, Jacques
NANSEN, Fridtjof
OCAMPO, Sebastian de
PALMER, Nathaniel

PARETO, Bartolomeo
PHIPPS, Constantine John
PINZON, Vicente Yanez
POWELL, William
RALEGH, Sir Walter
SERRAO, Francisco
TASMAN, Abel
TORRES, Luis Vaez de
WILKES, Charles
XAVIER, St Francis

7 ABRUZZI, Duke of the
AGUIRRE, Lope de
ALMAGRO, Diego de
BARENTS, Willem
BEECHEY, F. W.
BINGHAM, Hiram
BOROUGH, Stephen
BOROUGH, William
CARTIER, Jacques
CORDOBA, Francisco de
COVILHA, Pero da
DAMPIER, William
D'ELCANO, Juan
DESHNEV, Semyon
DOUGLAS, David
ESCOLAR, Pedro de
FREMONT, John
GALLEGO, Hernan
GILBERT, Sir Humphrey
GOSNOLD,
Bartholomew
HAWKINS, Richard
HOUTMAN, Cornelis
HOUTMAN, Frederik
JACKMAN, Charles
JOLLIET, Louis

7 LA SALLE, Rene-Robert,
sieur de
LEGAZPE, Miguel
Lopez, de
LEGAZPI, Miguel
Lopez, de
LE MAIRE, Jacob
MENDANA, Alvaro de
NARVAEZ, Panfilo de
NEWBURY, John
NICOLET, Jean
PACHECO, Duarte
PAREIRA, Duarte Pacheco
PARKMAN, Francis
PIZARRO, Francisco
RALEIGH, Sir Walter
SIMPSON, Thomas
STANLEY, Sir Henry
WALLACE, Alfred
WEDDELL, James
ZHENG HE

8 AMUNDSEN, Roald
BASTIDAS, Rodrigo de
CABRILLO, Juan
COLUMBUS,
Bartholomew
COLUMBUS, Christopher
ERICSSON, Leif
FLINDERS, Matthew
FRANKLIN, Sir John
GRIVALVA, Juan de
GUNBJORN
KINGSLEY, Mary
MAGELLAN, Ferdinand
ORELLANA, Francisco de
PRIBYLOV, Gerasim

RADISSON, Pierre Esprit
SANTAREM, Joao de
SCHOUTEN, Willem
Corneliszoon
SCORESBY, William
SEQUEIRA, Ruy de
SPALDING, Eliza
SPALDING, Narcissa
THOMPSON, Edward
VARENNES, Pierre, de
VARTHEMA, Ludovico di
VESPUCCI, Amerigo
WARWIJCK, Wijbrand
van
WAYMOUTH, George

9 ARMSTRONG, Neil
CADAMOSTO, Alvise de
CHAMPLAIN, Samuel de
CORTE-REAL, Gaspar de
FERNANDEZ, Juan
FROBISHER, Sir Martin
FRONTENAC, Louis de
Buade, Comte de
GIL EANNES
GONCALVES, Lopo
GRENVILLE, Sir Richard
HAWAII-LOA
LANCASTER, James
MACKENZIE, Sir
Alexander
MARQUETTE, Jacques
PIGAFETTA, Antonio
RODRIGUES, Francisco
VANCOUVER, George
VERMUYDEN, John
BRANSFIELD, Edward

10 CHANCELLOR, Richard
CHARLEVOIX, Pierre de
ERIC THE RED
KEMPTHORNE, John
LINSCHOTEN, Jan
   Huyghen van
RICHTHOFEN,
   Ferdinand
SHACKLETON, Sir Ernest
WILLIBRORD,
   Archbishop
WILLOUGHBY, Sir Hugh

11 BOURNEVILLE,
   Benjamin de
GREENLANDER, Jon
GROSEILLERS, Chouart
IBN BATTUTAH
LA VERENDRYE, Sieur de
LIVINGSTONE, David
PONCE DE LEON, Juan

12 LEO AFRICANUS
NORDENSKJOLD, Nils
   Adolf Erik

14 BELLINGSHAUSEN,
   Fabian, Baron von

15 DIAZ DEL CASTILLO,
   Bernal

20 COSMAS
   INDICOPLEUSTES

FISH
Marine and Freshwater species

Marine Species

3 ASP
AYU
COD
DAB
EEL
RAY

4 BASS
BRIT
CHUB
DACE
DRUM
GISU
GOBY
HAKE
HUSS
LING
MAKO
OPAH
ORFE
POUT
SCAD
SHAD
TOPE
TUNA
ZOPE

5 BADEN
BLEAK
BREAM
BRILL

COLEY
GUPPY
LOACH
MANTA
MOLLY
PERCH
PORGY
SAURY
SKATE
SMELT

6 BARBEL
BELUGA
BICHIR
BLENNY
BONITO
CLINID
CONGER
CUTTLE
GUNNEL
MARLIN
MULLET
PLAICE
REMORA
SAITHE
SALMON
TARPON
TURBOT
WEEVER
WRASSE

7 ALEWIFE
ANCHOVY
BATFISH
CAVALLA
CROAKER
DOGFISH
DOLPHIN
EELFISH
ESPARDA
GARFISH
GARPIKE
GROUPER
GURNARD
HADDOCK
HALIBUT
HERRING
OARFISH
POLLACK
POLLOCK
POMPANO
RAGFISH
RONQUIL
SARDINE
SAWFISH
SUNFISH
TILAPIA
WHITING

8 ALBACORE
BLUE LING
BONEFISH
CHIMAERA
COALFISH
DEVIL RAY
EAGLE RAY
FLATFISH
FLOUNDER
GRAYLING

HAWKFISH
JOHN DORY
LADYFISH
LIONFISH
LUNGFISH
MACKEREL
MAHI MAHI
MANTA RAY
MONKFISH
PILCHARD
PIPEFISH
PORPOISE
SEAHORSE
SEA TROUT
SNAKE EEL
STING RAY
STURGEON
TOADFISH
WITCH EEL
WOLFFISH

9 ANGELFISH
BARRACUDA
BEARDFISH
CLINGFISH
CLOWNFISH
CONGER EEL
DOVER SOLE
GOOSE-FISH
GRENADIER
LEMON SOLE
PAPAGALLO
PEARLFISH
PORBEAGLE
QUILLFISH
RED MULLET
SANDSHARK
SARGASSUM

9
SEA DRAGON
SNIPE FISH
STARGAZER
STONEFISH
SWALLOWER
SWORDFISH
VIPER FISH
WHITEBAIT

10
ANGEL SHARK
ANGLERFISH
BLACK BREAM
BLUE MARLIN
COELACANTH
GHOST SHARK
GIPPERFISH
GUITARFISH
LANCETFISH
MUDSKIPPER
NEEDLEFISH
PADDLEFISH
PARROTFISH
PUFFER FISH
SMOOTHHEAD
SPOTTED RAY
STONE LOACH
TIGERSHARK
TRIPODFISH
TUB GURNARD
WHALESHARK

11
COW-NOSED RAY
ELECTRIC EEL
ELECTRIC RAY
GIZZARD SHAD
GOBLIN SHARK
GRID-EYE FISH
HATCHETFISH
MOORISH IDOL
PRICKLEBACK

SALMON TROUT
SMOOTH HOUND
TRIGGERFISH
TRUMPET FISH
WHALESUCKER

12
BASKING SHARK
BLUENOSE TUNA
BUTTERFLY RAY
CARDINAL FISH
FOUR-EYED FISH
ORANGE ROUGHY
PINE-CONE FISH
REQUIEM SHARK
SCORPION FISH
SKIPJACK TUNA
THORNBACK RAY

13
BARNDOOR SKATE
BLACK SCABBARD
DUCKBILLED EEL
GILTHEAD BREAM
HORSE MACKEREL
PORCUPINE FISH
SHORE ROCKLING
THRESHER SHARK
YELLOWFIN TUNA

15
GREAT WHITE SHARK
HAMMERHEAD SHARK
LEOPARD TOADFISH

17
STARRY
 SMOOTHHOUND

19
SIAMESE FIGHTING
 FISH

Freshwater Species

3 GAR
IDE
KOI

4 CARP
CHAR
PIKE
RUDD

5 LOACH
PERCH
ROACH
TENCH

6 BURBOT
DISCUS
LAMPREY
MINNOW
SUCKER

7 CATFISH
CICHLID
CRUCIAN
GARFISH
GARPIKE
GUDGEON
PIRANHA
SLEEPER
SUNFISH

8 BULLHEAD
CHARACIN
GOLDFISH
MOONFISH
RIVER COD

9 ANGELFISH
GRASS CARP
HOG SUCKER
NILE PERCH

10 BROWN TROUT
COMMON CARP

11 STICKLEBACK

12 RAINBOW TROUT

16 BLACKBELT CICHLID
BLACKMOUTH
SHINER

17 SHORTNOSE
STURGEON

18 SPOTTED
HATCHETFISH

FLOWERS & PLANTS

3
HOP
IVY
RYE

4
ALOE
ARUM
DOCK
FERN
FLAG
FLAX
HEMP
HOYA
IRIS
IXIA
JUTE
LILY
PINK
RAPE
REED
RICE
ROSE
RUSH
TARE
UPAS
WOAD

5
AGAVE
ASTER
AVENS
BRIAR
CANNA

CAREX
CYCAD
DAISY
GALAX
GAURA
HENNA
HOSTA
INULA
JALAP
KUDZU
LOTUS
LUPIN
MAIZE
OXLIP
PANSY
PEONY
PHLOX
POPPY
RHEUM
SEDGE
SEDUM
SENNA
SISAL
STIPA
TULIP
VIOLA
WHEAT

6
ALLIUM
ALSIKE
BALSAM

6

BLUETS
BRYONY
BURNET
CACTUS
CALTHA
CLOVER
COLEUS
COSMOS
COTTON
COWPEA
CROCUS
DAHLIA
DARNEL
FESCUE
GALEGA
HYSSOP
IBERIS
LAMIUM
MADDER
MALLOW
MEDICK
MILLET
ORCHID
PETREA
RATTAN
SALVIA
SCILLA
SPURGE
SQUILL
SUNDEW
TEASEL
THRIFT
TWITCH
VIOLET
YARROW
ZINNIA
ACONITE

7

ALFALFA
ALKANET
ALTHAEA
ALYSSUM
ANCHUSA
ARUNCUS
ASTILBE
BEGONIA
BISTORT
BRACKEN
BUGLOSS
BULRUSH
BURDOCK
CAMPION
CATMINT
CLARKIA
COMFREY
COWSLIP
DOGBANE
FIGWORT
FREESIA
FUCHSIA
GAZANIA
GENTIAN
GLADDON
GODETIA
HEMLOCK
HENBANE
HONESTY
IPOMOEA
JONQUIL
KINGCUP
LINARIA
LOBELIA
LYCASTE
LYCHNIS
MILFOIL

7

MIMULUS	BINDWEED
MULLEIN	BLECHNUM
MUSCARI	BLUEBELL
NEMESIA	BRUNNERA
NIGELLA	CATBRIER
OPUNTIA	CHARLOCK
PAEONIA	CLEAVERS
PAPAVER	CLEMATIS
PAPYRUS	CYCLAMEN
PETUNIA	DAFFODIL
PRIMULA	DIANTHUS
RAGWORT	ECHINOPS
ROSELLE	ENDYMION
SAGUARO	ERANTHIS
SANICLE	ERIGERON
SPURREY	ERYNGIUM
STACHYS	EUCHARIS
TAGETES	FLEABANE
THISTLE	FLEAWORT
TOBACCO	FOXGLOVE
TREFOIL	FUMITORY
URSINIA	GALTONIA
VERBENA	GERANIUM
VERVAIN	GLOXINIA
	GOUT WEED

8

ABUTILON	HAREBELL
ACANTHUS	HAWKWEED
ACHILLEA	HELENIUM
ADIANTUM	HENEQUEN
AGERATUM	HEUCHERA
AGRIMONY	HIBISCUS
ARUM LILY	HYACINTH
ASPHODEL	ICE PLANT
AUBRETIA	KNAPWEED
AURICULA	LARKSPUR
BEDSTRAW	LATHYRUS
BERGENIA	LAVATERA

8

LAVENDER
LEUCOJUM
LUNGWORT
MARIGOLD
MILKWEED
MILKWORT
MYOSOTIS
PHALARIS
PHORMIUM
PLANTAIN
PLUMBAGO
POLYPODY
PRIMROSE
SAMPHIRE
SCABIOUS
SHAMROCK
SNOWDROP
SOLIDAGO
SWEET PEA
TOADFLAX
VALERIAN
VERONICA
WOODBINE
WOODRUSH
WORMWOOD

BUCKWHEAT
BUTTERCUP
CALENDULA
CAMPANULA
CANDYTUFT
CARNATION
CELANDINE
CENTAUREA
CHICKWEED
CINERARIA
COCKLEBUR
COLUMBINE
COREOPSIS
CORYDALIS
COTYLEDON
CROCOSMIA
CYMBIDIUM
DICENTRUM
DIGITALIS
DORONICUM
ECHINACEA
EDELWEISS
EGLANTINE
EUPHORBIA
GALANTHUS
GLADIOLUS

9

AARON'S ROD
AGRIMONIA
AMARYLLIS
ANAPHALIS
ANTHURIUM
AQUILEGIA
ARROWROOT
ASPLENIUM
BLUEGRASS
BROOMRAPE
BRYOPHYTE

GOLDEN ROD
GROUNDSEL
HELIOPSIS
HELLEBORE
HOLLYHOCK
HORSETAIL
IMPATIENS
KNIPHOFIA
MARE'S-TAIL
MONBRETIA
MONEYWORT

9 MONK'S-HOOD
NARCISSUS
NEMOPHILA
NICOTIANA
OENOTHERA
PATCHOULI
PENSTEMON
PIMPERNEL
PYRETHRUM
RUDBECKIA
SAXIFRAGE
SPEEDWELL
STONECROP
SUNFLOWER
TORMENTIL
VERBASCUM
WATER LILY
WITCHWEED
WOUNDWORT

10 AGAPANTHUS
ALCHEMILLA
AMARANTHUS
AMAZON LILY
ASPIDISTRA
BELLADONNA
BRACHYCOME
BUSY LIZZIE
BUTTERWORT
CINQUEFOIL
CITRONELLA
CLIFFBREAK
CORNCOCKLE
COUCHGRASS
COW PARSLEY
CRANESBILL
CUCKOO-PINT

DELPHINIUM
DRAGONROOT
DYER'S BROOM
FRITILLARY
GAILLARDIA
GOOSEGRASS
GRANADILLA
GYPSOPHILA
HELIANTHUS
HELIOTROPE
HERB ROBERT
JIMSONWEED
LADY'S SMOCK
MARGUERITE
MIGNONETTE
MOONFLOWER
NASTURTIUM
PELAGONIUM
PENNISETUM
PERIWINKLE
POLYANTHUS
POTENTILLA
RANUNCULUS
SNAKE'S HEAD
SNAPDRAGON
SPLEENWORT
STITCHWORT
THUNBERGIA
WALLFLOWER
WATERCRESS
WILLOWHERB
WOOD SORREL

11 ANTIRRHINUM
ASPHODELINE
BISHOP'S WEED
BLADDERWORT

11
CALANDRINIA
CALCEOLARIA
CONVOLVULUS
FORGET-ME-NOT
HELICHRYSUM
HONEYSUCKLE
LADY'S MANTLE
LEOPARD LILY
LONDON PRIDE
LOVE-IN-A-MIST
MARRAM GRASS
MARSH MALLOW
PAMPAS GRASS
POLYGONATUM
RAGGED ROBIN
RED HOT POKER
SHRIMP PLANT
SPIDER PLANT
WELWITSCHIA

12
ALSTROEMERIA
AUTUMN CROCUS
CALLISTEPHUS
CENTURY PLANT
COMPASS PLANT
DACTYLORHIZA
ESCHSCHOLZIA
GLOBE THISTLE
HEMEROCALLIS
LADY'S SLIPPER
MONKEYFLOWER
MORNING GLORY
OLD MAN'S BEARD
PHALAENOPSIS
PRICKLY POPPY
SCHIZOSTYLIS
SNOW IN SUMMER

SOLOMON'S SEAL
SWEET WILLIAM
VENUS FLYTRAP

13
AFRICAN VIOLET
BLEEDING HEART
CHRISTMAS ROSE
CHRYSANTHEMUM
CREEPING JENNY
ECCREMOCARPUS
ELEPHANT GRASS
GRAPE HYACINTH
MARSH MARIGOLD
PASSIONFLOWER
ROSE OF JERICO
TRAVELLER'S JOY
WINTER ACONITE

14
BIRD OF PARADISE
CANTERBURY BELL
CASTOR OIL PLANT
LORDS AND LADIES
MAIDENHAIR FERN
TRUMPET CREEPER

15
ACANTHOCALYCIUM
LILY OF THE VALLEY
MICHAELMAS DAISY
STAR OF BETHLEHEM
TURPENTINE PLANT
WOODY NIGHTSHADE

16
MESEMBRYANTHEMUM

17
SNOW ON THE
  MOUNTAIN

FOOTBALL TEAMS
International, including home grounds

TEAM	GROUND
4	
CORK	Turner's Cross Stadium
5	
BASEL	St Jakob Park
DERRY	Brandywell Stadium
PORTO	Estadio do Dragao
6	
BRUGGE	Jan Breydel Stadion
CELTIC	Celtic Park
HEARTS	Tynecastle Stadium
SANTOS	Estadio Urbano Caldeira
UJPEST	Megyeri uti Stadion
7	
AC MILAN	San Siro
BENFICA	Estadio da Luz
RANGERS	Ibrox Stadium
SK BRANN	Brann Stadium
8	
ABERDEEN	Pittodrie Street
BOAVISTA	Estadio de Bessa XXI
CAGLIARI	Stadio Sant'Elia
JUVENTUS	Stadio Delle Alpi
LINFIELD	Windsor Park
(AS) MONACO	Stade Louis II
NAC BREDA	MyCom Stadion
SERVETTE	Stade de Geneve
VALENCIA	Estadio Mestalla

TEAM	GROUND

9

AJ AUXERRE	Stade de l'Abbe-Deschamps
BARCELONA	Camp Nou
EINDHOVEN	Philips Stadion
FEYENOORD	De Kuip
SAMPDORIA	Stadio Luigi Ferraris
ST-ETIENNE	Stade Geoffroy Guichard
STURM GRAZ	Arnold Schwarzenegger Stadion

10

FENERBAHCE	Sukru Saracoglu Stadi
FIORENTINA	Stadio Artemio Franchi
OLYMPIAKOS	Karaiskaki Stadium
QUEENS PARK	Hampden Park
REAL MADRID	Estadio Santiago Bernabeu
RIVER PLATE	El Monumental

11

BOCA JUNIORS	La Bombonera
FERENCVAROS	Stadion Ulloi Ut
GALATASARAY	Ali Sami Yen
HAJDUK SPLIT	Poljud Stadion
HJK HELSINKI	Finnair Stadion
LEVSKI SOFIA	Georgi Asparuhov
ROSENBERG BK	Lerkendal Stadium

12

(AIK) STOCKHOLM	Rasunda Stadion
BANIK OSTRAVA	Bazaly
DINAMO ZAGREB	Maksimir Stadion
DUNDEE UNITED	Tannadice Park
REAL SOCIEDAD	Estadio Anoeta
REAL ZARAGOZA	Estadio La Romareda
SPARTA PRAGUE	Toyota Arena
WERDER BREMEN	Weserstadion

TEAM	GROUND

13

ANDERLECHT RSC	Constant Vanden Stock Stadion
PANATHINAIKOS	Apostolos Nikolaidis Stadium
SK RAPID VIENNA	Gerhard Hanappi Stadion
STANDARD LIEGE	Stade de Sclessin
VITESSE ARNHAM	Gelredome

14

KAISERSLAUTERN	Fritz Walter Stadion
PARIS ST-GERMAIN	Parc des Princes
RAPID BUCHAREST	Giulesti

15

ATLETICO MADRID	Estadio Vicente Calderon
BAYER LEVERKUSEN	Bay Arena
DYNAMO BUCHAREST	Stefan cel Mare

16

| BORUSSIA DORTMUND | Westfalenstadion |
| SLOVAN BRATISLAVA | Tehelne Pole |

17

| DEPORTIVO LA CORUNA | Estadio Riazor |

18

| OLYMPIQUE MARSEILLE | Stade Velodrome |
| ZURICH GRASSHOPPERS | Hardturm |

FOOTBALL TEAMS
UK – including nickname and home ground

FOOTBALL TEAM	NICKNAME	HOME GROUND
4		
BURY	Shakers	Gigg Lane
6		
FULHAM	Cottagers	Craven Cottage
MK DONS	Dons	National Hockey Stadium, Milton Keynes
7		
ARSENAL	Gunners	Arsenal Stadium, Highbury
BURNLEY	Clarets	Turf Moor
CHELSEA	Blues, Pensioners	Stamford Bridge
EVERTON	Toffees	Goodison Park
READING	Biscuitmen Royals	Madejski Stadium
WATFORD	Hornets	Vicarage Road
WALSALL	Saddlers	Bescot Stadium
WREXHAM	Robins	Racecourse Ground
8		
BARNSLEY	Reds, Tykes	Oakwell
HULL CITY	Tigers	Kingston Communications Stadium
MILLWALL	Lions	New Den
PORT VALE	Valiants	Vale Park
ROCHDALE	Dale	Spotland
9		
BLACKPOOL	Seasiders	Bloomfield Road
BRENTFORD	Bees	Griffin Park

FOOTBALL TEAM	NICKNAME	HOME GROUND

9

FOOTBALL TEAM	NICKNAME	HOME GROUND
LIVERPOOL	Pool, Reds	Anfield
LUTON TOWN	Hatters	Kenilworth Road
STOKE CITY	Potters	Britannia Stadium

10

FOOTBALL TEAM	NICKNAME	HOME GROUND
ASTON VILLA	Villans	Villa Park
DARLINGTON	Quakers	Feethams Ground
GILLINGHAM	Gills	Priestfield Stadium
PORTSMOUTH	Pompey	Fratton Park
SUNDERLAND	Black Cats, Rokerites	Stadium of Light
YEOVIL TOWN	Glovers	Huish Park

11

FOOTBALL TEAM	NICKNAME	HOME GROUND
BRISTOL CITY	Robins	Ashton Gate
CARDIFF CITY	Bluebirds	Ninian Park
CHESTER CITY	Blues	Deva Stadium
DERBY COUNTY	Rams	Pride Park
GRIMSBY TOWN	Mariners	Blundell Park
IPSWICH TOWN	Blues, Town, Tractor Boys	Portman Road
LEEDS UNITED	Peacocks United Whites,	Elland Road
LINCOLN CITY	Red Imps	Sincil Bank
NORWICH CITY	Canaries	Carrow Road
NOTTS COUNTY	Magpies	County Ground, Meadow Lane
SOUTHAMPTON	Saints	St Mary's Stadium
SWANSEA CITY	Swans	Vetch Field
SWINDON TOWN	Robins	County Ground

12

FOOTBALL TEAM	NICKNAME	HOME GROUND
BOSTON UNITED	Pilgrims	York Street Stadium

FOOTBALL TEAM	NICKNAME	HOME GROUND

12

FOOTBALL TEAM	NICKNAME	HOME GROUND
BRADFORD CITY	Bantams	Valley Parade
CHESTERFIELD	Blues, Spireites	Recreation Ground, Saltergate
COVENTRY CITY	Sky Blues	Highfield Road (Jaguar Arena from 2005/2006)
LEYTON ORIENT	O's	Leyton Stadium, Brisbane Road
OXFORD UNITED	U's	Kassam Stadium

13

FOOTBALL TEAM	NICKNAME	HOME GROUND
BRISTOL ROVERS	Pirates	Memorial Ground
CRYSTAL PALACE	Eagles	Selhurst Park
LEICESTER CITY	Foxes	Walkers Stadium
MANSFIELD TOWN	Stags	Field Mill
MIDDLESBROUGH	Boro	Riverside Stadium
TORQUAY UNITED	Gulls	Plainmoor
WEST HAM UNITED	Hammers	Boleyn Ground, Upton Park
WIGAN ATHLETIC	Latics	JJB Stadium

14

FOOTBALL TEAM	NICKNAME	HOME GROUND
AFC BOURNEMOUTH	Cherries	Dean Court
BIRMINGHAM CITY	Blues	St Andrews
CHELTENHAM TOWN	Robins	Whaddon Road
CREWE ALEXANDRA	Railwaymen	Gresty Road
MANCHESTER CITY	Blues	City of Manchester Stadium
OLDHAM ATHLETIC	Latics	Boundary Park
PLYMOUTH ARGYLE	Pilgrims	Home Park
SHREWSBURY TOWN	Shrews	Gay Meadow
SOUTHEND UNITED	Shrimpers	Roots Hall
TRANMERE ROVERS	Rovers	Prenton Park

FOOTBALL TEAM	NICKNAME	HOME GROUND

15

FOOTBALL TEAM	NICKNAME	HOME GROUND
BLACKBURN ROVERS	Rovers	Ewood Park
BOLTON WANDERERS	Trotters	Reebok Stadium
CAMBRIDGE UNITED	U's	Abbey Stadium
DONCASTER ROVERS	Rovers	Belle Vue
NEWCASTLE UNITED	Magpies	St James' Park
NORTHAMPTON TOWN	Cobblers	Sixfields Stadium
PRESTON NORTH END	Lilywhites	Deepdale
ROTHERHAM UNITED	Merry Millers	Millmoor
SHEFFIELD UNITED	Blades	Bramall Lane
STOCKPORT COUNTY	County, Hatters	Edgeley Park

16

FOOTBALL TEAM	NICKNAME	HOME GROUND
CHARLTON ATHLETIC	Addicks, Valiants, Robins	The Valley
COLCHESTER UNITED	U's	Layer Road
HARTLEPOOL UNITED	Pool	Victoria Ground
HUDDERSFIELD TOWN	Terriers	Alfred McAlpine Stadium
MACCLESFIELD TOWN	Silkmen	Moss Rose
MANCHESTER UNITED	Red Devils	Old Trafford
NOTTINGHAM FOREST	Forest, Reds	City Ground
RUSHDEN & DIAMONDS	Diamonds	Nene Park
SCUNTHORPE UNITED	Irons	Glanford Park
TOTTENHAM HOTSPUR	Spurs	White Hart Lane
WYCOMBE WANDERERS	Blues, Chairboys	Causeway Stadium

17

FOOTBALL TEAM	NICKNAME	HOME GROUND
QUEENS PARK RANGERS	Rangers	Rangers Stadium, Loftus Road

FOOTBALL TEAM	NICKNAME	HOME GROUND
18		
PETERBOROUGH UNITED	Posh	London Road
SHEFFIELD WEDNESDAY	Owls	Hillsborough
WEST BROMWICH ALBION	Albion, Baggies, Throstles	The Hawthorns
21		
BRIGHTON AND HOVE ALBION	Seagulls	Withdean Stadium
KIDDERMINSTER HARRIERS	Harriers	Aggborough Stadium
22		
WOLVERHAMPTON WANDERERS	Wolves	Molineux

FRUIT

3 FIG

4 AKEE
ANON
DATE
KEPE
LIME
PEAR
PLUM
SALA
UGLI

5 APPLE
ARAZA
GUAVA
GUAVE
KEPEL
LEMON
MANGO
MELON
NANCE
OLIVE
PEACH
PLUOT
SALAK
XIGUA

6 ABABAI
BANANA
BIGNAY
BIRIBA

CASABA
CHALTA
CHERRY
DURIAN
FEIJOA
ILLAMA
KETUPA
KIWANO
LONGAN
LOQUAT
LUCUMA
LYCHEE
NANGKA
ORANGE
PAPAYA
PAW-PAW
PITAYA
QUINCE
RAMBAI
SHARYN
SWEETY
TOMATO

7 APRICOT
ATEMOYA
AVOCADO
BILIMBI
CAPULIN
GENIPAP
HOGPLUM
ITAPLUM

7
KECHAPI
KUMQUAT
MORINDA
PLUMCOT
PUMMELO
SANTOLI
SATSUMA
SONCOYA
SOURSOP
TANGELO

8
ASAM JAWA
BILBERRY
CALABASH
CANISTEL
GANDARIA
MANDARIN
MINNEOLA
MONSTERA
NET MELON
PITAHAYA
PLANTAIN
RAMBUTAN
SEA GRAPE
SWEETSOP
VOAVANGA
WAS MELON

9
ALIBERTIA
BAELFRUIT
BLUEBERRY
CARAMBOLA
CHAMPEDAK
CHERIMOYA
CRANBERRY
JACKFRUIT
KIWI FRUIT

LEECH LIME
MELON-PEAR
MUSK MELON
NASHI PEAR
NECTARINE
OGEN MELON
PEACH PALM
PERSIMMON
PINEAPPLE
RASPBERRY
RED BANANA
ROSE APPLE
SAPODILLA
STAR APPLE
STAR FRUIT
TANGERINE
WOOD APPLE

10
BABY BANANA
BLACKBERRY
BREADFRUIT
CLEMENTINE
ELDERBERRY
GALIA MELON
GOOSEBERRY
GRAPEFRUIT
JABOTICABA
MALAY APPLE
MANGOSTEEN
REDCURRANT
ROUGH LEMON
STRAWBERRY
SUGARAPPLE
SWEET MELON
TREE TOMATO
UZBEK MELON
WATER APPLE
WATER MELON

11
APPLE BANANA
ASAM GELUGOR
BLACK SAPOTE
CANARY MELON
FRUIT BANANA
GOLDEN APPLE
HORNED MELON
HUCKLEBERRY
MAMMEY APPLE
MONKEY BREAD
PEPINO MELON
POMEGRANATE
PRICKLY PEAR
PRINCE MELON
STAR NUT PALM
WINTER MELON

12
BAKING BANANA
CUSTARD APPLE
DERISHI MELON
INDIAN JUJUBE
MAMMEY SAPOTE
PASSION FRUIT
PERSIAN MELON
WHITECURRANT

13
CRENSHAW MELON
HONEYDEW MELON
JAMAICA CHERRY
SURINAM CHERRY

14
BARBADOS CHERRY
CAPE GOOSEBERRY
CHOCOLATE-FRUIT
CHRISTMAS MELON
VELVET TAMARIND

15
CANNON BALL FRUIT
CANTALOUPE MELON
CHARANTAIS MELON
MOUNTAIN SOURSOP
SANTA CLAUS MELON
SWEET GRENADILLA

16
CEYLON GOOSEBERRY
YELLOW WATERMELON

18
OTAHEITE GOOSEBERRY

19
PHILIPPINE ROSEAPPLE

FUNGI
UK and EUROPEAN

5 MOREL
YEAST

6 AGARIC
INK CAP
MILLER

7 AMANITA
BLUSHER
BOLETUS
CANDIDA
JEW'S EAR
TRUFFLE

8 CLUB-FOOT
DECEIVER
EARTH FAN
GRIZETTE
PENNY BUN
PUFFBALL

9 CUP FUNGUS
EARTHSTAR
FAIRY RING
FLY AGARIC
FUNNEL CAP
POISON PIE
STINKHORN
TOADSTOOL

10 CRAMP BALLS

FALSE MOREL
LIBERTY CAP
OAK MILKCAP
PANTHER CAP
WOOD BLEWIT

11 ASCOMYCETES
ASPERGILLUS
BIRCH BOLETE
CANDLE SNUFF
CHANTERELLE
FIELD BLEWIT
HONEY FUNGUS
JELLY BABIES
LAWYER'S RING
SULPHUR TUFT
UGLY MILK CAP

12 BITTER BOLETE
DOG STINKHORN
DRYAD'S SADDLE
HORN OF PLENTY
ORANGE BOLETE
OYSTER FUNGUS
ROOTING SHANK
SHAGGY INK CAP
SLIPPERY JACK
SPINDLE SHANK
TINDER FUNGUS
WEEPING WIDOW
WITCH'S BUTTER
WOOD HEDGEHOG

13
BRACKET FUNGUS
CLOUDED AGARIC
DUNG ROUND HEAD
GIANT PUFFBALL
HORSE MUSHROOM
MAGIC MUSHROOM
RUFOUS MILK CAP
SHAGGY PARASOL
TAWNY GRIZETTE
WOOLLY MILK CAP

14
BASIDIOMYCETES
CHARCOAL BURNER
HERALD OF WINTER
SAFFRON MILK-CAP
TRUMPET OF DEATH
WOOD WOOLLY-FOOT

15
BLUSHING BRACKET
COMMON EARTHBALL
DESTROYING ANGEL
PLUMS AND CUSTARD
PORCELAIN FUNGUS

16
FALSE CHANTERELLE
KING ALFRED'S CAKES
ORANGE PEEL FUNGUS

17
BLACKENING RUSSULA
CAULIFLOWER FUNGUS
CHICKEN OF THE WOODS
POOR MAN'S BEEFSTEAK
SPOTTED TOUGH SHANK
ST GEORGE'S MUSHROOM

21
BLACK AND PURPLE RUSSULA

FURNITURE

3 BED
COT
PEW

4 DESK
SOFA

5 BENCH
CHAIR
CHEST
COUCH
SHELF
STOOL
TABLE

6 BUFFET
BUREAU
COFFER
CRADLE
LOWBOY
MIRROR
POUFFE
SETTEE
SETTLE
THRONE
TRIPOD

7 ARMOIRE
ART DECO (style)
BAROQUE (style)
BUNK BED

CABINET
COMMODE
CONSOLE
DRESSER
HIGHBOY
OTTOMAN
REGENCY (style)
SOFABED
TABOURET
TALLBOY
TROLLEY
WHATNOT

8 ARMCHAIR
BENTWOOD
BOOKCASE
CABIN BED
CELLARET
CUPBOARD
DOVER BED
HATSTAND
LOVE SEAT
PRIE-DIEU
SHERATON (style)
TABOURET
WARDROBE

9 BATH CHAIR
BED SETTEE
CAMELBACK
DAVENPORT

9
DRUM TABLE
FOLD STOOL
FOOTSTOOL
HIGHBOARD
LLOYD LOOM (style)
QUEEN ANNE (style)
SIDEBOARD

10
ART NOUVEAU (style)
BANJO CLOCK
CHIFFONIER
CORNER UNIT
ESCRITOIRE
JOINT STOOL
LINEN PRESS
SECRETAIRE
SHELF CLOCK
SUTHERLAND
TRUNDLE-BED

11
BALLOON BACK
CHIPPENDALE (style)
COFFEE TABLE
DINING TABLE
HEPPLEWHITE (style)
ROLL-TOP DESK
SWIVEL CHAIR
WORKSTATION

12
CARLTON HOUSE (style)
CHAISE LONGUE
CHESTERFIELD
CLOTHES PRESS
GATELEG TABLE
PARSONS TABLE
PEDESTAL DESK
ROCKING CHAIR

TILT-TOP TABLE
WELSH DRESSER
WINDSOR CHAIR

13
ARTS AND CRAFTS
   (style)
DRESSING TABLE
DROP-LEAF TABLE
FILING CABINET
LONGCASE CLOCK
PEMBROKE TABLE
PILLAR-AND-CLAW
RECLINER CHAIR
SCISSORS CHAIR
UMBRELLA STAND
WAINSCOT CHAIR

14
CORNER CUPBOARD
DISPLAY CABINET

15
COMPUTER TROLLEY
LADDERBACK CHAIR
OCCASIONAL TABLE
WINCHESTER CHEST

16
CARLTON HOUSE
   DESK
GRANDFATHER
   CLOCK

GAMES, HOBBIES
& PASTIMES

3 ART
DIY

4 JUDO
GOLF
POOL
X-BOX
YOGA

5 BINGO
CARDS
CHESS
CRAPS
DARTS
MAGIC
MUSIC
OPERA
SPOOF
WHIST

6 ACTING
CAVING
CINEMA
FLYING
SEWING

7 CAMPING
COOKING
CROQUET
CYCLING
DANCING

FISHING
GLIDING
JOGGING
KEEP FIT
ORIGAMI
PILATES
POTTERY
PUZZLES
READING
SAILING
SINGING
SURFING
THEATRE
TOPIARY
WRITING

8 AEROBICS
ANTIQUES
CLIMBING
DRAUGHTS
FRETWORK
KNITTING
LAPIDARY
RAMBLING
SCRABBLE
SPINNING
SWIMMING
WAR GAMES
    (PAINTBALL)
WOODWORK

9
ASTRONOMY
BILLIARDS
CARPENTRY
DECOUPAGE
GARDENING
GENEALOGY
LANGUAGES
METALWORK
PHILATELY
SCULPTING

10
BALLOONING
CONCHOLOGY
CROCHETING
CROSSWORDS
DOG AGILITY
EMBROIDERY
ENTOMOLOGY
TRAVELLING

11
ARCHAEOLOGY
BELL-RINGING
CALLIGRAPHY
CARAVANNING
DRESS-MAKING
HORSE RACING
HORSE RIDING
MOTOR RACING
PHOTOGRAPHY
PLAY STATION
SHOW JUMPING
WATERSKIING
WINDSURFING

12
AMATEUR RADIO
BIRD WATCHING
CANAL BOATING
LOCAL HISTORY
ORIENTEERING
POINT-TO-POINT

13
COMPUTER GAMES
IN-LINE SKATING
MODEL RAILWAYS
RACING PIGEONS
ROLLER SKATING
SKATEBOARDING
TABLE FOOTBALL
TRAIN-SPOTTING

14
COIN COLLECTING
METAL DETECTING
MOUNTAINEERING
PIGEON FANCYING
WEIGHT TRAINING

15
FLOWER ARRANGING
STAMP COLLECTING

19
AUTOGRAPH
    COLLECTING
WATERCOLOUR
    PAINTING

GEMSTONES

4 JADE
ONYX
OPAL
RUBY

5 AGATE
AMBER
BERYL
CORAL
PEARL
TOPAZ

6 GARNET
IOLITE
JASPER
QUARTZ
SPINEL
ZIRCON

7 CITRINE
DIAMOND
EMERALD
KUNZITE
PERIDOT

8 AMATRINE
AMETHYST
FIRE-OPAL
SAPPHIRE

9 MOONSTONE

MORGANITE
TANZANITE
TURQUOISE

10 ANDALUSITE
AQUAMARINE
BLOODSTONE
TOURMALINE

11 ALEXANDRITE
CHRYSOBERYL
LAPIS LAZULI

14 BLUE TOURMALINE
CHROME DIPOSIDE
MANDARIN GARNET

15 DEMANTOID GARNET
GREEN TOURMALINE
TSAVORITE GARNET

16 YELLOW TOURMALINE

17 PARAIBA TOURMALINE

19 RUBELLITE
TOURMALINE

20 MULTICORED
TOURMALINE

GIRLS' NAMES

2

DI
EM
JO
VI

3

ADA
AMY
ANN
AVA
BEA
BEE
CIS
DEB
DEE
DOT
EDA
ENA
EVA
EVE
FAY
FLO
GAY
IDA
INA
ISA
IVY
JAN
JAY
JEN
JOY
KAY

KIM
LEE
LIL
LIZ
LOU
LYN
MAE
MAI
MAY
MEG
MEL
MIA
NAN
PAM
PAT
PEG
PEN
PIA
PRU
RAE
RIA
ROS
SAL
SAM
SUE
UMA
UNA
VAL
VIV
WIN
ZOE

4

ABBY	EMMY
ADDY	ENID
AIME	ERIN
ALEX	ERYL
ALLY	ESME
ALMA	ETTA
ALYS	EVIE
AMIE	FAYE
ANNA	FERN
ANNE	FIFE
ANYA	FRAN
AVIS	GABI
BABS	GABY
BEAT	GAIL
BESS	GALE
BETH	GAYE
BETT	GERT
CARA	GILL
CASS	GINA
CATH	GLAD
CERI	GWEN
CHER	HEBE
CISS	HEDY
CLEM	HOPE
CLEO	ILSE
CORA	INEZ
DANA	IONA
DAWN	IRIS
DOLL	IRMA
DORA	ISLA
EDIE	JADA
EDNA	JADE
ELLA	JANE
ELMA	JEAN
ELSA	JESS
ELSE	JILL
EMMA	JOAN

4

JODI	MOLL
JODY	MONA
JOSS	MYRA
JUDI	NADA
JUDY	NELL
JUNE	NINA
KARA	NITA
KATE	NOLA
KATH	NORA
KATY	NOVA
KAYE	OLGA
KERI	OONA
KYLE	PETA
LANA	PHIL
LARA	PHYL
LEAH	POLL
LELA	PRUE
LENA	RENA
LILA	RENE
LILY	RHEA
LISA	RINA
LITA	RITA
LOIS	ROMA
LOLA	RONA
LORA	ROSA
LORI	ROSE
LORN	ROSY
LUCY	ROXY
LULU	RUBY
LYNN	RUMI
MAIR	RUTH
MARY	SANA
MAUD	SARA
MAYA	SIAN
META	SUKY
MIMI	SUSY
MINA	SUZY

4	TANA	ANITA
	TARA	ANNIE
	TESS	ANWEN
	THEA	APRIL
	TINA	AVERY
	TRIX	AVRIL
	TYNE	BARBI
	VERA	BECCI
	VIDA	BECKY
	VIKI	BELLA
	WYNN	BELLE
	XANA	BERNY
	XENA	BERYL
	YOKO	BESSY
	ZARA	BETSY
	ZENA	BETTE
	ZITA	BETTY
	ZOLA	BIDDY
		BOBBY
5	ABBEY	BONNY
	ABBIE	BRITT
	ADDIE	BUNTY
	ADELA	CANDY
	ADELE	CARLA
	AGGIE	CARLY
	AGNES	CAROL
	ALISA	CARYS
	AIMEE	CASEY
	AISHA	CATHY
	ALANA	CELIA
	ALEXA	CERYS
	ALICE	CHLOE
	ALINA	CHRIS
	ALINE	CILLA
	ALLIE	CINDY
	AMBER	CISSY
	ANGIE	CLARA

5

CLARE	FREDA
CORAL	FREYA
CORIN	GABBY
DAISY	GAYLE
DEBRA	GEMMA
DELIA	GERDA
DELLA	GERTY
DIANA	GILDA
DIANE	GINNY
DILYS	GRACE
DINAH	GREER
DIONE	GRETA
DODIE	GUSSY
DOLCE	HALEY
DOLLY	HANNA
DONNA	HATTY
DORIA	HAZEL
DORIS	HEDDA
DOTTY	HEIDI
EDITH	HELEN
EFFIE	HELGA
ELENA	HENNY
ELISA	HETTY
ELISE	HILDA
EMILY	HOLLY
EMMIE	HONOR
ERICA	HULDA
ESMEE	HYLDA
ETHEL	ILONA
ETTIE	IRENE
EVITA	ISMAY
FAITH	ISOLD
FANNY	JACKY
FARON	JANET
FIONA	JANEY
FLORA	JANIE
FLOSS	JANIS

5

JAYNE	LORNA
JEMMA	LORNE
JENNA	LOTTY
JENNY	LUCIA
JESSY	LUCIE
JINNY	LYDIA
JODIE	LYNDA
JOSIE	LYNNE
JOYCE	MABLE
JULIA	MADGE
JULIE	MAEVE
KAREN	MAGDA
KARIN	MAMIE
KATEY	MANDY
KATHY	MANEL
KATIA	MARGE
KATIE	MARGO
KAYIA	MARIA
KELLY	MARIE
KERRY	MARTA
KIRBY	MARTI
KITTY	MARTY
KYLIE	MATTY
LAURA	MAUDE
LAURI	MAVIS
LEIGH	MEAVE
LEILA	MEGAN
LEONE	MERCY
LETTY	MERLE
LIBBY	MERYL
LIESL	MILLY
LILLA	MITZI
LILLY	MOIRA
LINDA	MOLLY
LINDY	MORAG
LIZZY	MOYNA
LOREN	MOYRA

5

MYRNA	RHIAN
NADIA	RHODA
NANCE	RHONA
NANCY	RILEY
NANNY	ROBYN
NAOMI	ROSIE
NELLY	SADIE
NERYS	SALLY
NESTA	SAMMY
NETTA	SANDY
NICKY	SARAH
NIKKI	SASHA
NOELE	SHANI
NORAH	SHARI
NORMA	SHENA
NYREE	SHIRL
OLIVE	SHONA
OLWEN	SISSY
OLWYN	SOFIA
ORIEL	SONIA
OWENA	SONJA
PAIGE	SONYA
PANSY	SOPHY
PATSY	STACY
PATTI	SUKEY
PATTY	SUSAN
PAULA	SUSIE
PEARL	SUZIE
PEGGY	SYBIL
PENNY	TAMMY
PETRA	TANIA
PHEBE	TANSY
PIPPA	TANYA
POLLY	TEGAN
POPPY	TERRI
RAINE	TERRY
RENEE	TESSA

5	
THORA	AMANDA
TILLY	AMELIA
TONIA	AMINTA
TONYA	ANABEL
TOPSY	ANDREA
TOYAH	ANGELA
TRACY	ANNIKA
TRUDI	ANTHEA
TRUDY	ARIANA
VALDA	ARLEEN
VANDA	ARMINA
VELDA	ASHLEY
VELMA	ASTRID
VERNA	AUDREY
VICKI	AURIEL
VICKY	AURIOL
VIKKI	AURORA
VILMA	AUTUMN
VINNY	AVERIL
VIOLA	BAILEY
WANDA	BARBIE
WENDY	BARBRA
WILMA	BEATTY
WYNNE	BENITA
XENIA	BERNIE
ZELDA	BERTHA
ZELMA	BESSIE
ZORAH	BETHAN
	BEULAH
6	BIANCA
ALEXIA	BIDDIE
ALEXIS	BILLIE
ALICIA	BIRGIT
ALISON	BLANCH
ALTHEA	BOBBIE
ALYSON	BONITA
ALYSSA	BONNIE
AMABEL	

6

BRENDA
BRIDIE
BRIGID
BRIGIT
BRIONY
BROOKE
BRYONY
CANICE
CARINA
CARMEL
CARMEN
CAROLA
CAROLE
CARRIE
CASSIE
CATRIN
CECILE
CECILY
CELINA
CELINE
CHERIE
CHERRY
CHERYL
CICELY
CISSIE
CLAIRE
CONNIE
DAGMAR
DAPHNE
DAVIDA
DEANNA
DEBBIE
DENISE
DIANNE
DIONNE
DORCAS
DOREEN

DORICE
DORITA
DORRIE
DOTTIE
DULCIE
DYMPNA
EARTHA
EDWINA
EILEEN
ELAINE
ELINOR
ELISHA
ELISSA
ELOISE
ELVIRA
EMILIA
ESTHER
EUNICE
EVADNE
EVELYN
EVONNE
FANNIE
FARREN
FATIMA
FEDORA
FELICE
FLAVIA
FRANCA
FRIEDA
GABBIE
GAENOR
GAYNOR
GERTIE
GINGER
GLADYS
GLENDA
GLENIS

6 GLENYS

GLINYS

GLORIA

GLYNIS

GOLDIE

GRACIE

GRETEL

GUSSIE

GWENDA

GWYNNE

HAILEY

HANNAH

HATTIE

HAYLEY

HELENA

HESTER

HILARY

HONORA

IMELDA

IMOGEN

INGRID

ISABEL

ISEULT

ISOBEL

ISOLDA

ISOLDE

JACKIE

JACQUI

JANICE

JANINE

JEANIE

JEANNE

JEMIMA

JENNIE

JESSIE

JOANNA

JOANNE

JOLINE

JORDAN

JUDITH

JULIET

KARINA

KAYLEE

KEELEY

KELLIE

KERRIE

KIRSTY

KRISTY

LALLIE

LAUREL

LAUREN

LAURIE

LAVINA

LEANNE

LEILAH

LENORE

LEONIE

LESLEY

LESLIE

LETTIE

LIAMME

LIANNE

LIESEL

LILIAN

LILLAH

LILLIE

LINNET

LIZZIE

LOLITA

LOTTIE

LOUELA

LOUISA

LOUISE

MADDIE

6 MAGGIE

MAISIE

MARCIA

MARCIE

MARGIE

MARGOT

MARIAN

MARINA

MARION

MARISA

MARITA

MARSHA

MARTHA

MARTHE

MARTIE

MATTIE

MAUDIE

MAXINE

MELITA

MELODY

MERIEL

MILLIE

MINNIE

MIRIAM

MOLLIE

MONICA

MORGAN

MUREEN

MURIEL

MYRTLE

NADINE

NELLIE

NETTIE

NICOLA

NICOLE

NOELLE

NOREEN

ODETTE

OLIVIA

PAMELA

PAMMIE

PATTIE

PATULA

PHOEBE

PORTIA

PSYCHE

RACHEL

RAMONA

RENATA

RHONDA

ROBBIE

ROBINA

ROSINA

ROSITA

ROSLYN

ROWENA

ROXANA

ROXANE

SABINA

SALENA

SALINA

SALOME

SANDIE

SANDRA

SELENA

SELINA

SERENA

SHARON

SHAUNA

SHEENA

SHEILA

SHELBY

SHELLY

SHERRI

6 SHERRY
SHERYL
SHIBAN
SIERRA
SILVIA
SIMONA
SIMONE
SINEAD
SOPHIA
SOPHIE
STACEY
STELLA
STEVIE
SYDNEY
SYLVIA
SYLVIE
TAMARA
TAMSIN
TAYLOR
TEAGAN
TERESA
THELMA
TRACEY
TRICIA
TRISHA
TRIXIE
TRUDIE
URSULA
VERENA
VERITY
VERONA
VICKIE
VINNIE
VIOLET
VIVIAN
VIVIEN
VYVYAN

WALLIS
WINNIE
XANTHE
YASMIN
YVETTE
YVONNE
ZANDRA
ZILLAH
ZINNIA

7 AALIYAH
ABIGAIL
ADELINA
ADELINE
ADRIANA
ALBERTA
ALEDWEN
ALFREDA
ALISSON
ALOISIA
ALOYSIA
ANNABEL
ANNETTE
ANOUSKA
ANTONIA
ARIADNE
ARIANNA
ARLETTA
ARLETTE
AUGUSTA
AURELIA
AUREOLA
AUREOLE
AVELINE
BARBARA
BEATRIX
BEATTIE

7

BELINDA	COLLEEN
BERNICE	CORALIE
BETHANY	CORINNA
BETTINA	CORRINE
BEVERLY	CRYSTAL
BILLY-JO	CYNTHIA
BLANCHE	DANIELA
BLODWEN	DARLENE
BLOSSOM	DAVINIA
BRANWEN	DEBORAH
BRIANNA	DEIDREE
BRIDGET	DELILAH
BRONWYN	DELORES
CAITLIN	DEMELZA
CAMILLA	DESIREE
CAMILLE	DESTINY
CANDICE	DOLORES
CANDIDA	DORINDA
CARLEEN	DOROTHY
CARLENE	DORRICE
CARMELA	DYMPHNA
CAROLYN	ELEANOR
CATRINA	ELFREDA
CECELIA	ELFRIDA
CECILIE	ELLENOR
CELESTE	ELLINOR
CHANTAL	ELSPETH
CHARITY	EMELINE
CHARLEY	ESTELLA
CHARLIE	ESTELLE
CHELSEA	EUGENIE
CHRISSY	EULALIA
CLARICE	EULALIE
CLARRIE	EVELINA
CLAUDIA	EVELINE
CLODAGH	FELICIA
COLETTE	FENELLA

7

FEODORA	KATELYN
FLORRIE	KATHRYN
FLOSSIE	KATRINA
FRANCES	KATRINE
FRANCIE	KIRSTEN
FRANKIE	KRISTEN
GEORGIA	KRISTIN
GEORGIE	LARISSA
GILLIAN	LAVINIA
GINETTE	LETTICE
GISELLE	LETTUCE
GWYNEDD	LILLIAN
GWYNETH	LINDSAY
HARRIET	LINDSEY
HEATHER	LINETTE
HELLENA	LISANNE
HELOISE	LISBETH
HILLARY	LIZBETH
HONORIA	LIZETTE
ISADORA	LORETTE
JACINTA	LORINDA
JACINTH	LOVEDAY
JANETTA	LUCIANA
JANETTE	LUCILLA
JASMINE	LUCILLE
JEANNIE	LUCINDA
JESSICA	LYNETTE
JILLIAN	MABELLA
JOCELYN	MADISON
JOHANNA	MAKAYLA
JONQUIL	MANUELA
JOSEPHA	MARGERY
JUANITA	MARILYN
JULIANA	MARISSA
JUSTINA	MARJORY
JUSTINE	MARLENE
KAITLYN	MARTINA

7

MARTINE	REBEKAH
MATILDA	RHONWEN
MAUREEN	RHYANNE
MELANIE	ROBERTA
MELINDA	ROMAINE
MELIORA	ROSALIE
MELISSA	ROSALYN
MELODIE	ROSANNA
MICHELE	ROSANNE
MILDRED	ROSEANN
MINERVA	ROSETTA
MIRABEL	ROWENNA
MIRANDA	ROXANNA
MODESTY	ROXANNE
MONIQUE	SABRINA
MYFANWY	SAFFRON
NANETTE	SANCHIA
NATALIA	SCARLET
NATALIE	SHANNON
NATASHA	SHARRON
NERISSA	SHEILAH
NICHOLA	SHELAGH
NOELINA	SHELLEY
OCTAVIA	SHIRLEY
OLYMPIA	SIBELLA
OPHELIA	SIBILLA
ORIANNA	SIBYLLA
PANDORA	SIOBHAN
PAULINA	SUSANNA
PAULINE	SUZANNE
PERDITA	SUZELLE
PETRINA	SYBILLA
PHYLLIS	TABITHA
PRISSIE	THERESA
RACHAEL	THERESE
RAFAELA	TIFFANY
REBECCA	TITANIA

7
TRINITY
TRISSIE
TUESDAY
VALERIE
VANESSA
WHITNEY
YOLANDA
ZENOBIA

8
ADELAIDE
ADRIANNE
ADRIENNE
ANGELICA
ANGELINA
ANGELINE
ANGHARAD
ARABELLA
ARAMINTA
BEATRICE
BERENICE
BEVERLEY
BIRGITTA
BRIGETTE
BRIGITTA
BRITTANY
BRUNETTA
CARLOTTA
CAROLINA
CAROLINE
CATHLEEN
CATRIONA
CHARLENE
CHRISSIE
CLARABEL
CLARISSA
CLAUDINE
CLEMENCY

CLOTILDA
CONCEPTA
CORDELIA
CORNELIA
COURTNEY
CRESSIDA
CYTHEREA
DANIELLE
DELPHINE
DIONYSIA
DOMINICA
DOROTHEA
DRUSILLA
ELEANORA
EMANUELA
EMMELINE
EUPHEMIA
EUSTACIA
FELICITY
FLORENCE
FLORETTA
FLORETTE
FLORINDA
FRANCINE
FREDRICA
FREDRIKA
GABRIELA
GEORGINA
GERMAINE
GERTRUDE
GRETCHEN
GRISELDA
GWYNNETH
HARRIETT
HERMIONE
HORTENSE
HYACINTH

8

IOLANTHE	MARIGOLD
ISABELLA	MARJORIE
ISABELLE	MELICENT
JACOBINA	MELISENT
JEANETTE	MELLONEY
JEANNINE	MERCEDES
JENNIFER	MEREDITH
JOSCELIN	MICHAELA
JOYCELYN	MICHELLE
JULIANNE	MURIELLE
JULIENNE	PATIENCE
JULIETTE	PATRICIA
KATHLEEN	PAULETTE
KATHRINE	PENELOPE
KIMBERLY	PHILIPPA
KRISTINA	PHYLLIDA
KRISTINE	PRIMROSE
LAURETTA	PRUDENCE
LAURETTE	PRUNELLA
LAURIANE	RAPHAELA
LAVENDER	RICHENDA
LORAINNE	ROSALEEN
LORRAINE	ROSALIND
LUCIENNE	ROSALINE
LUCRETIA	ROSAMOND
LUCREZIA	ROSAMUND
LYNNETTE	ROSEANNE
MADELINA	ROSELINE
MADELINE	ROSEMARY
MAGDALEN	SAMANTHA
MAGNOLIA	SAPPHIRA
MARCELLA	SAPPHIRE
MARCELLE	SAVANNAH
MARGARET	SCARLETT
MARIANNE	SHARLENE
MARIETTA	SHEELAGH
MARIETTE	STEFANIE

8

SUSSANAH
TALLULAH
TAMASINE
THEODORA
THOMASIN
TIMOTHEA
VERONICA
VICTORIA
VIOLETTA
VIRGINIA
VIVIENNE
WINIFRED

9

ALBERTINA
ALBERTINE
ALEXANDRA
AMARYLLIS
AMBROSINA
AMBROSINE
ANASTASIA
ANGELIQUE
ANNABELLA
ANNABELLE
ARTEMISIA
ARTHURINA
ARTHURINE
BATHSHEBA
BENEDICTA
BERNADINE
CASSANDRA
CATHARINE
CATHERINE
CELESTINA
CELESTINE
CHANTELLE
CHARLOTTE
CHARMAINE

CHRISTINA
CHRISTINE
CLAUDETTE
CLEOPATRA
CLOTHILDE
COLUMBINE
CONSTANCE
CONSTANCY
DESDEMONA
DOMINIQUE
ELISABETH
ELIZABETH
EMMANUELA
ERNESTINE
ESMERELDA
FRANCESCA
FRANCISCA
FREDERICA
FREDERIKA
GABRIELLA
GABRIELLE
GENEVIEVE
GEORGETTE
GEORGIANA
GERALDINE
GWENDOLYN
GWENLLIAN
HARRIETTE
HENRIETTA
HENRIETTE
HILDEGARD
HORTENSIA
HYACINTHA
JACQUETTA
JAQUELLYN
JEANNETTE
JOSEPHINE

275

9

KATHARINE
KATHERINE
KIMBERLEY
MACKENZIE
MADELEINE
MAGDALENA
MAGDALENE
MARGARETA
MARGARITA
MELISANDE
MILLICENT
MIRABELLA
NICOLETTE
PHILLIPPA
PHILOMENA
POLLYANNA
PRISCILLA
ROSABELLE
ROSALINDA
ROSEMARIE
STEPHANIE
THOMASINA
THOMASINE
VALENTINE
VERONIQUE
WINNIFRED

10

ANTOINETTE
BERNADETTE
BERNARDINE
CHRISTABEL
CHRISTIANA
CHRISTOBEL
CLEMENTINA
CLEMENTINE
CONSTANTIA
DULCIBELLA

ERMINTRUDE
ERMYNTRUDE
ETHELDREDA
EVANGELINA
EVANGELINE
GWENDOLINE
HILDEGARDE
JACQUELINE
MARGARETTA
MARGUERITE
PETRONELLA
WILHELMINA

11

ALEXANDRINA
CHRISTIANIA

GRAND NATIONAL WINNERS
including jockey and year

HORSE	JOCKEY	YEAR
3		
E.S.B.	D.V. Dick	1956
OXO	M. Scudamore	1959
4		
ILEX	A. Nightingall	1890
TEAL	A.P. Thompson	1952
5		
ANGLO	T. Norman	1966
AYALA	P. Buckley	1963
JERRY	Mr B. Bretherton	1840
REGAL	J. Cannon	1876
RUBIO	H.B. Bletsoe	1908
SPRIG	T.E. Leader	1927
6		
ANATIS	Mr T. Pickernell	1860
EMBLEM	G. Stevens	1863
EREMON	A. Newey	1907
FORBRA	J. Hamey	1932
GAY LAD	T. Olliver	1842
GRAKLE	R. Lyall	1931
GRUDON	A. Nightingall	1901
JERRY M	E. Piggott	1912
LUCIUS	R. Davies	1978
MOIFAA	A.Birch	1904
MR WHAT	A.R. Freeman	1958
OLD JOE	T. Skelton	1886
RED RUM	B. Fletcher	1973
RED RUM	B. Fletcher	1974
RED RUM	T. Stack	1977

HORSE	JOCKEY	YEAR

6

HORSE	JOCKEY	YEAR
REUGNY	Mr J.M. Richardson	1874
SEAMAN	Lord Manners	1882
SUNDEW	F. Winter	1957
WHY NOT	A. Nightingall	1894

7

HORSE	JOCKEY	YEAR
BOBBYJO	P. Carberry	1999
BOGSKAR	M. Jones	1940
BOURTON	J. Tasker	1854
CAUGHOO	E. Dempsey	1947
CHARITY	Mr H. Powell	1841
CURE-ALL	Mr W.G. Loft	1845
EMPRESS	Mr T. Beasley	1880
FRIGATE	Mr T. Beasley	1889
GAY TRIP	P. Taaffe	1970
GRITTAR	Mr R. Saunders	1982
KILMORE	F. Winter	1962
LOTTERY	Jem Mason	1839
MATTHEW	D. Wynne	1847
MR FRISK	Mr M. Armytage	1990
PIONEER	W. Taylor	1846
RUBSTIC	M. Barnes	1979
SEAGRAM	N. Hawke	1991
SHIFNAL	J. Jones	1878
SPECIFY	J. Cook	1971
SUNLOCH	W.J. Smith	1914
THE DUKE	Mr H. Potts	1837
THE LAMB	Mr G. Ede-Edwards	1868
THE LAMB	Mr T. Pickernell	1871
WEST TIP	R. Dunwoody	1986
WORKMAN	T. Hyde	1939
ZOEDONE	Count K. Kinsky	1883

HORSE	JOCKEY	YEAR

8

HORSE	JOCKEY	YEAR
ALDANITI	R. Champion	1981
AMBUSH II	A. Anthony	1900
BEN NEVIS	Mr C. Fenwick	1980
BINDAREE	J. Culloty	2002
CHANDLER	Capt Josey Little	1848
CLOISTER	W. Dollery	1893
COME AWAY	Mr H. Beasley	1891
CORBIERE	B. De Haan	1983
DISCOUNT	Mr H. Crickmere	1844
DROGHEDA	J. Gourley	1898
DRUMCREE	P. Woodland	1903
EMIGRANT	C. Boyce	1857
FOINAVON	J. Buckingham	1967
GAMECOCK	W. Daniels	1887
GLENSIDE	J.R. Anthony	1911
HUNTSMAN	H. Lamplugh	1862
JAY TRUMP	Mr C. Smith	1965
JEALOUSY	J. Kendall	1861
KIRKLAND	F. Mason	1905
PAPILLON	R. Walsh	2000
PLAYFAIR	C. Mawson	1888
POETHLYN	E. Piggott	1919

(Also won in 1918 but race was held at Gatwick not Aintree)

RAG TRADE	J. Burke	1976
ROYAL TAN	B. Marshall	1954
TROYTOWN	J.R. Anthony	1920
VANGUARD	T. Olliver	1843
VERMOUTH	J. Reardon	1916

(This race was held at Gatwick not Aintree)

WANDERER	J. Hanlon	1855
WELL TO DO	G. Thorner	1972

9

ALCIBIADE	Capt H. Coventry	1865

HORSE	JOCKEY	YEAR

9

HORSE	JOCKEY	YEAR
CASSE TETE	J. Page	1872
CORTOLVIN	J. Page	1867
EARLY MIST	B. Marshall	1953
GREGALACH	R. Everett	1929
HALF CASTE	C. Green	1859
L'ESCARGOT	T. Carberry	1975
MANIFESTO	T. Kavanagh	1897
MANIFESTO	G. Williamson	1899
MINNEHOMA	R. Dunwoody	1994
MUSIC HALL	F.B. Rees	1922
ROQUEFORT	Mr E.P. Wilson	1885
ROYAL MAIL	E. Williams	1937
SGT MURPHY	Capt G.H. Bennett	1923
THE SOARER	D. Campbell	1896
WOODBROOK	Mr T. Beasley	1881

10

HORSE	JOCKEY	YEAR
ABD-EL-KADER	C. Green	1850
ABD-EL-KADER	T. Abbot	1851
ALLY SLOPER	J.R. Anthony	1915
AUSTERLITZ	Mr F.G. Hobson	1877
BALLYMACAD	E. Driscoll	1917
(This race was held at Gatwick not Aintree)		
BATTLESHIP	Bruce Hobbs	1938
COVERTCOAT	P. Woodland	1913
EMBLEMATIC	G. Stevens	1864
FREEBOOTER	J. Power	1950
FREETRADER	G. Stevens	1856
HALLO DANDY	N. Doughty	1984
JACK HORNER	W. Watkinson	1926
LUTTEUR III	G. Parfrement	1909
MERRYMAN II	G. Scott	1960
MONTY'S PASS	B. Geraghty	2003
NICKEL COIN	J.A. Bullock	1951

HORSE	JOCKEY	YEAR

10

HORSE	JOCKEY	YEAR
PATHFINDER	Mr T. Pickernell	1875
QUARE TIMES	P. Taaffe	1955
ROUGH QUEST	M. Fitzgerald	1996
SALAMANDER	Mr A. Goodman	1866
SIR WILLIAM	A. McDonough	1838
TEAM SPIRIT	W. Robinson	1964
THE COLONEL	G. Stevens	1869
THE COLONEL	G. Stevens	1870
VOLUPTUARY	Mr E.P. Wilson	1884

11

HORSE	JOCKEY	YEAR
DISTURBANCE	Mr J.M. Richardson	1873
EARTH SUMMIT	C. Llewellyn	1998
HEDGE HUNTER	R. Walsh	2005
JENKINSTOWN	R. Chadwick	1910
LAST SUSPECT	H. Davies	1985
LORD GYLLENE	A. Dobbin	1997
MISS MOWBRAY	Mr A. Goodman	1852
PETER SIMPLE	T. Cunningham	1849
PETER SIMPLE	T. Olliver	1853
RED MARAUDER	R. Guest	2001
RUSSIAN HERO	L. McMorrow	1949
SHANNON LASS	D. Read	1902
SHAUN GOILIN	T. Cullinan	1930
SHAUN SPADAH	F.B. Rees	1921

12

HORSE	JOCKEY	YEAR
DOUBLE CHANCE	Major J. Wilson	1925
FATHER O'FLYNN	Capt R. Owen	1892
GOLDEN MILLER	G. Wilson	1934
MAORI VENTURE	S. Knight	1987
MASTER ROBERT	R. Trudgill	1924
RED ALLIGATOR	B. Fletcher	1968
REYNOLDSTOWN	Mr F.C. Furlong	1935

HORSE	JOCKEY	YEAR

12

REYNOLDSTOWN	Mr F.T. Walwyn	1936
RHYME 'N' REASON	B. Powell	1988
ROYAL ATHLETE	J. Titley	1995
THE LIBERATOR	Mr G. Moore	1879
TIPPERARY TIM	Mr W.P. Dutton	1928

13

KELLSBORO JACK	D. Williams	1933
LITTLE CHARLEY	W. Archer	1858
LITTLE POLVEIR	J. Frost	1989
LOVELY COTTAGE	Capt. R. Petre	1946
PARTY POLITICS	C. Llewellyn	1992

14

ASCETIC'S SILVER	Hon. A. Hastings	1906
NICOLAUS SILVER	R. Beasley	1961
SHEILA'S COTTAGE	A.P. Thompson	1948

15

AMBERLEIGH HOUSE	G. Lee	2004
HIGHLAND WEDDING	E. Harty	1969

17

WILD MAN FROM BORNEO	Mr J. Widger	1895

HERALDIC TERMS

3
BAR
DUN
HUE
PER

4
BEND
ENTY
FRET
GAMB
HELM
ORLE
PALY
PATY
PEAN
PILE
UNDY
URDY
VAIR
VERT
WAVY

5
AZURE
BARRY
BENDY
CADET
CHIEF
CREST
CROIZ
CROSS
DANCE
DANCY

FESSE
FIELD
FLANK
FLORY
FORMY
FUSIL
GEMEL
GIRON
GULES
GYRON
LABEL
MOLET
MOTTO
PALED
PARTY
PLAIN
RAZED
SABLE
STAKE
TENNE
TORSE
VAIRY

6
ARGENT
BANNER
BARRED
BASTON
BEZANT
BILLET
BORDER
BURELY

283

6 CANTEL
CANTON
CHARGE
CHECKY
COUPED
DEXTER
ERMINE
FITCHY
FLEURY
GOBONY
MANTLE
MASCLE
MAUNCH
MOLINE
MURREY
NEBULY
PARTED
PENNON
POTENT
RAGGED
RAGULY
ROLLAR
SHIELD
VOIDED
WYVERN

FORCENE
FUSILLY
GIRONNY
GRAFTED
GYRONNY
IMPALED
LEOPARD
LIONCEL
LOZENGE
MARTLET
NOMBRIL
PARTING
PASSANT
PATONCE
PIERCED
POTENTE
PURPURE
QUARTER
RAMPANT
ROUNDEL
SALIENT
SALTIRE
SCALLOP
STATANT
SURCOAT
TREFOIL
UNGULED
WILD MAN

7 ANNELET
ATTIRED
BENDLET
BEZANTY
CHARGED
CHECKER
CHEVRON
CLECHEE
CRUSILY
DORMANT
ERMINES

8 ADDORSED
ARMORIAL
BENDWISE
BLAZONED
BLAZONER
BLAZONRY
COUCHANT
DANCETTY

8
DEMI-LION
ERMINOIS
FIXABILL
FLOWERED
FOUNTAIN
INDENTED
INVECTED
MANTLING
ORDINARY
SANGUINE
SCOCHEON
SEGREANT
SINISTER
SYNOBILL
TINCTURE
TRESSURE
TRIPPANT

9
CHECKERED
CHEVRONNY
DIMIDATED
DISPLAYED
EMBATTLED
ENGRAILED
ERMINITES
FLEURETTY
QUARTERED
QUARTERLY
RECERCELE
SUPPORTER

10
CINQUEFOIL
COMBATTANT
CROSSLETED
DOVETAILED
ESCUTCHEON
FLEUR-DE-LYS

LAMBREQUIN
QUARTERING
REGUARDANT

11
COMPARTMENT
COUNTER VAIR
MARSHALLING
SURMOUNTING
VAIR EN POINT

12 INESCUTCHEON

13
COUNTERPOTENT
CROSS-CROSSLET
INNERSCOCHEON

14 COUNTER COMPONY

15
COUNTER-COLOURED
COUNTERFLOWERED

HERBS & SPICES

3
BAY
HOP
RUE

4
BALM
DILL
MACE
MINT
ROSE
SAGE
SALT

5
AJMUD
ANISE
BASIL
CAPER
CHAYA
CLOVE
CRESS
CUMIN
ELDER
TANSY
THYME

6
AJWAIN
BORAGE
CASSIA
CHILLI
CHIVES
FENNEL
GARLIC

GINGER
HYSSOP
KHELLA
LOVAGE
MAMANG
NETTLE
NUTMEG
PEPPER
SAVORY
SESAME
YARROW
YOMOGI

7
ANISEED
CARAWAY
CAYENNE
CHERVIL
CHICORY
COMFREY
EPAZOTE
GINSENG
HARISSA
JUNIPER
MUGWORT
MUSTARD
OREGANO
PAPRIKA
PARSLEY
PERILLA
ROSEHIP
SAFFRON

7 VANILLA
VERBENA

8 ALLSPICE
ANGELICA
BERGAMOT
CARDAMOM
CINNAMON
DONG QUAI
FEVERFEW
GALANGAL
LAVENDER
LUNGWORT
MARIGOLD
MARJORAM
PURSLANE
ROSEMARY
SAND LEEK
TAMARIND
TARRAGON
TURMERIC
VALERIAN
WOODRUFF

9 AKASHISHO
ARROWROOT
CHAMOMILE
CORIANDER
CURRY LEAF
DANDELION
EYEBRIGHT
FENUGREEK
HOREHOUND
LEMON BALM
ROCAMBOLE
SPEARMINT
STAR ANISE

SWEET ROOT

10 ASAFOETIDA
LEMON GRASS
NASTURTIUM
PENNYROYAL
PEPPERMINT
WATERCRESS
WITCH HAZEL

11 AVOCADO LEAF
CURRY POWDER
ELDERFLOWER
GARAM MASALA
HORSERADISH
MARSH MALLOW
ST JOHN'S WORT
SWEET CICELY
WINTERGREEN

12 LEMON VERBENA
SOUTHERNWOOD

HORSE BREEDS
**from all
over the world**

3
COB
DON
JAF

4
ARAB
BALI
BARB
DALE
DØLE
FELL
JAVA

5
BATAK
BURMA
FJORD
HUCUL
IOMUD
KONIK
LOKAI
PINTO
SHIRE
SPITI
SUMBA
TIMOR
TORIC

6
ALBINO
AUXIOS
AZTECA
BASQUE
BASUTO

BHUTIA
BRETON
BRUMBY
DULMEN
EXMOOR
GIDRAN
KAZAKH
MORGAN
PENEIA
PINDOS
PLEVEN
SKYROS
TARPAN
TERSKY
VIATKA

7
ARIEGOS
BASHKIR
BEETEWK
BOSNIAN
BRABANT
CASPIAN
COMTOIS
CRIOLLO
CRIOULO
FURIOSA
GARRANO
GOTLAND
HACKNEY
JUTLAND
KELPPER

288

7
LANDAIS
LLANERO
MANIPUR
MARWARI
MURGESE
MUSTANG
NORIKER
SALERNO
SORRAIA

8
ARDENNES
ASTURIAN
BALEARIC
BAVARIAN
BUDYONNY
CAMARGUE
DANUBIAN
DARTMOOR
FRIESIAN
GALICENO
GALICIAN
HIGHLAND
HOKKAIDO
HOLSTEIN
KABARDIN
KARABAIR
KARABAKH
KUSTANAI
LUSITANO
MURAKOSI
NIGERIAN
PAHLAVAN
PALOMINO
PASO FINO
POITEVIN

SHETLAND
SICILIAN
SOKOLSKY
TURKOMAN
WELSH COB

9
AKHAL-TEKE
ALTER-REAL
ANGLO-ARAB
APPALOOSA
ARDENNAIS
BEBERBECK
CALABRESE
CAMPOLINO
CONNEMARA
FALABELLA
GRONINGEN
HAFLINGER
ICELANDIC
KARACABEY
KLADRUBER
KNABSTRUP
MAREMMANA
NEW FOREST
NORMAN COB
NORTHLAND
OLDENBURG
PERCHERON
PINZGAUER
SARDINIAN
TRAKEHNER
WELSH PONY

10
ANDALUSIAN
ASSATEAGUE
AVELIGNESE
BARDIGIANO

10
BOULONNAIS
BURGUNDIAN
CARTHUSIAN
CLYDESDALE
DARASHOURI
EINSIEDLER
GELDERLAND
HANOVERIAN
KATHIAWARI
LIPIZZANER
MALOPOLSKI
MANGALARGA
MARCHADOR
POLISH ARAB
PRZEWALSKI
SADDLEBRED
SANDALWOOD
SHAGYA ARAB
TCHENARANI

11
DØLE TROTTER
MECKLENBURG
NOVOKIRGHIZ
PERSIAN ARAB
SAN FRATELLO
TRAIT DU NORD
WEST PHALIAN
WURTTEMBURG

12
CHINCOTEAGUE
CLEVELAND BAY
DUTCH DRAUGHT
EAST FRIESIAN
EGYPTIAN ARAB
IRISH DRAUGHT
KIGER MUSTANG
METIS TROTTER

ORLOV TROTTER
PERUVIAN PASO
STANDARDBRED
SUFFOLK PUNCH
THOROUGHBRED
WIELKOPOLSKI

13
EAST BULGARIAN
FREDERIKSBORG
FRENCH TROTTER
IRISH HALF-BRED
NATIVE TIBETAN
ROCKY MOUNTAIN
SELLE FRANCAIS
SWISS HALFBRED
WELSH MOUNTAIN
WORKING HUNTER

14
DUTCH WARMBLOOD
ITALIAN COW PONY
PLATEAU PERSIAN
RUSSIAN TROTTER
SWISS WARMBLOOD

15
SABLE ISLAND PONY
SWEDISH ARDENNES
SWEDISH HALFBRED

16
AMERICAN SHETLAND
BRITISH DALES PONY
BRITISH WARMBLOOD
CAYUSE INDIAN PONY
DANISH SPORT HORSE
DOLE-GUDBRANDSDAL
FINNISH UNIVERSAL
HISPANO ANGLO-ARAB

17
AMERICAN WARMBLOOD
FRANCHES MONTAGNES
FRENCH SADDLE HORSE
HESSEN RHEINLANDER
PONY OF THE AMERICAS

18
BRITISH SPORTS HORSE
CHICKSAW INDIAN PONY
MISSOURI FOX TROTTER
MONGOLIAN WILD HORSE
SARDINIAN ANGLO-ARAB
SOVIET HEAVY DRAUGHT

19
AMERICAN PERFORMANCE
BELGIAN HEAVY DRAUGHT
ITALIAN HEAVY DRAUGHT
LATVIAN HEAVY DRAUGHT
NORTH SWEDISH TROTTER
RUSSIAN HEAVY DRAUGHT

20
AMERICAN QUARTER-HORSE
AUSTRALIAN STOCK HORSE
CANADIAN CUTTING HORSE
VLADIMIR HEAVY DRAUGHT

21
RHINELAND HEAVY DRAUGHT
TENNESSEE WALKING HORSE

22
LITHUANIAN HEAVY DRAUGHT
AMERICAN MINIATURE HORSE

23
SCHLESWIGER HEAVY DRAUGHT

INSECTS

3 ANT
BEE
BUG
FLY

4 FLEA
GNAT
MOTH
WASP

5 APHID
DRONE
LOUSE
MIDGE

6 BEDBUG
BEETLE
BOT FLY
CAPSID
CHAFER
CHIGOE
CICADA
EARWIG
GAD FLY
HORNET
IO MOTH
LAPPET
LOCUST
LOOPER
MAGGOT
MANTID

MANTIS
MAYFLY
PSOCID
SAWFLY
THRIPS
WEEVIL

7 ANTLION
ARMY ANT
BILLBUG
BLOWFLY
CHALCID
CRICKET
CUTWORM
DIPTERA
FIG WASP
FIRE ANT
KATYDID
PROTURA
SANDFLY
STYLOPS
TERMITE
WAX MOTH

8 ALDERFLY
ARMY WORM
BLACKFLY
BOOKWORM
BRACONID
CRANEFLY
DIPLURAN

8
DIPTERAN
FIREBRAT
FRUIT FLY
GALL WASP
GLOW-WORM
GOAT MOTH
GREENFLY
HAWK MOTH
HONEY ANT
HONEYBEE
HORNTAIL
HORSEFLY
HOUSEFLY
HOVERFLY
LACEWING
LADYBIRD
LUNA MOTH
MASON BEE
MEALWORM
MEALYBUG
MOSQUITO
PHASMIDA
PLANT BUG
PUSS MOTH
SAND WASP
SHEEP KED
SILKWORM
SNAKEFLY
STINK BUG
STONEFLY
WATER BUG
WHITE FLY
WIREWORM
WOODWASP
WOODWORM

9
AMAZON ANT
AMBUSH BUG
ALOE APHID
BLOODWORM
BOOKLOUSE
BUMBLEBEE
CADDIS FLY
CHINCH BUG
COCKROACH
COREID BUG
CORN BORER
DAMSELFLY
DOBSONFLY
DOR BEETLE
DRAGONFLY
DRIVER ANT
ELIA BROWN
FLOUR MOTH
GALL MIDGE
GROUND BUG
GYPSY MOTH
ICHNEUMON
OIL BEETLE
OWLET MOTH
ROBBER FLY
SCREW WORM
SHIELD BUG
SWIFT MOTH
TIGER MOTH
TSETSE FLY
VELVET ANT
WARBLE FLY
WHIRLIGIG
YUCCA MOTH

10
APTERYGOTE
BARK BEETLE

10 BESS BEETLE
BLUEBOTTLE
BOLL WEEVIL
CACTUS MOTH
COCKCHAFER
CUCKOO WASP
DROSOPHILA
DUNG BEETLE
FLEA BEETLE
FROGHOPPER
FUNGUS GNAT
HESSIAN FLY
JUNE BEETLE
LEAF BEETLE
LEAF HOPPER
LEAF INSECT
LYGAEID BUG
POND SKATER
POTTER WASP
ROVE BEETLE
SEED BEETLE
SILVERFISH
SPANISH FLY
SPIDER WASP
SPITTLEBUG
SPRINGTAIL
STAG BEETLE
TINEID MOTH
TREEHOPPER
VINEGAR FLY
WEBSPINNER
ZODIAC MOTH

11 ASSASSIN BUG
BACKSWIMMER
BAGWORM MOTH
BITING MIDGE

BLACK BEETLE
BRISTLETAIL
BUFFALO GNAT
BUSH CRICKET
CANTHARIDAN
CATERPILLAR
CLICK BEETLE
CLOTHES MOTH
CODLING MOTH
COLEOPTERAN
EMPEROR MOTH
GRASSHOPPER
MOLE CRICKET
PLANT HOPPER
PYRALID MOTH
SCORPION FLY
STICK INSECT
TACHINID FLY
TIGER BEETLE
TUSSOCK MOTH
WATER BEETLE
WITJUTI GRUB

12 CACTOBLASTIS
CARPENTER BEE
CARPET BEETLE
CINNABAR MOTH
DIVING BEETLE
FLOWER CHAFER
FORESTER MOTH
GROUND BEETLE
HERCULES MOTH
HYMENOPTERAN
PEPPERED MOTH
PLUM CURCULIO
SCARAB BEETLE
SEXTON BEETLE

12
SPIDER BEETLE
WALKINGSTICK
WATER BOATMAN
WATER STRIDER

HERCULES BEETLE
JAPANESE BEETLE
LADYBIRD BEETLE
SLAVE-MAKING ANT
TORTOISE BEETLE

13
ALFALFA WEEVIL
ANTHOMYIID FLY
BLISTER BEETLE
BLUE BUTTERFLY
BURYING BEETLE
CARRION BEETLE
CLEARWING MOTH
COTTON STAINER
DADDY LONGLEGS
ELM BARK BEETLE
GELECHIID MOTH
GEOMETRID MOTH
GIANT WATER BUG
GOLIATH BEETLE
LEAFCUTTER ANT
LEAFCUTTER BEE
MEASURING WORM
REDBACK SPIDER
SATURNIID MOTH
SOLDIER BEETLE
STREPSIPTERAN
TORTOISESHELL
UNDERWING MOTH
UNICORN BEETLE
WATER SCORPION

14
AMBROSIA BEETLE
CABBAGE ROOT FLY
COLORADO BEETLE
CUCUMBER BEETLE
DARKLING BEETLE
DEATH'S-HEAD MOTH

15
CHECKERED BEETLE
COPPER BUTTERFLY
DERMESTID BEETLE
DIAMONDBACK
   MOTH
FUNNELWEB SPIDER
GRAPE PHYLLOXERA
NET-WINGED BEETLE
OLETHREUTID MOTH
PRIMITIVE BEETLE
SULFUR BUTTERFLY
WHIRLIGIG BEETLE

16
BOMBARDIER BEETLE
CUCKOO-SPIT INSECT
DEATHWATCH BEETLE
DEVIL'S COACH
   HORSE
LONG-HORNED
   BEETLE
NYMPHALIS ANTIOPA
   (CAMBERWELL
   BEAUTY BUTTERFLY)
PEACOCK BUTTERFLY
RHINOCEROS BEETLE
RINGLET BUTTERFLY
SATYRID BUTTERFLY
SKIPPER BUTTERFLY
XERODES PLUME
   MOTH
ZEBRA SWALLOWTAIL

17 CASEBEARING BEETLE
LEAF-ROLLING BEETLE
MILKWEED BUTTERFLY
SHINING LEAF CHAFER
THREAD-WAISTED WASP
XANTHOMERA SKIPPER

18 BLADDER GRASSHOPPER
BRANCH AND TWIG BORER
BRIMSTONE BUTTERFLY
ORANGE TIP BUTTERFLY

19 GATEKEEPER BUTTERFLY
HAIRSTREAK BUTTERFLY
PAPILIONID BUTTERFLY
RED ADMIRAL BUTTERFLY

20 BRUSH-FOOTED BUTTERFLY
NYMPHALIS POLYCHLOROS
(LARGE TORTOISESHELL BUTTERFLY)
PAINTED LADY BUTTERFLY
TUMBLING FLOWER BEETLE
WATER SCAVENGER BEETLE

21 CABBAGE WHITE BUTTERFLY

22 TORTOISESHELL BUTTERFLY

31 SILVER-WASHED FRITILLARY BUTTERFLY

ISLANDS
Atlantic Ocean

3 SAL

4 BRAC
FAGO
HERM
MAIO
PICO
SARK

5 BAIXO
BIOKO
BLOCK
BUGIO
CORVO
FAIAL
GOUGH
KUNOY
LEWIS
PRAIA
SAZAN
SUMBA
VAGAR
VIDAY

6 BAFFIN
BORDUY
BOUVET
FLORES
FUGLOY
GIMSOY
GOMERA

GRANDE
HARRIS
HESTUR
HIERRO
JERSEY
KALSOY
KOLTUR
NOLSOY
SANDOY
SKUVOV
SVINOY

7 ANNOBON
BERMUDA
CABRERA
CHAUSEY
DRVENIK
ICELAND
ILE DE RE
ILE D'YEU
IRELAND
LA PALMA
MADEIRA
PEREJIL

8 ALDERNEY
BELLE-ILE
BOA VISTA
DEER ISLE
EYSTUROY
GRACIOSA

8
GUERNSEY
JAN MAYEN
MONHEGAN
SAO JORGE
SAO TIAGO
ST HELENA
STREYMOY
TENERIFE
TERCEIRA
TRINDADE

9
AUSTVAGOY
BENBECULA
GREENLAND
ISLE OF MAN
LANZAROTE
MATINICUS
NORTH RONA
NORTH UIST
SAO MIGUEL
SOUTH UIST
SULA SEGIR
TRAVERSAY
VESTVAGOY

10
CAPE BRETON
FLAKSTADOY
GRAND MANAN
ILE D'OLERON
ISLE AU HAUT
ISLE OF MULL
ISLE OF SKYE
KILLY GOWAN
LITLA DIMUN
LONG ISLAND
PORTO SANTO
SANTA MARIA

SANTO ANTAO
SAO NICOLAU
STORA DIMUN
VINALHAVEN

11
GRAN CANARIA
ISLA ALBORAN
ISLE OF LEWIS
MOUNT DESERT
NIGHTINGALE
SABLE ISLAND
SAO VINCENTE

12
BRITISH ISLES
ILE-AUX-MOINES
NEWFOUNDLAND

13
FUERTEVENTURA

14
TRISTAN DA CUNHA

15
MARTHA'S VINEYARD
NANTUCKET ISLAND
WEST SPITSBERGEN

16
ILE DE LA MADELEINE
ILE DE NOIRMOUTIER

18
PRINCE EDWARD
ISLAND

ISLANDS
Caribbean Sea

3 CAT

4 CUBA
LONG
SABA

5 ARUBA
EXUMA
HAITI
NEVIS
UTILA

6 ANDROS
CANCUN
NASSAU
ROATAN
RUM CAY
ST JOHN
TOBAGO

7 ACKLINS
ANEGADA
ANTIGUA
BARBUDA
BONAIRE
COZUMEL
CROOKED
CURACAO
GRENADA
GUANAJA
JAMAICA

NAVASSA
ST BARTS
ST CROIX
ST KITTS
ST LUCIA
TORTOLA

8 ANGUILLA
BARBADOS
DOMINICA
ST MARTIN
ST THOMAS
TRINIDAD

9 GRAND TURK
ISLA COLON
MAYAGUANA
ST VINCENT

10 CAYMAN BRAC
GREAT ABACO
GUADELOUPE
HISPANIOLA
MARTINIQUE
MONTSERRAT
PUERTO RICO
SAN ANDREAS

11 BASTIMENTOS
GRAND BAHAMA

11 GRAND CAYMAN
ISLA MUJERES
ISLE OF YOUTH
LITTLE ABACO
PROVIDENCIA
SAN SALVADOR
ST CATHERINE
ST EUSTATIUS
VIRGIN GORDA

12
LITTLE CAYMAN
LITTLE INAGUA
MARIE-GALANTE
NECKER ISLAND

13
NEW PROVIDENCE
SAN BLAS DE CUNA

15
ISLA DE MARGARITA

17
DOMINICAN REPUBLIC

ISLANDS
Greek

3
COS (Alt. spelling KOS)
IOS
KEA
LOS

4
EVIA
HIOS (Alt. spelling Chios)
TZIA

5
CORFU
DOKOS
HYDRA
LEROS
LIPSI
NAXOS
PAROS
POROS
SAMOS
SYROS
TENOS (Alt. spelling
    TINOS)
ZANTE

6
AEGINA
ANDROS
EUBAEA (Alt. spelling
    EVIA)
IKARIA
ITHACA
KASSOS
LEMNOS
LESVOS (Alt. spelling
    LESBOS)
LEUCAS
LIMNOS
PATMOS

POTHIA
RHODES (Alt. sp.
    RODOS)
SIFNOS
SKIROS
SKYROS

7
AMORGOS
KEFALOS
KITHNOS
KYTHRIA
LEFKADA
MYKONOS
NISYROS
SERIFOS
SIKINOS
SPETSES
THASSOS

8
ANGISTRI
KALIMNOS
SALAMINA
SERIPHOS
SKIATHOS
SKOPELOS

9
ALONISSOS
ASTIPALEA
CARPATHOS
KEFALONIA
SANTORINI
ZAKINTHOS

10
CEPHALONIA
SAMOTHRACE

ISLANDS
Indian Ocean

4
BALI
BIRD
CERF
JAVA
KING
MAHE
NIAS
SHAG

5
ARIDE
DENIS
HEARD
TIMOR

6
BARROW
COUSIN
DANGER
MOHELI (alt. spelling
   MWALI)
PHUKET
SIPURA
ST PAUL

7
ALDABRA
ANJOUAN
BOMPOKA
COMOROS
FREGATE
LA DIGUE
MAYOTTE
PRASLIN

REUNION
SIBERUT
SOCOTRA
SUMATRA
THERESE

8
ALPHONSE
ARI ATOLL
BATHURST
CURIEUSE
FELICITE
FLINDERS
KANGAROO
KATCHALL
MELVILLE
NANCOWRY
SIMEULUE
SRI LANKA
TROMELIN
ZANZIBAR

9
ADDU ATOLL
CHRISTMAS
DESROCHES
MALE' ATOLL
MAURITIUS
RODRIGUES

10
CAPE BARREN
CAR NICOBAR
MADAGASCAR

10 SILHOUETTE
TARASA DWIP

11 DIEGO GARCIA
MALAKU ATOLL

12 GOIDHOO ATOLL
GREAT NICOBAR
LOWER ANDAMAN
NORTH ANDAMAN

13 FELIDHOO ATOLL
HUVADHOO ATOLL
LITTLE ANDAMAN
LITTLE NICOBAR
MIDDLE ANDAMAN
NELSONS ISLAND

14 HADHDHUNMATHEE
NILANDHOO ATOLL

15 CARGADOS CARAJOS

16 KOLHUMADULU ATOLL

17 FAADHIPPOLHU ATOLL
MAAMAKUNUHOO ATOLL

18 MAALHOSMADULU ATOLL

19 MILADHUNMAFULU ATOLL

20 IHAVANDHIPPOLHU ATOLL
THILADHUNMATHEE ATOLL

ISLANDS
Mediterranean Sea

4 ELBA
GOZO

5 CAPRI
IBIZA
MALTA
SAZAN

6 COMINO
CYPRUS
LIPARI
SALINA
SICILY (Alt. spelling
SICILLIA)
ZEMBRA

7 ALBORAN
CABRERA
CAPRAIA
CORSICA (Alt. spelling
CORSE)
JALITAH
MENORCA (Alt.
spelling MINORCA)
PARSLEY
VULCANO

8 MALLORCA (Alt.
spelling MAJORCA)
PONZIANE

SARDINIA (Alt. spelling
SARDEGNA)

9 LAMPEDUSA
SAN PIETRO
STROMBOLI

10 FORMENTERA

11 PANTELLERIA
SANT' ANTIOCO

ISLANDS
Oceana/Pacific

3
EUA
GAU
OFU
ONO
RAT
TAU
YAP

4
AITU
BEGA
CEBU
ELAO
GIZO
GUAM
KIOA
KORO
KURE
MARE
MAUI
NIUE
OAHU
PITT
RABI
ROTA
UVEA
WAYA

5
ALOFI
AUNUU
BAKER
BOHOL

CHUUK
EFATE
FAIOA
JAPAN
KAUAI
LANAI
LIFOU
LUZON
MANUA
MAUKE
MOALA
NAURU
NIHOA
OUVEA
PAGAN
PALAU
PANAY
SAMAR
SAMOA
TAHAA
TANNA
TONGA
TUPAI
UA POA
UPOLU

6
AMBRYM
BANABA
BIKINI
CABRAS
FUTUNA

6
HAINAN
HATUTU
HAWAII (aka Big Island)
HIVA OA
HIYA OA
HONSHU
KADAVU
KARKAR
KODIAK
KOSRAE
KYUSHU
LAKEBA
LAYSAN
MALOLO
MATUKU
MOOREA
NAIRAI
NASSAU
NAVITI
NECKER
NEGROS
NEPEAN
NIIHAU
OVALAU
PANGAI
PHILIP
ROTUMA
SAIPAN
SAVAI'I
ST PAUL
TAHITI
TAIWAN
TARAWA
TINIAN
TOYOTA
TUBUAI
TUVALU

UA HUKA
VAIAKU
YASAWA

7
ABALANG
CHATHAM
CHEJU DO
HOWLAND
HUAHINE
MALAITA
MANGAIA
MATA UTU
MAUPITI
MINDORO
MITIARO
MOLOKAI
NUNIVAK
OKINAWA
OLASEGA
PALAWAN
PENRHYN
POHNPEI
RAIATEA
SHIKOKU
STEWART
TAHUATA
TAIOHAE
TAKUTEA
TAVEUNI
TOKELAU
TUTUILA
VANUATU
WAIHEKE

8
AITUTAKI
BORA BORA
CAMPBELL

8
CHOISEUL
FATU HIVA
HONG KONG
ISLA PUNA
KIRIBATI
MALEKULA
MANIHIKI
MINDANAO
MOHOTANI
NIUAFO'OU
NUKUAETA
NUKU HIVA
PITCAIRN
PUKAPUKA
RANGIROA
SAKHALIN
SAN FELIX
SUWARROW
TASMANIA
TETIAROA
'UTA VAVA'U
VATULELE
VITI LEVU

9
AUSTRALIA
ERROMANGO
ISLA PINTA
KAHOOLAWE
KWAJALEIN
MILI ATOLL
MUTU AOTEA (aka Great
   Barrier Island)
NEW GUINEA
RAKAHANGA
RAROTONGA
SAN MIGUEL
SANTA CRUZ

SANTA ROSA
ST MATTHEW
TABUAERAN
TONGATAPU
VANCOUVER
VANUA LEVU

10
ATAFU ATOLL
BABELTHUAP
GRAND TERRE
GUADACANAL
KIRITAMATI
NEW BRITAIN
NEW IRELAND
NEW ZEALAND
PALMERSTON
PITT ISLAND
SAN NICOLAS
SANTA CLARA
ST LAWRENCE
WAKE ISLAND

11
ISLE OF PINES
JALUIT ATOLL
MAJURO ATOLL
NORTH ISLAND
   (NEW ZEALAND)
SAN CLEMENTE
SANTA ISABEL
SOUTH ISLAND
   (NEW ZEALAND)
VANUA BALAVU

12
BOUGAINVILLE
EASTER ISLAND
FAKAOFO ATOLL
ISLA ESPANOLA

12 ISLA GENOVESA
ISLA ISABELLA
ISLA MARCHENA
NANUMEA ATOLL
NIUATOPUTAPU
PALMYRA ATOLL
SAN CRISTOBAL

13 ESPIRITU SANTO
FUNAFUTI ATOLL
ISLA SANTA CRUZ
JOHNSTON ATOLL
MALOELAP ATOLL
NUKUNONO ATOLL
RONGELAP ATOLL
SANTA CATALINA

14 ISLA FERNANDINA
ISLA SANTA MARIA
KWAJALEIN ATOLL
NIULAKITA ATOLL
NUKUFETAU ATOLL
OSTROV SAKHALIN

15 ISLA SAN SALVADOR
NUKULAELAE ATOLL

16 ISLA SAN CRISTOBAL

17 FARALLON DE PAJAROS

20 ROBINSON CRUSOE ISLAND

ISLAND GROUPS

Atlantic Ocean

6 AZORES

8 HEBRIDES

11 SCILLY ISLES

13 CANARY ISLANDS
FAEROE ISLANDS
ORKNEY ISLANDS

14 ANDAMAN ISLANDS
CHANNEL ISLANDS
TRISTAN DA CUNHA

15 FALKLAND ISLANDS
SANDWICH ISLANDS
SHETLAND ISLANDS

16 CAPE VERDE ISLANDS
MARTIN VAS ISLANDS

Caribbean Sea

10 THE BAHAMAS
WEST INDIES

12 BAY OF ISLANDS

13 BIMINI ISLANDS
CAICOS ISLANDS
CAYMAN ISLANDS

14 LESSER ANTILLES
SAN BLAS ISLANDS

15 GREATER ANTILLES

16 FRENCH WEST INDIES

19 NETHERLANDS
ANTILLES

Greek Islands

13 IONIAN ISLANDS

15 CYCLADES ISLANDS
SPORADES ISLANDS

17 DODECANESE ISLANDS

Indian Ocean

9 INDONESIA

10 SEYCHELLES

12 COCOS ISLANDS
EAGLE ISLANDS

13 CROZET ISLANDS
EGMONT ISLANDS
THREE BROTHERS

14 AGALEGA ISLANDS
ANDAMAN ISLANDS
NICOBAR ISLANDS

15 MCDONALD ISLANDS

17 CHAGOS
ARCHIPELAGO

18 LAKSHADWEEP
ISLANDS

19 MILADHUNMAFULU
ATOLL
PRINCE EDWARD
ISLANDS

Mediterranean Sea

11 ILES D'HYERES

14 AEOLIAN ISLANDS
MALTESE ISLANDS

15 BALEARIC ISLANDS

Pacific Ocean – North

10 MICRONESIA

11 NEAR ISLANDS

12 BONIN ISLANDS

13 MIDWAY ISLANDS

14 CHANNEL ISLANDS
(US)
DIOMEDE ISLANDS
VOLCANO ISLANDS

15 ALEUTIAN ISLANDS
CAROLINE ISLANDS
HAWAIIAN ISLANDS
MARSHALL ISLANDS

16 ALEXANDER ISLANDS
ANDREANOF ISLANDS
NORTHERN MARIANAS

21 QUEEN CHARLOTTE
ISLANDS

Pacific Ocean – South

14 LOYALTY ISLANDS
SOLOMAN ISLANDS

16 GALAPAGOS ISLANDS

20 JUAN FERNANDEZ
ISLANDS

Oceana

8 LAU GROUP

9 ANTIPODES
MELANESIA
POLYNESIA

10 MANU'A GROUP

11 COOK ISLANDS
FIJI ISLANDS
LINE ISLANDS
YASAWA GROUP

12 HORNE ISLANDS
NIUAS ISLANDS

13 BOUNTY ISLANDS
WALLIS ISLANDS

14 AUSTRAL ISLANDS
CHATHAM ISLANDS
GAMBIER ISLANDS
GILBERT ISLANDS
LOYALTY ISLANDS
NORFOLK ISLANDS
PHOENIX ISLANDS
SOCIETY ISLANDS
SOLOMON ISLANDS
TUAMOTU ISLANDS

15 AUCKLAND ISLANDS
CORAL SEA ISLANDS
FRENCH POLYNESIA
WALLIS AND FUTUNA

16 ADMIRALTY ISLANDS
MARQUISES ISLANDS
SANTA CRUZ ISLANDS
VAVA'U ISLAND
GROUP

17 HA'APAI ISLAND
GROUP
NEW GEORGIA
ISLANDS
NOMUKA ISLAND
GROUP
WHITSUNDAY
ISLANDS

KINGS and QUEENS of ENGLAND

3 INE

4 AESC
ANNE
COEL
EDWY
JANE
JOHN
MARK
MARY
OCTA
OFFA
OISC
OSWY
SVEN (Sweyn)

5 AELLE
CISSA
EDGAR
EDRED
EDWIN
HENRY
JAMES
NUNNA
PENDA
SWEYN (Sven)
URIEN

6 ALFRED
ARTHUR
CANUTE

CERDIC
EDMUND
EDWARD
EGBERT
GEORGE
HAROLD
OSWALD

7 CEAWLIN
CHARLES
COMMIUS
GERAINT
HENGIST
MAELGWN
REDWALD
RICHARD
STEPHEN
WILLIAM

8 ALLECTUS
BOUDICCA
ETHELRED
VICTORIA

9 AMBROSIUS
ATHELSTAN

9 CARATACUS
CARAUSIUS
ELIZABETH
EORMENRIC
ETHELBALD
ETHELBERT
MARY TUDOR
SEAXBURGH
VORTIGERN

10 COGIDUBNUS
HARTHACNUT

11 CARTIMANDUA
CUNOBELINUS
HARDICANUTE (Harthacnut)

12 LADY JANE GREY

14 EDMUND IRONSIDE
EDWARD THE ELDER
WILLIAM AND MARY

18 EDWARD THE CONFESSOR

KITCHEN UTENSILS
and equipment

3
AGA
CUP
HOB
JAR
JUG
LID
MAT
MUG
PAN
POT
TIN
WOK

4
BOWL
DISH
EWER
FORK
MILL
RACK
SINK
SPIT
TRAY

5
BASIN
BOARD
CLOTH
CROCK
FLUTE
GRILL
KNIFE
LADLE

MIXER
MOULD
PLATE
PRESS
RICER
RUSSE
SIEVE
SPOON
STRAW
TONGS
WHISK

6
BOTTLE
BUCKET
BUN TIN
BURNER
CARAFE
COOLER
FILTER
FUNNEL
GRATER
JUICER
KETTLE
MINCER
MORTAR
MUSLIN
PESTLE
SAUCER
SCALES
SKEWER
TAJINE

6 TUREEN
ZESTER

7 BLENDER
CAKE TIN
CHIP PAN
DRAINER
FLAN TIN
GAS RING
GRIDDLE
GRINDER
MARMITE
PITCHER
POACHER
SKILLET
SPATULA
SYRINGE
TOASTER

8 CAULDRON
COLANDER
CRUET SET
FLAN RING
MEAT DISH
SAUCEPAN
SCISSORS
STOCKPOT
STRAINER
TRENCHER

9 BAIN-MARIE
BAKING TIN
CAFETIERE
CASSEROLE
CORKSCREW
CRUMB TRAY
FISH SLICE

FRYING PAN
KILNER JAR
OVEN TIMER
PASTRY BAG
PIPING BAG
SALAD BOWL
SAUCEBOAT

10 APPLE-CORER
BREAD MAKER
CRUET STAND
FISH KETTLE
HEATED TRAY
LIQUIDIZER
MUSTARD POT
PERCOLATOR
ROLLING PIN
SALT CELLAR
SLOW COOKER
STERILIZER
WAFFLE IRON

11 BAKING SHEET
BRAISING PAN
CARVING FORK
COFFEE MAKER
DOUGH TROUGH
GARLIC PRESS
NUTCRACKERS
OYSTER KNIFE
PASTRY BRUSH
PASTRY WHEEL
PIZZA CUTTER
PLATE WARMER
SERVING DISH
THERMOMETER
TURBOT KNIFE

12
CARVING KNIFE
CHERRY STONER
DEEP FAT FRYER
MARMALADE POT
MEASURING JUG
PALETTE KNIFE
PASTRY CUTTER
POTATO MASHER
SMOOTHY MAKER
YOGHURT MAKER

13
BUTCHER'S BLOCK
FOOD PROCESSOR
GARLIC CRUSHER
ICE-CREAM MAKER
KITCHEN SCALES
NUTMEG GRINDER
PEPPER GRINDER
PRESERVING JAR
VEGETABLE DISH

14
JUICE EXTRACTOR
KNIFE SHARPENER
PRESSURE COOKER
TRUSSING NEEDLE

15
VEGETABLE PEELER

LAKES and LOCHS

LAKE/LOCH	COUNTRY
3	
AWE	Scotland
VAN	Turkey
4	
ARAL	Kazakhstan, Uzbekistan
BALA	Wales
CHAD	Chad, Niger, Nigeria, Cameroon
COMO	Italy
ERIE	Canada, USA
EYRE	Australia
KIVU	Zaire, Rwanda
NEMI	Italy
NESS	Scotland
TANA	Ethiopia
5	
FOYLE	Ireland
GARDA	Italy
GREAT	Australia
GREAT	Canada, USA
HURON	Canada, USA
KIOGA	Uganda
KYOGA	Uganda
LEMAN	Switzerland, France
LEVEN	Scotland
LOCHY	Scotland
MAREE	Scotland
NEAGH	N. Ireland

LAKE/LOCH	COUNTRY

5

NYASA	Malawi, Tanzania, Mozambique
ONEGA	Russia
TAUPO	New Zealand
URMIA	Iran

6

ALBERT	Uganda, Zaire
BAIKAL	Russia
EDWARD	Uganda, Zaire
GENEVA	Switzerland, France
KARIBA	Zambia, Zimbabwe
LADOGA	Russia
LOMOND	Scotland
LOP NOR	China
MALAWI	Malawi, Tanzania, Mozambique
MOBUTU	Uganda, Zaire
MURITZ	Germany
NASSER	Egypt
NATRON	Tanzania
PEIPUS	Russia
POYANG	China
RUDOLF	Kenya, Ethiopia
SAIMAA	Finland
VANERN	Sweden

7

BALATON	Hungary
DERWENT	England
KATRINE	Scotland
KOKO NOR	China
LACANAU	France
LUCERNE	Switzerland
NIPIGON	Canada
NU JIANG	China, Myanmar (Burma)

LAKE/LOCH	COUNTRY

7

ONTARIO	Canada, USA
QINGHAI	China
ST CLAIR	Canada, USA
TORRENS	Australia
TURKANA	Kenya, Ethiopia

8

BALKHASH	Kazakhstan
CHIEMSEE	Germany
CONISTON	England
DONGTING	China
GRASMERE	England
ISSYK KUL	Kyrgyzstan
MANITOBA	Canada
MAGGIORE	Italy
MAZURIAN	Poland
MICHIGAN	USA
MOHNESEE	Germany
NEUSIEDL	Austria, Hungary
REINDEER	Canada
SUPERIOR	USA, Canada
TITICACA	Peru, Bolivia
TONLE SAP	Kampuchea
TUNG-T'ING	China
VICTORIA	Uganda, Tanzania, Kenya
WINNIPEG	Canada

9

ATHABASCA	Canada
BANGWEULU	Zambia
CHAMPLAIN	USA
COCIBOLCA	Nicaragua
CONSTANCE	Germany
ENNERDALE	England

LAKE/LOCH	COUNTRY

9

GREAT BEAR	Canada
GREAT SALT	USA
MARACAIBO	Venezuela
NEUCHATEL	France
NICARAGUA	Nicaragua
THIRLMERE	England
TRASIMENO	Italy
ULLSWATER	England

10

BUTTERMERE	England
GREAT SLAVE	Canada
IJSSELMEER	Netherlands
NETTILLING	Canada
OKEECHOBEE	USA
TANGANYIKA	Tanzania
WINDERMERE	England

11

BISCARROSSE	France
SEBKHA D'ORAN	Algeria

12

KARA-BOGAZ-GOL	Russia
WINNIPEGOSIS	Canada

14

MOBUTU SESE SEKO	Uganda

18

VIERWALDSTATTERSEE	Switzerland

LANGUAGES

LANGUAGE	MAIN COUNTRIES SPOKEN
2	
WU	China
3	
MON	Mayanmar (Burma)
TWI	Ghana
4	
BUHI	Philippines
DARI (Persian)	Afghanistan
URDU	India, Pakistan
ZARI	Nigeria
ZULU	Botswana, Lesotho, Malawi, Mozambique, South Africa, Swaziland
5	
AYMAR	Peru
BATAK	Philippines
BIKYA (aka Furu)	Cameroon
CZECH	Czech Republic
DUTCH	The Netherlands
FARSI (Persian)	Iran
GAFAT	Ethiopia
GREEK	Greece
HAUSA	Nigeria, Sudan, south of the Sahara
HINDI	Goa, Northern India
HMONG	Thailand

LANGUAGE	MAIN COUNTRIES SPOKEN

5

LANGUAGE	MAIN COUNTRIES SPOKEN
JINYU	China
KAKWA	Congo, Sudan, Uganda
KAMBA	Kenya
MAORI	New Zealand
MAYAN	S.E. Mexico & Central America down to Honduras
TAMIL	India, Malyasia, Singapore, Sri Lanka
TIGRE	Ethiopia
XIANG	China

6

LANGUAGE	MAIN COUNTRIES SPOKEN
ARABIC	Djibouti, Jordan, Kuwait, Libya, Mauritania, Morocco, Oman, Qatar, Saudi Arabia, Somalia, Sudan, Syria, Tunisia, UAE, Yemen
BASQUE (aka Euskera)	Basque Country (N.W. Spain/ S.W. France)
BERBER	Morocco, Algeria
DANISH	Denmark
DUNGAN	Spoken by the Dungan of Asia
FIJIAN	Islands of Fiji
FRENCH	Official language of France and 24 other countries, many of which are in Africa and Quebec (Canada)
GEN-GBE	Benin, Togo
GERMAN	Only official language of Austria, Germany and Liechtenstein. It shares official status in Belgium, Denmark, Italy, Luxembourg and Switzerland

LANGUAGE	MAIN COUNTRIES SPOKEN

6

LANGUAGE	MAIN COUNTRIES SPOKEN
MINNAN	China, Indonesia, Philippines
NEPALI	Nepal
PASHTU	Afghanistan
POLISH	Poland
SLOVAK	Slovakia
TELUGU	Southern India
TICUNA	Brazil, Colombia, Peru
ZAPARO	Ecuador

7

LANGUAGE	MAIN COUNTRIES SPOKEN
AMHARIC	Ethiopia
BENGALI	Bangladesh
BOSNIAN	Bosnia & Herzegovina
BURMESE	Burma
CATALAN	Catalonian region of Spain
CHINESE *Mandarin/ Cantonese*	China, Hong Kong, Malaysia, Singapore, Taiwan
ENGLISH *American English* *Australian English* *British English* *Caribbean English* *Jamaican English* *New Zealand English*	Antigua, Australia, Bahamas, Barbados, Bermuda, Dominica, Gibraltar, Grenada, Guyana, Jamaica, Malta, New Zealand Saint Lucia, Saint Kitts and Nevis, Saint Vincent and the Grenadines, Trinidad and Tobago, United Kingdom and the United States of America
FINNISH	Finland
ITALIAN	Italy, San Marino, Switzerland, Vatican City
KURDISH	Iran, Iraq, Syria, Turkey
LAKHOTA	Native American Lakota people
LATVIAN	Latvia
MALTESE	Malta
MARATHI	Indian state of Maharashra, Israel and Mauritius

LANGUAGE	MAIN COUNTRIES SPOKEN

7

OCCITAN	Romance language of France
PERSIAN (Iranian)	Iran
PUNJABI	India and Pakistan
QASHQAI	Iran
QUECHUA	American Indian, South America
RUSSIAN	All former Soviet Union countries
SENTANI	Indonesia
SLOVENE	Slovenia
SPANISH	Argentina, Bolivia, Chile, Colombia, Costa Rica, Cuba, Dominican Republic, Ecuador, El Salvador, Equatorial Guinea, Guatemala, Honduras, Mexico, Nicaragua, Panama, Paraguay, Peru, Puerto Rico, Spain, Uruguay and Venezuela
SWAHILI	Congo, The Democratic Republic of
SWEDISH	Sweden
TAGALOG	Philippines
TURKISH	Turkey
YIDDISH	Jewish race throughout the world
ZAPOTEC	South and Central America

8

ALSATIAN	France
ASSURIAN	N.W. Spain
ASSYRIAN	N.W. Iran
BHOJPURI	Certain Indian states
CHICHEWA	Malawi
DHUNDARI	India
ESTONIAN	Estonia
GUJARATI	Kenya, Western India
HAWAIIAN	Hawaiian islands
JAPANESE	Japan, Java (Indonesia)

LANGUAGE	MAIN COUNTRIES SPOKEN

8

MARAGHEI	Iran
ROMANIAN	Moldova and Romania
SANSKRIT	India
YAWANAWA	Brazil

9

BULGARIAN	Bulgaria
DONGXIANG	N.W. China
LONWOLWOL	Vanuatu
NORWEGIAN	Norway
SLOVENIAN	Slovenia
UKRAINIAN	Moldova, Ukraine

10

BWANA BWANA	Papua New Guinea
LITHUANIAN	Lithuania
MACEDONIAN	Republic of Macedonia
PORTUGUESE	Brazil, Portugal

11

BELARUSSIAN	Belarus

12

LEGA-SHABUNDA	Congo, The Democratic Republic of

17

KATCHA-KADUGLI-MIRI	Sudan

LITERARY TERMS

3 PUN

4 TONE

5 CANON
GENRE
IDIOM
METRE
RHYME
SLANG

6 ACTIVE
CLICHE
EPONYM
GERUND
HYBRID
ITALIC
PARODY
RHYTHM
SATIRE
SIMILE
SYMBOL
ZEUGMA

7 ACRONYM
ANAGRAM
ANALOGY
ANTONYM
APOCOPE
CAESURA
COUPLET

ELISION
LITOTES
MEIOSIS
PARADOX
PASSIVE
PRONOUN
REVIVAL
RHYMING
SYNCOPE
SYNONYM

8 ACROSTIC
ALLEGORY
APOLOGUE
ELLIPSIS
EUPHUISM
METAPHOR
PEDANTRY
PLEONASM
SAXONISM
TRAVESTY

9 ASSONANCE
BARBARISM
BURLESQUE
DIAERESIS
EUPHEMISM
FREE VERSE
GALLICISM
HACKNEYED
HEXAMETER

9
HYPERBOLE
SOBRIQUET
SOLILOQUY
SYLLEPSIS
TAUTOLOGY

10
ANTITHESIS
APHAERESIS
BLANK VERSE
BOWDLERISM
CONSONANCE
DENOTATION
GENTEELISM
METATHESIS
PALINDROME
PARTICIPLE
SPOONERISM
STEREOTYPE
SYNECDOCHE
TRANSITIVE

11
CANNIBALISM
CONNOTATION
LEGERDEMAIN
MALAPROPISM
PARENTHESIS
PERIPHRASIS
STOCK PATHOS
SUBJUNCTIVE

12
ABBREVIATION
ALLITERATION
ANTI-SAXONISM
INTRANSITIVE
ONOMATOPOEIA
POLYSYLLABIC
SIAMESE TWINS

13
BACK-FORMATION
COLLOQUIALISM
DRAMATIC IRONY
HEROIC COUPLET
MIXED METAPHOR
ORATIO OBLIQUA
WORD PATRONAGE
WORN-OUT HUMOUR

14 WALLED-UP OBJECT

15
PATHETIC FALLACY
PERSONIFICATION
PORTMANTEAU WORD
SPLIT INFINITIVE

16
ELEGANT VARIATION
HYSTERON PROTERON
IAMBIC PENTAMETER
REDUPLICATED WORD

18
METAPHYSICAL
POETRY

MATHEMATICAL TERMS

2 PI

3 ADD
ARC
DIE
ODD
SET
SIN

4 APEX
AREA
AXES
AXIS
BASE
CODE
CONE
DATA
DICE
EDGE
EVEN
FACE
GRID
KITE
LINE
LOOP
MAZE
MEAN
MODE
OVAL
PLUS
ROOT

ROSE
SINE
STAR
TAKE
UNIT
VENN
ZERO

5 ACUTE
ANGLE
CHORD
COUNT
CURVE
DEPTH
DIGIT
EQUAL
GRAPH
GROUP
HELIX
LOCUS
LOGIC
NAPPE
ORBIT
ORDER
PLANE
PRIME
PRISM
PROOF
RATIO
SHAPE
SHARE

5
- SOLID
- SPACE
- TABLE
- UNION
- VALUE
- WEDGE
- WIDTH

6
- BINARY
- CENTRE
- CIRCLE
- CONOID
- CONVEX
- COSINE
- CUBOID
- CYPHER
- DIVIDE
- FOLIUM
- HEIGHT
- LAMINA
- LENGTH
- LINEAR
- MATRIX
- MEDIAN
- METRIC
- NORMAL
- NOUGHT
- OBLONG
- OBTUSE
- RADIUS
- RANDOM
- SECANT
- SECTOR
- SPHERE
- SPIRAL
- SQUARE
- SYMBOL

6
- SYSTEM
- TENSOR
- THEORY
- VECTOR

7
- ALGEBRA
- AVERAGE
- CONCAVE
- CONCEPT
- DECAGON
- DECIMAL
- FORMULA
- FRACTAL
- FRUSTUM
- GELOSIA multiplication
- HEXAGON
- INTEGER
- INVERSE
- LATTICE
- MEASURE
- NONAGON
- NTH TERM
- NUMERAL
- OCTAGON
- ORDINAL
- PARADOX
- PATTERN
- POLYGON
- PROBLEM
- PRODUCT
- PYRAMID
- REGULAR
- RHOMBUS
- RUSSIAN multiplication
- SCALENE
- SURFACE
- TANGENT

7 THEOREM

8 ADDITION
ADJACENT
ANALYSIS
BINOMIAL
CALCULUS
CARDINAL
CUBE ROOT
CYLINDER
DIAGONAL
DISTANCE
DIVISION
EGYPTIAN
   multiplication
ELLIPSES
EQUALITY
EQUATION
ESTIMATE
FORMULAE
FRACTION
FUNCTION
IMPERIAL
INFINITY
INTERVAL
MATRICES
MULTIPLY
NEGATIVE
NOTATION
PARABOLA
PARALLEL
PENTAGON
POSITION
POSITIVE
PROPERTY
QUADRANT
RATIONAL

ROTATION
SEPTAGON
SEQUENCE
SYMMETRY
TOPOLOGY
TRIANGLE
VERTICAL
VERTICES

9 ALGEBRAIC
ASYMMETRY
CALCULATE
DIVERGENT
DODECAGON
HYPERBOLA
ISOSCELES
LINE GRAPH
NUMERICAL
OPERATION
PARAMETER
PENTAGRAM
PERIMETER
PICTOGRAM
POLYHEDRA
REASONING
RECTANGLE
TRAPEZIUM

10 ARITHMETIC
BLOCK GRAPH
CONCENTRIC
CONVERGENT
COORDINATE
HEMISPHERE
HORIZONTAL
OCTAHEDRON
PERCENTAGE

10
PLACE VALUE
POLYNOMIAL
PROJECTION
PROPORTION
REFLECTION
RIGHT ANGLE
SEMICIRCLE
SQUARE ROOT

11
CALCULATION
COEFFICIENT
DENOMINATOR
DIGITAL ROOT
EQUIANGULAR
EQUILATERAL
GOLDEN RATIO
ICOSAHEDRON
MAGIC SQUARE
MOBIUS STRIP
PENTAHEDRON
PROBABILITY
SUBTRACTION
TETRAHEDRON
VENN DIAGRAM
WHOLE NUMBER

12
COMMON FACTOR
DIFFERENTIAL
DISTRIBUTION
DODECAHEDRON
INTERSECTION
NAPIER'S BONES
PARTITIONING
RELATIONSHIP
RHOMBOHEDRON
SQUARE NUMBER
TRIGONOMETRY

13
CIRCUMFERENCE
GOLDEN SECTION
MIXED FRACTION
PARALLELOGRAM
PERPENDICULAR

14
COMPUTATIVE LAW
FREQUENCY TABLE
MULTIPLICATION
TRANSFORMATION
VULGAR FRACTION

15
DISTRIBUTIVE LAW

16
ELLIPTIC GEOMETRY
TRIANGULAR
    NUMBER

17
COMMON
    DENOMINATOR
EUCLIDEAN
    GEOMETRY
FIBONACCI
    SEQUENCE
ICOSIDODECAHEDRON
QUADRATIC
    EQUATION

18
EQUIVALENT
    FRACTION
HYPERBOLIC
    GEOMETRY

19
HIGHEST COMMON
    FACTOR

MILITARY LEADERS

3 LEE, General Robert E.
MAR, Earl of
NEY, Marshal Michel

4 CNUT
FOCH, Marshal
Ferdinand
GIAP, General Vo
Nguyen
HAIG, Field Marshal
Douglas
JEHU
JODL, General Alfred
KING, Admiral Ernest
MOLA, General Emilio
NOGI, General
TOGO, Count
Heihachiro, Admiral
TOJO, General Hideki

5 AKBAR
BLEDA
BOTHA, General Louis
CHAKA
CLIVE, Robert
CYRUS
DAVID
DIETL, Brig-General
Eduard
GOWON, General
Yakubu

GRANT, Ulysses S.
HORSA
LEACH, Admiral Sir
Henry
LENIN, Vladimir
MAHDI, The
ROLLO
SAITO, Lt-General
Yoshitsugo
SHAKA
SHORT, Lt-General
Walter
SMUTS, General Jan
SULLA
SWEYN
WOLFE, James

6 AHMOSE
ALARIC
ALFRED
ARGYLL, Duke of
ARTHUR
ATTILA
BEATTY, Admiral Sir
David
BUTLER, James
CANUTE
CLOVIS
CUSTER, General
George
DARIUS

6

DARLAN, Admiral Jean
EUGENE, Prince of
 Savoy
FRANCO, General
 Francisco
GINKEL, General
 Godert de
GORDON, General
GRIVAS, Colonel
 George
HARRIS, Air Marshal
 Arthur
HECTOR
JOFFRE, General Joseph
MARIUS
NEGUIB, General
 Mohammed
NELSON, Horatio, Lord
NIMITZ, Admiral
 Chester
O'NEILL, Hugh
PATTON, General
 George S.
PETAIN, Marshal
 Philippe
POMPEY
RAGLAN, Fitzroy
 Somerset, Lord
STUART, Prince Charles
TOSTIG
WAVELL, General
 Archibald
XERXES
ZEDONG, Mao

7

ALLENBY, General
 Edmund

BAN CHAO
BLUCHER, Field
 Marshal Gebhard von
BOLIVAR, Simon
CHOLITZ, General
 Dietrich von
COLLINS, Michael
DENIKIN, General
 Anton
DON JOHN
DUPLEIX, Marquis de
FAIRFAX, Sir Thomas
GALLERY, Admiral
 Daniel
GUTHRUM
HADRIAN
HENGEST
HENGIST
HERBERT, Admiral
 Arthur
HOUSTON, Sam
JACKSON, Andrew
KOLCHAK, Admiral
LE CLERC, General
 Jacques-Philippe
LEPIDUS
PERSEUS
RIDGWAY, General
 Matthew
ROBERTS, Frederick
 Sleigh, Lord
ROMMELL, Field
 Marshal Erwin
SALADIN
SPINOLA, General
 Antonio

7 STURDEE, Rear Admiral
Sir Frederick
TEMUJIN
TROTSKY, Leon
WINGATE, General
Orde
WRANGEL, Baron Peter

8 ACHILLES
AGRICOLA
AUGUSTUS
BOUDICCA
CAMPBELL, Archibald
(Earl of Argyll)
CARDIGAN, James
Brudenell, Lord
CETEWAYO
CONNOLLY, James
COTENTIN, Anne de
(Comte de Tourville)
CROMWELL, Oliver
DEVEREUX, Robert
GAISERIC
GALTIERI, General
Leopoldo
HAMILTON, General
Sir Ian
HANNIBAL
LANSDORF, Captain
Hans
LAWRENCE, Captain
T. E.
LUCULLUS
LYSANDER
MANSTEIN, Field
Marshal Erich von
MONMOUTH, Duke of

MONTCALM,
Marquis de
NAPOLEON
OCTAVIAN
PERSHING, General
John
RADETZKY, Count
Johann
RAMESES
STILICHO
TAILLARD, Camille de
TASSIGNY, General
Jean de
TECUMSEH
VAN TROMP, Cornelius

9 AGAMEMNON
ALEXANDER
ALEXANDER, General
Sir Harold
AQUILLIUS, Marcus
BONAPARTE, Napoleon
BRIAN BORU
BRUDENELL, James
(Lord Cardigan)
CARATACUS
CHURCHILL, John
EARL OF MAR
FLAMINIUS
GARIBALDI, Giuseppe
HASDRUBAL
HO CHI-MINH
KING DAVID
KITCHENER, Horatio
Herbert, Lord
MACARTHUR, General
MARCELLUS

9 MCAULIFFE, Anthony
MERNEPTAH
METACOMET
PACHACUTI
PILSUDSKI, Josef
RUNDSTEDT, Field
   Marshal Gerd von
SAN MARTIN, Jose de
SANTA ANNA, General
SARSFIELD, Patrick
   (Lord Lucan)
SCHLIEBEN, General
   Karl von
SPARTACUS
STRONGBOW
TAMERLANE
VESPASIAN
WELLESLEY, Arthur
WU SAN-KUEI
YAMASHITA, General
   Tomoyuki

10 BRAUCHITSH, Field
   Marshal Heinrich
CLAUSEWITZ, General
   Karl von
CORNWALLIS, General
CUMBERLAND,
   Duke of
EISENHOWER, General
   Dwight
HINDENBURG,
   General Paul von
KOMOROWSKI,
   General Tadeusz
KUBLAI KHAN
MARK ANTONY

MEHEMIT ALI
MONTGOMERY, Field
   Marshal Bernard
   (Viscount
   Montgomery)
WASHINGTON,
   George
VOROSHILOV, General
WELLINGTON, Duke of

11 BLACK PRINCE
DE LA VALETTE, Jean
DUKE OF PARMA
EARL OF ESSEX
EPAMINONDAS
GENGHIS KHAN
JOHN OF GAUNT
MARLBOROUGH,
   Duke of
RENNENKAMPF,
   General Paul
SITTING BULL

12 DUKE OF ARGYLL
JULIUS CAESAR
MUSTAFA KEMAL
TUKHACHEVSKI,
   Marshal Mikhail

13 CHARLES MARTEL
CHIANG KAI-SHEK
PETER THE GREAT
SADDAM HUSSEIN
VERCINGETORIX

14 CASSIVELLAUNUS
JUDAS MACCABEUS

MOUNTAINS
and mountain ranges

MOUNTAIN/RANGE	COUNTRY/CONTINENT
3	
ASO	Japan
DOM	Switzerland
IDA	Turkey
4	
ALPS	Europe
BLUE	Australia
COOK	New Zealand
ETNA	Sicily
HARZ	Germany
JAYA	Indonesia
JURA	France
OSSA	Australia
RIGI	Switzerland
5	
ALTAI	E. Asia
ANDES	S. America
ATHOS	Greece
ATLAS	N. Africa
BLACK	Wales
COAST	Canada
EIGER	Switzerland
ELGON	Uganda
GHATS	India
KAMET	India
KENYA	Kenya

MOUNTAIN/RANGE	COUNTRY/CONTINENT
5	
LENIN	Russia
LOGAN	Canada
PELEE	Martinique
ROCKY	N. America
SAYAN	Russia
SNOWY	Australia
TATRA	E. Europe
URALS	Russia
6	
ARARAT	Turkey
BALKAN	Bulgaria
BROOKS	Alaska
CARMEL	Israel
CHUSKA	USA
EGMONT	New Zealand
ELBERT	USA
ELBRUS	Russia
ELBURZ	Russia
HERMON	Syria
HOGGAR	Algeria
KUNLUN	China
LADAKH	India
LHOTSE	Nepal
MAKALU	Nepal
MOURNE	N. Ireland
OLIVES	Israel
OTZTAL	Austria
PAMIRS	Asia
PINDUS	Greece
TASMAN	New Zealand
TAURUS	Turkey
VOSGES	France
ZAGROS	Iran

MOUNTAIN/ RANGE	COUNTRY/CONTINENT

7

AHAGGAR	Algeria
BERNINA	Switzerland
BROCKEN	Germany
CHIANTI	Italy
CHUGACH	Alaska
EVEREST	Nepal
MANASLU	Nepal
OLYMPUS	Greece
PALOMAR	USA
RAINIER	USA
RORAIMA	S. America
RUAPEHU	New Zealand
SKIDDAW	England
SNOWDON	Wales
ST ELIAS	Alaska
TIBESTI	Chad

8

ARDENNES	Europe
BEN NEVIS	Scotland
CAMBRIAN	Wales
CAUCASUS	Russia
CEVENNES	France
COLUMBIA	USA
COTOPAXI	Ecuador
FLINDERS	Australia
FUJIYAMA	Japan
HYMETTUS	Greece
JUNGFRAU	Switzerland
KAIKOURA	New Zealand
MAUNA LOA	USA
MCKINLEY	USA
MUSGRAVE	Australia
PENNINES	England

MOUNTAIN/RANGE	COUNTRY/CONTINENT

PYRENEES	Europe
STANOVOI	Russia
TATEYAMA	Japan
TIEN SHAN	Asia
VESUVIUS	Italy

9

ACONCAGUA	Argentina
ALLEGHENY	USA
ANNAPURNA	Nepal
APENNINES	Italy
BEN LAWERS	Scotland
BROAD PEAK	Pakistan
CAIRNGORM	Scotland
DOLOMITES	Italy
DUNSINANE	Scotland
GRAMPIANS	Scotland
HAMERSLEY	Australia
HELVELLYN	England
HIMALAYAS	S. Asia
HINDU KUSH	Central Asia
HUASCARAN	Peru
KARAKORAM	Asia
KOSCIUSKO	Australia
MACKENZIE	USA
MONT BLANC	France
NANDA DEVI	India
PACARAIMA	S. America
PARICUTIN	Mexico
PARNASSUS	Greece
RUWENZORI	Uganda
TIRICH MIR	Pakistan
TONGARIRO	New Zealand
ZUGSPITZE	Germany

MOUNTAIN/ RANGE	COUNTRY/CONTINENT

10

ADIRONDACK	USA
CADER IDRIS	Wales
CANTABRIAN	Spain
CARPATHIAN	E. Europe
CHIMBORAZO	Ecuador
DHAULAGIRI	Nepal
ERZGEBIRGE	E. Europe
GASHERBRUM	Pakistan
KEBNEKAISE	Sweden
MACDONNELL	Australia
MATTERHORN	Switzerland
MIDDLEBACK	Australia
MONTSERRAT	Spain
MOUNT LOFTY	Australia

11

ANTI-LEBANON	Lebanon
APPALACHIAN	USA
DRAKENSBERG	South Africa
JOTUNHEIMEN	Norway
KILIMANJARO	Tanzania
MONADHLIATH	Scotland
NANGA PARBAT	Pakistan
SCAFELL PIKE	England
SIERRA MADRE	Mexico

12

CITLALTEPETL	Mexico
GODWIN AUSTEN	Pakistan
GOLAN HEIGHTS	Syria
GRAN PARADISO	Italy
IZTACCIHUATI	Mexico
KANCHENJUNGA	Nepal
POPOCATEPETL	Mexico

MOUNTAIN/RANGE	COUNTRY/CONTINENT

12

SIDING SPRING	Australia
SIERRA MORENA	Spain
SIERRA NEVADA	Spain, USA
THREE SISTERS	Canada
VINSON MASSIF	Antarctica
WARRUMBUNGLE	Australia

13

COMMUNISM PEAK	Tajikistan
GROSSGLOCKNER	Austria
KOMMUNIZMA PIK	Russia
OJOS DEI SALADO	S America
SIERRA MAESTRA	Cuba

14

FICHTELGEBIRGE	Germany
FINSTERAARHORN	Switzerland
SHIRE HIGHLANDS	Malawi

15

| BERNESE OBERLAND | Switzerland |

18

| GREAT DIVIDING RANGE | Australia |

MUSICAL INSTRUMENTS

3 LUR

4 BELL
FIFE
GONG
HARP
HORN
LUTE
LYRE
OBOE
TUBA
VIOL
WHIP

5 ANVIL
AULOS
BANJO
BUGLE
CELLO
CLAVE
FLUTE
ORGAN
PIANO
REBEC
SHAWM
SITAR
VIOLA

6 CORNET
CYMBAL
GUITAR

RACKET
RATTLE
SPINET
TAM-TAM
TOM-TOM
VIOLIN
ZITHER

7 BAGPIPE
BASSOON
CELESTA
CEMBALO
CITTERN
CLAVIER
MARACAS
OCARINA
PANPIPE
PIANOLA
PICCOLO
ROTO-TOM
SACKBUT
SERPENT
SISTRUM
TAMBOUR
THEORBO
TIMPANI
TRUMPET
UKELELE

8 BASS DRUM
BASS HORN

8
CASTANET
CIMBALOM (or
   CEMBALON)
CLARINET
DULCIMER
JEW'S HARP
KEYBOARD
MANDOLIN
PSALTERY
RECORDER
SIDE DRUM
TRIANGLE
TROMBONE
VIRGINAL

9
ACCORDION
ALPEN HORN
ALTO FLUTE
BALALAIKA
BASS FLUTE
BOMBARDON
CASSATION
EUPHONIUM
HARMONICA
HARMONIUM
SAXOPHONE
SNARE DRUM
TENOR DRUM
VIRGINALS
WOOD BLOCK
XYLOPHONE

10
ARPEGGIONE
BASSET-HORN
CHAIR ORGAN
CLAVICHORD
CONCERTINA

COR ANGLAIS
DOUBLE BASS
FLUGELHORN
FRENCH HORN
HURDY-GURDY
KETTLEDRUM
OBOE D'AMORE
OPHICLEIDE
PIANOFORTE
SOUSAPHONE
TAMBOURINE
VIBRAPHONE
WAGNER TUBA

11
APOLLONICON
BARREL ORGAN
HARPSICHORD
TEMPLE BLOCK
TUBULAR BELL
VIOLA D'AMORE
VIOLONCELLO

12
ALTO TROMBONE
BASS CLARINET
BASS TROMBONE
GLOCKENSPIEL
SARRUSOPHONE
VIOLA DA GAMBA

13
ALTO SAXOPHONE
DOUBLE BASSOON
ONDES MARTENOT

14
TENOR SAXOPHONE
VIOLINO PICCOLO

MUSICAL TERMS

3 AIR
BAR
KEY

4 ALTO
ARCO
ARIA
BASS
CLEF
CODA
DUMP
LOCO
OPUS
SOLO

5 AD LIB
ASSAI
CANON
CAROL
CATCH
CHANT
CHOIR
CHORD
DOLCE
FORTE
FUGUE
GIGUE
LARGO
MAJOR
MEZZO
MINIM

MINOR
MOTET
NONET
OCTET
OSSIA
PIANO
PITCH
PRIMA
RONDO
SCALE
SCORE
SEGUE
SHAKE
SHARP
SOL-FA
SOTTO
SUITE
TACET
TEMPO
TENOR
THEME
TRILL

6 ACCENT
ADAGIO
AL FINE
ANTHEM
ARIOSO
A TEMPO
ATONAL
AUBADE

6
BALLAD
BRANLE
CHORAL
CHORUS
FINALE
LEGATO
MELODY
MINUET
OCTAVE
QUAVER
REPEAT
RHYTHM
RUBATO
SEMPRE
SEPTET
SEXTET
SONATA
TENUTO
TREBLE
UNISON
VIVACE

7
AGITATO
ALLEGRO
AMOROSO
ANDANTE
ARIETTA
BALLADE
BOURREE
CADENCE
CADENZA
CANTATA
CANZONA
CHANTER
CHORALE
CUT TIME
DESCANT

DISCORD
DOLENTE
HARMONY
MAZURKA
MELISMA
MORENDO
PESANTE
PORTATO
PRELUDE
QUARTET
RECITAL
REPRISE
SCHERZO
SOLOIST
SOPRANO
STRETTO
TREMOLO
TRIPLET
VIBRATO

8
ABGESANG
A CAPELLA
ALBORADA
ANTIPHON
ARPEGGIO
AUSDRUCK
BARITONE
CAVATINA
CHACONNE
COL LEGNO
CONCERTO
CROTCHET
FANTASIA
GALLIARD
INTERVAL
MADRIGAL
MAESTOSO

8

MOVEMENT
NOCTURNE
OVERTURE
REGISTER
RISOLUTO
RITENUTO
SEMITONE
SEMPLICE
SERENADE
STACCATO
SYMPHONY
VIRTUOSO

9

ADAGIETTO
AD LIBITUM
ALLA TURCA
ALLA ZOPPA
ANDANTINO
ATONALITY
BAGATELLE
CANTABILE
CAPRICCIO
COME PRIMA
COME SOPRA
CRESCENDO
DRONE BASS
GLISSANDO
IMPROMPTU
LARGHETTO
LEITMOTIV
OBBLIGATO
PIZZICATO
PLAINSONG
POLYPHONY
SEMIBREVE
SFORZANDO
SOSTENUTO

STENTANDO
VOLUNTARY

10

ACCIDENTAL
ADAGISSIMO
ALBUMBLATT
ALLARGANDO
ALLEGRETTO
ANTIPHONAL
BARCAROLLE
CANZONETTA
COLORATURA
DA CAPO ARIA
DIMINUENDO
DISSONANCE
FORTISSIMO
INCALZANDO
INTERMEZZO
INTONATION
LARGAMENTE
MODULATION
PEDAL POINT
PIANISSIMO
PORTAMENTO
PRIMA DONNA
QUADRIVIUM
RECITATIVE
REPETITEUR
RESOLUTION
RITARDANDO
SCHERZANDO
SCORDATURA
SEMIQUAVER
STRINGENDO
TREMOLANDO

11 ACCELERANDO
AFFRETTANDO
BATTLE MUSIC
DECRESCENDO
PASSACAGLIA
QUARTER-TONE
RALLENTANDO
SINFONIETTA
SYNCOPATION
TENERAMENTE

12 ACCIACCATURA
APPASSIONATO
BISBIGLIANDO
CHAMBER MUSIC
COUNTERPOINT
COUNTER-TENOR
DIVERTIMENTO
DODECAPHONIC
REGISTRATION

13 ABSOLUTE MUSIC
ABSOLUTE PITCH
ACCOMPANIMENT
FORTISSISSIMO
IMPROVISATION
PIANISSISSIMO

15 INCIDENTAL MUSIC

MUSICALS

4
CATS
FAME
HAIR
RENT

MOVIN' OUT
OKLAHOMA
SHOW BOAT
SPAMALOT

5
ANNIE
CHESS
DIL SE
EVITA
GYPSY
STOMP
TOMMY

9
ALTAR BOYZ
DESSA ROSE
EIGHT MILE
FUNNY FACE
FUNNY GIRL
HAIRSPRAY
ON THE TOWN

6
GREASE
LENNON
OLIVER
SHOLAY
TOP HAT
WICKED

10
ALL SHOOK UP
BRIGHT EYES
CINDERELLA
DR DOLITTLE
GRAND HOTEL
JUNGLE BOOK
KISS ME KATE
MISS SAIGON
MY FAIR LADY

7
AVENUE Q
CABARET
CAMELOT
CHICAGO
CRY BABY
MAMA MIA
SCROOGE

11
A CHORUS LINE
A STAR IS BORN
ALL THAT JAZZ
BILLY ELLIOT
BUGSY MALONE
CARMEN JONES
HIGH SOCIETY
LITTLE WOMEN

8
CAROUSEL
GODSPELL
LABYRINTH

11
MARY POPPINS
MOULIN ROUGE
SWEENEY TODD
THE KING AND I
THE LION KING

12
ANYTHING GOES
CALAMITY JANE
EASTER PARADE
GUYS AND DOLLS
LET'S MAKE LOVE
LONE STAR LOVE
PORGY AND BESS
SHALL WE DANCE
SOUTH PACIFIC
SWEET CHARITY
THE PRODUCERS
WE'RE STILL HOT

13
ACORN ANTIQUES
BLOOD BROTHERS
BREAKING GLASS
FOR ME AND MY GAL
HALF A SIXPENCE
JAILHOUSE ROCK
LES MISERABLES
SUMMER HOLIDAY
THE COTTON CLUB
THE JAZZ SINGER
THE MAMBO KINGS
THE WIZARD OF OZ
WEST SIDE STORY
WE WILL ROCK YOU
WONDERFUL TOWN

14
SIMPLY HEAVENLY
UNDER THE BRIDGE
WHITE CHRISTMAS

15
DANCER IN THE DARK
LA CAGE AUX FOLLES
MEET ME IN ST LOUIS
SINGIN' IN THE RAIN
THE FAR PAVILIONS
THE SOUND OF
  MUSIC
THE WOMAN IN
  WHITE
ZIEGFELD FOLLIES

16
FIDDLER ON THE
  ROOF
PACIFIC OVERTURES
STARLIGHT EXPRESS

17
A LITTLE NIGHT
  MUSIC
AN AMERICAN IN
  PARIS
BEAUTY AND THE
  BEAST
FORTY SECOND
  STREET
LULLABY OF
  BROADWAY
PHANTOM OF THE
  OPERA
YANKEE DOODLE
  DANDY

18 BROOKLYN, THE MUSICAL
SATURDAY NIGHT FEVER
WHISTLE DOWN THE WIND

19 LITTLE SHOP OF HORRORS
THE LIGHT IN THE PIAZZA

20 CHITTY CHITTY BANG BANG
EVERYONE SAYS I LOVE YOU
FORBIDDEN BROADWAY SVU
JESUS CHRIST SUPERSTAR
MILLION DOLLAR MERMAID
MUPPETS TAKE MANHATTEN

21 BILLY ELLIOT THE MUSICAL
DIRTY ROTTEN SCOUNDRELS
HEDWIG AND THE ANGRY
    INCH
JERRY SPRINGER: THE OPERA

23 JAILHOUSE ROCK THE MUSICAL

NAUTICAL TERMS

3
AFT
AMA
BOW
EBB
LEE
LOG
RUN
SET
WAY
YAW

4
ALEE
BALE
BEAM
BOAT
BUOY
COIL
DECK
DOCK
FLOW
HEAD
HELM
HOLD
HULL
KEEL
KNOT
LINE
PIER
PILE
PORT
RODE

ROPE
SHIP
SOLE
STEM
STOW
TIDE
TRIM
WAKE

5
ABACK
ABAFT
ABEAM
AHEAD
ALOFT
AVAST
BARGE
BELOW
BERTH
BIGHT
BILGE
CABIN
CARGO
CHART
CHINE
CHOCK
CLEAT
CUDDY
DRAFT
FLARE
FLEET
FLOOD

5
FLUKE
HATCH
HITCH
JETTY
SCOPE
SCREW
SLACK
STERN
SWAMP

6
ABOARD
ADRIFT
ANCHOR
ASTERN
AWEIGH
BECKET
BIMINI
BRIDGE
BRIDLE
COURSE
DINGHY
FATHOM
FENDER
FOULED
GALLEY
JETSAM
LEEWAY
PILING
RUDDER
SECURE
SQUALL
TILLER

7
ABREAST
AGROUND
BAILERS
BALANCE

BALLAST
BATTENS
BEARING
BLANKET
BOOT TOP
BOW LINE
CAPSIZE
CAST OFF
COAMING
COCKPIT
CURRENT
DOLPHIN
FLOTSAM
FORWARD
GANGWAY
GUNWALE
HEADING
HEADWAY
INBOARD
LEEWARD
MIDSHIP
MOORING
PLANING
QUARTER
RIGGING
SEACOCK
SEA ROOM
SEXTANT
TRANSOM
V BOTTOM

8
BACKSTAY
BOAT HOOK
BULKHEAD
FOREPEAK
LATITUDE
MASTHEAD

8
OUTBOARD
PILOTING
QUADRANT
SCUPPERS
SOUNDING
TOPSIDES
TRIMARAN
UNDERWAY
WINDWARD

9
ABOUT SHIP
ABOVE DECK
ADMEASURE
AMIDSHIPS
ANCHORAGE
AUTOPILOT
AUXILIARY
BAROMETER
BILGE PUMP
BITTER END
BOATSWAIN
CATAMARAN
DEAD AHEAD
FREEBOARD
GRAB RAILS
HARD CHINE
LAZARETTO
LONGITUDE
OVERBOARD
SEAWORTHY
STARBOARD

10
ANCHOR BEND
ANEMOMETER
BALLOON JIB
BARBER HAUL
BATTEN DOWN

CLOVE HITCH
DEAD ASTERN
FORE-AND-AFT
FORECASTLE
LUBBER LINE
MIDSHIPMAN
NAVIGATION
SEAMANSHIP
SPRING LINE
SQUARE KNOT

11
ANCHOR LIGHT
CHAFING GEAR
FLOORBOARDS
MARLINSPIKE
PLANING HULL
THWARTSHIPS

12
ABAFT THE BEAM
ADMIRALTY LAW
ANCHOR LOCKER
ANCHOR ROLLER
ATHWARTSHIPS
BAGGY WINKLES
DISPLACEMENT
FOLLOWING SEA
GROUND TACKLE
JACOB'S LADDER
NAUTICAL MILE
PLIMSOLL LINE
PLIMSOLL MARK
STANDING PART

13
BEAUFORT SCALE
GIVE-WAY VESSEL
QUARTERING SEA
QUARTERMASTER

NAUTICAL TERMS

NOBEL PRIZE LAUREATES
CHEMISTRY – 1901–2004

LAUREATE(S)	YEAR WON
3	
LEE, Yuan T	1986
4	
AGRE, Peter	2003
BERG, Paul	1980
CECH, Thomas R.	1989
CRAM, Donald J.	1987
CURL, Robert F. Jr	1996
HAHN, Otto	1944
KLUG, Sir Aaron	1982
KOHN, Walter	1998
KUHN, Richard	1938
LEHN, Jean-Marie	1987
OLAH, George A.	1994
ROSE, Irwin A.	2004
SKOU, Jens C.	1997
TODD, Lord Alexander R.	1957
UREY, Harold Clayton	1934
5	
ALDER, Kurt	1950
ASTON, Francis William	1922
BOSCH, Carl	1931
BOYER, Paul D.	1997
BROWN, Herbert C.	1979
COREY, Elias James	1990
CURIE, Marie	1911
DEBYE, Petrus Josephus Wilhelmus	1936

LAUREATE(S)	YEAR WON

5

DIELS, Otto Paul Hermann	1950
EIGEN, Manfred	1967
ERNST, Richard R.	1991
FLORY, Paul J.	1974
FUKUI, Kenichi	1981
HABER, Fritz	1918
HUBER, Robert	1988
KARLE, Jerome	1985
KROTO, Sir Harold W.	1996
LIBBY, Willard Frank	1960
MOORE, Stanford	1972
MULIS, Kary B.	1993
NATTA, Giulio	1963
POPLE, John A.	1998
PREGL, Fritz	1923
SMITH, Michael	1993
SODDY, Frederick	1921
STEIN, William H.	1972
SYNGE, Richard Laurence Millington	1952
TAUBE, Henry	1983

6

ALTMAN, Sydney	1989
BARTON, Sir Derek H. R.	1969
CALVIN, Melvin	1961
HARDEN, Sir Arthur	1929
HASSEL, Odd	1969
HEEGER, Alan J.	2000
KARRER, Paul	1937
LELOIR, Luis F.	1970
MARCUS, Rudolph A.	1992
MARTIN, Archer John Porter	1952
MICHEL, Hartmut	1988
MOLINA, Mario	1995

LAUREATE(S)	YEAR WON

6

NERNST, Walther Hermann	1920
NOYORI, Ryoji	2001
PERUTZ, Max Ferdinand	1962
PORTER, Lord George	1967
PRELOG, Vladimir	1975
RAMSAY, Sir William	1904
SANGER, Frederick	1958
SANGER, Frederick	1980
SUMNER, James Batcheller	1946
TANAKA, Koichi	2002
WALKER, John E.	1997
WERNER, Alfred	1913
WITTIG, Georg	1979
ZEWAIL, Ahmed H.	1999

7

BERGIUS, Friedrich	1931
BUCHNER, Eduard	1907
CRUTZEN, Paul	1995
FISCHER, Ernst Otto	1973
FISCHER, Hans	1930
FISCHER, Emil Hermann	1902
GIAUQUE, William Francis	1949
GILBERT, Walter	1980
HAWORTH, Sir Walter Norman	1937
HERSHKO, Avram	2004
HODGKIN, Dorothy Mary	1964
KENDREW, Sir John Cowdery	1962
KNOWLES, William S.	2001
MOISSAN, Henri	1906
NORRISH, Ronald George Wreyford	1967
ONSAGER, Lars	1968
OSTWALD, Friedrich Wilhelm	1909

LAUREATE(S)	YEAR WON

7

PAULING, Linus Carl	1954
POLANYI, John C.	1986
ROWLAND, F. Sherwood	1995
RUZICKA, Leopold	1939
SEABORG, Glenn Theodore	1951
SEMENOV, Nikolai Nikilaevich	1956
STANLEY, Wendell Meredith	1946
WALLACH, Otto	1910
WIELAND, Heinrich Otto	1927
WINDAUS, Adolf Otto Reinhold	1928
ZIEGLER, Karl	1963

8

ANFINSEN, Christian B.	1972
DE HEVESY, George	1943
GRIGNARD, Victor	1912
HAUPTMAN, Herbert A.	1985
HERZBERG, Gerhard	1971
HOFFMANN, Roald	1981
LANGMUIR, Irving	1932
LIPSCOMB, William N.	1976
MCMILLAN, Edwin Mattison	1951
MITCHELL, Peter D.	1978
MULLIKEN, Robert S.	1966
NORTHROP, John Knudson	1946
PEDERSON, Charles J.	1987
RICHARDS, Theodore William	1914
ROBINSON, Sir Robert	1947
SABATIER, Paul	1912
SVEDBERG, Theodor	1926
TISELIUS, Arne Wilhelm Kaurin	1948
VAN T'HOFF, Jacobus Henricus	1901
VIGNEAUD, Vincent du	1955
VIRTANEN, Artturi Ilmari	1945

LAUREATE(S)	YEAR WON

8

| WOODWARD, Robert Burns | 1965 |
| WUTHRICH, Kurt | 2002 |

9

ARRHENIUS, Svante August	1903
BUTENANDT, Adolf Friedrich Johann	1939
CORNFORTH, Sir John Warcup	1975
HEYROVSKY, Jaroslav	1959
MACKINNON, Roderick	2003
PRIGOGINE, Ilya	1977
SHARPLESS, K. Barry	2001
SHIRAKAWA, Hideki	2000
VON BAEYER, Johann Friedrich Wilhelm Adolf	1905
WILKINSON, Sir Geoffrey	1973
ZSIGMONDY, Richard Adolf	1925

10

HERSCHBACH, Dudley R.	1986
MACDIARMID, Alan G.	2000
MERRIFIELD, Robert Bruce	1984
RUTHERFORD, Lord Ernest	1908
STAUDINGER, Hermann	1953

11

CIECHANOVER, Aaron	2004
DEISENHOFER, Johann	1988
HINSHELWOOD, Sir Cyril Norman	1956
JOLIOT-CURIE, Irene	1935
JOLIOT-CURIE, Jean Frederic	1935
WILLSTATTER, Richard Martin	1915

12

| VON EULER-CHELPIN, Hans Karl August Simon | 1929 |

NOBEL PRIZE LAUREATES
ECONOMICS – 1969–2004

LAUREATE(S)	YEAR WON
3	
SEN, Amartya	1998
4	
NASH, John E.	1994
5	
ARROW, Kenneth J.	1972
COASE, Ronald H.	1991
ENGLE, Robert F.	2003
FOGEL, Robert W.	1993
HAYEK, Friedrich August von	1974
HICKS, Sir John R.	1972
KLEIN, Lawrence R.	1980
LEWIS, Sir Arthur	1979
LUCAS, Robert	1995
MEADE, James E.	1977
NORTH, Douglass C.	1993
OHLIN, Bertil	1977
SIMON, Herbert A.	1978
SMITH, Vernon L.	2002
SOLOW, Robert M.	1987
STONE, Sir Richard	1984
TOBIN, James	1981
6	
ALLAIS, Maurice	1988
BECKER, Gary S.	1992
DEBREU, Gerard	1983

LAUREATE(S)	YEAR WON

6

FRISCH, Ragnar	1969
MERTON, Robert C.	1997
MILLER, Merton M.	1990
MYRDAL, Gunnar	1974
SELTEN, Reinhard	1994
SHARPE, William F.	1990
SPENCE, A. Michael	2001

7

AKERLOF, George A.	2001
GRANGER, Clive W. J.	2003
HECKMAN, James J.	2000
KUZNETS, Simon	1971
KYDLAND, Finn E.	2004
MUNDELL, Robert A.	1999
SCHOLES, Myron S.	1997
SCHULTZ, Theodore W.	1979
STIGLER, George J.	1982
VICKREY, William	1996

8

BUCHANAN, James M. Jr	1986
FRIEDMAN, Milton	1976
HAAVELMO, Trygve	1989
HARSANYI, John	1994
KAHNEMAN, Daniel	2002
KOOPMANS, Tjalling C.	1975
LEONTIEF, Wassily	1973
MCFADDEN, Daniel L.	2000
MIRRLEES, James A.	1996
PRESCOTT, Edward C.	2004
STIGLITZ, Joseph E.	2001

LAUREATE(S)	YEAR WON
9	
MARKOVITZ, Harry M.	1990
SAMUELSON, Paul A.	1970
TINBERGEN, Jan	1969
10	
MODIGLIANI, Franco	1985
11	
KANTOROVICH, Leonid Vitaliyevich	1975

NOBEL PRIZE LAUREATES
LITERATURE – 1901–2004

LAUREATE(S)	YEAR WON
2	
FO, Dario	1997
OE, Kenzaburo	1994
3	
GAO, Xingjian	2000
PAZ, Octavio	1990
4	
BUCK, Pearl	1938
CELA, Camilo Jose	1989
GIDE, Andre Paul Guillaume	1947
MANN, Thomas	1929
SHAW, George Bernard	1925
5	
AGNON, Shmuel Yosef	1966
BOELL, Heinrich	1972
BUNIN, Ivan Alexeievich	1933
CAMUS, Albert	1957
ELIOT, Thomas Stearns	1948
GRASS, Gunter	1999
HESSE, Hermann	1946
HEYSE, Paul Johann Ludwig von	1910
LEWIS, Sinclair	1930
PERSE, Saint-John	1960
SACHS, Nelly	1966
SIMON, Claude	1985
WHITE, Patrick	1973

LAUREATE(S)	YEAR WON

5

YEATS, William Butler	1923

6

ANDRIC, Ivo	1961
BELLOW, Saul	1976
DU GARD, Roger Martin	1937
ELYTIS, Odysseus	1979
EUCKEN, Rudolf Christoph	1908
FRANCE, Anatole	1921
HAMSUN, Knut Pedersen	1920
HEANEY, Seamus	1995
JENSEN, Johannes Vilhelm	1944
MILOSZ, Czeslaw	1980
NERUDA, Pablo	1971
O'NEILL, Eugene Gladstone	1936
SARTRE, Jean-Paul	1964
SINGER, Isaac Bashevis	1978
TAGORE, Rabindranath	1913
UNDSET, Sigrid	1928

7

BECKETT, Samuel	1969
BERGSON, Henri	1927
BRODSKY, Joseph	1987
CANETTI, Elias	1981
COETZEE, John Maxwell	2003
DELEDDA, Grazia	1926
GOLDING, Sir William	1983
JELINEK, Elfriede	2004
JIMENEZ, Juan Ramon	1956
JOHNSON, Eyvind	1974
KERTESZ, Imre	2002
KIPLING, Rudyard	1907
LAXNESS, Halldor Kiljan	1955

LAUREATE(S)	YEAR WON

7

MAHFOUZ, Naguib	1988
MARQUEZ, Gabriel Garcia	1982
MAURIAC, Francois	1952
MISTRAL, Frederic	1904
MISTRAL, Gabriela	1945
MOMMSEN, Christian Matthias Theodor	1902
MONTALE, Eugenio	1975
NAIPAUL, Sir V. S.	2001
REYMONT, Wladyslaw Stanislaw	1924
ROLLAND, Romain	1915
RUSSELL, Earl Bertrand Arthur William	1950
SEFERIS, Giorgos	1963
SEIFERT, Jaroslav	1984
SOYINKA, Wole	1986
WALCOTT, Derek	1992

8

ASTURIAS, Miguel Angel	1967
BJORNSON, Bjornstjerne Martinius	1903
CARDUCCI, Giosue	1906
FAULKNER, William	1949
GORDIMER, Nadine	1991
MORRISON, Toni	1993
SARAMAGO, Jose	1998
YASUNARI, Kawabata,	1968

9

BENAVENTE, Jacinto	1922
CHURCHILL, Sir Winston Leonard Spencer	1953
GJELLERUP, Karl Adolph	1917
HAUPTMANN, Gerhart Johann Robert	1912
HEMINGWAY, Ernest Millar	1954
KARLFELDT, Erik Axel	1931
LAGERLOEF, Selma Ottiliana Lovisa	1909
MARTINSON, Harry	1974
PASTERNAK, Boris Leonidovich	1958

LAUREATE(S)	YEAR WON

9

QUASIMODO, Salvatore	1959
SHOLOKHOV, Mickail Alexandrovich	1965
SILLANPAA, Frans Eemil	1939
SPITTELER, Carl Friedrich Georg	1919
STEINBECK, John	1962

10

ALEIXANDRE, Vicente	1977
EIZAGUIRRE, Jose Echegaray y	1904
GALSWORTHY, John	1932
LAGERKVIST, Par Fabian	1951
PIRANDELLO, Luigi	1934
SZYMBORSKA, Wislawa	1996

11

MAETERLINCK, Count Maurice Polydore Marie Bernard	1911
PONTOPPIDAN, Henrik	1917
SIENKIEWICZ, Henryk	1905

12

SOLZHENITSYN, Alexandr Isayevich	1970

13

VON HEIDENSTAM, Karl Gustav Verner	1916

14

SULLY-PRUDHOMME, Rene	1901

NOTE – THIS PRIZE WAS NOT AWARDED BETWEEN 1940 AND 1943. THE PRIZE MONEY WAS ALLOCATED TO THE MAIN FUND AND THE SPECIAL FUND.

NOBEL PRIZE LAUREATES
PEACE – 1901–2004
(Up to 31 characters)

LAUREATE(S)	YEAR WON
3	
KYI, Aung San Suu	1991
THO, Le Duc	1973
4	
BELO, Carlos Filipe Ximenes	1996
HULL, Cordell	1945
HUME, John	1998
KING, Martin Luther Jr	1964
MOTT, John Raleigh	1946
PIRE, Georges Henri	1958
ROOT, Elihu	1912
TUTU, Desmond Mpilo	1984
5	
ANNAN, Kofi	2001
ASSER, Tobias Michael Carel	1911
BAJER, Fredrik	1908
BALCH, Emily Greene	1946
BEGIN, Menachem	1978
CECIL, Lord Edgar Algernon Robert Gascoyne	1937
DAWES, Charles Gates	1925
EBADI, Shirin	2003
FRIED, Alfred Hermann	1911
GOBAT, Charles Albert	1902
LAMAS, Carlos Saavedra	1936
LANGE, Christian Louis	1921
PASSY, Frederic	1901
PERES, Shimon	1994
RABIN, Yitshak	1994

LAUREATE(S)	YEAR WON
5	
SADAT, Mohammed Anwar El	1978
6	
ADDAMS, Jane	1931
ANGELL, Sir Norman	1933
ARAFAT, Yasser	1994
BRANDT, Willy	1971
BRIAND, Aristide	1926
BUNCHE, Ralphe	1950
BUTLER, Nicholas Murray	1931
CARTER, Jimmy Jr	2002
CASSIN, Rene	1968
CREMER, Sir William Randall	1903
DUNANT, Jean Henri	1901
EISAKU, Sato,	1974
MENCHU, Rigoberta	1992
MONETA, Ernesto Teodoro	1907
MYRDAL, Alva	1982
NANSEN, Fridtjof	1922
QUIDDE, Ludwig	1927
ROBLES, Alfonso Garcia	1982
WALESA, Lech	1983
WIESEL, Elie	1986
WILSON, Thomas Woodrow	1919
7	
BORLAUG, Norman	1970
BUISSON, Ferdinand	1927
DE KLERK, Frederik Willem	1993
JOUHAUX, Leon	1951
KELLOGG, Frank Billings	1929
LUTHULI, Albert John	1960
MAATHAI, Wangari	2004
MANDELA, Nelson	1993
PAULING, Linus Carl	1962

LAUREATE(S)	YEAR WON

7

PEARSON, Lester Bowles	1957
RENAULT, Louis	1907
ROTBLAT, Joseph	1995
SANCHEZ, Oscar Arias	1987
TRIMBLE, David	1998

8

BRANTING, Karl Hjalmar	1921
CORRIGAN, Mairead	1976
DUCOMMUN, Elie	1902
ESQUIVEL, Adolfo Perez	1980
MACBRIDE, Sean	1974
MARSHALL, George Catlett	1953
SAKHAROV, Andrei Dimitrievich	1975
WILLIAMS, Betty	1976
WILLIAMS, Jody	1997

9

ARNOLDSON, Klas Pontus	1908
BEERNAERT, Auguste Marie Francois	1909
BOURGEOIS, Leon Victor Auguste	1920
DALAI LAMA	1989
GORBACHEV, Mikhail Sergeyevich	1990
HENDERSON, Arthur	1934
KISSINGER, Henry A.	1973
NOEL-BAKER, Philip J.	1959
ROOSEVELT, Theodore	1906

10

DE CONSTANT, Paul Henribenjamin Baron d'Estournelles	1909
KIM DAE-JUNG	2000
LAFONTAINE, Henri	1913
RAMOS-HORTA, Jose	1996
SCHWEITZER, Albert	1952
SOEDERBLOM, Lars Olaf Nathan	1930

LAUREATE(S)	YEAR WON

10

STRESEMANN, Gustav	1926
VON SUTTNER, Baroness Bertha Sophie Felicita	1905

11

CHAMBERLAIN, Sir Austen	1925

12

VON OSSIETZKY, Carl	1935

13

HAMMARSKJOELD, Dag Hjalmar Agne Carl	1961
MOTHER THERESA	1979
UNITED NATIONS	2001

16

BOYD ORR OF BRECHIN, Lord John	1949

20

AMNESTY INTERNATIONAL	1977

21

DOCTORS WITHOUT BORDERS	1999

26

UNITED NATIONS CHILDREN'S FUND	1965

30

INTERNATIONAL RED CROSS COMMITTEE	1963

31

AMERICAN FRIENDS SERVICE COMMITTEE	1947

NOBEL PRIZE LAUREATES
PHYSICS – 1901–2004

LAUREATE(S)	YEAR WON
3	
CHU, Steven	1997
LEE, David M.	1996
LEE, Tsung-Dao	1957
4	
BOHR, Aage	1975
BOHR, Niels	1922
BORN, Max	1954
HESS, Victor Franz	1936
LAMB, Willis Eugene Jr	1955
MOTT, Sir Nevill F.	1977
NEEL, Louis	1970
PAUL, Wolfgang	1989
PERL, Martin L.	1995
RABI, Isidor Isaac	1944
RYLE, Sir Martin	1974
TAMM, Igor Yevgenyevich	1958
TING, Samuel C. C.	1976
TSUI, Daniel C.	1998
WIEN, Wilhelm	1911
YANG, Chen Ning	1957
5	
BASOV, Nicolai Gennadiyevich	1964
BETHE, Hans Albrecht	1967
BLOCH, Felix	1952
BOTHE, Walther	1954
BRAGG, Sir William Henry	1915

LAUREATE(S)	YEAR WON

5

BRAGG, Sir William Lawrence	1915
BRAUN, Carl Ferdinand	1909
CURIE, Marie	1903
CURIE, Pierre	1903
DALEN, Nils Gustav	1912
DAVIS, Raymond Jr	2002
DIRAC, Paul Adrien Maurice	1933
ESAKI, Leo	1973
FERMI, Enrico	1938
FITCH, Val L.	1980
FRANK, Ilya Mikhailovich	1958
GABOR, Dennis	1971
GROSS, David	2004
HERTZ, Gustav	1925
HOOFT, Gerardhus'T	1999
HULSE, Russell A.	1993
KILBY, Jack S.	2000
KUSCH, Polykarp	1955
PAULI, Wolfgang	1945
RAMAN, Sir Chandrasekhara Venkata	1930
RUSKA, Ernst	1986
SALAM, Abdus	1979
SEGRE, Emilio Gino	1959
SHULL, Clifford G.	1994
STARK, Johannes	1919
STERN, Otto	1943

6

ALFVEN, Hannes	1970
BARKLA, Charles Glover	1917
BINNIG, Gerd	1986
COOPER, Leon N.	1972
CRONIN, James W.	1980
FOWLER, William A.	1983

LAUREATE(S)	YEAR WON

6

FRANCK, James	1925
GLASER, Donald A.	1960
HEWISH, Antony	1974
JENSEN, J. Hans D.	1963
LANDAU, Lev Davidovich	1962
LENARD, Philipp Eduard Anton	1905
MULLER, K. Alexander	1987
PERRIN, Jean Baptiste	1926
PLANCK, Max Karl Ernst Ludwig	1919
POWELL, Cecil Frank	1950
RAMSEY, Norman F.	1989
REINES, Frederick	1995
ROHRER, Heinrich	1986
RUBBIA, Carlo	1984
TAYLOR, Joseph H. Jr	1993
TAYLOR, Richard E.	1990
TOWNES, Charles H.	1964
WALTON, Ernest Thomas Sinton	1951
WIEMAN, Carl E.	2001
WIGNER, Eugene P.	1963
WILSON, Charles Thomson Rees	1927
WILSON, Kenneth G.	1982
WILSON, Robert W.	1978
YUKAWA, Hideki	1949
ZEEMAN, Pieter	1902

7

ALFEROV, Zhores L.	2000
ALVAREZ, Luis W.	1968
BARDEEN, John	1956
BARDEEN, John	1972
BEDNORZ, J. Georg	1987
CHARPAK, Georges	1992
COMPTON, Arthur Holly	1927

LAUREATE(S)	YEAR WON

7

CORNELL, Eric A.	2001
DEHMELT, Hans G.	1989
FEYNMAN, Richard P.	1965
GIAEVER, Ivar	1973
GLASHOW, Sheldon L.	1979
KAPITZA, Pyotr Leonidovich	1978
KASTLER, Alfred	1966
KENDALL, Henry W.	1990
KOSHIBA, Masatoshi	2002
KROEMER, Herbert	2000
LEGGETT, Anthony J.	2003
LORENTZ, Hendrik Antoon	1902
MARCONI, Guglielmo	1909
PENZIAS, Arno A.	1978
PURCELL, Edward Mills	1952
RICHTER, Burton	1976
STORMER, Horst	1998
THOMSON, Sir George Paget	1937
THOMSON, Sir Joseph John	1906
VELTMAN, Martinus J. G.	1999
VON LAUE, Max	1914
WILCZEK, Frank	2004
ZERNIKE, Frits	1953

8

ANDERSON, Carl David	1936
ANDERSON, Philip W.	1977
APPLETON, Sir Edward Victor	1947
BLACKETT, Lord Patrick Maynard Stuart	1948
BRATTAIN, Walter Houser	1956
BRIDGMAN, Percy Williams	1946
CHADWICK, Sir James	1935
DAVISSON, Clinton Joseph	1937
DE GENNES, Pierre-Gilles	1991

LAUREATE(S)	YEAR WON

8

EINSTEIN, Albert	1921
FRIEDMAN, Jerome I.	1990
GELL-MANN, Murray	1969
GIACCONI, Riccardo	2002
GINZBURG, Vitaly L.	2003
KETTERLE, Wolfgang	2001
LAUGHLIN, Robert B.	1998
LAWRENCE, Ernest Orlando	1939
LEDERMAN, Leon M.	1988
LIPPMANN, Gabriel	1908
MILLIKAN, Robert Andrews	1923
OSHEROFF, Douglas D.	1996
PHILLIPS, William D.	1997
POLITZER, H. David	2004
RAYLEIGH, Lord John William Strutt	1904
ROENTGEN, Wilhelm Conrad	1901
SCHAWLOW, Arthur L.	1981
SCHWARTZ, Melvin	1988
SHOCKLEY, William	1956
SIEGBAHN, Kai M.	1981
SIEGBAHN, Karl Manne Georg	1924
TOMONAGA, Sinichiro	1965
VAN VLECK, John H.	1977
WEINBERG, Steven	1979

9

ABRIKOSOV, Alexei A.	2003
BECQUEREL, Antoine Henri	1903
CHERENKOV, Pavel Alekseevich	1958
COCKCROFT, Sir John Douglas	1951
DE BROGLIE, Prince Louis-Victor	1929
GUILLAUME, Charles Edouard	1920
JOSEPHSON, Brian D.	1973
MICHELSON, Albert Abraham	1907

LAUREATE(S)	YEAR WON

9

MOTTELSON, Ben	1975
PROKHOROV, Aleksandr Mikhailovich	1964
RAINWATER, James	1975
SCHWINGER, Julian	1965

10

BROCKHOUSE, Bertram N.	1994
HEISENBERG, Werner	1932
HOFSTADTER, Robert	1961
MOESSBAUER, Rudolf Ludwig	1961
RICHARDSON, Robert C.	1996
RICHARDSON, Sir Owen Williams	1928
SCHRIEFFER, J. Robert	1972
VAN DER MEER, Simon	1984

11

BLOEMBERGEN, Nicolas	1981
CHAMBERLAIN, Owen	1959
STEINBERGER, Jack	1988
VAN DER WAALS, Johannes Diderik	1910
VON KLITZING, Klaus	1985

12

SCHROEDINGER, Erwin	1933

13

CHANDRASEKHAR, Subrahmanyan	1983
GOEPPERT-MEYER, Maria	1963

14

COHEN-TANNOUDJI, Claude	1997

15

KAMERLINGH ONNES, Heike	1913

NOBEL PRIZE LAUREATES
PHYSIOLOGY & MEDICINE – 1901–2004

LAUREATE(S)	YEAR WON
3	
DAM, Carl Peter Henrik	1940
4	
AXEL, Richard	2004
BUCK, Linda B.	2004
CORI, Carl Ferdinand	1947
CORI, Gerty Theresa	1947
DALE, Sir Henry Hallett	1936
HESS, Walter Rudolf	1949
HILL, Sir Archibald Vivian	1922
HUNT, R. Timothy	2001
KATZ, Sir Bernard	1970
KOCH, Robert	1905
ROSS, Sir Ronald	1902
ROUS, Francis Peyton	1966
VANE, Sir John R.	1982
WALD, George	1967
5	
ARBER, Werner	1978
BLACK, Sir James W.	1988
BLOCH, Konrad	1964
BOVET, Daniel	1957
BROWN, Michael S.	1985
CHAIN, Sir Ernst Boris	1945
COHEN, Stanley	1986
CRICK, Francis Harry Compton	1962
DOISY, Edward Adelbert	1940
ELION, Gertrude B.	1988
GOLGI, Camillo	1906

LAUREATE(S)	YEAR WON

5

HENCH, Philip Showalter	1950
HUBEL, David H.	1981
JACOB, Francois	1965
JERNE, Niels K.	1984
KREBS, Edwin G.	1992
KREBS, Sir Hans Adolf	1953
KROGH, Schack August Steenberg	1920
LEWIS, Edward B.	1995
LOEWI, Otto	1936
LURIA, Salvador E.	1969
LWOFF, Andre	1965
LYNEN, Feodor	1964
MINOT, George Richards	1934
MONOD, Jacques	1965
MURAD, Ferid	1998
NEHER, Erwin	1991
NURSE, Paul M.	2001
OCHOA, Severo	1959
SHARP, Phillip A.	1993
SMITH, Hamilton O.	1978
SNELL, George D.	1980
TATUM, Edward Lawrie	1958
TEMIN, Howard Martin	1975
YALOW, Rosalyn	1977

6

ADRIAN, Lord Edgar Douglas	1932
BARANY, Robert	1914
BEADLE, George Wells	1958
BISHOP, J Michael	1989
BLOBEL, Gunter	1999
BORDET, Jules	1919
BURNET, Sir Frank Macfarlane	1960
CARREL, Alexis	1912
CLAUDE, Albert	1974
DE DUVE, Christian	1974

LAUREATE(S)	YEAR WON

6

DOMAGK, Gerhard	1939
ECCLES, Sir John Carew	1963
ENDERS, John Franklin	1954
FINSEN, Niels Ryberg	1903
FISHER, Edmund H.	1992
FLOREY, Lord Howard Walter	1945
GASSER, Herbert Spencer	1944
GILMAN, Alfred G.	1994
GRANIT, Ragnar	1967
HOLLEY, Robert W.	1968
HUXLEY, Sir Andrew Fielding	1963
KANDEL, Eric R.	2000
KOCHER, Emil Theodor	1909
KOSSEL, Albrecht	1910
LORENZ, Konrad	1973
MORGAN, Thomas Hunt	1933
MULLER, Hermann Joseph	1946
MULLER, Paul Hermann	1948
MURPHY, William Parry	1934
MURRAY, Joseph E.	1990
PALADE, George E.	1974
PAVLOV, Ivan Petrovich	1904
PORTER, Rodney R.	1972
RICHET, Charles Robert	1913
SPERRY, Roger W.	1981
THOMAS, E. Donnall	1990
VARMUS, Harold E.	1989
WATSON, James Dewey	1962
WELLER, Thomas Huckle	1954
WIESEL, Torsten N.	1981

7

AXELROD, Julius	1970
BANTING, Sir Frederick Grant	1923
BRENNER, Sydney	2002
CORMACK, Allan M.	1979

LAUREATE(S)	YEAR WON

7

DAUSSET, Jean	1980
DOHERTY, Peter C.	1996
EDELMAN, Gerald M.	1972
EHRLICH, Paul	1908
EIJKMAN, Christiaan	1929
FIBIGER, Johannes Andreas Grib	1926
FLEMING, Sir Alexander	1945
HERSHEY, Alfred D.	1969
HEYMANS, Corneille Jean Francois	1938
HODGKIN, Sir Alan Lloyd	1963
HOPKINS, Sir Frederick Gowland	1929
HORVITZ, H. Robert	2002
HOUSSAY, Bernardo Alberto	1947
HUGGINS, Charles Brenton	1966
IGNARRO, Louis J.	1998
KENDALL, Edward Calvin	1950
KHORANA, Har Gobind	1968
KOEHLER, Georges J. F.	1984
LAVERAN, Charles Louis Alphonse	1907
LIPMANN, Fritz Albert	1953
MACLEOD, John James Rickard	1923
MEDAWAR, Sir Peter Brian	1960
NATHANS, Daniel	1978
NICOLLE, Charles Jules Henri	1928
ROBBINS, Frederick Chapman	1954
ROBERTS, Richard J.	1993
RODBELL, Martin	1994
SAKMANN, Bert	1991
SCHALLY, Andrew V.	1977
SPEMANN, Hans	1935
SULSTON, Sir John E.	2002
THEILER, Max	1951
WAKSMAN, Selman Abraham	1952
WARBURG, Otto Heinrich	1931
WHIPPLE, George Hoyt	1934
WILKINS, Maurice Hugh Frederick	1962

LAUREATE(S)	YEAR WON

8

BLUMBERG, Baruch S.	1976
CARLSSON, Arvid	2000
COURNAND, Andre Frederic	1956
DELBRUCK, Max	1969
DULBECCO, Renato	1975
ERLANGER, Joseph	1944
GAJDUSEK, D. Carleton	1976
HARTLINE, Haldan Keffer	1967
HARTWELL, Leland H.	2001
KORNBERG, Arthur	1959
MEYERHOF, Otto Fritz	1922
MILSTEIN, Cesar	1984
PRUSINER, Stanley B.	1997
RICHARDS, Dickinson W.	1956
THEORELL, Axel Hugo Theodor	1955
TONEGAWA, Susumu	1987
VON EULER, Ulf	1970

9

BALTIMORE, DAVID	1975
EGAS MONIZ, Antonio (Caetano de Abreu Freire)	1949
EINTHOVEN, Willem	1924
FORSSMANN, Werner	1956
FURCHGOTT, Robert F.	1998
GOLDSTEIN, Joseph L.	1985
GREENGARD, Paul	2000
GUILLEMIN, Roger	1977
HITCHINGS, George H.	1988
LAUTERBUR, Paul C.	2003
LEDERBERG, Joshua	1958
MANSFIELD, Sir Peter	2003
MECHNIKOV, Ilya Ilich	1908
NIRENBERG, Marshall W.	1968
TINBERGEN, Nikolaas	1973
VON BEKESY, Georg	1961

LAUREATE(S)	YEAR WON

9

VON FRISCH, Karl	1973
WIESCHAUS, Eric F.	1995

10

BENACERRAF, Baruj	1980
BERGSTROEM, Sune K.	1982
GULLSTRAND, Allvar	1911
HOUNSFIELD, Sir Godfrey N.	1979
MCCLINTOCK, Barbara	1983
REICHSTEIN, Tadeusz	1950
SAMUELSSON, Bengt I.	1982
SUTHERLAND, Earl W. Jr	1971
VON BEHRING, Emil Adolf	1901

11

LANDSTEINER, Karl	1930
RAMON Y CAJAL, Santiago	1906
SHERRINGTON, Sir Charles Scott	1932
ZINKERNAGEL, Rolf M.	1996

13

WAGNER-JAUREGG, Julius	1927

14

LEVI-MONTALCINI, Rita	1986

16

NUESSLEIN-VOLHARD, Christiane	1995

OCEANS AND SEAS

3 IYO
RED

4 ARAL
AZOV
BALI
DEAD
JAVA
KARA
KORO
ROSS
SAVU
SETO
SULU

5 BANDA
BLACK
BOHOL
CERAM
CHINA
CORAL
CRETE
DAVIS
IRISH
JAPAN
NORTH
SUNDA
TIMOR
WHITE

6 AEGEAN
ARCTIC
BALTIC
BERING
CELTIC
FLORES
HARIMA
INDIAN
INLAND
IONIAN
LAPTEV
NANHAI
SAGAMI
SCOTIA
TASMAN
YELLOW

7 AMAKUSA
ANDAMAN
ARABIAN
ARAFURA
BARENTS
BEHRING
BOTHIAN
CAMOTES
CASPIAN
CELEBES
CHUKCHI
DONG HAI
GALILEE

7 MARMARA
MOLUCCA
OKHOTSK
PACIFIC
SIBUYAN
SOLOMAN
VISAYAN
WEDDELL

8 ADRIATIC
AMUNDSEN
ATLANTIC
BALEARIC
BEAUFORT
BISMARCK
CHUCKCHI
HUANG HAI
LABRADOR
LIGURIAN
MINDANAO
SARGASSO
THRACIAN
TIBERIAS

9 ANTARCTIC
BAFFIN BAY
CARIBBEAN
EAST CHINA
GREENLAND
HALMAHERA
HUDSON BAY
LACCADIVE
NORWEGIAN
ZUIDERZEE

10 PHILIPPINE
SETO-NAIKAI

SOUTH CHINA
TYRRHENIAN

11 BAY OF BENGAL
BAY OF BISCAY

12 BELLIGHAUSEN
EAST SIBERIAN
GULF OF ALASKA
GULF OF GUINEA
GULF OF MEXICO

13 GULF OF BOTHNIA
MEDITERRANEAN

14 ENGLISH CHANNEL

OPERAS

3 CID, Le

4 AIDA
LULU

5 FAUST
FEDRA
GREEK
JUIVE, La
ZAMPA

6 ALCINA
AMADIS
ARMIDA
ARMIDE
CONSUL, The
DAPHNE
GAWAIN
JENUFA
JOSEPH
KOANGA
LOUISE
OBERON
ORPHEE
RIENZI
SCIPIO

7 ALCESTE
ALMEIDA
ARIANNA, L'
BRONWEN

DALIBOR
ELEKTRA
FIDELIO
IRMELIN
IVANHOE
MACBETH
MAZEPPA
NEW YEAR
PHAETON
TABARRO, Il
TEMPEST, The
TROJANS, The
TROYENS, Les
WALKURE, Die

8 AKHNATEN
ANACREON
ARABELLA
ATALANTA
COMTE ORY, Le
EURIDICE, L'
FALSTAFF
FAVORITE, La
IDOMENEO
IOLANTHE
PURITANI, I
SERAGLIO, Il
SORCERER, The
TANCREDI
TRAVIATA, La
TURANDOT
VALKYRIE, The

8 WINFRITH

9 AGRIPPINA
ALCHYMIST, Der
BASSARIDS, The
BILLY BUDD
CERT A KACA
COX AND BOX
DON CARLOS
EURYANTHE
FEUERSNOT
GRAND DUKE, The
HUGUENOTS, Les
I PURITANI
KING PRIAM
LOHENGRIN
RE PASTORE, Il
RHEINGOLD, Das
RICCARDO I
RIGOLETTO
RING CYCLE
RUDDIGORE
SIEGFRIED
TAMERLANO
TROVATORE, Il

10 CINDERELLA
CORREGIDOR, Der
DON QUIXOTE
FAIRY QUEEN, The
FRA DIAVOLO
FREISCHUTZ, Der
GONDOLIERS, The
KING ARTHUR
KNOT GARDEN, The
L'AFRICAINE
LALLA-ROOKH

MAGIC FLUTE, The
MERRY MOUNT
OEDIPUS REX
SONNAMBULA, La
TANNHAUSER

11 BELLE HELENE, La
BELLEROPHON
CENERENTOLA, La
CURLEW RIVER
DAME BLANCHE, La
DOKTOR FAUST
DON GIOVANNI
DON PASQUALE
FRA GHERARDO
HMS PINAFORE
MAID OF PSKOV, The
NOYE'S FLUDDE
PERFECT FOOL, The
PETER GRIMES
SVANDA DUDAK
WILLIAM TELL
ZAUBERFLOTE, Die

12 BEGGAR'S OPERA, The
BORIS GODUNOV
DEBORA E JAELE
EUGENE ONEGIN
IMMORTAL HOUR, The
KAMENNYI GOST
LIEBESVERBOT, Das
MANON LESCAUT
MOSES IN EGYPT
MOSES UND ARON
NIXON IN CHINA
OWEN WINGRAVE
PEARLFISHERS, The

12 PORGY AND BESS
QUEEN OF SHEBA
SERVA PADRONA, La
SILVER TASSIE, The

13 ALBERT HERRING
AMORE DEI TRE RE, L'
BARTERED BRIDE, The
DEATH IN VENICE
DIDO AND AENEAS
GUILLAUME TELL
HUGH THE DROVER
KATYA KABANOVA
LIEBE DER DANAE, Die
MEISTERSINGER, Die
MOSES AND AARON
PETER IBBETSON
QUEEN OF SPADES,
The
ROSENKAVALIER, Der
SIR JOHN IN LOVE

14 BOATSWAIN'S MATE,
The
CLEMENZA DI TITO, La
DEVIN DU VILLAGE, Le
GIANNI SCHICCHI
GOLDEN COCKEREL,
The
LILY OF KILARNEY, The
MATHIS DER MALER
RIDERS TO THE SEA
ROBERT LE DIABLE
TURN OF THE SCREW,
The

15 ARIADNE AUF NAXOS

BALLO IN MASCHERA,
Un
BARBER OF SEVILLE,
The
CONTES
D'HOFFMANN, Les
HANSEL AND GRETEL
IVAN THE TERRIBLE
MADAMA BUTTERFLY
SICILIAN VESPERS, The
SIMON BOCCANEGRA
TALES OF
HOFFMANN, The
THREEPENNY OPERA,
The

16 BENVENUTO CELLINI
CADMUS ET
HERMIONE
DREIGROSCHENOPER,
Die
ECHO AND
NARCISSUS
FANCIULLA DEL WEST,
La
FINTA GIARDINIERA,
La
FRAU OHNE
SCHATTEN, Die
HISTOIRE DU SOLDAT
ITALIANA IN ALGERI, L'
PECHEURS DE PERLES,
Les
PILGRIM'S PROGRESS,
The
YEOMEN OF THE
GUARD, The

17 FENNIMORE AND
GERDA
HIPPOLYTE ET ARICIE
IPHIGENIE EN AULIDE
JOLIE FILLE DE PERTH,
La
MIDSUMMER
MARRIAGE, The
PIRATES OF
PENZANCE, The
RING DES
NIBELUNGEN, Der
VILLAGE
SOOTHSAYER, The

18 ALFONSO UND
ESTRELLA
ARIANE ET BARBE-
BLEUE
BARBIERE DI SIVIGLIA,
Il
FLIEGENDE
HOLLANDER, Der
IPHIGENIE EN
TAURIDE
MAMELLES DE
TIRESIAS, Les
PELLEAS ET
MELISANDE
PETIT CHAPERON
ROUGE, Le
TROILUS AND
CRESSIDA

19 CAVALLERIA
RUSTICANA

JONGLEUR DE NOTRE-
DAME, Le
LITTLE RED RIDING
HOOD
LOVE FOR THREE
ORANGES, The
MERRY WIVES OF
WINDSOR, The
SCHWANDA THE
BAGPIPER

20 GIULIO CESARE IN
EGITTO
MIDSUMMER NIGHT'S
DREAM, A

21 ENFANT ET LES
SORTILEGES, L'
FOUR SAINTS IN
THREE ACTS
INCORONAZIONE DI
POPPEA, L'
VILLAGE ROMEO AND
JULIET, A

23 LADY MACBETH OF
THE MTSENSK

POISONS

3 IVY
YEW

4 LEAD

6 BRYONY

7 ARSENIC
CYANIDE
HEMLOCK
HENBANE
MERCURY
PHORATE
URANIUM

8 ALDICARB
ATROPINE
DEATH CAP
FOXGLOVE
LABURNUM
METHOMYL
NICOTINE
PARAQUAT

9 BANEBERRY
BUCKTHORN
BUTTERCUP
COLUMBINE
FLY AGARIC
MISTLETOE
MONKSHOOD

POISON PIE
THIOMETON

10 BELLADONNA
CIGUATERRA
DICHLORVOS
DOMOIC ACID
ENDOSULFAN
NITRIC ACID
STRYCHNINE
TRIAZAPHOS
WEEVER FISH

11 MEPHOSFOLAN
SPINDLE TREE
SURGEON FISH

12 CHLOROPICRIN
FOOL'S PARSLEY
FORMALDEHYDE

13 AMANITA VIROSA
Destroying Angel
DEMETON-S-METHYL
FENTIN ACETATE
MEADOW SAFFRON
METHYL BROMIDE
RUSSULA MAIREI
SODIUM CYANIDE
SULPHURIC ACID
ZINC PHOSPHIDE

14 SODIUM FLUORIDE
TETRAODONTOXIN

15 ALPHACHLORALOSE
AMANITA MUSCARIA   Fly Agaric
CHLORFENVINPHOS
DESTROYING ANGEL
FENTIN HYDROXIDE

16 DEADLY NIGHTSHADE Belladonna
DISULFUTON OXAMYL
HYDROCHLORIC ACID

17 AMANITA PHALLOIDES Death Cap
CLITOCYBE DEALBATA Toadstool

18 ALUMINIUM PHOSPHIDE
AMMONIUM BIFLUORIDE
MAGNESIUM PHOSPHIDE

20 INOCYBE PATOUILLARDII Toadstool

POLITICAL LEADERS –
of the twentieth century

3
ITO, Prince
MAX, Prince of Baden

TITO, Marshal Josip
TODD, Garfield
TUTU, Bishop Desmond

4
AMIN, Idi
BENN, Tony
BLUM, Leon
BUSH, George
BUSH, George W.
COOK, Arthur
DIAZ, Porfirio
DYER, General
EDEN, Anthony
FAHD, King of Saudi
   Arabia
FOOT, Michael
FORD, Gerald
FUAD, King
GREY, Sir Edward
HESS, Rudolf
HOLT, Harold
KARL, Emperor
KENT, Bruce
KING, Martin Luther
KOHL, Helmut
KRIM, Abdel
MEIR, Golda
MORO, Aldo
NAGY, Imre
PU YI, Emperor
RHEE, Syngman
TAFT, William

5
AGNEW, Spiro
ASTOR, Nancy,
   Viscountess
BEGIN, Menachem
BERIA, Lavrenti
BEVAN, Aneurin
BEVIN, Ernest
BLAIR, Tony
BOTHA, General Louis
BOTHA, P. W.
BROWN, George
COHEN, Sir Andrew
DAOUD, Mohammed
DAYAN, Moshe
DESAI, Morarji
DOBBS, Sir Henry
EVREN, General Kenan
GOWON, General
   Yakubu
HEATH, Edward
HOARE, Sir Samuel
KIROV, Sergei
LAVAL, Pierre
LENIN, Vladimir
LUBBE, Marinus van der
LYNCH, Jack
MALAN, Daniel

5 NEHRU, Jawaharlal
NKOMO, Joshua
OBOTE, Milton
PALME, Olof
PERES, Shimon
PERON, Eva
PERON Isabel
PERON, Juan
PETER, King of Serbia
PUTIN, Vladimir
RYKOV, Aleksei
SADAT, Anwar
SALAN, General
SMITH, Ian
SMUTS, General Jan
TINIO, General
VILLA, Pancho

6 ADOULA, Cyrille
AITKEN, Max (Lord
   Beaverbrook)
AQUINO, Corazon
ARAFAT, Yasser
ATTLEE, Clement
BISHOP, Maurice
BHUTTO, Benazir
BHUTTO, Zulfikar Ali
BRANDT, Willi
BRESCI, Angelo
BUHARI, Muhammed
CARSON, Sir Edward
CARTER, Jimmy
CASTRO, Fidel
CHIRAC, Jacques
CUNHAL, Alvaro
CURZON, Lord
DARLAN, Admiral Jean

DOUMER, Paul
DULLES, John Foster
ERHARD, Ludwig
ESHKOL, Levi
FAISAL, King of Saudi
   Arabia
FRANCO, Francisco
GANDHI, Indira
GANDHI, Mohandas
   (Mahatma Gandhi)
GANDHI, Rajiv
GBENYE, Christophe
GIRAUD, General
   Henri
GRIVAS, Colonel
   George
HARDIE, James Keir
HEALEY, Denis
HITLER, Adolf
HOOVER, Herbert
HOOVER, John Edgar
   (J. Edgar Hoover)
JINNAH, Mohammed
   Ali
KARAMI, Rashid
KAUNDA, Kenneth
KHALED, King of Saudi
   Arabia
KRUGER, Paul
LEMASS, Sean
MALAN, D. F.
MANDEL, Georges
MARCOS, Ferdinand
MASHIN, Colonel
MENDEZ, Costa
MOBUTU, General
   Joseph-Desire

6

MOLLET, Guy
MOSLEY, Oswald
MOULIN, Jean
MUGABE, Robert
NASSER, Colonel
    Gamal
NIXON, Richard
OJUKWE, Colonel
    Odumegwu
O'KELLY, Sean
O'NEILL, Terence
OUEDDI, Goukoni
PINEAU, Christian
POL POT
POWELL, Enoch
RAHMAN, Shaikh
    Mujibur
REAGAN, Ronald
RHODES, Cecil
RIVERA, Primo de
ROMERO, Archbishop
    Arnulfo
SHAMIR, Yitzhak
SOARES, Mario
SOMOZA, Anastasia
STALIN, Josif (or Josef or
    Yosip)
STOPES, Marie
SUSLOV, Mikhail
THOMAS, James
TSU-HSI, Empress
U THANT
WALESA, Lech
WARREN, Earl
WILSON, Harold
WILSON, Woodrow
YAGODA, Gehrikh

YAMANI, Sheikh
ZAMORA, Niceto
ZEDONG, Mao

7

ASQUITH, Herbert
BALDWIN, Stanley
BALFOUR, Arthur
BARZANI, Mustafa
BATISTA, General
    Fulgencio
BAVADRA, Timoci
BOKASSA, Jean-Bedel
BOYD ORR, John
CLINTON, Bill
COLLINS, Michael
DOENITZ, Karl
GADDAFI, Colonel
    Muammar
GAMELIN, General
GEMAYAL, Amin
GIZIKIS, Phaeton
GUEVARA, Ernesto
    'Che'
HALIFAX, Lord
HARDING, Warren
HAUGHEY, Charles
HIMMLER, Heinrich
HUSSEIN, King of
    Jordan
JENKINS, Roy
JOHNSON, Lyndon
JOUHAUD, General B.
KAROLYI, Count
    Michael
KENNEDY, Edward
KENNEDY, John F.
KENNEDY, Robert
KOSYGIN, Alexei

7

LEOPOLD, King of
Belgium
LIN PIAO
LUMUMBA, Patrice
LUTHULI, Albert
MANDELA, Nelson
MASARYK, Tomas
MENZIES, Robert
MICHAEL, Grand Duke
MISCHNES, Colonel
MOLOTOV, Vyacheslav
MUBARAK, Hosni
NKRUMAH, Kwame
PAISLEY, Ian
PRINCIP, Gavrilo
RAZMARA, General Ali
RUDDOCK, Joan
RUSSELL, Bertrand
(Lord Russell)
SALAZAR, Antonio
SHASTRI, Lal
SPINOLA, Antonio
SUKARNO, Ahmad
TOLSTOY, Count Leo
TROTSKY, Leon
TRUDEAU, Pierre
TSHOMBE, Moise
URRUTIA, Manuel
WALLACE, George
WHITLAM, Gough
WOJTYLA, Karol (Pope
John Paul II)
YELTSIN, Boris

8

ABDULLAH, King of
Jordan
ADENAUER, Konrad

ALFONSIN, Raul
ANDROPOV, Yuri
BADOGLIO, Marshal
BAUDOUIN, King of
the Belgians
BEN BELLA, Ahmed
BERNHARD, Prince of
The Netherlands
BONAR LAW, Andrew
BREZHNEV, Leonid
BUKHARIN, Nikolai
BULGANIN, Marshal
Nikolai
CLERIDES, Grafkos
CONNOLLY, James
COOLIDGE, Calvin
COSGRAVE, W. T.
DALADIER, Edouard
DE GAULLE, General
Charles
DENKTASH, Rauf
DE VALERA, Eamon
DINIZULU, Chief
DOLLFUSS, Engelbert
DUVALIER, Francois
DUVALIER, Jean-Claude
FAULKNER, Brian
GALTIERI, Leopoldo
GONZALEZ, Felipe
GRIFFITH, Arthur
HEYDRICH, Reinhard
HIROHITO, Emperor
KASAVUBU, Joseph
KENYATTA, Jomo
KERENSKY, Alexander
KHOMEINI, Ayatollah
Ruhollah

8

MAKARIOS, Archbishop
MALENKOV, Georgi
MARSHALL, George
MORRISON, Herbert
MUZOREWA, Bishop
  Abel
NICHOLAS, Tsar
PODGORNY, Nikolai
POINCARE, Raymond
POMPIDOU, Georges
QUISLING, Vidkun
RAWLINGS, Jerry
SATYA PAL
SHINWELL, Emmanuel
SIKORSKI, General
  Wladislaw
STOLYPIN, Peter
THATCHER, Margaret
VERWOERD, Hendrik
WALDHEIM, Kurt
WEIZMANN, Chaim
WELENSKY, Sir Roy
ZINOVIEV, Grigoriy

9

ALEXANDER, King of
  Yugoslavia
BEN-GURION, David
CHERNENKO,
  Constantin
CHOU EN-LAI
CHURCHILL, Winston
DALAI LAMA
GOERDELER, Karl
GOLDWATER, Barry
GORBACHEV, Mikhail
HENDERSON, Arthur
HO CHI MINH

JIANG QING
KIM IL-SUNG
KISSINGER, Henry
KITCHENER, Lord
MACDONALD, Ramsay
MACMILLAN, Harold
MACSWINEY, Terence
MATTEOTTI, Giacomo
MOSSADEGH,
  Mohammed
MUSSOLINI, Benito
NOEL-BAKER, Philip
PANKHURST, Emmeline
ROOSEVELT, Franklin
  Delano
ROOSEVELT, Theodore
ROSENBERG, Alfred
SAINT JEAN, Alfredo
SALISBURY, Lord
STEVENSON, Adlai
STREICHER, Julius
SUN YAT-SEN
TALAAT BEY
VENIZELOS, Eleutherios
VISHINSKY, Andrei
WHITEHEAD, Edgar
YIN JU-KANG

10

BEN KHEDDAH,
  Benyoussef
BERLINGUER, Enrico
CARRINGTON, Lord
CLEMENCEAU, Georges
FITZGERALD, Dr
  Garrett
FRANZ JOSEF, Emperor

10 HINDENBURG, Field-
Marshal Paul von
HUA KUO-FENG
JUAN CARLOS, King of
Spain
KEMAL PASHA
KHRUSHCHEV, Nikita
LENNOX-BOYD, Alan
LIU SHAO-TSI
LUXEMBOURG, Rosa
MINDSZENTY, Cardinal
Josef
PAPANDREOU,
Georgios
RIBBENTROP, Joachim
von
RICHTHOFEN, Baron
von
WILHELMINA, Queen
of Netherlands

11 ALI REZA KHAN (Shah
of Persia)
BEAVERBROOK, Lord
CHAMBERLAIN, Joseph
CHAMBERLAIN,
Neville
CONSTANTINE, King of
Greece
DOUGLAS-HOME, Sir
Alec
LLOYD-GEORGE,
David
MIHAILOVICH, Draja
MOUNTBATTEN, Lord
Louis
NGO DINH DIEM

PRAJADHIPOK, King of
Siam
SHARIF-EMANI, Jaffer
YUAN SHIH-KAI

12 HAMMARSKJOLD, Dag
MENDES-FRANCE,
Pierre
PAPADOPOULOS,
Colonel Georges

13 CHIANG KAI-SHEK
KAISER WILHELM
SADDAM HUSSEIN

14 SOUVANNA
PHOUMA, Prince
VICTOR EMMANUEL,
King

15 CHICHESTER-CLARK,
James

17 BROCKDORFF-
RANTZAU, Count
Ulrich von
CAMPBELL-
BANNERMAN,
Andrew

POPES

3 LEO

4 JOHN
PAUL
PIUS

5 CAIUS
CONON
DONUS
FELIX
LINUS
PETER
SOTER
URBAN

6 ADRIAN
AGATHO
ALBERT
CLETUS
EUGENE
FABIAN
HILARY
JULIUS
LANDUS
LUCIUS
MARCUS
MARTIN
PHILIP
SIXTUS
VICTOR

7 ANTERUS
CLEMENT
DAMASUS
GREGORY
HYGINUS
MARINUS
PASCHAL
PONTIAN
ROMANUS
SERGIUS
STEPHEN
URSINUS
ZACHARY
ZOSIMUS

8 AGAPETUS
ANICETUS
BENEDICT
BONIFACE
EULALIUS
EUSEBIUS
FORMOSUS
GELASIUS
HONORIUS
INNOCENT
JOHN PAUL
LAWRENCE
LIBERIUS
NICHOLAS
NOVATIAN
PELAGIUS

8 SABINIAN
SIRICIUS
THEODORE
VIGILIUS
VITALIAN

9 ADEODATUS
ALEXANDER
ANACLETUS
CALLISTUS
CELESTINE
CORNELIUS
DEUSDEDIT
DIONYSIUS
DIOSCORUS
EUTYCHIAN
EVARISTUS
HORMISDAS
MARCELLUS
SEVERINUS
SILVERIUS
SISINNIUS
SYLVESTER
SYMMACHUS
THEODORIC
VALENTINE

10 ANASTASIUS
HIPPOLYTUS
MELCHIADES
SIMPLICIUS
ZEPHYRINUS

11 CHRISTOPHER
CONSTANTINE
ELEUTHERIUS
MARCELLINUS
TELESPHORUS

13 JOHN THE MARTYR

15 MARTIN THE MARTYR

PORTS
Worldwide

PORT	COUNTRY
3	
BAR	Montenegro
ILO	Peru
4	
ACRE	Israel
ADEN	Yemen
AKKO	Israel
AMOY	China
BAKU	Azerbaijan
BARI	Italy
CEBU	Philippines
COBH	Ireland
CORK	Ireland
ELAT	Israel
ERIE	USA
HULL	England
KIEL	Germany
KOBE	Japan
ORAN	Algeria
OSLO	Norway
PARA	Brazil
RIGA	Latvia
SAFI	Morocco
SUEZ	Egypt
TAIN	Scotland
TEMA	Ghana
WICK	Scotland

PORT	COUNTRY
5	
AKYAB	Myanmar (Burma)
BASRA	Iraq
BEIRA	Mozambique
BELEM	Brazil
BREST	France
CANEA	Greece
CEUTA	Morocco
COLON	Panama
CORFU	Greece
DAKAR	Senegal
DELFT	Netherlands
DOVER	England
EILAT	Israel
EMDEN	Germany
GAETA	Italy
GALLE	Sri Lanka
GENOA	Italy
HAIFA	Israel
IZMIR	Turkey
KOCHI	Japan
KOTOR	Montenegro
LAGOS	Nigeria
LEITH	Scotland
LULEA	Sweden
MALMO	Sweden
MOCHA	Yemen
OSAKA	Japan
OSTIA	Italy
PALMA	Spain
PALOS	Spain
PUSAN	S. Korea
RABAT	Morocco
RYEKA	Croatia
SCAPA	Scotland

PORT	COUNTRY

5

TRANI	Italy
VARNA	Bulgaria
WISBY	Sweden
YSTAD	Sweden

6

ABADAN	Iran
AGADIR	Morocco
AHMEDI	Yemen
ANCONA	Italy
ASHDOD	Israel
BALBOA	Panama
BASTIA	Corsica
BEIRUT	Lebanon
BERGEN	Norway
BILBAO	Spain
BOMBAY	India
BREMEN	Germany
CALAIS	France
CALLAO	Peru
CANNES	France
CHALNA	Pakistan
CHEFOO	China
COCHIN	India
DANZIG	Poland
DIEPPE	France
DOUALA	Cameroon
DUNBAR	Scotland
DUNDEE	Scotland
DURBAN	S. Africa
FERROL	Spain
GDANSK	Poland
GDYNIA	Poland
HALDIA	India

PORT	COUNTRY

6

HANKOW	China
HAVANA	Cuba
JEDDAH	Saudi Arabia
KALMAR	Sweden
KANDLA	India
LARVIK	Norway
LISBON	Portugal
LOBITO	Angola
LONDON	England
LUANDA	Angola
MADRAS	India
MALAGA	Spain
MANILA	Philippines
MAPUTO	Mozambique
MATADI	Zaire
MTWARA	Tanzania
NAPLES	Italy
NARVIK	Norway
NELSON	New Zealand
ODENSE	Denmark
ODESSA	Ukraine
OPORTO	Portugal
OSTEND	Belgium
PADANG	Indonesia
PATRAS	Greece
PENANG	Malaysia
RECIFE	Brazil
RHODES	Greece
SANTOS	Brazil
SKIKDA	Algeria
SMYRNA	Turkey
SUAKIN	Sudan
SWATOW	China

PORT	COUNTRY

6

PORT	COUNTRY
SYDNEY	Australia
TAINAN	Taiwan
TETUAN	Morocco
TOULON	France
TROMSO	Norway
VENICE	Italy
WEIHAI	China
WISMAR	Germany

7

PORT	COUNTRY
AALBORG	Denmark
ABIDJAN	Ivory Coast
AJACCIO	Corsica
ALGIERS	Algeria
ANTWERP	Belgium
BELFAST	N. Ireland
BUSHIRE	Iran
CARDIFF	Wales
CHATHAM	England
COLOMBO	Sri Lanka
CORUNNA	Spain
COTONOU	Benin
DAMPIER	Australia
DETROIT	USA
DONEGAL	Ireland
DUNDALK	Ireland
DUNKIRK	France
FOOCHOW	China
FUNCHAL	Spain
GEELONG	Australia
GRIMSBY	England
GUAYMAS	Mexico
HALIFAX	Canada
HAMBURG	Germany

PORT	COUNTRY

7

PORT	COUNTRY
HARWICH	England
HORSENS	Denmark
HOUSTON	USA
JAKARTA	Indonesia
KARACHI	Pakistan
KEELUNG	Taiwan
KITIMAT	Canada
LA PLATA	Argentina
LARNACA	Cyprus
LEGHORN	Italy
LE HAVRE	France
MARSALA	Italy
MELILLA	Morocco
MESSINA	Italy
MOGADOR	Morocco
MOMBASA	Kenya
NEW YORK	USA
NORFOLK	USA
PALERMO	Italy
PIRAEUS	Greece
ROSTOCK	Germany
SALERNO	Italy
SAN JUAN	Puerto Rico
SEATTLE	USA
STETTIN	Poland
SWANSEA	Wales
TALLINN	Estonia
TANGIER	Morocco
TILBURY	England
TOBARAO	Brazil
TRAPANI	Italy
TRIESTE	Italy
TRIPOLI	Libya
YING KOW	China

PORT	COUNTRY

7

YOUGHAL	Ireland

8

ADELAIDE	Australia
ALICANTE	Spain
ARRECIFE	Spain
AUCKLAND	New Zealand
BENGHAZI	Libya
BORDEAUX	France
BOULOGNE	France
BRINDISI	Italy
BRISBANE	Australia
BUDAPEST	Hungary
CALCUTTA	India
CAPE TOWN	S Africa
COCANADA	India
COQUIMBO	Chile
DAMIETTA	Egypt
DUNLEARY	Ireland
ELSINORE	Denmark
FALMOUTH	England
FLUSHING	Netherlands
FREETOWN	Sierra Leone
GISBORNE	New Zealand
GOTEBORG	Sweden
GREENOCK	Scotland
HAKODATE	Japan
HALMSTAD	Sweden
HELSINKI	Finland
HOLYHEAD	Wales
HONFLEUR	France
HONOLULU	Hawaii
ISTANBUL	Turkey
KAKINADA	India
KINGSTON	Jamaica

PORT	COUNTRY

8

PORT	COUNTRY
LA CORUNA	Spain
LA GUIARA	Venezuela
LLANELLI	Wales
LIMASSOL	Cyprus
MACASSAR	Indonesia
MAKASSAR	Indonesia
MATARINI	Peru
MONTREAL	Canada
NAGASAKI	Japan
NAVARINO	Greece
NEW HAVEN	USA
NEWHAVEN	England
NYKOPING	Sweden
PARADEEP	Indonesia
PEMBROKE	Wales
PENZANCE	England
PLYMOUTH	England
PORT SAID	Egypt
SHANGHAI	China
SZCZECIN	Poland
TAMATAVE	Madagascar
TIENTSIN	China
VERU CRUZ	Mexico
WEYMOUTH	England
YOKOHAMA	Japan

9

PORT	COUNTRY
ALGECIRAS	Spain
AMSTERDAM	Netherlands
ARCHANGEL	Russia
ARDROSSAN	Scotland
AVONMOUTH	England
BALTIMORE	USA
BARCELONA	Spain
CARTAGENA	Columbia

PORT	COUNTRY

9

PORT	COUNTRY
CARTAGENA	Spain
CHERBOURG	France
CHURCHILL	Canada
CRISTOBAL	Panama
DEVONPORT	England
DUBROVNIK	Croatia
ESQUIMALT	Canada
ESSAOUIRA	Morocco
EUROPOORT	Netherlands
GALVESTON	USA
GRAVESEND	England
GUAYAQUIL	Ecuador
HELSINGOR	Denmark
HIROSHIMA	Japan
KAGOSHIMA	Japan
KAOHSIUNG	Taiwan
KOLOBRZEG	Poland
LAS PALMAS	Spain
LENINGRAD	Russia
LIVERPOOL	England
LYTTELTON	New Zealand
MARSEILLE	France
MBUJI-MAYI	Zaire
MELBOURNE	Australia
MOSSEL BAY	S. Africa
NANTUCKET	USA
NEWCASTLE	Australia
NEWCASTLE	England
OWEN SOUND	Canada
PENSACOLA	USA
PORT ARZEW	Algeria
PORT KLANG	Malaysia
PORT LOUIS	Mauritius
PORTMADOC	Wales

PORT	COUNTRY

9

PORT NATAL	S. Africa
PORT ROYAL	Jamaica
PORT SUDAN	Sudan
PORTO NOVO	Benin
ROTTERDAM	Netherlands
SCAPA FLOW	Scotland
STAVANGER	Norway
STOCKHOLM	Sweden
STORNAWAY	Scotland
TRONDHEIM	Norway
VANCOUVER	Canada
ZEEBRUGGE	Belgium

10

BRIDGEPORT	USA
CASABLANCA	Morocco
CHARLESTON	USA
CHRISTIANA	Norway
CONSTANTSA	Romania
EAST LONDON	S. Africa
FELIXSTOWE	England
FOLKESTONE	England
FREEMANTLE	Australia
GEORGE TOWN	Malaysia
GOTHENBURG	Sweden
HAMMERFEST	Norway
HARTLEPOOL	England
HERMOPOLIS	Greece
JERSEY CITY	USA
LA ROCHELLE	France
LOS ANGELES	USA
MARSEILLES	France
MONTEGO BAY	Jamaica
MONTEVIDEO	Uruguay

PORT	COUNTRY

10

NEW BEDFORD	USA
NEW ORLEANS	USA
PERNAMBUCO	Brazil
PERTH AMBOY	USA
PORTSMOUTH	England
PORTSMOUTH	USA
ROCK HARBOR	USA
SAN JUAN BAY	Peru
SIMONSTOWN	S. Africa
SUNDERLAND	England
TRAVEMUNDE	Germany
VALPARAISO	Chile
VLISSINGEN	Netherlands

11

BREMERHAVEN	Germany
BUENOS AIRES	Argentina
DAR ES SALAAM	Tanzania
GRANGEMOUTH	Scotland
HELSINGBORG	Sweden
HERMOUPOLIS	Greece
MASULIPATAM	India
PEARL HARBOR	Hawaii
PORT GLASGOW	Scotland
PORT JACKSON	Australia
PORT MORESBY	Papua New Guinea
PORT-OF-SPAIN	Trinidad and Tobago
RICHARD'S BAY	S. Africa
SAINT HELIER	Jersey
SHIMONOSEKI	Japan
SOUTHAMPTON	England
ST PETER PORT	Guernsey
THREE RIVERS	Canada
VLADIVOSTOK	Russia

PORT	COUNTRY

12

BARRANQUILLA	Columbia
BUENAVENTURA	Columbia
DUN LAOGHAIRE	Ireland
KOTAKINABALU	Malaysia
MILFORD HAVEN	Wales
MINA AL- AHMADI	Kuwait
NORTH SHIELDS	England
PORT ADELAIDE	Australia
PORT HARCOURT	Nigeria
PORT SUNLIGHT	England
PUERTO HIERRO	Venezuela
RIO DE JANEIRO	Brazil
SAN FRANCISCO	USA

13

CHRISTIANSUND	Norway
FREDERIKSHAVN	Denmark
MIDDLESBROUGH	England
PETROPAVLOVSK	Russia
PORT ELIZABETH	S. Africa
PUERTO CABELLO	Venezuela
WILHELMSHAVEN	Germany

14

CONSTANTINOPLE	Turkey
SANTIAGO DE CUBA	Cuba

PRIME MINISTERS of BRITAIN

4
BUTE, Earl of (or Lord Bute)
CECIL, Robert Gascoyne (Marquess of Salisbury)
EDEN, Anthony
GREY, Earl
PEEL, Robert
PITT, William

CANNING, George
CHATHAM, Earl of
FITZROY, Augustus (Duke of Grafton)
GRAFTON, Duke of
RUSSELL, Earl
RUSSELL, Lord John
STANLEY, Edward (Earl of Derby)
WALPOLE, Sir Robert

5
BLAIR, Tony
DERBY, Earl of
HEATH, Edward
MAJOR, John
NORTH, Lord
PETTY, William (Earl of Shelburne)

8
ABERDEEN, Earl of
BONAR LAW, Andrew
DISRAELI, Benjamin
GODERICH, Viscount
PERCEVAL, Spencer
PORTLAND, Duke of
ROSEBERY, Earl of
THATCHER, Margaret (Baroness Thatcher)

6
ATTLEE, Clement
GORDON, George (Earl of Aberdeen)
PELHAM, Henry
STUART, John (Earl of Bute)
TEMPLE, Henry (Lord Palmerston)
WILSON, Harold

9
ADDINGTON, Henry (Viscount Sidmouth)
CALLAGHAN, James
CAVENDISH, William (Duke of Portland)
CHURCHILL, Winston Spencer
GLADSTONE, William Ewart
GRENVILLE, George

7
ASQUITH, Herbert
BALDWIN, Stanley
BALFOUR, Arthur

412

9 GRENVILLE, William (Baron Grenville)
LIVERPOOL, Earl of
MACDONALD, (James) Ramsay
MACMILLAN, Harold (Earl of Stockton)
MELBOURNE, Viscount
NEWCASTLE, Duke of
SALISBURY, Marquess of
SHELBURNE, Earl of
WENTWORTH, Charles (Earl of Rockingham)

10 DEVONSHIRE, Duke of
PALMERSTON, Viscount
ROCKINGHAM, Earl of
WELLINGTON, Duke of
WILMINGTON, Earl of

11 CHAMBERLAIN, Neville
DOUGLAS-HOME, Sir Alec (Lord Hume)
LLOYD GEORGE, David

17 CAMPBELL-BANNERMAN, Henry

RACE COURSES
UK

3 AYR

4 BATH
YORK

5 ASCOT
EPSOM
RIPON

6 EXETER
HEXHAM
LUDLOW
REDCAR
THIRSK

7 AINTREE
CARTMEL
CHESTER
NEWBURY
TAUNTON
WARWICK
WINDSOR

8 BEVERLEY
BRIGHTON
CARLISLE
CHEPSTOW
FAKENHAM
GOODWOOD
HEREFORD
PLUMPTON
YARMOUTH

9 CATTERICK
DONCASTER
LEICESTER
NEWCASTLE
NEWMARKET
SALISBURY
SOUTHWELL
TOWCESTER
UTTOXETER
WINCANTON
WORCESTER

10 CHELTENHAM
FOLKESTONE
HUNTINGDON
NOTTINGHAM
PONTEFRACT
SEDGEFIELD

11 BANGOR-ON-DEE
HAYDOCK PARK
KEMPTON PARK
MARKET RASEN
NEWTON ABBOT
SANDOWN PARK

12 FONTWELL PARK

13 LINGFIELD PARK
WOLVERHAMPTON

15 STRATFORD-ON-AVON

414

REPTILES & AMPHIBIANS

3
ASP
BOA
OLM

4
FROG
TOAD

5
ADDER
AGAMA
ANOLE
COBRA
GECKO
KRAIT
MAMBA
RACER
SIREN
SKINK
TOKAY
VIPER

6
CAIMAN/ CAYMAN
ELAPID
GAVIAL
IGUANA
LIZARD
MOLOCH
MUGGER
PYTHON
TAIPAN
ZALTYS

7
AXOLOTL
GHARAIL
REPTILE
TADPOLE
TUATARA

8
ANACONDA
BASILISK
BULLFROG
COLUBRID
MATAMATA
MOCCASIN
MUD PUPPY
PIT VIPER
RAT SNAKE
RINGHALS
SLOW WORM
TERRAPIN
TORTOISE
TREE FROG

9
ALLIGATOR
BLINDWORM
BOOMSLANG
BOX TURTLE
CAECILIAN
CHAMELEON
COACHWHIP
CROCODILE
HAIRY FROG
MUD TURTLE

9
PUFF ADDER
SEA TURTLE
TREE SNAKE
VINE SNAKE
WART SNAKE

10
BLACK SNAKE
BUSHMASTER
CHUCKWALLA
CLAWED FROG
COPPERHEAD
CORAL SNAKE
FER-DE-LANCE
GLASS SNAKE
GREEN SNAKE
HELLBENDER
HORNED TOAD
MUSK TURTLE
NATTERJACK
RACERUNNER
SALAMANDER
SAND LIZARD
SIDEWINDER
SMOOTH NEWT
WATER SNAKE
WOOD TURTLE
WORM LIZARD

11
AMPHISBAENA
CONSTRICTOR
COTTONMOUTH
DIAMONDBACK
FLYING SNAKE
GABOON VIPER
GARTER SNAKE
GILA MONSTER
GOLIATH FROG
GREEN TURTLE

HORNED VIPER
INDIGO SNAKE
LEOPARD FROG
MIDWIFE TOAD
PALMATE NEWT
RATTLESNAKE
SMOOTH SNAKE
SURINAM TOAD

12
COMMON LIZARD
FLYING LIZARD
HORNED LIZARD
KOMODO DRAGON

13
BEARDED LIZARD
FRILLED LIZARD
GIANT TORTOISE
MANGROVE SNAKE
MONITOR LIZARD
PAINTED TURTLE
RUSSELL'S VIPER
SPADEFOOT TOAD
WATER MOCCASIN

14
EGG-EATING SNAKE
FIRE SALAMANDER
NATTERJACK TOAD
SNAPPING TURTLE

15
ARROW-POISON FROG
BLANDING'S TURTLE
FIRE-BELLIED TOAD
HAWKSBILL TURTLE
SHIELDTAIL SNAKE

17
LEATHERBACK TURTLE

RIVERS
Africa, Asia, Australasia, Europe, N. America and S. America

Africa

3
OMO

4
BOMU
DRAA
JUBA
KANA
KLIP
KOTO
LOFA
MILO
MONO
NAHR
NILE
SAVE
TANA
TANO
VAAL

5
ABBAI
BENUE
CHARI
DONGA
KASAI
KEBBI
KOMOE
LUNGA
LURIO
NIGER
SHIRE

SOUSS
VOLTA
WEBBE

6
BAFING
CUANZA
CUNENE
DINDER
GAMBIA
GURAVA
KAGERA
KAMEUR
KUNENE
LOGONE
LOMAMI
LOMELA
MAOULE
MAPUTO
MARIGA
MODDER
NGADDA
ORANGE
SHASHI
ST JOHN
UBANGI

7
BANDAMA
CALEDON
CORUBAL
CUBANGO
GONGOLA

7 KABOMPO
KATSINA
LUALABA
LUILAKA
OUERRHA
SANKURU
SENEGAL
SHIBELI
TSHUAPA
ZAMBEZI

8 BLUE NILE
GREAT KEI
NUANETSI
OKAVANGO

9 GREAT FISH
OUBANGOUI
OUM-ER-RBIA
SASSANDRA
WHITE NILE

10 ALBERT NILE
BLACK VOLTA
KOMADOUGOU
WHITE VOLTA

11 BAHR EL AZRAQ
BAHR EL JEBEL

Asia

2 OB

3 CHU
ILI
KET

PUR
SEV
TAZ
TYM
UDA
USA

4 ADUR
AMGA
AMUR
ARAS
EMBA
KAMA
LENA
MAYA
MOMA
TARA
TULA
TURA
ULYA
VAKH
VIVI
YANA
ZEYA

5 ALDAN
AMGUN
ANYNY
BHIMA
CHONA
CHUNA
DICLE
FIRAT
GANGA
GONAM
INDUS
IRKUT

5
ISHIM
JUMNA
KALAR
KAZYM
KHETA
KOTUY
LOZVA
MURAT
NOIRE
ORHON
SOSVA
SUGOY
TAPTI
TARIM
TAVDA
TOBOL
TYUNG
UCHUR
VITIM

6
ANADYR
ANGARA
BUREYA
GANGES
INGODA
IRTYSH
KELKIT
KOLYMA
LIAO HE
LINDYA
MARKHA
MEKONG
MURGAB
OLEKMA
OLENEK
OMOLON
SARYSU

SHILKA
SUTLEJ
TIGRIS
VILYUY
YAMANU
YUDOMA

7
BIRYUSA
CHAMBAL
DUDYPTA
HARIRUD
HELMAND
HUANG HE
JIANG HE
KERULEN
KRISHNA
KUREYKA
MEANDER
MORKOKA
MOYYERO
NARMADA
NU JIANG
SALWEEN
SELENGE
SUNGARI
TAYMURA
YENISEI
YORKAUT

8
AMUDARYA
FARAH RUD
GHAGHARA
GODAVARI
HONGSHUI
KORKODON
MAHANADI
QARQAN HE

8 SYR DARYA
TUNGUSKA
VASYUGAN

9 EUPHRATES
INDIGIRKA
IRRAWADDY
NIZHNYAYA
SCAMANDER
SELEMDZHA

10 CHANG JIANG
KIZIL IRMAK

11 BRAHMAPUTRA
JINSHA JIANG
ULUNGUR YUAN
YALONG JIANG
YELLOW RIVER

12 LANCANG JIANG
YANGTZE KIANG

Australasia

3 ORD

4 AVON
DALY
GREY
HILL
LORT
MEDA
SHAW
SWAN

5 ETHEL
FINKE
IRWIN
LYONS
MOORE
ROPER
TURON
YANKO
YARRA
YOUNG

6 BARCOO
BARWON
CULGOA
DAWSON
DURACK
KALGAN
MURRAY
WAIRAU

7 BALONNE
COONGAN
DARLING
FITZROY
GARDNER
GILBERT
LACHLAN
LENNARD
OAKOVER
SALMOND
SANFORD
THOMSON
TORRENS
WAITAKI
WARREGO

8 BRISBANE
BURDEKIN
CLARENCE
DRYSDALE
DUMARESQ
FLINDERS
GAIRDNER
GASCOYNE
GEORGINA
GOULBURN
JURGURVA
MITCHELL
OLDFIELD
PALLINUP
VICTORIA
WILLIAMS
WOORAMEL

9 ALLIGATOR
ASHBURTON
BLACKWOOD
CHRISTMAS
CLONCURRY
FORTESCUE
FRANKLAND
GREENOUGH
MACQUARIE
MURCHISON
NICHOLSON
WARBURTON

10 BLACKWATER
CUNNINGHAM
DIAMANTINA
KING EDWARD
SERPENTINE
STURT CREEK

WEST BAINES

11 CHAMBERLAIN
FITZMAURICE
KALLAKOOPAH

12 MURRUMBIDGEE

Europe

2 PO

3 AAR
BUG
DAL
DEE
DON
EMS
FAX
INN
KEM
LOT
MUR
OKA
TAY
UME
URE
VAH
VAR

4 ADUR
AIRE
ALTA
ARNO
ARUN
AVON
BANN

4

EARN	**5**	BYSKE
EBRO		CLYDE
EDEN		DNEPR
ELBE		DONAU
GUNZ		DOURO
KAMA		DVINA
KEMI		FORTH
KLAR		FROME
LAHN		ILLER
LECH		INDAL
LULE		JUCAR
MAAS		LOIRE
MAIN		LOVAT
MINO		MARNE
NENE		MEUSE
NIDD		MEZEN
ODER		NEMAR
ODRA		ONEGA
OISE		OYKEL
RISS		PONOY
RUHR		RANCE
SAVA		REUSS
SIEG		RHINE
SPEY		RHONE
SUCK		SAONE
SVIR		SEINE
TAFF		SPREE
TANA		SWALE
TARN		TAGUS
TEES		TAMAR
TEJO		TEIFI
TYNE		TIBER
URAL		TISZA
WEAR		TRENT
WURM		TWEED
ADIGE		VOLGA
BOYNE		WARTA

5
WESER
WISLA (Vistula)

6
ALFIOS
ALLIER
BARROW
CALDER
CHIARI
DANUBE
DNESTR
KENNET
KHOPER
LIFFEY
MANYCH
MARICA
MEDWAY
MERSEY
MINDEL
NECKAR
PINEGA
PINIOS
RIBBLE
ROTHER
SLANEY
TANARO
TICINO
VIJOSE
VYATKA
WHARFE
WITHAM

7
BRADANO
DERWENT
DURANCE
EUROTAS
GARONNE
LJUSNAN

MARITSA
PAMISOS
PECHORA
SHANNON
VISTULA
VOLKHOV
WAVENEY
WELLAND
YSTWYTH

8
AKHELOOS
ANGERMAN
CUCKMERE
FINDHORN
GUADIANA
KALAJOKI
OULUJOKI
PYHAJOKI
SIMOJOKI
VYCHEGDA

9
GREAT OUSE
PERHOJOKI
SKELLEFTE

11
YEROPOTAMOS

12
GUADALQUIVIR

North America & Canada

3
FOX
PIC
RED

4
ANNA
BACK

4

CREE	POLAR
FAWN	RAINY
FORD	REESE
LEAF	RESNO
LOON	SLAVE
MILK	SMITH
OHIO	STEEL
PEAR	TROUT
PEEL	WAGER
SEAL	WHITE
SWAN	WOODY
TOMS	YAZOO
WOLF	YUKON

5

BELLY
CAINS
CLYDE
CREEK
CROIX
EKWAN
ELBOW
GRASS
GREEN
HAYES
HORSE
HOUSE
JAMES
KAKWA
LIARD
MIAMI
NIPIN
NOIRE
OGOKI
OTTER
PEACE
PECOS
PELLY

6

ALBANY
ANTLER
ARNAUD
BATTLE
BERENS
BRAZOS
CANAAN
CARROL
CAYUTA
CLINCH
DILLON
FINLAY
FRASER
FREMAN
GANDER
GEORGE
HUDSON
HUMBER
INKLIN
INNOKA
KANSAS
LAURIE
MAGPIE

6

MOREAU	NIPIGON
NECHES	NORDEGG
NOATAK	NOWITNA
OTTAWA	OLOMANE
PAGATA	PASSAIC
PIGEON	PEMBINA
PLATTE	POTOMAC
POWDER	RED DEER
RUPERT	RONDOUT
SABINE	SALINAS
SALMON	SPOHANE
SEVERN	STEWART
SHEKAK	STIKINE
SKEENA	ST MARYS
ST JOHN	ST REGIS
TESLIN	SUSITNA
THAMES	SWATARA
THELON	TAUNTON
TONGUE	TRINITY
TURKEY	WABASCA
WINISK	WACOUNO

7

	8	
ABITIBI		ANDERSON
ALABAMA		ARKANSAS
AU SABLE		BELANGER
BERLAND		BIG PINEY
BRAZEAU		BIG SANDY
CACAPAN		CANADIAN
CHESTER		CHEYENNE
CLARION		CHIPPEWA
ELKHORN		CIMARRON
FEATHER		COLORADO
GUNISAO		COLUMBIA
KOYUKUK		COLVILLE
LICKING		COULONGE
MAURICE		CUYAHOGA
MOTAGUA		DELAWARE

8

ESCAMBIA
FLAMBEAU
ILLINOIS
KEDGWICK
MCCUSKER
MEDICINE
MISSOURI
MONTREAL
MUKUTAWA
NOUVILLE
NUSHAGAK
OUACHITA
PENBONCA
PORTNEUF
RAQUETTE
RINOUSKI
SAGUENAY
SANDUSKY
SHEENJEK
THOMPSON
VICTORIA

9

ALLEGHENY
ARCTIC RED
AROOSTOOK
ATHABASCA
BURNTWOOD
CHURCHILL
CONESTOGA
DES MOINES
GROUNDHOG
HARRICANA
KALAMAZOO
KUSHOKWIM
LITTLE BOW
MACKENZIE
MACMILLAN

MADAWASKA
MATTAGAMI
MEZQUITAL
MINNESOTA
MOKELUMNE
MULCHATNA
PENOBSCOT
PORCUPINE
QU'APPELLE
RIO GRANDE
SCHUYKILL
TENNESSEE
TERRA NOVA
TOMBIGBEE
VERMILION
WHITE BEAR
WHITE BULL
WISCONSIN

10

BLACKSTONE
CASCAPEDIA
CLEARWATER
COPPERMINE
COWPASTURE
GREENBRIER
HACKENSACK
LITTLE GREY
MIDDLE LOUP
SACRAMENTO
SAN JOAQUIN
THORNAPPLE

11

CONNECTICUT
HOUSATONNIC
LITTLE SIOUX
LITTLE SMOKY
LITTLE SNAKE

11
MANICOUAGAN
MISSISSIPPI
OVERFLOWING
SUSQUEHANNA
YELLOWSTONE

12
ATTAWAPISKAT
BELLE FOURCHE
LITTLE WABASH
SASKATCHEWAN

13
CHATTAHOOCHEE
SAINT AUGUSTIN

14
LITTLE MEVATINA

South America

4
BENI
BERM
DOCE
ITUI
JARI
META
PARU
TEFE

5
APURE
CAUCA
CURUA
IRIRI
JURUA
JUTAI
NEGRO
PURUS
TEUCO
VERDE

XINGU

6
AMAZON
ARAUCA
ATRATO
BALSAS
BRANCO
CABIXI
CHUBUT
DEMINI
GURUPI
JAPURA
MAMORE
PARANA
PILAYA
SALADO
UATUMA
YAVARI

7
APURITA
BERMEJO
CURACAO
DESEADO
GUAPORE
INIRIDA
JURUENA
MADEIRA
MAPUERA
MARANON
ORINOCO
TAPAJOZ
TAQUARI
UCAYALI
URUGUAY

8
ARAGUAIA
ARIPUANA

8
COLORADO
GURGUEIA
HUALLAGA
JIPARANA
PARAGUAY
PARNAIBA
SANTIAGO
SOLIMOES

9
ITACAIUNA
MAGDALENA
PILCOMAYO
RIO GRANDE
SAN MARTIN
SANTA CRUZ
TOCANTINS
TROMBETAS

10
USUMACINTA

11
MADRE DE DIOS

12
SAO FRANCISCO

17
THEODORE
   ROOSEVELT

SAINTS

3 LEO

4 ANNE
CEDD
CHAD
HUGH of Avalon
JOAN of Arc
JUDE
LUCY
LUKE
MALO
MARK
PAUL

5 AGNES
AIDAN
ALBAN
BASIL
CLARE
CYRIL
DAVID
DENIS (or Denys)
FAITH
GILES
HILDA
JAMES, Brother of Jesus
LEOBA
LOUIS
PETER
SIMON Stylites
SIMON Zelotes

6 AGATHA
ANDREW
ANSELM
BLAISE
EDMUND, King and
    Martyr
EDMUND Rich
EDWARD, King and
    Martyr
FABIAN
GEORGE
GERMAN
HELENA
HILARY
JEROME
JOSEPH
LUCIAN
MARTIN
MONICA
OSWALD
PETROC
PRISCA
SAMSON
TERESA
THOMAS of Canterbury
URSULA

7 ALPHEGE
AMBROSE
ANTHONY
BERNARD of Clairvaux

7
BIRINUS
BLASIUS
BRIDGET (Bride)
BRITIUS
CECILIA
CHARLES, King and
    Martyr
CLEMENT
COLUMBA
CRISPIN
CYPRIAN
DOMINIC
DUNSTAN
EUSTACE
FRANCIS
GREGORY the Great
LAMBERT
LEONARD
MATTHEW
PANCRAS
PATRICK
RICHARD of Chichester
STEPHEN
SWITHIN
VINCENT
WILFRED
WILFRID

8
BARNABAS
BENEDICT
BIRINIUS
BONIFACE
CUTHBERT
GERMANUS
GERTRUDE
LAURENCE
MACHUTUS (Malo)

MARGARET
MATTHIAS
NICHOLAS
NICOMEDE
PADRE PIO (Pio de
    Pietrelcina)
PAULINUS
PERPETUA
POLYCARP
REMIGIUS
VERONICA
WULFSTAN

9
AUGUSTINE of
    Canterbury
AUGUSTINE of Hippo
CATHERINE
DUBRICIUS
ELIZABETH
EUNURCHUS
JOAN OF ARC
SEBASTIAN
SYLVESTER
VALENTINE

10
ATHANASIUS
BERNADETTE
CRISPINIAN
ETHELDREDA
FRIDESWIDE
JEANNE D'ARC
PHILIP NERI

11
BARTHOLOMEW
CHRISTOPHER
SCHOLASTICA

12 JAMES THE LESS
SIMON ZELOTES
THOMAS BECKET

13 FRANCIS XAVIER
JAMES THE GREAT
JOHN THE DIVINE
MARY MAGDALENE
MARY THE VIRGIN
THOMAS AQUINAS
VENERABLE BEDE

14 IGNATIUS LOYOLA
JOHN THE BAPTIST
SIMEON STYLITES

15 FRANCIS OF ASSISI

16 JOSEMARIA ESCRIVA
THOMAS THE APOSTLE

17 JOHN THE EVANGELIST
JOSEPH OF ARIMATHEA

18 EDWARD THE CONFESSOR

SEASHELLS

3
PEN
SUN
TUN

4
CLAM
HARP

5
CHANK
CONCH
TULIP
WHELK

6
CHITON
COCKLE
COWRIE
LIMPET
MARINE
MUSSEL
NUTMEG
OYSTER
WINKLE

7
ABALONE
COQUINA
JUNONIA
SCALLOP
SLIPPER
SUNDIAL

8
BABY'S EAR
DYE MUREX
LION'S PAW
NAUTILUS

NOBLE PEN
PAPER FIG
PHEASANT
SHARK EYE
TURK'S CUP

9
BAT VOLUTE
BURSA FROG
BUTTERCUP
EGG COCKLE
GASTROPOD
GIANT CLAM
LACE MUREX
MOON SNAIL
PEAR WHELK
PINK CONCH
ROTA MUREX
SEA GOPHER
SEA URCHIN
SPINY VASE
TELESCOPE
TENT OLIVE
TONE TULIP
WEDGE CLAM

10
ANGEL WINGS
APPLE MUREX
BLUE MUSSEL
CALICO CLAM
COAT OF MAIL
CROWN CONCH
DELPHINULA
ECHINOIDEA

10
EYED COWRIE
HORSE CONCH
KING HELMET
KING'S CROWN
KITTEN'S PAW
QUAHOG CLAM
SAND DOLLAR
SOZON'S CONE
TURKEY WING
WENTLETRAP

11
BANDED TULIP
CAMEO HELMET
FLAME HELMET
FLORIDA CONE
GAUDY NATICA
GREEN TURBAN
HEART COCKLE
MUSIC VOLUTE
ONYX SLIPPER
OSTRICH FOOT
QUEEN HELMET
ROLLER CONCH
SACRED CHANK
SUNRAY VENUS
TIGER COWRIE

12
ALPHABET CONE
AMORIA VOLUTE
ATLANTIC CONE
FLORIDA AUGER
FLORIDA MITER
GAUDY ASAPHIS
GOLDEN COWRIE
GOLDEN TELLIN
LIMA FILE CLAM
PACIFIC AUGER
PARTRIDGE TUN
PELICAN'S FOOT

SCOTCH BONNET
SPIKED LIMPET
SPINDLE TIBIA
WORM SEASHELL

13
ANGULAR VOLUTE
BABYLON TURRID
BLEEDING TOOTH
CALICO SCALLOP
CARDINAL MITER
COSTATE COCKLE
EMPEROR HELMET
FIGHTING CONCH
FLORIDA CERITH
GEOGRAPHY CONE
IMPERIAL VENUS
JACKKNIFE CLAM
LETTERED OLIVE
PAPER NAUTILUS
SPINY JEWEL BOX
SPIRAL BABYLON
SUNRISE TELLIN
TRITON'S HELMET
VENUS COMB CLAM
ZIGZAG SCALLOP

14
ATLANTIC BUBBLE
CHANNELED WHELK
DISTAFF SPINDLE
ELEGANT DOSINIA
ELEGANT FIMBRIA
FLAMINGO TONGUE
JUJUBE TOP-SHELL
LEUCODON COWRIE
LIGHTNING WHELK
PANAMANIAN CONE
PECTEN RAVENELI
TAPESTRY TURBAN
TRITON'S TRUMPET
VENUS COMB MUREX

15
BITTERSWEET CLAM
BULL-MOUTH HELMET
JAPANESE CARRIER
NEW ENGLAND WHELK
PANAMANIAN AUGER
PILGRIM'S SCALLOP
ROSE PETAL TELLIN
SUNBURST CARRIER
TURRITELLA SNAIL
WATERING POT CLAM
WEST AFRICAN CONE
WEST INDIAN CHANK

16
ASIAN MOON SCALLOP
ATLANTIC SURF CLAM
BEADED PERIWINKLE
DONKEY EAR ABALONE
EDIBLE BAY SCALLOP
FLY SPECKED CERITH
FRILLED DOGWINKLE
GLORY-OF-INDIA CONE
ORANGE-MOUTH OLIVE
PAGODA PERIWINKLE
PERPLICATE VOLUTE
PINK-MOUTHED MUREX
ROOSTERTAIL CONCH
VAN HYNING'S
  COCKLE
WEDDING CAKE
  VENUS

17
AUSTRALIAN
  TRUMPET
CHAMBERED
  NAUTILUS
CHANNELED DUCK
  CLAM
FLORIDA HORSE
  CONCH

MACULATED BABY'S
  EAR
PACIFIC WING OYSTER
SANTA CRUZ LATIAXIS
VIOLET SPIDER
  CONCH

18
ANGULATE
  PERIWINKLE
ATLANTIC DEER
  COWRIE
BROAD RIBBED
  CARDITA
GIANT KNOBBED
  CERITH
GLORY-OF-THE-SEAS
  CONE
GREAT KEYHOLE
  LIMPET
PACIFIC GRINNING
  TUN
PRECIOUS
  WENTLETRAP
WHITE-SPOTTED
  MARGIN

19
TANKERVILLE'S
  ANCILLA

20
ARTHRITIC SPIDER
  CONCH
ATLANTIC PARTRIDGE
  TUN
ATLANTIC THORNY
  OYSTER

SHAKESPEARE'S PLAYS

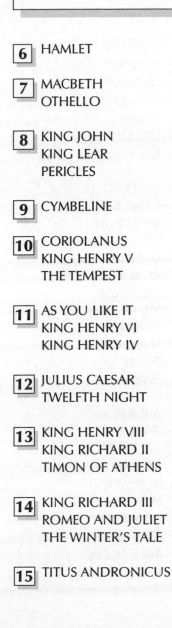

6 HAMLET

7 MACBETH
OTHELLO

8 KING JOHN
KING LEAR
PERICLES

9 CYMBELINE

10 CORIOLANUS
KING HENRY V
THE TEMPEST

11 AS YOU LIKE IT
KING HENRY VI
KING HENRY IV

12 JULIUS CAESAR
TWELFTH NIGHT

13 KING HENRY VIII
KING RICHARD II
TIMON OF ATHENS

14 KING RICHARD III
ROMEO AND JULIET
THE WINTER'S TALE

15 TITUS ANDRONICUS

16 LOVE'S LABOUR'S LOST

17 MEASURE FOR MEASURE
THE COMEDY OF ERRORS

18 ANTONY AND
CLEOPATRA
THE TWO NOBLE
KINSMEN
TROILUS AND CRESSIDA

19 MUCH ADO ABOUT
NOTHING
THE MERCHANT OF
VENICE
THE TAMING OF THE
SHREW

20 ALL'S WELL THAT ENDS
WELL
TWO GENTLEMEN OF
VERONA

21 A MIDSUMMER NIGHT'S
DREAM

22 THE MERRY WIVES OF
WINDSOR

23 THE TWO GENTLEMEN
OF VERONA

SPORTS

4 GOLF
JUDO
POLO
SUMO

5 BANDY
BOCCE
BOWLS
DARTS
FIVES
KENDO

6 BOULES
BOXING
HOCKEY
KARATE
PILOTA
QUOITS
ROWING
SKIING
SQUASH

7 ANGLING
ARCHERY
CRICKET
CROQUET
CURLING
CYCLING
FENCING
HURLING
JAI ALAI

KABADDI
MARBLES
NETBALL
RACKETS
SAILING
SNOOKER
SURFING

8 BASEBALL
CANOEING
DUCKPINS
GOALBALL
HANDBALL
KORFBALL
LACROSSE
MUAY THAI
ROUNDERS
SHOOTING
SOFTBALL
SWIMMING

9 AIR RACING
ATHLETICS
BADMINTON
BILLIARDS
BOBSLEIGH
BOOMERANG
ICE HOCKEY
STOOLBALL
TRIATHLON
WATER POLO

9 WRESTLING

10 BASKETBALL
EQUESTRIAN
GYMNASTICS
ICE SKATING
KICKBOXING
LAWN TENNIS
PADDLEBALL
RACKETBALL
REAL TENNIS
RUGBY UNION
THAI BOXING
VOLLEYBALL

11 HORSE-RACING
MARTIAL ARTS
MOTOR RACING
RUGBY LEAGUE
SHOW JUMPING
TABLE TENNIS
WATER SKIING
WINDSURFING

12 BODY BOARDING
ETON WALL GAME
MOTORCYCLING
ORIENTEERING
PADDLE TENNIS
PIGEON RACING
TRAMPOLINING
WAKE BOARDING

13
BATON TWIRLING
ROLLER SKATING
TENPIN BOWLING
WEIGHTLIFTING

14 FIVE-PIN BOWLING
FOOTBALL (GAELIC)

15 ADVENTURE RACING
BEACH VOLLEYBALL
GREYHOUND RACING
POWERBOAT RACING

16 AMERICAN FOOTBALL

19 ASSOCIATION
FOOTBALL

437

SPORTS PERSONALITIES

NAME	SPORT

3

ALI, Muhammad	Boxing
COE, Seb	Athletics
ELS, Ernie	Golf
HOY, Chris	Cycling
LAW, Denis	Football (Association)

4

ASHE, Arthur	Lawn tennis
BALL, Alan	Football (Association)
BELL, Colin	Football (Association)
BENN, Nigel	Boxing
BEST, George	Football (Association)
BIRD, Larry	Basketball
BORG, Bjorn	Lawn tennis
BOWE, Riddick	Boxing
BUDD, Zola	Athletics
COLE, Ashley	Football (Association)
COOK, Stephanie	Pentathlon
CRAM, Steve	Athletics
DEAN, Christopher	Figure skating
DEAN, Dixie	Football (Association)
DUKE, Geoff	Road racing
FARR, Tommy	Boxing
FIGO, Luis	Football (Association)
GRAF, Steffi	Lawn tennis
HARE Dusty	Rugby union
HILL, Damon	Motor racing
HILL, Graham	Motor racing

NAME	SPORT

4

HUNT, Geoff	Squash
HUNT, James	Motor racing
HUNT, Roger	Football (Association)
ICKX, Jacky	Motor racing
JOHN, Barry	Rugby union
KHAN, Jansher	Squash
KING, Billie-Jean	Lawn tennis
LARA, Brian	Cricket
LOMU, Jonah	Rugby union
LOWE, John	Darts
LYLE, Sandy	Golf
MOSS, Stirling	Motor racing
OWEN, Michael	Football (Association)
PELE	Football (Association)
(Edson Arantes do Nascimento)	
RAUL	Football (Association)
(Raul Gonzalez Blanco)	
READ, Phil	Road racing
RUSH, Ian	Football (Association)
RUTH, George Herman ('Babe')	Baseball
RYUN, Jim	Athletics
SNOW, John	Cricket
WATT, Jim	Boxing
ZICO	Football (Association)
(Artur Antunes Coimbra)	
ZOFF, Dino	Football (Association)
ZOLA, Gianfranco	Football (Association

5

ADAMS, Neil	Judo
ADAMS, Tony	Football (Association)
BANKS, Gordon	Football (Association)
BRUNO, Frank	Boxing
BUSBY, Matt	Football (Association)

NAME	SPORT
5	
CAPES, Geoff	Athletics
CLARK, Jim	Motor racing
COHEN, George	Football (Association)
COOKE, Alan	Table tennis
COURT, Margaret	Lawn tennis
DAVIS, Joe	Snooker
DAVIS, Steve	Snooker
DAWES, John	Rugby union
DURAN, Roberto	Boxing
EBDON, Peter	Snooker
FALDO, Nick	Golf
FLOYD, Ray	Golf
GIGGS, Ryan	Football (Association)
GOOCH, Graham	Cricket
GOUGH, Darren	Cricket
GOULD, Shane	Swimming
GOWER, David	Cricket
GRACE, William Gilbert (W.G.)	Cricket
GREIG, John	Football (Association)
GREIG, Tony	Cricket
GROSS, Michael	Swimming
HAGEN, Walter	Golf
HAMED, Naseem	Boxing
HENRY, Thierry	Football (Association)
HOBBS, Jack	Cricket
HOGAN, Ben	Golf
HURST, Geoff	Football (Association)
JONES, Bobby	Golf
JONES, Marion	Athletics
JONES, Michael	Rugby union
KEANE, Roy	Football (Association)
KEINO, Kip	Athletics
KERLY, Sean	Hockey
KILLY, Jean-Claude	Skiing
LAKER, Jim	Cricket

NAME	SPORT

5

LAUDA, Niki	Motor racing
LAVER, Rod	Lawn tennis
LENDL, Ivan	Lawn tennis
LEWIS, Carl	Athletics
LEWIS, Geoff	Horse racing
LEWIS, Lennox	Boxing
LLOYD, Clive	Cricket
LOCKE, Bobby	Golf
LOPEZ, Nancy	Golf
LOUIS, Joe	Boxing
LYDON, Joe	Rugby league
MAHRE, Phil	Skiing
MCCOY, Tony	Horse racing
MCKAY, Heather	Squash
MEADS, Colin	Rugby union
MOORE, Bobby	Football (Association)
MOSES, Ed	Athletics
NICOL, Peter	Squash
OBERG, Margo	Surfing
OTTEY, Merlene	Athletics
OVETT, Steve	Athletics
OWENS, Jesse	Athletics
PERRY, Fred	Lawn tennis
PRICE, Nick	Golf
PROST, Alain	Motor racing
REVIE, Don	Football (Association)
SAFIN, Marat	Lawn tennis
SELES, Monica	Lawn tennis
SENNA, Ayrton	Motor racing
SINGH, Vijay	Golf
SNEAD, Sam	Golf
SNELL, Peter	Athletics
SPITZ, Mark	Swimming
STEIN, Jock	Football (Association)

NAME	SPORT

5

TOMBA, Alberto	Skiing
TYSON, Frank	Cricket
TYSON, Mike	Boxing
VIREN, Lasse	Athletics
WALSH, Courtney	Cricket
WARNE, Shane	Cricket
WAUGH, Steve	Cricket
WELLS, Allan	Athletics
WHITE, Jimmy	Snooker
WOODS, Tiger	Golf

6

AGASSI, Andre	Lawn tennis
ANDREW, Rob	Rugby union
AOUITA, Said	Athletics
ASHTON, Eric	Rugby league
BAGGIO, Roberto	Football (Association)
BARNES, John	Football (Association)
BAXTER, Jim	Football (Association)
BEAMON, Bob	Athletics
BECKER, Boris	Lawn tennis
BEDSER, Alec	Cricket
BENAUD, Richie	Cricket
BORDER, Allan	Cricket
BORZOV, Valery	Athletics
BOSTON, Billy	Rugby league
BOTHAM, Ian	Cricket
BRIGGS, Barry	Speedway
BRYANT, David	Bowls
BURTON, Beryl	Cycling
BUTTON, Jenson	Motor racing
CARSON, Willie	Horse racing
CARTER, Kenny	Speedway
CASPER, Billy	Golf

NAME	SPORT

6

NAME	SPORT
CLARKE, Darren	Golf
CLOUGH, Brian	Football (Association)
CONTEH, John	Boxing
COTTON, Fran	Rugby union
COTTON, Henry	Golf
COOPER, Henry	Boxing
CRUYFF, Johan	Football (Association)
CULLIS, Stan	Football (Association)
DAVIES, Gerald	Rugby union
DAVIES, Jonathan	Rugby union
DAVIES, Laura	Golf
DAVIES, Lynn	Athletics
DAVIES, Sharron	Swimming
DEXTER, Ted	Cricket
DOOHAN, Michael	Road racing
DOUGAN, Derek	Football (Association)
EDDERY, Pat	Horse racing
EUBANK, Chris	Boxing
FALLON, Kieren	Horse racing
FANGIO, Juan Manuel	Motor racing
FINNEY, Tom	Football (Association)
FISHER, Allison	Snooker
FOSTER, Brendan	Athletics
FOSTER, Tim	Rowing
FRASER, Dawn	Swimming
GARCIA, Sergio	Golf
GIBSON, Mike	Rugby union
GULLIT, Ruud	Football (Association)
HADLEE, Richard	Cricket
HAGLER, Marvin	Boxing
HANLEY, Ellery	Rugby league
HANSEN, Alan	Football (Association)
HARRIS, Reg	Cycling
HARVEY, Neil	Cricket
HAYNES, Johnny	Football (Association)

NAME	SPORT

6

NAME	SPORT
HEARNS, Thomas	Boxing
HEMERY, David	Athletics
HENDRY, Stephen	Snooker
HENMAN, Tim	Lawn tennis
HEWITT, Lleyton	Lawn tennis
HINGIS, Martina	Lawn tennis
HODDLE, Glenn	Football (Association)
HOLMES, Kelly	Athletics
HOLMES, Larry	Boxing
HUGHES, Emlyn	Football (Association)
HUGHES, Mark	Football (Association)
HUTTON, Len	Cricket
IRVINE, Andrew	Rugby union
JORDAN, Michael	Basketball
KEEGAN, Kevin	Football (Association)
KORBUT, Olga	Gymnastics
LANGER, Bernhard	Golf
LAWTON, Tommy	Football (Association)
LEMOND, Greg	Cycling
LILLEE, Dennis	Cricket
LYNAGH, Michael	Rugby union
MACKAY, Dave	Football (Association)
MAUGER, Ivan	Speedway
MERCKX, Eddy	Cycling
MILLER, Keith	Cricket
MINTER, Alan	Boxing
MORGAN, Cliff	Rugby union
MULLER, Gerd	Football (Association)
MURPHY, Alex	Rugby league
NORMAN, Greg	Golf
O'BRIEN, Vincent	Horse racing
OFFIAH, Martin	Rugby league
O'NEILL, Jonjo	Horse racing
PALMER, Arnold	Golf
PETERS, Martin	Football (Association)

NAME	SPORT

6

PETERS, Mary	Athletics
PLAYER, Gary	Golf
PORTER, Hugh	Cycling
PUSKAS, Ferenc	Football (Association)
RAMSEY, Alf	Football (Association)
RIPLEY, Andrew	Rugby union
RIVERA, Gianni	Football (Association)
ROBSON, Bobby	Football (Association)
ROBSON, Bryan	Football (Association)
ROONEY, Wayne	Football (Association)
SEELER, Uwe	Football (Association)
SHEENE, Barry	Road racing
SLATER, Kelly	Surfing
SOBERS, Garfield	Cricket
STILES, Nobby	Football (Association)
TAAFFE, Pat	Horse racing
TAYLOR, Dennis	Snooker
TAYLOR, Phil	Darts
THORPE, Ian	Swimming
VIEIRA, Patrick	Football (Association)
WATSON, Tom	Golf
WEEKES, Everton	Cricket
WILKIE, David	Swimming
WILLIS, Bob	Cricket
WILSON, Ray	Football (Association)
WINTER, Fred	Horse racing
WINTER, Russel	Surfing
WRIGHT, Billy	Football (Association)
WRIGHT, Ian	Football (Association)
YASHIN, Lev	Football (Association)
ZIDANE, Zinedine	Football (Association)

7

AINSLIE, Ben	Sailing
AKABUSI, Kriss	Athletics
ALBERTO, Carlos	Football (Association)

NAME	SPORT

7

AMBROSE, Curtly	Cricket
ARDILES, Ossie	Football (Association)
ASHFORD, Evelyn	Athletics
BACKLEY, Steve	Athletics
BECKHAM, David	Football (Association)
BENNETT, Phil	Rugby union
BOYCOTT, Geoffrey	Cricket
BRABHAM, Jack	Motor racing
BRADMAN, Don	Cricket
BRASHER, Chris	Athletics
BREMNER, Billy	Football (Association)
BRISTOW, Eric	Darts
CAMPESE, David	Rugby union
CANTONA, Eric	Football (Association)
CAUTHEN, Steve	Horse racing
CHARLES, Bob	Golf
CHARLES, John	Football (Association)
COMPTON, Denis	Cricket
CONNORS, Jimmy	Lawn tennis
CORBETT, James	Boxing
COWDREY, Colin	Cricket
DEMPSEY, Jack	Boxing
DETTORI, Frankie	Horse racing
DOUGLAS, Desmond	Table tennis
EDWARDS, Duncan	Football (Association)
EDWARDS, Gareth	Rugby union
ELLIOTT, Herb	Athletics
EUSEBIO	Football (Association)
(Eusebio da Silva Ferreira)	
FEDERER, Roger	Lawn tennis
FLOWERS, Ron	Football (Association)
FOGARTY, Carl	Road racing
FOREMAN, George	Boxing
FOSBURY, Dick	Athletics
FRANCIS, Trevor	Football (Association)

NAME	SPORT

7

NAME	SPORT
FRAZIER, Joe	Boxing
FREEMAN, Cathy	Athletics
FUNNELL, Philippa	Equestrian
GIFFORD, Josh	Horse racing
GOODHEW, Duncan	Swimming
GREAVES, Jimmy	Football (Association)
GREGORY, Mike	Darts
GUNNELL, Sally	Athletics
HAMMOND, Walter	Cricket
HEADLEY, George	Cricket
HIGGINS, Alex	Snooker
HOLDING, Michael	Cricket
HUSSAIN, Nasser	Cricket
JACKLIN, Tony	Golf
JACKSON, Colin	Athletics
JOHNSON, Michael	Athletics
LAMPARD, Frank	Football (Association) -
LARWOOD, Harold	Cricket
LEONARD, Sugar Ray	Boxing
LINEKER, Gary	Football (Association)
LITTLER, Gene	Golf
LOCHORE, Sir Brian	Rugby union
MANSELL, Nigel	Motor racing
MCBRIDE, Willie John	Rugby union
MCENROE, John	Lawn tennis
MCGRATH, Glenn	Cricket
MCNEILL, Billy	Football (Association)
MILBURN, Jackie	Football (Association)
MONTANA, Joe	American football
MONTOYA, Juan Pablo	Motor racing
NASTASE, Ilie	Lawn tennis
PAISLEY, Bob	Football (Association)
PARROTT, John	Snooker
PIGGOTT, Lester	Horse racing
PINSENT, Matthew	Rowing

NAME	SPORT

7

NAME	SPORT
PLATINI, Michel	Football (Association)
POLLOCK, Graeme	Cricket
REARDON, Ray	Snooker
ROBERTS, Andy	Cricket
ROBERTS, Kenny	Road racing
RODDICK, Andy	Lawn tennis
RONALDO, Cristiano	Football (Association)
RONALDO (Luiz Nazario de Lima)	Football (Association)
SAMPRAS, Pete	Lawn tennis
SARAZEN, Gene	Golf
SCHOLES, Paul	Football (Association)
SHANKLY, Bill	Football (Association)
SHEARER, Alan	Football (Association)
SHILTON, Peter	Football (Association)
SIMPSON, Bobby	Cricket
SPENCER, John	Snooker
STADLER, Craig	Golf
STATHAM, Brian	Cricket
STEWART, Jackie	Motor racing
STEWART, Payne	Golf
STRANGE, Curtis	Golf
SURTEES, John	Road racing
THOMSON, Peter	Golf
TORVILL, Jayne	Figure skating
TREVINO, Lee	Golf
TRUEMAN, Fred	Cricket
VAUGHAN, Michael	Cricket
WALCOTT, Clyde	Cricket
WOOLLEY, Frank	Cricket
WOOSNAM, Ian	Golf
WORRELL, Frank	Cricket
ZATOPEK, Emil	Athletics

NAME	SPORT

8

ABRAHAMS, Harold	Athletics
AGOSTINI, Giacomo	Road racing
ANDERSEN, Lisa	Surfing
ATHERTON, Michael	Cricket
BEAUMONT, Bill	Rugby union
BERGKAMP, Dennis	Football (Association)
BOARDMAN, Chris	Cycling
BREASLEY, Scobie	Horse racing
BROOKING, Trevor	Football (Association)
CALZAGHE, Joe	Boxing
CAMPBELL, Darren	Athletics
CAPRIATI, Jennifer	Lawn tennis
CHAMPION, Bob	Horse racing
CHAPPELL, Ian	Cricket
CHARLTON, Bobby	Football (Association)
CHARLTON, Eddie	Snooker
CHARLTON, Jack	Football (Association)
CHRISTIE, Linford	Athletics
COMANECI, Nadia	Gymnastics
CONNOLLY, Maureen	Lawn tennis
DALGLISH, Kenny	Football (Association)
DEVONISH, Marlon	Athletics
DIMAGGIO, Jo	Baseball
DUNWOODY, Richard	Horse racing
FAULKNER, Max	Golf
FERGUSON, Alex	Football (Association)
FRANCOME, John	Horse racing
GARDENER, Jason	Athletics
GAVASKAR, Sunil	Cricket
GRAVENEY, Tom	Cricket
HAILWOOD, Mike	Road racing
HASTINGS, Gavin	Rugby union
INDURAIN, Miguel	Cycling
JENNINGS, Pat	Football (Association)
KAPIL DEV	Cricket

NAME	SPORT

8

LINDWALL, Ray	Cricket
MARADONA, Diego	Football (Association)
MARCIANO, Rocky	Boxing
MARSHALL, Malcolm	Cricket
MATTHEWS, Stanley	Football (Association)
MCCOLGAN, Liz	Athletics
MCGUIGAN, Barry	Boxing
MILLWARD, Roger	Rugby league
NICKLAUS, Jack	Golf
OLAZABAL, Jose Maria	Golf
REDGRAVE, Steve	Rowing
REYNOLDS, Butch	Athletics
RICHARDS, Barry	Cricket
RICHARDS, Sir Gordon	Horse racing
RICHARDS, Vivian	Cricket
ROBINSON, Sugar Ray	Boxing
STENMARK, Ingemar	Skiing
SWINBURN, Walter	Horse racing
THOMPSON, Daley	Athletics
THORBURN, Cliff	Snooker
TORRENCE, Gwen	Athletics
WESTWOOD, Lee	Golf
WILANDER, Mats	Lawn tennis
WILLIAMS, J. P. R.	Rugby union
WILLIAMS, Rex	Snooker & billiards
WILLIAMS, Serena	Lawn tennis
WILLIAMS, Venus	Lawn tennis

9

ARMSTRONG, Lance	Cycling
BANNISTER, Sir Roger	Athletics
BEARDSLEY, Peter	Football (Association)
CRACKNELL, James	Rowing
DALLAGLIO, Lawrence	Rugby union
DI STEFANO, Alfredo	Football (Association)

NAME	SPORT

9

FARR-JONES, Nick	Rugby union
GARRINCHA, Manoel Francisco dos Santos	Football (Association)
GASCOIGNE, Paul	Football (Association)
GILCHRIST, Adam	Cricket
GREENIDGE, Gordon	Cricket
GRIFFITHS, Terry	Snooker
HOLYFIELD, Evander	Boxing
IMRAN KHAN	Cricket
JAIRZINHO (Jair Ventura Filho)	Football (Association)
KLINSMANN, Jurgen	Football (Association)
LAWRENSON, Mark	Football (Association)
LOFTHOUSE, Nat	Football (Association)
MACARTHUR, Ellen	Sailing
MICKELSON, Phil	Golf
MOORCROFT, David	Athletics
NICHOLSON, Bill	Football (Association)
NICHOLSON, David	Horse racing
O'SULLIVAN, Ronnie	Snooker
O'SULLIVAN, Sonia	Athletics
PATTERSON, Floyd	Boxing
RADCLIFFE, Paula	Athletics
SANDERSON, Tessa	Athletics
SCUDAMORE, Peter	Horse racing
SHOEMAKER, Willie	Horse racing
SORENSTAM, Annika	Golf
TENDULKAR, Sachin	Cricket
TRAUTMANN, Bert	Football (Association)
UNDERWOOD, Derek	Cricket
UNDERWOOD, Rory	Rugby union
WHITBREAD, Fatima	Athletics
WILKINSON, Jonny	Rugby union

NAME	SPORT

10

BARRINGTON, Jonah	Squash
FITTIPALDI, Emerson	Motor racing
IVANISEVIC, Goran	Lawn tennis
JUANTORENA, Alberto	Athletics
RONALDINHO (Ronaldo de Assis Moreira)	Football (Association)
SCHMEICHEL, Peter	Football (Association)
SCHUMACHER, Michael	Motor racing
VILLENEUVE, Gilles	Motor racing
WASIM AKRAM	Cricket

11

BALLESTEROS, Seve	Golf
BECKENBAUER, Franz	Football (Association)
BIDDLECOMBE, Terry	Horse racing
KRISTIANSEN, Ingrid	Athletics
MONTGOMERIE, Colin	Golf
NAVRATILOVA, Martina	Lawn tennis

12

BLANCHFLOWER, Danny	Football (Association)
BLANKERS-KOEN, Fanny	Athletics
JOYNER-KERSEE, Jackie	Athletics
LEWIS-FRANCIS, Mark	Athletics
MURALITHARAN, Muttiah	Cricket

13

| HENIN-HARDENNE, Justine | Lawn tennis |
| ROBERTO CARLOS | Football (Association) |

14

| GRIFFITH-JOYNER, Florence | Athletics |

SPORTING TROPHIES

TROPHY	SPORT

5

ASHES	Cricket

7

COLE CUP	Fencing
UBER CUP	Badminton
UEFA CUP	Association football

8

DAVIS CUP	Tennis
DEWAR CUP	Rifle shooting
RYDER CUP	Golf

9

CANADA CUP	Golf
CURRIE CUP	Rugby union
CURTIS CUP	Golf
HAMBLETON	Harness racing
HOPMAN CUP	Tennis
SWALEC CUP	Rugby union
THOMAS CUP	Badminton
WALKER CUP	Golf

10

ARMADA DISH	Equestrian
CARLING CUP	Association football
SOLHEIM CUP	Golf
STANLEY CUP	Ice hockey

TROPHY	SPORT

11

ADMIRAL'S CUP	Sailing
AMERICA'S CUP	Sailing
BOWRING BOWL	Rugby union
CALCUTTA CUP	Rugby union
IROQUOIS CUP	Lacrosse
KINNAIRD CUP	Eton fives
MARCHANT CUP	Rugby fives
PALMA TROPHY	Shooting
POWERGEN CUP	Rugby union
PURA MILK CUP	Cricket
QUEEN'S PRIZE	Rifle shooting
REGAL TROPHY	Rugby league
STEWARDS CUP	Rowing
TENNENT'S CUP	Rugby union
TRIPLE CROWN	Surfing
WIGHTMAN CUP	Tennis

12

BLEDISLOE CUP	Rugby union
LAPHAM TROPHY	Squash
LONSDALE BELT	Boxing
MIDDLETON CUP	Bowls
WOLFE-NOEL CUP	Squash

13

BOLOGNA TROPHY	Swimming
DIAMOND SCULLS	Rowing
FEDERATION CUP	Tennis
JOHN PLAYER CUP	Rugby league
LEONARD TROPHY	Bowls
PILKINGTON CUP	Rugby union
PRESIDENTS' CUP	Golf
SEAWANHAKA CUP	Sailing
STRATHCONA CUP	Curling

TROPHY	SPORT

13

SUBALTERNS' CUP	Polo
SWAYTHLING CUP	Table tennis
VOLVO WORLD CUP	Show jumping
WORRELL TROPHY	Cricket

14

GEORGE HEARN CUP	Diving
LANCE TODD AWARD	Rugby league
LONDONDERRY CUP	Squash
RANFURLY SHIELD	Rugby union
TALBOT HANDICAP	Crown green bowls
WESTCHESTER CUP	Polo

15

BRITANNIA SHIELD	Speedway
VAL BARKER TROPHY	Boxing
WEBB ELLIS TROPHY	Rugby union

16

BRENDAN MARTIN CUP	Gaelic football
EISENHOWER TROPHY	Golf
HALFORD HEWITT CUP	Golf
HARMSWORTH TROPHY	Powerboat racing
JULES RIMET TROPHY	Association football
LIAM MACCARTHY CUP	Hurling
PRINCE OF WALES CUP	Sailing
PRINCE RAINIER CUP	Fencing
TETLEY'S BITTER CUP	Rugby union

17

AFRICAN NATIONS CUP	Association football
GRAND CHALLENGE CUP	Rowing
JAMES NORRIS TROPHY	Ice hockey
SAM MACGUIRE TROPHY	Gaelic football

TROPHY	SPORT

18

COWDRAY PARK GOLD CUP	Polo
KING GEORGE V GOLD CUP	Show jumping
MARCEL CORBILLON CUP	Table tennis
WYFOLD CHALLENGE CUP	Rowing

19

ESPIRITO SANTO TROPHY	Golf
GORDON BENNETT TROPHY	Motor racing
HARRY BENJAMIN TROPHY	Swimming & water polo
PHILADELPHIA GOLD CUP	Rowing
QUEEN ELIZABETH II CUP	Show jumping
SIR WILLIAM BURTON CUP	Sailing

20

| DOGGETT'S COAT AND BADGE | Rowing |

23

| BARON MATSUI INTER-CLUB CUP | Judo |

STARS
and constellations

3
ARA
LEO
SUN

4
APUS
GRUS
LYNX
LYRA
MIRA
PAVO
VEGA
VELA

5
ACRUX
AGENA
AIGAL
ALCOR
ALGOL
ARGUS
ARIES
CETUS
CYGNI
DENEB
DRACO
HYDRA
INDUS
LEPUS
LIBRA
LUPUS
MALUS
MENSA

MIZAR
MUSCA
NORMA
ORION
PYXIS
RIGEL
SPICA
VIRGO

6
AL FARD
ALTAIR
ANTLIA
AQUILA
AURIGA
BOOTES
CAELUM
CANCER
CARINA
CASTOR
CORVUS
CRATER
DORADO
FORNAX
GEMINI
HYDRUS
LEONIS
MARKAB
MIMOSA
NORMOE
OCTANS
PICTOR

6
PISCES
POLLUX
PUPPIS
SCUTUM
SIRIUS
TAURUS
TOUCAN
TUCANA
VOLANS

7
ALCYONE
ALGENIB
ALNILAM
ALNITAK
ANTARES
CANOPUS
CAPELLA
CEPHEUS
COLUMBA
LACERTA
MINTAKA
MIRPHAK
PEGASUS
PERSEUS
PHOENIX
POLARIS
PROCYON
REGULUS
SAGITTA
SCORPIO
SERPENS
SEXTANS

8
ACHERNAR
AQUARIUS
ARCTURUS
CERBERUS

CIRCINUS
DENEBOLA
EQUULEUS
ERIDANUS
HERCULES
LEO MINOR
MIRA CETI
PICTORIS
PLEIADES
RED GIANT
RETICULI
SCULPTOR
VOTANTIS

9
ALDEBARAN
ALPHERATZ
ANDROMEDA
BELLATRIX
CAPRICORN
CENTAURUS
COR CAROLI
DELPHINUS
FOMALHAUT
MONOCEROS
OPHIUCHUS
RETICULUM
SEXTANTIS
SUPERNOVA
URSA MAJOR
URSA MINOR
VULPECULA

10
BETELGEUSE
CANIS MAJOR
CANIS MINOR
CASSIOPEIA
CHAMAELEON

10 HOROLOGIUM
MONS MENSAE
TELESCOPUS
TRIANGULUM
URSUS MAJOR
URSUS MINOR
WHITE DWARF

19 APPARATUS
SCULPTORIS

11 CAPRICORNUS
MICROSCOPUS
SAGITTARIUS
TELESCOPIUM

12 BARNARD'S STAR
MICROSCOPIUM
PYXIS NAUTICA

13 ALPHA CENTAURI
ALPHA DRACONIS
CANES VENATICI
CHAMOELEONTIS
COLUMBA NOACHI
COMA BERENICES
FORNAX CHEMICA

14 CAMELOPARDALIS
CORONA BOREALIS

15 CORONA AUSTRALIS
PISCIS AUSTRALIS
PISCIS AUSTRINUS

16 ANTLIA PNEUMATICA
CLOUDS OF MAGELLAN
MAGELLANIC CLOUDS
VULPECULA ET ANSER

TREES & SHRUBS

3
ASH
BAY
BOX
ELM
FIG
FIR
GUM
IVY
MAY
OAK
YEW

4
ACER
COCA
COLA
DATE
GEAN
HEBE
ILEX
KOLA
LIME
LING
PALM
PEAR
PINE
PLUM
RHUS
ROSE
SLOE
TEAK
TOLU

5
ABELE
ALDER
APPLE
ASPEN
BEECH
BIRCH
BROOM
CACAO
CAPER
CAROB
CEDAR
EBONY
ELDER
ERICA
FAGUS
FURZE
GORSE
HAZEL
HOLLY
JUDAS
KARRI
LARCH
LEMON
LILAC
MALUS
MAPLE
NYSSA
OLIVE
OSIER
PEACH
PECAN

5
PICEA
PINUS
PLANE
PYRUS
RIBES
ROWAN
SALIX
TULIP
YUCCA

6
ACACIA
ARABIS
AZALEA
BAMBOO
BANYAN
BAOBAB
BONSAI
BO TREE
CASSIA
CHERRY
CISTUS
CORNEL
CORNUS
DAPHNE
DATURA
DEODAR
DRAGON
GINKGO
GOMUTI
JARRAH
JINBUL
JOSHUA
JUJUBE
KERRIA
LAUREL
LOCUST
MEDLAR

MIMOSA
MOOLAR
MYRTLE
ORANGE
PIERIS
POPLAR
PRIVET
PROTEA
PRUNUS
REDBUD
RED GUM
RUBBER
SALLOW
SORBUS
SPRUCE
SUMACH
WALNUT
WILLOW

7
AMBOYNA
APRICOT
ARBUTUS
BEBEERU
BULLACE
CALLUNA
CAMELIA
CAMPHOR
CHOISYA
CORK OAK
CYPRESS
DEUTZIA
DOGWOOD
FUCHSIA
GENISTA
HEATHER
HEMLOCK
HICKORY

7

HOLM OAK
JASMINE
JUNIPER
MAHONIA
PHLOMIS
REDWOOD
ROBINIA
SEQUOIA
SERVICE
SKIMMIA
SOURSOP
SPINDLE
SPIRAEA
SYRINGA
WEIGELA
WYCH ELM

8

ALBIZZIA
BARBERRY
BASSWOOD
BAYBERRY
BERBERIS
BERGAMOT
BLACKBOX
BUDDLEIA
CALABASH
CAMELLIA
CARPINUS
CINCHONA
COOLABAR
EUONYMUS
HAWTHORN
HORNBEAM
IRONWOOD
JAPONICA
LABURNUM
LONICERA

MAGNOLIA
MAHOGANY
OLEANDER
QUANDONG
RAMBUTAN
SAGO PALM
SILKY OAK
SWEET GUM
SYCAMORE
TAMARISK
VIBURNUM
WISTERIA
WOODBINE

9

ARAUCARIA
BUCKTHORN
CEANOTHUS
CORDYLINE
CRAB APPLE
CRATAEGUS
CUPRESSUS
EUPHORBIA
FIRETHORN
FORSYTHIA
GREVILLEA
HYDRANGEA
HYPERICUM
JACARANDA
KALANCHOE
LAVANDULA
MANGROVES
MISTLETOE
SANTOLINA
SASSAFRAS
SCOTS PINE
SILVER FIR
STINKWOOD

9
STONE PINE
SWEETWOOD
SYMPHOCOS
TURKEY OAK
WAYFARING
WHITEBEAM

10
BIRD CHERRY
BLACKTHORN
BRAZILWOOD
COTTONWOOD
DOUGLAS FIR
ESCALLONIA
EUCALYPTUS
FIELD MAPLE
FRANGIPANI
INDIAN BEAN
LIBOCEDRUS
MANGOSTEEN
POTENTILLA
PYRACANTHA
STRAWBERRY
WILD CHERRY
WITCH HAZEL

11
BOTTLEBRUSH
CHAULMOOGRA
COTONEASTER
CRACK WILLOW
DWARF CHERRY
GUELDER ROSE
LIQUIDAMBAR
MOUNTAIN ASH
PHYLLANTHUS
PITTOSPORUM
PUSSY WILLOW
STEPHANOTIS

TALIPOT PALM
WHITE WILLOW

12
AUSTRIAN PINE
ENGLISH MAPLE
LIRIODENDRON
PHILADELPHUS
RHODODENDRON
WOOLLY WILLOW

13
BOUGAINVILLEA
HORSE CHESTNUT
JAPANESE MAPLE
LAWSON CYPRESS
PAPER MULBERRY
SWEET CHESTNUT

14
CEDAR OF LEBANON
LOMBARDY POPLAR
SYMPHORICARPOS

15
VIRGINIA CREEPER

VEGETABLES

3 YAM

4 KALE
LEEK
OKRA
PEAS
TARO

5 ANISE
CHARD
MAIZE
ONION
RAMPS
SWEDE

6 CARROT
CELERY
CHIVES
DAIKON
ENDIVE
FENNEL
FRISEE
GARLIC
GINGER
JICAMA
KAI-LAN
MARROW
POTATO
RADISH
RAPINI
ROCKET

TATSOI
TOMATO
TURNIP
WASABI

7 AVOCADO
CABBAGE
CASSAVA
CHICORY
LENTILS
LETTUCE
NETTLES
PAPRIKA
PARSLEY
PARSNIP
PUMPKIN
RHUBARB
SALSIFY
SHALLOT
SKIRRET
SPINACH
TABASCO

8 BEETROOT
BROCCOLI
CELERIAC
CUCUMBER
HABANERO
JALAPENO
KOHLRABI
PIMIENTO

8 SOYBEANS

9 ARTICHOKE
ASPARAGUS
AUBERGINE
CALABRESE
CECI BEANS
CHICKPEAS
CORIANDER
CORN SALAD
COURGETTE
GARBANZOS
GEM SQUASH
MUNG BEANS
MUSHROOMS
NAVY BEANS
PATTY PANS
RADICCHIO
RED PEPPER
SWEETCORN

10 AZUKI BEANS
BELL PEPPER
BLACK BEANS
BREADFRUIT
BROAD BEANS
BROCCOLINI
FIDDLEHEAD
GREEN BEANS
LEMON GRASS
WATERCRESS

11 ACORN SQUASH
BEAN SPROUTS
BITTER MELON
BUTTER BEANS
CAULIFLOWER

GREEN PEPPER
KIDNEY BEANS
RUNNER BEANS
SPRING ONION
SWEET POTATO
WHITE RADISH
WINTER MELON

12 BROCCOFLOWER
CHILLI PEPPER
MANGEL-WURZEL
SPRING GREENS

13 BORLOTTI BEANS
CAYENNE PEPPER
CHINESE LEAVES
MANGETOUT PEAS
MUSTARD GREENS
SUGAR SNAP PEAS
WATER CHESTNUT

14 ALFALFA SPROUTS
BLACK-EYED BEANS

15 BRUSSELS SPROUTS
BUTTERNUT SQUASH
SPAGHETTI SQUASH

17 NEW ZEALAND
SPINACH

18 JERUSALEM
ARTICHOKE

WATERFALLS

WATERFALL	COUNTRY
4	
SKOK	Slovakia
5	
ANGEL	Venezuela
DELLA	Canada
GRAND	Canada
KJELL	Norway
MONGE	Norway
6	
FEIGUM	Norway
HUNLEN	Canada
KAHIWA	Hawaii, USA
PIEMAN	Australia
RIBBON	USA
SENDAT	Malaysia
TUGELA	S. Africa
VETTIS	Norway
WAIPIO	Hawaii, USA
7	
FACHODA	Tahiti
KALAMBO	Australia
NIAGARA	USA/ Canada
TIN MINE	Australia
UTIGORD	Norway

WATERFALL	COUNTRY

8

CUQUENAN	Venezuela
CUYAHOGA	USA
GAVARNIE	France
GERSOPPA	India
KAIETEUR	Guyana
KALIUWAA	Hawaii, USA
KRIMMLER	Austria
MUTARAZI	Zimbabwe
PAPALAUA	Hawaii, USA
SENTINEL	USA
TAKKAKAW	Canada
VICTORIA	Zambia/Zimbabwe
WALLAMAN	Australia
YOSEMITE	USA

9

DETTIFOSS	Iceland
DUDHSAGAR	India
ESPELANDS	Norway
GIESSBACH	Switzerland
HONOKOHAU	Hawaii, USA
HORSESHOE	Canada
MONTEZUMA	Australia

10

SALTO ANGEL	Venezuela
SUTHERLAND	New Zealand
WOLLOMOMBI	Australia

11

BASASEACHIC	Mexico
KIJANG JATUH	Malaysia
SPRAY STREAM	Switzerland

WATERFALL	COUNTRY

12

KING GEORGE VI	Guyana
LATA BEREMBUN	Malaysia
PAULO ALFONSO	Brazil
SALTO DEL LAJA	Chile
SILVER STRAND	USA

14

KING EDWARD VIII	Guyana
LOWER MAR VALLEY	Norway
TYSSESTRENGENE	Norway
UPPER MAR VALLEY	Norway

17

CACHOEIRA DA FUMACA	Brazil

23

CACHOEIRA DE SANTO ANTONIO	Brazil

DICTIONARY SECTION
A–Z : three to ten letter words

3	AWL	BUN	DAH	EAT	FEY
	AWN	BUS	DAM	EBB	FEZ
ACT	AXE	BUT	DAN	EEL	FIB
ADD	AYE	BUY	DAP	EFT	FID
ADO	BAA	BYE	DAY	EGG	FIG
AFT	BAD	CAB	DEE	EGO	FIR
AGA	BAG	CAD	DEN	EKE	FIT
AGE	BAH	CAM	DEW	ELD	FIX
AFT	BAN	CAN	DID	ELF	FLY
AGO	BAP	CAP	DIE	ELK	FOB
AHA	BAR	CAR	DIG	ELL	FOE
AID	BAT	CAT	DIM	ELM	FOG
AIL	BAY	CAW	DIN	EMU	FOP
AIM	BED	CAY	DIP	END	FOR
AIR	BEE	CEP	DIT	ERA	FOX
ALE	BEG	COB	DOB	ERG	FRO
ALL	BET	COD	DOE	ERK	FRY
ALP	BIB	COG	DOG	ERR	FUG
AMP	BID	COP	DOH	ETH	FUN
AND	BIG	COS	DOM	EVE	FUR
ANT	BIN	COT	DON	EWE	GAB
ANY	BIT	COW	DOP	EYE	GAD
APE	BOA	COX	DOR	FAD	GAG
APT	BOB	CRY	DOT	FAG	GAP
ARC	BOD	CUB	DRY	FAH	GAS
ARM	BOG	CUD	DUB	FAN	GAY
ART	BOO	CUE	DUD	FAR	GEL
ASH	BOP	CUM	DUE	FAT	GEM
ASK	BOW	CUP	DUG	FAX	GET
ASP	BOX	CUR	DUN	FAY	GIB
ASS	BOY	CUT	DUO	FEE	GIG
ATE	BRA	DAB	DUX	FEN	GIN
AUK	BUD	DAD	DYE	FEU	GOB
AWE	BUG	DAG	EAR	FEW	GOD

GOO	IRE	LET	NEE	PAL	RAP
GUM	IVY	LEY	NET	PAN	RAT
GUN	JAB	LID	NEW	PAP	RAW
GUT	JAG	LIE	NIB	PAR	RAY
GUY	JAM	LIP	NIL	PAS	RED
GYM	JAR	LOB	NIP	PAT	REP
GYP	JAT	LOG	NIT	PAW	RET
HAG	JAW	LOO	NIX	PAX	REX
HAT	JAY	LOP	NOB	PAY	RIB
HAW	JET	LOT	NOD	PEA	RID
HAY	JEW	LOW	NOH	PEE	RIG
HEM	JIB	LOX	NOR	PEG	RIM
HEN	JIG	LUG	NOT	PEN -	RIP
HEX	JOB	LUX	NOW	PFP	ROB
HIP	JOG	LYE	NUB	PER	ROC
HIT	JOT	MAD	NUN	PET	ROD
HOB	JOY	MAN	NUT	PEW	ROE
HOD	JUG	MAP	OAF	PIE	ROT
HOE	JUT	MAR	OAK	PIG	ROW
HOG	KED	MAT	OAR	PIN	RUB
HOM	KEF	MAW	OAT	PIP	RUE
HOP	KEG	MAY	OBI	PIT	RUG
HOT	KEN	MEN	ODD	PLY	RUM
HOW	KEY	MEW	ODE	POD	RUN
HOY	KID	MIL	OFF	POP	RUT
HUB	KIN	MIX	OIK	POT	RYE
HUE	KIP	MOB	OIL	POX	SAC
HUG	KIT	MOD	OLD	PRY	SAD
HUM	KOI	MOO	ONE	PUG	SAG
HUN	KOP	MOP	OPT	PUN	SAP
HUT	LAD	MOR	ORB	PUP	SAT
ICE	LAG	MOT	ORE	PUS	SAW
ICY	LAH	MOW	OUR	PUT	SAX
IDO	LAP	MUD	OUT	PUY	SAY
ILK	LAW	MUG	OVA	PYX	SEA
ILL	LAX	NAB	OWE	RAD	SEE
IMP	LAY	NAG	OWL	RAG	SET
INK	LEA	NAN	OWN	RAJ	SEW
INN	LEE	NAP	OWT	RAM	SEX
ION	LEG	NAY	PAD	RAN	SHE

SHY	THE	WEY	ACES	ANON	AWRY
SIC	THY	WHO	ACHE	ANTE	AXED
SIN	TIC	WHY	ACID	ANTS	AXES
SIP	TIE	WIG	ACME	ANUS	AXIS
SIR	TIN	WIN	ACNE	APED	AXLE
SIT	TIP	WIT	ACRE	APES	AYES
SIX	TIT	WOE	ACTS	APEX	BABE
SKI	TOE	WOK	ADZE	APSE	BABY
SKY	TOG	WOO	AEON	AQUA	BACK
SLY	TOM	WOW	AFAR	ARAB	BADE
SOB	TON	WRY	AGED	ARAN	BAGS
SOD	TOO	YAK	AGES	ARCH	BAIL
SOH	TOP	YAM	AGOG	ARCS	BAIT
SOL	TOR	YAP	AGRA	ARDS	BAKE
SON	TOT	YAW	AGUE	AREA	BALD
SOP	TOW	YEA	AHOY	ARIA	BALE
SOT	TOY	YEN	AIDE	ARID	BALL
SOU	TRY	YES	AIDS	ARKS	BALM
SOW	TUB	YET	AIMS	ARMS	BAND
SOY	TUG	YEW	AIRE	ARMY	BANE
SPA	TWO	YIN	AIRS	ARSE	BANG
SPY	URN	YOB	AIRY	ARTS	BANK
STY	USE	YOD	AJAR	ARTY	BANS
SUE	VAN	YON	AKIN	ASHY	BARB
SUM	VAT	YOU	ALAR	ASPS	BARD
SUN	VEX	ZAG	ALAS	ATOM	BARE
SUP	VIA	ZAP	ALLY	ATOP	BARK
TAB	VIE	ZED	ALMS	AUBE	BARN
TAD	VIM	ZEN	ALOE	AUDE	BARS
TAG	VOW	ZIG	ALPS	AUKS	BASE
TAN	WAD	ZIP	ALSO	AUNT	BASH
TAP	WAG	ZOO	ALTO	AURA	BASK
TAR	WAN	**4**	ALUM	AUTO	BASS
TAT	WAR		AMEN	AVER	BATH
TAW	WAX	ABED	AMID	AVID	BATS
TAX	WAY	ABET	AMOK	AVON	BAWD
TEA	WEB	ABLE	AMOY	AVOW	BAWL
TEE	WED	ABLY	AMPS	AWAY	BAYS
TEG	WEE	ABUT	ANAL	AWED	BEAD
TEN	WET	ACER	ANEW	AWLS	BEAK

BEAM	BLIP	BRAN	CAFE	CHOW	CONE
BEAN	BLOB	BRAS	CAGE	CHUG	CONK
BEAR	BLOC	BRAT	CAKE	CHUM	CONS
BEAT	BLOT	BRAY	CALF	CITE	CONY
BEAU	BLOW	BREW	CALL	CITY	COOK
BECK	BLUE	BRIM	CALM	CLAD	COOL
BEDS	BLUR	BROW	CAME	CLAM	COON
BEEF	BOAR	BUDS	CAMP	CLAN	COOP
BEER	BOAS	BUFF	CAMS	CLAP	COOS
BEES	BOAT	BUGS	CANE	CLAW	COOT
BEET	BOBS	BULB	CANS	CLAY	COPE
BELL	BODE	BULK	CANT	CLEW	COPS
BEND	BODS	BULL	CAPE	CLIP	COPY
BENS	BODY	BUMF	CAPS	CLOD	CORD
BENT	BOER	BUMP	CARD	CLOG	CORE
BERK	BOGS	BUMS	CARE	CLOP	CORK
BEST	BOIL	BUNG	CARP	CLOT	CORM
BETA	BOLD	BUNK	CARS	CLOY	CORN
BETS	BOLT	BUNS	CART	CLUB	COSH
BEVY	BOMB	BUOY	CASE	CLUE	COST
BIAS	BOND	BURK	CASH	COAL	COSY
BIBS	BONE	BURN	CASK	COAT	COTS
BIDE	BONY	BURR	CAST	COAX	COUP
BIDS	BOOB	BURS	CATS	COBS	COVE
BIER	BOOK	BURY	CAVE	COCK	COWL
BIFF	BOOM	BUSH	CAWS	CODE	COWS
BIKE	BOON	BUSK	CEDE	CODS	COZY
BILE	BOOR	BUSS	CELL	COGS	CRAB
BILL	BOOS	BUST	CENT	COIF	CRAG
BIND	BOOT	BUSY	CHAP	COIL	CRAM
BINS	BOPS	BUTE	CHAR	COIN	CRAP
BIRD	BORE	BUTS	CHAT	COIR	CREW
BIRO	BORN	BUTT	CHEF	COKE	CRIB
BITE	BOSH	BUYS	CHER	COLA	CROP
BITS	BOSS	BUZZ	CHEW	COLD	CROW
BLAB	BOUT	BYES	CHIC	COLT	CRUX
BLAG	BOWL	BYRE	CHIN	COMA	CUBA
BLAH	BOWS	BYTE	CHIP	COMB	CUBE
BLED	BOYS	CABS	CHIT	COME	CUBS
BLEW	BRAG	CADS	CHOP	COMO	CUED

CUES	DEAD	DISK	DRUM	ECRU	EYED
CUFF	DEAF	DISS	DUAL	EDAM	FACE
CULL	DEAL	DIVE	DUCK	EDDY	FACT
CULT	DEAN	DOCK	DUCT	EDGE	FADE
CUPS	DEAR	DODO	DUDE	EDGY	FADS
CURB	DEBS	DOER	DUDS	EDIT	FAFF
CURD	DEBT	DOES	DUEL	EELS	FAGS
CURE	DECK	DOFF	DUES	EGGS	FAIL
CURL	DEED	DOGS	DUET	EGOS	FARE
CURS	DEEM	DOLE	DUFF	EIRE	FAKE
CURT	DEEP	DOLL	DUGS	ELAN	FALL
CUSP	DEER	DOLT	DUKE	ELBE	FAME
CUSS	DEFT	DOME	DULL	ELKS	FANG
CUTE	DEFY	DONE	DULY	ELMS	FANS
CUTS	DELL	DONS	DUMB	ELSE	FARE
CYAN	DEMO	DOOM	DUMP	EMIR	FARM
CYST	DENS	DOOR	DUNE	EMIT	FART
CZAR	DENT	DOPE	DUNG	EMUS	FAST
DABS	DENY	DORY	DUNK	ENDS	FATE
DADO	DESK	DOSE	DUNS	ENVY	FATS
DADS	DEWY	DOSH	DUOS	EONS	FAUX
DAFT	DHOW	DOSS	DUPE	EPEE	FAWN
DAGO	DIAL	DOTE	DUSK	EPIC	FAZE
DAIS	DICE	DOTS	DUST	ERAS	FEAR
DALE	DIED	DOUR	DUTY	ERGO	FEAT
DAME	DIET	DOVE	DYED	ERGS	FEED
DAMN	DIGS	DOWN	DYER	ERIE	FEEL
DAMP	DIKE	DOZE	DYES	ERNE	FEES
DAMS	DILL	DOZY	DYKE	ERSE	FEET
DANK	DIME	DRAB	EACH	ESPY	FELL
DARE	DINE	DRAG	EARL	ETCH	FELT
DARN	DINK	DRAM	EARN	EVEN	FEND
DART	DINS	DRAT	EARS	EVER	FENS
DASH	DINT	DRAW	EASE	EVES	FERN
DATA	DIPS	DRAY	EAST	EVIL	FEST
DATE	DIRE	DREW	EASY	EWER	FETE
DAUB	DIRK	DRIP	EATS	EWES	FEUD
DAWN	DIRT	DROP	EBBS	EXAM	FIBS
DAYS	DISC	DRUB	ECGS	EXES	FIGS
DAZE	DISH	DRUG	ECHO	EXIT	FILE

FILL	FOLD	GAIT	GIRD	GRAN	HANK
FILM	FOLK	GALA	GIRL	GREW	HARD
FILO	FOND	GALE	GIRO	GREY	HARE
FIND	FONT	GALS	GIRT	GRID	HARK
FINE	FOOD	GAME	GISH	GRIM	HARL
FINS	FOOL	GAMY	GIST	GRIN	HARM
FIRE	FOOT	GANG	GIVE	GRIP	HARP
FIRM	FOPS	GAOL	GLAD	GRIT	HART
FIRS	FORD	GAPE	GLEE	GROG	HASH
FISH	FORE	GAPS	GLEN	GROW	HASP
FIST	FORK	GARB	GLIB	GRUB	HATE
FITS	FORM	GARD	GLOW	GUFF	HATH
FIVE	FORT	GARY	GLUE	GULF	HATS
FIZZ	FOUL	GASH	GLUM	GULL	HAUL
FLAB	FOUR	GASP	GLUT	GULP	HAVE
FLAG	FOWL	GATE	GNAT	GUMS	HAWK
FLAK	FOXY	GAVE	GNAW	GUNN	HAZE
FLAP	FRAY	GAWD	GNUS	GUNS	HAZY
FLAT	FREE	GAWK	GOAD	GURN	HEAD
FLAW	FRET	GAUP	GOAL	GURU	HEAL
FLAX	FRIT	GAYS	GOAT	GUSH	HEAP
FLAY	FROE	GAZE	GOBS	GUST	HEAR
FLEA	FROG	GEAR	GODS	GUTS	HEAT
FLED	FROM	GEEK	GOER	GUYS	HEBE
FLEE	FUEL	GELD	GOES	GYBE	HECK
FLEW	FULL	GELS	GOLD	GYMS	HEED
FLEX	FUME	GEMS	GOLF	HACK	HEEL
FLIP	FUMY	GENE	GONE	HAFT	HEFT
FLIT	FUND	GINK	GONG	HAGS	HEIR
FLOG	FUNK	GENT	GOOD	HAIL	HELD
FLOP	FURL	GERM	GOOF	HAIR	HELL
FLOW	FURS	GHEE	GOON	HAKE	HELM
FLUE	FURY	GIBE	GOOP	HALE	HEMP
FLUX	FUSE	GIFT	GORE	HALF	HEMS
FOAL	FUSS	GIGS	GORY	HALL	HENS
FOAM	FUZZ	GILD	GOSH	HALO	HERB
FOBS	GAFF	GILL	GOUT	HALT	HERD
FOES	GAGA	GILT	GOWN	HAMS	HERE
FOGS	GAGS	GIMP	GRAB	HAND	HERM
FOIL	GAIN	GINS	GRAM	HANG	HERO

HERS	HOPE	ILLS	JOIN	KIPS	LAWN
HEST	HOPS	INCA	JOKE	KIRK	LAWS
HEWN	HORN	INCH	JOLT	KISS	LAYS
HICK	HOSE	INKS	JOSH	KITE	LAZE
HIDE	HOST	INKY	JOVE	KITH	LAZY
HI-FI	HOUR	INNS	JOWL	KITS	LEAD
HIGH	HOVE	INTO	JOYS	KIWI	LEAF
HIKE	HOWL	IONS	JUDO	KNEE	LEAK
HILL	HUBS	IOTA	JUGS	KNEW	LEAN
HILT	HUES	IRIS	JULY	KNIT	LEAP
HIND	HUFF	IRON	JUMP	KNOB	LEAS
HINT	HUGE	ISLE	JUNE	KNOT	LEEK
HIPS	HUGS	ITCH	JUNK	KNOW	LEER
HIRE	HULA	ITEM	JURY	KOHL	LEES
HISS	HULK	JABS	JUST	LACE	LEFT
HIST	HULL	JACK	JUTE	LACK	LEGS
HITS	HUMP	JADE	KALE	LACY	LEND
HIVE	HUMS	JAGS	KALI	LADE	LENS
HOAR	HUNG	JAIL	KAME	LADS	LENT
HOAX	HUNK	JAMB	KEEL	LADY	LESS
HOBO	HUNT	JAMS	KEEN	LAGS	LEST
HOBS	HURL	JAPE	KEEP	LAID	LETS
HOCK	HURT	JARS	KEGS	LAIN	LEVY
HODS	HUSH	JAWS	KELP	LAIR	LEWD
HOED	HUSK	JAYS	KENS	LAKE	LIAR
HOER	HUSS	JAZZ	KEPI	LAMB	LICE
HOES	HUTS	JEEP	KEPT	LAME	LICK
HOGS	HYMN	JEER	KERB	LAMP	LIDO
HOLD	IAMB	JELL	KERN	LAND	LIDS
HOLE	IBEX	JERK	KEYS	LANE	LIED
HOLM	IBIS	JEST	KICK	LANK	LIEF
HOLT	ICED	JETS	KIDS	LAPS	LIEN
HOLY	ICES	JIBE	KILL	LARD	LIEU
HOME	ICON	JIBS	KILN	LARK	LIFE
HONK	IDEA	JIGS	KILO	LASH	LIFT
HOOD	IDES	JILT	KILT	LASS	LIKE
HOOF	IDLE	JINX	KIND	LAST	LILO
HOOK	IDLY	JIVE	KINE	LATE	LILT
HOOP	IDOL	JOBS	KING	LAUD	LILY
HOOT	ILEX	JOGS	KINK	LAVA	LIMB

LIME	LOSS	MARK	MINE	MUGS	NICE
LIMP	LOST	MARL	MINI	MULE	NICK
LINE	LOTS	MARS	MINK	MULL	NIDE
LING	LOUD	MART	MINT	MURK	NIFF
LINK	LOUR	MASH	MINX	MUSE	NIGH
LINT	LOUT	MASK	MIRE	MUSH	NINE
LION	LOVE	MASS	MIRY	MUSK	NIPS
LIPS	LOWS	MAST	MISO	MUSS	NISI
LIRA	LUCK	MATE	MISS	MUST	NITS
LIRE	LUDO	MATS	MIST	MUTE	NOBS
LISP	LUFF	MATT	MITE	MUTT	NODE
LIST	LUGS	MAUL	MITT	MYTH	NODS
LIVE	LULL	MAZE	MOAN	NAGS	NOEL
LOAD	LUMP	MAZY	MOAT	NAIL	NONE
LOAF	LUNG	MEAD	MOBS	NAME	NOOK
LOAM	LURE	MEAL	MOCK	NANA	NOON
LOAN	LURK	MEAN	MODE	NAPE	NOSE
LOBE	LUSH	MEAT	MOKE	NAPS	NOSH
LOBS	LUST	MEEK	MOLE	NARD	NOSY
LOCH	LUTE	MEET	MOLL	NARK	NOTE
LOCK	LYNX	MELD	MOLY	NAVE	NOUN
LOCO	LYRE	MELT	MONK	NAVY	NOUS
LODE	MACE	MEMO	MOOD	NAYS	NOVA
LOFT	MADE	MEND	MOON	NEAP	NOWT
LOGO	MAGI	MENU	MOOR	NEAR	NUBS
LOGS	MAID	MERE	MOOS	NEAT	NUDE
LOIN	MAIL	MESH	MOOT	NECK	NULL
LOLL	MAIM	MESS	MOPE	NEED	NUMB
LONE	MAIN	METE	MOPS	NEEM	NUNS
LONG	MAKE	MEWS	MORN	NEEP	NUTS
LOOK	MALE	MICA	MORT	NEON	OAFS
LOOM	MALL	MICE	MOSS	NERD	OAKS
LOON	MALM	MIDI	MOST	NESS	OARS
LOOP	MALT	MIEN	MOTE	NEST	OAST
LOOT	MAMA	MILD	MOTH	NETS	OATH
LOPE	MANE	MILE	MOVE	NETT	OATS
LORD	MANX	MILK	MOWN	NEWS	OBEY
LORE	MANY	MILL	MUCH	NEWT	OBOE
LORN	MAPS	MILT	MUCK	NEXT	ODDS
LOSE	MARE	MIME	MUFF	NIBS	ODES

OGEE	PACK	PEEL	PLOY	PROW	RAIL
OGLE	PACT	PEEP	PLUG	PUBS	RAIN
OGRE	PACY	PEER	PLUM	PUCE	RAKE
OILS	PADS	PEGS	PLUS	PUCK	RAMP
OILY	PAGE	PELT	PODS	PUFF	RAMS
OINK	PAID	PENS	POEM	PUGS	RAND
OKRA	PAIL	PERK	POET	PULE	RANG
OMEN	PAIN	PERT	POGO	PULL	RANK
OMIT	PAIR	PESO	POKE	PULP	RANT
ONCE	PALE	PEST	POKY	PUMA	RAPE
ONES	PALL	PETS	POLE	PUMP	RAPS
ONLY	PALM	PEWS	POLL	PUNK	RAPT
ONTO	PALP	PICA	POLO	PUNS	RARE
ONUS	PANE	PICK	POME	PUNT	RASH
ONYX	PANG	PIED	POND	PUNY	RASP
OOZE	PANS	PIER	PONE	PUPA	RATA
OOZY	PANT	PIGS	PONG	PUPS	RATE
OPAL	PAPA	PIKA	PONY	PURE	RATS
OPEN	PAPS	PIKE	POOF	PURL	RAVE
OPUS	PARE	PILE	POOL	PURR	RAYS
ORAL	PARK	PILL	POOP	PUSH	RAZE
ORBS	PARR	PIMP	POOR	PUSS	READ
ORES	PART	PINE	POPE	PUTT	REAL
ORGY	PASS	PING	POPS	PYRE	REAM
ORLE	PAST	PINK	PORE	QUAD	REAP
ORYX	PATE	PINS	PORK	QUAY	REAR
OURS	PATH	PINT	PORT	QUID	RECK
OUST	PATS	PINY	POSE	QUIN	REDO
OUZO	PAVE	PIPE	POSH	QUIP	REDS
OVAL	PAWL	PIPS	POST	QUIT	REED
OVEN	PAWN	PISS	POSY	QUIZ	REEF
OVER	PAWS	PITH	POTS	QUOD	REEK
OVUM	PEAK	PITS	POUR	RACE	REEL
OWED	PEAL	PITY	POUT	RACK	REIN
OWES	PEAN	PLAN	PRAM	RACY	RELY
OWLS	PEAR	PLAY	PRAY	RAFT	REND
OXEN	PEAS	PLEA	PREY	RAGA	RENT
OYEZ	PEAT	PLOD	PRIG	RAGE	REST
PACA	PECK	PLOP	PROD	RAGS	RHEA
PACE	PEEK	PLOT	PROP	RAID	RIBS

RICE	ROPY	SAGS	SEEN	SIFT	SLIT
RICH	ROSE	SAIL	SEEP	SIGH	SLOB
RICK	ROSY	SAKE	SEER	SIGN	SLOE
RIDE	ROTA	SAKI	SEES	SIKH	SLOG
RIFE	ROTE	SALE	SEGO	SILK	SLOP
RIFF	ROTS	SALT	SELF	SILL	SLOT
RIFT	ROUE	SAME	SELL	SILO	SLOW
RIGS	ROUP	SAMP	SEME	SILT	SLUB
RILE	ROUT	SAND	SEMI	SIMA	SLUG
RILL	ROUX	SANE	SEND	SINE	SLUM
RIME	ROVE	SANG	SENT	SING	SLUR
RIMS	ROWS	SANK	SERA	SINH	SLUT
RIND	RUBE	SAPS	SERE	SINK	SMOG
RING	RUBS	SARD	SERF	SINS	SMUG
RINK	RUBY	SARI	SETS	SIPS	SMUT
RIOT	RUCK	SASH	SEWN	SIRE	SNAG
RIPE	RUDE	SATE	SEXT	SIRS	SNAP
RIPS	RUDD	SAVE	SEXY	SITE	SNIG
RISE	RUED	SAWN	SHAD	SIZE	SNIP
RISK	RUFF	SAWS	SHAG	SKEG	SNOB
RITE	RUGS	SAYS	SHAH	SKEP	SNOG
RIVE	RUIN	SCAB	SHAM	SKEW	SNOT
ROAD	RULE	SCAD	SHED	SKID	SNOW
ROAM	RUMP	SCAM	SHEW	SKIM	SNUB
ROAN	RUNE	SCAN	SHIM	SKIN	SNUG
ROAR	RUNG	SCAR	SHIN	SKIP	SOAK
ROBE	RUNS	SCAT	SHIP	SKIS	SOAP
ROCK	RUNT	SCOT	SHIT	SKIT	SOAR
RODE	RUSA	SCUD	SHOD	SKUA	SOBS
RODS	RUSE	SCUM	SHOE	SLAB	SOCK
ROES	RUSH	SCUT	SHOO	SLAG	SODA
ROLE	RUSK	SEAL	SHOP	SLAM	SODS
ROLL	RUST	SEAM	SHOT	SLAP	SOFA
ROMP	RUTS	SEAR	SHOW	SLAT	SOFT
ROOD	RYOT	SEAS	SHUN	SLAY	SOIL
ROOF	SACK	SEAT	SHUT	SLED	SOLD
ROOK	SAFE	SECT	SIAL	SLEW	SOLE
ROOM	SAGA	SEED	SICE	SLID	SOLO
ROOT	SAGE	SEEK	SICK	SLIM	SOMA
ROPE	SAGO	SEEM	SIDE	SLIP	SOME

SONE	STEW	TACT	TEST	TOFT	TROD
SONG	STIR	TAGS	TEXT	TOGA	TROT
SONS	STOA	TAHR	THAN	TOGS	TROY
SOON	STOP	TAIL	THAT	TOIL	TRUE
SOOT	STOW	TAKE	THAW	TOLD	TRUG
SOPS	STUB	TALC	THEE	TOLL	TSAR
SORA	STUD	TALE	THEM	TOMB	TUBA
SORB	STUM	TALK	THEN	TOME	TUBE
SORE	STUN	TALL	THEY	TONE	TUBS
SORT	STYE	TAME	THIN	TONS	TUCK
SOTS	SUCH	TAMP	THIS	TOOK	TUFA
SOUL	SUCK	TANG	THOU	TOOL	TUFF
SOUP	SUDS	TANH	THUD	TOOT	TUFT
SOUR	SUED	TANK	THUG	TOPE	TUGS
SOWN	SUER	TANS	THUS	TOPS	TUNA
SOWS	SUET	TAPE	TICK	TORC	TUNE
SOYA	SUIT	TAPS	TICS	TORE	TURD
SPAM	SULK	TARE	TIDE	TORN	TURF
SPAN	SUMP	TARN	TIDY	TORR	TURN
SPAR	SUMS	TARO	TIED	TORS	TUSH
SPAS	SUNG	TARS	TIER	TORT	TUSK
SPAT	SUNK	TART	TIES	TOSA	TUTU
SPAY	SUNS	TASK	TIFF	TOSH	TWAT
SPED	SUPS	TAUT	TILE	TOSS	TWEE
SPEW	SURE	TAXI	TILL	TOTE	TWIG
SPIN	SURF	TEAK	TILT	TOTS	TWIN
SPIT	SWAB	TEAL	TIME	TOUR	TWIT
SPIV	SWAG	TEAM	TINE	TOUT	TWOS
SPOT	SWAM	TEAR	TING	TOWN	TYKE
SPRY	SWAN	TEAS	TINS	TOWS	TYPE
SPUD	SWAP	TEAT	TINT	TOYS	TYRE
SPUN	SWAT	TEED	TINY	TRAM	TYRO
SPUR	SWAY	TEES	TIPS	TRAP	TZAR
STAB	SWIG	TEFF	TIRE	TRAY	UDAL
STAG	SWIM	TELL	TITI	TREE	UGLY
STAR	SWOP	TEND	TITS	TREK	ULNA
STAY	SWOT	TENS	TOAD	TREY	UNDO
STEM	TABS	TENT	TOED	TRIM	UNIT
STEP	TACK	TERM	TOES	TRIO	UNTO
STET	TACO	TERN	TOFF	TRIP	UPON

URDU	VIOL	WEAN	WINS	YAWL	**5**
UREA	VISA	WEAR	WIPE	YAWN	
URGE	VOID	WEBS	WIRE	YAWS	ABACK
URIC	VOLE	WEED	WIRY	YEAN	ABAFT
URNS	VOLT	WEEK	WISE	YEAR	ABASE
URUS	VOTE	WEEP	WISH	YEAS	ABASH
USED	VOWS	WEFT	WISP	YELL	ABATE
USER	WADE	WEIR	WITH	YELP	ABBEY
USES	WADI	WELD	WITS	YENS	ABBOT
UVEA	WADS	WELL	WOAD	YETI	ABEAM
VAIN	WAFT	WELS	WOES	YEWS	ABHOR
VALE	WAGE	WELT	WOKE	YOBS	ABIDE
VAMP	WAGS	WEND	WOKS	YOGA	ABODE
VANE	WAIF	WENT	WOLD	YOGI	ABORT
VANS	WAIL	WEPT	WOLF	YOKE	ABOUT
VARY	WAIN	WEST	WOMB	YOLK	ABOVE
VASE	WAIT	WETA	WONT	YOMP	ABSTR
VAST	WAKE	WETS	WOOD	YORE	ABUSE
VATS	WALK	WHAT	WOOF	YOUR	ABYSM
VEAL	WALL	WHEN	WOOL	YOWL	ABYSS
VEER	WAND	WHET	WORD	YO-YO	ACORN
VEIL	WANE	WHEY	WORE	YUAN	ACRID
VEIN	WANK	WHIG	WORK	YUCK	ACTOR
VELD	WANT	WHIM	WORM	YULE	ACUTE
VEND	WARD	WHIP	WOVE	ZANY	ADAGE
VENT	WARM	WHIT	WORT	ZEAL	ADAPT
VERB	WARP	WHOA	WRAP	ZEBU	ADDER
VERT	WARS	WHOM	WREN	ZEDS	ADDLE
VEST	WART	WHYS	WRIT	ZEIN	ADDNL
VETO	WARY	WICK	WROT	ZERO	ADEPT
VIAL	WASH	WIDE	WYND	ZEST	ADIEU
VICE	WASP	WIFE	XMAS	ZINC	ADIOS
VIED	WATT	WIGS	X-RAY	ZIPS	ADMAN
VIES	WAUL	WILD	YAKS	ZITS	ADMIN
VIEW	WAVE	WILL	YAMS	ZIZZ	ADMIT
VILE	WAVY	WILT	YANG	ZONE	ADMIX
VILL	WAXY	WIMP	YANK	ZOOM	ADOBE
VINA	WAYS	WIND	YAPS	ZOOS	ADOPT
VINE	WEAK	WING	YARD	ZOUK	ADORE
VINT	WEAL	WINK	YARN	ZULU	ADORN

ADULT	ALOOF	APORT	AURAR	BASSO	BEVEL
AEGIS	ALOUD	APPLE	AUXIN	BASTE	BEZEL
AERIE	ALTAR	APPLY	AVAIL	BATCH	BHANG
AFFIX	ALTER	APRIL	AVAST	BATHE	BIBLE
AFIRE	AMAIN	APRON	AVERT	BATIK	BIDDY
AFOOT	AMASS	ARENA	AVIAN	BATON	BIDET
AFTER	AMAZE	ARGON	AVOID	BATTY	BIGHT
AGAIN	AMBER	ARGOT	AWAIT	BAWDY	BIGOT
AGAPE	AMBLE	ARGUE	AWAKE	BAYOU	BILGE
AGATE	AMEND	ARISE	AWARD	BEACH	BILLY
AGAVE	AMISS	ARITH	AWARE	BEANO	BINGE
AGENT	AMITY	AROMA	AWASH	BEARD	BINGO
AGILE	AMONG	ARRAS	AWFUL	BEAST	BIPED
AGLOW	AMOUR	ARRAY	AXIAL	BEDEW	BIRCH
AGONY	AMPLE	ARROW	AXIOM	BEECH	BIRTH
AGORA	AMPUL	ARSON	AZTEC	BEEFY	BISON
AGREE	AMUCK	ARYAN	AZURE	BEFIT	BITCH
AHEAD	AMUSE	ASCOT	BABEL	BEFOG	BLACK
AISLE	ANENT	ASHEN	BACON	BEGET	BLADE
ALARM	ANGEL	ASIAN	BADGE	BEGIN	BLAIN
ALBUM	ANGER	ASIDE	BAGEL	BEGUM	BLAME
ALDER	ANGLE	ASKEW	BAGGY	BEIGE	BLAND
ALERT	ANGLO	ASPEN	BAIRN	BEING	BLANK
ALIAS	ANGRY	ASPIC	BAIZA	BELAY	BLARE
ALIBI	ANGST	ASSAY	BAIZE	BELCH	BLASÉ
ALIEN	ANION	ASSET	BALKY	BELIE	BLAST
ALIGN	ANISE	ASTER	BALMY	BELLE	BLAZE
ALIKE	ANKLE	ASTIR	BALSA	BELLS	BLEAK
ALIVE	ANNEX	ATILT	BANAL	BELLY	BLEAR
ALKYD	ANNOY	ATLAS	BANDY	BELOW	BLEAT
ALLAH	ANNUL	ATOLL	BANJO	BENCH	BLEED
ALLAY	ANODE	ATONE	BANNS	BENNY	BLEND
ALLEY	ANTIC	ATTAR	BANTU	BERET	BLESS
ALLOT	ANVIL	ATTIC	BARGE	BERRY	BLIMP
ALLOW	AORTA	AUDIO	BARON	BERTH	BLIND
ALLOY	APACE	AUDIT	BASAL	BERYL	BLINK
ALOFT	APART	AUGER	BASIC	BESET	BLISS
ALOHA	APEAK	AUGHT	BASIL	BESOM	BLITZ
ALONE	APHID	AUGUR	BASIN	BESOT	BLOAT
ALONG	APHIS	AURAL	BASIS	BETEL	BLOCK

BLOND	BOXER	BRUTE	CANAL	CHARY	CHURN
BLOOD	BRACE	BUDDY	CANDY	CHASE	CHUTE
BLOOM	BRACT	BUDGE	CANNA	CHASM	CIDER
BLOWY	BRAID	BUGGY	CANNY	CHEAP	CIGAR
BLUES	BRAIN	BUGLE	CANOE	CHEAT	CINCH
BLUET	BRAKE	BUILD	CANON	CHECK	CIRCA
BLUFF	BRAND	BULGE	CANTO	CHEEK	CIVET
BLUNT	BRASH	BULKY	CAPER	CHEEP	CIVIC
BLURB	BRASS	BULLY	CAPON	CHEER	CIVIL
BLURT	BRAVE	BUNCH	CARAT	CHELA	CLACK
BLUSH	BRAVO	BUNCO	CARET	CHERT	CLAIM
BOARD	BRAWL	BUNNY	CARGO	CHESS	CLAMP
BOAST	BRAWN	BURGH	CARNY	CHEST	CLANG
BOBBY	BRAZE	BURLY	CAROL	CHEWY	CLANK
BOGEY	BREAD	BURRO	CAROM	CHIAO	CLASH
BOGUS	BREAK	BURST	CARRY	CHICK	CLASP
BOLUS	BREAM	BUSBY	CARVE	CHIDE	CLASS
BONER	BREED	BUTTE	CASTE	CHIEF	CLEAN
BONGO	BRIAR	BUTUT	CATCH	CHILD	CLEAR
BONNY	BRIBE	BUXOM	CATER	CHILL	CLEAT
BONUS	BRICK	BYLAW	CATTY	CHIME	CLEFT
BONZE	BRIDE	BYWAY	CAULK	CHIMP	CLERK
BOOBY	BRIEF	CABAL	CAUSE	CHINA	CLICK
BOOST	BRIER	CABBY	CAVIL	CHINE	CLIFF
BOOTH	BRINE	CABIN	CEASE	CHINK	CLIMB
BOOTY	BRING	CABLE	CECUM	CHINO	CLIME
BOOZE	BRINK	CACAO	CEDAR	CHIRP	CLING
BORAX	BRISK	CACHE	CELLO	CHIVE	CLINK
BORNE	BROAD	CADDY	CHAFE	CHOCK	CLOAK
BORON	BROIL	CADET	CHAFF	CHOIR	CLOCK
BOSKY	BROKE	CADGE	CHAIN	CHOKE	CLOSE
BOSOM	BROOD	CADRE	CHAIR	CHOMP	CLOTH
BOSUN	BROOK	CAGEY	CHALK	CHOPS	CLOUD
BOTCH	BROOM	CAIRN	CHAMP	CHORD	CLOUT
BOUGH	BROTH	CAJUN	CHANT	CHORE	CLOVE
BOULE	BROWN	CALLA	CHAOS	CHOSE	CLOWN
BOUND	BRUIN	CALVE	CHAPS	CHUCK	CLUCK
BOURN	BRUIT	CALYX	CHARD	CHUMP	CLUMP
BOWEL	BRUNT	CAMEL	CHARM	CHUNK	CLUNG
BOWER	BRUSH	CAMEO	CHART	CHURL	COACH

COAST	CRAPE	CRUSE	DEFOG	DOGGY	DROOP
COBRA	CRAPS	CRUSH	DEGAS	DOGIE	DROSS
COCKY	CRASH	CRUST	DEICE	DOGMA	DROVE
COCOA	CRASS	CRYPT	DEIFY	DOILY	DROWN
CODEX	CRATE	CRYST	DEIGN	DOLLY	DRUID
COLIC	CRAVE	CUBAN	DEISM	DOLOR	DRUNK
COLON	CRAWL	CUBIC	DEITY	DONOR	DRUPE
COMBO	CRAZE	CUBIT	DELAY	DONUT	DRYAD
COMER	CRAZY	CUPID	DELFT	DOPEY	DRYER
COMET	CREAK	CURIA	DELTA	DOUBT	DUCAL
COMFY	CREAM	CURIO	DELVE	DOUGH	DUCAT
COMIC	CREDO	CURRY	DEMON	DOUSE	DUCHY
COMMA	CREED	CURSE	DEMUR	DOWDY	DUMMY
CONCH	CREEK	CURVE	DENIM	DOWEL	DUMPS
CONEY	CREEL	CYCLE	DENSE	DOWER	DUMPY
CONGA	CREEP	CYNIC	DEPOT	DOWNY	DUNCE
CONIC	CREME	CZECH	DEPTH	DOWRY	DUPLE
COPRA	CREPE	DACHA	DERBY	DOWSE	DUSKY
COPSE	CRESC	DADDY	DERIV	DOYEN	DUTCH
CORAL	CRESS	DAFFY	DETER	DOZEN	DWARF
CORNY	CREST	DAILY	DEUCE	DRAFT	DWELL
CORPS	CRICK	DAIRY	DEVIL	DRAIN	DYING
COUCH	CRIER	DAISY	DIARY	DRAKE	EAGER
COUGH	CRIME	DALLY	DIGIT	DRAMA	EAGLE
COULD	CRIMP	DANCE	DINAR	DRANK	EARED
COUNT	CRISP	DANDY	DINER	DRAPE	EARLY
COUPE	CROAK	DATED	DINGO	DRAWL	EARTH
COURT	CROCK	DATUM	DINGY	DREAD	EASEL
COVEN	CRONE	DAUNT	DINKY	DREAM	EAVES
COVER	CRONY	DAVIT	DIODE	DREAR	EBONY
COVET	CROOK	DEATH	DIRGE	DRESS	ECLAT
COVEY	CROON	DEBAR	DIRTY	DRIER	EDEMA
COWER	CROSS	DEBIT	DISCO	DRIFT	EDICT
COYPU	CROUP	DEBUT	DITCH	DRILL	EDUCE
COZEN	CROWD	DECAL	DITTO	DRILY	EERIE
CRACK	CROWN	DECAY	DITTY	DRINK	EGRET
CRAFT	CRUDE	DECOR	DIVAN	DRIVE	EIDER
CRAMP	CRUEL	DECOY	DIVOT	DROLL	EIGHT
CRANE	CRUET	DECRY	DIZZY	DRONE	EJECT
CRANK	CRUMB	DEFER	DODGE	DROOL	ELAND

ELATE	ESSAY	FEAST	FLANK	FORGO	FUZZY
ELBOW	ESTER	FEAZE	FLARE	FORTE	GABBY
ELDER	ETHER	FEIGN	FLASH	FORTH	GABLE
ELECT	ETHOS	FEINT	FLASK	FORTY	GAFFE
ELEGY	ETHYL	FELON	FLECK	FORUM	GAILY
ELIDE	ETUDE	FEMUR	FLEER	FOUND	GAMIN
ELITE	EVADE	FENCE	FLEET	FOUNT	GAMUT
ELOPE	EVENT	FERAL	FLESH	FOXED	GAUDY
ELUDE	EVERY	FERRY	FLICK	FOYER	GAUGE
ELVER	EVICT	FETAL	FLIED	FRAIL	GAUNT
ELVES	EVOKE	FETCH	FLIER	FRAME	GAUSS
EMBED	EXACT	FETID	FLING	FRANC	GAUZE
EMBER	EXALT	FEVER	FLINT	FRANK	GAVEL
EMCEE	EXCEL	FEWER	FLIRT	FRAUD	GAWKY
EMEND	EXERT	FIBRE	FLOAT	FREAK	GEESE
EMERY	EXILE	FICHE	FLOCK	FRESH	GELID
EMOTE	EXIST	FICHU	FLOOD	FRIAR	GENIE
EMPTY	EXPEL	FIELD	FLOOR	FRILL	GENRE
ENACT	EXTOL	FIEND	FLORA	FRISK	GENUS
ENDOW	EXTRA	FIERY	FLOSS	FRIZZ	GEODE
ENDUE	EXUDE	FIFTH	FLOUR	FROCK	GETUP
ENEMA	EXULT	FIFTY	FLOUT	FROND	GHOST
ENEMY	EXURB	FIGHT	FLOWN	FRONT	GHOUL
ENJOY	EYRIE	FILAR	FLUFF	FROST	GIANT
ENNUI	EYRIR	FILCH	FLUID	FROTH	GIDDY
ENSUE	FABLE	FILLY	FLUKE	FROWN	GIMPY
ENTER	FACET	FILTH	FLUME	FROZE	GIPSY
ENTRY	FAGOT	FINAL	FLUNG	FRUIT	GIRTH
ENVOI	FAINT	FINCH	FLUNK	FRYER	GIVEN
ENVOY	FAIRY	FINIS	FLUSH	FUDGE	GIZMO
EPOCH	FAITH	FINNY	FLUTE	FUGUE	GLADE
EPOXY	FAKIR	FIRST	FLYBY	FULLY	GLAND
EQUAL	FALSE	FIRTH	FLYER	FUNKY	GLANS
EQUIP	FANCY	FISHY	FOCUS	FUNNY	GLARE
ERASE	FARCE	FIXED	FOIST	FUROR	GLASS
ERECT	FATAL	FJORD	FOLIO	FURRY	GLAZE
ERGOT	FATED	FLAIL	FOLLY	FURZE	GLEAM
ERODE	FATTY	FLAIR	FORAY	FUSEE	GLEAN
ERROR	FAULT	FLAKE	FORCE	FUSSY	GLEBE
ERUPT	FAUNA	FLAME	FORGE	FUSTY	GLIDE

GLINT	GREEK	GUSTO	HERTZ	ICTUS	IVORY
GLOAT	GREEN	GUTTY	HINDI	IDEAL	JABOT
GLOBE	GREET	GUYOT	HINGE	IDIOM	JADED
GLOOM	GRIEF	GYPSY	HITCH	IDIOT	JALAP
GLORY	GRILL	HABIT	HIVES	IDYLL	JAPAN
GLOSS	GRIME	HADES	HOARD	IGLOO	JAUNT
GLOVE	GRIND	HAIKU	HOARY	ILEUM	JAZZY
GLOZE	GRIPE	HAIRY	HOBBY	IMAGE	JEANS
GNARL	GRIST	HALER	HOGAN	IMAGO	JELLY
GNASH	GRITS	HALLO	HOIST	IMBED	JENNY
GNOME	GROAN	HALVE	HOKUM	IMBUE	JETTY
GODLY	GROAT	HANDY	HOLLO	IMPEL	JEWEL
GONAD	GROIN	HAPLY	HOLLY	IMPER	JEWRY
GONER	GROOM	HAPPY	HOMER	IMPLY	JIFFY
GOODY	GROPE	HARDY	HOMEY	INANE	JIHAD
GOFFY	GROSS	HAREM	HONEY	INCOG	JIMMY
GOOSE	GROSZ	HARPY	HOOEY	INCUR	JOINT
GORGE	GROUP	HARRY	HORDE	INCUS	JOIST
GORSE	GROUT	HARSH	HORSE	INDEF	JOKER
GOUDA	GROVE	HASTE	HOTEL	INDEX	JOLLY
GOUGE	GROWL	HATCH	HOUND	INDUE	JOUST
GOURD	GRUEL	HAUNT	HOUSE	INEPT	JUDGE
GRACE	GRUFF	HAVEN	HOVEL	INERT	JUICE
GRADE	GRUNT	HAVOC	HOVER	INFER	JUICY
GRAFT	GUANO	HAZEL	HUMAN	INGLE	JULEP
GRAIL	GUARD	HEADY	HUMID	INGOT	JUMBO
GRAIN	GUAVA	HEART	HUMUS	INLAY	JUMPY
GRAND	GUESS	HEATH	HUNCH	INLET	JUNCO
GRANT	GUEST	HEAVE	HURON	INNER	JUNTA
GRAPE	GUIDE	HEAVY	HURRY	INPUT	JUNTO
GRAPH	GUILD	HEDGE	HUSKY	INSET	JUROR
GRASP	GUILE	HEFTY	HUSSY	INTER	KABOB
GRASS	GUILT	HEIST	HUTCH	INURE	KAPOK
GRATE	GUISE	HELIX	HYDRA	INURN	KAPUT
GRAVE	GULCH	HELLO	HYDRO	IRATE	KARAT
GRAVY	GULLY	HELOT	HYENA	IRISH	KARMA
GRAZE	GUMBO	HELVE	HYING	IRONY	KARST
GREAT	GUNNY	HENCE	HYMEN	ISLAM	KAYAK
GREBE	GUPPY	HENNA	ICHOR	ISLET	KAZOO
GREED	GUSHY	HERON	ICING	ISSUE	KEBAB

KEDGE	LARCH	LINEN	LUSTY	MAYOR	MORAL
KETCH	LARGE	LINER	LYING	MECCA	MORAY
KHAKI	LARGO	LINGO	LYMPH	MEDAL	MOREL
KIOSK	LARVA	LINKS	LYNCH	MEDIA	MORES
KIOWA	LASER	LISLE	LYRIC	MEDIC	MORON
KITTY	LASSO	LISTS	MACAW	MELEE	MOSEY
KNACK	LATCH	LITHE	MACRO	MELON	MOTEL
KNAVE	LATEX	LIVEN	MADAM	MERCY	MOTET
KNEAD	LATHE	LITRE	MAFIA	MERGE	MOTIF
KNEEL	LATIN	LIVER	MAGIC	MERIT	MOTOR
KNELL	LAUGH	LIVES	MAGMA	MERRY	MOTTO
KNIFE	LAYER	LIVID	MAIZE	METAL	MOULD
KNISH	LAZAR	LLAMA	MAJOR	METRE	MOULT
KNOCK	LEACH	LLANO	MALAY	METRO	MOUND
KNOLL	LEARN	LOATH	MAMBO	MIAMI	MOUNT
KNOUT	LEASE	LOBBY	MANES	MICRO	MOURN
KNURL	LEASH	LOCAL	MANGE	MIDDY	MOUSE
KOALA	LEAST	LOCUS	MANGO	MIDGE	MOUSY
KOOKY	LEAVE	LODGE	MANIA	MIDST	MOUTH
KORAN	LEDGE	LOESS	MANIC	MIGHT	MOVER
KRAAL	LEECH	LOFTY	MANLY	MILCH	MOVIE
KRAUT	LEERY	LOGIC	MANNA	MIMIC	MUCUS
KRONA	LEGAL	LONER	MANOR	MINCE	MUFTI
KRONE	LEGGY	LOONY	MANSE	MINIM	MUGGY
KUDOS	LEMON	LOOSE	MANTA	MINOR	MULCH
KULAK	LEMUR	LORRY	MANUF	MINUS	MULCT
KURUS	LEONE	LOTUS	MAORI	MIRTH	MUMMY
LABEL	LEPER	LOUSE	MAPLE	MISER	MUMPS
LADEN	LEVEE	LOUSY	MARCH	MISTY	MUNCH
LADLE	LEVEL	LOWER	MARRY	MITRE	MURAL
LAGER	LEVER	LOWLY	MARSH	MODEL	MUSHY
LAIRD	LIBEL	LOYAL	MASER	MOGUL	MUSIC
LAITY	LICIT	LUCID	MASON	MOIRE	MUSTY
LAMIA	LIEGE	LUCKY	MATCH	MOIST	MYRRH
LANAI	LIFER	LUCRE	MATZO	MOLAR	NABOB
LANCE	LIGHT	LUNAR	MAUVE	MONEY	NACRE
LANKY	LIKEN	LUNCH	MAVEN	MONGO	NADIR
LAPEL	LILAC	LUNGE	MAVIS	MONTH	NAIAD
LAPIN	LIMBO	LURCH	MAXIM	MOODY	NAIVE
LAPSE	LIMIT	LURID	MAYBE	MOOSE	NAKED

NARIS	NOTCH	OUGHT	PASTA	PIECE	PLUSH
NASAL	NOTED	OUNCE	PASTE	PIETY	PLUTO
NASTY	NOVEL	OUTDO	PASTY	PIGMY	POACH
NATAL	NUDGE	OUTER	PATCH	PIKER	POESY
NATTY	NUMIS	OUTGO	PATEN	PILAF	POILU
NAVAL	NURSE	OUTRE	PATIO	PILES	POINT
NAVEL	NUTTY	OVARY	PATSY	PILOT	POISE
NEATH	NYLON	OVATE	PATTY	PINCH	POKER
NEEDS	NYMPH	OVERT	PAUSE	PINON	POLAR
NEEDY	OAKUM	OVOID	PEACE	PINTO	POLIO
NEGRO	OASIS	OVULE	PEACH	PINUP	POLIT
NEGUS	OBESE	OWLET	PEARL	PIOUS	POLKA
NEIGH	OCCUR	OXBOW	PECAN	PIQUE	POLYP
NERVE	OCEAN	OXIDE	PEDAL	PITCH	POOCH
NERVY	OCHRE	OZONE	PEEVE	PITHY	POPPY
NEVER	OCTET	PACER	PIKOE	PITON	PORCH
NEVUS	ODIUM	PADDY	PENAL	PIVOT	POSER
NEWEL	OFFAL	PADRE	PENCE	PIXIE	POSIT
NEWLY	OFFER	PAEAN	PENIS	PIZZA	POSSE
NEWSY	OFTEN	PAGAN	PENNY	PLACE	POUCH
NEXUS	OLDEN	PAINT	PEONY	PLAID	POULT
NICHE	OLDIE	PAISA	PERCH	PLAIN	POUND
NIECE	OLIVE	PALMY	PERIL	PLAIT	POWER
NIFTY	OMAHA	PALSY	PESKY	PLANE	PRANK
NIGHT	ONION	PAMPA	PETAL	PLANK	PRATE
NINNY	ONSET	PANDA	PETER	PLANT	PRAWN
NIPPY	OPERA	PANEL	PETTY	PLASH	PREEN
NISEI	OPINE	PANIC	PEWEE	PLATE	PRESS
NITRE	OPIUM	PANSY	PHAGE	PLATY	PRICE
NITRO	OPTIC	PANTS	PHARM	PLAYA	PRICK
NOBLE	ORATE	PAPAL	PHASE	PLAZA	PRIDE
NODDY	ORBIT	PAPAW	PHIAL	PLEAD	PRIME
NOISE	ORDER	PAPER	PHLOX	PLEAT	PRIMP
NOISY	ORGAN	PARCH	PHONE	PLEBE	PRINK
NOMAD	ORIEL	PARKA	PHONO	PLEBS	PRINT
NONCE	ORRIS	PARRY	PHONY	PLUCK	PRIOR
NONES	OSAGE	PARSE	PHOTO	PLUMB	PRISM
NOOSE	OSIER	PARTY	PIANO	PLUME	PRIVY
NORSE	OTHER	PASHA	PICKY	PLUMP	PRIZE
NORTH	OTTER	PASSE	PICOT	PLUNK	PROBE

PROEM	QUASI	RAZOR	RIPEN	SALVE	SCRIM
PRONE	QUEAN	REACH	RISER	SALVO	SCRIP
PRONG	QUEEN	REACT	RIVAL	SANIT	SCROD
PROOF	QUEER	READY	RIVER	SAPPY	SCRUB
PROSE	QUELL	REALM	RIVET	SASSY	SCUBA
PROSY	QUERY	REBEL	RIYAL	SATAN	SCUFF
PROUD	QUEST	REBUS	ROACH	SATIN	SCULL
PROVE	QUEUE	REBUT	ROAST	SATYR	SCURF
PROWL	QUICK	RECAP	ROBIN	SAUCE	SEAMY
PROXY	QUIET	RECIP	ROBOT	SAUCY	SEATO
PRUDE	QUILL	RECTO	RODEO	SAUNA	SEDAN
PRUNE	QUILT	RECUR	ROGER	SAUTE	SEDGE
PSALM	QUINT	REEVE	ROGUE	SAVVY	SEEDY
PSEUD	QUIRE	REFER	ROMAN	SCALD	SEINE
PSYCH	QUIRK	REGAL	ROOST	SCALE	SEISM
PUBES	QUIRT	REIGN	ROSIN	SCALP	SEIZE
PUBIC	QUITE	RELAX	ROTOR	SCAMP	SEMEN
PUBIS	QUITS	RELAY	ROUGE	SCAND	SENNA
PUDGY	QUOIT	RELIC	ROUGH	SCANT	SENSE
PUKKA	QUOTA	RELIG	ROUND	SCARE	SENTI
PULSE	QUOTE	REMIT	ROUSE	SCARF	SEPAL
PUNCH	QUOTH	RENAL	ROUTE	SCARP	SEPIA
PUPIL	RABBI	RENEW	ROWDY	SCENE	SERGE
PUPPY	RABID	REPAY	ROWEL	SCENT	SERUM
PUREE	RADAR	REPEL	ROYAL	SCION	SERVE
PURGE	RADII	REPLY	RUBLE	SCOFF	SERVO
PURIM	RADIO	RERUN	RUDDY	SCOLD	SETUP
PURSE	RADON	RESIN	RUGBY	SCONE	SEVEN
PUSHY	RAISE	RETCH	RULER	SCOOP	SEVER
PUSSY	RALLY	REVEL	RUMBA	SCOOT	SEWER
PUTTY	RAMIE	REVUE	RUMMY	SCOPE	SHACK
PYGMY	RANCH	RHEUM	RUNNY	SCORE	SHADE
PYLON	RANGE	RHINO	RUPEE	SCORN	SHAFT
QUACK	RANGY	RHYME	RURAL	SCOTS	SHAKE
QUAFF	RAPID	RIDER	SABLE	SCOUR	SHAKY
QUAIL	RATIO	RIDGE	SABRE	SCOUT	SHALE
QUAKE	RATTY	RIFLE	SAINT	SCOWL	SHALL
QUALM	RAVEL	RIGHT	SALAD	SCRAM	SHAME
QUART	RAVEN	RIGID	SALLY	SCRAP	SHANK
QUASH	RAYON	RINSE	SALON	SCREW	SHAPE

SHARD	SHUCK	SLICE	SNIPS	SPIEL	STALE
SHARE	SHUNT	SLICK	SNOOP	SPIKE	STALK
SHARK	SIBYL	SLIDE	SNORE	SPILL	STALL
SHARP	SIDLE	SLIER	SNORT	SPINE	STAMP
SHAVE	SIEGE	SLIME	SNOUT	SPIRE	STAND
SHAWL	SIEVE	SLING	SNOWY	SPIRT	STANK
SHEAF	SIGHT	SLINK	SNUCK	SPITE	STARE
SHEAR	SILLY	SLOOP	SNUFF	SPLAY	STARK
SHEEN	SINCE	SLOPE	SOBER	SPLIT	START
SHEEP	SINEW	SLOSH	SOGGY	SPOIL	STASH
SHEER	SINGE	SLOTH	SOLAR	SPOKE	STATE
SHEET	SINUS	SLUMP	SOLID	SPOOF	STAVE
SHELF	SIOUX	SLUNG	SOLON	SPOOK	STEAD
SHELL	SIREN	SLUNK	SOLVE	SPOOL	STEAK
SHIER	SIRUP	SLURP	SONAR	SPOON	STEAL
SHIFT	SISAL	SLUSH	SONIC	SPOOR	STEAM
SHILL	SISSY	SMACK	SOOTH	SPORE	STEED
SHINE	SITAR	SMALL	SORRY	SPORT	STEEL
SHINY	SIXTY	SMART	SOUGH	SPOUT	STEEP
SHIPT	SKATE	SMASH	SOUND	SPRAT	STEER
SHIRE	SKEET	SMEAR	SOUPY	SPRAY	STEIN
SHIRK	SKEIN	SMELL	SOUSE	SPREE	STERE
SHIRR	SKIFF	SMELT	SOUTH	SPRIG	STERN
SHIRT	SKILL	SMILE	SPACE	SPUME	STICK
SHOAL	SKIMP	SMIRK	SPADE	SPUNK	STIFF
SHOAT	SKIRT	SMITE	SPANK	SPURN	STILE
SHOCK	SKULK	SMITH	SPARE	SPURT	STILL
SHONE	SKULL	SMOCK	SPARK	SQUAB	STILT
SHOOK	SKUNK	SMOKE	SPASM	SQUAD	STING
SHOOT	SLACK	SMOTE	SPATE	SQUAT	STINK
SHORE	SLAIN	SNACK	SPAWN	SQUAW	STINT
SHORN	SLAKE	SNAIL	SPEAK	SQUIB	STOAT
SHORT	SLANG	SNAKE	SPEAR	SQUID	STOCK
SHOUT	SLANT	SNARE	SPECK	STACK	STOIC
SHOVE	SLASH	SNARL	SPEED	STAFF	STOKE
SHOWY	SLATE	SNEAK	SPELL	STAGE	STOLE
SHRED	SLAVE	SNEER	SPEND	STAID	STOMP
SHREW	SLEEK	SNIDE	SPENT	STAIN	STONE
SHRUB	SLEEP	SNIFF	SPERM	STAIR	STOOD
SHRUG	SLEET	SNIPE	SPICE	STAKE	STOOL

STOOP	SWAMI	TALON	THICK	TOAST	TRIAL
STORE	SWAMP	TALUS	THIEF	TODAY	TRIBE
STORK	SWANK	TANGO	THIGH	TODDY	TRICE
STORM	SWARD	TANSY	THINE	TOKAY	TRICK
STORY	SWARM	TAPER	THING	TOKEN	TRIED
STOUT	SWART	TAPIR	THINK	TONGS	TRILL
STOVE	SWASH	TARDY	THIRD	TONIC	TRINE
STRAP	SWATH	TAROT	THOLE	TOOTH	TRIPE
STRAW	SWEAR	TARRY	THONG	TOPAZ	TRITE
STRAY	SWEAT	TASTE	THORN	TOPER	TROLL
STREW	SWEDE	TASTY	THORP	TOPIC	TROMP
STRIA	SWEEP	TAUNT	THOSE	TOQUE	TROOP
STRIP	SWEET	TAUPE	THREE	TORAH	TROPE
STROP	SWELL	TAWNY	THREW	TORCH	TROTH
STRUM	SWEPT	TEACH	THROB	TORSO	TROUT
STRUT	SWIFT	TEASE	THROE	TOTAL	TRUCE
STUCK	SWILL	TEENS	THROW	TOTEM	TRUCK
STUDY	SWINE	TEENY	THRUM	TOUCH	TRUMP
STUFF	SWING	TEETH	THUMB	TOUGH	TRUNK
STUMP	SWIPE	TELEG	THUMP	TOWEL	TRUSS
STUNG	SWIRL	TEMPO	THYME	TOWER	TRUST
STUNK	SWISH	TEMPT	TIARA	TOXIC	TRUTH
STUNT	SWISS	TENET	TIBIA	TOXIN	TRYST
STYLE	SWOON	TENON	TICAL	TRACE	TUBER
SUAVE	SWOOP	TENOR	TIGER	TRACK	TULIP
SUCRE	SWORD	TENSE	TIGHT	TRACT	TULLE
SUEDE	SWORE	TEPEE	TILDE	TRADE	TUMID
SUGAR	SWORN	TEPID	TILTH	TRAIL	TUMMY
SUITE	SWUNG	TERRY	TIMES	TRAIN	TUNIC
SULFA	SYLPH	TERSE	TIMID	TRAIT	TUNNY
SULKY	SYNOD	TESTY	TINCT	TRAMP	TUQUE
SULLY	SYRUP	THANE	TINGE	TRANS	TURPS
SUMAC	TABBY	THANK	TINNY	TRAPS	TUTOR
SUNUP	TABLE	THEAT	TIPSY	TRASH	TWAIN
SUPER	TABOO	THEFT	TIRED	TRAWL	TWANG
SUPRA	TACIT	THEIR	TITAN	TREAD	TWEAK
SURGE	TACKY	THEME	TITHE	TREAT	TWEED
SURLY	TAINT	THERE	TITLE	TREND	TWEEN
SWAGE	TALER	THERM	TIZZY	TRESS	TWEET
SWAIN	TALLY	THESE	TOADY	TRIAD	TWICE

TWILL	USUAL	VIRAL	WEEDY	WITCH
TWINE	USURP	VIRTU	WEENY	WITHE
TWIRL	USURY	VIRUS	WEEPY	WITHY
TWIST	UTILE	VISIT	WEIGH	WITTY
TWIXT	UTTER	VISOR	WEIRD	WIVES
TYING	UVULA	VISTA	WELCH	WOKEN
UDDER	VAGUE	VITAL	WELSH	WOMAN
ULCER	VALET	VIVID	WENCH	WOODY
ULTRA	VALID	VIXEN	WHACK	WOOZY
UMBEL	VALSE	VIZOR	WHALE	WORDY
UMBER	VALUE	VOCAL	WHARF	WORLD
UMBRA	VALVE	VODKA	WHEAL	WORRY
UMIAK	VAPID	VOGUE	WHEAT	WORSE
UNARM	VARIA	VOICE	WHEEL	WORST
UNBAR	VASTY	VOILE	WHELK	WORTH
UNCAP	VATIC	VOMIT	WHELM	WOULD
UNCLE	VAULT	VOUCH	WHELP	WOUND
UNCUT	VAUNT	VOWEL	WHERE	WOVEN
UNDER	VEERY	VULVA	WHICH	WRACK
UNDUE	VELAR	VYING	WHIFF	WRATH
UNFIT	VELUM	WACKY	WHILE	WREAK
UNFIX	VENAL	WADER	WHINE	WRECK
UNIFY	VENOM	WAFER	WHIRL	WREST
UNION	VENUE	WAGER	WHISH	WRING
UNITE	VENUS	WAGON	WHISK	WRIST
UNITY	VERGE	WAHOO	WHIST	WRITE
UNMAN	VERSE	WAIST	WHITE	WRONG
UNPEG	VERSO	WAIVE	WHOLE	WROTE
UNPIN	VERST	WAKEN	WHOOP	WROTH
UNSAY	VERVE	WALTZ	WHORE	WRUNG
UNTIE	VETCH	WASHY	WHORL	WURST
UNTIL	VIAND	WASTE	WHOSE	XEBEC
UNZIP	VIBES	WATCH	WIDEN	XENON
UPEND	VICAR	WATER	WIDOW	XERIC
UPPER	VIDEO	WAVER	WIDTH	XYLEM
UPSET	VIGIL	WAXEN	WIELD	YACHT
URBAN	VILLA	WEALD	WIGHT	YAHOO
URINE	VINYL	WEARY	WINCE	YEARN
USAGE	VIOLA	WEAVE	WINCH	YEAST
USHER	VIPER	WEDGE	WINDY	YIELD

YODEL	ABJECT	ACCEDE	ADAGIO	ADVENT
YOKEL	ABJURE	ACCENT	ADAPTS	ADVERB
YOUNG	ABLATE	ACCEPT	ADDEND	ADVERT
YOURS	ABLAUT	ACCESS	ADDERS	ADVICE
YOUTH	ABLAZE	ACCORD	ADDICT	ADVISE
YUCCA	ABLEST	ACCOST	ADDING	ADYTUM
YUMMY	ABLINS	ACCRUE	ADDLED	ADZUKI
ZAIRE	ABLOOM	ACCUSE	ADDLES	AECIAL
ZEBRA	ABLUSH	ACEDIA	ADDUCE	AECIUM
ZIPPY	ABMHOS	ACETAL	ADDUCT	AEDILE
ZLOTY	ABOARD	ACETIC	ADEEMS	AEDINE
ZONAL	ABODED	ACETIN	ADENYL	AENEUS
	ABODES	ACETUM	ADEPTS	AEONIC
6	ABOHMS	ACETYL	ADHERE	AERATE
	ABOLLA	ACHENE	ADIEUS	AERIAL
AARRGH	ABOMAS	ACHIER	ADIEUX	AERIED
ABACAS	ABORAL	ACHING	ADIPIC	AERIER
ABACUS	ABORTS	ACIDIC	ADJOIN	AERIES
ABAMPS	ABOUND	ACIDLY	ADJURE	AERIFY
ABASED	ABOVES	ACINAR	ADJUST	AERILY
ABASER	ABRADE	ACINIC	ADMASS	AEROBE
ABASES	ABROAD	ACINUS	ADMIRE	AERUGO
ABASIA	ABRUPT	ACKEES	ADMITS	AETHER
ABATED	ABSEIL	ACNODE	ADMIXT	AFEARD
ABATER	ABSENT	ACORNS	ADNATE	AFFAIR
ABATES	ABSORB	ACQUIT	ADNEXA	AFFECT
ABATIS	ABSURD	ACROSS	ADNOUN	AFFINE
ABATOR	ABULIA	ACTING	ADOBES	AFFIRM
ABBACY	ABULIC	ACTINS	ADOBOS	AFFLUX
ABBESS	ABUSED	ACTION	ADONIS	AFFORD
ABBEYS	ABUSER	ACTIVE	ADOPTS	AFFRAY
ABBOTS	ABUSES	ACTORS	ADORED	AFGHAN
ABDUCE	ABVOLT	ACTUAL	ADORER	AFIELD
ABDUCT	ABWATT	ACUATE	ADORES	AFLAME
ABELES	ABYING	ACUITY	ADORNS	AFLOAT
ABELIA	ABYSMS	ACULEI	ADRIFT	AFRAID
ABHORS	ACACIA	ACUMEN	ADROIT	AFREET
ABIDED	ACAJOU	ACUTER	ADSORB	AFRESH
ABIDER	ACARID	ACUTES	ADULTS	AFRITS
ABIDES	ACARUS	ADAGES	ADVECT	AFTERS

AFTOSA	AGRIAS	ALANDS	ALINED	ALMUGS
AGAMAS	AGUISH	ALANIN	ALINER	ALNICO
AGAMIC	AHCHOO	ALANTS	ALINES	ALODIA
AGAPAE	AHIMSA	ALANYL	ALIPED	ALOHAS
AGAPAI	AHOLDS	ALARMS	ALIYAH	ALOINS
AGARIC	AHORSE	ALARUM	ALIYAS	ALPACA
AGATES	AIDERS	ALASKA	ALIYOS	ALPHAS
AGAVES	AIDFUL	ALATED	ALIYOT	ALPHYL
AGEDLY	AIDING	ALATES	ALKALI	ALPINE
AGEING	AIDMAN	ALBATA	ALKANE	ALSIKE
AGEISM	AIDMEN	ALBEDO	ALKENE	ALTARS
AGEIST	AIGLET	ALBEIT	ALKIES	ALTERS
AGENCY	AIGRET	ALBINO	ALKINE	ALTHEA
AGENDA	AIKIDO	ALBITE	ALKOXY	ALUDEL
AGENES	AILING	ALBUMS	ALKYDS	ALULAE
AGENTS	AIMERS	ALCADE	ALKYLS	ALULAR
AGGERS	AIMFUL	ALCAIC	ALKYNE	ALUMIN
AGGIES	AIMING	ALCIDS	ALLAYS	ALUMNA
AGGROS	AIOLIS	ALCOVE	ALLEES	ALUMNI
AGHAST	AIRBUS	ALDERS	ALLEGE	ALVINE
AGINGS	AIRERS	ALDOLS	ALLELE	ALWAYS
AGISMS	AIREST	ALDOSE	ALLEYS	AMADOU
AGISTS	AIRIER	ALDRIN	ALLIED	AMARNA
AGLARE	AIRILY	ALEGAR	ALLIES	AMATOL
AGLEAM	AIRING	ALEPHS	ALLIUM	AMAZED
AGLETS	AIRMAN	ALERTS	ALLODS	AMAZES
AGNAIL	AIRMEN	ALEVIN	ALLOTS	AMAZON
AGNATE	AIRTED	ALEXIA	ALLOWS	AMBAGE
AGNIZE	AIRTHS	ALEXIN	ALLOYS	AMBARI
AGONAL	AIRWAY	ALFAKI	ALLUDE	AMBARY
AGONES	AISLED	ALGINS	ALLURE	AMBEER
AGONIC	AISLES	ALGOID	ALLYLS	AMBERS
AGORAE	AIVERS	ALGORS	ALMAHS	AMBERY
AGORAS	AJIVAS	ALGUMS	ALMEHS	AMBITS
AGOROT	AJOWAN	ALIBIS	ALMNER	AMBLED
AGOUTI	AJUGAS	ALIBLE	ALMOND	AMBLER
AGOUTY	AKELAS	ALIDAD	ALMOST	AMBLES
AGRAFE	AKENES	ALIENS	ALMUCE	AMBUSH
AGREED	AKIMBO	ALIGHT	ALMUDE	AMEBAE
AGREES	ALAMOS	ALIGNS	ALMUDS	AMEBAN

AMEBAS	ANABAS	ANNALS	ANYWAY	ARBORS
AMEBIC	ANADEM	ANNEAL	AORIST	ARBOUR
AMEERS	ANALLY	ANNEXE	AORTAE	ARBUTE
AMENDS	ANALOG	ANNOYS	AORTAL	ARCADE
AMENTS	ANANKE	ANNUAL	AORTAS	ARCANA
AMERCE	ANARCH	ANNULI	AORTIC	ARCANE
AMICES	ANATTO	ANNULS	AOUDAD	ARCHED
AMICUS	ANCHOR	ANODAL	APACHE	ARCHER
AMIDES	ANCONE	ANODES	APATHY	ARCHES
AMIDIC	ANEARS	ANODIC	APERCU	ARCHIL
AMIDIN	ANELED	ANOINT	APEXES	ARCHLY
AMIDOL	ANELES	ANOLES	APHIDS	ARCHON
AMIDST	ANEMIA	ANOMIC	APHTHA	ARCING
AMIGAS	ANEMIC	ANOMIE	APIARY	ARCKED
AMIGOS	ANENST	ANONYM	APICAL	ARCTIC
AMINES	ANERGY	ANOPIA	APICES	ARDEBS
AMINIC	ANGARY	ANORAK	APIECE	ARDENT
AMMINE	ANGELS	ANOXIA	APLITE	ARDORS
AMMINO	ANGERS	ANOXIC	APLOMB	ARDOUR
AMMONO	ANGINA	ANSATE	APNEAL	ARECAS
AMNION	ANGLED	ANSWER	APNEAS	ARENAS
AMOEBA	ANGLER	ANTEED	APNEIC	AREOLA
AMOLES	ANGLES	ANTHEM	APNOEA	AREOLE
AMORAL	ANGORA	ANTHER	APODAL	ARETES
AMOUNT	ANGSTS	ANTIAR	APOGEE	ARGALA
AMOURS	ANILIN	ANTICK	APOLLO	ARGALI
AMPERE	ANIMAL	ANTICS	APOLOG	ARGALS
AMPLER	ANIMAS	ANTING	APPALL	ARGENT
AMPULE	ANIMES	ANTLER	APPALS	ARGILS
AMPULS	ANIMIS	ANTRAL	APPEAL	ARGLED
AMRITA	ANIMUS	ANTRES	APPEAR	ARGLES
AMTRAC	ANIONS	ANTRUM	APPELS	ARGOLS
AMUCKS	ANISES	ANURAL	APPEND	ARGONS
AMULET	ANISIC	ANURAN	APPLES	ARGOSY
AMUSED	ANKLED	ANURIA	APPOSE	ARGOTS
AMUSER	ANKLES	ANURIC	APRONS	ARGUED
AMUSES	ANKLET	ANUSES	APTEST	ARGUER
AMUSIA	ANKUSH	ANVILS	ARABIC	ARGUES
AMYLIC	ANLACE	ANYHOW	ARABLE	ARGUFY
AMYLUM	ANLAGE	ANYONE	ARAMID	ARGYLE

ARGYLL	ARREST	ASPENS	ATONAL	AUNTIE
ARHATS	ARRIVE	ASPERS	ATONED	AUNTLY
ARIDER	ARROBA	ASPICS	ATONER	AURATE
ARIDLY	ARROWS	ASPIRE	ATONES	AUREUS
ARIELS	ARROWY	ASPISH	ATONIC	AURIST
ARIGHT	ARROYO	ASSAIL	ATOPIC	AURORA
ARILED	ARSENO	ASSAIS	ATRIAL	AUROUS
ARIOSE	ARSHIN	ASSAYS	ATRIUM	AURUMS
ARIOSI	ARSINE	ASSENT	ATTACH	AUSPEX
ARIOSO	ARSINO	ASSERT	ATTACK	AUSUBO
ARISEN	ARSONS	ASSESS	ATTAIN	AUTEUR
ARISES	ARTELS	ASSETS	ATTARS	AUTHOR
ARISTA	ARTERY	ASSIGN	ATTEND	AUTISM
ARISTO	ARTFUL	ASSIST	ATTENT	AUTOED
ARKOSE	ARTIER	ASSIZE	ATTEST	AUTUMN
ARMADA	ARTILY	ASSOIL	ATTICS	AUXINS
ARMERS	ARTIST	ASSORT	ATTIRE	AVAILS
ARMETS	ASANAS	ASSUME	ATTORN	AVATAR
ARMFUL	ASARUM	ASSURE	ATTUNE	AVAUNT
ARMIES	ASCEND	ASTERN	ATWAIN	AVENGE
ARMING	ASCENT	ASTERS	ATWEEN	AVENUE
ARMLET	ASCOTS	ASTHMA	ATYPIC	AVERSE
ARMORS	ASDICS	ASTONY	AUBADE	AVERTS
ARMORY	ASHCAN	ASTRAL	AUBURN	AVIANS
ARMOUR	ASHIER	ASTRAY	AUCUBA	AVIARY
ARMPIT	ASHING	ASTUTE	AUDADS	AVIATE
ARMURE	ASHLAR	ASWARM	AUDIAL	AVIDIN
ARNICA	ASHLER	ASWIRL	AUDILE	AVIDLY
AROIDS	ASHMAN	ASWOON	AUDING	AVIONS
AROINT	ASHMEN	ASYLUM	AUDIOS	AVISOS
AROMAS	ASHORE	ATABAL	AUDITS	AVOCET
AROUND	ASHRAM	ATAMAN	AUGEND	AVOIDS
AROUSE	ASIDES	ATAVIC	AUGERS	AVOSET
AROYNT	ASKANT	ATAXIA	AUGHTS	AVOUCH
ARPENS	ASKERS	ATAXIC	AUGITE	AVOWAL
ARPENT	ASKING	ATELIC	AUGURS	AVOWED
ARRACK	ASLANT	ATLATL	AUGURY	AVOWER
ARRANT	ASLEEP	ATMANS	AUGUST	AVULSE
ARRAYS	ASLOPE	ATOLLS	AUKLET	AWAITS
ARREAR	ASPECT	ATOMIC	AULDER	AWAKED

AWAKEN	BAALIM	BAILED	BANDOG	BARIUM
AWAKES	BAASES	BAILEE	BANGED	BARKED
AWARDS	BABBLE	BAILER	BANGER	BARKER
AWEARY	BABELS	BAILEY	BANGLE	BARLEY
AWEIGH	BABIED	BAILIE	BANIAN	BARLOW
AWEING	BABIES	BAILOR	BANING	BARMAN
AWHILE	BABKAS	BAIRNS	BANISH	BARMEN
AWHIRL	BABOOL	BAITED	BANJAX	BARMIE
AWLESS	BABOON	BAITER	BANJOS	BARONG
AWMOUS	BABOOS	BAIZAS	BANKED	BARONS
AWNING	BABULS	BAIZES	BANKER	BARONY
AWOKEN	BACCAE	BAKERS	BANNED	BARQUE
AXEMAN	BACHED	BAKERY	BANNER	BARRED
AXEMEN	BACHES	BAKING	BANNET	BARREL
AXENIC	BACKED	BALATA	BANTAM	BARREN
AXILLA	BACKER	BALBOA	BANTER	BARRES
AXIOMS	BACKUP	BALDED	BANYAN	BARRET
AXIONS	BACONS	BALDER	BANZAI	BARRIO
AXISED	BACULA	BALDLY	BAOBAB	BARROW
AXISES	BADASS	BALEEN	BARBAL	BARTER
AXITES	BADDER	BALERS	BARBED	BARYES
AXLIKE	BADDIE	BALING	BARBEL	BARYON
AXONAL	BADGED	BALKED	BARBER	BARYTA
AXONES	BADGER	BALKER	BARBES	BARYTE
AXONIC	BADGES	BALLAD	BARBET	BASALT
AXSEED	BADMAN	BALLED	BARBUT	BASELY
AZALEA	BADMEN	BALLER	BARDED	BASEST
AZIDES	BAFFED	BALLET	BARDES	BASHAW
AZINES	BAFFLE	BALLON	BARDIC	BASHED
AZLONS	BAGASS	BALLOT	BAREGE	BASHER
AZOLES	BAGELS	BALLSY	BARELY	BASHES
AZONAL	BAGFUL	BALSAM	BAREST	BASICS
AZONIC	BAGGED	BALSAS	BARFED	BASIFY
AZOTED	BAGGER	BAMBOO	BARFLY	BASILS
AZOTES	BAGGIE	BAMMED	BARGED	BASING
AZOTHS	BAGMAN	BANANA	BARGEE	BASINS
AZOTIC	BAGMEN	BANCOS	BARGES	BASION
AZURES	BAGNIO	BANDED	BARHOP	BASKED
AZYGOS	BAGUET	BANDER	BARING	BASKET
BAAING	BAGWIG	BANDIT	BARITE	BASQUE

BASSES	BAZARS	BEDLAM	BEHEAD	BEMUSE
BASSET	BAZOOS	BEDPAN	BEHELD	BENAME
BASSLY	BEACHY	BEDRID	BEHEST	BENDAY
BASSOS	BEACON	BEDRUG	BEHIND	BENDED
BASTED	BEADED	BEDSIT	BEHOLD	BENDEE
BASTER	BEADLE	BEDUIN	BEHOOF	BENDER
BASTES	BEAGLE	BEDUMB	BEHOVE	BENDYS
BATBOY	BEAKED	BEEBEE	BEHOWL	BENIGN
BATEAU	BEAKER	BEECHY	BEIGES	BENNES
BATHED	BEAMED	BEEFED	BEINGS	BENNET
BATHER	BEANED	BEEPED	BEKISS	BENNIS
BATHES	BEANIE	BEEPER	BEKNOT	BENUMB
BATHOS	BEANOS	BEETLE	BELADY	BENZAL
BATIKS	BEARDS	BEEVES	BELAUD	BENZIN
BATING	BEARER	BEEZER	BELAYS	BENZOL
BATMAN	BEASTS	BEFALL	BELDAM	BENZYL
BATMEN	BEATEN	BEFELL	BELEAP	BERAKE
BATONS	BEATER	BEFITS	BELFRY	BERATE
BATTED	BEAUTS	BEFLAG	BELGAS	BEREFT
BATTEN	BEAUTY	BEFLEA	BELIED	BERETS
BATTER	BEAVER	BEFOGS	BELIEF	BERIME
BATTIK	BEBOPS	BEFOOL	BELIER	BERLIN
BATTLE	BECALM	BEFORE	BELIES	BERMES
BATTUE	BECAME	BEFOUL	BELIKE	BERTHA
BAUBEE	BECAPS	BEFRET	BELIVE	BERTHS
BAUBLE	BECKED	BEGALL	BELLED	BERYLS
BAULKS	BECKET	BEGAZE	BELLES	BESEEM
BAULKY	BECKON	BEGETS	BELLOW	BESETS
BAWBEE	BECLOG	BEGGAR	BELONG	BESIDE
BAWDRY	BECOME	BEGGED	BELOWS	BESMUT
BAWLED	BEDAMN	BEGINS	BELTED	BESNOW
BAWLER	BEDAUB	BEGIRD	BELTER	BESOMS
BAWTIE	BEDBUG	BEGIRT	BELUGA	BESOTS
BAYAMO	BEDDED	BEGLAD	BEMATA	BESTED
BAYARD	BEDDER	BEGONE	BEMEAN	BESTIR
BAYING	BEDECK	BEGRIM	BEMIRE	BESTOW
BAYMAN	BEDELL	BEGULF	BEMIST	BESTUD
BAYMEN	BEDELS	BEGUMS	BEMIXT	BETAKE
BAYOUS	BEDEWS	BEHALF	BEMOAN	BETELS
BAZAAR	BEDIMS	BEHAVE	BEMOCK	BETHEL

BETIDE	BIBBED	BILLED	BIRLES	BLEARS
BETIME	BIBBER	BILLER	BIRRED	BLEARY
BETISE	BIBLES	BILLET	BIRSES	BLEATS
BETONS	BICARB	BILLIE	BIRTHS	BLEBBY
BETONY	BICEPS	BILLON	BISECT	BLEEDS
BETOOK	BICKER	BILLOW	BISHOP	BLEEPS
BETRAY	BICORN	BIMAHS	BISONS	BLENCH
BETTAS	BICRON	BIMBOS	BISQUE	BLENDE
BETTED	BIDDEN	BINARY	BISTER	BLENDS
BETTER	BIDDER	BINATE	BISTRE	BLENNY
BETTOR	BIDERS	BINDER	BISTRO	BLIGHT
BEVELS	BIDETS	BINDIS	BITCHY	BLIMEY
BEVIES	BIDING	BINDLE	BITERS	BLIMPS
BEVORS	BIELDS	BINGED	BITING	BLINDS
BEWAIL	BIFACE	BINGER	BITTED	BLINIS
BEWARE	BIFFED	BINGES	BITTEN	BLINKS
BEWEEP	BIFFIN	BINGOS	BITTER	BLINTZ
BEWEPT	BIFLEX	BINITS	BIZONE	BLITES
BEWIGS	BIFOLD	BINNED	BIZZES	BLITHE
BEWORM	BIFORM	BINOCS	BLABBY	BLOATS
BEWRAP	BIGAMY	BIOGAS	BLACKS	BLOCKS
BEWRAY	BIGEYE	BIOGEN	BLADED	BLOCKY
BEYLIC	BIGGER	BIOMES	BLADES	BLOKES
BEYLIK	BIGGIE	BIONIC	BLAINS	BLONDE
BEYOND	BIGGIN	BIONTS	BLAMED	BLONDS
BEZANT	BIGHTS	BIOPIC	BLAMER	BLOODS
BEZAZZ	BIGOTS	BIOPSY	BLAMES	BLOODY
BEZELS	BIGWIG	BIOTAS	BLANCH	BLOOEY
BEZILS	BIJOUS	BIOTIC	BLANKS	BLOOIE
BEZOAR	BIJOUX	BIOTIN	BLARED	BLOOMS
BHAKTA	BIKERS	BIPACK	BLARES	BLOOMY
BHAKTI	BIKIES	BIPEDS	BLASTS	BLOOPS
BHANGS	BIKING	BIPODS	BLASTY	BLOTCH
BHARAL	BIKINI	BIRDED	BLAWED	BLOTTO
BHOOTS	BILBOA	BIRDER	BLAZED	BLOTTY
BIALIS	BILBOS	BIRDIE	BLAZER	BLOUSE
BIALYS	BILGED	BIREME	BLAZES	BLOUSY
BIASED	BILGES	BIRKIE	BLAZON	BLOWBY
BIASES	BILKED	BIRLED	BLEACH	BLOWED
BIAXAL	BILKER	BIRLER	BLEAKS	BLOWER

BLOWSY	BODING	BONGOS	BORATE	BOUNCY
BLOWUP	BODKIN	BONIER	BORDEL	BOUNDS
BLOWZY	BOFFIN	BONING	BORDER	BOUNTY
BLUELY	BOFFOS	BONITA	BOREAL	BOURGS
BLUEST	BOGANS	BONITO	BOREEN	BOURNE
BLUESY	BOGEYS	BONKED	BORERS	BOURNS
BLUETS	BOGGED	BONNES	BORIDE	BOURSE
BLUEYS	BOGGLE	BONNET	BORING	BOUSED
BLUFFS	BOGIES	BONNIE	BORONS	BOUSES
BLUING	BOGLES	BONSAI	BORROW	BOUTON
BLUISH	BOHEAS	BONZER	BORSCH	BOVIDS
BLUMED	BOHUNK	BONZES	BORSHT	BOVINE
BLUMES	BOILED	BOOBED	BORZOI	BOWELS
BLUNGE	BOILER	BOOBIE	BOSHES	BOWERS
BLUNTS	BOITES	BOOBOO	BOSKER	BOWERY
BLURBS	BOLDER	BOODLE	BOSKET	BOWFIN
BLURRY	BOLDLY	BOOGER	BOSOMS	BOWING
BLURTS	BOLERO	BOOGEY	BOSOMY	BOWLED
BLYPES	BOLETE	BOOGIE	BOSONS	BOWLEG
BOARDS	BOLETI	BOOHOO	BOSQUE	BOWLER
BOARTS	BOLIDE	BOOING	BOSSED	BOWMAN
BOASTS	BOLLED	BOOKED	BOSSES	BOWMEN
BOATED	BOLLIX	BOOKER	BOSTON	BOWPOT
BOATEL	BOLLOX	BOOKIE	BOSUNS	BOWSED
BOATER	BOLSHY	BOOMED	BOTANY	BOWSES
BOBBED	BOLSON	BOOMER	BOTCHY	BOWYER
BOBBER	BOLTED	BOOSTS	BOTELS	BOXCAR
BOBBIN	BOLTER	BOOTED	BOTFLY	BOXERS
BOBBLE	BOMBAX	BOOTEE	BOTHER	BOXFUL
BOBCAT	BOMBED	BOOTHS	BOTTLE	BOXIER
BOCCES	BOMBER	BOOTIE	BOTTOM	BOXING
BOCCIA	BOMBES	BOOZED	BOUBOU	BOYARD
BOCCIE	BOMBYX	BOOZER	BOUCLE	BOYARS
BOCCIS	BONACI	BOOZES	BOUFFE	BOYISH
BOCHES	BONBON	BOPEEP	BOUGHS	BOYLAS
BODEGA	BONDED	BOPPED	BOUGHT	BRACED
BODICE	BONDER	BOPPER	BOUGIE	BRACER
BODIED	BONDUC	BORAGE	BOULES	BRACES
BODIES	BONERS	BORALS	BOULLE	BRACHS
BODILY	BONGED	BORANE	BOUNCE	BRACTS

BRAGGY	BREADY	BRINKS	BRUISE	BUGGER
BRAHMA	BREAKS	BRIONY	BRUITS	BUGLED
BRAIDS	BREAMS	BRISKS	BRULOT	BUGLER
BRAILS	BREAST	BRITTS	BRUMAL	BUGLES
BRAINS	BREATH	BROACH	BRUMBY	BUGSHA
BRAINY	BREDES	BROADS	BRUMES	BUILDS
BRAISE	BREECH	BROCHE	BRUNCH	BULBAR
BRAIZE	BREEDS	BROCKS	BRUNET	BULBED
BRAKED	BREEKS	BROGAN	BRUNTS	BULBEL
BRAKES	BREEZE	BROGUE	BRUSHY	BULBIL
BRANCH	BREEZY	BROILS	BRUTAL	BULBUL
BRANDS	BREGMA	BROKEN	BRUTED	BULGED
BRANDY	BRENTS	BROKER	BRUTES	BULGER
BRANKS	BREVES	BROLLY	BRYONY	BULGES
BRANNY	BREVET	BROMAL	BUBALE	BULGUR
BRANTS	BREWED	BROMES	BUBALS	BULKED
BRASHY	BREWER	BROMIC	BUBBLE	BULLAE
BRASIL	BREWIS	BROMID	BUBBLY	BULLED
BRASSY	BRIARD	BROMIN	BUBOED	BULLET
BRATTY	BRIARS	BROMOS	BUBOES	BUMBLE
BRAVAS	BRIARY	BRONCO	BUCCAL	BUMKIN
BRAVED	BRIBED	BRONCS	BUCKED	BUMMED
BRAVER	BRIBEE	BRONZE	BUCKER	BUMMER
BRAVES	BRIBER	BRONZY	BUCKET	BUMPED
BRAVOS	BRIBES	BROOCH	BUCKLE	BUMPER
BRAWER	BRICKS	BROODS	BUCKRA	BUMPHS
BRAWLS	BRICKY	BROODY	BUDDED	BUNCHY
BRAWLY	BRIDAL	BROOKS	BUDDER	BUNCOS
BRAWNS	BRIDES	BROOMS	BUDDLE	BUNDLE
BRAWNY	BRIDGE	BROOMY	BUDGED	BUNDTS
BRAYED	BRIDLE	BROSES	BUDGER	BUNGED
BRAYER	BRIEFS	BROTHS	BUDGES	BUNGEE
BRAZAS	BRIERS	BROTHY	BUDGET	BUNGLE
BRAZED	BRIERY	BROWED	BUDGIE	BUNION
BRAZEN	BRIGHT	BROWNS	BUFFED	BUNKED
BRAZER	BRILLS	BROWNY	BUFFER	BUNKER
BRAZES	BRINED	BROWSE	BUFFET	BUNKOS
BRAZIL	BRINER	BRUCIN	BUFFOS	BUNKUM
BREACH	BRINES	BRUGHS	BUGEYE	BUNTED
BREADS	BRINGS	BRUINS	BUGGED	BUNTER

BUNYAS	BURSAR	BUYERS	CACHED	CALESA
BUOYED	BURSAS	BUYING	CACHES	CALICO
BUPPIE	BURSES	BUYOUT	CACHET	CALIFS
BUQSHA	BURSTS	BUZUKI	CACHOU	CALIPH
BURANS	BURTON	BUZZED	CACKLE	CALKED
BURBLE	BUSBAR	BUZZER	CACTUS	CALKER
BURBLY	BUSBOY	BUZZES	CADDIE	CALKIN
BURBOT	BUSHED	BWANAS	CADDIS	CALLAN
BURDEN	BUSHEL	BYELAW	CADENT	CALLAS
BURDIE	BUSHER	BYGONE	CADETS	CALLED
BUREAU	BUSHES	BYLAWS	CADGED	CALLER
BURETS	BUSHWA	BYLINE	CADGER	CALLET
BURGEE	BUSIED	BYNAME	CADGES	CALLOW
BURGER	BUSIER	BYPASS	CADMIC	CALLUS
BURGHS	BUSIES	BYPAST	CADRES	CALMED
BURGLE	BUSILY	BYPATH	CAECAL	CALMER
BURGOO	BUSING	BYPLAY	CAECUM	CALMLY
BURIAL	BUSKED	BYRLED	CAEOMA	CALORY
BURIED	BUSKER	BYRNIE	CAESAR	CALPAC
BURIER	BUSKIN	BYROAD	CAFTAN	CALQUE
BURIES	BUSMAN	BYSSUS	CAGERS	CALVED
BURINS	BUSMEN	BYTALK	CAGIER	CALVES
BURKED	BUSSED	BYWAYS	CAGILY	CALXES
BURKER	BUSSES	BYWORD	CAGING	CAMAIL
BURKES	BUSTED	BYWORK	CAHIER	CAMASS
BURLAP	BUSTER	BYZANT	CAHOOT	CAMBER
BURLED	BUSTIC	CABALA	CAHOWS	CAMBIA
BURLER	BUSTLE	CABALS	CAIMAN	CAMELS
BURLEY	BUTANE	CABANA	CAIQUE	CAMEOS
BURNED	BUTENE	CABBED	CAIRDS	CAMERA
BURNER	BUTEOS	CABBIE	CAIRNS	CAMION
BURNET	BUTLED	CABERS	CAIRNY	CAMISA
BURNIE	BUTLER	CABINS	CAJOLE	CAMISE
BURPED	BUTLES	CABLED	CAKIER	CAMLET
BURRED	BUTTED	CABLES	CAKING	CAMPED
BURRER	BUTTER	CABLET	CALAMI	CAMPER
BURROS	BUTTES	CABMAN	CALASH	CAMPOS
BURROW	BUTTON	CABMEN	CALCAR	CAMPUS
BURSAE	BUTUTS	CABOBS	CALCES	CANALS
BURSAL	BUTYLS	CACAOS	CALCIC	CANAPE

CANARD	CANYON	CARKED	CASEIN	CAUGHT
CANARY	CAPERS	CARLES	CASERN	CAULDS
CANCAN	CAPFUL	CARLIN	CASHAW	CAULES
CANCEL	CAPIAS	CARMAN	CASHED	CAULIS
CANCER	CAPITA	CARMEN	CASHES	CAULKS
CANCHA	CAPLET	CARNAL	CASHEW	CAUSAL
CANDID	CAPLIN	CARNET	CASHOO	CAUSED
CANDLE	CAPONS	CARNEY	CASING	CAUSER
CANDOR	CAPOTE	CARNIE	CASINI	CAUSES
CANERS	CAPPED	CAROBS	CASINO	CAUSEY
CANFUL	CAPPER	CAROCH	CASITA	CAVEAT
CANGUE	CAPRIC	CAROLI	CASKED	CAVERN
CANIDS	CAPRIS	CAROLS	CASKET	CAVERS
CANINE	CAPSID	CAROMS	CASQUE	CAVIAR
CANING	CAPTAN	CARPAL	CASSIA	CAVIES
CANKER	CAPTOR	CARPED	CASSIS	CAVING
CANNAS	CARACK	CARPEL	CASTER	CAVITY
CANNED	CARAFE	CARPER	CASTES	CAVORT
CANNEL	CARATE	CARPET	CASTLE	CAWING
CANNER	CARATS	CARPUS	CASTOR	CAYMAN
CANNIE	CARBON	CARREL	CASUAL	CAYUSE
CANNON	CARBOS	CARROM	CATALO	CEASED
CANNOT	CARBOY	CARROT	CATCHY	CEASES
CANOED	CARCEL	CARSES	CATENA	CEBIDS
CANOES	CARDED	CARTED	CATERS	CEBOID
CANOLA	CARDER	CARTEL	CATGUT	CEDARN
CANONS	CARDIA	CARTER	CATION	CEDARS
CANOPY	CAREEN	CARTES	CATKIN	CEDERS
CANSOS	CAREER	CARTON	CATLIN	CEDING
CANTED	CARERS	CARTOP	CATNAP	CEDULA
CANTER	CARESS	CARVED	CATNIP	CEIBAS
CANTHI	CARETS	CARVEL	CATSUP	CEILED
CANTIC	CARFUL	CARVEN	CATTED	CEILER
CANTLE	CARGOS	CARVER	CATTIE	CELEBS
CANTON	CARHOP	CARVES	CATTLE	CELERY
CANTOR	CARIBE	CASABA	CAUCUS	CELIAC
CANTOS	CARIED	CASAVA	CAUDAD	CELLAE
CANTUS	CARIES	CASBAH	CAUDAL	CELLAR
CANULA	CARINA	CASEFY	CAUDEX	CELLED
CANVAS	CARING	CASEIC	CAUDLE	CELLOS

CELOMS	CHAIRS	CHEAPO	CHIELD	CHOKER
CEMENT	CHAISE	CHEAPS	CHIELS	CHOKES
CENOTE	CHAKRA	CHEATS	CHIGOE	CHOKEY
CENSED	CHALAH	CHECKS	CHILDE	CHOLER
CENSER	CHALET	CHEDER	CHILES	CHOLLA
CENSES	CHALKS	CHEEKS	CHILLI	CHOLOS
CENSOR	CHALKY	CHEEKY	CHILLS	CHOMPS
CENSUS	CHALLA	CHEEPS	CHILLY	CHOOKS
CENTAL	CHALLY	CHEERO	CHIMBS	CHOOSE
CENTER	CHALOT	CHEERS	CHIMED	CHOOSY
CENTOS	CHAMMY	CHEERY	CHIMER	CHOPIN
CENTRA	CHAMPS	CHEESE	CHIMES	CHOPPY
CENTRE	CHAMPY	CHEESY	CHIMPS	CHORAL
CENTUM	CHANCE	CHELAE	CHINAS	CHORDS
CERATE	CHANCY	CHELAS	CHINCH	CHOREA
CERCIS	CHANGE	CHEMIC	CHINED	CHORED
CERCUS	CHANGS	CHEMOS	CHINES	CHORES
CEREAL	CHANTS	CHEQUE	CHINKS	CHORIC
CERIPH	CHANTY	CHERRY	CHINOS	CHORUS
CERISE	CHAPEL	CHERTS	CHINTZ	CHOSEN
CERITE	CHAPES	CHERTY	CHIPPY	CHOSES
CERTES	CHARAS	CHERUB	CHIRAL	CHOTTS
CERUSE	CHARDS	CHESTS	CHIRKS	CHOUGH
CERVID	CHARED	CHESTY	CHIRMS	CHOUSE
CERVIX	CHARES	CHETAH	CHIROS	CHOUSH
CESIUM	CHARGE	CHEVRE	CHIRPS	CHOWED
CESSED	CHARKA	CHEWED	CHIRPY	CHOWSE
CESSES	CHARKS	CHEWER	CHIRRE	CHRISM
CESTAS	CHARMS	CHIASM	CHIRRS	CHROMA
CESURA	CHARTS	CHIAUS	CHISEL	CHROME
CETANE	CHASED	CHICER	CHITAL	CHROMO
CHADAR	CHASER	CHICHI	CHITIN	CHUBBY
CHADOR	CHASES	CHICKS	CHITON	CHUCKS
CHAFED	CHASMS	CHICLE	CHITTY	CHUCKY
CHAFER	CHASMY	CHICLY	CHIVES	CHUFAS
CHAFES	CHASSE	CHICOS	CHIVVY	CHUFFS
CHAFFS	CHASTE	CHIDED	CHOCKS	CHUFFY
CHAFFY	CHATTY	CHIDER	CHOICE	CHUKAR
CHAINE	CHAUNT	CHIDES	CHOIRS	CHUKKA
CHAINS	CHAWED	CHIEFS	CHOKED	CHUMMY

CHUMPS	CITRIC	CLERID	CLOSED	COBALT
CHUNKS	CITRIN	CLERKS	CLOSER	COBBER
CHUNKY	CITRON	CLEVER	CLOSES	COBBLE
CHURCH	CITRUS	CLEVIS	CLOSET	COBIAS
CHURLS	CIVETS	CLEWED	CLOTHE	COBLES
CHURNS	CIVICS	CLICHE	CLOTHS	COBNUT
CHURRS	CIVIES	CLICKS	CLOTTY	COBRAS
CHUTED	CIVISM	CLIENT	CLOUDS	COBWEB
CHUTES	CLACKS	CLIFFS	CLOUDY	COCAIN
CHYLES	CLADES	CLIFFY	CLOUGH	COCCIC
CHYMES	CLAIMS	CLIFTS	CLOUTS	COCCID
CHYMIC	CLAMMY	CLIMAX	CLOVEN	COCCUS
CICADA	CLAMPS	CLIMBS	CLOVES	COCCYX
CICALA	CLANGS	CLIMES	CLOWNS	COCHIN
CICALE	CLANKS	CLINAL	CLOYED	COCKED
CICELY	CLAQUE	CLINCH	CLOZES	COCKER
CICERO	CLARET	CLINES	CLUBBY	COCKLE
CIDERS	CLAROS	CLINGS	CLUCKS	COCKUP
CIGARS	CLASPS	CLINGY	CLUING	COCOAS
CILICE	CLASSY	CLINIC	CLUMPS	COCOON
CILIUM	CLASTS	CLINKS	CLUMPY	CODDED
CINDER	CLAUSE	CLIQUE	CLUMSY	CODDER
CINEMA	CLAVER	CLITIC	CLUNKS	CODDLE
CINQUE	CLAVES	CLIVIA	CLUNKY	CODECS
CIPHER	CLAVUS	CLOACA	CLUTCH	CODEIA
CIRCLE	CLAWED	CLOAKS	COACTS	CODEIN
CIRCUS	CLAWER	CLOCHE	COALAS	CODENS
CIRQUE	CLAYED	CLOCKS	COALED	CODERS
CIRRUS	CLAYEY	CLODDY	COALER	CODGER
CISCOS	CLEANS	CLOGGY	COAPTS	CODIFY
CISTUS	CLEARS	CLOMPS	COARSE	CODING
CITERS	CLEATS	CLONAL	COASTS	CODLIN
CITHER	CLEAVE	CLONED	COATED	CODONS
CITIED	CLEFTS	CLONER	COATEE	COEDIT
CITIES	CLENCH	CLONES	COATER	COELOM
CITIFY	CLEOME	CLONIC	COATIS	COEMPT
CITING	CLEPED	CLONKS	COAXAL	COERCE
CITOLA	CLEPES	CLONUS	COAXED	COEVAL
CITOLE	CLERGY	CLOOTS	COAXER	COFFEE
CITRAL	CLERIC	CLOQUE	COAXES	COFFER

COFFIN	COLTER	CONFIT	COPIED	COSETS
COGENT	COLUGO	CONGAS	COPIER	COSEYS
COGGED	COLUMN	CONGOS	COPIES	COSHED
COGITO	COLURE	CONINE	COPING	COSHES
COGNAC	COLZAS	CONING	COPLOT	COSIED
COGONS	COMADE	CONINS	COPPED	COSIER
COGWAY	COMAKE	CONIUM	COPPER	COSIES
COHEAD	COMATE	CONKED	COPRAH	COSIGN
COHEIR	COMBAT	CONKER	COPRAS	COSILY
COHERE	COMBED	CONNED	COPSES	COSINE
COHOGS	COMBER	CONSUL	COQUET	COSMIC
COHORT	COMBES	CONTES	CORALS	COSMOS
COHOST	COMBOS	CONTOS	CORBAN	COSSET
COHUNE	COMEDY	CONTRA	CORBEL	COSTAE
COIFED	COMELY	CONVEX	CORBIE	COSTAL
COIFFE	COMERS	CONVEY	CORDED	COSTAR
COILED	COMETH	CONVOY	CORDER	COSTED
COILER	COMETS	COOEED	CORDON	COSTER
COINED	COMFIT	COOERS	CORERS	COSTLY
COINER	COMICS	COOEYS	CORGIS	COTING
COITAL	COMING	COOING	CORING	COTTAE
COITUS	COMITY	COOKED	CORKED	COTTAR
COJOIN	COMMAS	COOKER	CORKER	COTTAS
COLDER	COMMIT	COOKIE	CORNEA	COTTER
COLDLY	COMMON	COOLED	CORNED	COTTON
COLEAD	COMPED	COOLER	CORNEL	COUGAR
COLEUS	COMPEL	COOLIE	CORNER	COUGHS
COLICS	COMPLY	COOLLY	CORNET	COULIS
COLIES	COMPOS	COOLTH	CORONA	COUNTS
COLINS	COMPTS	COOMBE	CORPSE	COUNTY
COLLAR	COMTES	COOMBS	CORPUS	COUPED
COLLET	CONCHA	COOPED	CORRAL	COUPES
COLLIE	CONCHS	COOPER	CORRIE	COUPLE
COLLOP	CONCHY	COOPTS	CORSAC	COUPON
COLOGS	CONCUR	COOTER	CORSET	COURSE
COLONE	CONDOM	COPALM	CORTEX	COURTS
COLONI	CONDOR	COPALS	CORTIN	COUSIN
COLONS	CONDOS	COPECK	CORVES	COUTHS
COLONY	CONFAB	COPENS	CORVET	COVENS
COLOUR	CONFER	COPERS	CORYZA	COVERS

COVERT	CRANKS	CREPON	CROZES	CULTCH
COVETS	CRANKY	CRESOL	CRUCES	CULTIC
COVING	CRANNY	CRESTS	CRUCKS	CULTUS
COVINS	CRAPED	CRETIC	CRUDDY	CULVER
COWAGE	CRAPES	CRETIN	CRUDES	CUMBER
COWARD	CRAPPY	CREWED	CRUETS	CUMINS
COWBOY	CRASES	CRICKS	CRUISE	CUMMIN
COWERS	CRATCH	CRIERS	CRUMBS	CUMULI
COWIER	CRATED	CRIKEY	CRUMBY	CUNEAL
COWING	CRATER	CRIMES	CRUMPS	CUNNER
COWLED	CRATES	CRIMPS	CRUNCH	CUPELS
COWMEN	CRAVAT	CRIMPY	CRUSES	CUPFUL
COWPAT	CRAVED	CRINGE	CRUSET	CUPIDS
COWPIE	CRAVEN	CRINUM	CRUSTS	CUPOLA
COWPOX	CRAVER	CRIPES	CRUSTY	CUPPAS
COWRIE	CRAVES	CRISIC	CRUTCH	CUPPED
COXING	CRAWLS	CRISIS	CRUXES	CUPPER
COYEST	CRAWLY	CRISPS	CRYING	CUPRIC
COYING	CRAYON	CRISPY	CRYPTO	CUPRUM
COYISH	CRAZED	CRITIC	CRYPTS	CUPULA
COYOTE	CRAZES	CROAKS	CUBAGE	CUPULE
COZENS	CREAKS	CROAKY	CUBERS	CURACY
COZEYS	CREAKY	CROCKS	CUBICS	CURATE
COZIED	CREAMS	CROCUS	CUBING	CURBED
COZIER	CREAMY	CROFTS	CUBISM	CURBER
COZIES	CREASE	CRONES	CUBIST	CURDED
COZILY	CREATE	CROOKS	CUBITS	CURDLE
CRABBY	CRECHE	CROONS	CUBOID	CURERS
CRACKS	CREDAL	CROSSE	CUCKOO	CURFEW
CRACKY	CREDIT	CROTCH	CUDDLE	CURIAL
CRADLE	CREEDS	CROTON	CUDDLY	CURIES
CRAFTS	CREEKS	CROUCH	CUDGEL	CURING
CRAFTY	CREELS	CROUPE	CUFFED	CURITE
CRAGGY	CREEPS	CROUPS	CULETS	CURIUM
CRAKES	CREEPY	CROUPY	CULLAY	CURLED
CRAMPS	CRENEL	CROWDS	CULLED	CURLER
CRANCH	CREOLE	CROWDY	CULLER	CURLEW
CRANED	CREPED	CROWED	CULLET	CURRAN
CRANES	CREPES	CROWNS	CULLIS	CURRED
CRANIA	CREPEY	CROZER	CULMED	CURSED

CURSER	CYCLOS	DAISES	DARNEL	DEANED
CURSES	CYDERS	DAKOIT	DARNER	DEARER
CURSOR	CYESES	DALLES	DARTED	DEARIE
CURTAL	CYESIS	DALTON	DARTER	DEARLY
CURTER	CYGNET	DAMAGE	DARTLE	DEARTH
CURTLY	CYMARS	DAMANS	DASHED	DEATHS
CURTSY	CYMBAL	DAMARS	DASHER	DEATHY
CURULE	CYMENE	DAMASK	DASHES	DEAVED
CURVED	CYMLIN	DAMMED	DASHIS	DEAVES
CURVES	CYMOID	DAMMER	DASSIE	DEBARK
CURVEY	CYMOLS	DAMNED	DATARY	DEBARS
CUSCUS	CYMOSE	DAMNER	DATCHA	DEBASE
CUSECS	CYMOUS	DAMPED	DATERS	DEBATE
CUSHAT	CYNICS	DAMPEN	DATING	DEBEAK
CUSHAW	CYPHER	DAMPER	DAUBED	DEBITS
CUSPED	CYPRUS	DAMPLY	DAUBER	DEBONE
CUSPIS	CYSTIC	DAMSEL	DAUBES	DEBRIS
CUSSED	CYTONS	DAMSON	DAUBRY	DEBTOR
CUSSER	DABBED	DANCED	DAUNTS	DEBUGS
CUSSES	DABBER	DANCER	DAUTED	DEBUNK
CUSSOS	DABBLE	DANCES	DAVENS	DEBUTS
CUSTOM	DACHAS	DANDER	DAVIES	DECADE
CUSTOS	DACKER	DANDLE	DAVITS	DECAFS
CUTELY	DACOIT	DANGER	DAWDLE	DECALS
CUTEST	DACTYL	DANGLE	DAWING	DECAMP
CUTESY	DADDLE	DANISH	DAWNED	DECANT
CUTIES	DADOED	DANKER	DAYBED	DECARE
CUTINS	DADOES	DANKLY	DAYFLY	DECAYS
CUTLAS	DAEDAL	DAPHNE	DAYLIT	DECEIT
CUTLER	DAEMON	DAPPED	DAZING	DECENT
CUTLET	DAFFED	DAPPER	DAZZLE	DECERN
CUTOFF	DAFTER	DAPPLE	DEACON	DECIDE
CUTOUT	DAFTLY	DARERS	DEADEN	DECILE
CUTTER	DAGGER	DARING	DEADER	DECKED
CUTTLE	DAGGLE	DARKED	DEADLY	DECKER
CYCADS	DAGOES	DARKEN	DEAFEN	DECKLE
CYCLED	DAHLIA	DARKER	DEAFER	DECLAW
CYCLER	DAIKON	DARKLE	DEAFLY	DECOCT
CYCLES	DAIMON	DARKLY	DEAIRS	DECODE
CYCLIC	DAINTY	DARNED	DEALER	DECORS

DECOYS	DEICES	DENIER	DESOXY	DIALOG
DECREE	DEIFIC	DENIES	DESPOT	DIBBED
DEDUCE	DEIGNS	DENIMS	DETACH	DIBBER
DEDUCT	DEISMS	DENNED	DETAIL	DIBBLE
DEEDED	DEISTS	DENOTE	DETAIN	DIBBUK
DEEJAY	DEIXIS	DENSER	DETECT	DICAST
DEEMED	DEJECT	DENTAL	DETENT	DICERS
DEEPEN	DEKARE	DENTED	DETERS	DICIER
DEEPER	DELATE	DENTIL	DETEST	DICING
DEEPLY	DELAYS	DENTIN	DETOUR	DICKED
DEFACE	DELEAD	DENUDE	DEUCED	DICKER
DEFAME	DELETE	DEPART	DEUCES	DICKEY
DEFANG	DELFTS	DEPEND	DEVEIN	DICKIE
DEFEAT	DELICT	DEPERM	DEVELS	DICOTS
DEFECT	DELIME	DEPICT	DEVEST	DICTUM
DEFEND	DELIST	DEPLOY	DEVICE	DIDACT
DEFERS	DELTAS	DEPONE	DEVILS	DIDDLE
DEFIED	DELTIC	DEPORT	DEVISE	DIDDLY
DEFIER	DELUDE	DEPOSE	DEVOID	DIDIES
DEFIES	DELUGE	DEPOTS	DEVONS	DIDOES
DEFILE	DELUXE	DEPTHS	DEVOTE	DIEING
DEFINE	DELVED	DEPUTE	DEVOUR	DIENES
DEFLEA	DELVER	DEPUTY	DEVOUT	DIESEL
DEFOAM	DELVES	DERAIL	DEWIER	DIESES
DEFOGS	DEMAND	DERATE	DEWILY	DIESIS
DEFORM	DEMARK	DERIDE	DEWING	DIETED
DEFRAY	DEMAST	DERIVE	DEWLAP	DIETER
DEFTER	DEMEAN	DERMAL	DEWOOL	DIFFER
DEFTLY	DEMENT	DERMIC	DEWORM	DIGEST
DEFUND	DEMISE	DERMIS	DEXTER	DIGGED
DEFUSE	DEMITS	DERRIS	DEXTRO	DIGGER
DEFUZE	DEMOBS	DESALT	DHARMA	DIGHTS
DEGAGE	DEMODE	DESCRY	DHARNA	DIGITS
DEGAME	DEMONS	DESERT	DHOBIS	DIGLOT
DEGERM	DEMOTE	DESIGN	DHOTIS	DIKTAT
DEGREE	DEMURE	DESIRE	DHURNA	DILATE
DEHORN	DENARY	DESIST	DIACID	DILDOS
DEHORT	DENGUE	DESMAN	DIADEM	DILLED
DEICED	DENIAL	DESMID	DIALED	DILUTE
DEICER	DENIED	DESORB	DIALER	DIMITY

DIMMED	DIRECT	DJINNI	DOLMAN	DOTTED
DIMMER	DIRELY	DJINNS	DOLMAS	DOTTEL
DIMOUT	DIREST	DJINNY	DOLMEN	DOTTER
DIMPLE	DIRGES	DOABLE	DOLOUR	DOTTLE
DIMPLY	DIRHAM	DOATED	DOMAIN	DOUBLE
DIMWIT	DIRKED	DOBBER	DOMINE	DOUBLY
DINARS	DIRLED	DOBBIN	DOMING	DOUBTS
DINDLE	DIRNDL	DOBIES	DOMINO	DOUCHE
DINERS	DISARM	DOBLAS	DONATE	DOUGHS
DINGED	DISBAR	DOBLON	DONEES	DOUGHT
DINGER	DISBUD	DOBRAS	DONKEY	DOUGHY
DINGES	DISCED	DOCENT	DONNAS	DOUMAS
DINGEY	DISCOS	DOCILE	DONNED	DOURER
DINGHY	DISCUS	DOCKED	DONORS	DOURLY
DINGLE	DISHED	DOCKER	DONUTS	DOUSED
DINING	DISHES	DOCKET	DOODLE	DOUSER
DINKED	DISKED	DOCTOR	DOOFUS	DOUSES
DINKEY	DISMAL	DODDER	DOOLIE	DOVENS
DINKLY	DISMAY	DODGED	DOOMED	DOVISH
DINKUM	DISMES	DODGEM	DOOZIE	DOWERY
DINNED	DISOWN	DODGER	DOPERS	DOWING
DINNER	DISPEL	DODGES	DOPIER	DOWNED
DINTED	DISSED	DOFFED	DOPING	DOWNER
DIOBOL	DISSES	DOFFER	DORADO	DOZENS
DIODES	DISTAL	DOGDOM	DORMER	DOZERS
DIOECY	DISTIL	DOGEAR	DORMIE	DOZIER
DIOXAN	DISUSE	DOGGED	DORSEL	DOZILY
DIOXID	DITHER	DOGGER	DORSER	DOZING
DIOXIN	DITTOS	DOGGIE	DORSUM	DRABLY
DIPLEX	DITZES	DOGIES	DOSAGE	DRAFTS
DIPLOE	DIVERS	DOGLEG	DOSERS	DRAFTY
DIPNET	DIVERT	DOGMAS	DOSING	DRAGEE
DIPODY	DIVEST	DOGNAP	DOSSED	DRAGGY
DIPOLE	DIVIDE	DOILED	DOSSER	DRAGON
DIPPED	DIVINE	DOINGS	DOSSES	DRAINS
DIPPER	DIVING	DOITED	DOTAGE	DRAKES
DIPSAS	DIVOTS	DOLING	DOTARD	DRAMAS
DIPSOS	DIXITS	DOLLAR	DOTERS	DRAPED
DIQUAT	DIZENS	DOLLED	DOTIER	DRAPER
DIRDUM	DJEBEL	DOLLOP	DOTING	DRAPES

DRAWER	DROWNS	DUMPER	EAGLES	EDGILY
DRAWLS	DROWSE	DUNCES	EAGLET	EDGING
DRAWLY	DROWSY	DUNGED	EAGRES	EDIBLE
DRAYED	DRUDGE	DUNITE	EARFUL	EDICTS
DREADS	DRUGGY	DUNKED	EARING	EDILES
DREAMS	DRUIDS	DUNKER	EARLAP	EDITED
DREAMT	DRUNKS	DUNNED	EARNED	EDITOR
DREAMY	DRUPES	DUNNER	EARNER	EERIER
DREARS	DRUSES	DUNTED	EARTHS	EERILY
DREARY	DRYERS	DUPERS	EARTHY	EFFACE
DREDGE	DRYEST	DUPERY	EARWAX	EFFECT
DREIDL	DRYING	DUPING	EARWIG	EFFETE
DRENCH	DRYISH	DUPLEX	EASELS	EFFIGY
DRESSY	DRYLOT	DUPPED	EASIER	EFFLUX
DRIERS	DUALLY	DURESS	EASIES	EFFORT
DRIEST	DUBBED	DURIAN	EASILY	EFFUSE
DRIFTS	DUBBER	DURING	EASING	EGGCUP
DRIFTY	DUCKED	DURION	EASTER	EGGING
DRILLS	DUCKER	DURNED	EATERS	EGGNOG
DRINKS	DUCKIE	DURRAS	EATERY	EGISES
DRIPPY	DUCTAL	DURRIE	EATING	EGRESS
DRIVEL	DUCTED	DURUMS	EBBING	EGRETS
DRIVEN	DUDING	DUSKED	ECARTE	EIGHTH
DRIVER	DUDISH	DUSTED	ECESIS	EIGHTS
DRIVES	DUELED	DUSTER	ECHING	EIGHTY
DROGUE	DUELER	DUSTUP	ECHINI	EITHER
DROITS	DUFFEL	DUTIES	ECHOED	EJECTA
DROLLS	DUFFER	DUVETS	ECHOER	EJECTS
DRONED	DUFFLE	DWARFS	ECHOES	ELAINS
DRONER	DUGOUT	DWEEBS	ECHOEY	ELAPSE
DRONES	DUKING	DWELLS	ECHOIC	ELATED
DRONGO	DULCET	DWINED	ECLAIR	ELATER
DROOLS	DULLED	DWINES	ECLATS	ELATES
DROOPS	DULLER	DYADIC	ECTYPE	ELBOWS
DROOPY	DULSES	DYEING	ECZEMA	ELDERS
DROPSY	DUMBED	DYINGS	EDDIED	ELDEST
DROSSY	DUMBER	DYNAMO	EDDIES	ELECTS
DROVED	DUMBLY	DYNAST	EDDOES	ELEVEN
DROVER	DUMDUM	DYNODE	EDGERS	ELFINS
DROVES	DUMPED	EAGERS	EDGIER	ELFISH

ELICIT	EMODIN	ENLACE	EPIGON	ESCUDO
ELIDED	EMOTED	ENLIST	EPIMER	ESKARS
ELIDES	EMOTER	ENMESH	EPIZOA	ESKERS
ELINTS	EMPERY	ENMITY	EPOCHS	ESPIAL
ELITES	EMPIRE	ENOUGH	EPODES	ESPIED
ELIXIR	EMPLOY	ENRAGE	EPONYM	ESPIES
ELODEA	ENABLE	ENRAPT	EPOSES	ESPRIT
ELOIGN	ENACTS	ENRICH	EQUALS	ESSAYS
ELOINS	ENAMEL	ENROBE	EQUATE	ESTATE
ELOPED	ENATIC	ENROLS	EQUIDS	ESTEEM
ELOPER	ENCAGE	ENROOT	EQUINE	ESTRAL
ELOPES	ENCAMP	ENSIGN	EQUIPS	ESTRAY
ELUDED	ENCASE	ENSUED	EQUITY	ESTRIN
ELUDER	ENCASH	ENSUES	ERASED	ESTRUM
ELUDES	ENCINA	ENSURE	ERASER	ESTRUS
ELUENT	ENCODE	ENTAIL	ERASES	ETCHED
ELUTED	ENCORE	ENTERS	ERECTS	ETCHER
ELUTES	ENDEAR	ENTICE	ERGATE	ETCHES
ELUVIA	ENDERS	ENTIRE	ERGOTS	ETERNE
ELVERS	ENDING	ENTITY	ERMINE	ETHANE
ELVISH	ENDITE	ENTOIL	ERODED	ETHENE
EMBALM	ENDIVE	ENTOMB	ERODES	ETHERS
EMBANK	ENDOWS	ENTRAP	EROSES	ETHICS
EMBARK	ENDRIN	ENTREE	EROTIC	ETHNIC
EMBEDS	ENDUED	ENVIED	ERRAND	ETHNOS
EMBERS	ENDUES	ENVIER	ERRANT	ETHOXY
EMBLEM	ENDURE	ENVIES	ERRING	ETHYLS
EMBODY	ENEMAS	ENVOYS	ERRORS	ETHYNE
EMBOSS	ENERGY	ENWIND	ERSATZ	ETOILE
EMBRYO	ENFACE	ENWOMB	ERUCTS	ETUDES
EMCEED	ENFOLD	ENWRAP	ERUGOS	EULOGY
EMCEES	ENGAGE	ENZYME	ERUPTS	EUNUCH
EMEERS	ENGILD	ENZYMS	ERVILS	EUREKA
EMERGE	ENGINE	EONIAN	ESCAPE	EVADED
EMESES	ENGIRD	EONISM	ESCARS	EVADER
EMESIS	ENGIRT	EOSINE	ESCHAR	EVADES
EMETIC	ENGULF	EOSINS	ESCHEW	EVENED
EMETIN	ENIGMA	EPACTS	ESCORT	EVENER
EMIGRE	ENISLE	EPHORS	ESCOTS	EVENLY
EMMERS	ENJOYS	EPICAL	ESCROW	EVENTS

EVICTS	EXPATS	FACTOR	FARCIE	FEASED
EVILER	EXPECT	FADERS	FARFAL	FEASES
EVILLY	EXPELS	FADING	FARFEL	FEASTS
EVINCE	EXPEND	FAECAL	FARINA	FECKLY
EVITED	EXPERT	FAECES	FARING	FECULA
EVITES	EXPIRE	FAENAS	FARLES	FECUND
EVOKED	EXPIRY	FAERIE	FARMED	FEDORA
EVOKER	EXPORT	FAGGED	FARMER	FEEBLE
EVOKES	EXPOSE	FAGINS	FARROW	FEEBLY
EVOLVE	EXTANT	FAILED	FARTED	FEEDER
EXACTA	EXTEND	FAINTS	FASCES	FEELER
EXACTS	EXTENT	FAIRED	FASCIA	FEEZES
EXALTS	EXTERN	FAIRER	FASTED	FEIGNS
EXAMEN	EXTOLL	FAIRLY	FASTEN	FEIJOA
EXARCH	EXTOLS	FAITHS	FASTER	FEIRIE
EXCEED	EXTORT	FAJITA	FATHER	FEISTS
EXCELS	EXTRAS	FAKERS	FATHOM	FEISTY
EXCEPT	EXUDED	FAKERY	FATING	FELINE
EXCESS	EXUDES	FAKING	FATTED	FELLAS
EXCIDE	EYASES	FAKIRS	FATTEN	FELLED
EXCISE	EYEBAR	FALCES	FATTER	FELLOW
EXCITE	EYECUP	FALCON	FATWAS	FELTED
EXCUSE	EYEFUL	FALLEN	FAUCAL	FEMALE
EXEDRA	EYEING	FALLER	FAUCES	FEMMES
EXEMPT	EYELET	FALLOW	FAUCET	FEMORA
EXEQUY	EYELID	FALSER	FAULDS	FEMURS
EXERTS	EYRIES	FALSIE	FAULTS	FENCED
EXHALE	FABLED	FALTER	FAULTY	FENCER
EXHORT	FABLER	FAMILY	FAUNAE	FENCES
EXHUME	FABLES	FAMINE	FAUNAL	FENDED
EXILED	FABRIC	FAMISH	FAUNAS	FENDER
EXILES	FACADE	FAMOUS	FAUVES	FENNEC
EXINES	FACERS	FANGED	FAVISM	FENNEL
EXISTS	FACETE	FANNED	FAVOUR	FEOFFS
EXITED	FACETS	FANNER	FAWNED	FERBAM
EXODUS	FACEUP	FANUMS	FAXING	FERIAE
EXOGEN	FACIAL	FARADS	FAYING	FERIAL
EXONIC	FACIES	FARCED	FAZING	FERIAS
EXOTIC	FACILE	FARCER	FEARED	FERINE
EXPAND	FACING	FARCES	FEARER	FERITY

FERLIE	FIDGED	FIRKIN	FLANES	FLOCKS
FERMIS	FIDGES	FIRMED	FLANGE	FLOODS
FERREL	FIDGET	FIRMER	FLANKS	FLOORS
FERRET	FIELDS	FIRMLY	FLAPPY	FLOOZY
FERRIC	FIENDS	FIRSTS	FLARED	FLOPPY
FERRUM	FIERCE	FIRTHS	FLARES	FLORAL
FERULA	FIESTA	FISCAL	FLASHY	FLORAS
FERULE	FIFERS	FISHED	FLASKS	FLORET
FERVID	FIFING	FISHER	FLATLY	FLORID
FESTAL	FIFTHS	FISHES	FLAUNT	FLORIN
FESTER	FIGGED	FISTED	FLAVIN	FLOSSY
FETIAL	FIGHTS	FISTIC	FLAWED	FLOURS
FETING	FIGURE	FITCHY	FLAXEN	FLOURY
FETISH	FILERS	FITFUL	FLAXES	FLOUTS
FETTED	FILETS	FITTED	FLAYED	FLOWED
FETTER	FILIAL	FITTER	FLAYER	FLOWER
FETTLE	FILING	FIVERS	FLECKS	FLUENT
FEUDAL	FILLED	FIXATE	FLECKY	FLUFFS
FEUDED	FILLER	FIXERS	FLEDGE	FLUFFY
FEVERS	FILLES	FIXING	FLEDGY	FLUIDS
FEWEST	FILLET	FIXURE	FLEECE	FLUKED
FEYEST	FILMED	FIZZED	FLEETS	FLUKES
FEZZED	FILMER	FIZZER	FLESHY	FLUKEY
FEZZES	FILMIC	FIZZES	FLEXED	FLUMED
FIANCE	FILTER	FIZZLE	FLEXES	FLUMES
FIASCO	FILTHS	FJORDS	FLICKS	FLUMPS
FIBBED	FILTHY	FLABBY	FLIERS	FLURRY
FIBBER	FINALE	FLACKS	FLIGHT	FLUTED
FIBRES	FINALS	FLAGON	FLIMSY	FLUTER
FIBRIL	FINDER	FLAILS	FLINCH	FLUTES
FIBRIN	FINELY	FLAIRS	FLINGS	FLUTEY
FIBULA	FINERY	FLAKED	FLINTS	FLUXED
FICHES	FINEST	FLAKER	FLINTY	FLUXES
FICHUS	FINGER	FLAKES	FLIPPY	FLYERS
FICINS	FINIAL	FLAKEY	FLIRTS	FLYING
FICKLE	FINING	FLAMBE	FLIRTY	FLYWAY
FICKLY	FINISH	FLAMED	FLITCH	FOALED
FICOES	FINITE	FLAMEN	FLOATS	FOAMED
FIDDLE	FIRERS	FLAMER	FLOATY	FOAMER
FIDDLY	FIRING	FLAMES	FLOCCI	FOBBED

FOETAL	FORGOT	FRESCO	FULMAR	GAINLY
FOETID	FORKED	FRIARS	FUMBLE	GALAXY
FOETUS	FORKER	FRIARY	FUMERS	GALLED
FOGIES	FORMAL	FRIDGE	FUMETS	GALLEY
FOIBLE	FORMAT	FRIEND	FUMIER	GALLON
FOILED	FORMED	FRIERS	FUMING	GALLOP
FOLATE	FORMER	FRIEZE	FUNDED	GALOOT
FOLDED	FORTES	FRIGHT	FUNGAL	GALOPS
FOLDER	FORUMS	FRIGID	FUNGUS	GALORE
FOLIAR	FOSSIL	FRILLS	FUNKED	GALOSH
FOLIOS	FOSTER	FRILLY	FUNNEL	GAMBAS
FOLKSY	FOUGHT	FRINGE	FUNNER	GAMBIT
FOLLOW	FOULED	FRINGY	FURIES	GAMBLE
FOMENT	FOULER	FRISKS	FURORE	GAMELY
FONDED	FOULLY	FRISKY	FURRED	GAMERS
FONDER	FOUNDS	FRIZZY	FURROW	GAMEST
FONDLE	FOURTH	FROCKS	FURZES	GAMINE
FONDLY	FOWLED	FROLIC	FUSING	GAMING
FONDUE	FOWLER	FRONTS	FUSION	GAMMER
FOODIE	FOXIER	FROSTS	FUSSED	GAMMON
FOOLED	FOXILY	FROSTY	FUSSER	GANDER
FOOTED	FOXING	FROTHS	FUSSES	GANGED
FOOTER	FOYERS	FROTHY	FUTILE	GANGLY
FOOTLE	FRACAS	FROWNS	FUTONS	GANNET
FOOTSY	FRAILS	FROZEN	FUTURE	GANOID
FOPPED	FRAISE	FRUGAL	FUZZED	GANTRY
FORAGE	FRAMED	FRUITS	GABBED	GAOLED
FORAYS	FRAMER	FRUITY	GABBER	GAOLER
FORBAD	FRAMES	FRUMPS	GABBLE	GAPERS
FORBID	FRANCS	FRUMPY	GADDED	GAPING
FORCED	FRAPPE	FRYERS	GADDER	GAPPED
FORCES	FRAUDS	FRYING	GADGET	GARAGE
FOREBY	FRAYED	FUDGED	GAFFER	GARBLE
FOREDO	FREAKS	FUDGES	GAFFES	GARCON
FOREGO	FREAKY	FUELED	GAGGED	GARDEN
FOREST	FREELY	FUELER	GAGGER	GARGLE
FORGED	FREERS	FUHRER	GAGGLE	GARISH
FORGER	FREEZE	FULFIL	GAGING	GARLIC
FORGES	FRENCH	FULHAM	GAIETY	GARNET
FORGET	FRENZY	FULLER	GAINED	GAROTE

GARRET	GENTIL	GLARES	GOBBLE	GRADED
GARTER	GENTLE	GLASSY	GOBLIN	GRADER
GASHED	GENTLY	GLAZED	GOGGLE	GRADES
GASHER	GENTRY	GLAZER	GOGGLY	GRAHAM
GASHES	GERBIL	GLAZES	GOINGS	GRAILS
GASKET	GERMAN	GLEAMS	GOLDEN	GRAINS
GASPED	GETTER	GLEANS	GOLDER	GRAINY
GASPER	GHETTO	GLIBLY	GOLFER	GRANDS
GASSED	GHOSTS	GLIDED	GONADS	GRANGE
GASSER	GHOSTY	GLIDER	GONERS	GRANNY
GASSES	GHOULS	GLIDES	GOODIE	GRANTS
GATEAU	GIANTS	GLIFFS	GOODLY	GRAPES
GATHER	GIBBON	GLINTS	GOOFED	GRAPHS
GATING	GIBLET	GLITCH	GOOGLY	GRASPS
GAUCHE	GIFTED	GLITZY	GOOGOL	GRASSY
GAUGED	GIGGLE	GLOATS	GOOIER	GRATED
GAUGER	GIGGLY	GLOBAL	GOONEY	GRATER
GAUGES	GIGOLO	GLOBBY	GOONIE	GRATES
GAUZES	GILDED	GLOBES	GOOSED	GRATIS
GAWKED	GILDER	GLOOMS	GOOSES	GRAVED
GAWKER	GILLED	GLOOMY	GOOSEY	GRAVEL
GAWPED	GINGER	GLORIA	GOPHER	GRAVEN
GAWPER	GIRDED	GLOSSY	GORGED	GRAVER
GAZEBO	GIRDER	GLOVED	GORGER	GRAVES
GAZERS	GIRDLE	GLOVES	GORGES	GRAYED
GAZING	GIRLIE	GLOWED	GORGON	GRAZED
GAZUMP	GIRNED	GLUERS	GORILY	GRAZER
GEARED	GIRTHS	GLUING	GORING	GRAZES
GEEING	GISMOS	GLUMLY	GORSES	GREASE
GEEZER	GIVENS	GLUMPY	GOSPEL	GREASY
GEISHA	GIVERS	GLUTEN	GOSSIP	GREAVE
GENDER	GIVING	GNARLS	GOTHIC	GREEDY
GENETS	GIZMOS	GNARLY	GOTTEN	GREENS
GENEVA	GLACES	GNATTY	GOURDE	GREENY
GENIAL	GLADES	GNAWED	GOURDS	GREYED
GENIES	GLADLY	GNAWER	GOVERN	GREYER
GENIUS	GLAIRE	GNOMES	GOWNED	GREYLY
GENOAS	GLANCE	GOALED	GOYISH	GRIEFS
GENOME	GLANDS	GOALIE	GRACED	GRIEVE
GENRES	GLARED	GOATEE	GRACES	GRIFTS

GRILLS	GUIDES	HAGGIS	HASTEN	HEEDED
GRIMED	GUILDS	HAGGLE	HASTES	HEEDER
GRIMES	GUILES	HAILED	HATERS	HEELED
GRIMLY	GUILTS	HAILER	HATFUL	HEELER
GRINDS	GUILTY	HAIRDO	HATING	HEIGHT
GRIPED	GUIMPE	HAIRED	HATRED	HEILED
GRISLY	GUINEA	HALTED	HAUGHS	HEISTS
GRITTY	GUISES	HALTER	HAULED	HELIAC
GROCER	GUITAR	HALVAH	HAUNCH	HELIUM
GROINS	GULFED	HALVAS	HAUNTS	HELLED
GROOMS	GULLED	HALVED	HAVING	HELLER
GROOVE	GULLET	HALVES	HAVOCS	HELLOS
GROOVY	GULLEY	HAMLET	HAWING	HELMED
GROPED	GULPED	HAMMER	HAWKED	HELMET
GROPER	GULPER	HAMPER	HAWKER	HELPED
GROPES	GUMMED	HANCES	HAZARD	HELPER
GROTTO	GUNDOG	HANDED	HAZELS	HERALD
GROTTY	GUNMAN	HANDLE	HAZIER	HERBAL
GROUCH	GUNMEN	HANGAR	HAZILY	HERBED
GROUND	GUNNED	HANGED	HEADED	HERDED
GROUPS	GUNNEL	HANGER	HEADER	HERDER
GROUSE	GUNNER	HANKER	HEALED	HEREBY
GROVED	GURGLE	HANKIE	HEALER	HEREON
GROVEL	GURNET	HANSOM	HEALTH	HERESY
GROVES	GURNEY	HANTLE	HEAPED	HERETO
GROWER	GUSHED	HAPPED	HEARER	HERMIT
GROWLS	GUSHER	HAPPEN	HEARSE	HERNIA
GROWTH	GUSHES	HARASS	HEARTH	HEROES
GRUBBY	GUSSET	HARDER	HEARTS	HEROIC
GRUDGE	GUTTED	HARDLY	HEARTY	HEROIN
GRUMPY	GUTTER	HAREEM	HEATED	HERONS
GRUNGE	GUZZLE	HARKEN	HEATER	HERPES
GRUNGY	GYPPED	HARLOT	HEATHS	HETERO
GRUNTS	GYPPER	HARMED	HEAVED	HIATUS
GUARDS	GYPSUM	HARPED	HEAVEN	HICCUP
GUAVAS	GYRATE	HARPER	HECKLE	HICKEY
GUESTS	HABITS	HARROW	HECTIC	HIDDEN
GUFFAW	HACKED	HASHED	HECTOR	HIDERS
GUIDED	HACKER	HASHES	HEDGED	HIDING
GUIDER	HAGGED	HASSLE	HEDGES	HIGHER

HIGHLY	HOLILY	HOPPED	HUMMED	IDIOMS
HIGHTS	HOLIST	HOPPER	HUMMUS	IDIOTS
HIJACK	HOLLOW	HORDES	HUMORS	IDLERS
HIKERS	HOMAGE	HORNED	HUMOUR	IDLEST
HIKING	HOMBRE	HORNET	HUMPED	IDLING
HINDER	HOMELY	HORRID	HUNGER	IDYLLS
HINGED	HOMIER	HORROR	HUNGRY	IFFIER
HINGER	HOMILY	HORSED	HUNTED	IGLOOS
HINGES	HONCHO	HORSES	HUNTER	IGNIFY
HINTED	HONEST	HORSEY	HURDLE	IGNITE
HIPPER	HONEYS	HOSING	HURLED	IGNORE
HIPPIE	HONIED	HOSTED	HURRAH	IGUANA
HIPPOS	HONING	HOSTEL	HURRAY	ILIADS
HIRERS	HONKED	HOSTLY	HURTLE	ILLEST
HIRING	HONKER	HOTBED	HUSHED	IMAGED
HISSED	HONKEY	HOTDOG	HUSHES	IMAGER
HISSER	HONKIE	HOTELS	HUSKED	IMAGES
HISSES	HONOUR	HOTROD	HUSKER	IMBIBE
HISTED	HOODED	HOTTER	HUSTLE	IMBUED
HITHER	HOODIE	HOUNDS	HUTZPA	IMMUNE
HITTER	HOOFED	HOURLY	HYAENA	IMMURE
HIVING	HOOKAH	HOUSED	HYBRID	IMPACT
HOARDS	HOOKAS	HOUSES	HYBRIS	IMPAIR
HOARSE	HOOKED	HOVELS	HYDROS	IMPALA
HOAXED	HOOKER	HOVERS	HYENAS	IMPALE
HOAXER	HOOKEY	HOWLED	HYMENS	IMPART
HOAXES	HOOKUP	HOWLER	HYMNED	IMPEDE
HOBBIT	HOOLIE	HUBBUB	HYPHEN	IMPELS
HOBBLE	HOOPED	HUBCAP	HYPING	IMPEND
HOCKED	HOOPER	HUDDLE	IBISES	IMPING
HOCKER	HOOPLA	HUGELY	ICEBOX	IMPISH
HOCKEY	HOORAH	HUGEST	ICECAP	IMPORT
HOEING	HOORAY	HUGGED	ICICLE	IMPOSE
HOISTS	HOOTCH	HUGGER	ICIEST	IMPOST
HOKING	HOOTED	HULKED	ICINGS	IMPROV
HOLDEN	HOOTER	HUMANE	ICKIER	IMPUGN
HOLDER	HOOVED	HUMANS	ICKILY	IMPURE
HOLDUP	HOOVES	HUMBLE	ICONIC	IMPUTE
HOLIER	HOPERS	HUMBLY	IDEALS	INBORN
HOLIES	HOPING	HUMBUG	IDIOCY	INBRED

INCAGE	INKIER	ISOBAR	JEWELS	JOYOUS
INCANT	INKING	ISSUED	JIBBED	JUDDER
INCASE	INKJET	ISSUER	JIBBER	JUDGED
INCEPT	INKPOT	ISSUES	JIGGED	JUDGER
INCEST	INLAID	ITALIC	JIGGLE	JUDGES
INCHED	INLAND	ITCHED	JIGGLY	JUGGLE
INCHES	INLAYS	ITCHES	JIGSAW	JUGULA
INCISE	INLETS	ITEMED	JIHADS	JUICED
INCITE	INMATE	ITSELF	JILTED	JUICER
INCOME	INNERS	JABBED	JINGLE	JUICES
INCURS	INNING	JACKAL	JINGLY	JUMBLE
INDEED	INPUTS	JACKET	JINXED	JUMBOS
INDENT	INROAD	JAGGED	JINXES	JUMPED
INDICT	INSANE	JAGUAR	JITTER	JUMPER
INDIES	INSECT	JAILED	JIVERS	JUNGLE
INDIGO	INSERT	JALOPY	JIVING	JUNGLY
INDITE	INSETS	JAMMED	JOBBED	JUNIOR
INDOLE	INSIDE	JANGLE	JOBBER	JUNKED
INDOOR	INSIST	JANGLY	JOCKEY	JUNKET
INDUCE	INSTEP	JAPERS	JOGGED	JUNKIE
INDUCT	INSTIL	JAPERY	JOGGER	JURIES
INERTS	INSULT	JARGON	JOINED	JURORS
INFAMY	INTACT	JARRED	JOINER	JUSTLY
INFANT	INTAKE	JASMIN	JOINTS	JUTTED
INFECT	INTEND	JASPER	JOISTS	KABABS
INFERS	INTENT	JAUNTS	JOJOBA	KABALA
INFEST	INTERN	JAUNTY	JOKERS	KAFTAN
INFIRM	INTERS	JAZZED	JOKIER	KAISER
INFLUX	INTURN	JAZZES	JOKILY	KAMALA
INFORM	INVADE	JEERED	JOKING	KARATE
INFUSE	INVENT	JEERER	JOLTED	KARMAS
INGEST	INVERT	JERKED	JOSHED	KARMIC
INGLES	INVEST	JERKIN	JOSHES	KAYAKS
INGOTS	INVITE	JERSEY	JOSTLE	KAYLES
INHALE	INVOKE	JESTED	JOTTED	KAZOOS
INHAUL	INWARD	JESTER	JOTTER	KEBABS
INJECT	IRKING	JESUIT	JOUSTS	KEELED
INJURE	IRONIC	JETSAM	JOVIAL	KEENED
INJURY	ISLAND	JETSOM	JOYFUL	KEENER
INKERS	ISLETS	JETTED	JOYING	KEENLY

KEEPER	KNEADS	LANCED	LAWYER	LEMONY
KENNEL	KNEELS	LANCER	LAXEST	LEMURS
KERNEL	KNIFED	LANCES	LAYING	LENDER
KETTLE	KNIFER	LANDED	LAYMAN	LENGTH
KEYING	KNIFES	LANKLY	LAYMEN	LENSED
KEYPAD	KNIGHT	LAPDOG	LAYOFF	LENSES
KHAKIS	KNIVES	LAPELS	LAYOUT	LENTIL
KIBOSH	KNOCKS	LAPPED	LAZIER	LEPERS
KICKED	KNOLLS	LAPPER	LAZILY	LESSEN
KICKER	KNOTTY	LAPSED	LAZING	LESSER
KICKUP	KNOWER	LAPSES	LEADED	LESSON
KIDDED	KOALAS	LAPTOP	LEADEN	LETHAL
KIDDER	KONKED	LARDER	LEADER	LETTED
KIDDIE	KOOKIE	LARGER	LEAFED	LETTER
KIDNAP	KOSHER	LARGES	LEAGUE	LETUPS
KIDNEY	KOWTOW	LARKED	LEAKED	LEVELS
KILLED	KRAKEN	LARKER	LEAPED	LEVIED
KILLER	KRATER	LARRUP	LEAPER	LEVIES
KILNED	KYBOSH	LARVAE	LEARNS	LEVITY
KILTED	LABELS	LARYNX	LEARNT	LEWDLY
KILTER	LABOUR	LASERS	LEASED	LIABLE
KIMONO	LACERS	LASHED	LEASES	LIAISE
KINDER	LACHES	LASHES	LEASTS	LIBELS
KINDLE	LACIER	LASSES	LEAVEN	LIBIDO
KINDLY	LACING	LASSIE	LEAVES	LICHEE
KINGLY	LACKED	LASTED	LECHED	LICHEN
KINKED	LADDER	LASTLY	LECHER	LICHTS
KIOSKS	LADIES	LATELY	LECHES	LICKED
KIPPER	LADLED	LATENT	LEDGER	LICKER
KISMET	LADLER	LATEST	LEDGES	LIDDED
KISSED	LADLES	LATHED	LEERED	LIFTED
KISSER	LAGERS	LATHER	LEEWAY	LIFTER
KISSES	LAGGED	LATINO	LEGACY	LIGHTS
KITERS	LAGGER	LAUDED	LEGALS	LIKELY
KITING	LAGOON	LAUDER	LEGATE	LIKENS
KITSCH	LAIRDS	LAUGHS	LEGEND	LIKERS
KITTED	LAMELY	LAUNCH	LEGERS	LIKEST
KITTEN	LAMENT	LAUREL	LEGGED	LIKING
KLAXON	LAMEST	LAVISH	LEGION	LILACS
KNAVES	LAMPED	LAWFUL	LEMONS	LILIES

LILTED	LIZARD	LOOTER	LUSTED	MAKING
LIMBED	LLAMAS	LOPERS	LUSTER	MALADY
LIMBER	LOADED	LOPING	LUSTRE	MALICE
LIMBOS	LOADER	LOPPED	LUTING	MALIGN
LIMENS	LOAFED	LORDLY	LUTIST	MALLED
LIMEYS	LOAFER	LOSERS	LUXURY	MALLET
LIMIER	LOANED	LOSING	LYCEUM	MALLOW
LIMING	LOATHE	LOSSES	LYCHEE	MALTED
LIMITS	LOAVES	LOTION	LYINGS	MAMMAL
LIMPED	LOBBED	LOUDER	LYMPHS	MANAGE
LIMPER	LOCALE	LOUDLY	LYNXES	MANGLE
LIMPET	LOCALS	LOUIES	LYRICS	MANIAC
LIMPID	LOCATE	LOUNGE	MACAWS	MANIAS
LIMPLY	LOCKED	LOVELY	MACHOS	MANICS
LINAGE	LOCKER	LOVERS	MADAME	MANNER
LINEAL	LOCKET	LOVING	MADAMS	MANTIS
LINEAR	LOCUST	LOWERS	MADCAP	MANTLE
LINENS	LODGED	LOWEST	MADDEN	MANTRA
LINERS	LODGER	LUGGED	MADDER	MANUAL
LINEUP	LODGES	LUGGER	MADMAN	MANURE
LINGER	LOGGED	LULLED	MADMEN	MAPLES
LINING	LOGGER	LUMBER	MADRAS	MAPPED
LINKED	LOGICS	LUMMOX	MAFFIA	MAPPER
LIPPED	LOITER	LUMPED	MAFIAS	MARAUD
LIPPER	LOLLED	LUMPEN	MAGGOT	MARBLE
LIQUID	LOLLOP	LUMPER	MAGIAN	MARGIN
LIQUOR	LONELY	LUNACY	MAGICS	MARINA
LISPED	LONERS	LUNARS	MAGMAS	MARINE
LISTED	LONGED	LUNGED	MAGNET	MARKED
LISTEN	LONGER	LUNGER	MAGNUM	MARKER
LITMUS	LONGLY	LUNGES	MAGPIE	MARKET
LITRES	LOOFAH	LUPINE	MAIDEN	MARKUP
LITTER	LOOKED	LUPINS	MAILED	MAROON
LITTLE	LOOKER	LURING	MAILER	MARRED
LIVELY	LOOKUP	LURKED	MAILES	MARSHY
LIVENS	LOOMED	LURKER	MAIMED	MARTIN
LIVERY	LOONEY	LUSHED	MAINLY	MARTYR
LIVEST	LOOPER	LUSHER	MAJORS	MARVEL
LIVIER	LOOSEN	LUSHES	MAKERS	MASCOT
LIVING	LOOTED	LUSHLY	MAKEUP	MASHED

MASHER	MELDER	MEWING	MINUET	MODISH
MASHES	MELEES	MEZCAL	MINUTE	MODULE
MASKED	MELLOW	MIAOWS	MINXES	MOGGED
MASKER	MELODY	MICKEY	MIOSIS	MOGGIE
MASONS	MELONS	MICROS	MIRAGE	MOGULS
MASQUE	MELTED	MIDDAY	MIRKER	MOHAIR
MASSED	MEMBER	MIDDEN	MIRROR	MOLARS
MASSES	MEMOIR	MIDDLE	MIRTHS	MOLDED
MASTER	MEMORY	MIDGES	MISATE	MOLDER
MATING	MENACE	MIDGET	MISERS	MOLEST
MATRIX	MENDED	MIDSTS	MISERY	MOLTED
MATRON	MENDER	MIDWAY	MISFIT	MOLTEN
MATTED	MENTAL	MIFFED	MISHAP	MOLTER
MATTER	MENTOR	MIGHTS	MISLAY	MOMENT
MATTES	MEOWED	MIGHTY	MISLED	MONEYS
MATURE	MERCER	MILDER	MISSED	MONGOL
MAULED	MERELY	MILDEW	MISSES	MONIED
MAUVES	MEREST	MILDLY	MISTED	MONIES
MAXIMS	MERGED	MILIEU	MISTER	MONKEY
MAYBES	MERGER	MILKED	MISUSE	MONTHS
MAYDAY	MERGES	MILKER	MITRAL	MOOING
MAYFLY	MERITS	MILLED	MITRED	MOONED
MAYHEM	MERLIN	MILLER	MITRES	MOORED
MAYORS	MERLOT	MIMERS	MITTEN	MOOTED
MEADOW	MERMAN	MIMICS	MIXERS	MOOTER
MEAGRE	MERMEN	MIMING	MIXING	MOPEDS
MEANER	MESCAL	MIMOSA	MIXUPS	MOPERS
MEANIE	MESHED	MINCED	MOANED	MOPING
MEANLY	MESHES	MINCER	MOANER	MOPPED
MEASLY	MESSED	MINCES	MOATED	MORALE
MEDALS	MESSES	MINDED	MOBBED	MORALS
MEDIAS	METALS	MINDER	MOBILE	MORBID
MEDICS	METEOR	MINERS	MOCKED	MORGUE
MEDIUM	METERS	MINGLE	MOCKER	MORONS
MEDLEY	METHOD	MINIMS	MOCKUP	MOROSE
MEDUSA	METHYL	MINING	MODELS	MORSEL
MEEKER	METRED	MINION	MODEMS	MORTAL
MEEKLY	METRES	MINNOW	MODERN	MORTAR
MEETER	METRIC	MINORS	MODEST	MOSAIC
MELDED	METROS	MINTED	MODIFY	MOSQUE

MOSSED	MUMBLE	NAPKIN	NEWTON	NOTIFY
MOSSES	MURDER	NAPPED	NIBBED	NOTING
MOSTLY	MUSCAT	NAPPER	NIBBLE	NOTION
MOTELS	MUSCLE	NARROW	NICELY	NOUGAT
MOTHER	MUSCLY	NASALS C	NICEST	NOUGHT
MOTIFS	MUSEUM	NATION	NICETY	NOVELS
MOTION	MUSHED	NATIVE	NICHES	NOVICE
MOTIVE	MUSING	NATURE	NICKED	NOZZLE
MOTLEY	MUSKET	NAUGHT	NIECES	NUANCE
MOTORS	MUSLIN	NAUSEA	NIGGLE	NUBILE
MOULDS	MUSTED	NAVELS	NIGHTS	NUDGED
MOULDY	MUSTER	NEARBY	NIGHTY	NUDGES
MOULIN	MUTANT	NEARED	NIMBLE	NUDISM
MOULTS	MUTATE	NEARER	NIMBLY	NUDIST
MOUNDS	MUTELY	NEARLY	NIMBUS	NUDITY
MOUNTS	MUTEST	NEATEN	NINETY	NUGGET
MOURNS	MUTING	NEATER	NINJAS	NULLED
MOUSED	MUTINY	NEATLY	NINTHS	NUMBED
MOUSER	MUTTON	NEBULA	NIPPED	NUMBER
MOUSES	MUTUAL	NECKED	NIPPER	NUMBLY
MOUSEY	MUZZLE	NECTAR	NIPPLE	NURSED
MOUSSE	MYOPIA	NEEDED	NOBBLE	NURSES
MOUTHS	MYOPIC	NEEDER	NOBLER	NUTLET
MOUTHY	MYOSIS	NEEDLE	NOBLES	NUTMEG
MOVERS	MYOTIC	NEGATE	NOBODY	NUTTED
MOVIES	MYRIAD	NEPHEW	NODDED	NUTTER
MOVING	MYRTLE	NERVED	NODULE	NUZZLE
MOWERS	MYSELF	NERVES	NOGGIN	NYLONS
MOWING	MYSTIC	NESTED	NOISES	NYMPHS
MUCHLY	MYTHIC	NESTER	NOMADS	OAFISH
MUCKED	NABBED	NESTLE	NORDIC	OAKUMS
MUDDLE	NAGGED	NETHER	NORTHS	OARING
MUESLI	NAGGER	NETTED	NOSHES	OATERS
MUFFIN	NAILED	NETTER	NOSIER	OBEYED
MUFFLE	NAILER	NETTLE	NOSILY	OBJECT
MUGFUL	NAMELY	NEURAL	NOSING	OBLATE
MUGGED	NAMERS	NEURON	NOTARY	OBLIGE
MUGGER	NAMING	NEUTER	NOTATE	OBLONG
MULLED	NAPALM	NEWEST	NOTERS	OBSESS
MULLET	NAPERY	NEWISH	NOTICE	OBTAIN

OBTUSE	ONSETS	ORIENT	OXYGEN	PAPAYA
OCCULT	ONSIDE	ORIGIN	OYSTER	PAPERS
OCCUPY	ONUSES	ORNATE	OZONES	PAPERY
OCCURS	ONWARD	ORPHAN	PACIFY	PAPIST
OCEANS	ONYXES	OSPREY	PACING	PARADE
OCELOT	OODLES	OSSIFY	PACKED	PARCEL
OCHRED	OOHING	OTHERS	PACKER	PARDON
OCHRES	OOMPAH	OTTERS	PACKET	PARENT
OCTANE	OOMPHS	OUNCES	PADDED	PARIAH
OCTAVE	OOZIER	OUSTED	PADDLE	PARISH
OCTOPI	OOZILY	OUTAGE	PAGANS	PARITY
OCULAR	OOZING	OUTASK	PAGERS	PARKED
OCULUS	OPAQUE	OUTBID	PAGING	PARKER
ODDEST	OPENED	OUTBOX	PAGODA	PARLAY
ODDISH	OPENER	OUTCRY	PAINED	PARODY
ODDITY	OPENLY	OUTDID	PAINTS	PAROLE
ODIOUS	OPERAS	OUTERS	PAINTY	PARROT
ODISTS	OPIATE	OUTFIT	PALACE	PARSON
ODIUMS	OPIUMS	OUTFOX	PALATE	PARTED
ODOURS	OPPOSE	OUTING	PALELY	PARTLY
OFFALS	OPTICS	OUTLAW	PALEST	PASCAL
OFFEND	OPTIMA	OUTLAY	PALLID	PASSED
OFFERS	OPTING	OUTLET	PALLOR	PASSES
OFFICE	OPTION	OUTPUT	PALMED	PASTAS
OFFING	OPUSES	OUTRUN	PALMER	PASTED
OFFISH	ORACLE	OUTSEE	PALTRY	PASTEL
OFFSET	ORANGE	OUTSET	PAMPER	PASTES
OILCAN	ORATED	OUTSIN	PANAMA	PASTRY
OILERS	ORATES	OUTSIT	PANDAS	PATCHY
OILIER	ORATOR	OUTWIT	PANDER	PATENT
OILING	ORBITS	OVERED	PANELS	PATHOS
OINKED	ORCHID	OVERLY	PANFRY	PATIOS
OKAYED	ORDAIN	OVULAR	PANFUL	PATOIS
OLDEST	ORDEAL	OVULES	PANGED	PATROL
OLDISH	ORDERS	OWLETS	PANICS	PATRON
OLIVES	ORGANA	OWLISH	PANNED	PATTED
OMEGAS	ORGANS	OWNERS	PANNES	PATTER
OMELET	ORGASM	OWNING	PANTED	PAUNCH
ONIONS	ORGIES	OXIDES	PANTRY	PAUPER
ONIONY	ORIBIS	OXTAIL	PAPACY	PAUSED

PAUSER	PELTER	PIAZZA	PIPING	PLEADS
PAUSES	PELVIC	PICKED	PIPKIN	PLEASE
PAVERS	PELVIS	PICKER	PIPPED	PLEATS
PAVING	PENCIL	PICKET	PIPPIN	PLEDGE
PAWING	PENIAL	PICKLE	PIQUED	PLENTY
PAWNED	PENILE	PICKUP	PIQUES	PLEURA
PAYDAY	PENNED	PICNIC	PIQUET	PLEXUS
PAYEES	PEONES	PIDGIN	PIRACY	PLIANT
PAYERS	PEOPLE	PIECED	PIRANA	PLIERS
PAYING	PEPPER	PIECES	PIRATE	PLIGHT
PAYOFF	PEPTIC	PIERCE	PISTES	PLINTH
PAYOUT	PERILS	PIFFLE	PISTOL	PLOUGH
PAZAZZ	PERISH	PIGEON	PISTON	PLOYED
PEACHY	PERMED	PIGGIE	PITIED	PLUCKY
PEAKED	PERMIT	PIGGIN	PITIES	PLUMBS
PEANUT	PERSON	PIGLET	PITTED	PLUMED
PEARLS	PERTLY	PIGSTY	PIVOTS	PLUMES
PEARLY	PERUSE	PIKING	PIXELS	PLUMMY
PEBBLE	PESTER	PILAFS	PIXIES	PLUNGE
PEBBLY	PESTLE	PILFER	PIZAZZ	PLURAL
PECANS	PETALS	PILING	PIZZAS	PLUSES
PECKED	PETITE	PILLAR	PLACED	PLYERS
PECKER	PETROL	PILLED	PLACES	PLYING
PEDALO	PETTED	PILLOW	PLACID	POACHY
PEDALS	PETTER	PILOTS	PLAGUE	POCKED
PEDANT	PEWTER	PIMPED	PLAICE	POCKET
PEDDLE	PHASED	PIMPLE	PLAINS	PODIUM
PEDLER	PHASES	PIMPLY	PLAITS	POETIC
PEEKED	PHIALS	PINATA	PLANED	POETRY
PEELED	PHLEGM	PINCER	PLANER	POINTS
PEELER	PHOBIA	PINEAL	PLANES	POINTY
PEEPED	PHOBIC	PINERY	PLANET	POISED
PEEPER	PHONED	PINGED	PLANKS	POISES
PEERED	PHONES	PINING	PLANTS	POISON
PEEVED	PHONIC	PINION	PLAQUE	POKERS
PEEVES	PHOTON	PINKED	PLASMA	POKIER
PEGGED	PHOTOS	PINKER	PLATED	POLARS
PELLET	PHRASE	PINNED	PLATES	POLEAX
PELMET	PHYSIC	PINUPS	PLAYED	POLERS
PELTED	PIANOS	PIPETS	PLAYER	POLICE

POLICY	POSTAL	PRICED	PRUNES	PURELY
POLING	POSTED	PRICER	PRYING	PUREST
POLISH	POSTER	PRICES	PSALMS	PURGED
POLITE	POTAGE	PRICEY	PSEUDO	PURGER
POLKAS	POTATO	PRICKS	PSYCHO	PURGES
POLLED	POTENT	PRIDES	PUBLIC	PURIFY
POLLEE	POTION	PRIEST	PUDDLE	PURISM
POLLEN	POTTED	PRIMAL	PUFFED	PURIST
POLLER	POTTER	PRIMED	PUFFER	PURITY
POLYPI	POUNCE	PRIMER	PUFFIN	PURLED
POLYPS	POUNDS	PRIMLY	PUGGED	PURPLE
POMADE	POURED	PRINCE	PUKING	PURPLY
PONCED	POURER	PRINTS	PULLED	PURRED
PONCES	POUTED	PRIORS	PULLER	PURSED
PONCHO	POUTER	PRIORY	PULLEY	PURSER
PONDER	POWDER	PRISES	PULLUP	PURSES
PONGED	POWERS	PRISMS	PULPED	PURSUE
PONIED	POWWOW	PRISON	PULPER	PUSHED
PONIES	POXING	PRISSY	PULPIT	PUSHER
POODLE	PRAISE	PRIVET	PULSAR	PUSHES
POOLED	PRANCE	PRIZED	PULSED	PUSHUP
POORER	PRANGS	PRIZES	PULSES	PUSSES
POORLY	PRANKS	PROBED	PUMICE	PUTOFF
POPERY	PRAWNS	PROBES	PUMMEL	PUTOUT
POPLAR	PRAYED	PROFIT	PUMPED	PUTRID
POPPED	PRAYER	PROMOS	PUMPER	PUTTER
POPPER	PREACH	PROMPT	PUNCHY	PUZZLE
POPPET	PREAMP	PRONGS	PUNDIT	PYLONS
POROUS	PREARM	PRONTO	PUNIER	PYTHON
PORTAL	PREENS	PROOFS	PUNILY	QUACKS
PORTED	PREFAB	PROPEL	PUNNED	QUAFFS
PORTER	PREFER	PROPER	PUNNET	QUAINT
PORTLY	PREFIX	PROTON	PUNTED	QUAKED
POSERS	PRELIM	PROVED	PUNTER	QUAKER
POSEUR	PREMED	PROVEN	PUPATE	QUAKES
POSHER	PREMIX	PROVES	PUPILS	QUALMS
POSHLY	PRESET	PROWLS	PUPPED	QUALMY
POSIES	PRETTY	PRUDES	PUPPET	QUARKS
POSING	PREYED	PRUNED	PUREED	QUARRY
POSSUM	PREYER	PRUNER	PUREES	QUARTZ

QUASAR	RACOON	RAPIER	REARER	REDYES
QUATRE	RADARS	RAPING	REASON	REEFED
QUAVER	RADIAL	RAPIST	REBAIT	REEFER
QUEASY	RADIOS	RAPPER	REBARS	REEKED
QUEENS	RADISH	RARELY	REBATE	REELED
QUELLS	RAFFIA	RAREST	REBELS	REELER
QUENCH	RAFFLE	RARIFY	REBORN	REEMIT
QUESTS	RAFTED	RARING	REBUFF	REFERS
QUEUED	RAFTER	RARITY	REBUKE	REFILE
QUEUER	RAGGED	RASCAL	REBURY	REFILL
QUEUES	RAGING	RASERS	REBUTS	REFINE
QUICHE	RAIDED	RASHES	RECALL	REFITS
QUICKS	RAIDER	RASHLY	RECANT	REFLEX
QUIETS	RAILED	RASPED	RECAPS	REFLUX
QUIFFS	RAILER	RASPER	RECAST	REFORM
QUILLS	RAINED	RATHER	RECEDE	REFUEL
QUILTS	RAISED	RATIFY	RECENT	REFUGE
QUINCE	RAISER	RATING	RECESS	REFUND
QUINTS	RAISES	RATION	RECIPE	REFUSE
QUIRKS	RAISIN	RATIOS	RECITE	REFUTE
QUIRKY	RAKERS	RATTED	RECOIL	REGAIN
QUIVER	RAKING	RATTER	RECOOK	REGALE
QUOTAS	RAMBLE	RATTLE	RECORD	REGARD
QUOTED	RAMIFY	RAUNCH	RECOUP	REGENT
QUOTER	RAMMED	RAVAGE	RECTAL	REGGAE
QUOTES	RAMMER S	RAVENS	RECTOR	REGILD
RABBIT	RAMPED	RAVERS	RECTUM	REGIME
RABBLE	RANCID	RAVINE	RECURS	REGINA
RABIES	RANCOR	RAVING	REDDEN	REGION
RACERS	RANDOM	RAVISH	REDDER	REGRET
RACHET	RANGED	RAWEST	REDDLE	REHABS
RACIAL	RANGER	RAZORS	REDEEM	REHASH
RACIER	RANGES	REACTS	REDEFY	REHEAT
RACILY	RANKED	READER	REDENY	REHIRE
RACING	RANKER	REALLY	REDEYE	REIGNS
RACISM	RANKLY	REALMS	REDIAL	REINED
RACIST	RANSOM	REALTY	REDONE	REJECT
RACKED	RANTED	REAPED	REDOUT	REJOIN
RACKER	RAPHIS	REAPER	REDUCE	REKNIT
RACKET	RAPIDS	REARED	REDYED	RELACE

RELAID	REPAYS	REUSED	RIFTED	ROARER
RELATE	REPEAL	REVAMP	RIGGED	ROBBED
RELAYS	REPEAT	REVEAL	RIGGER	ROBBER
RELENT	REPELS	REVERB	RIGHTS	ROBBIN
RELICS	REPENT	REVERE	RILING	ROBOTS
RELICT	REPLAY	REVERT	RILLED	ROBUST
RELIED	REPORT	REVIEW	RILLES	ROCHET
RELIEF	REPOSE	REVILE	RIMMED	ROCKED
RELIES	REPUGN	REVISE	RINGED	ROCKER
RELISH	REPUTE	REVIVE	RINGER	ROCKET
RELIVE	REREAD	REVOKE	RINSED	ROCOCO
RELOAD	RERISE	REVOLT	RINSER	RODDED
RELOAN	RESALE	REVUES	RINSES	RODENT
RELUCT	RESCUE	REVVED	RIOTED	RODEOS
REMADE	RESEAL	REWARD	RIOTER	ROGUED
REMAIN	RESELL	REWIND	RIPELY	ROGUES
REMAKE	RESEND	REWIRE	RIPENS	ROLLED
REMAND	RESENT	REWORK	RIPEST	ROLLER
REMARK	RESIDE	RHINOS	RIPING	ROMANS
REMEDY	RESIGN	RHYMER	RIPOFF	ROMEOS
REMEND	RESIST	RHYMES	RIPOST	ROMPED
REMIND	RESIZE	RHYTHM	RIPPED	ROMPER
REMITS	RESOLD	RIALTO	RIPPER	ROOFED
REMOTE	RESORB	RIBALD	RIPPLE	ROOFER
REMOVE	RESORT	RIBAND	RIPPLY	ROOKED
RENAIL	RESOWN	RIBBED	RISERS	ROOKIE
RENAME	RESTED	RIBBON	RISING	ROOMED
RENDED	RESULT	RICHER	RISKED	ROOMER
RENDER	RESUME	RICHES	RISKER	ROOSED
RENEGE	RETAIL	RICHLY	RISQUE	ROOSTS
RENEWS	RETAIN	RICING	RITUAL	ROOTED
RENNET	RETAKE	RIDDLE	RITZES	ROOTER
RENOWN	RETAPE	RIDERS	RIVALS	ROPERS
RENTAL	RETARD	RIDGED	RIVERS	ROPERY
RENTED	RETINA	RIDGES	RIVETS	ROPIER
RENTER	RETIRE	RIDING	RIVING	ROPING
REOPEN	RETOLD	RIFFED	ROADIE	ROSARY
REPAID	RETORT	RIFLED	ROAMED	ROSETS
REPAIR	RETROS	RIFLER	ROAMER	ROSIER
REPAVE	RETURN	RIFLES	ROARED	ROSILY

ROSTRA	RULING	SALAAM	SAUCER	SCOLDS
ROTARY	RUMBLE	SALADS	SAUCES	SCOLEX
ROTATE	RUMOUR	SALALS	SAUTED	SCONCE
ROTTER	RUMPUS	SALAMI	SAUTES	SCONES
ROTUND	RUNNER	SALARY	SAVAGE	SCOOPS
ROUCHE	RUNOFF	SALEPS	SAVANT	SCOOTS
ROUENS	RUNOUT	SALINE	SAVATE	SCOPED
ROUGED	RUNWAY	SALIVA	SAVERS	SCOPES
ROUGES	RUPEES	SALLOW	SAVING	SCORCH
ROUGHS	RUSHED	SALMON	SAVINS	SCORED
ROUNDS	RUSHER	SALONS	SAVOUR	SCORER
ROUSED	RUSHES	SALOON	SAXONY	SCORES
ROUSER	RUSSET	SALSAS	SAYERS	SCORIA
ROUSES	RUSTED	SALTED	SAYING	SCORNS
ROUSTS	RUSTIC	SALTER	SCABBY	SCOTCH
ROUTED	RUTTED	SALUTE	SCALDS	SCOTIA
ROUTER	SABINE	SALVED	SCALED	SCOURS
ROUTES	SABLES	SALVES	SCALER	SCOUSE
ROVERS	SACHET	SAMARA	SCALES	SCOUTS
ROVING	SACKED	SAMBAR	SCALPS	SCOWLS
ROWANS	SACKER	SAMBAS	SCAMPI	SCRAGS
ROWING	SACRED	SAMOSA	SCAMPS	SCRAPE
ROYALS	SADDEN	SAMPLE	SCANTY	SCRAPS
ROZZER	SADDER	SANDAL	SCAPED	SCRAWL
RUBBED	SADDLE	SANDER	SCAPES	SCREAM
RUBBER	SADHUS	SANDHI	SCARAB	SCREED
RUBBLE	SADISM	SANELY	SCARCE	SCREEN
RUBIES	SADIST	SANEST	SCARED	SCREES
RUCKUS	SAFARI	SANGAR	SCARES	SCREWS
RUDDER	SAFELY	SANGHA	SCAREY	SCRIBE
RUDELY	SAFEST	SANITY	SCATHE	SCRIMP
RUDEST	SAFETY	SARGES	SCATTY	SCRIMS
RUEFUL	SAGELY	SARONG	SCENDS	SCRIPS
RUFFED	SAGEST	SASHAY	SCENES	SCRIPT
RUFFLE	SAGGED	SATAYS	SCENIC	SCRIVE
RUGGED	SAHIBS	SATEEN	SCENTS	SCRODS
RUINED	SAILED	SATINY	SCHEME	SCROLL
RUINER	SAILER	SATIRE	SCHISM	SCRUFF
RULERS	SAILOR	SATYRS	SCHIZO	SCULPT
RULIER	SAINTS	SAUCED	SCHOOL	SCUMMY

SCURFS	SEIZED	SERVER	SHAPED	SHIRTY
SCURFY	SEIZER	SERVES	SHAPEN	SHOALS
SCURRY	SEIZES	SESAME	SHAPER	SHOCKS
SCURVY	SEJANT	SETTEE	SHAPES	SHODDY
SCUTCH	SELDOM	SETTER	SHARDS	SHOGUN
SCUTES	SELECT	SETTLE	SHARED	SHOOTS
SCUZZY	SELFED	SEVENS	SHARER	SHORED
SCYTHE	SELLER	SEVERE	SHARES	SHORES
SEABED	SELVES	SEVERS	SHARIF	SHORTS
SEADOG	SENATE	SEWAGE	SHARKS	SHORTY
SEALED	SENDED	SEWERS	SHARPS	SHOULD
SEALER	SENDER	SEWING	SHAVED	SHOUTS
SEAMAN	SENDUP	SEXIER	SHAVEN	SHOVED
SEAMED	SENILE	SEXILY	SHAVER	SHOVEL
SEAMEN	SENIOR	SEXING	SHAVES	SHOVER
SEANCE	SENNET	SEXISM	SHAWLS	SHOVES
SEARCH	SENSED	SEXIST	SHEAFS	SHOWED
SEARED	SENSES	SEXTET	SHEALS	SHOWER
SEARER	SENSOR	SEXTON	SHEARS	SHRANK
SEASON	SENTRY	SEXUAL	SHEATH	SHREDS
SEATED	SEPALS	SHABBY	SHEENS	SHREWD
SEATER	SEPTET	SHACKS	SHEERS	SHREWS
SECEDE	SEPTIC	SHADED	SHEETS	SHRIEK
SECOND	SEPTUM	SHADES	SHEIKH	SHRIFT
SECRET	SEQUEL	SHADOW	SHELLS	SHRILL
SECTOR	SEQUIN	SHAFTS	SHELLY	SHRIMP
SECURE	SERAPH	SHAGGY	SHELVE	SHRINE
SEDATE	SERENE	SHAKEN	SHERPA	SHRINK
SEDILE	SERIAL	SHAKER	SHERRY	SHROUD
SEDUCE	SERIES	SHAKES	SHIELD	SHRUBS
SEEDED	SERIFS	SHALED	SHIEST	SHRUGS
SEEDER	SERINE	SHALES	SHIFTS	SHUNTS
SEEING	SERING	SHALOM	SHIFTY	SHUTED
SEEKER	SERINS	SHAMAN	SHIMMY	SHUTES
SEELED	SERMON	SHAMED	SHINED	SHYEST
SEEMED	SEROSA	SHAMES	SHINER	SHYING
SEEMLY	SEROUS	SHAMMY	SHINES	SIBYLS
SEEPED	SEROWS	SHANDY	SHIRES	SICKED
SEESAW	SERUMS	SHANKS	SHIRKS	SICKEN
SEETHE	SERVED	SHANTY	SHIRTS	SICKER

SICKLE	SINEWY	SKIVER	SLIMES	SMELLS
SICKLY	SINFUL	SKIVES	SLIMLY	SMELLY
SIDING	SINGED	SKIVVY	SLIMSY	SMELTS
SIDLED	SINGER	SKULKS	SLINGS	SMERKS
SIDLER	SINGES	SKULLS	SLINKS	SMIDGE
SIDLES	SINGLE	SKUNKS	SLINKY	SMILED
SIEGED	SINGLY	SLAKED	SLIPED	SMILER
SIEGES	SINKER	SLAKER	SLIPES	SMILES
SIENNA	SINNED	SLAKES	SLIPPY	SMILEY
SIERRA	SINNER	SLALOM	SLIPUP	SMIRKS
SIESTA	SIPPED	SLANGS	SLIVER	SMIRKY
SIEVED	SIPPER	SLANGY	SLOBBY	SMITER
SIEVES	SIRENS	SLANTS	SLOGAN	SMITES
SIFTED	SIRING	SLANTY	SLOPED	SMITHY
SIFTER	SIRUPS	SLATED	SLOPER	SMOCKS
SIGHED	SIRUPY	SLATES	SLOPES	SMOGGY
SIGHER	SISTER	SLAVED	SLOPPY	SMOKED
SIGHTS	SITARS	SLAVER	SLOSHY	SMOKER
SIGNAL	SITCOM	SLAVES	SLOTHS	SMOKES
SIGNED	SITING	SLAYED	SLOUCH	SMOKEY
SIGNEE	SITTER	SLAYER	SLOWED	SMOOCH
SIGNER	SITUPS	SLEAVE	SLOWER	SMOOTH
SIGNET	SIXTHS	SLEAZE	SLOWLY	SMUDGE
SILAGE	SIZING	SLEAZY	SLUDGE	SMUDGY
SILANE	SIZZLE	SLEDGE	SLUDGY	SMUGLY
SILENT	SKALDS	SLEEPS	SLUMMY	SMUTTY
SILICA	SKATED	SLEEPY	SLUMPS	SNACKS
SILKED	SKATER	SLEETY	SLURPS	SNAGGY
SILKEN	SKATES	SLEEVE	SLURRY	SNAILS
SILTED	SKETCH	SLEIGH	SLUSHY	SNAKED
SILVER	SKEWED	SLEUTH	SLUTTY	SNAKES
SIMIAN	SKEWER	SLICED	SLYEST	SNAPPY
SIMILE	SKIERS	SLICER	SMACKS	SNARED
SIMMER	SKIFFS	SLICES	SMALLS	SNARES
SIMONY	SKIING	SLICKS	SMARMS	SNARLS
SIMOOM	SKILLS	SLIDER	SMARMY	SNARLY
SIMPER	SKIMPY	SLIDES	SMARTS	SNATCH
SIMPLE	SKINNY	SLIEST	SMARTY	SNAZZY
SIMPLY	SKIRTS	SLIGHT	SMEARS	SNEAKS
SINEWS	SKIVED	SLIMED	SMEARY	SNEAKY

SNEERS	SODIUM	SOVIET	SPIRIT	SPRITZ
SNEEZE	SOFTEN	SPACED	SPITAL	SPROUT
SNEEZY	SOFTER	SPACER	SPITED	SPRUCE
SNIFFS	SOFTIE	SPACES	SPITES	SPRUNG
SNIFFY	SOFTLY	SPACEY	SPLASH	SPRYER
SNIPED	SOILED	SPADES	SPLAYS	SPRYLY
SNIPER	SOIREE	SPARED	SPLEEN	SPURTS
SNIPES	SOLACE	SPARES	SPLICE	SPUTUM
SNITCH	SOLDER	SPARKS	SPLINT	SPYING
SNIVEL	SOLELY	SPARKY	SPLITS	SQUADS
SNOBBY	SOLEMN	SPARSE	SPOILS	SQUALL
SNOOPS	SOLIDS	SPASMS	SPOILT	SQUARE
SNOOTY	SOLUTE	SPATES	SPOKEN	SQUASH
SNOOZE	SOLVED	SPAWNS	SPOKES	SQUATS
SNOOZY	SOLVER	SPAYED	SPONGE	SQUAWK
SNORED	SOMBRE	SPEAKS	SPONGY	SQUAWS
SNORER	SOMITE	SPEARS	SPOOFS	SQUEAK
SNORES	SONARS	SPECKS	SPOOFY	SQUEAL
SNORTS	SONATA	SPEECH	SPOOKS	SQUIDS
SNOTTY	SONICS	SPEEDO	SPOOKY	SQUINT
SNOUTS	SONNET	SPEEDS	SPOOLS	SQUIRE
SNOWED	SOONER	SPEEDY	SPOONS	SQUIRM
SNUBBY	SOOTED	SPELLS	SPOONY	SQUISH
SNUGLY	SOOTHE	SPENDS	SPORTS	STABLE
SOAKED	SOOTHS	SPEWED	SPORTY	STABLY
SOAKER	SORBET	SPHERE	SPOTTY	STACKS
SOAPED	SORDID	SPHINX	SPOUSE	STAGED
SOAPER	SORELY	SPICED	SPOUTS	STAGES
SOARED	SORREL	SPICES	SPRAIN	STAGEY
SOARER	SORROW	SPIDER	SPRANG	STAGGY
SOAVES	SORTED	SPIERS	SPRATS	STAINS
SOBBED	SORTER	SPIKED	SPRAWL	STAIRS
SOBBER	SORTIE	SPIKER	SPRAYS	STALKS
SOBERS	SOUGHT	SPIKES	SPREAD	STALKY
SOCAGE	SOUNDS	SPIKEY	SPRIER	STALLS
SOCCER	SOURCE	SPINAL	SPRIGS	STAMEN
SOCIAL	SOURED	SPINES	SPRING	STAMPS
SOCKED	SOURER	SPIRAL	SPRINT	STANCE
SOCKET	SOURLY	SPIRED	SPRITE	STANCH
SODDEN	SOUSED	SPIRES	SPRITS	STANDS

532

STANZA	STINGY	STREAM	SUBSET	SUPPLY
STAPLE	STINKS	STREET	SUBTLE	SURELY
STARCH	STINKY	STRESS	SUBTLY	SUREST
STARED	STINTS	STREWN	SUBURB	SURETY
STARER	STIPED	STREWS	SUBWAY	SURFED
STARES	STIPES	STRICT	SUCKED	SURFER
STARRY	STITCH	STRIDE	SUCKER	SURGED
STARTS	STOATS	STRIFE	SUCKLE	SURGES
STARVE	STOCKS	STRIKE	SUCRES	SURREY
STASIS	STOCKY	STRING	SUDDEN	SURTAX
STATED	STODGE	STRIPE	SUFFER	SURVEY
STATER	STODGY	STRIPS	SUFFIX	SUSSED
STATES	STOKES	STRIVE	SUGARS	SUSSES
STATIC	STOLEN	STROBE	SUGARY	SUTRAS
STATUE	STOMPS	STRODE	SUITED	SVELTE
STATUS	STONED	STROKE	SUITES	SWAGED
STAYED	STONER	STROLL	SUITOR	SWAGER
STAYER	STONES	STRONG	SULFUR	SWAMPS
STEADY	STONEY	STROVE	SULKED	SWAMPY
STEAKS	STOOGE	STROWN	SULKER	SWANKS
STEALS	STOOLS	STRUCK	SULLEN	SWANKY
STEAMS	STOOPS	STRUNG	SULTAN	SWARMS
STEAMY	STORAX	STUBBY	SULTRY	SWATCH
STEEDS	STORED	STUDIO	SUMMED	SWATHE
STEELY	STORES	STUFFY	SUMMER	SWAYED
STEEPS	STOREY	STUMPS	SUMMIT	SWEARS
STEERS	STORKS	STUMPY	SUMMON	SWEATS
STELLA	STORMS	STUNTS	SUNDAE	SWEATY
STENCH	STORMY	STUPID	SUNDER	SWEDES
STEREO	STOUPS	STUPOR	SUNDRY	SWEEPS
STEWED	STOURS	STURDY	SUNKEN	SWEETS
STICKS	STOURY	STYLED	SUNLIT	SWELLS
STICKY	STOUTS	STYLES	SUNNED	SWERVE
STIFFS	STOVES	STYLUS	SUNSET	SWIFTS
STIFLE	STOWED	STYRAX	SUNTAN	SWILLS
STIGMA	STRAIN	SUAVER	SUPERB	SWINGS
STILLS	STRAND	SUBBED	SUPERS	SWINGY
STILLY	STRAPS	SUBDUE	SUPPED	SWIPED
STILTS	STRAYS	SUBLET	SUPPER	SWIPES
STINGS	STREAK	SUBMIT	SUPPLE	SWIRLS

SWIRLY	TALKED	TATARS	TEMPTS	THENCE
SWISHY	TALKER	TATTER	TENACE	THEORY
SWITCH	TALKIE	TATTIE	TENANT	THESIS
SWIVEL	TALLER	TATTLE	TENDED	THICKS
SWOONS	TALLIS	TATTOO	TENDER	THIEVE
SWOOPS	TALLOW	TAUGHT	TENDON	THIGHS
SWOOSH	TAMALS	TAUNTS	TENETS	THINGS
SWORDS	TAMELY	TAUTLY	TENNER	THINKS
SYMBOL	TAMERS	TAVERN	TENNIS	THINLY
SYNODS	TAMEST	TAWDRY	TENORS	THIRDS
SYNTAX	TAMING	TAWNEY	TENSED	THIRST
SYNTHS	TAMPER	TAXERS	TENSER	THIRTY
SYPHON	TAMPON	TAXIED	TENSES	THONGS
SYRUPS	TANDEM	TAXIES	TENSOR	THORAX
SYRUPY	TANGLE	TAXING	TENTED	THORNS
SYSTEM	TANGLY	TAXMAN	TENTHS	THORNY
TABARD	TANKED	TAXMEN	TENURE	THOUGH
TABBED	TANKER	TEACUP	TERAPH	THRASH
TABLED	TANNED	TEAMED	TERGAL	THREAD
TABLES	TANNER	TEAPOT	TERGUM	THREAT
TABLET	TANTRA	TEARED	TERMED	THREES
TABOOS	TAPERS	TEARER	TERMLY	THRICE
TABORS	TAPING	TEASED	TERROR	THRIFT
TACHES	TAPPED	TEASER	TESTED	THRILL
TACKED	TARGET	TEASES	TESTER	THRIVE
TACKER	TARIFF	TEATED	TESTES	THROAT
TACKLE	TARMAC	TECHIE	TETCHY	THROBS
TACTIC	TAROTS	TEDIUM	TETHER	THRONE
TAGGED	TARRED	TEEING	THANES	THRONG
TAGGER	TARTAN	TEEMED	THANKS	THROWN
TAHINI	TARTAR	TEENSY	THATCH	THROWS
TAILED	TARTED	TEEPEE	THAWED	THRUMS
TAILER	TARTER	TEETER	THAWER	THRUSH
TAILOR	TARTLY	TEETHE	THEFTS	THRUST
TAINTS	TARZAN	TELLER	THEINE	THUMBS
TAKERS	TASKED	TELLYS	THEIRS	THUMPS
TAKEUP	TASSET	TEMPED	THEISM	THWART
TAKING	TASTED	TEMPER	THEIST	THYMES
TALCUM	TASTER	TEMPLE	THEMED	TIARAS
TALENT	TASTES	TEMPOS	THEMES	TIBIAE

TIBIAL	TINTED	TONNER	TOXINS	TRIERS
TIBIAS	TIPPED	TONNES	TOYING	TRIFID
TICKED	TIPPER	TONSIL	TOYISH	TRIFLE
TICKER	TIPPET	TOOLED	TRACED	TRIKES
TICKET	TIPPLE	TOOTED	TRACER	TRILBY
TICKLE	TIPTOE	TOOTHY	TRACES	TRILLS
TIDBIT	TIPTOP	TOOTLE	TRACKS	TRIMER
TIDDLY	TIRADE	TOOTSY	TRACTS	TRIMLY
TIDIED	TIRING	TOPICS	TRADED	TRIPES
TIDIER	TISSUE	TOPPED	TRADER	TRIPLE
TIDIES	TITHER	TOPPLE	TRADES	TRIPLY
TIDILY	TITLED	TORAHS	TRAGIC	TRIPOD
TIDING	TITLES	TORIES	TRAILS	TRIPPY
TIERCE	TITRES	TORPID	TRAINS	TRIVIA
TIERED	TITTER	TORQUE	TRAITS	TROLLS
TIFFIN	TITTLE	TORRID	TRAMPS	TROLLY
TIGERS	TOASTS	TORSOS	TRANCE	TROMPE
TIGHTS	TOASTY	TORTES	TRASHY	TROMPS
TILERS	TODDLE	TOSSED	TRAUMA	TROOPS
TILING	TOEING	TOSSES	TRAVEL	TROPES
TILTED	TOFFEE	TOTALS	TRAVES	TROPHY
TIMBER	TOGGED	TOTEMS	TRAWLS	TROUGH
TIMBRE	TOGGLE	TOTING	TREADS	TROUPE
TIMELY	TOILED	TOTTED	TREATS	TROUTS
TIMERS	TOILER	TOTTER	TREATY	TROUTY
TIMING	TOILET	TOUCAN	TREBLE	TROVER
TINDER	TOKAYS	TOUCHE	TREBLY	TROVES
TINGED	TOKENS	TOUCHY	TREMOR	TROWEL
TINGES	TOKERS	TOUPEE	TRENCH	TRUANT
TINGLE	TOKING	TOURED	TRENDS	TRUCED
TINGLY	TOLLED	TOURER	TRENDY	TRUCES
TINIER	TOMATO	TOUSLE	TREPID	TRUCKS
TINILY	TOMBED	TOUTED	TRIADS	TRUDGE
TINKER	TOMBOY	TOWAGE	TRIAGE	TRUEST
TINKLE	TOMCAT	TOWARD	TRIALS	TRUING
TINKLY	TONERS	TOWELS	TRIBAL	TRUISM
TINMAN	TONGED	TOWERS	TRIBES	TRUMPS
TINMEN	TONGUE	TOWING	TRICKS	TRUNKS
TINNED	TONICS	TOWNIE	TRICKY	TRUSTS
TINSEL	TONING	TOXICS	TRICOT	TRUSTY

TRUTHS	TUTORS	UHLANS	UNEVEN	UNPAID
TRYING	TUTTED	UKASES	UNFAIR	UNPICK
TRYOUT	TUXEDO	ULCERS	UNFELT	UNPLUG
TRYSTS	TWANGS	ULEMAS	UNFITS	UNREAD
TSETSE	TWANGY	ULLAGE	UNFOLD	UNREAL
TSKTSK	TWANKY	ULSTER	UNFURL	UNREST
TUBBED	TWEAKS	ULTRAS	UNGLUE	UNRIPE
TUBBER	TWEAKY	UMBERS	UNGUAL	UNRULY
TUBING	TWEEDS	UMBLES	UNHAND	UNSAFE
TUBULE	TWEEDY	UMLAUT	UNHELM	UNSAID
TUCKED	TWEENY	UMPING	UNHEWN	UNSEEN
TUCKER	TWEETS	UMPIRE	UNHOLY	UNSENT
TUFFET	TWEEZE	UNABLE	UNHOOK	UNSEXY
TUFTED	TWELVE	UNAGED	UNIFIC	UNSUNG
TUFTER	TWENTY	UNAKIN	UNIONS	UNSUNK
TUGGED	TWERPS	UNARMS	UNIPOD	UNSURE
TUGGER	TWIGGY	UNAWED	UNIQUE	UNTIDY
TULIPS	TWILIT	UNBARS	UNISEX	UNTIED
TUMBLE	TWILLS	UNBEND	UNISON	UNTIES
TUMOUR	TWINED	UNBENT	UNITED	UNTOLD
TUMULT	TWINES	UNBIND	UNITES	UNTROD
TUNDRA	TWINGE	UNBOLT	UNJUST	UNTRUE
TUNERS	TWIRLS	UNBORN	UNKEPT	UNTUCK
TUNICS	TWIRLY	UNBRED	UNKIND	UNUSED
TUNING	TWIRPS	UNCAGE	UNKNOT	UNVEIL
TUNNEL	TWISTS	UNCLAD	UNLACE	UNWARY
TURBAN	TWISTY	UNCLES	UNLAID	UNWELL
TURBID	TWITCH	UNCLIP	UNLEAD	UNWIND
TURBIT	TYCOON	UNCLOG	UNLESS	UNWISE
TUREEN	TYPHUS	UNCOIL	UNLIKE	UNWORN
TURFED	TYPIFY	UNCOOL	UNLINK	UNWRAP
TURGID	TYPING	UNCURL	UNLOAD	UNZIPS
TURKEY	TYPIST	UNDEAD	UNLOCK	UPBEAT
TURNED	TYRANT	UNDIES	UNMADE	UPCAST
TURNER	UBIETY	UNDOER	UNMAKE	UPCURL
TURNIP	UBIQUE	UNDOES	UNMASK	UPENDS
TURRET	UDDERS	UNDONE	UNMESH	UPFLOW
TURTLE	UGLIER	UNDULY	UNMOWN	UPGAZE
TUSKED	UGLIES	UNEASE	UNOPEN	UPHELD
TUSSLE	UGLIFY	UNEASY	UNPACK	UPHILL

UPHOLD	VAGARY	VENDOR	VIGOUR	VOTERS
UPKEEP	VAGILE	VENEER	VIKING	VOTING
UPLIFT	VAGINA	VENIAL	VILELY	VOWELS
UPLOAD	VAGUER	VENOMS	VILEST	VOWING
UPMOST	VAINER	VENTED	VILIFY	VOYAGE
UPPERS	VAINLY	VENTER	VILLAS	VOYEUR
UPPILE	VALETS	VENUES	VINERY	VULGAR
UPPING	VALLEY	VERBAL	VINIER	VULVAE
UPPISH	VALOUR	VERGED	VINIFY	VULVAL
UPPITY	VALUED	VERGER	VINING	VULVAS
UPRISE	VALUER	VERGES	VINYLS	WACKOS
UPROAR	VALUES	VERIFY	VIOLAS	WADDED
UPROOT	VAMPED	VERILY	VIOLET	WADDLE
UPROSE	VANDAL	VERITY	VIOLIN	WADERS
UPSETS	VANISH	VERNAL	VIPERS	WADING
UPSHOT	VANITY	VERNIX	VIRAGO	WAFERS
UPSIDE	VAPOUR	VERSUS	VIRGIN	WAFFLE
UPTAKE	VARIED	VERVES	VIRILE	WAFTED
UPTOWN	VARIES	VERVET	VIRTUE	WAGERS
UPWARD	VASTER	VESPER	VISAGE	WAGGED
URBANE	VASTLY	VESSEL	VISION	WAGGER
URCHIN	VATFUL	VESTAL	VISITS	WAGGLE
URGENT	VAULTS	VESTAS	VISORS	WAGGLY
URGING	VAULTY	VESTED	VISTAS	WAGING
URINAL	VEALER	VESTRY	VISUAL	WAGONS
URINES	VECTOR	VETOED	VITALS	WAIFED
USABLE	VEERED	VETOES	VIXENS	WAILED
USABLY	VEGANS	VETTED	VOCALS	WAILER
USAGES	VEGGIE	VEXERS	VODKAS	WAISTS
USEFUL	VEILED	VEXING	VOGUED	WAITED
USHERS	VEINAL	VIABLE	VOGUES	WAITER
USUALS	VEINED	VIABLY	VOICED	WAKENS
UTERUS	VELDTS	VIALED	VOICER	WAKERS
UTMOST	VELLUM	VICARS	VOICES	WAKING
UTOPIA	VELOCE	VICTIM	VOIDED	WALKED
UTTERS	VELOUR	VICTOR	VOLLEY	WALKER
VACANT	VELVET	VIDEOS	VOLUME	WALLED
VACATE	VENDED	VIEWED	VOMITS	WALLET
VACUUM	VENDEE	VIEWER	VOODOO	WALLOP
VADOSE	VENDER	VIGILS	VORTEX	WALLOW

WALNUT	WAXERS	WELTER	WHITER	WINKED
WALRUS	WAXIER	WENDED	WHITES	WINKLE
WANDER	WAXILY	WETHER	WHOLES	WINNER
WANGLE	WAXING	WETTED	WHOLLY	WINNOW
WANING	WAYLAY	WETTER	WHOOFS	WINTER
WANNED	WEAKEN	WHACKO	WHOOPS	WINTLE
WANNER	WEAKER	WHACKS	WHORLS	WINTRY
WANTED	WEAKLY	WHACKY	WICKED	WIPERS
WANTON	WEALDS	WHALED	WICKER	WIPING
WAPPED	WEALTH	WHALER	WICKET	WIRERS
WARBLE	WEANED	WHALES	WIDELY	WIRIER
WARDED	WEANER	WHAMMY	WIDENS	WIRILY
WARDEN	WEAPON	WHARFS	WIDEST	WIRING
WARDER	WEARER	WHEATS	WIDGET	WISDOM
WARIER	WEASEL	WHEELS	WIDOWS	WISELY
WARILY	WEAVED	WHEEZE	WIELDS	WISEST
WARING	WEAVER	WHEEZY	WIELDY	WISHED
WARMED	WEAVES	WHELKS	WIFELY	WISHER
WARMER	WEBBED	WHELKY	WIGGLE	WISHES
WARMLY	WEDDED	WHELMS	WIGGLY	WITCHY
WARMTH	WEDDER	WHELPS	WIGHTS	WITHAL
WARNED	WEDGED	WHENCE	WIGWAM	WITHER
WARPED	WEDGES	WHERES	WILDER	WITHES
WARRED	WEEDED	WHIFFS	WILDLY	WITHIN
WARREN	WEEDER	WHILST	WILFUL	WITTED
WASHED	WEEKLY	WHIMSY	WILLED	WIVERS
WASHER	WEENED	WHINED	WILLER	WIVING
WASHES	WEEPER	WHINER	WILLET	WIZARD
WASTED	WEEPIE	WHINES	WILLOW	WOBBLE
WASTER	WEEVIL	WHINEY	WILTED	WOBBLY
WASTES	WEIGHS	WHINGE	WIMPLE	WOEFUL
WATERS	WEIGHT	WHIRLS	WINCED	WOLFED
WATERY	WEIRDO	WHIRLY	WINCES	WOLVES
WATTLE	WEIRDS	WHIRRS	WINDED	WOMANS
WAVERS	WEIRDY	WHIRRY	WINDER	WOMBAT
WAVERY	WELDED	WHISKS	WINDLE	WOMBED
WAVEYS	WELDER	WHISKY	WINDOW	WONDER
WAVIER	WELLED	WHISTS	WINERY	WOODED
WAVILY	WELLIE	WHITED	WINGED	WOODEN
WAVING	WELTED	WHITEN	WINING	WOOERS

WOOFED	XYLOSE	ZEALOT	ABSCESS	ACTUALS
WOOFER	XYLYLS	ZEBRAS	ABSCOND	ACTUATE
WOOING	XYSTER	ZENITH	ABSENCE	ACUTELY
WOOLED	XYSTOI	ZEPHYR	ABSENTS	ACYCLIC
WOOLEN	XYSTOS	ZIGZAG	ABSOLVE	ADAGIOS
WOOLLY	XYSTUS	ZILLAH	ABSORBS	ADAMANT
WORDED	YABBER	ZINGED	ABSTAIN	ADAPTED
WORKED	YACHTS	ZINGER	ABUSING	ADAPTER
WORKER	YACKED	ZIPPED	ABUSIVE	ADAPTOR
WORLDS	YAHOOS	ZIPPER	ABUTTED	ADDENDA
WORMED	YANKED	ZITHER	ABUTTER	ADDICTS
WORSEN	YAPPED	ZODIAC	ABYSMAL	ADDRESS
WORTHS	YARNED	ZOMBIE	ABYSSES	ADDUCED
WORTHY	YARROW	ZONING	ACADEMY	ADDUCES
WOUNDS	YAWNED	ZONKED	ACCEDED	ADDUCTS
WOVENS	YEARLY	ZOOMED	ACCEDES	ADHERED
WOWING	YEARNS		ACCENTS	ADHERER
WRAITH	YEASTS	7	ACCEPTS	ADHERES
WRATHS	YEASTY		ACCLAIM	ADJOINS
WREATH	YELLED	ABANDON	ACCORDS	ADJOURN
WRECKS	YELLER	ABASHED	ACCOSTS	ADJUDGE
WRENCH	YELLOW	ABASHES	ACCOUNT	ADJUNCT
WRESTS	YELPED	ABASING	ACCURED	ADJURED
WRETCH	YELPER	ABDOMEN	ACCRUES	ADJURES
WRIGHT	YENNED	ABDUCTS	ACCUSAL	ADJUSTS
WRISTS	YESTER	ANETTED	ACCUSED	ADMIRAL
WRITER	YIELDS	ABETTER	ACCUSES	ADMIRED
WRITES	YOBBOS	ABIDING	ACETATE	ADMIRER
WRONGS	YODELS	ABILITY	ACETONE	ADMIRES
WRYEST	YODLED	ADJURED	ACHIEVE	ADMIXED
WRYING	YODLER	ABJURES	ACIDITY	ADMIXES
WUSSES	YOGURT	ABLATED	ACOLYTE	ADOPTED
XENIAL	YOKELS	ABLATES	ACQUIRE	ADOPTER
XENIAS	YOLKED	ABOLISH	ACQUITS	ADORNED
XENONS	YONDER	ABORTED	ACREAGE	ADRENAL
XYLANS	YOUTHS	ABOUNDS	ACROBAT	ADSORBS
XYLEMS	YUPPIE	ABRADD	ACRONYM	ADULATE
XYLENE	ZANIER	ABRADES	ACRYLIC	ADVANCE
XYLOID	ZANILY	ABREAST	ACTIONS	ADVERBS
XYLOLS	ZAPPED	ABRIDGE	ACTRESS	ADVERSE

ADVOSED	AIRPORT	AMATORY	ANILINE
ADVOSEE	AIRSHIP	AMAZERS	ANIMATE
ADVOSER	AIRWAYS	AMAZING	ANIMISM
ADVOSES	ALARMED	AMBIENT	ANIONIC
ADVOSPR	ALBUMIN	AMBLING	ANNEXED
AERATED	ALCHEMY	AMENDED	ANNEXES
AERATES	ALCOHOL	AMENITY	ANNOYED
AERATOR	ALCOVES	AMIABLE	ANNOYER
AERIALS	ALERTED	AMMONIA	ANNUALS
AEROBIC	ALERTER	AMNESTY	ANNUITY
AEROSOL	ALERTLY	AMOEBAE	ANNULAR
AFFABLE	ALFALFA	AMOEBAS	ANNULAR
AFFAIRS	ALGEBRA	AMONGST	ANNULUS
AFFECTS	ALIASED	AMORIST	ANODIZE
AFFIRMS	ALIASES	AMOROUS	ANOINTS
AFFIXED	ALIGNED	AMOUNTS	ANOMALY
AFFIXES	ALIMONY	AMPERES	ANOTHER
AFFLICT	ALKALIS	AMPLIFY	ANSWERS
AFFORDS	ALLAYED	AMPOULE	ANTENNA
AFFRONT	ALLEGED	AMULETS	ANTHEM
AGAINST	ALLEGES	AMUSERS	ANTIGEN
AGELESS	ALLERGY	AMUSING	ANTIQUE
AGENDAS	ALLOWED	ANAGRAM	ANXIETY
AGILELY	ALLUDED	ANALOGY	ANXIOUS
AGILITY	ALLUDES	ANALYST	ANYBODY
AGITATE	ALLYING	ANALYZE	ANYMORE
AGONIES	ALMANAC	ANARCHY	ANYTIME
AGONIZE	ALMONDS	ANATOMY	APHASIA
AGREERS	ALMONER	ANCHORS	APHASIC
AILMENT	ALMSMAN	ANCHOVY	APHONIC
AIMLESS	ALREADY	ANCIENT	APLENTY
AIRBAGS	ALTERED	ANEMONE	APOGEES
AIRFLOW	ALTERER	ANGELIC	APOLOGY
AIRFOIL	ALUMNAE	ANGERED	APOSTLE
AIRINGS	ALUMNUS	ANGLERS	APOSTLE
AIRLESS	ALVEOLI	ANGLING	APPAREL
AIRLIFT	AMALGAM	ANGRIER	APPEALS
AIRLINE	AMASSED	ANGRILY	APPEARS
AIRLOCK	AMASSES	ANGUISH	APPEASE
AIRMAIL	AMATEUR	ANGULAR	APPENDS

APPLAUD	ARRIVED	ASUNDER	AVERRER
APPLIED	ARRIVES	ATHEISM	AVERTED
APPLIER	ARROWED	ATHEIST	AVIATOR
APPLIES	ARSENAL	ATHLETE	AVIDITY
APPOINT	ARSENIC	ATOMICS	AVIONIC
APPRISE	ARTICLE	ATOMIZE	AVOCADO
APPROV E	ARTISAN	ATROPHY	AVOIDED
APRICOT	ARTISTS	ATTACHE	AVOIDER
APROPOS	ARTLESS	ATTACKS	AWAITED
APTNESS	ARTWORK	ATTAINS	AWAKENS
AQUARIA	ASCENDS	ATTEMPT	AWAKING
AQUATIC	ASCETIC	ATTENDS	AWARDED
AQUEOUS	ASCRIBE	ATTESTS	AWARDER
ARBITER	ASEPTIC	ATTIRED	AWESOME
ARCADED	ASHAMED	ATTIRES	AWFULLY
ARCADES	ASHTRAY	ATTRACT	AWKWARD
ARCHAIC	ASININE	ATTUNED	AWNINGS
ARCHERS	ASKANCE	ATTUNES	AXIALLY
ARCHERY	ASOCIAL	AUCTION	AXOLOTL
ARCHING	ASPECTS	AUDIBLE	AZALEAS
ARCHIVE	ASPHALT	AUDIBLY	AZIMUTH
ARCLIKE	ASPIRED	AUDITED	BABBLED
ARCSINE	ASPIRES	AUDITOR	BABBLER
ARDUOUS	ASPIRIN	AUGMENT	BABBLES
ARGUERS	ASSAILS	AURALLY	BABOONS
ARGUING	ASSAULT	AUREOLE	BABYING
ARIDITY	ASSAYED	AUSPICE	BABYISH
ARISING	ASSENTS	AUSTERE	BABYSIT
ARMHOLE	ASSERTS	AUTHORS	BACILLI
ARMLOAD	ASSIGNS	AUTOPSY	BACKERS
ARMPITS	ASSISTS	AUTUMNS	BACKING
AROUSAL	ASSORTS	AVAILED	BACKLOG
AROUSED	ASSUAGE	AVAILER	BACKUPS
AROUSES	ASSUMED	AVARICE	BADGERS
ARRAIGN	ASSUMES	AVENGED	BADNESS
ARRANGE	ASSURED	AVENGER	BAFFLED
ARRAYED	ASSURER	AVENGES	BAFFLER
ARREARS	ASSURES	AVENUES	BAGGAGE
ARRESTS	ASOUND	AVERAGE	BAGGERS
ARRIVAL	ASTRIDE	AVERRED	BAGGING

BAGPIPE	BARGING	BEAKERS	BELCHES
BAILIFF	BARKERS	BEAMERS	BELIEFS
BAILING	BARKINGS	BEAMING	BELIEVE
BAITING	BAROQUE	BEANBAG	BELLBOY
BAKLAVA	BARRACK	BEANING	BELLHOP
BALANCE	BARRAGE	BEARDED	BELLIES
BALCONY	BARRELS	BEARERS	BELLMAN
BALDING	BARRIER	BEARING	BELLOWS
BALEFUL	BARRING	BEARISH	BELONGS
BALKING	BARTERS	BEASTLY	BELOVED
BALLADS	BASEMAN	BEATING	BELTING
BALLAST	BASHFUL	BEATNIK	BELYING
BALLERS	BASHING	BEAVERS	BEMOANS
BALLETS	BASKETS	BECALMS	BENCHED
BALLING	BASKING	BECAUSE	BENCHES
BALLOON	BASTARD	BECKONS	BENDERS
BALLOTS	BASTING	BECOMES	BENDING
BANALLY	BASTION	BEDBUGS	BENEATH
BANANAS	BATCHED	BEDDING	BENEFIT
BANDAGE	BATCHES	BEDEVIL	BEQUEST
BANDIED	BATHERS	BEDFAST	BERATED
BANDING	BATHING	BEDPOST	BERATES
BANDITS	BATHRUB	BEDROCK	BEREAVE
BANEFUL	BATTENS	BEDROOM	BERRIES
BANGING	BATTERS	BEDSIDE	BERSERK
BANDITS	BATTERY	BEDTIME	BESEECH
BANEFUL	BATTING	BEEFING	BESIDES
BANGING	BATTLED	BEEHIVE	BESIEGE
BANGLES	BATTLER	BEETLED	BESPEAK
BANKERS	BATTLES	BEETLES	BESPOKE
BANGING	BAUBLES	BEFALLS	BESTIAL
BANNERS	BAWLING	BEFOULS	BESTING
BANNING	BAYONET	BEGGARS	BETRAYS
BANQUET	BAZAARS	BEGGING	BETROTH
BANSHEE	BEACHED	BEGUILE	BETTERS
BANTERS	BEACHES	BEHAVED	BETTING
BAPTISM	BEACONS	BEHOLDS	BETWEEN
BAPTIZE	BEADING	BELATED	BETWIXT
BARBELL	BEADLES	BELAYED	BEWAILS
BARGAIN	BEAGLES	BELCHED	BEWITCH

BIASING	BLABBED	BLOTTED	BOOKIES
BIBBING	BLACKEN	BLOUSES	BOOKING
BICKERS	BLACKER	BLOWING	BOOKISH
BICYCLE	BLACKLY	BLOWOUT	BOOKLET
BIDDERS	BLADDER	BLUBBER	BOOMING
BIDDIES	BLAMERS	BLUNDER	BOORISH
BIDDING	BLAMING	BLUNTED	BOOSTED
BIFOCAL	BLANDLY	BLUNTER	BOOSTER
BIGGEST	BLANKED	BLUNTLY	BOOTING
BIGNESS	BLANKER	BLURRED	BOOTLEG
BIGOTED	BLANKET	BLURTED	BORATES
BIGOTRY	BLANKLY	BLUSHED	BORDERS
BIKINIS	BLARING	BLUSHES	BOREDOM
BILLETS	BLASTED	BOARDED	BOROUGH
BILLING	BLASTER	BOARDER	BOROWS
BILLION	BLATANT	BOASTED	BOTCHED
BIMODAL	BLAZERS	BOASTER	BOTCHER
BINDERS	BLAZING	BOATING	BOTCHES
BINDING	BLEAKER	BOATMAN	BOTHERS
BIOLOGY	BLEAKLY	BOBBING	BOTTLED
BIPLANE	BLEEDER	BOBBINS	BOTTLER
BIPOLAR	BLEMISH	BOGGLED	BOTTLES
BIRCHEN	BLENDED	BOGGLES	BOTTOMS
BIRCHES	BLENDER	BOILERS	BOULDER
BIRDIED	BLESSED	BOILING	BOUNCED
BIRDIES	BLINDED	BOLDEST	BOUNCER
BIRTHED	BLINDLY	BOLSTER	BOUNCES
BISCUIT	BLINKED	BOLTING	BOUNDED
BISECTS	BLINKER	BOMBARD	BOUQUET
BISHOPS	BLISTER	BOMBAST	BOURBON
BISMUTH	BLITZES	BOMBERS	BOVINES
BISQUES	BLOATED	BOMBING	BOWLERS
BISTATE	BLOATER	BONANZA	BOWLINE
BITCHES	BLOCKED	BONDAGE	BOWLING
BITTERS	BLOCKER	BONDERS	BOXTOPS
BITUMEN	BLONDES	BONDING	BOXWOOD
BITWISE	BLOODED	BONFIRE	BOYCOTT
BIVALVE	BLOOMED	BONNETS	BOYHOOD
BIVOUAC	BLOOPER	BONUSES	BRACING
BIZARRE	BLOSSOM	BOOKERS	BRACKET

BRAGGED	BRIDLED	BUCKETS	BUNDLES
BRAGGER	BRIDLES	BUCKING	BUNGLED
BRAIDED	BRIEFED	BUCKLED	BUNGLER
BRAINED	BRIEFER	BUCKLER	BUNGLES
BRAKING	BRIEFLY	BUCKLES	BUNIONS
BRAMBLE	BRIGADE	BUCOLIC	BUNKERS
BRAMBLY	BRIMFUL	BUDDIES	BUNNIES
BRANDED	BRIMMED	BUDDING	BUNTERS
BRASHLY	BRINDLE	BUDGETS	BUNTING
BRASSES	BRINGER	BUDGING	BUOYANT
BRAVADO	BRISKER	BUFFALO	BURDERS
BRAVELY	BRISKLY	BUFFERS	BUREAUS
BRAVERY	BRISTLE	BUFFETS	BURGEON
BRAVEST	BRITTLE	BUFFOON	BURGHER
BRAVING	BROADEN	BUGGIES	BURNERS
BRAWLER	BROADER	BUGGING	BURNING
BRAYING	BROADLY	BUGLING	BURNISH
BRAZIER	BROCADE	BUILDER	BURNTLY
BRAZING	BROILED	BUILDUP	BURPING
BREADED	BROILER	BULGING	BURROWS
BREADTH	BROKERS	BULLDOG	BURYING
BRAKER	BROMIDE	BULLETS	BUSHELS
BREAKUP	BRONCHI	BULLIES	BUSHING
BREASTS	BRONZED	BULLIES	BUSIEST
BREATHE	BRONZES	BULLING	BUSSING
BREATHS	BROODER	BULLION	BUSTARD
BREEDER	BROOKED	BULLISH	BUTCHER
BREEZES	BROTHEL	BULLOCK	BUTLERS
BREVETS	BROTHER	BULWARK	BUTTERS
BREVITY	BROUGHT	BUMBLED	BUTTERY
BREWERS	BROWNED	BUMBLER	BUTTING
BREWERY	BROWNER	BUMBLES	BUTTOCK
BREWING	BROWNIE	BUMMING	BUTTONS
BRIBERS	BRUISED	BUMPERS	BUZZING
BRIBERY	BRUSHED	BUMPING	BYLINES
BRIBING	BRUSHES	BUMPERS	BYWORDS
BRICKED	BRUSQUE	BUMPING	CABARET
BRICKER	BRUTISH	BUNCHED	CABBAGE
BRIDGED	BUBBLED	BUNCHES	CABINET
BRIDGES	BUBBLES	BUNDLED	CABLING

CABOOSE	CAPABLE	CASSOCK	CHAIRED
CACHING	CAPABLY	CASTERS	CHALICE
CACKLED	CAPITAL	CASTING	CHALKED
CACKLER	CAPITOL	CASTLED	CHAMBER
CACKLES	CAPPING	CASTLES	CHANCED
CADAVER	CAPSULE	CASUALS	CHANCES
CADENCE	CAPTAIN	CATCHER	CHANGED
CAJOLED	CAPTION	CATCHES	CHANGER
CAJOLES	CAPTIVE	CATERED	CHANGES
CALCIFY	CAPTORS	CATERER	CHANNEL
CALCIUM	CAPTURE	CATHODE	CHANTED
CALIBRE	CARAMEL	CATLIKE	CHANTER
CALIPHS	CARAVAN	CATTAIL	CHAOTIC
CALLERS	CARAWAY	CAUSING	CHAPELS
CALLING	CARBONS	CAUSTIC	CHAPTER
CALLOUS	CARCASS	CAUTION	CHARGED
CALMEST	CARDIAC	CAVALRY	CHARGER
CALMING	CAREERS	CAVEATS	CHARIOT
CALORIC	CAREFUL	CAVEMAN	CHARITY
CALORIE	CARGOES	CAVERNS	CHARMED
CALUMNY	CARIBOU	CEASING	CHARMER
CALYPSO	CARLOAD	CEILING	CHARTED
CAMERAS	CARNAGE	CELLARS	CHARTER
CAMPERS	CARPETS	CELLIST	CHASERS
CAMPING	CARPORT	CEMENTS	CHASING
CANCELS	CARRIED	CENSORS	CHASSIS
CANCERS	CARRIER	CENSURE	CHATEAU
CANDIED	CARRIES	CENTAUR	CHATTEL
CANDIES	CARRION	CENTRAL	CHATTER
CANDLES	CARRROTS	CENTRED	CHEAPEN
CANNERS	CARTERS	CENTRES	CHEAPLY
CANNERY	CARTING	CENTURY	CHEATED
CANNING	CARTONS	CERAMIC	CHECKED
CANNONS	CARTOON	CEREALS	CHEERED
CANONIC	CARVING	CERTAIN	CHEERER
CANTEEN	CASCADE	CERTIFY	CHEESES
CANTONS	CASHIER	CHAFING	CHEETAH
CANTORS	CASHING	CHAGRIN	CHEMISE
CANVASS	CASINGS	CHAINED	CHERISH
CANYONS	CASKETS	CHAIRED	CHERUBS

CHEWERS	CLAMBER	CLONING	COEXIST
CHEWING	CLAMPED	CLOSELY	COFFEES
CHICKEN	CLANGED	CLOSERS	COFFERS
CHIDING	CLARIFY	CLOSEST	COFFINS
CHIEFLY	CLARITY	CLOSETS	COHERED
CHIFFON	CLASHED	CLOSING	COHERES
CHILLED	CLASHES	CLOSURE	COILING
CHILLER	CLASPED	CLOTHED	COINAGE
CHIMERA	CLASSED	CLOTHES	COLDEST
CHIMNEY	CLASSES	CLOTURE	COLICKY
CHINKED	CLASSIC	CLOUDED	COLLARS
CHINNED	CLATTER	CLUBBED	COLLATE
CHIRPED	CLAUSES	CLUCKED	COLLECT
CHISELS	CLAWING	CLUMPED	COLLEGE
CHOICES	CLEANED	CLUSTER	COLLIDE
CHOKERS	CLEANER	CLUTTER	COLLIES
CHOKING	CLEANLY	COACHED	COLONEL
CHOLERA	CLEANSE	COACHES	COLUMNS
CHOOSER	CLEARED	COARSEN	COMBATS
CHOOSES	CLEARER	COARSER	COMBERS
CHOPPED	CLEARLY	COASTAL	COMBINE
CHOPPER	CLEAVED	COASTED	COMBING
CHORDED	CLEAVER	COASTER	COMEDIC
CHORING	CLEMENT	COATING	COMFORT
CHORTLE	CLERKED	COAXIAL	COMICAL
CHOWDER	CLICHES	COAXING	COMINGS
CHRONIC	CLICKED	COBBLER	COMMAND
CHUCKLE	CLIENTS	COBWEBS	COMMEND
CHURNED	CLIMATE	COCAINE	COMMENT
CINDERS	CLIMBED	COCKING	COMMITS
CIPHERS	CLIMBER	COCKPIT	COMMONS
CIRCLED	CLINICS	COCONUT	COMMUNE
CIRCLES	CLINKED	COCOONS	COMMUTE
CIRCLET	CLINKER	CODEINE	COMPACT
CIRCUIT	CLIPPED	CODFISH	COMPANY
CISTERN	CLIPPER	CODICIL	COMPARE
CITADEL	CLIQUES	CODINGS	COMPASS
CITIZEN	CLOBBER	COEQUAL	COMPELS
CIVILLY	CLOCKED	COERCED	COMPETE
CLAIMED	CLOGGED	COERCES	COMPILE

COMPLEX	CONSULT	COSINES	CRADLES
COMPOSE	CONSUME	COSTING	CRAFTED
COMPOST	CONTACT	COSTUME	CRAFTER
COMPUTE	CONTAIN	COTTAGE	CRANIUM
COMRADE	CONTENT	COTTONS	CRANKED
CONCAVE	CONTEST	COUCHED	CRASHED
CONCEAL	CONTEXT	COUGHED	CRASHES
CONCEDE	CONTOUR	COUNCIL	CRATERS
CONCEIT	CONTROL	COUNSEL	CRAVATS
CONCEPT	CONVECT	COUNTED	CRAVING
CONCERN	CONVENE	COUNTER	CRAWLED
CONCERT	CONVENT	COUNTRY	CRAWLER
CONCISE	CONVERT	COUPLED	CRAZIER
CONCOCT	CONVEYS	COUPLER	CRAZILY
CONCORD	CONVICT	COUPLES	CRAZING
CONCURS	CONVOKE	COUPONS	CREAKED
CONDEMN	CONVOYS	COURAGE	CREAMED
CONDONE	COOKERY	COURIER	CREAMER
CONDUCE	COOKIES	COURSES	CREASED
CONDUCT	COOKING	COURSER	CREASES
CONDUIT	COOLERS	COURSES	CREATED
CONFERS	COOLEST	COURTED	CREATES
CONFESS	COLLIES	COURTER	CREATOR
CONFIDE	COOLING	COURTLY	CREDITS
CONFINE	COOPERS	COUSINS	CREEPER
CONFORM	COPIERS	COVERED	CREMATE
CONFUSE	COPINGS	COVETED	CRESTED
CONGEST	COPIOUS	COWBOYS	CREVICE
CONIFER	COPPERS	COWERED	CREWCUT
CONJURE	COPYING	COWERER	CREWING
CONNECT	CORDIAL	COWHERD	CRICKET
CONNIVE	CORKERS	COWHIDE	CRIMSON
CONNOTE	CORKING	COWLICK	CRINGED
CONQUER	CORNERS	COWLING	CRINGES
CONSENT	CORNING	COWSLIP	CRIPPLE
CONSIGN	CORONER	COYOTES	CRISPLY
CONSIST	CORPSES	CRACKED	CRITICS
CONSOLE	CORRECT	CRACKER	CRITTER
CONSORT	CORRODE	CRACKLE	CROAKED
CONSULS	CORRUPT	CRADLED	CROCHET

CROOKED	CURBING	DAMPENS	DECIDES
CROPPED	CURFEWS	DAMPING	DECIMAL
CROPPER	CURIOUS	DAMSELS	DECKING
CROSSED	CURLERS	DANCERS	DECLARE
CROSSER	CURLING	DANCING	DECLINE
CROSSES	CURRANT	DANGERS	DECODED
CROSSLY	CURRENT	DANGLED	DECODER
CROWDED	CURRIED	DARESAY	DECODES
CROWDER	CURRIES	DARKEST	DECORUM
CROWING	CURSING	DARLING	DECREED
CROWNED	CURSIVE	DARNING	DECREES
CRUCIAL	CURSORS	DARTING	DECRYPT
CRUCIFY	CURSORY	DASHING	DEDUCED
CRUDELY	CURTAIL	DAUNTED	DEDUCER
CRUDEST	CURTAIN	DAWNING	DEDUCES
CRUELLY	CURTATE	DAYTIME	DEEDING
CRUELTY	CURVING	DAZZLED	DEEMING
CRUISER	CUSHION	DAZZLER	DEEPENS
CRUISES	CUSTARD	DAZZLES	DEEPEST
CRUMBLE	CUSTODY	DEACONS	DEFAULT
CRUMBLY	CUSTOMS	DEAFEST	DEFEATS
CRUMPLE	CUTBACK	DEALERS	DEFECTS
CRUNCHY	CUTLASS	DEALING	DEFENDS
CRUSADE	CUTTERS	DEAREST	DEFENCE
CRUSHED	CUTTING	DEARTHS	DEFIANT
CRUSHER	CYANIDE	DEATHLY	DEFICIT
CRUSHES	CYCLONE	DEBACLE	DEFINED
CRYPTIC	CYMBALS	DEBATED	DEFINES
CRYSTAL	CYNICAL	DEBATER	DEFLATE
CUCKOOS	CYPRESS	DEBATES	DEFLECT
CUDDLED	DABBLED	DEBAUCH	DEFOCUS
CUDGELS	DABBLER	DEBITED	DEFRAUD
CUISINE	DABBLES	DEBRIEF	DEFROST
CULLING	DAILIES	DECADES	DEFUNCT
CULPRIT	DAISIES	DECAYED	DEFYING
CULTURE	DAMAGED	DECEASE	DEGRADE
CUNNING	DAMAGER	DECEIVE	DEGREES
CUPPING	DAMAGES	DECENCY	DEIGNED
CURABLE	DAMMING	DECIBEL	DEITIES
CURABLY	DAMNING	DECIDED	DELAYED

DELETED	DERIVES	DICTUMS	DISLIKE
DELETER	DERVISH	DIEHARD	DISMISS
DELETES	DESCEND	DIETARY	DISOBEY
DELIGHT	DESCENT	DIETERS	DISOWNS
DELIMIT	DESERTS	DIFFERS	DISPELL
DELIVER	DESERVE	DIFFUSE	DISPELS
DELUDED	DESIGNS	DIGEST	DISPLAY
DELUDES	DESIRED	DIGGERS	DISPOSE
DELUGED	DESIRES	DIGGING	DISPUTE
DELUGES	DESKTOP	DIGITAL	DISRUPT
DELVING	DESPAIR	DIGNIFY	DISSECT
DEMANDS	DESPISE	DIGNITY	DISSENT
DEMERIT	DESPITE	DIGRESS	DISTAFF
DEMIGOD	DESPOIL	DILATED	DISTANT
DEMONIC	DESPOTS	DILATES	DISTILL
DENIALS	DESSERT	DILEMMA	DISTORT
DENIZEN	DESTINY	DILUTED	DISTURB
DENOTED	DESTROY	DILUTES	DITCHES
DENOTES	DETAILS	DIMMERS	DIURNAL
DENSELY	DETECTS	DIMMEST	DIVERGE
DENSEST	DETRACT	DIMMING	DIVERSE
DENSITY	DEVELOP	DIMNESS	DIVERTS
DENTING	DEVIANT	DINNERS	DIVESTS
DENTIST	DEVIATE	DIOXIDE	DIVIDED
DENTURE	DEVICES	DIPLOMA	DIVIDER
DENYING	DEVIOUS	DIPPERS	DIVIDES
DEPARTS	DEVISED	DIPPING	DIVINER
DEPENDS	DEVISES	DIRECTS	DIVISOR
DEPICTS	DEVOLVE	DIRTIER	DIVORCE
DEPLETE	DEVOTED	DIRTILY	DIVULGE
DEPLORE	DEVOTEE	DISABLE	DOCTORS
DEPLOYS	DEVOURS	DISARMS	DODGERS
DEPOSED	DEWDROP	DISBAND	DODGING
DEPOSES	DIAGRAM	DISCERN	DOGGING
DEPOSIT	DIALECT	DISCORD	DOLDRUM
DEPRAVE	DIAMONG	DISCUSS	DOLEFUL
DEPRESS	DIAPERS	DISDAIN	DOLLARS
DEPRIVE	DIARIES	DISEASE	DOLLIES
DETAILS	DOCTATE	DISGUST	DOLPHIN
DERIVED	DICTION	DISHING	DOMAINS

DONATED	DRILLER	DYNAMIC	ELEVENS
DONATES	DRINKER	DYNASTY	ELICITS
DONKEYS	DRIVERS	EAGERLY	ELISION
DOOMING	DRIVING	EARDRUM	ELITIST
DOORMAN	DRIZZLE	EARLIER	ELLIPSE
DOORWAY	DRIZZLY	EARMARK	ELUDING
DORMANT	DROOPED	EARNERS	ELUSIVE
DOSSIER	DROPLET	EARNEST	EMANATE
DOTTING	DROPOUT	EARNING	EMBARGO
DOUBLED	DROPPED	EARRING	EMBARKS
DOUBLES	DROPPER	EARTHEN	EMBASSY
DOUBLET	DROUGHT	EARTHLY	EMBRACE
DOUBTED	DROVERS	EASIEST	EMBROIL
DOWAGER	DROWNED	EASTERN	EMBRYOS
DOWNERS	DRUMMED	EATINGS	EMERALD
DRAFTED	DRUMMER	ECHELON	EMERGED
DRAFTEE	DRUNKEN	ECHOING	EMERGES
DRAFTER	DRUNKLY	ECLIPSE	EMINENT
DRAGGED	DUALISM	ECOLOGY	EMITTED
DRAGNET	DUALITY	ECONOMY	EMITTER
DRAGONS	DUBIOUS	ECSTASY	EMOTION
DRAGOON	DUCHESS	EDIFICE	EMPATHY
DRAINED	DUCKING	EDITING	EMPEROR
DRAINER	DULLEST	EDITION	EMPIRES
DRAPERS	DUMBEST	EDITORS	EMPLOYS
DRAPERY	DUMMIES	EDUCATE	EMPOWER
DRASTIC	DUMPING	EFFECTS	EMPRESS
DRAUGHT	DUNGEON	EFFORTS	EMPTIED
DRAWERS	DURABLE	EGOTISM	EMPTIER
DRAWING	DURABLY	EGOTIST	EMPTIES
DRAWLED	DUSTBIN	EJECTED	EMPTILY
DREADED	DUSTERS	ELAPSED	EMULATE
DREAMED	DUSTIER	ELASTIC	ENABLES
DREAMER	DUSTING	ELDERLY	ENACTED
DRESSED	DUTIFUL	ELECTED	ENAMELS
DRESSER	DWARFED	ELECTOR	ENCAMPS
DRESSES	DWARVES	ELECTRO	ENCASED
DRIFTED	DWELLED	ELEGANT	ENCHANT
DRIFTER	DWELLER	ELEMENT	ENCLOSE
DRILLED	DWINDLE	ELEVATE	ENCODED

ENCODER	ENTERED	ESQUIRE	EXERTED
ENCODES	ENTICER	ESSAYED	EXHALED
ENCRUST	ENTICES	ESSENCE	EXHALES
ENCRYPT	ENTITLE	ESTATES	EXHAUST
ENDEARS	ENTREAT	ESTEEMS	EXHIBIT
ENDEMIC	ENTRIES	ETCHING	EXILING
ENDGAME	ENTROPY	ETERNAL	EXISTED
ENDINGS	ENTRUST	ETHICAL	EXITING
ENDLESS	ENVELOP	EUNUCHS	EXPANDS
ENDORSE	ENVIOUS	EVADING	EXPANSE
ENDOWED	ENVIRON	EVASION	EXPECTS
ENDURED	EPAULET	EVASIVE	EXPENDS
ENDURES	EPIGRAM	EVENING	EXPENSE
ENEMIES	EPISODE	EVICTED	EXPERTS
ENFORCE	EPISTLE	EVIDENT	EXPIRED
ENGAGED	EPITAPH	EVINCED	EXPIRES
ENGAGES	EPITHET	EVINCES	EXPLAIN
ENGINES	EPSILON	EVOKING	EXPLODE
ENGRAVE	EQUALLY	EVOLUTE	EXPLOIT
ENGROSS	EQUATED	EVOLVED	EXPLORE
ENHANCE	EQUATOR	EVOLVES	EXPORTS
ENJOINS	EQUINOX	EXACTED	EXPOSED
ENJOYED	ERASERS	EXACTLY	EXPOSER
ENLARGE	ERASING	EXALTED	EXPOSES
ENLISTS	ERASURE	EXAMINE	EXPOUND
ENLIVEN	ERECTED	EXAMPLE	EXPRESS
ENNOBLE	ERECTOR	EXCEEDS	EXPUNGE
ENQUIRE	ERGODIC	EXCEPTS	EXTENDS
ENQUIRY	ERMINES	EXCERPT	EXTENTS
ENRAGED	EROSION	EXCISED	EXTINCT
ENRAGES	EROTICA	EXCISES	EXTRACT
ENROLLS	ERRATIC	EXCITED	EXTREME
ENSIGNS	ERRATUM	EXCITES	EYEBALL
ENSLAVE	ERUDITE	EXCLAIM	EYEBROW
ENSNARE	ESCAPED	EXCLUDE	EYELASH
ENSUING	ESCAPEE	EXCRETE	EYELIDS
ENSURED	ESCAPES	EXCUSED	FABRICS
ENSURER	ESCHEWS	EXCUSES	FACADED
ENSURES	ESCORTS	EXECUTE	FACADES
ENTAILS	ESPOUSE	EXEMPTS	FACETED

FACINGS	FASTING	FICTION	FITTERS
FACTION	FATALLY	FIDDLED	FITTING
FACTORS	FATEFUL	FIDDLER	FIXATED
FACTORY	FATHERS	FIDDLES	FIXATES
FACULTY	FATHOMS	FIEFDOM	FIXEDLY
FADEOUT	FATIGUE	FIELDED	FIXINGS
FAILING	FATNESS	FIELDER	FIXTURE
FAILURE	FATTENS	FIERCER	FIZZLED
FAINTED	FATTEST	FIFTEEN	FLAGGED
FAINTER	FAULTED	FIFTIES	FLAKING
FAINTLY	FAWNING	FIGHTER	FLAMERS
FAIREST	FEARFUL	FIGURED	FLAMING
FAIRIES	FEARING	FIGURES	FLANKED
FAIRING	FEASTED	FILINGS	FLANKER
FALCONS	FEATHER	FILLERS	FLANNEL
FALLACY	FEDERAL	FILLING	FALRING
FALLING	FEEBLER	FILMING	FLASHED
FALLOUT	FEEDERS	FILTERS	FLASHER
FALSELY	FEEDING	FINALLY	FLASHES
FALSITY	FEELERS	FINANCE	FLATBED
FAMINES	FEELING	FINDERS	FLATTEN
FANATIC	FEIGNED	FINDING	FLATTER
FANCIED	FELLING	FINESSE	FLAUNTS
FANCIER	FELLOWS	FINGERS	FLEDGED
FANCIES	FEMALES	FINICKY	FLEECES
FANCILY	FENCERS	FIREARM	FLEEING
FANFARE	FENCING	FIREBUG	FLESHED
FANFOLD	FERMENT	FIREFLY	FLESHES
FANGLED	FERRIED	FIREMAN	FLESHLY
FANNING	FERRIES	FIREMEN	FLICKED
FANTASY	FERRITE	FIRINGS	FLICKER
FARAWAY	FERTILE	FIRMEST	FLIGHTS
FARMERS	FERVENT	FIRMING	FLIPPED
FARMING	FESTIVE	FIRSTLY	FLIRTED
FARTHER	FETCHED	FISHERS	FLOATED
FASCISM	FETCHES	FISHERY	FLOATER
FASCIST	FETTERS	FISHING	FLOCKED
FASHION	FEVERED	FISSION	FLOODED
FASTENS	FIANCEE	FISSURE	FLOORED
FASTEST	FIBBING	FITNESS	FLORIST

552

FLOSSED	FORBIDS	FRAUGHT	FURLONG
FLOSSES	FORCING	FRAYING	FURFACE
FLOURED	FOREARM	FRAZZLE	FURNISH
FLOWERS	FOREIGN	FRECKLE	FURRIER
FLOWERY	FOREMAN	FREEDOM	FURROWS
FLOWING	FORESEE	FREEING	FURTHER
FLUENCY	FORESTS	FREEWAY	FURTIVE
FLUIDLY	FOREVER	FREEZER	FUSSING
FLUSHED	FORFEIT	FREEZES	FUTURES
FLUSHES	FORGAVE	FREIGHT	FUZZIER
FLUTING	FORGERY	FRESHEN	GABBING
FLUTTER	FORGETS	FRESHER	GADGETS
FLYABLE	FORGING	FRESHLY	GAGGING
FOAMING	FORGIVE	FRETFUL	GAINERS
FOBBING	FORKING	FRIDAYS	GAINFUL
FOCALLY	FORLORN	FRIENDS	GAINING
FOCUSED	FORMANT	FRIEZES	GAITERS
FOCUSES	FORMATS	FRIGATE	GALLANT
FOGGIER	FORMING	FRINGED	GALLERY
FOGGILY	FORMULA	FRISBEE	GALLEYS
FOGGING	FORREST	FRISKED	GALLING
FOILING	FORSAKE	FRITTER	GALLONS
FOLDERS	FORTIER	FROLICS	GALLOPS
FOXTROT	FORTIES	FRONTAL	GALLOWS
FOLDOUT	FORTIFY	FRONTED	GAMBLED
FOLIAGE	FORTUNE	FROSTED	GAMBLER
FOLLIES	FORWARD	FROWNED	GAMBLES
FOLLOWS	FOSTERS	FUCHSIA	GANNETT
FONDLED	FOULEST	FULCRUM	GARAGED
FONDLES	FOULING	FULFILL	GARAGES
FOOLING	FOUNDED	FULLEST	GARBAGE
FOOLISH	FOUNDER	FUMBLED	GARBLED
FOOTAGE	FOUNDRY	FUNCTOR	GARDENS
FOOTERS	FRAGILE	FUNDERS	GARGLED
FOOTING	FRAILTY	FUNDING	GARGLES
FOOTMAN	FRAMING	FUNERAL	GARLAND
FORAGED	FRANKED	FUNNELS	GARMENT
FORAGES	FRANKER	FUNNIER	GARNISH
FORBADE	FRANKLY	FUNNILY	GARTERS
FORBEAR	FRANTIC	FURIOUS	GASEOUS

GASPING	GLANCED	GOODBYE	GRAZING
GASSING	GLANCES	GOODIES	GREASED
GASTRIC	GLARING	GORGING	GREASES
GATEWAY	GLASSED	GORILLA	GREATER
GATHERS	GLASSES	GOSPELS	GREATLY
GAYNESS	GLAZING	GOSSIPS	GREENER
GAZELLE	GLEAMED	GOUGING	GREENLY
GAZETTE	GLEANED	GOURMET	GREETED
GEARING	GLEANER	GOVERNS	GREETER
GELLING	GLEEFUL	GRABBED	GRENADE
GENDERS	GLIDERS	GRABBER	GREYEST
GENERAL	GLIMMER	GRACING	GREYING
GENERIC	GLIMPSE	GRADERS	GRIDDLE
GENETIC	GLINTED	GRADUAL	GRIEVED
GENTEEL	GLISTEN	GRAFTED	GRIEVER
GENTILE	GLITTER	GRAFTED	GRIEVES
GENTLER	GLORIES	GRAINED	GRILLED
GENUINE	GLORIFY	GRAMMAR	GRIMAC E
GEOLOGY	GLOSSED	GRANARY	GRINDER
GESTURE	GLOSSES	GRANDER	GRIPPED
GETAWAY	GLOTTAL	GRANDLY	GRIZZLY
GETTERS	GLOVERS	GRANDMA	GROANED
GETTING	GLOVING	GRANDPA	GROANER
GHASTLY	GLOWERS	GRANITE	GROCERS
GHOSTED	GLOWING	GRANOLA	GROCERY
GHOSTLY	GLUTTON	GRANTED	GROOMED
GIBBONS	GNAWING	GRANTEE	GROOVED
GIGABIT	GOATEES	GRANTER	GROPING
GIGGLED	GOBBLED	GRANTOR	GROSSED
GIGGLES	GOBBLER	GRAPHED	GROSSER
GILDING	GOBBLES	GRAPHIC	GRASSES
GIMMICK	GOBLETS	GRAPPLE	GROSSLY
GINGHAM	GOBLINS	GRASPED	GROTTOS
GUIPSIES	GODDESS	GRASSED	GROUNDS
GIRDERS	GODLIKE	GRASSES	GROUPED
GLACIAL	GODSEND	GRATIFY	GROVELS
GLACIER	GOGGLES	GRATING	GROVERS
GLADDEN	GOLFERS	GRAVELY	GROWERS
GLADDER	GOLFING	GRAVEST	GROWING
GLAMOUR	GONDOLA	GRAVITY	GROWLED

GROWNUP	HALTERS	HARSHLY	HEELERS
GROWTHS	HALTING	HARVEST	HEELING
GRUDGES	HALVING	HASHING	HEIGHTS
GRUFFLY	HAMLETS	HASHISH	HEINOUS
GRUMBLE	HAMMERS	HASTENS	HEIRESS
GRUNTED	HAMMING	HASTILY	HELICAL
GUARDED	HAMMOCK	HATCHED	HELLISH
GUESSED	HAMPERS	HATCHET	HELMETS
GUESSES	HAMSTER	HATEFUL	HELPERS
GUIDING	HANDBAG	HAUGHTY	HELPFUL
GUILDER	HANDFUL	HAULING	HELPING
GUITARS	HANDGUN	HAUNTED	HEMLOCK
GULCHES	HANDIER	HAUNTER	HENPECK
GULLIES	HANDILY	HAZARDS	HERALDS
GULLING	HANDING	HEADERS	HERDING
GUMMING	HANDLED	HEADING	HERETIC
GUNFIRE	HANDLER	HEADSET	HERMITS
GUNNERS	HANDLES	HEADWAY	HEROICS
GUNNERY	HANDOUT	HEALERS	HEROINE
GUNNING	HANGARS	HEADING	HEROISM
GUNPLAY	HANGERS	HEADSET	HERRING
GUNSHOT	HANGING	HEADWAY	HERSELF
GUSHING	HANGMAN	HEALERS	HEXAGON
GUTTERS	HANGOUT	HEALING	HICKORY
GYMNAST	HAPLESS	HEALTHY	HIDEOUS
GYPSIES	HAPPENS	HEAPING	HIDEOUT
HABITAT	HAPPIER	HEARERS	HIGHEST
HACKERS	HAPPILY	HEARING	HIGHWAY
HACKING	HARDEST	HEARKEN	HILLOCK
HACKSAW	HARLOTS	HEARSAY	HILLTOP
HADDOCK	HARMFUL	HEARTEN	HIMSELF
HAGGARD	HARMING	HEATERS	HINDERS
HAILING	HARMONY	HEATHEN	HINTING
HAIRCUT	HARNESS	HEATHER	HIRINGS
HAIRIER	HARPERS	HEATING	HISSING
HAIRPIN	HARPING	HEAVENS	HISTORY
HALCYON	HARRIED	HEAVERS	HITCHED
HALFWAY	HARRIER	HEAVIER	HITTERS
HALLWAY	HARROWS	HEAVILY	HITTING
HALOGEN	HARSHER	HEAVING	HOARDER

HOBBIES	HUMIDLY	IMPAIRS	INDUCED
HOBBLED	HUMMING	IMPARTS	INDUCER
HOBBLES	HUNCHED	IMPASSE	INDUCES
HOGGING	HUNCHES	IMPEACH	INDUCTS
HOISTED	HUNDRED	IMPEDED	INDULGE
HOLDERS	HUNGERS	IMPEDES	INERTIA
HOLDING	HUNTERS	IMPERIL	INERTLY
HOLIDAY	HUNTING	IMPETUS	INEXACT
HOLLOWS	HURLERS	IMPINGE	INFANCY
HONESTY	HURLING	IMPIOUS	INFANTS
HOODLUM	HURRIED	IMPLANT	INFARCT
HOOKERS	HURRIES	IMPLIED	INFECTS
HOOKING	HURTING	IMPLIES	INFERNO
HOOKUPS	HUSBAND	IMPLORE	INFESTS
HOOTING	HUSHING	IMPORTS	INFIDEL
HOPEFUL	HUSKING	IMPOSED	INFLATE
HOPPERS	HUSTLED	IMPOSES	INFLICT
HOPPING	HUSTLER	IMPOUND	INFORMS
HORIZON	HUSTLES	IMPRESS	INFUSED
HORMONE	HYDRANT	IMPRINT	INFUSES
HORNETS	HYGIENE	IMPROVE	INGRATE
HORRIFY	HYPHENS	IMPULSE	INGROWN
HORRORS	ICEBERG	IMPUTED	INHABIT
HOSTAGE	ICINESS	INBOARD	INHALED
HOSTESS	IDEALLY	INBOUND	INHALER
HOSTILE	IDIOTIC	INBREED	INHALES
HOSTING	IGNOBLE	INCENSE	INHERES
HOTNESS	IGNORED	INCHING	INHERIT
HOTTEST	IGNORES	INCITED	INHIBIT
HOUNDED	ILLEGAL	INCITES	INHUMAN
HOUSING	ILLICIT	INCLINE	INITIAL
HOVERED	ILLNESS	INCLOSE	INJECTS
HOWEVER	IMAGERY	INCLUDE	INJURES
HOWLING	IMAGINE	INCOMES	INKINGS
HUDDLED	IMAGING	INDENTS	INKLING
HUGGING	IMITATE	INDEXED	INMATES
HUMANLY	IMMENSE	INDEXES	INNARDS
HUMBLED	IMMERSE	INDIANS	INNINGS
HUMBLER	IMMORAL	INDICES	INQUEST
HUMERUS	IMPACTS	INDOORS	INQUIRE

INQUIRY	INVOKED	JINGLED	KEYNOTE
INROADS	INVOKER	JITTERY	KEYPADS
INSECTS	INVOKES	JOGGING	KEYWORD
INSERTS	INVOLVE	JOINERS	KICKERS
INSIDER	INWARDS	JOINING	KICKING
INSIDES	IRANIZE	JOINTLY	KICKOFF
INSIGHT	IRATELY	JOLTING	KIDDING
INSIPID	IRKSOME	JOSTLED	KIDNAPS
INSISTS	IRONIES	JOSTLES	KIDNEYS
INSOFAR	IRONING	JOTTING	KILLERS
INSPECT	ISLANDS	JOURNAL	KILLING
INSPIRE	ISOLATE	JOURNEY	KILLJOY
INSTALL	ISOTOPE	JOUSTED	KILOBIT
INSTANT	ISSUERS	JOYRIDE	KILOTON
INSTEAD	ISSUING	JUBILEE	KINDEST
INSTILL	ISTHMUS	JUDAISM	KINDLED
INSULAR	ITALICS	JUDDERS	KINDLES
INSULIN	ITCHING	JUDGING	KINDRED
INSULTS	ITEMIZE	JUGGLER	KINETIC
INSURED	ITERATE	JUGGLES	KINGDOM
INSURES	ITERATE	JUMBLED	KINGPIN
INTEGER	JABBING	JUMBLES	KINSHIP
INTENDS	JACKASS	JUMPERS	KINSMAN
INTENSE	JACKETS	JUMPING	KISSERS
INTENTS	JACKING	JUNGLES	KISSING
INTERIM	JACKPOT	JUNIORS	KITCHEN
INTERNS	JAILERS	JUNIPER	KITTENS
INTRUDE	JAILING	JUNKERS	KNEECAP
INTRUST	JAMMING	JUPITER	KNEEING
INVADED	JANITOR	JUSTICE	KNEELED
INVADER	JANUARY	JUSTIFY	KNIFING
INVADES	JARRING	JUTTING	KNIGHTS
INVALID	JAVELIN	KEELING	KNOCKED
INVENTS	JAWBONE	KEENEST	KNOCKER
INVERSE	JEALOUS	KEEPERS	KNOTTED
INVERTS	JELLIES	KENNELS	KNOWHOW
INVESTS	JERKING	KERNELS	KNOWING
INVITED	JERSEYS	KETCHUP	KNUCKLE
INVITES	JESTING	KETTLES	LACKING
INVOICE	JETTING	KEYHOLE	LACQUER

LAGOONS	LEANING	LIBERAL	LOBSTER
LAMBDAS	LEAPING	LIBERTY	LOCALLY
LAMENTS	LEARNED	LIBRARY	LOCATED
LAMINAR	LEARNER	LICENSE	LOCATES
LAMPOON	LEASHES	LICHENS	LOCATOR
LAMPREY	LEASING	LICKING	LOCKERS
LANCERS	LEATHER	LIFTERS	LOCKING
LANDERS	LEAVING	LIFTING	LOCKOUT
LANDING	LECHERY	LIGHTED	LOCKUPS
LANGUID	LECTURE	LIGHTEN	LOCUSTS
LANTERN	LEDGERS	LIGHTER	LODGING
LAPPING	LEECHES	LIGHTLY	LOGGERS
LARGEST	LEEWARD	LIKENED	LOGGING
LASHING	LEFTIST	LIMITED	LOGICAL
LASTING	LEGALLY	LIMITER	LOITERS
LATCHED	LEGENDS	LIMPING	LONGEST
LATCHES	LEGIBLE	LINGERS	LONGING
LATENCY	LEGIBLY	LININGS	LOOKERS
LATERAL	LEGIONS	LINKAGE	LOOKING
LATRINE	LEISURE	LINKING	LOOKOUT
LAUGHED	LEMMING	LINSEED	LOOMING
LAUNDER	LENDERS	LIONESS	LOOPING
LAUNDRY	LENDING	LIQUIDS	LOOSELY
LAURELS	LENGTHS	LIQUORS	LOOSENS
LAWSUIT	LENGTHY	LISPING	LOOSEST
LAWYERS	LENIENT	LISTENS	LOOSING
LAYERED	LENTILS	LISTERS	LOOTING
LAYOFFS	LEOPARD	LISTING	LOTTERY
LAYOUTS	LEPROSY	LITERAL	LOUDEST
LAZIEST	LESBIAN	LITTERS	LOUNGED
LEADERS	LESSENS	LIVABLE	LOUNGES
LEADING	LESSONS	LIVABLY	LOVABLE
LEAFING	LETTERS	LIZARDS	LOVABLY
LEAFLET	LETTING	LOADERS	LOWERED
LEAGUED	LETTUCE	LOADING	LOWLAND
LEAGUER	LEVELLY	LOANING	LOWNESS
LEAGUES	LEVYING	LOATHED	LOYALLY
LEAKAGE	LEXICAL	LOATHLY	LOYALTY
LEAKING	LEXICON	LOBBIED	LUCKIER
LEANEST	LIAISON	LOBBIES	LUCKILY

LUGGAGE	MANAGES	MASONIC	MENTORS
ILULLABY	MANDATE	MASONRY	MERCURY
LUMPING	MANGERS	MASSAGE	MERGERS
LUNATIC	MANGLED	MASSING	MERGING
LUNCHED	MANGLER	MASSIVE	MERITED
LUNCHES	MANGLES	MASTERS	MERMAID
LURCHED	MANHOLE	MASTERY	MERRILY
LURCHES	MANHOOD	MATCHED	MESSAGE
LURKING	MANIACS	MATCHER	MESSIAH
LUSTFUL	MANKIND	MATCHES	MESSIER
LUSTILY	MANNERS	MATINGS	MESSILY
LYNCHED	MANNING	MATTERS	MESSING
LYNCHER	MANSION	MATURED	METEORS
LYNCHES	MANTELS	MATURES	METHANE
MACHINE	MANTLES	MAXIMAL	METHODS
MADAMES	MANUALS	MAXIMUM	METRICS
MADDEST	MAPPING	MAYORAL	MEXICAN
MADNESS	MARBLES	MEADOWS	MIDDLES
MAGENTA	MARCHED	MEANDER	MIDWEEK
MAGGOTS	MARCHER	MEANEST	MIDWEST
MAGICAL	MARCHES	MEANING	MIDWIFE
MAGNETO	MARGINS	MEASLES	MIGRANT
MAGNIFY	MARINER	MEASURE	MIGRATE
MAIDENS	MARINES	MEDDLED	MILDEST
MAILBOX	MARITAL	MEDDLER	MILEAGE
MAILING	MARKERS	MEDDLES	MILITIA
MAILMAN	MARKETS	MEDIATE	MILKERS
MAILMEN	MARKING	MEDICAL	MILKING
MAIMING	MARQUIS	MEDIUMS	MILLING
MAJESTY	MARRIED	MEEKEST	MILLION
MAJORED	MARRIES	MEETING	MINARET
MAKABLE	MARSHAL	MEGABIT	MINCING
MAKEUPS	MARSHES	MELTING	MINDFUL
MAKINGS	MARTIAL	MEMBERS	MINDING
MALARIA	MARTIAN	MEMENTO	MINERAL
MALLETS	MARTYRS	MEMOIRS	MINGLED
MAMMALS	MARVELS	MENACED	MINGLES
MAMMOTH	MASCARA	MENDING	MINIMAL
MANAGED	MASHING	MENIALS	MINIMUM
MANAGER	MASKING	MENTION	MINNOWS

MINTING	MONITOR	MUGGING	NATURED
MINUTES	MONKEYS	MUMBLED	NATURES
MIRACLE	MONKISH	MUMBLER	NAUGHTY
MIRRORS	MONSOON	MUMBLES	NAUSEUM
MISERLY	MONSTER	MUMMIES	NAVALLY
MISFITS	MONTHLY	MUNCHED	NEAREST
MISHAPS	MOONING	MUNDANE	NEARING
MISLEAD	MOONLIT	MURDERS	NEATEST
MISSILE	MOORING	MURMURS	NEBULAR
MISSING	MOORISH	MUSCLED	NECKING
MISSION	MORALLY	MUSCLES	NEEDFUL
MISSIVE	MORNING	MUSEUMS	NEEDING
MISTAKE	MORSELS	MUSICAL	NEEDLED
MISTERS	MORTALS	MUSINGS	NEEDLER
MISTING	MORTARS	MUSKETS	NEEDLES
MISTYPE	MORTIFY	MUSKRAT	NEGATED
MISUSED	MOSAICS	MUSLIMS	NEGATES
MISUSES	MOSLEMS	MUSSELS	NEGATOR
MITTENS	MOTHERS	MUSTARD	NEGLECT
MIXTURE	MOTIONS	MUTABLE	NEGROES
MOBSTER	MOTIVES	MUTATED	NEGROID
MOCKERY	MOTTOES	MUTATES	NEITHER
MOCKING	MOULTON	MUTTERS	NEPHEWS
MODALLY	MOUNDED	MUZZLES	NEPTUNE
MODERNS	MOUNTED	MYSTERY	NERVOUS
MODESTY	MOUNTER	MYSTICS	NESTING
MODICUM	MOURNED	MYSTIFY	NESTLED
MODULAR	MOURNER	NAILING	NESTLES
MODULES	MOUTHED	NAIVELY	NETTING
MODULUS	MOVABLE	NAIVETE	NETTLED
MOISTEN	MOVINGS	NAKEDLY	NETWORK
MOISTLY	MUCKING	NAPKINS	NEURONS
MOLESTS	MUDDIED	NARRATE	NEUTRAL
MOLLIFY	MUDDLED	NARROWS	NEUTRON
MOLLUSK	MUDDLER	NASALLY	NEWBORN
MOMENTS	MUDDLES	NASTIER	NEWNESS
MONADIC	MUFFINS	NASTILY	NEWSMAN
MONARCH	MUFFLED	NATIONS	NEWSMEN
MONDAYS	MUFFLER	NATIVES	NIBBLED
MONEYED	MUFFLES	NATURAL	NIBBLER

NIBBLES	NUPTIAL	OMITTED	ORIFICE
NICKELS	NURSERY	OMNIBUS	ORIGINS
NICKING	NURSING	ONANISM	ORPHANS
NIGHTLY	NURTURE	ONENESS	OSMOSIS
NIMBLER	OATMEAL	ONEROUS	OSMOTIC
NITROUS	OBELISK	ONESELF	OTTOMAN
NOBLEST	OBEYING	ONETIME	OURSELF
NODDING	OBJECTS	ONGOING	OUTCAST
NODULAR	OBLIGED	ONWARDS	OUTCOME
NOISIER	OBLIGES	OPACITY	OUTDOOR
NOISILY	OBLIQUE	OPENERS	OUTFITS
NOMINAL	OBSCENE	OPENING	OUTGREW
NOMINEE	OBSCURE	OPERATE	OUTGROW
NOONDAY	OBSERVE	OPINION	OUTLAST
NOSTRIL	OBTAINS	OPOSSUM	OUTLAWS
NOTABLE	OBVIATE	OPPOSED	OUTLAYS
NOTABLY	OBVIOUS	OPPOSES	OUTLETS
NOTCHED	OCCLUDE	OPPRESS	OUTLINE
NOTCHES	OCEANIC	OPTICAL	OUTLIVE
NOTHING	OCTAGON	OPTIMAL	OUTLOOK
NOTHING	OCTAVES	OPTIMUM	OUTPOST
NOTICED	OCTOBER	OPTIONS	OUTPUTS
NOTICES	OCTOPUS	OPULENT	OUTRAGE
NOTIONS	ODDNESS	ORACLES	OUTRUNS
NOURISH	ODOROUS	ORANGES	OUTSIDE
NOVELTY	ODYSSEY	ORATION	OUTVOTE
NOVICES	OFFENDS	ORATORS	OUTWARD
NOWHERE	OFFENSE	ORATORY	OUTWITS
NOXIOUS	OFFERED	ORBITAL	OVARIES
NUANCES	OFFERER	ORBITED	OVERALL
NUCLEAR	OFFHAND	ORBITER	OVERDUE
NUCLEIC	OFFICER	ORCHARD	OVERJOY
NUCLEUS	OFFICES	ORCHIDS	OVERLAP
NUCLIDE	OFFLOAD	ORDAINS	OVERLAY
NULLARY	OFFSETS	ORDERED	OVERRUN
NULLIFY	OILIEST	ORDERLY	OVERSEE
NUMBERS	OLDNESS	ORDINAL	OVERTLY
NUMBING	OLYMPIC	OREGANO	OVERUSE
NUMERAL	OMICRON	ORGANIC	OXIDIZE
NUMERIC	OMINOUS	ORIENTS	OYSTERS

PACKAGE	PARENTS	PATTERS	PERCENT
PACKERS	PARINGS	PATTIES	PERCHED
PACKETS	PARKERS	PAUCITY	PERCHES
PACKING	PARKING	PAUNCHY	PERFECT
PADDING	PARKWAY	PAUSING	PERFORM
PADDOCK	PAROLED	PAYABLE	PERFUME
PADLOCK	PAROLES	PAYMENT	PERHAPS
PAGEANT	PARRIED	PAYOFFS	PERIODS
PAINFUL	PARRISH	PAYROLL	PERJURE
PAINTED	PARROTS	PEACHES	PERJURY
PAINTER	PARSERS	PEACOCK	PERMITS
PAIRING	PARSING	PEALING	PERMUTE
PALACES	PARSLEY	PEANUTS	PERPLEX
PALATES	PARSONS	PEASANT	PERSIST
PALFREY	PARTAKE	PEBBLES	PERSONS
PALMING	PARTERS	PECCARY	PERTAIN
PANACEA	PARTIAL	PECKING	PERTURB
PANCAKE	PARTIES	PEDDLER	PERUSAL
PANGAEA	PARTING	PEEKING	PERUSED
PANICKY	PARTNER	PEELING	PERUSER
PANNING	PARTOOK	PEEPING	PERUSES
PANSIES	PASSAGE	PEERING	PERVADE
PANTHER	PASSERS	PELICAN	PERVERT
PANTIES	PASSING	PELTING	PETTERS
PANTING	PASSION	PENALTY	PETTING
PAPERED	PASSIVE	PENANCE	PHANTOM
PAPERER	PASTIME	PENCILS	PHASERS
PAPOOSE	PASTING	PENDANT	PHASING
PAPYRUS	PASTORS	PENDING	PHOENIX
PARADED	PASTURE	PENGUIN	PHONING
PARADES	PATCHED	PENISES	PHRASED
PARADOX	PATCHES	PENNIES	PHRASES
PARAGON	PATENTS	PENNING	PHYSICS
PARAMUS	PATENTS	PENSION	PIANIST
PARAPET	PATHWAY	PENSIVE	PICCOLO
PARASOL	PATIENT	PEOPLED	PICKAXE
PARBOIL	PATRIOT	PEOPLES	PICKERS
PARCELS	PATROLS	PEPPERS	PICKETS
PARCHED	PATRONS	PEPPERY	PICKING
PARDONS	PATTERN	PEPTIDE	PICKLED

PICKLES	PITIERS	PLOTTED	POPPING
PICKMAN	PITIFUL	PLOTTER	POPULAR
PICKUPS	PITYING	PLUCKED	PORCHES
PICNICS	PIVOTAL	PLUGGED	PORCINE
PICTURE	PLACARD	PLUMAGE	PORTAGE
PIECING	PLACATE	PLUMBED	PORTALS
PIERCED	PLACEBO	PLUMMET	PORTEND
PIERCES	PLACING	PLUMPED	PORTENT
PIGEONS	PLAGUED	PLUNDER	PORTERS
PIGGISH	PLAGUES	PLUNGED	PORTICO
PIGMENT	PLAINER	PLUNGER	PORTING
PIGSKIN	PLAINLY	PLUNGES	PORTION
PIGTAIL	PLANERS	PLURALS	PORTRAY
PILGRIM	PLANETS	PLYWOOD	POSITED
PILINGS	PLANING	POACHER	POSSESS
PILLAGE	PLANNED	POACHES	POSSUMS
PILLARS	PLANNER	POCKETS	POSTAGE
PILLOWS	PLANTED	POETICS	POSTERS
PINBALL	PLANTER	POINTED	POSTING
PINCHED	PLASTER	POINTER	POSTMAN
PINCHES	PLASTIC	POISONS	POSTURE
PINHEAD	PLATEAU	POISSON	POTABLE
PINHOLE	PLATENS	POLECAT	POTHOLE
PINKEST	PLATING	POLEMIC	POTTERS
PINKISH	PLATOON	POLICED	POTTERY
PINNING	PLATTER	POLICES	POTTING
PIONEER	PLAYBOY	POLITER	POUCHES
PIOUSLY	PLAYERS	POLITIC	POULTRY
PIPETTE	PLAYFUL	POLLING	POUNCED
PIRATES	PLAYING	POLLUTE	POUNCES
PISTILS	PLAYOFF	POLYGON	POUNDED
PISTOLS	PLEADED	POLYMER	POUNDER
PISTONS	PLEADER	POMPOUS	POURERS
PITCHED	PLEASED	PONDERS	POURING
PITCHER	PLEASES	PONTIAC	POUSSIN
PITCHES	PLEBIAN	PONTIFF	POUTING
PITEOUS	PLEDGED	POOLING	POVERTY
PITFALL	PLEDGES	POOREST	POWDERS
PITHIER	PLENARY	POPCORN	POWDERY
PITHING	PLIABLE	POPPIES	POWERED

PRAIRIE	PRIDING	PROPANE	PUMPING
PRAISED	PRIMACY	PROPELS	PUMPKIN
PRAISER	PRIMARY	PROPHET	PUNCHED
PRAISES	PRIMATE	PROPOSE	PUNCHER
PRANCED	PRIMERS	PRORATE	PUNCHES
PRANCER	PRIMING	PROSPER	PUNGENT
PRAYERS	PRINCES	PROTECT	PUNTING
PRAYING	PRINTED	PROTEGE	PUPPETS
PRECEDE	PRINTER	PROTEIN	PUPPIES
PRECEPT	PRISONS	PROTEST	PURGING
PRECESS	PRIVACY	PROTONS	PURITAN
PRECISE	PRIVATE	PROUDER	PURPLER
PREDATE	PRIVIES	PROUDLY	PURPORT
PREDICT	PRIZERS	PROVERB	PURPOSE
PREEMPT	PRIZING	PROVERS	PURRING
PREFACE	PROBATE	PROVIDE	PURSUED
PREFERS	PROBING	PROVING	PURSUER
PRELATE	PROBITY	PROVISO	PURSUES
PRELUDE	PROBLEM	PROVOKE	PURSUIT
PREMIER	PROCEED	PROVOST	PURVIEW
PREMISE	PROCESS	PROWESS	PUSHERS
PREMIUM	PROCURE	PROWLED	PUSHING
PREPARE	PRODIGY	PROWLER	PUTTERS
PREPEND	PRODUCE	PRUDENT	PUTTING
PRESENT	PRODUCT	PRUNERS	PUZZLED
PRESIDE	PROFANE	PRUNING	PUZZLER
PRESSED	PROFESS	PSYCHES	PUZZLES
PRESSER	PROFFER	PSYCHIC	PYGMIES
PRESSES	PROFILE	PUBERTY	PYJAMAS
PRESUME	PROFITS	PUBLISH	PYRAMID
PRETEND	PROFUSE	PUCKERS	PYRRHIC
PRETEXT	PROGENY	PUDDING	QUACKED
PREVAIL	PROJECT	PUDDLES	QUAKERS
PREVENT	PROLATE	PUFFING	QUAKING
PREVIEW	PROLONG	PULLEYS	QUALIFY
PREYING	PROMISE	PULLING	QUALITY
PRICERS	PROMOTE	PULPING	QUANTUM
PRICING	PROMPTS	PULPITS	QUARREL
PRICKED	PRONGED	PULSATE	QUARTER
PRICKLY	PRONOUN	PULSING	QUARTET

QUASHED	RAIDING	RAUCOUS	RECEDES
QUASHES	RAILERS	RAVAGED	RECEIPT
QUAVERS	RAILING	RAVAGER	RECEIVE
QUEENLY	RAILWAY	RAVAGES	RECIPES
QUEERER	RAIMENT	RAVINES	RECITAL
QUEERLY	RAINBOW	RAVINGS	RECITED
QUERIED	RAINIER	RAWNESS	RECITER
QUERIES	RAINING	REACHED	RECITES
QUESTED	RAISERS	REACHER	RECKONS
QUESTER	RAISING	REACHES	RECLAIM
QUEUERS	RALLIED	REACTED	RECLINE
QUEUING	RALLIES	REACTOR	RECODED
QUIBBLE	RAMBLER	READERS	RECODES
QUICKEN	RAMBLES	READIED	RECOILS
QUICKER	RAMPAGE	READIER	RECORDS
QUICKIE	RAMPANT	READIES	RECOUNT
QUICKLY	RAMPART	READILY	RECOVER
QUIETED	RANCHED	READING	RECRUIT
QUIETER	RANCHER	READOUT	RECTIFY
QUIETLY	RANCHES	REALEST	RECTORS
QUILTED	RANGERS	REALIGN	RECTUMS
QUININE	RANGING	REALISM	RECURSE
QUINTET	RANKERS	REALIST	RECYCLE
QUITTER	RANKEST	REALITY	REDCOAT
QUIVERS	RANKING	REALIZE	REDDEST
QUIZZED	RANSACK	REALTOR	REDDISH
QUIZZES	RANSOMS	REAPING	REDEEMS
QUOTING	RANTERS	REARING	REDHEAD
RABBITS	RANTING	REASONS	REDNECK
RACCOON	RAPIDLY	REBATES	REDNESS
RACKETS	RAPPORT	REBINDS	REDRAWN
RACKING	RAPTURE	REBOOTS	REDRESS
RADIANT	RARITAN	REBOUND	REDUCED
RADIATE	RASCALS	REBUILD	REDUCER
RADICAL	RASPING	REBUILT	REDUCES
RADICES	RATINGS	REBUKED	REDWOOD
RADIOED	RATIONS	REBUKES	REFLECT
RAFTERS	RATTLED	RECALLS	REELING
RAGWEED	RATTLER	RECASTS	REENTER
RAIDERS	RATTLES	RECEDED	REFEREE

REFILLS	RELAXER	REPLICA	RESTORE
REFINED	RELAXES	REPLIED	RESULTS
REFINER	RELAYED	REPLIES	RESUMED
REFINES	RELEASE	REPORTS	RESUMES
REFLECT	RELENTS	REPOSED	RETAINS
REFORMS	RELIANT	REPOSES	RETICLE
REFRACT	RELIEVE	REPRESS	RETINAL
REFRAIN	RELIVES	REPRINT	RETINAS
REFRESH	RELOADS	REPROOF	RETINUE
REFUELS	RELYING	REPROVE	RETIRED
REFUGE	REMAINS	REPTILE	RETIREE
REFUSAL	REMARKS	REPULSE	RETIRES
REFUSED	REMINDS	REPUTED	RETORTS
REFUSES	REMNANT	REPUTES	RETRACE
REFUTED	REMODEL	REQUEST	RETRACT
REFUTER	REMORSE	REQUIRE	RETRAIN
REFUTES	REMOVAL	REROUTE	RETREAT
REGAINS	REMOVED	RESCIND	RETRIED
REGALED	REMOVER	RESCUED	RETRIER
REGALLY	REMOVES	RESCUER	RETRIES
REGARDS	RENAMED	RESCUES	RETURNS
REGATTA	RENAMES	RESENTS	RETYPED
REGENTS	RENDERS	RESERVE	RETYPES
REGIMEN	RENDING	RESIDED	REUNION
REGIMES	RENEWAL	RESIDED	REUNITE
REGIONS	RENEWED	RESIDES	REUSING
REGRESS	RENEWER	RESIDUE	REVAMPS
REGRETS	RENTALS	RESIGNS	REVEALS
REGROUP	RENTING	RESISTS	REVELRY
REGULAR	REOCCUR	RESOLVE	REVENGE
REIGNED	REOPENS	RESORTS	REVENUE
REJECTS	REORDER	RESOUND	REVERED
REJOICE	REPAIRS	RESPECT	REVERES
REJOINS	REPASTS	RESPITE	REVERIE
RELABEL	REPEALS	RESPOND	REVERSE
RELAPSE	REPEATS	RESTART	REVERTS
RELATED	REPENTS	RESTATE	REVIEWS
RELATER	REPLACE	RESTFUL	REVILED
RELATES	REPLAYS	RESTING	REVILER
RELAXED	REPLETE	RESTIVE	REVISED

REVISER	RIOTING	ROTATES	RUPTURE
REVISES	RIOTOUS	ROTATOR	RURALLY
REVISIT	RIPPING	ROTTING	RUSHING
REVIVAL	RIPPLED	ROTUNDA	RUSTING
REVIVED	RIPPLES	ROUGHED	RUSTLED
REVIVER	RISINGS	ROUGHEN	RUSTLER
REVIVES	RISKING	ROUGHER	SABBASH
REVOKED	RITUALS	ROUGHLY	SACKING
REVOKER	RIVALRY	ROUNDED	SADDENS
REVOKES	RIVETER	ROUNDER	SADDEST
REVOLTS	RIVIERA	ROUNDLY	SADDLED
REVOLVE	RIVULET	ROUNDUP	SADDLES
REWARDS	ROADWAY	ROUSING	SADISTS
REWINDS	ROAMING	ROUTERS	SADNESS
REWORKS	ROARING	ROUTINE	SAFFRON
REWOUND	ROASTED	ROUTING	SAGGING
REWRITE	ROASTER	ROWBOAT	SAGUARO
RHOMBIC	ROBBERS	ROYALLY	SAILING
RHOMBUS	ROBBERY	ROYALTY	SAILORS
RHUBARB	ROBBING	RUBBERS	SAINTED
RHYMING	ROBOTIC	RUBBERY	SAINTLY
RHYTHMS	ROCKERS	RUBBING	SALABLE
RIBBING	ROCKETS	RUBBISH	SALIENT
RIBBONS	ROCKING	RUBDOWN	SALLIES
RICHEST	RODENTS	RUDDERS	SALOONS
RICKETS	ROLLERS	RUFFIAN	SALTERS
RICKETY	ROLLING	RUFFLED	SALTIER
RIDDING	ROMANCE	RUFFLES	SALTING
RIDDLED	ROMPING	RUINING	SALUTED
RIDDLES	ROOFING	RUINOUS	SALUTES
RIFLING	ROOFTOP	RULINGS	SALVAGE
RIGGING	ROOMERS	RUMBLED	SAMPLED
RIGHTED	ROOMFUL	RUMBLER	SAMPLER
RIGHTER	ROOMING	RUMBLES	SAMPLES
RIGHTLY	ROOSTER	RUMMAGE	SANCTUM
RIGIDLY	ROOTING	RUMPLED	SANDALS
RINGERS	ROSEBUD	RUNAWAY	SANDBAG
RINGING	ROSETTE	RUNDOWN	SANDING
RINSING	ROSTRUM	RUNNERS	SANDMAN
RIOTERS	ROTATED	RUNNING	SAPIENS

SAPLING	SCHEMER	SEAMING	SELLOUT
SARCASM	SCHEMES	SEAPORT	SELTZER
SARDINE	SCHOLAR	SEARING	SEMINAL
SARGENT	SCHOOLS	SEASIDE	SEMINAR
SATANIC	SCIENCE	SEASONS	SENATES
SATCHEL	SCISSOR	SEATING	SENATOR
SATIRES	SCOFFED	SEAWARD	SENDERS
SATIRIC	SCOFFER	SEAWEED	SENDING
SATISFY	SCOLDED	SECEDED	SENIORS
SAUCERS	SCOPPED	SECEDES	SENSING
SAUNTER	SCOPING	SECLUDE	SENSORS
SAUSAGE	SCORERS	SECONDS	SENSORY
SAVAGED	SCORING	SECRECY	SENSUAL
SAVAGER	SCORNED	SECRETE	SEQUELS
SAVAGES	SCORNER	SECRETS	SERIALS
SAVINGS	SCORPIO	SECTION	SERIOUS
SAVIOUR	SCOURGE	SECTORS	SERMONS
SAWDUST	SCOUTED	SECULAR	SERPENT
SAWFISH	SCOWLED	SECURED	SERVANT
SAWMILL	SCRAPED	SECURES	SERVERS
SAYINGS	SCRAPER	SEDUCED	SERVICE
SCALARS	SCRAPES	SEDUCER	SERVILE
SCALDED	SCRATCH	SEDUCES	SERVING
SCALING	SCRAWLS	SEEDERS	SESSION
SCALLOP	SCRAWNY	SEEDING	SETBACK
SCAMPER	SCREAMS	SEEKERS	SETTERS
SCANDAL	SCREECH	SEEKING	SETTING
SCANNED	SCREENS	SEEMING	SETTLED
SCANNER	SCREWED	SEEPAGE	SETTLER
SCANTLY	SCRIBES	SEEPING	SETTLES
SCARCER	SCRIPTS	SEETHED	SEVENTH
SCARING	SCROLLS	SEETHES	SEVENTY
SCARLET	SCRUPLE	SEGMENT	SEVERAL
SCARVES	SCUFFLE	SEISMIC	SEVERED
SCATTER	SCULPTS	SEIZING	SEVERER
SCENERY	SCUTTLE	SEIZURE	SEXTANS
SCENTED	SCYTHES	SELECTS	SHACKED
SCEPTER	SEAFOOD	SELFISH	SHACKLE
SCHEMAS	SEAGULL	SELLERS	SHADIER
SCHEMED	SEALING	SELLING	SHADILY

SHADING	SHOCKED	SIGNIFY	SKILLED
SHADOWS	SHOCKER	SIGNING	SKILLET
SHADOWY	SHOEING	SILENCE	SKIMMED
SHAKERS	SHOOTER	SILICON	SKIMPED
SHAKING	SHOPPED	SILKIER	SKINNED
SHALLOW	SHOPPER	SILKILY	SKINNER
SHAMING	SHORTED	SILTING	SIPPED
SHAMPOO	SHORTEN	SILVERS	SKIPPER
SHAPELY	SHORTER	SILVERY	SKIRTED
SHAPERS	SHORTLY	SIMILAR	SKULKED
SHAPING	SHOTGUN	SIMMERS	SKULKER
SHARERS	SHOUTED	SIMPLER	SKYHOOK
SHARING	SHOUTER	SIMPLEX	SKYJACK
SHARPEN	SHOVELS	SINCERE	SKYLARK
SHARPER	SHOVING	SINGERS	SKYLINE
SHARPLY	SHOWERS	SINGING	SLACKEN
SHATTER	SHOWING	SINGLED	SLACKER
SHAVING	SHRIEKS	SINGLES	SLACKLY
SHEARED	SHRILLY	SINGLET	SLAMMED
SHEATHS	SHRINES	SINKERS	SLANDER
SHEAVES	SHRINKS	SINKING	SLANTED
SHEERED	SHRIVEL	SINNERS	SLAPPED
SHEETED	SHUDDER	SINNING	SLASHED
SHELLED	SHUFFLE	SINUOUS	SLASHES
SHELLER	SHUTOFF	SIPPING	SLAVERY
SHELTER	SHUTOUT	SISTERS	SLAVISH
SHELVED	SHUTTER	SITTERS	SLAYERS
SHELVES	SHUTTLE	SITTING	SLAYING
SHERBET	SHYNESS	SITUATE	SLEDGES
SHERIFF	SIBLING	SIXFOLD	SLEEPER
SHIFTED	SICKEST	SIXTEEN	SLEEVES
SHIFTER	SIDEARM	SIXTIES	SLEIGHS
SHIMMER	SIDECAR	SIZABLE	SLEIGHT
SHINERS	SIDINGS	SIZINGS	SLENDER
SHINGLE	SIFTING	SKATERS	SLEWING
SHINING	SIGHING	SKATING	SLICERS
SHIPPED	SIGHTED	SKEPTIC	SLICING
SHIPPER	SIGHTLY	SKETCHY	SUCKER
SHIRKER	SIGNALS	SKEWERS	SLIDERS
SHIVERS	SIGNERS	SKEWING	SLIDING

SLIGHTS	SNIFFED	SONNETS	SPAWNED
SLIPPED	SNIFFLE	SOONEST	SPEAKER
SLIPPER	SNIFTER	SOOTHED	SPEARED
SLITHER	SNIGGER	SOOTHER	SPECIAL
SLOGANS	SNIPPET	SOOTHES	SPECIES
SLOPERS	SNOOPED	SOPRANO	SPECIFY
SLOPING	SNORING	SORCERY	SPECKLE
SLOPPED	SNORKEL	SORGHUM	SPECTRE
SLOTTED	SNORTED	SORRIER	SPEEDED
SLOWEST	SNOWIER	SORROWS	SPEEDER
SLOWING	SNOWILY	SORTERS	SPEEDUP
SLUMBER	SNOWMAN	SORTING	SPELLED
SLUMPED	SNUFFED	SOULFUL	SPELLER
SMACKED	SNUFFER	SOUNDED	SPENDER
SMALLER	SNUGGLE	SOUNDER	SPHERES
SMARTED	SOAKING	SOUNDLY	SPIDERS
SMARTER	SOAPING	SOURCES	SPIDERY
SMARTLY	SOARING	SOUREST	SPILLED
SMASHED	SOBBING	SOURING	SPILLER
SMASHER	SOBERED	SOVIETS	SPINACH
SMASHES	SOBERLY	SOYBEAN	SPINDLE
SMEARED	SOCIETY	SPACERS	SPINNER
SMELLED	SOCKETS	SPACING	SPINOTT
SMELTER	SOCKING	SPADING	SPIRITS
SMILING	SOFTENS	SPANIEL	SPITING
SMITTEN	SOFTEST	SPANKED	SPITTLE
SMOKERS	SOILING	SPANNED	SPLASHY
SMOKIES	SOJOURN	SPANNER	SPLICED
SMOKING	SOLACED	SPARELY	SPLICER
SMOTHER	SOLDIER	SPAREST	SPLINES
SMUGGLE	SOLICIT	SPARING	SPLURGE
SNAPPED	SOLIDLY	SPARKED	SPOILED
SNAPPER	SOLUBLE	SPARKLE	SPOILER
SNARING	SOLVENT	SPARROW	SPONGED
SNARLED	SOLVERS	SPARSER	SPONGER
SNEAKED	SOLVING	SPARTAN	SPONGES
SNEAKER	SOMATIC	SPASTIC	SPONSOR
SNEERED	SOMEDAY	SPATIAL	SPOOLED
SNEEZED	SOMEHOW	SPATTER	SPOOLER
SNEEZES	SOMEONE	SPATUAL	SPOONED

SPORTED	STAGGER	STEEPLE	STORMED
SPOTTED	STAGING	STEEPLY	STOUTER
SPOTTER	STAINED	STEERED	STOUTLY
SPOUSES	STALKED	STELLAR	STRAINS
SPOUTED	STALLED	STEMMED	STRAITS
SPRAWLS	STAMENS	STENCIL	STRANDS
SPRAYED	STAMINA	STEPPED	STRANGE
SPRAYER	STAMMER	STEPPER	STRATUM
SPREADS	STAMPED	STEPSON	STRAYED
SPRINGS	STAMPER	STEREOS	STREAKS
SPRINGY	STANDBY	STERILE	STREAMS
SPRINTS	STANZAS	STERNLY	STREETS
SPRUCED	STAPLER	STEWARD	STRETCH
SPURNED	STAPLES	STICKER	STRIDER
SPURTED	STARDOM	STIFFEN	STRIDES
SPUTTER	STARING	STIFFER	STRIKER
SQUALID	STARKLY	STIFFLY	STRIKES
SQUALLS	STARLET	STIFLED	STRINGS
SQUARED	STARRED	STIFLES	STRINGY
SQUARER	STARTED	STILLED	STRIPED
SQUARES	STARTER	STILLER	STRIPES
SQUAWKS	STARTLE	STIMULI	STRIVEN
SQUEAKS	STARTUP	STINKER	STRIVES
SQUEAKY	STARVED	STIPEND	STROBED
SQUEALS	STARVES	STIRRED	STROBES
SQUEEZE	STATELY	STIRRER	STROKED
SQUELCH	STATING	STIRRUP	STROKER
SQUIRES	STATION	STOCKED	STROKES
SQUIRMS	STATUES	STOCKER	STROLLS
SQUIRMY	STATURE	STOMACH	STUBBLE
SQUISHY	STATUTE	STONING	STUDENT
STABBED	STAUNCH	STOOPED	STUDIED
STABILE	STAYING	STOPGAP	STUDIES
STABLED	STEALER	STOPPED	STUDIOS
STABLER	STEALTH	STOPPER	STUFFED
STABLES	STEAMED	STORAGE	STUMBLE
STACKED	STEAMER	STOREYS	STUMPED
STADIUM	STEELED	STORIED	STUPEFY
STAFFED	STEEPED	STORIES	STUTTER
STAFFER	STEEPER	STORING	STYLERS

STYLING	SULKING	SWATTED	TAILORS
STYLISH	SULPHUR	SWAYING	TAINTED
SUBDUED	SULTANS	SWEARER	TAKINGS
SUBDUES	SUMMAND	SWEATED	TALENTS
SUBFILE	SUMMARY	SWEATER	TALKERS
SUBGOAL	SUMMING	SWEEPER	TALKING
SUBJECT	SUMMONS	SWEETEN	TALLEST
SUBLIME	SUNBEAM	SWEETER	TAMPERS
SUBLIST	SUNBURN	SWEETLY	TANGENT
SUBMITS	SUNDAYS	SWELLED	TANGLED
SUBMODE	SUNDIAL	SWELTER	TANKERS
SUBNETS	SUNDOWN	SWERVED	TANNERS
SUBSSETS	SUNNING	SWERVES	TANTRUM
SUBSIDE	SUNRISE	SWIFTER	TAPERED
SUBSIDY	SUNSPOT	SWIFTLY	TAPINGS
SUBSIST	SUPPERS	SWIMMER	TAPPERS
SUBSLOT	SUPPORT	SWINDLE	TAPPING
SUBSUME	SUPPOSE	SWINGER	TAPROOT
SUBTASK	SUPREME	SWIRLED	TARGETS
SUBTLER	SURFACE	SWISHED	TARIFFS
SUBTREE	SURGEON	SWIZZLE	TASKING
SUBUNIT	SURGERY	SWOLLEN	TASSELS
SUBURBS	SURGING	SWOOPED	TASTERS
SUBVERT	SURMISE	SYMBOLS	TASTING
SUBWAYS	SURNAME	SYMPTOM	TATTOOS
SUCCEED	SURPASS	SYNAPSE	TAUNTED
SUCCESS	SURPLUS	SYNERGY	TAUNTER
SUCCUMB	SURREAL	SYNONYM	TAVERNS
SUCKERS	SURVEYS	SYRINGE	TAXABLE
SUCKING	SURVIVE	TABLEAU	TAXICAB
SUCTION	SUSPECT	TABLETS	TAXIING
SUDSING	SUSPEND	TABLING	TEACHER
SUFFERS	SUSTAIN	TABULAR	TEACHES
SUFFICE	SUTURES	TACITLY	TEAMING
SUGARED	SWAGGER	TACKING	TEARFUL
SUGGEST	SWALLOW	TACKLES	TEARING
SUICIDE	SWAMPED	TACTICS	TEASING
SUITERS	SWAPPED	TACTILE	TEDIOUS
SUITING	SWARMED	TAGGING	TEEMING
SUITORS	SWARTHY	TAILING	TEENAGE

TEETHED	THERETO	TIDYING	TOPMOST
TEETHES	THERMAL	TIGHTEN	TOPPLED
TELLERS	THICKEN	TIGHTER	TOPPLES
TELLING	THICKER	TIGHTLY	TORCHES
TEMPERS	THICKET	TILLERS	TORMENT
TEMPEST	THICKLY	TILLING	TORNADO
TEMPLES	THIEVES	TILTING	TORPEDO
TEMPTED	THIMBLE	TIMBERS	TORRENT
TEMPTER	THINKER	TIMEOUT	TORTURE
TENANTS	THINNER	TIMIDLY	TORUSES
TENDERS	THIRDLY	TIMINGS	TOSSING
TENDING	THIRSTS	TINGLED	TOTALLY
TENFOLD	THIRSTY	TINGLES	TOTTERS
TENSELY	THISTLE	TINIEST	TOUCHED
TENSEST	THOUGHT	TINKERS	TOUCHES
TENSING	THREADS	TINKLED	TOUGHEN
TENSION	THREADS	TINKLES	TOUGHER
TENTING	THREATS	TINNIER	TOUGHLY
TERMING	THRIFTY	TINNILY	TOURING
TERNARY	THRILLS	TINTING	TOURIST
TERRACE	THRIVED	TIPPERS	TOWARDS
TERRAIN	THRIVES	TIPPING	TOWERED
TERRIER	THROATS	TIREDLY	TRACERS
TERRIFY	THRONES	TISSUES	TRACING
TERRORS	THRONGS	TITHING	TRACKED
TESTERS	THROUGH	TITTERS	TRACKER
TESTIFY	THROWER	TOASTED	TRACTOR
TESTING	THRUSTS	TOASTER	TRADERS
TEXTILE	THUMBED	TOBACCO	TRADING
TEXTUAL	THUMPED	TOGGLED	TRAFFIC
TEXTURE	THUNDER	TOGGLES	TRAGEDY
THANKED	THWARTS	TOILETS	TRAILED
THAWING	THYSELF	TOILING	TRAILER
THEATRE	TICKERS	TONGUED	TRAINED
THEOREM	TICKETS	TONGUES	TRAINEE
THERAPY	TICKING	TONIGHT	TRAITOR
THEREBY	TICKLED	TONNAGE	TRAMPED
THEREIN	TICKLES	TOOLERS	TRAMPLE
THEREOF	TIDALLY	TOOLING	TRANCES
THEREON	TIDINGS	TOPICAL	TRANSIT

TRAPPED	TRUSTEE	UNBOUND	UNWRAPS
TRAPPER	TUCKING	UNCANNY	UPBRAID
TRAVAIL	TUESDAY	UNCLEAN	UPDATED
TRAVELS	TUITION	UNCLEAR	UPDATER
TREASON	TUMBLED	UNCOUTH	UPDATES
TREATED	TUMBLER	UNCOVER	UPGRADE
TREETOP	TUMBLES	UNDERGO	UPHOLDS
TREMBLE	TUMULTS	UNDOING	UPLANDS
TREMORS	TUNABLE	UNDRESS	UPLINKS
TRESSES	TUNNELS	UNEQUAL	UPRIGHT
TRIBUTE	TURBANS	UNFOLDS	UPROOTS
TRICKED	TURKEYS	UNHAPPY	UPSHOTS
TRICKLE	TURMOIL	UNHEARD	UPTURNS
TRIFLER	TURNERS	UNICORN	UPWARDS
TRIFLES	TURNING	UNIFIED	URCHINS
TRIGGER	TURNIPS	UNIFIER	URGINGS
TRIGRAM	TURRETS	UNIFIES	URINATE
TRILLED	TURTLES	UNIFORM	USELESS
TRIMMED	TUTORED	UNITIES	USHERED
TRIMMER	TWELFTH	UNITING	USUALLY
TRINKET	TWELVES	UNKNOWN	USURPED
TRIPLED	TWINKLE	UNLEASH	USURPER
TRIPLES	TWIRLED	UNLINKS	UTENSIL
TRIPLET	TWIRLER	UNLOADS	UTILITY
TRIUMPH	TWISTED	UNLOCKS	UTILIZE
TRIVIAL	TWISTER	UNLUCKY	UTOPIAN
TROLLEY	TWITTER	UNMOVED	UTTERED
TROOPER	TWOFOLD	UNNAMED	UTTERLY
TROPICS	TYPHOID	UNNERVE	VACANCY
TROUBLE	TYPICAL	UNPACKS	VACATED
TROUSER	TYPISTS	UNRAVEL	VACATES
TROWELS	TYRANNY	UNROLLS	VACUOUS
TRUANTS	TYRANTS	UNSOUND	VAGINAS
TRUCKED	UGLIEST	UNTRIED	VAGRANT
TRUCKER	UMBRAGE	UNTYING	VAGUELY
TRUDGED	UMPIRES	UNUSUAL	VAGUEST
TRUISMS	UNAIDED	UNVEILS	VALENCE
TRUMPED	UNARMED	UNWINDS	VALIANT
TRUMPET	UNAWARE	UNWISER	VALIDLY
TRUSTED	UNBLOCK	UNWOUND	VALLEYS

VALUERS	VILLAGE	WALKERS	WEAPONS
VALUING	VILLAIN	WALKING	WEARIED
VAMPIRE	VINEGAR	WALLETS	WEARIER
VANILLA	VINTAGE	WALLING	WEARILY
VANTAGE	VIOLATE	WALLOWS	WEARING
VARIANT	VIOLENT	WALNUTS	WEASELS
VARIETY	VIOLETS	WALTZED	WEATHER
VARIOUS	VIOLINS	WALTZES	WEAVING
VARNISH	VIRGINS	WANDERS	WEDDING
VARYING	VIRTUAL	WANTING	WEDGING
VASTEST	VIRTUES	WARBLED	WEDLOCK
VAULTED	VIRUSES	WARBLER	WEEKEND
VAULTER	VISCOUS	WARBLES	WEEPING
VAUNTED	VISIBLE	WARDENS	WEIGHED
VECTORS	VISIBLY	WARFARE	WEIGHTS
VEERING	VISIONS	WARLIKE	WEIGHTY
VEHICLE	VISITED	WARMERS	WEIRDLY
VEILING	VISITOR	WARMEST	WELCOME
VEINING	VITALLY	WARMING	WELDING
VENDORS	VIVIDLY	WARNING	WELFARE
VENISON	VOCALLY	WARPING	WELLING
VENTURE	VOICERS	WARRANT	WENCHES
VERBOSE	VOICING	WARRING	WESTERN
VERDICT	VOIDING	WARRIOR	WETNESS
VERDURE	VOLCANO	WARSHIP	WETTEST
VERSING	VOLTAGE	WARTIME	WETTING
VERSION	VOLUMES	WASHERS	WHACKED
VESSELS	VOMITED	WASHING	WHALING
VESTIGE	VOUCHER	WASTING	WHARVES
VETERAN	VOUCHES	WATCHED	WHEATEN
VIBRATE	VOYAGED	WATCHER	WHEELED
VICEROY	VOYAGER	WATCHES	WHEELER
VICIOUS	VULTURE	WATERED	WHEREAS
VICTIMS	WAFFLES	WAYSIDE	WHEREBY
VICTORS	WAGONER	WAYWARD	WHEREIN
VICTORY	WAILING	WEAKENS	WHETHER
VICTUAL	WAITERS	WEAKEST	WHIMPER
VIEWERS	WAITING	WEALTHS	WHINING
VIEWING	WAIVING	WEALTHY	WHIPPED
VIKINGS	WAKENED	WEANING	WHIPPER

WHIRLED	WITCHES	YEARNED	ABSENCES
WHISKED	WITHERS	YELLING	ABSENTED
WHISKER	WITHOUT	YELLOWS	ABSENTEE
WHISKEY	WITNESS	YELPING	ABSENTIA
WHISPER	WIZARDS	YIELDED	ABSENTLY
WHISTLE	WOMANLY	YOUNGER	ABSINTHE
WHITELY	WONDERS	YOUNGLY	ABSOLUTE
WHITENS	WOODMAN	ZEALOUS	ABSOLVED
WHITEST	WOOFERS	ZEROING	ABSOLVES
WHITING	WOOFING	ZONALLY	ABSORBED
WHITTLE	WORDILY		ABSORBER
WHIZZED	WORDING	**8**	ABSTAINS
WHIZZES	WORKERS		ABSTRACT
WHOEVER	WORKING	ABANDONS	ABSTRUSE
WHOOPED	WORKMAN	ABASHING	ABSURDLY
WIDENED	WORLDLY	ABDOMENS	ABUNDANT
WIDENER	WORMING	ABDUCTED	ABUTMENT
WIDOWED	WORRIED	ABDUCTOR	ABUTTERS
WIDOWER	WORRIER	ABERRANT	ABUTTING
WIELDED	WORRIES	ABETTING	ACADEMIA
WIELDER	WORSHIP	ABEYANCE	ACADEMIC
WILDCAT	WORSTED	ABHORRED	ACCENTED
WILDEST	WOUNDED	ABHORRER	ACCEPTED
WILLFUL	WRANGLE	ABJECTLY	ACCEPTER
WILLING	WRAPPED	ABJURING	ACCEPTOR
WILLOWS	WRAPPER	ABLATING	ACCESSED
WILTING	WRECKED	ABLATION	ACCESSES
WINCING	WRECKER	ABLATIVE	ACCIDENT
WINDERS	WRESTLE	ABNORMAL	ACCLAIMS
WINDING	WRIGGLE	ABORTING	ACCOLADE
WINDOWS	WRITERS	ABORTIVE	ACCORDED
WINGING	WRITHED	ABOUNDED	ACCORDER
WINKING	WRITHES	ABRADING	ACCOSTED
WINNERS	WRITING	ABRASION	ACCOUNTS
WINNING	WRITTEN	ABRIDGED	ACCREDIT
WISDOMS	WRONGED	ABRIDGES	ACCRUING
WISHERS	WRONGLY	ABROGATE	ACCURACY
WISHFUL	WROUGHT	ABRUPTLY	ACCURATE
WISHING	YANKING	ABSCISSA	ACCURSED
WISTFUL	YAWNING	ABSCONDS	ACCUSING

ACCUSTOM	ADHESIVE	AFFERENT	ALBACORE
ACHIEVED	ADJACENT	AFFINITY	ALCOHOLS
ACHIEVER	ADJOINED	AFFIRMED	ALDERMAN
ACHIEVES	ADJOURNS	AFFIXING	ALERTERS
ACHILLES	ADJUDGED	AFFLICTS	ALERTING
ACOYLYTES	ADJUDGES	AFFLUENT	ALEUTIAN
ACOUSTIC	ADJUNCTS	AFFORDED	ALFRESCO
ACQUAINT	ADJURING	AFFRIGHT	ALGEBRAS
ACQUIRED	ADJUSTED	AFFRONTS	ALGERIAN
ACQUIRES	ADJUSTER	AGENCIES	ALGINATE
ACRIMONY	ADJUSTOR	AGGRIEVE	ALHAMBRA
ACROBATS	ADJUTANT	AGITATED	ALIASING
ACRONYMS	ADMIRALS	AGITATES	ALIENATE
ACTINUM	ADMIRERS	AGITATOR	ALKALINE
ACTIVATE	ADMIRING	AGNOSTIC	ALKALOID
ACTIVELY	ADMITTED	AGNIZED	ALLAYING
ACTIVISM	ADMITTER	AGONIZES	ALLEGING
ACTIVIST	ADMONISH	AGREEING	ALLEGORY
ACTIVITY	ADOPTERS	AILMENTS	ALLERGIC
ACTUALLY	ADOPTING	AIRBORNE	ALLEYWAY
ACTUATED	ADOPTION	AIRCRAFT	ALLIANCE
ACTUATES	ADOPTIVE	AIRDROPS	ALLOCATE
ACTUATOR	ADORABLE	AIREDALE	ALLOTTED
ADAPTERS	ADSORBED	AIRFIELD	ALLOTTER
ADAPTING	ADULTERY	AIRFOILS	ALLOWING
ADAPTIVE	ADVANCED	AIRFRAME	ALLUDING
ADAPTORS	ADVANCES	AIRLIFTS	ALLURING
ADDENDUM	ADVISEES	AIRLINER	ALLUSION
ADDICTED	ADVISERS	AIRLINES	ALLUSIVE
ADDITION	ADVISING	AIRLOCKS	ALMANACS
ADDITIVE	ADVISORS	AIRMAILS	ALMIGHTY
ADDUCING	ADVISORY	AIRPLANE	ALPHABET
ADDUCTED	ADVOCACY	AIRPORTS	ALSATIAN
ADDUCTOR	ADVOCATE	AIRSHIPS	ALTERERS
ADEQUACY	AERATING	AIRSPACE	ALTERING
ADEQUATE	AERATION	AIRSPEED	ALTHOUGH
ADHERENT	AERATORS	AIRTIGHT	ALTITUDE
ADHERERS	AEROBICS	ALACRITY	ALTRUISM
ADHERING	AEROSOLS	ALARMING	ALTRUIST
ADHESION	AFFECTED	ALARMIST	ALVEOLAR

ALVEOLUS	ANCHORED	ANYWHERE	AQUARIUS
AMALGAMS	ANCIENTS	APERTURE	AQUEDUCT
AMARETTO	ANECDOTE	APHELION	ARABIANS
AMASSING	ANECHOIC	APHORISM	ARACHNID
AMATEURS	ANGELICA	APIARIES	ARBITERS
AMAZEDLY	ANGLICAN	APOLOGIA	ARBOREAL
AMBIANCE	ANGRIEST	APOSTATE	ARCHAISM
AMBITION	ANGSTROM	APOSTLES	ARCHIVAL
AMBUSHED	ANIMATED	APOTHEGM	ARCHIVED
AMBUSHES	ANIMATES	APPALLED	ARCHIVER
AMENABLE	ANIMATOR	APPANAGE	ARCHIVES
AMENDING	ANIMIZED	APPARENT	ARDENTLY
AMERICAN	ANNEXING	APPEALED	ARGONAUT
AMICABLE	ANNOTATE	APPEALER	ARGUABLE
AMICABLY	ANNOUNCE	APPEARED	ARGUABLY
AMMONIAC	ANNOYERS	APPEARER	ARGUMENT
AMMONIUM	ANNOYING	APPEASED	ARISINGS
AMORTIZE	ANNUALLY	APPEASES	ARMAGNAC
AMOUNTED	ANNULLED	APPENDED	ARMAMENT
AMOUNTER	ANODIZED	APPENDER	ARMCHAIR
AMPERAGE	ANODIZES	APPENDIX	ARMENIAN
AMPOULES	ANOINTED	APPETITE	AROMATIC
AMPUTATE	ANOREXIA	APPLAUDS	AROUSING
AMUSEDLY	ANSWERED	APPLAUSE	ARPEGGIO
ANACONDA	ANSWERER	APPLIERS	ARRAIGNS
ANAGRAMS	ANTEATER	APPLIQUE	ARRANGED
ANALOGUE	ANTEDATE	APPLYING	ARRANGER
ANALYSES	ANTELOPE	APPOINTS	ARRANGES
ANALYSIS	ANTENNAE	APPOSITE	ARRESTED
ANBALYSTS	ANTENNAS	APPRAISE	ARRESTER
ANALYTIC	ANTERIOR	APPRISED	ARRESTOR
ANALYZED	ANTIBODY	APPRISES	ARRIVALS
ANALYZER	ANTIDOTE	APPROACH	ARRIVING
ANALYZES	ANTIGENS	APPROVAL	ARROGANT
ANAPHORA	ANTIMONY	APPROVED	ARSENALS
ANARCHIC	ANTIPODE	APPROVER	ARTERIAL
ANATHEMA	ANTIQUES	APPROVES	ARTERIES
ANATOMIC	ANTISERA	APRICOTS	ARTFULLY
ANCESTOR	ANTLERED	APTITUDE	ARTICLES
ANCESTRY	ANYTHING	AQUARIUM	ARTIFACT

ARTIFICE	ASTERISK	AUTHORED	BACKLOGS
ARTISANS	ASTEROID	AUTISTIC	BACKPACK
ARTISTIC	ASTONISH	AUTOCRAT	BACKSIDE
ARTISTRY	ASTOUNDS	AUTOMATA	BACKSTOP
ASBESTOS	ASTUTELY	AUTOMATE	BACKWARD
ASCENDED	ASUNCION	AUTONOMY	BACKYARD
ASCENDER	ATHEISTS	AUTUMNAL	BACTERIA
ASCETICS	ATHLETES	AVAILERS	BADGERED
ASCRIBED	ATHLETIC	AVAILING	BAFFLERS
ASCRIBES	ATOMIZED	AVENGING	BAFFLING
ASHTRAYS	ATOMIZES	AVERAGED	BAGPIPES
ASPHYXIA	ATONALLY	AVERAGES	BAILIFFS
ASPIRANT	ATROCITY	AVERRING	BAKERIES
ASPIRATE	ATROPHIC	AVERSION	BALANCED
ASPIRING	ATTACHED	AVERTING	BALANCER
ASPIRINS	ATTACHER	AVARIES	BALANCES
ASSAILED	ATTACHES	AVIATION	BALDNESS
ASSASSIN	ATTACKED	AVIATORS	BALLARDS
ASSAULTS	ATTACKER	AVIONICS	BALLASTS
ASSAYING	ATTAINED	AVOCADOS	BALLGOWN
ASSEMBLE	ATTAINER	AVOIDERS	BALLOONS
ASSEMBLY	ATTEMPTS	AVOIDING	BALLPARK
ASSENTED	ATTENDED	AWAITING	BALLROOM
ASSENTER	ATTENDER	AWAKENED	BALLYHOO
ASSERTED	ATTESTED	AWARDERS	BANDAGED
ASSERTER	ATTIRING	AWARDING	BANDAGES
ASSESSED	ATTITUDE	AXOLOTLS	BANDPASS
ASSESSES	ATTORNEY	AZIMUTHS	BANDYING
ASSESSOR	ATTRACTS	BABBLING	BANISHED
ASSIGNED	ATTUNING	BABALIZE	BANISHES
ASSIGNEE	ATYPICAL	BABYHOOD	BANISTER
ASSIGNER	AUDACITY	BACHELOR	BANKRUPT
ASSONANT	AUDIENCE	BACILLUS	BANQUETS
ASSORTED	AUDITING	BACKACHE	BANSHEES
ASSUAGED	AUDITION	BACKBEND	BANTERED
ASSUAGES	AUDITORS	BACKBONE	BAPTISMS
ASSUMING	AUDITORY	BACKDROP	BAPTISTE
ASSURERS	AUGMENTS	BACKFILL	BAPTISTS
ASSURING	AUGUSTLY	BACKHAND	BAPTIZED
ASTATINE	AUSPICES	BACKLASH	BAPTIZES

BARBARIC	BEATNIKS	BELONGED	BILLETED
BARBECUE	BEAUTIES	BEMOANED	BILLIARD
BARBELLS	BEAUTIFY	BENDABLE	BILLINGS
BARBITAL	BECALMED	BENEFITS	BILLIONS
BAREFOOT	BECKONED	BENIGNLY	BILLOWED
BARENESS	BECOMING	BEQUEATH	BINARIES
BARFLIES	BEDAZZLE	BEQUESTS	BINAURAL
BARGAINS	BEDEVILS	BERATING	BINDINGS
BARITONE	BEDPOSTS	BEREAVED	BINOMIAL
BARNYARD	BEDROOMS	BEREAVES	BIOPSIES
BARONESS	BEDSTEAD	BERIBERI	BIPLANES
BARONIAL	BEEHIVES	BESIEGED	BIRACIAL
BARONIES	BEETLING	BESIEGER	BIRDBATH
BARRACKS	BEFALLEN	BESMIRCH	BIRDLIKE
BARRAGES	BEFITTED	BESOTTED	BIRTHDAY
BARRIERS	BEFOGGED	BESOTTER	BISCUITS
BARTERED	BEFOULED	BESOUGHT	BISECTED
BASEBALL	BEFRIEND	BESPEAKS	BISECTOR
BASEBAND	BEFUDDLE	BESSEMER	BISTABLE
BASELESS	BEGGARLY	BESTOWAL	BITINGLY
BASELINE	BEGINNER	BESTOWED	BITTERER
BASEMENT	BEGOTTEN	BETRAYAL	BITTERLY
BASENESS	BEGRUDGE	BETRAYED	BIVALVES
BASSINET	BEGUILED	BETRAYER	BIVOUACS
BASTARDS	BEGUILES	BETTERED	BIWEEKLY
BASTIONS	BEHAVING	BEVERAGE	BLABBING
BATHROBE	BEHEMOTH	BEWAILED	BLACKENS
BATHROOM	BEHOLDEN	BEWILDER	BLACKEST
BATHTUBS	BEHOLDER	BIANNUAL	BLACKING
BATTERED	BEHOOVES	BIBLICAL	BLACKMAN
BATTLERS	BELAYING	BICKERED	BLACKOUT
BATTLING	BELCHING	BICONVEX	BLADDERS
BAYONETS	BELFRIES	BICYCLED	BLAMABLE
BEACHING	BELIEVED	BICYCLER	BLANCHED
BEARABLE	BELIEVER	BICYCLES	BLANCHES
BEARABLY	BELIEVES	BIDDABLE	BLANKEST
BEARINGS	BELITTLE	BIENNIAL	BLANKETS
BEATABLE	BELLBOYS	BIENNIUM	BLANKING
BEATABLY	BELLHOPS	BIFOCALS	BLASTERS
BEATINGS	BELLOWED	BILINEAR	BLASTING

BLEACHED	BOARDING	BOTULISM	BRETHREN
BLEACHER	BOASTERS	BOUFFANT	BREVETED
BLEACHES	BOASTFUL	BOULDERS	BRIDGING
BLEATING	BOASTING	BOUNCING	BRIDLING
BLEEDING	BOATLOAD	BOUNDARY	BRIEFEST
BLENDING	BOATSMAN	BOUNDING	BRIEFING
BLESSING	BOATYARD	BOUNTIES	BRIGADES
BLIGHTED	BOBOLINK	BOUQUETS	BRIGHTEN
BLINDERS	BOGEYMEN	BOUTIQUE	BRIGHTER
BLINDING	BOGGLING	BOWLINES	BRIGHTLY
BLINKERS	BOHEMIAN	BOYCOTTS	BRIMMING
BLINKING	BOLDNESS	BRACELET	BRINDLED
BLISSFUL	BOLSTERS	BRACKETS	BRINGERS
BLISTERS	BOMBARDS	BRACKISH	BRINGING
BLITHELY	BOMBINGS	BRAGGING	BRISTLED
BLIZZARD	BONANZAS	BRAIDING	BRISTLES
BLOATING	BONDSMAN	BRAINING	BRITCHES
BLOCKADE	BONFIRES	BRAMBLES	BROACHED
BLOCKAGE	BONNETED	BRANCHED	BROACHES
BLOCKERS	BOOKCASE	BRANCHES	BROADENS
BLOCKING	BOOKINGS	BRANDING	BROADEST
BLOODIED	BOOKLETS	BRANDISH	BROCADED
BLOOMERS	BOOKMARK	BRAWLING	BROCCOLI
BLOOMING	BOOKWORM	BRAZENLY	BROCHURE
BLOSSOMS	BOOSTING	BRAZIERS	BROILERS
BLOTTING	BOOTABLE	BREACHED	BROILING
BLOWFISH	BOOTLEGS	BREACHER	BROKENLY
BLUDGEON	BORDELLO	BREACHES	BROMIDES
BLUEBIRD	BORDERED	BREADBOX	BRONCHUS
BLUENESS	BOROUGHS	BREADING	BROOCHES
BLUFFING	BORROWED	BREAKAGE	BROODING
BLUNDERS	BORROWER	BREAKERS	BROTHELS
BLUNTEST	BOSPORUS	BREAKING	BROTHERS
BLUNTING	BOTANIST	BREASTED	BROWBEAT
BLURRING	BOTCHERS	BREATHED	BROWNEST
BLURTING	BOTCHING	BREATHER	BROWNIES
BLUSHING	BOTHERED	BREATHES	BROWNING
BLUSTERS	BOTTLERS	BREECHES	BROWNISH
BLUSTERY	BOTTLING	BREEDING	BROWNING
BOARDERS	BOTTOMED	BREEZILY	BRUISING

BRUNCHES	BUSTARDS	CAPSTONE	CATHETER
BRUNETTE	BUSTLING	CAPTAINS	CATHODES
BRUSHING	BUTCHERS	CAPTIONS	CATHOLIC
BRUTALLY	BUTCHERY	CAPTURED	CAULDRON
BUBBLING	BUTTERED	CAPTURER	CAUSALLY
BUCKLING	BUTTERER	CAPTURES	CAUSEWAY
BUCKSHOT	BUTTOCKS	CAPYBARA	CAUSTICS
BUCKSKIN	BUTTONED	CARAVANS	CAUTIONS
BUDGETED	BUTTRESS	CARBOLIC	CAUTIOUS
BUDGETER	BUZZARDS	CARBONES	CAVALIER
BUFFETTED	BUZZWORD	CARBONIC	CAVITIES
BUFFOONS	BYPASSED	CARDINAL	CEILINGS
BUILDERS	BYPASSES	CAREFREE	CELEBRITY
BUILDING	CABINETS	CARELESS	CELLISTS
BUILDUPS	CACKLING	CARESSED	CELLULAR
BULLDOGS	CADENCED	CARESSER	CEMENTED
BULLDOZE	CADILLAC	CARESSES	CEMETERY
BULLETIN	CAJOLING	CARNIVAL	CENSORED
BULLFROG	CALAMITY	CARPETED	CENSURED
BULLSEYE	CALCULUS	CARRIAGE	CENSURER
BULLYING	CALENDER	CARRIERS	CENSURES
BUMBLERS	CALFSKIN	CARRYING	CENSUSES
BUMBLING	CALIBRES	CARTOONS	CENTRIST
BUNCHING	CALLABLE	CARVINGS	CENTROID
BUNDLING	CALLIOPE	CASCADED	CEREBRAL
BUNGALOW	CALMNESS	CASCADES	CEREMONY
BUNGLERS	CALORIES	CASEMENT	CHAFFING
BUNGLING	CAMPFIRE	CASEWORK	CHAINING
BUNKERED	CAMPSITE	CASHIERS	CHAIRING
BUOYANCY	CAMPUSES	CASHMERE	CHAIRMAN
BURDENED	CANARIES	CASSETTE	CHALICES
BURGHERS	CANDIDLY	CASUALLY	CHALKING
BURGLARS	CANISTER	CASUALTY	CHALMERS
BURGLARY	CANNABIS	CATALYST	CHAMPION
BURNINGS	CANNIBAL	CATAPULT	CHANCERY
BURROWED	CANVASES	CATARACT	CHANCING
BURROWER	CAPACITY	CATCHERTS	CHANGERS
BURSITIS	CAPITALS	CATCHING	CHANGING
BURSTING	CAPITOLS	CATEGORY	CHANNELS
BUSINESS	CAPSICUM	CATERING	CHANTING

CHAPERON	CHIMNEYS	CLAIMANT	CLINGING
CHAPLAIN	CHINAMAN	CLAIMING	CLINICAL
CHAPTERS	CHINNERS	CLAMBERS	CLIPPERS
CHARCOAL	CHINNING	CLAMPING	CLIPPING
CHARGERS	CHIPMUNK	CLANGING	CLITORIS
CHARGING	CHIRPING	CLANNISH	CLOBBERS
CHARIOTS	CHIVALRY	CLAPPING	CLOCKERS
CHARISMA	CHLORINE	CLARINET	CLOCKING
CHARMERS	CHOICEST	CLASHING	CLOISTER
CHARMING	CHOOSERS	CLASPING	CLOSETED
CHARTERS	CHOOSING	CLASSICS	CLOSURES
CHARTING	CHOPPERS	CLASSIFY	CLOTHING
CHASTELY	CHOPPING	CLEANERS	CLOTTING
CHASTISE	CHORDATE	CLEANEST	CLOUDIER
CHASTITY	CHORDING	CLEANING	CLOUDING
CHATEAUS	CHORUSED	CLEANSED	CLOWNING
CHATTERS	CHORUSES	CLEANSER	CLUBBING
CHATTING	CHRISTEN	CLEANSES	CLUBROOM
CHEAPENS	CHROMIUM	CLEAREST	CLUCKING
CHEAPEST	CHUBBIER	CLEARING	CLUMPING
CHEATERS	CHUCKLED	CLEAVAGE	CLUMSILY
CHEATING	CHUCKLES	CLEAVERS	CLUSTERS
CHECKERS	CHURCHES	CLEAVING	CLUTCHED
CHECKING	CHURCHLY	CLEMENCY	CLUTCHES
CHECKOUT	CHURNING	CLENCHED	CLUTTERS
CHEERFUL	CINERAMA	CLENCHES	COACHING
CHEERILY	CINNAMON	CLERICAL	COACHMAN
CHEERING	CIRCLING	CLERKING	COACHMEN
CHEMICAL	CIRCUITS	CLEVERER	COALESCE
CHEMISTS	CIRCULAR	CLEVERLY	COARSELY
CHEROKEE	CIRCUSES	CLICKING	COARSEST
CHERRIES	CISTERNS	CLIMATES	COASTERS
CHERUBIM	CITADELS	CLIMATIC	COASTING
CHESTNUT	CITATION	CLIMAXED	COATINGS
CHICKENS	CITIZENS	CLIMAXES	COAUTHOR
CHILDISH	CITYWIDE	CLIMBERS	COBBLERS
CHILDREN	CIVILIAN	CLIMBING	COCKTAIL
CHILLERS	CIVILITY	CLINCHED	COCONUTS
CHILLIER	CIVILIZE	CLINCHER	CODEWORD
CHILLING	CLADDING	CLINCHES	CODIFIED

CODIFIER	COMMANDO	CONCERTO	CONSENTS
CODIFIES	COMMANDS	CONCERTS	CONSERVE
CODPIECE	COMMENCE	CONCLAVE	CONSIDER
COEDITOR	COMMENDS	CONCLUDE	CONSIGNS
COERCING	COMMENTS	CONCORDE	CONSISTS
COERCION	COMMERCE	CONCRETE	CONSOLED
COERCIVE	COMMONER	CONDEMNS	CONSOLER
COEXISTS	COMMONLY	CONDENSE	CONSOLES
COFACTOR	COMMUNES	CONDONES	CONSORTS
COGENTLY	COMMUTED	CONDONES	CONSPIRE
COGITATE	COMMUTER	CONDUCTS	CONSTANT
COHERENT	COMMUTES	CONFEREE	CONSTRUE
COHERING	COMPACTS	CONFIDED	CONSULAR
COHESION	COMPARED	CONFIDES	CONSULTS
COHESIVE	COMPARES	CONFINED	CONSUMED
COINCIDE	COMPETED	CONFINER	CONSUMER
COLANDER	COMPETES	CONFINES	CONSUMES
COLDNESS	COMPILED	CONFIRMS	CONTACTS
COLISEUM	COMPILER	CONFLICT	CONTAINS
COLLAGEN	COMPILES	CONFOCAL	CONTEMPT
COLLAPSE	COMPLAIN	CONFIRMS	CONTENDS
COLLARED	COMPLETE	CONFLICT	CONTENTS
COLLECTS	COMPLIED	CONFOCAL	CONTESTS
COLLEGES	COMPOSED	CONFORMS	CONTEXTS
COLLIDED	COMPOSER	CONFOUND	CONTINUE
COLLIDES	COMPOSES	CONFRONT	CONTOURS
COLONELS	COMPOUND	CONFUSED	CONTRACT
COLONIAL	COMPRESS	CONFUSER	CONTRARY
COLONIES	COMPRISE	CONFUSES	CONTRAST
COLONIST	COMPUTED	CONGRESS	CONTRITE
COLONIZE	COMPUTER	CONJUGAL	CONTRIVE
COLOSSAL	COMPUTES	CONJUNCT	CONTROLS
COMBATED	COMRADES	CONJURED	CONVENED
COMBINED	CONCEALS	CONJURER	CONVENES
COMBINES	CONCEDED	CONJURES	CONVENTS
COMEBACK	CONCEDES	CONNECTS	CONVERGE
COMEDIAN	CONCEITS	CONNOTED	CONVERSE
COMEDIES	CONCEIVE	CONNOTES	CONVERTS
COMETARY	CONCEPTS	CONQUERS	CONVEYED
COMFORTS	CONCERNS	CONQUEST	CONVEYER

CONVEYOR	COVENANT	CREDIBLY	CRUSADES
CONVICTS	COVERAGE	CREDITED	CRUSHERS
CONVINCE	COVERING	CREDITOR	CRUSHING
CONVOYED	COVERLET	CREEPERS	CRUTCHES
CONVULSE	COVERTLY	CREEPING	CRYSTALS
COOKBOOK	COVETING	CREMATED	CUCUMBER
COOLNESS	COVETOUS	CREMATES	CUFFLINK
COQUETTE	COWARDLY	CRESCENT	CULINARY
CORNERED	COWERERS	CREVICES	CULPABLE
CORNMEAL	COWERING	CRICKETS	CULPRITS
CORONARY	COWORKER	CRIMINAL	CULTURAL
CORONETS	COWSLIPS	CRINGING	CULTURED
CORPORAL	COZINESS	CRIPPLED	CULTURES
CORRECTS	CRACKERS	CRIPPLES	CUPBOARD
CORRIDOR	CRACKING	CRITERIA	CURLICUE
CORRUPTS	CRACKLED	CRITICAL	CURRANTS
CORTICAL	CRACKLES	CRITIQUE	CURRENCY
COSMETIC	CRACKPOT	CROAKING	CURRENTS
COSTUMED	CRAFTING	CROCHETS	CURRYING
COSTUMER	CRAMMING	CROCKERY	CURTAILS
COSTUMES	CRANKIER	CROPPERS	CURTAINS
COTTAGER	CRANKILY	CROPPING	CURTNESS
COTTAGES	CRANKING	CROSSBAR	CURTSIES
COUCHING	CRASHERS	CROSSERS	CUSHIONS
COUGHING	CRASHING	CROSSING	CUSTOMER
COUNCILS	CRAWLERS	CROUCHED	CUTTINGS
COUNSELS	CRAWLING	CROWDING	CYANAMID
COUNTERS	CRAZIEST	CROWNING	CYCLADES
COUNTESS	CREAKING	CRUCIBLE	CYCLOIDS
COUNTIES	CREAMERS	CRUCIFIX	CYCLONES
COUNTING	CREAMERY	CRUELEST	CYLINDER
COUPLERS	CREAMING	CRUISERS	CYRILLIC
COUPLING	CREASING	CRUISING	CYTOLOGY
COURIERS	CREATING	CRUMBLED	DABBLING
COURSING	CREATION	CRUMBLES	DACTYLIC
COURTERS	CREATIVE	CRUMPLED	DAFFODIL
COURTESY	CREATORS	CRUMPLES	DAINTILY
COURTIER	CREATURE	CRUNCHED	DAMAGERS
COURTING	CREDENCE	CRUNCHES	DAMAGING
COVALENT	CREDIBLE	CRUSADER	DAMPNESS

DANGLING	DECLARED	DELICACY	DERRIERE
DARINGLY	DECLARER	DELICATE	DESCENDS
DARKNESS	DECLARES	DELIGHTS	DESCENTS
DARKROOM	DECLINED	DELIMITS	DESCRIBE
DARLINGS	DECLINER	DELIRIUM	DESERTED
DATABASE	DECLINES	DELIVERS	DESERTER
DATAGRAM	DECODERS	DELIVERY	DESERVED
DAUGHTER	DECODING	DELUDING	DESERVES
DAYBREAK	DECORATE	DELUSION	DESIGNED
DAYDREAM	DECOUPLE	DEMANDED	DESIGNER
DAYLIGHT	DECREASE	DEMANDER	DESIRING
DAZZLING	DECRYPTS	DEMENTED	DESIROUS
DEADLOCK	DEDICATE	DEMOCRAT	DESOLATE
DEADNESS	DEDUCING	DEMOLISH	DESPAIRS
DEADWOOD	DEDUCTED	DEMONIAC	DESPATCH
DEAFNESS	DEEPENED	DENATURE	DESPISED
DEALINGS	DEFAULTS	DENIABLE	DESPISES
DEATHBED	DEFEATED	DENOTING	DESPOTIC
DEBATERS	DEFECTED	DENOUNCE	DESSERTS
DEBATING	DEFENDED	DENTALLY	DESTINED
DEBILITY	DEFENDER	DENTISTS	DESTROYS
DEBUGGED	DEFENSES	DEPARTED	DESTRUCT
DEBUGGER	DEFERRED	DEPENDED	DESTUFFS
DECADENT	DEFERRER	DEPICTED	DETACHED
DECAYING	DEFIANCE	DEPLETED	DETACHER
DECEASED	DEFICITS	DEPLETES	DETACHES
DECEASES	DEFILING	DEPLORED	DETAILED
DECEDENT	DEFINING	DEPLORES	DETAINED
DECEIVED	DEFINITE	DEPLOYED	DETECTED
DECEIVER	DEFLATER	DEPORTEE	DETECTOR
DECEIVES	DEFOREST	DEPOSITS	DETERRED
DECEMBER	DEFORMED	DEPRAVED	DETESTED
DECENTLY	DEGRADED	DEPRIVED	DETRACTS
DECIDING	DEGRADES	DEPRIVES	DEVELOPS
DECIMALS	DEIGNING	DEPUTIES	DEVIANTS
DECIMATE	DEJECTED	DEQUEUED	DEVIATED
DECIPHER	DELAYING	DEQUEUES	DEVIATES
DECISION	DELEGATE	DERAILED	DEVILISH
DECISIVE	DELETING	DERISION	DEVISING
DECKINGS	DELETION	DERIVING	DEVOTEES

DEVOTING	DINOSAUR	DISMAYED	DIVIDERS
DEVOTION	DIPLOMAS	DISMOUNT	DIVIDING
DEVOURED	DIPLOMAT	DISOBEYS	DIVINELY
DEVOURER	DIPPINGS	DISORDER	DIVINING
DEVOUTLY	DIRECTED	DISOWNED	DIVINITY
DEWDROPS	DIRECTLY	DISPATCH	DIVISION
DIABETES	DIRTIEST	DISPENSE	DIVISIVE
DIABETIC	DISABLED	DISPERSE	DIVISORS
DIABOLIC	DISABLER	DISPLACE	DIVORCED
DIAGNOSE	DISABLES	DISPLAYS	DIVORCEE
DIAGONAL	DISAGREE	DISPOSAL	DIVULGED
DIAGRAMS	DISALLOW	DISPOSED	DIVULGES
DIALECTS	DISARMED	DISPOSER	DOBERMAN
DIALOGUE	DISASTER	DISPOSES	DOCKSIDE
DIALYSIS	DISBANDS	DISPROVE	DOCKYARD
DIAMETER	DISBURSE	DISPUTED	DOCTORAL
DIAMONDS	DISCARDS	DISPUTER	DOCTORED
DIATRIBE	DISCERNS	DISPUTES	DOCTRINE
DICTATED	DISCIPLE	DISQUIET	DOCUMENT
DICTATES	DISCLAIM	DISRUPTS	DOGGEDLY
DICTATOR	DISCLOSE	DISSECTS	DOGHOUSE
DIDACTIC	DISCOUNT	DISSENTS	DOGMATIC
DIETETIC	DISCOVER	DISSOLVE	DOLPHINS
DIFFERED	DISCREET	DISSUADE	DOMESDAY
DIFFERER	DISCRETE	DISTALLY	DOMESTIC
DIFFRACT	DISDAINS	DISTANCE	DOMICILE
DIFFUSED	DISEASED	DISTASTE	DOMINANT
DIFFUSER	DISEASES	DISTILLS	DOMINATE
DIFFUSES	DISGORGE	DISTINCT	DOMINEER
DIGESTED	DISGRACE	DISTORTS	DOMINION
DIGGINGS	DISGUISE	DISTRACT	DONATING
DIGITIZE	DISGUSTS	DISTRESS	DONATION
DIHEDRAL	DISHEVEL	DISTRICT	DOOMSDAY
DILATING	DISJOINT	DISTRUST	DOORBELL
DILATION	DISJUNCT	DISTURBS	DOORSTEP
DILEMMAS	DISKETTE	DIVERGED	DOORWAY
DILIGENT	DISLIKED	DIVERGES	DOSSIERS
DILUTING	DISLIKES	DIVERTED	DOTINGLY
DILUTION	DISLODGE	DIVESTED	DOUBLERS
DIMINISH	DISMALLY	DIVIDEND	DOUBLETS

DOUBLING	DRILLING	ECLECTIC	ELLIPSIS
DOUBLOON	DRINKERS	ECLIPSED	ELLIPTIC
DOUBTERS	DRINKING	ECLIPSES	ELOQUENT
DOUBTFUL	DRIPPING	ECLIPTIC	EMACIATE
DOUBTING	DRIVEWAY	ECSTATIC	EMBARKED
DOUGHNUT	DROOPING	EDIFICES	EMBEDDED
DOVETAIL	DROPPERS	EDITIONS	EMBEZZLE
DOWNCAST	DROPPING	EDUCABLE	EMBODIED
DOWNFALL	DROUGHTS	EDUCATED	EMBEZZLE
DOWNHILL	DROWNING	EDUCATES	EMBODIED
DOWNLINK	DRUBBING	EDUCATOR	EMBODIES
DOWNLOAD	DRUDGERY	EELGRASS	EMBOLDEN
DOWNPLAY	DRUGGIST	EFFECTED	EMBRACED
DOWNPOUR	DRUMMERS	EFFECTOR	EMBRACES
DOWNSIDE	DRUMMING	EFFICACY	EMERALDS
DOWNTOWN	DRUNKARD	EGGPLANT	EMERGENT
DOWNTURN	DUCKLING	EGGSHELL	EMERGING
DOWNWARD	DULLNESS	EGYPTIAN	EMERITUS
DRAFTERS	DUMBBELL	EGYPTIZE	EMIGRANT
DRAFTING	DUMBNESS	EIGHTEEN	EMIGRATE
DRAGGING	DUNGEONS	EIGHTIES	EMINENCE
DRAGOONS	DURATION	EJECTING	EMISSARY
DRAINAGE	DUSTIEST	ELAPSING	EMISSION
DRAINING	DUTCHESS	ELBOWING	EMITTING
DRAMATIC	DWELLERS	ELECTING	EMOTIONS
DRAUGHTS	DWELLING	ELECTION	EMPERORS
DRAWBACK	DWINDLES	ELECTIVE	EMPHASES
DRAWINGS	DYNAMICS	ELECTORS	EMPHASIS
DRAWLING	DYNAMISM	ELECTRIC	EMPHATIC
DREADFUL	DYNAMITE	ELECTRON	EMPLOYED
DREADING	DYNASTIC	ELEGANCE	EMPLOYEE
DREAMERS	EARLIEST	ELEMENTS	EMPLOYER
DREAMILY	EARMARKS	ELEPHANT	EMPORIUM
DREAMING	EARNINGS	ELEVATED	EMPOWERS
DRENCHED	EARPHONE	ELEVATES	EMPTIEST
DRENCHES	EARRINGS	ELEVATOR	EMPTYING
DRESSERS	EARTHMAN	ELEVENTH	EMULATED
DRESSING	EASEMENT	ELICITED	EMULATES
DRIFTERS	EASINESS	ELIGIBLE	EMULATOR
DRIFTING	EASTWARD	ELLIPSES	ENABLERS

ENABLING	ENLARGES	ENVIRONS	EUPHORIA
ENACTING	ENLISTED	ENVISAGE	EUPHORIC
ENAMELED	ENLIVENS	ENVISION	EUROPEAN
ENCAMPED	ENMITIES	EPAULETS	EVACUATE
ENCHANTS	ENNOBLED	EPIDEMIC	EVALUATE
ENCIPHER	ENNOBLES	EPILOGUE	EVENINGS
ENCIRCLE	ENORMITY	EPIPHANY	EVENNESS
ENCLOSED	ENORMOUS	EPISODES	EVENTFUL
ENCLOSES	ENQUEUED	EPISTLES	EVENTUAL
ENCODERS	ENQUEUES	EPITAPHS	EVERMORE
ENCODING	ENQUIRED	EQUALITY	EVERYDAY
ENCROACH	ENQUIRER	EQUALIZE	EVERYONE
ENCRYPTS	ENQUIRES	EQUATING	EVICTING
ENCUMBER	ENRAGING	EQUATION	EVICTION
ENDANGER	ENRICHED	EQUATORS	EVIDENCE
ENDEARED	ENRICHES	EQUIPPED	EVOLUTES
ENDORSED	ENROLLED	ERASABLE	EVOLVING
ENDORSES	ENSEMBLE	ERECTING	EXACTING
ENDOWING	ENSLAVED	ERECTION	EXACTION
ENDPOINT	ENSLAVES	ERECTORS	EXALTING
ENDURING	ENSNARED	ERRINGLY	EXAMINED
ENERGIES	ENSNARES	ERUPTION	EXAMINER
ENERGIZE	ENSURERS	ESCALATE	EXAMINES
ENERVATE	ENSURING	ESCAPADE	EXAMPLES
ENFEEBLE	ENTAILED	ESCAPEES	EXCAVATE
ENFORCED	ENTANGLE	ESCAPING	EXCEEDED
ENFORCER	ENTERING	ESCHEWED	EXCELLED
ENFORCES	ENTICERS	ESCORTED	EXCEPTED
ENGAGING	ENTICING	ESOTERIC	EXCERPTS
ENGENDER	ENTIRELY	ESPAGNOL	EXCESSES
ENGINEER	ENTIRETY	ESPECIAL	EXCHANGE
ENGRAVED	ENTITIES	ESPOUSED	EXCISING
ENGRAVER	ENTITLED	ESPOUSES	EXCISION
ENGRAVES	ENTITLES	ESQUIRES	EXCITING
ENHANCED	ENTRANCE	ESSENCES	EXCLAIMS
ENHANCES	ENTREATY	ESTEEMED	EXCLUDED
ENJOINED	ENTRENCH	ESTIMATE	EXCLUDES
ENJOYING	ENTRUSTS	ETERNITY	EXCRETED
ENLARGED	ENVELOPE	ETHERFAL	EXCRETED
ENLARGER	ENVELOPS	ETHERNET	EXCRETES

EXCUSING	EXPOUNDS	FARTHEST	FIDDLING
EXECUTED	EXPUNGED	FARTHING	FIDELITY
EXECUTES	EXPUNGES	FASCICLE	FIDUCIAL
EXECUTOR	EXTENDED	FASHIONS	FIELDERS
EXEMPLAR	EXTERIOR	FASTENED	FIELDING
EXEMPTED	EXTERNAL	FASTENER	FIENDISH
EXERCISE	EXTORTED	FASTNESS	FIERCELY
EXERTING	EXTRACTS	FATALITY	FIERCEST
EXERTION	EXTREMAL	FATHERED	FIFTEENS
EXHALING	EXTREMES	FATHOMED	FIFTIETH
EXHAUSTS	EYEBROWS	FATIGUED	FIGHTERS
EXHIBITS	EYESIGHT	FATIGUES	FIGHTING
EXIGENCY	FABULOUS	FATTENED	FIGURING
EXISTENT	FACILELY	FATTENER	FILAMENT
EXISTING	FACILITY	FAULTING	FILLABLE
EXORCISM	FACTIONS	FEARLESS	FILLINGS
EXORCIST	FACTIOUS	FEARSOME	FILTERED
EXPANDED	FACTORED	FEASIBLE	FILTHIER
EXPANDER	FAILINGS	FEASTING	FINALITY
EXPANSES	FAILURES	FEATHERS	FINALIZE
EXPECTED	FAINTEST	FEATHERY	FINANCED
EXPEDITE	FAINTING	FEATURED	FINANCES
EXPELLED	FAIRNESS	FEATURES	FINDINGS
EXPENDED	FAITHFUL	FEBRUARY	FINENESS
EXPENSES	FALCONER	FEDERALS	FINESSED
EXPERTLY	FALLIBLE	FEEBLEST	FINGERED
EXPIRING	FALTERED	FEEDBACK	FINISHED
EXPLAINS	FAMILIAL	FEEDINGS	FINISHER
EXPLODED	FAMILIAR	FEELINGS	FINISHES
EXPLODES	FAMILIES	FEIGNING	FINITELY
EXPLOITS	FAMILISM	FEMININE	FIREARMS
EXPLORED	FAMOUSLY	FEMINISM	FIRESIDE
EXPLORER	FANATICS	FEMINIST	FIREWALL
EXPLORES	FANCIERS	FERMENTS	FIREWOOD
EXPONENT	FANCIEST	FEROCITY	FIRMNESS
EXPORTED	FANCIFUL	FESTIVAL	FISCALLY
EXPORTER	FANCYING	FETCHING	FISHPOND
EXPOSERS	FAREWELL	FETTERED	FISSURED
EXPOSING	FARMLAND	FEVERISH	FITFULLY
EXPOSURE	FARMYARD	FICTIONS	FITTINGS

590

FIVEFOLD	FLOURISH	FORESTER	FREEZING
FIXATING	FLOWERED	FORESTRY	FREIGHTS
FIXATION	FLUENTLY	FORETELL	FRENETIC
FIXTURES	FLUFFIER	FORETOLD	FRENZIED
FLAGGING	FLUIDITY	FOREWARN	FREQUENT
FLAGPOLE	FLURRIED	FORGIVEN	FRESCOES
FLAGRANT	FLUSHING	FORGIVES	FRESHENS
FLANKING	FLUTTERS	FORKLIFT	FRESHEST
FLANNELS	FOCUSING	FORMALLY	FRESHMAN
FLASHERS	FOCUSSED	FORMANTS	FREUDIAN
FLASHING	FOGGIEST	FORMERLY	FRICTION
FLATNESS	FOLKLORE	FORMULAE	FRIENDLY
FLATTERY	FOLKSONG	FORMULAS	FRIGATES
FLATTEST	FOLLOWED	FORSAKEN	FRIGHTEN
FLATWORM	FOLLOWER	FORSAKES	FRISKING
FLAUNTED	FONDLING	FORTIETH	FRONTAGE
FLAWLESS	FONDNESS	FORTRESS	FRONTIER
FLEETEST	FOOTBALL	FORTUNES	FRONTING
FLEETING	FOOTFALL	FORWARDS	FROSTING
FLESHING	FOOTHILL	FOSTERED	FROTHING
FLEXIBLE	FOOTHOLD	FOULNESS	FROWNING
FLEXIBLY	FOOTNOTE	FOUNDERS	FROZENLY
FLICKING	FOOTPATH	FOUNDING	FRUGALLY
FLINCHED	FOOTSTEP	FOUNTAIN	FRUITFUL
FLINCHES	FORAGING	FOURFOLD	FUGITIVE
FLIPFLOP	FORBEARS	FOURSOME	FULFILLS
FLIRTING	FORCEFUL	FOURTEEN	FULLNESS
FLITTING	FORCIBLE	FRACTION	FUMBLING
FLOATING	FORCIBLY	FRAGMENT	FUNCTION
FLOCKING	FOREARMS	FRAGRANT	FUNCTORS
FLOGGING	FORECAST	FRAILEST	FUNERALS
FLOODING	FOREGOES	FRANKEST	FUNEREAL
FLOODLIT	FOREGONE	FRANKING	FUNGIBLE
FLOORING	FOREHEAD	FREAKISH	FUNNIEST
FLOPPIES	FOREIGNS	FRECKLED	FURLOUGH
FLOPPILY	FOREMOST	FRECKLES	FURNACES
FLOPPING	FORENSIC	FREEDOMS	FURROWED
FLOSSING	FORESEEN	FREEINGS	FURTHERS
FLOTILLA	FORESEES	FREENESS	FURTHEST
FLOUNDER	FORESTED	FREEZERS	FUTILITY

GADGETRY	GIGABITS	GRABBING	GRINDING
GAIETIES	GIGABYTE	GRACEFUL	GRINNING
GALACTIC	GIGANTIC	GRACIOUS	GRIPPING
GALAXIES	GIGAVOLT	GRADIENT	GROANERS
GALLANTS	GIGAWATT	GRADINGS	GROANING
GALLOPED	GIGGLING	GRADUATE	GROOMING
GALLOPER	GIMMICKS	GRAFTING	GROSSEST
GAMBLERS	GINGERLY	GRAINING	GROSSING
GAMBLING	GINGHAMS	GRAMMARS	GROUNDED
GAMENESS	GIRAFFES	GRANDEST	GROUNDER
GANGLAND	GIVEAWAY	GRANDEUR	GROUPING
GANGLING	GLADDEST	GRANDSON	GROWLING
GANGRENE	GLADNESS	GRANTING	GROWNUPS
GANGSTER	GLANCING	GRAPHICS	GRUESOME
GARBAGES	GLAUCOMA	GRAPHING	GRUMBLED
GARDENED	GLEAMING	GRAPHITE	GRUMBLES
GARDENER	GLIMMERS	GRAPPLED	GRUNTING
GARGLING	GLIMPSED	GRASPING	GUARDIAN
GARMENTS	GLIMPSES	GRASSERS	GUESSING
GARNERED	GLINTING	GRASSIER	GUIDANCE
GARRISON	GLISTENS	GRATEFUL	GUILDERS
GASLIGHT	GLITTERS	GRATINGS	GUILFORD
GASOLINE	GLOBALLY	GRATUITY	GUILTIER
GASSINGS	GLOBULAR	GRAVELLY	GUILTILY
GATEWAYS	GLOOMILY	GRAYNESS	GUMPTION
GATHERED	GLORIOUS	GREATEST	GUTTERED
GATHERER	GLORYING	GREEDILY	GUTTURAL
GAUNTLEY	GLOSSARY	GREENERY	GYMNASTS
GELATINE	GLOSSING	GREENEST	HABITATS
GENERALS	GOBBLERS	GREENING	HABITUAL
GENERATE	GOLDENLY	GREENISH	HAIRCUTS
GENEROUS	GOLDFISH	GREETING	HAIRLESS
GENIALLY	GOODNESS	GRENADES	HALLMARK
GENIUSES	GOODWILL	GRIDIRON	HALLOWED
GENTLEST	GORGEOUS	GRIEVERS	HALLWAYS
GEOMETRY	GORILLAS	GRIEVING	HAMMERED
GEORGIAN	GOSSIPED	GRIEVOUS	HAMMOCKS
GERANIUM	GOVERNED	GRILLING	HAMPERED
GESTURED	GOVERNOR	GRIMNESS	HANDBAGS
GESTURES	GRABBERS	GRINDERS	HANDBOOK

HANDCUFF	HEDONISM	HOBBYIST	HUMBLING
HANDFULS	HEDONIST	HOISTING	HUMIDIFY
HANDICAP	HEEDLESS	HOLDINGS	HUMIDITY
HANDIEST	HEGEMONY	HOLIDAYS	HUMILITY
HANDLERS	HEIGHTEN	HOLINESS	HUMOROUS
HANDLING	HELLENIC	HOLISTIC	HUMPBACK
HANDMAID	HELLFIRE	HOLLOWED	HUNDREDS
HANDSOME	HELMSMAN	HOLLOWLY	HUNGERED
HANGOVER	HELPLESS	HEARSAY	HUNGRIER
HAPPENED	HELPMATE	HOLOGRAM	HUNGRILY
HAPPIEST	HEMLOCKS	HOMELESS	HUNTSMAN
HARASSES	HENCHMAN	HOMEMADE	HURRYING
HARDNESS	HERALDED	HOMESPUN	HURTLING
HARDSHIP	HEREDITY	HOMEWARD	HUSBANDS
HARDWARE	HERETICS	HOMEWORK	HUSTLING
HARMLESS	HEREWITH	HOMICIDE	HYACINTH
HARMONIC	HERITAGE	HONESTLY	HYDROGEN
HARROWED	HERMETIC	HONEYBEE	HYPNOSIS
HARVESTS	HEROINES	HONEYDEW	HYPNOTIC
HASTENED	HERRINGS	HONORARY	ICEBERGS
HATCHETS	HESITANT	HOODWINK	IDEALISM
HATCHING	HESITATE	HOPEFULS	IDEALIZE
HAUNCHES	HESSIANS	HOPELESS	IDENTIFY
HAUNTING	HEXAGONS	HORIZONS	IDENTITY
HAYSTACK	HIDEOUTS	HORMONES	IDEOLOGY
HAZINESS	HIGHLAND	HORRIBLE	IDLENESS
HEADACHE	HIGHNESS	HORRIDLY	IDOLATRY
HEADGEAR	HIGHWAYS	HORSEFLY	IGNITION
HEADINGS	HIJACKED	HORSEMAN	IGNORANT
HEADLAND	HILLSIDE	HOSPITAL	IGNORING
HEADLONG	HILLTOPS	HOSTAGES	ILLUSION
HEADROOM	HINDERED	HOUNDING	ILLUSIVE
HEARINGS	HINDUSIM	HOUSEFLY	ILLUSORY
HEARTILY	HISPANIC	HOUSETOP	IMAGINED
HEATABLE	HISTORIC	HOVERING	IMAGINES
HEATEDLY	HITCHING	HUDDLING	IMBECILE
HEAVENLY	HITHERTO	HUGENESS	IMITATED
HEAVIEST	HOARDING	HUMANELY	IMITATES
HEDGEHOG	HOARSELY	HUMANITY	IMMATURE
HEDONISM	HOBBLING	HUMBLEST	IMMERSED

IMMERSES	INCLINED	INFORMED	INSPIRES
IMMINENT	INCLINES	INFORMER	INSTALLS
IMMODEST	INCLOSED	INFRARED	INSTANCE
IMMORTAL	INCLOSES	INFRINGE	INSTINCT
IMMUNITY	INCLUDED	INFUSING	INSTRUCT
IMPACTED	INCLUDES	INFUSION	INSULATE
IMPACTOR	INCOMING	INHABITS	INSULTED
IMPAIRED	INCREASE	INHALING	INSURERS
IMPARTED	INCUBATE	INHERENT	INSURING
IMPEDING	INCURRED	INHERITS	INTEGRAL
IMPELLED	INDEBTED	INHIBITS	INTENDED
IMPERIAL	INDECENT	INHUMANE	INTENTLY
IMPINGED	INDENTED	INIMICAL	INTERACT
IMPINGES	INDEXING	INIQUITY	INTERCOM
IMPLANTS	INDICATE	INITIALS	INTERIOR
IMPLICIT	INDIRECT	INITIATE	INTERMIX
IMPLORED	INDOLENT	INJECTED	INTERNAL
IMPLYING	INDUCING	INJURIES	INTERNED
IMPOLITE	INDUCTED	INJURING	INTERNET
IMPORTED	INDUCTEE	INKLINGS	INTERVAL
IMPORTER	INDUCTOR	INNATELY	INTIMACY
IMPOSING	INDULGED	INNOCENT	INTIMATE
IMPOSTER	INDUSTRY	INNOVATE	INTREPID
IMPOTENT	INEQUITY	INNUENDO	INTRIGUE
IMPRINTS	INERTIAL	INQUIRED	INTRUDED
IMPRISON	INFANTRY	INQUIRER	INTRUDER
IMPROPER	INFECTED	INQUIRES	INTRUDES
IMPROVED	INFERIOR	INSANELY	INTUBATE
IMPROVES	INFERNAL	INSANITY	INUNDATE
IMPUDENT	INFERNOS	INSCRIBE	INVADERS
IMPULSES	INFERRED	INSECURE	INVADING
IMPUNITY	INFESTED	INSERTED	INVALIDS
IMPURITY	INFIDELS	INSIDERS	INVASION
INACTION	INFINITE	INSIGHTS	INVENTED
INACTIVE	INFINITY	INSIGNIA	INVENTOR
INASMUCH	INFLAMED	INSISTED	INVERSES
INCENSED	INFLATED	INSOLENT	INVERTED
INCENSES	INFLATER	INSOMNIA	INVERTER
INCIDENT	INFLATES	INSPECTS	INVESTED
INCISIVE	INFLICTS	INSPIRED	INVESTOR
INCITING	INFORMAL	INSPIRER	INVITING

INVOICED	JOSTLING	KNOCKOUT	LAVISHLY
INVOICES	JOURNALS	KNOWABLE	LAWFULLY
INVOKING	JOURNEYS	KNUCKLED	LAWGIVER
INVOLVED	JOUSTING	KNUCKLES	LAWSUITS
INVOLVES	JOYFULLY	LABELLED	LAXATIVE
INWARDLY	JOYOUSLY	LABELLER	LAYERING
IONICIZE	JOYSTICK	LABRADOR	LAZINESS
IRISHMAN	JUDDERED	LACERATE	LEADINGS
IRONICAL	JUDICIAL	LACQUERS	LEAFIEST
IRONINGS	JUGGLERS	LACROSSE	LEAFLESS
IRRIGATE	JUGGLING	LADYLIKE	LEAFLETS
IRRITANT	JUCIEST	LAMENESS	LEAGUERS
IRRITATE	JUNCTION	LANDFILL	LEAKAGES
ISLANDER	JUNCTURE	LANDINGS	LEANNESS
ISOLATED	JURASSIC	LANDLADY	LEAPFROG
ISOLATES	JUSTICES	LANDLORD	LEARNERS
ISOTOPES	JUSTNESS	LANDMARK	LEARNING
ISSUANCE	JUVENILE	LANGUAGE	LEATHERS
ITEMIZED	KAMIKAZE	LANGUISH	LEAVENED
ITEMIZES	KANGAROO	LANTERNS	LEAVINGS
ITERATED	KEENNESS	LASHINGS	LECTURED
ITERATES	KERCHIEF	LATCHING	LECTURER
ITERATOR	KEROSENE	LATENESS	LECTURES
JACKETED	KEYBOARD	LATINATE	LEFTISTS
JACOBEAN	KEYWORDS	LATINITY	LEFTMOST
JACOBIAN	KILLINGS	LATINIZE	LEFTOVER
JACOBITE	KILOBITS	LATITUDE	LEFTWARD
JAMAICAN	KILOBYTE	LATRINES	LEGACIES
JANITORS	KILOGRAM	LATTERLY	LEGALITY
JAPANESE	KILOVOLT	LATTICES	LEGALIZE
JAUNDICE	KILOWATT	LAUDABLE	LEGGINGS
JAVANESE	KINDLING	LAUGHING	LEMMINGS
JAVELINS	KINDNESS	LAUGHTER	LEMONADE
JEALOUSY	KINGDOMS	LAUNCHED	LENGTHEN
JEOPARDY	KITCHENS	LAUNCHER	LENGTHLY
JERKINGS	KNAPSACK	LAUNCHES	LENIENCY
JEROBOAM	KNEELING	LAUNDERS	LEOPARDS
JETLINER	KNIGHTED	LAUREATE	LESBIANS
JEWELLED	KNIGHTLY	LAVATORY	LESSENED
JINGLING	KNOCKERS	LAVENDER	LETTERED
JOKINGLY	KNOCKING	LAVISHED	LETTERER

LEUKEMIA	LINOLEUM	LOUDNESS	MALENESS
LEVELLED	LIPSTICK	LOUNGING	MANAGERS
LEVERAGE	LISTENED	LOVELIER	MANAGING
LEVIABLE	LISTENER	LOVELIES	MANDARIN
LEWDNESS	LISTINGS	LOVELORN	MANDATED
LEXICONS	LITERACY	LOVINGLY	MANDATES
LIAISONS	LITERALS	LOWERING	MANDIBLE
LIBELOUS	LITERARY	LOWLANDS	MANGLING
LIBERALS	LITERATE	LOWLIEST	MANIACAL
LIBERATE	LITIGANT	LUCKIEST	MANICURE
LIBRETTO	LITIGATE	LUCKLESS	MANIFEST
LICENSEE	LITTERED	LUKEWARM	MANIFOLD
LICENSES	LITTLEST	LUMBERED	MANNERED
LICENSOR	LIVENESS	LUMINOUS	MANNERLY
LICORICE	LIVERIED	LUNCHEON	MANPOWER
LIFEBOAT	LOADINGS	LUNCHING	MANSIONS
LIFELESS	LOATHING	LURCHING	MANUALLY
LIFELIKE	LOBBYING	LUSCIOUS	MAPPABLE
LIFELONG	LOBSTERS	LUSTROUS	MAPPINGS
LIFESPAN	LOCALITY	LUTHERAN	MARATHON
LIFETIME	LOCALIZE	LUXURIES	MARBLING
LIGAMENT	LOCATING	MACASSAR	MARCHING
LIGATURE	LOCATION	MACHINED	MARGINAL
LIGHTENS	LOCATIVE	MACHINES	MARIGOLD
LIGHTERS	LOCATORS	MACKEREL	MARINADE
LIGHTEST	LOCKINGS	MADHOUSE	MARINATE
LIGHTING	LOCKOUTS	MAGAZINE	MARITIME
LIKELIER	LODGINGS	MAGICIAN	MARKABLE
LIKENESS	LOGICIAN	MAGNETIC	MARKEDLY
LIKENING	LOGISTIC	MAGNOLIA	MARKETED
LIKEWISE	LOITERED	MAHOGANY	MARKINGS
LILLIPUT	LOITERER	MAILABLE	MARRIAGE
LIMERICK	LONDONER	MAILINGS	MARRYING
LIMITERS	LONELIER	MAINLAND	MARSHALL
LIMITING	LONESOME	MAINLINE	MARSHALS
LIMPNESS	LONGHAND	MAINSTAY	MARTIANS
LINEARLY	LONGINGS	MAINTAIN	MARXISMS
LINGERED	LOOPHOLE	MAJESTIC	MASKABLE
LINGERIE	LOOSENED	MAJORING	MASKINGS
LINGUIST	LOPSIDED	MAJORITY	MASONITE
LINKAGES	LORDSHIP	MALADIES	MASSACRE

MASSAGES	MEMBRANE	MINISTER	MOLECULE
MASTERED	MEMORIAL	MINISTRY	MOLEHILL
MASTERLY	MEMORIES	MINORING	MOLESTED
MATCHERS	MEMORIZE	MINORITY	MOMENTUM
MATCHING	MENACING	MINOTAUR	MONARCHS
MATERIAL	MENTALLY	MINSTREL	MONARCHY
MATERNAL	MENTIONS	MINUTELY	MONASTIC
MATRICES	MERCHANT	MIRACLES	MONETARY
MATRONLY	MERCIFUL	MIRRORED	MONGOOSE
MATTERED	MERIDIAN	MISCARRY	MONITORS
MATTRESS	MERINGUE	MISCHIEF	MONKEYED
MATURELY	MERITING	MISERIES	MONOGAMY
MATURING	MERRIEST	MISLEADS	MONOGRAM
MATURITY	MESSAGES	MISMATCH	MONOLITH
MAVERICK	MESSIEST	MISNOMER	MONOPOLY
MAXIMIZE	METALLIC	MISPLACE	MONOTONE
MAXIMUMS	METAPHOR	MISSILES	MONOTONY
MEAGERLY	METEORIC	MISSIONS	MONSTERS
MEALTIME	METERING	MISSPELL	MONUMENT
MEANDERS	METRICAL	MISTAKEN	MOONLIKE
MEANINGS	MIDDLING	MISTAKES	MOORINGS
MEANNESS	MIDNIGHT	MISTRESS	MORALITY
MEANTIME	MIDPOINT	MISTRUST	MORBIDLY
MEASURED	MIDRANGE	MISTYPED	MOREOVER
MEASURER	MIDSCALE	MISTYPES	MORIBUND
MEASURES	MIDWIVES	MISUSING	MORNINGS
MECHANIC	MIGHTIER	MITIGATE	MORPHINE
MEDDLING	MIGHTILY	MIXTURES	MORPHISM
MEDIATES	MIGRAINE	MNEMONIC	MORTALLY
MEDIATOR	MIGRATED	MOBILITY	MORTARED
MEDICINE	MIGRATES	MOCCASIN	MORTGAGE
MEDIEVAL	MILDNESS	MODALITY	MOSQUITO
MEDIOCRE	MILITANT	MODERATE	MOTHBALL
MEDITATE	MILITARY	MODERNLY	MOTHERED
MEEKNESS	MILKMAID	MODESTLY	MOTHERER
MEETINGS	MILLIONS	MODIFIED	MOTHERLY
MEGABITS	MIMICKED	MODIFIER	MOTIONED
MEGABYTE	MINDLESS	MODIFIES	MOTIVATE
MEGAVOLT	MINERALS	MODULATE	MOTORCAR
MELLOWED	MINGLING	MOISTURE	MOTORING
MELODIES	MINIMIZE	MOLASSES	MOTORIST

MOTORIZE	NAMESAKE	NIGHTCAP	OBITUARY
MOULDING	NARCOTIC	NIHILISM	OBJECTED
MOUNTAIN	NARROWED	NINEFOLD	OBJECTOR
MOUNTING	NARROWER	NINETEEN	OBLIGING
MOURNERS	NARROWLY	NINETIES	OBLIVION
MOURNFUL	NASTIEST	NITROGEN	OBSCURED
MOURNING	NATIONAL	NOBILITY	OBSCURER
MOUTHFUL	NATIVELY	NOBLEMAN	OBSCURES
MOUTHING	NATIVITY	NOMINATE	OBSERVED
MOVEMENT	NATURALS	NONSENSE	OBSERVER
MUDDLERS	NAUSEATE	NOONTIDE	OBSERVES
MUDDLING	NAVIGATE	NOONTIME	OBSOLETE
MUFFLING	NEARNESS	NORMALCY	OBSTACLE
MULTIPLE	NEATNESS	NORMALLY	OBSTRUCT
MULTIPLY	NEBULOUS	NORTHERN	OBTAINED
MUMBLERS	NECKLACE	NOSTRILS	OBVIATED
MUMBLING	NECKLINE	NOTABLES	OBVIATES
MUNCHING	NECROSIS	NOTARIZE	OCCASION
MUNITION	NEEDLERS	NOTATION	OCCIDENT
MURDERED	NEEDLESS	NOTCHING	OCCLUDED
MURDERER	NEEDLING	NOTEBOOK	OCCLUDES
MURMURED	NEGATING	NOTHINGS	OCCUPANT
MURMURER	NEGATION	NOTICING	OCCUPIED
MUSCLING	NEGATIVE	NOTIFIED	OCCUPIER
MUSCULAR	NEGLECTS	NOTIFIER	OCCUPIES
MUSHROOM	NEGLIGEE	NOTIFIES	OCCURRED
MUSICALS	NEONATAL	NOVELIST	OCTOBERS
MUSICIAN	NESTLING	NOVEMBER	ODDITIES
MUSKRATS	NETWORKS	NOWADAYS	ODIOUSLY
MUTATING	NEURITIS	NUISANCE	OFFENDED
MUTATION	NEUROSES	NUMBERED	OFFENDER
MUTATIVE	NEUROSIS	NUMBERER	OFFENSES
MUTENESS	NEUROTIC	NUMBNESS	OFFERERS
MUTILATE	NEWCOMER	NUMERALS	OFFERING
MUTINIES	NEWLYWED	NUMERICS	OFFICERS
MUTTERED	NEWSCAST	NUMEROUS	OFFICIAL
MUTTERER	NIBBLERS	NURTURED	OFFSHORE
MUTUALLY	NIBBLING	NURTURES	OILCLOTH
MYSTICAL	NICENESS	NUTRIENT	OINTMENT
MYTHICAL	NICKNAME	NUTSHELL	OLYMPICS
NAMEABLE	NICOTINE	OBEDIENT	OMISSION

OMITTING	OUTBURST	OVERLOOK	PANORAMA
OMNIVORE	OUTCASTS	OVERRIDE	PANTHEON
ONCOLOGY	OUTCOMES	OVERRODE	PANTHERS
ONLOOKER	OUTCRIES	OVERRULE	PANTRIES
ONTOLOGY	OUTDATED	OVERRUNS	PAPERERS
OPAQUELY	OUTDOORS	OVERSEAS	PAPERING
OPENINGS	OUTGOING	OVERSEER	PARABOLA
OPENNESS	OUTGROWN	OVERSEES	PARADIGM
OPERABLE	OUTGROWS	OVERSHOT	PARADING
OPERANDI	OUTLASTS	OVERTAKE	PARADISE
OPERATED	OUTLAWED	OVERTIME	PARAFFIN
OPERATES	OUTLINED	OVERTONE	PARAGONS
OPERETTA	OUTLINES	OVERTOOK	PARAKEET
OPINIONS	OUTLIVED	OVERTURE	PARALLAX
OPPONENT	OUTLIVES	OVERTURN	PARALLAX
OPPOSING	OUTLYING	OVERVIEW	PARALLEL
OPPOSITE	OUTPOSTS	OVERWORK	PARALYZE
OPTIMISM	OUTRAGED	OXIDIZED	PARANOIA
OPTIMIST	OUTRAGES	PACIFIED	PARANOID
OPTIMIZE	OUTRIGHT	PACIFIER	PARAPETS
OPULENCE	OUTSIDER	PACIFIER	PARASITE
ORATIONS	OUTSTRIP	PACIFIES	PARDONED
ORBITERS	OUTVOTED	PACIFISM	PARDONER
ORBITING	OUTVOTES	PACIFIST	PARENTAL
ORCHARDS	OUTWEIGH	PACKAGED	PARISHES
ORDAINED	OVERALLS	PACKAGER	PARKLAND
ORDERING	OVERCAME	PACKAGES	PARKLIKE
ORDINARY	OVERCOAT	PAGEANTS	PARMESAN
ORDINATE	OVERCOME	PAGINATE	PAROLING
ORGANISM	OVERDONE	PAINLESS	PARSIFAL
ORGANIST	OVERDOSE	PAINTERS	PARSINGS
ORGANIZE	OVERFLOW	PAINTING	PARTAKER
ORIENTAL	OVERHANG	PAIRINGS	PARTAKES
ORIENTED	OVERHAUL	PALENESS	PARTICLE
ORIFICES	OVERHEAD	PALLIATE	PARTINGS
ORIGINAL	OVERHEAR	PALPABLE	PARTISAN
ORNAMENT	OVERKILL	PAMPHLET	PARTNERS
ORPHANED	OVERLAND	PANACEAS	PASSAGES
ORTHODOX	OVERLAPS	PANCAKES	PASSIONS
OUTBOUND	OVERLAYS	PANDEMIC	PASSOVER
OUTBREAK	OVERLOAD	PANICKED	PASSPORT

PASSWORD	PENITENT	PHOSPHOR	PLASTERS
PASTIMES	PENSIONS	PHYSICAL	PLASTICS
PASTNESS	PENTAGON	PHYSIQUE	PLATEAUS
PASTORAL	PENUMBRA	PICKETED	PLATELET
PASTURES	PEPPERED	PICKETER	PLATFORM
PATCHING	PERCEIVE	PICKINGS	PLATINUM
PATENTED	PERCENTS	PICKLING	PLATONIC
PATENTER	PERCHING	PICTURED	PLATTERS
PATENTLY	PERCIVAL	PICTURES	PLAYABLE
PATERNAL	PERFECTS	PIERCING	PLAYBACK
PATHETIC	PERFORCE	PIGMENTS	PLAYMATE
PATHOGEN	PERFORMS	PILLAGED	PLAYROOM
PATHWAYS	PERFUMED	PILLARED	PLAYTIME
PATIENCE	PERFUMES	PILOTING	PLEADING
PATIENTS	PERILOUS	PINAFORE	PLEASANT
PATRIOTS	PERIODIC	PINCHING	PLEASING
PATTERED	PERISHED	PINKNESS	PLEASURE
PATTERNS	PERISHER	PINNACLE	PLEBEIAN
PAVEMENT	PERISHES	PINNINGS	PLETHORA
PAVILION	PERMEATE	PINPOINT	PLEURISY
PAWNSHOP	PERMUTED	PINWHEEL	PLODDING
PAYCHECK	PERMUTES	PIONEERS	PLOTTERS
PAYMENTS	PEROXIDE	PIPELINE	PLOTTING
PEACEFUL	PERSISTS	PITCHERS	PLUCKING
PEACOCKS	PERSONAL	PITCHING	PLUGGING
PEASANTS	PERSPIRE	PITFALLS	PLUMBING
PECTORAL	PERSUADE	PITHIEST	PLUNDERS
PECULIAR	PERTAINS	PITIABLE	PLUNGERS
PEDAGOGY	PERUSERS	PITILESS	PLUNGING
PEDANTIC	PERUSING	PIVOTING	POCKETED
PEDANTRY	PERVADED	PLACARDS	POETICAL
PEDDLERS	PERVADES	PLACENTA	POETRIES
PEDESTAL	PERVERTS	PLACIDLY	POIGNANT
PEDIGREE	PETITION	PLAGUING	POINTERS
PEEPHOLE	PETULANT	PLAINEST	POINTING
PEERLESS	PHANTOMS	PLANKING	POISONED
PEGBOARD	PHARMACY	PLANKTON	POISONER
PENALIZE	PHEASANT	PLANNERS	POLARITY
PENCHANT	PHONEMIC	PLANNING	POLEMICS
PENDULUM	PHONETIC	PLANTERS	POLICIES
PENGUINS	PHOSGENE	PLANTING	POLICING

POLISHED	PRACTICE	PRESUMES	PROFILES
POLISHER	PRAISERS	PRETENCE	PROFITED
POLISHES	PRAISING	PRETENDS	PROFOUND
POLITELY	PRANCING	PRETEXTS	PROGRAMS
POLITEST	PREACHED	PRETTIER	PROGRESS
POLITICS	PREACHER	PRETTILY	PROHIBIT
POLLUTED	PREACHES	PREVAILS	PROJECTS
POLLUTES	PREAMBLE	PREVENTS	PROLIFIC
POLYGONS	PRECEDED	PREVIEWS	PROLOGUE
POLYMERS	PRECEDES	PREVIOUS	PROLONGS
PONDERED	PRECEPTS	PRICKING	PROMISED
PONTIFIC	PRECINCT	PRIGGISH	PROMISES
POORNESS	PRECIOUS	PRIMEVAL	PROMOTED
POPSICLE	PRECLUDE	PRIMROSE	PROMOTER
POPULACE	PREDATED	PRINCELY	PROMOTES
POPULATE	PREDATES	PRINCESS	PROMPTED
POPULOUS	PREDICTS	PRINTERS	PROMPTER
PORPOISE	PREEMPTS	PRINTING	PROMPTLY
PORRIDGE	PREFACED	PRINTOUT	PRONOUNS
PORTABLE	PREFACES	PRIORITY	PROPERLY
PORTENDS	PREFIXED	PRISONER	PROPERTY
PORTIONS	PREFIXES	PRISTINE	PROPHECY
PORTRAIT	PREGNANT	PRIVATES	PROPHESY
PORTRAYS	PREJUDGE	PROBABLE	PROPHETS
POSITION	PRELUDES	PROBABLY	PROPOSAL
POSITIVE	PREMIERS	PROBATED	PROPOSED
POSSIBLE	PREMISES	PROBATES	PROPOSER
POSSIBLY	PREMIUMS	PROBINGS	PROPOSES
POSTCARD	PRENATAL	PROBLEMS	PROPOUND
POSTMARK	PRENTICE	PROCEEDS	PRORATED
POSTPONE	PREPARED	PROCLAIM	PRORATES
POSTURES	PREPARES	PROCURED	PROSODIC
POTATOES	PRESENCE	PROCURER	PROSPECT
POTBELLY	PRESENTS	PROCURES	PROSPERS
POULTICE	PRESERVE	PRODIGAL	PROSTATE
POUNCING	PRESIDED	PRODUCED	PROTECTS
POUNDERS	PRESIDES	PRODUCER	PROTEGES
POUNDING	PRESSING	PRODUCES	PROTEINS
POWDERED	PRESSURE	PRODUCTS	PROTESTS
POWERFUL	PRESTIGE	PROFFERS	PROTOCOL
POWERING	PRESUMED	PROFILED	PROTOZOA

PROTRACT	PURSUING	QUITTING	RAVAGERS
PROTRUDE	PURSUITS	QUIVERED	RAVAGING
PROUDEST	PURVEYOR	QUIXOTIC	RAVENING
PROVABLE	PUSHDOWN	QUIZZING	RAVENOUS
PROVABLY	PUSSYCAT	QUOTIENT	REACHING
PROVENCE	PUZZLERS	RACCOONS	REACTING
PROVERBS	PUZZLING	RACIALLY	REACTION
PROVIDED	PYRAMIDS	RADIALLY	REACTIVE
PROVIDER	QUACKERY	RADIANCE	REACTORS
PROVIDES	QUADRANT	RADIATED	READABLE
PROVINCE	QUAGMIRE	RADIATES	READIEST
PROVOKED	QUAINTLY	RADIATOR	READINGS
PROVOKES	QUANDARY	RADICALS	READOUTS
PROWLERS	QUANTIFY	RADIOING	READYING
PROWLING	QUANTILE	RADISHES	REALIGNS
PROXIMAL	QUANTITY	RAGGEDLY	REALISTS
PRUDENCE	QUANTIZE	RAILROAD	REALIZED
PRURIENT	QUARRELS	RAILWAYS	REALIZES
PUBLICLY	QUARRIES	RAINCOAT	REALNESS
PUCKERED	QUARTERS	RAINDROP	REAPPEAR
PUDDINGS	QUARTETS	RAINFALL	REARREST
PUDDLING	QUARTILE	RAINIEST	REASONED
PULLINGS	QUASHING	RALLYING	REASONER
PULLOVER	QUAVERED	RAMBLING	REASSIGN
PUMPKINS	QUEEREST	RANCHERS	REASSURE
PUNCHING	QUELLING	RANCHING	REAWAKEN
PUNCTUAL	QUENCHED	RANDOMLY	REBELLED
PUNCTURE	QUENCHES	RANKINGS	REBOOTED
PUNISHED	QUERYING	RANKNESS	REBOUNDS
PUNISHES	QUESTERS	RANSACKS	REBUFFED
PUNITIVE	QUESTING	RANSOMER	REBUILDS
PURCHASE	QUESTION	RAPIDITY	REBUKING
PURIFIED	QUEUEING	RAPTURES	REBUTTAL
PURIFIER	QUICKENS	RARENESS	REBUTTED
PURIFIES	QUICKEST	RASCALLY	RECALLED
PURPLEST	QUIETEST	RASHNESS	RECEDING
PURPORTS	QUIETING	RATIFIED	RECEIPTS
PURPOSED	QUIETUDE	RATIFIES	RECEIVED
PURPOSES	QUILTING	RATIONAL	RECEIVER
PURSUANT	QUIRINAL	RATTLERS	RECEIVES
PURSUERS	QUITTERS	RATTLING	RECENTLY

RECEPTOR	REFINERY	RELIABLE	REPAYING
RECESSED	REFINING	RELIABLY	REPEALED
RECESSES	REFLECTS	RELIANCE	REPEALER
RECITALS	REFLEXES	RELIEVED	REPEATED
RECITING	REFORMAT	RELIEVER	REPEATER
RECKLESS	REFORMED	RELIEVES	REPELLED
RECKONED	REFORMER	RELIGION	REPENTED
RECKONER	REFRAINS	RELISHED	REPHRASE
RECLAIMS	REFUELED	RELISHES	REPLACED
RECODING	REFUGEES	RELIVING	REPLACER
RECOILED	REFUSING	RELOADED	REPLACES
RECORDED	REFUTING	RELOADER	REPLAYED
RECORDER	REGAINED	RELOCATE	REPLICAS
RECOUNTS	REGARDED	REMAINED	REPLYING
RECOURSE	REGIMENT	REMARKED	REPORTED
RECOVERS	REGIONAL	REMEDIAL	REPORTER
RECOVERY	REGISTER	REMEDIED	REPOSING
RECREATE	REGISTRY	REMEDIES	REPRIEVE
RECRUITS	REGULARS	REMEMBER	REPRINTS
RECURSED	REGULATE	REMINDED	REPRISAL
RECURSES	REHEARSE	REMINDER	REPROACH
RECYCLED	REIGNING	REMNANTS	REPROVER
RECYCLES	REINDEER	REMODELS	REPTILES
REDDENED	REINVENT	REQUEST	REPUBLIC
REDEEMED	REJECTED	REMOTELY	REPULSED
REDEEMER	REJECTOR	REMOTEST	REPULSES
REDEFINE	REJOICED	REMOVALS	REQUESTS
REDESIGN	REJOICER	REMOVING	REQUIRED
REDIRECT	REJOICES	RENAMING	REQUIRES
REDOUBLE	REJOINED	RENDERED	REROUTED
REDSTONE	RELABELS	RENEGADE	REROUTES
REDUCERS	RELATING	RENEWING	RESCUERS
REDUCING	RELATION	RENOUNCE	RESCUING
REELECTS	RELATIVE	RENOVATE	RESEARCH
REENTERS	RELAXING	RENOWNED	RESELECT
REFEREED	RELAYING	RENUMBER	RESEMBLE
REFEREES	RELEASED	REOPENED	RESENTED
REFERENT	RELEASES	REORDERS	RESERVED
REFERRAL	RELEGATE	REPAIRED	RESERVER
REFERRED	RELENTED	REPAIRER	RESERVES
REFILLED	RELEVANT	REPARTEE	RESIDENT

RESIDING	RETRACTS	REWORKED	ROTATION
RESIDUAL	RETRAINS	REWRITES	ROUGHEST
RESIDUES	RETREATS	RHAPSODY	ROULETTE
RESIGNED	RETRIERS	RHETORIC	ROUNDEST
RESISTED	RETRIEVE	RHYTHMIC	ROUNDING
RESISTOR	RETRYING	RICHNESS	ROUNDOFF
RESOLUTE	RETURNED	RICKSHAW	ROUTINES
RESOLVED	RETURNER	RICOCHET	ROUTINGS
RESOLVER	RETYPING	RIDDANCE	ROYALIST
RESOLVES	REUNIONS	RIDDLING	REQUEST
RESONANT	REUNITED	RIDICULE	RUDENESS
RESONATE	REUSABLE	RIFLEMAN	RUDIMENT
RESORTED	REVAMPED	RIGHTING	RUEFULLY
RESOUNDS	REVEALED	RIGIDITY	RUFFIANS
RESOURCE	REVELING	RIGOROUS	RUGGEDLY
RESOURCE	REVENGER	RINGINGS	RUMBLING
RESPECTS	REVENUES	RINGSIDE	RUNNABLE
RESPONDS	REVEREND	RIPENESS	RUPTURED
RESPONSE	REVERENT	RIPPLING	RUPTURES
RESTARTS	REVERIFY	RITUALLY	RUSTLERS
RESTATED	REVERING	RIVALLED	RUSTLING
RESTATES	REVERSAL	RIVULETS	RUTHLESS
RESTLESS	REVERSED	ROADSIDE	SABOTAGE
RESTORED	REVERSER	ROADSTER	SACREDLY
RESTORER	REVERSES	ROADWAYS	SADDENED
RESTORES	REVERTED	ROASTING	SADISTIC
RESTRAIN	REVIEWED	ROBOTICS	SAFENESS
RESTRICT	REVIEWER	ROBUSTLY	SAFETIES
RESTROOM	REVILING	ROCKETED	SAGACITY
RESULTED	REVISING	ROLLBACK	SAGITTAL
RESUMING	REVISION	ROMANCER	SAILBOAT
RETAILER	REVISITS	ROMANCES	SAILORLY
RETAINED	REVIVALS	ROMANTIC	SALARIED
RETAINER	REVIVING	ROOMMATE	SALARIES
RETARDED	REVOKING	ROOSTERS	SALESMAN
RETARDER	REVOLTED	ROSEBUDS	SALIVARY
RETICLES	REVOLTER	ROSEBUSH	SALIVATE
RETIRING	REVOLVED	ROSEMARY	SALLYING
RETORTED	REVOLVER	ROSINESS	SALTIEST
RETRACED	REVOLVES	ROTARIAN	SALUTARY
RETRACES	REWARDED	ROTATING	SALUTING

SALVAGED	SCANNERS	SCREAMER	SEEDINGS
SALVAGER	SCANNING	SCREENED	SEEDLING
SALVAGES	SCANTIER	SCREWING	SEETHING
SAMENESS	SCANTILY	SCRIBBLE	SEGMENTS
SAMPLERS	SCARCELY	SCRIBING	SEIZURES
SAMPLING	SCARCITY	SCROLLED	SELECTED
SANCTIFY	SCATTERS	SCROUNGE	SELECTOR
SANCTION	SCENARIO	SCRUTINY	SELENIUM
SANCTITY	SCEPTRES	SCUFFLED	SEMANTIC
SANGUINE	SCHEDULE	SCUFFLES	SEMESTER
SANITARY	SCHEMATA	SCULPTED	SEMINARS
SANSKRIT	SCHEMERS	SCULPTOR	SEMINARY
SAPLINGS	SCHEMING	SCURRIED	SEMINOLE
SAPPHIRE	SCHOLARS	SCUTTLED	SEMITIZE
SARACENS	SCHOOLED	SCUTTLES	SENATORS
SARCASMS	SCHOOLER	SEABOARD	SENSIBLE
SARDONIC	SCHOONER	SEAHORSE	SENSIBLY
SATANISM	SCIENCES	SEAPORTS	SENSUOUS
SATANIST	SCISSORS	SEARCHED	SENTENCE
SATCHELS	SCOFFING	SEARCHER	SENTINEL
SATURATE	SCOLDING	SEARCHES	SENTRIES
SATURDAY	SCOOPING	SEASHORE	SEPARATE
SAUCEPAN	SCORCHED	SEASONAL	SEQUENCE
SAUSAGES	SCORCHER	SEASONED	SERENELY
SAVAGELY	SCORCHES	SEASONER	SERENITY
SAVAGERS	SCORINGS	SECEDING	SERGEANT
SAVAGING	SCORNFUL	SECLUDED	SERIALLY
SAVANNAH	SCORNING	SECONDED	SERPENTS
SAVORING	SCORPION	SECONDER	SERVANTS
SAWMILLS	SCOTSMAN	SECONDLY	SERVICED
SAWTOOTH	SCOTTISH	SECRETED	SERVICES
SAXONIZE	SCOURING	SECRETES	SERVINGS
SCABBARD	SCOUTING	SECRETLY	SESSIONS
SCABROUS	SCOWLING	SECTIONS	SETTABLE
SCAFFOLD	SCRAMBLE	SECURELY	SETTINGS
SCALABLE	SCRAPERS	SECURING	SETTLERS
SCALDING	SCRAPING	SECURITY	SETTLING
SCALINGS	SCRAPPED	SEDIMENT	SEVERELY
SCALLOPS	SCRATCHY	SEDITION	SEVEREST
SCAMPERS	SCRAWLED	SEDUCERS	SEVERING
SCANDALS	SCREAMED	SEDUCING	SEVERITY

SEXTUPLE	SHIVERED	SHUTTLED	SIXPENCE
SEXUALLY	SHIVERER	SHUTTLES	SIXTEENS
SHACKLED	SHOCKERS	SIBLINGS	SIXTIETH
SHACKLES	SHOCKING	SICKNESS	SKELETAL
SHADIEST	SHOEHORN	SICKROOM	SKELETON
SHADINGS	SHOELACE	SIDEBAND	SKEPTICS
SHADOWED	SHOOTERS	SIDELINE	SKETCHED
SHAKABLE	SHOOTING	SIDEREAL	SKETCHES
SHAKABLY	SHOPPERS	SIDESHOW	SKIDDING
SHAMBLES	SHOPPING	SIDESTEP	SKILLFUL
SHAMEFUL	SHOPWORN	SIDEWALK	SKIMMING
SHAMROCK	SHORTAGE	SIDEWAYS	SKIMPING
SHANTIES	SHORTCUT	SIDEWISE	SKINDIVE
SHARABLE	SHORTENS	SIGHTING	SKINNERS
SHARPENS	SHORTEST	SIGNALED	SKINNING
SHARPEST	SHORTING	SIGNALLY	SKIPPERS
SHATTERS	SHORTISH	SILENCED	SKIPPING
SHAVINGS	SHOTGUNS	SILENCER	SKIRMISH
SHEARING	SHOULDER	SILENCES	SKIRTING
SHEDDING	SHOUTERS	SILENTLY	SKULKING
SHEETING	SHOUTING	SILICATE	SKULLCAP
SHELLING	SHOVELED	SILICONE	SKYLARKS
SHELTERS	SHOWBOAT	SILKIEST	SKYLIGHT
SHELVING	SHOWCASE	SILLIEST	SLACKING
SHEPHERD	SHOWDOWN	SILVERED	SLAMMING
SHERIFFS	SHOWERED	SIMMERED	SLANDERS
SHIELDED	SHOWINGS	SIMPLEST	SLANTING
SHIFTERS	SHOWROOM	SIMPLIFY	SLAPPING
SHIFTIER	SHRAPNEL	SIMULATE	SLASHING
SHIFTILY	SHREDDER	SINFULLY	SLAVIZES
SHIFTING	SHREWDLY	SINGABLE	SLEEPERS
SHILLING	SHRIEKED	SINGLING	SLEEPILY
SHINBONE	SHRILLED	SINGSONG	SLEEPING
SHINGLES	SHROUDED	SINGULAR	SLICKERS
SHIPMATE	SHRUNKEN	SINISTER	SLIGHTED
SHIPMENT	SHUDDERS	SINKHOLE	SLIGHTER
SHIPPERS	SHUFFLED	SINUSOID	SLIGHTLY
SHIPPING	SHUFFLES	SISTERLY	SLINGING
SHIPYARD	SHUTDOWN	SITTINGS	SLIPPAGE
SHIRKING	SHUTTERS	SITUATED	SLIPPERS
SHIRTING	SHUTTING	SITUATES	SPINSOFT

SLIPPERY	SNEAKING	SOMETIME	SPEEDUPS
SLIPPING	SNEERING	SOMEWHAT	SPELLERS
SLOPPING	SNEEZING	SOOTHING	SPELLING
SLOTHFUL	SNIFFING	SORCERER	SPENDERS
SLOTTING	SNOBBERY	SORDIDLY	SPENDING
SLOUCHED	SNOBBISH	SORENESS	SPILLING
SLOUCHES	SNOOPING	SORORITY	SPINALLY
SLOWDOWN	SNORTING	SORRIEST	SPINDLED
SLOWNESS	SNOWBALL	SOUNDEST	SPINNERS
SLUGGISH	SNOWFALL	SOUNDING	SPINNING
SLUMMING	SNOWIEST	SOURNESS	SPINSTER
SLURRING	SNOWSHOE	SOUTHERN	SPIRALLY
SMACKING	SNUFFING	SOUVENIR	SPIRITED
SMALLEST	SNUGGLED	SPACEWAR	SPITEFUL
SMALLISH	SNUGGLES	SPACINGS	SPITFIRE
SMALLPOX	SNUGNESS	SPACIOUS	SPITTING
SMARTEST	SOBERING	SPANDREL	SPLASHED
SMASHERS	SOBRIETY	SPANKING	SPLASHES
SMASHING	SOCIABLE	SPANNERS	SPLENDID
SMEARING	SOCIABLY	SPANNING	SPLICERS
SMELLING	SOCIALLY	SPARKING	SPLICING
SMOCKING	SOCIETAL	SPARRING	SPLINTER
SMOKABLE	SOFTBALL	SPARROWS	SPLITTER
SMOOTHED	SOFTENED	SPARSELY	SPOILAGE
SMOOTHER	SOFTNESS	SPARSEST	SPOILERS
SMOOTHES	SOFTWARE	SPAWNING	SPOILING
SMOOTHLY	SOLDERED	SPEAKERS	SPONGERS
SMOTHERS	SOLDIERS	SPEAKING	SPONGING
SMUGGLED	SOLEMNLY	SPECIALS	SPONSORS
SMUGGLER	SOLENOID	SPECIFIC	SPOOLERS
SMUGGLES	SOLICITS	SPECIMEN	SPOOLING
SNAPPERS	SOLIDIFY	SPECIOUS	SPOONFUL
SNAPPILY	SOLIDITY	SPECKLED	SPOONING
SNAPPING	SOLITARY	SPECKLES	SPORADIC
SNAPSHOT	SOLITUDE	SPECTRAL	SPORTING
SNARLING	SOLSTICE	SPECTRES	SPORTIVE
SNATCHED	SOLUTION	SPECTRUM	SPOTLESS
SNATCHES	SOLVABLE	SPEECHES	SPOTTERS
SNEAKERS	SOLVENTS	SPEEDERS	SPOTTING
SNEAKIER	SOMBERLY	SPEEDILY	SPOUTING
SNEAKILY	SOMEBODY	SPEEDING	SPRAWLED

SPRAYING	STAMMERS	STERLING	STRAINED
SPREADER	STAMPEDE	STETSONS	STRAINER
SPRINGER	STAMPERS	STEWARDS	STRAITEN
SPRINKLE	STAMPING	STICKERS	STRANDED
SPRINTED	STANDARD	STICKIER	STRANGER
SPRINTER	STANDING	STICKILY	STRANGLE
SPROCKET	STANDISH	STICKING	STRATEGY
SPROUTED	STANDOFF	STIFFENS	STRATIFY
SPURIOUS	STAPLING	STIFFEST	STREAKED
SPURNING	STARCHED	STIFLING	STREAMED
SPURTING	STARFISH	STIGMATA	STREAMER
SPYGLASS	STARLING	STILETTO	STRENGTH
SQUABBLE	STARRING	STILLEST	STRESSED
SQUADRON	STARTERS	STILLING	STRESSES
SQUANDER	STARTING	STIMULUS	STRICKEN
SQUARELY	STARTLED	STINGING	STRICTER
SQUAREST	STARTLES	STINKERS	STRICTLY
SQUARING	STARTUPS	STINKING	STRIDING
SQUASHED	STARVING	STIPENDS	STRIKERS
SQUAWKED	STATIONS	STIRLING	STRIKING
SQUEAKED	STATUSES	STIRRERS	STRINGED
SQUEALED	STATUTES	STIRRING	STRINGER
SQUEEZED	STEADIED	STITCHED	STRIPPED
SQUEEZER	STEADIER	STITCHES	STRIPPER
SQUEEZES	STEADIES	STOCKADE	STRIVING
SQUINTED	STEADILY	STOCKERS	STROKERS
SQUIRMED	STEALING	STOCKING	STROKING
SQUIRREL	STEALTHY	STOOPING	STROLLED
STABBING	STEAMERS	STOPCOCK	STROLLER
STABLING	STEAMING	STOPOVER	STRONGER
STACKING	STEELERS	STOPPAGE	STRONGLY
STAFFING	STEELING	STOPPERS	STRUGGLE
STAGGERS	STEEPEST	STOPPING	STUBBORN
STAGNANT	STEEPING	STORAGES	STUDENTS
STAGNATE	STEEPLES	STOREYED	STUDIOUS
STAINING	STEERING	STORMIER	STUDYING
STAIRWAY	STEMMING	STORMING	STUFFIER
STALKING	STENCHES	STOUTEST	STUFFING
STALLING	STENCILS	STRADDLE	STUMBLED
STALLION	STEPPING	STRAGGLE	STUMBLES
STALWART	STEPWISE	STRAIGHT	STUMPING

STUNNING	SUFFIXED	SURMISES	SWITCHES
STUPIDLY	SUFFIXER	SURMOUNT	SWOOPING
STURGEON	SUFFIXES	SURNAMES	SYCAMORE
STYLIZED	SUFFRAGE	SURPRISE	SYLLABLE
SUBCLASS	SUGARING	SURROUND	SYMBOLIC
SUBCYCLE	SUGGESTS	SURVEYED	SYMMETRY
SUBFILES	SUICIDAL	SURVEYOR	SYMPATHY
SUBGOALS	SUICIDES	SURVIVAL	SYMPHONY
SUBGRAPH	SUITABLE	SURVIVED	SYMPOSIA
SUBGROUP	SUITABLY	SURVIVES	SYMPTOMS
SUBJECTS	SUITCASE	SURVIVOR	SYNAPSES
SUBLIMED	SULFURIC	SUSPECTS	SYNAPTIC
SUBLISTS	SULLENLY	SUSPENDS	SYNDROME
SUBMERGE	SULPHATE	SUSPENSE	SYNONYMS
SUBMODES	SUMMITRY	SUSTAINS	SYNOPSES
SUBPARTS	SUMMONED	SWABBING	SYNOPSIS
SUBPOENA	SUMMONER	SWALLOWS	SYNOPSYS
SUBPROOF	SUNBEAMS	SWAMPING	SYNTAXES
SUBSIDED	SUNBURNT	SWANLIKE	SYRACUSE
SUBSIDES	SUNDRIES	SWAPPING	SYRINGES
SUBSISTS	SUNGLASS	SWARMING	SYSTEMIC
SUBSUMED	SUNLIGHT	SWASTIKA	TABLEAUS
SUBSUMES	SUNSHINE	SWEARING	TABULATE
SUBTASKS	SUPERBLY	SWEATERS	TAILORED
SUBTITLE	SUPEREGO	SWEATING	TALENTED
SUBTLEST	SUPERIOR	SWEEPERS	TALLNESS
SUBTLETY	SUPPLANT	SWEEPING	TAMENESS
SUBTOTAL	SUPPLIED	SWEETENS	TAMPERED
SUBTRACT	SUPPLIER	SWEETEST	TANGENTS
SUBURBAN	SUPPLIES	SWEETISH	TANGIBLE
SUBURBIA	SUPPORTS	SWELLING	TANGIBLY
SUBVERTS	SUPPOSED	SWERVING	TANTRUMS
SUCCEEDS	SUPPOSES	SWIFTEST	TAPERING
SUCCINCT	SUPPRESS	SWIMMERS	TAPESTRY
SUCCUMBS	SURENESS	SWIMMING	TARGETED
SUCKLING	SURETIES	SWIMSUIT	TARTNESS
SUDDENLY	SURFACED	SWINGERS	TASTEFUL
SUFFERED	SURFACES	SWINGING	TATTERED
SUFFERER	SURGEONS	SWIRLING	TATTOOED
SUFFICED	SURGICAL	SWITCHED	TAUNTING
SUFFICES	SURMISED	SWITCHER	TAUTNESS

TAXATION	TEXTURES	THUMPING	TOTTERED
TAXICABS	THANKFUL	THUNDERS	TOUCHIER
TAXONOMY	THANKING	THURSDAY	TOUCHILY
TAXPAYER	THATCHES	THWARTED	TOUCHING
TEACHERS	THEATERS	TICKLING	TOURISTS
TEACHING	THEMATIC	TICKLISH	TOWELING
TEASPOON	THEOLOGY	TIDINESS	TOWELLED
TEENAGED	THEOREMS	TIGHTENS	TOWERING
TEENAGER	THEORIES	TIGHTEST	TOWNSHIP
TEETHING	THEORIST	TILLABLE	TRACINGS
TELEGRAM	THEORIZE	TIMBERED	TRACKERS
TELETYPE	THICKENS	TIMELESS	TRACKING
TELEVISE	THICKEST	TIMEOUTS	TRACTIVE
TEMPERED	THICKETS	TIMIDITY	TRACTORS
TEMPLATE	THIEVING	TINCTURE	TRADEOFF
TEMPORAL	THIMBLES	TINGLING	TRAFFICS
TEMPTERS	THINKERS	TININESS	TRAILERS
TEMPTING	THINKING	TINKERED	TRAILING
TENDENCY	THINNESS	TINKLING	TRAINEES
TENDERLY	THINNEST	TINNIEST	TRAINERS
TENEMENT	THIRSTED	TIRELESS	TRAINING
TENSIONS	THIRTEEN	TIRESOME	TRAITORS
TENTACLE	THIRTIES	TOASTING	TRAMPING
TERMINAL	THOROUGH	TOGETHER	TRAMPLED
TERMINUS	THOUGHTS	TOGGLING	TRAMPLER
TERMWISE	THOUSAND	TOLERANT	TRAMPLES
TERRACED	THRASHED	TOLERATED	TRANQUIL
TERRACES	THRASHER	TOMAHAWK	TRANSACT
TERRAINS	THRASHES	TOMATOES	TRANSFER
TERRIBLE	THREADED	TOMORROW	TRANSMIT
TERRIBLY	THREADER	TOPOLOGY	TRAPPERS
TERRIERS	THREATEN	TOPPLING	TRAPPING
TERRIFIC	THRILLED	TORRENTS	TRAVERSE
TERTIARY	THRILLER	TORTOISE	TRAVESTY
TESTABLE	THRIVING	TORTURED	TREADING
TESTICLE	THROATED	TORTURER	TREASURE
TESTINGS	THROBBED	TORTURES	TREASURY
TEUTONIC	THROTTLE	TOTALING	TREATIES
TEXTBOOK	THROWING	TOTALITY	TREATING
TEXTILES	THRUSTER	TOTALLED	TREATISE
TEXTURED	THUMBING	TOTALLER	TREETOPS

TREMBLED	TUMBLERS	UNFOLDED	UNSTEADY
TREMBLES	TUMBLING	UNGUIDED	UNSUITED
TRENCHER	TUNNELED	UNHARMED	UNTAGGED
TRENCHES	TURGIDLY	UNHEEDED	UNTAPPED
TRENDING	TURMOILS	UNICORNS	UNTESTED
TRESPASS	TURNABLE	UNICYCLE	UNTIMELY
TRIANGLE	TURNINGS	UNIFIERS	UNTOWARD
TRIASSIC	TURNOVER	UNIFORMS	UNUSABLE
TRIBUNAL	TUTORIAL	UNIFYING	UNVEILED
TRIBUNES	TUTORING	UNIONIZE	UNWANTED
TRIBUTES	TWENTIES	UNIQUELY	UNWIELDY
TRICKIER	TWILIGHT	UNIVALVE	UNWINDER
TRICKING	TWINKLED	UNIVERSE	UNWISELY
TRICKLED	TWINKLER	UNJUSTLY	UNWISEST
TRICKLES	TWINKLES	UNKINDLY	UNWORTHY
TRIFLING	TWIRLING	UNKNOWNS	UPCOMING
TRIGGERS	TWISTERS	UNLAWFUL	UPDATING
TRIGRAMS	TWISTING	UNLIKELY	UPGRADED
TRILLION	TWITCHED	UNLINKED	UPGRADES
TRIMMEST	TYPIFIED	UNLOADED	UPHOLDER
TRIMMING	TYPIFIES	UNLOCKED	UPRISING
TRIMNESS	UBIQUITY	UNMANNED	UPROOTED
TRINKETS	UGLINESS	UNMARKED	UPSTAIRS
TRIPLETS	ULTIMATE	UNMASKED	UPSTREAM
TRIPLING	UMBRELLA	UNNEEDED	UPTURNED
TRIUMPHS	UNABATED	UNNERVED	URGENTLY
TROLLEYS	UNAWARES	UNNERVES	URINATED
TROOPERS	UNBIASED	UNOPENED	URINATES
TROPHIES	UNBLOCKS	UNPACKED	USEFULLY
TROPICAL	UNBROKEN	UNPARSED	USHERING
TROUBLED	UNCAUGHT	UNPROVEN	UTENSILS
TROUBLES	UNCLOSED	UNQUOTED	UTILIZED
TROUSERS	UNCOMMON	UNRAVELS	UTILIZES
TRUCKERS	UNCOVERS	UNROLLED	UTOPIANS
TRUCKING	UNDERLIE	UNSAFELY	UTTERING
TRUNCATE	UNDERWAY	UNSEEDED	VACANTLY
TRUSTEES	UNDOINGS	UNSHAKEN	VACATING
TRUSTFUL	UNEASILY	UNSHARED	VACATION
TRUSTING	UNENDING	UNSIGNED	VACUUMED
TRUTHFUL	UNEVENLY	UNSOLVED	VAGABOND
TUESDAYS	UNFAIRLY	UNSTABLE	VAGARIES

VALENCES	VIBRATOR	WALLOWED	WHIMSIES
VALIDATE	VICINITY	WALRUSES	WHIPPERS
VALIDITY	VICTUALS	WALTZING	WHIPPING
VALUABLE	VIGILANT	WANDERED	WHIRLING
VALUABLY	VIGNETTE	WANDERER	WHIRRING
VANGUARD	VIGOROUS	WANTONLY	WHISKERS
VANISHED	VILENESS	WARBLING	WHISKING
VANISHER	VILIFIED	WARDROBE	WHISPERS
VANISHES	VILIFIES	WARINESS	WHISTLED
VANITIES	VILLAGER	WARNINGS	WHISTLER
VANQUISH	VILLAGES	WARRANTS	WHISTLES
VARIABLE	VILLAINS	WARRANTY	WHITENED
VARIABLY	VILLAINY	WARRIORS	WHITENER
VARIANCE	VINEYARD	WARSHIPS	WHITTIER
VARIANTS	VIOLATED	WASHINGS	WHITTLED
VARITYPE	VIOLATES	WASTEFUL	WHITTLES
VARYINGS	VIOLATOR	WATCHERS	WHIZZING
VASTNESS	VIOLENCE	WATCHFUL	WHOMEVER
VAULTING	VIRTUOSO	WATCHING	WHOOPING
VEGANISM	VIRTUOUS	WATCHMAN	WICKEDLY
VEGETATE	VIRULENT	WATERING	WIDEBAND
VEHEMENT	VISCOUNT	WATERWAY	WIDENING
VEHICLES	VISITING	WEAKENED	WIDOWERS
VELOCITY	VISITORS	WEAKNESS	WIELDING
VENOMOUS	VISUALLY	WEARABLE	WIGHTMAN
VENTURED	VITALITY	WEARIEST	WILDNESS
VENTURER	VOCATION	WEARYING	WILINESS
VENTURES	VOLATILE	WEATHERS	WINDMILL
VERACITY	VOLCANIC	WEDDINGS	WINNINGS
VERANDAS	VOLCANOS	WEEKENDS	WINTERED
VERBALLY	VOLITION	WEIGHING	WIRELESS
VERIFIED	VOLTAGES	WEIGHTED	WIRINESS
VERIFIER	VOMITING	WELCOMED	WITCHING
VERIFIES	VOUCHERS	WELCOMES	WITHDRAW
VERSIONS	VOUCHING	WESTWARD	WITHDREW
VERTICAL	VOYAGERS	WHACKING	WITHHELD
VERTICES	VOYAGING	WHATEVER	WITHHOLD
VESTIGES	VULGARLY	WHEELING	WOEFULLY
VETERANS	VULTURES	WHENEVER	WONDERED
VEXATION	WAITRESS	WHEREVER	WONDROUS
VIBRATED	WAKENING	WHIMPERS	WOODCOCK

WOODENLY	YOUNGEST	ABSURDITY	ACTIVATES
WOODLAND	YOURSELF	ABUNDANCE	ACTIVATOR
WOODWORK	YOUTHFUL	ABYSMALLY	ACTIVISTS
WORKABLE	ZILLIONS	ACADEMICS	ACTRESSES
WORKABLY		ACADEMIES	ACTUALITY
WORKBOOK	**9**	ACCENTING	ACTUARIAL
WORKINGS		ACCENTUAL	ACTUATING
WORKLOAD	ABASEMENT	ACCEPTERS	ACTUATORS
WORKSHOP	ABATEMENT	ACCEPTING	ACUTENESS
WORRIERS	ABDOMINAL	ACCEPTORS	ADAMANTLY
WORRYING	ABDUCTION	ACCESSING	ADAPTABLE
WORSHIPS	ABDUCTORS	ACCESSION	ADDICTING
WOUNDING	ABHORRENT	ACCESSORS	ADDICTION
WRANGLED	ABHORRING	ACCESSORY	ADDITIONS
WRANGLER	ABILITIES	ACCIDENTS	ADDITIVES
WRAPPERS	ABJECTION	ACCLAIMED	ADDRESSED
WRAPPING	ABOLISHED	ACCLIMATE	ADDRESSEE
WREATHED	ABOLISHER	ACCOLADES	ADDRESSER
WREATHES	ABOLISHES	ACCOMPANY	ADDRESSES
WRECKAGE	ABOLITION	ACCORDERS	ADDUCIBLE
WRECKERS	ABOMINATE	ACCORDING	ADDUCTING
WRECKING	ABORIGINE	ACCORDION	ADDUCTION
WRENCHED	ABORTIONS	ACCOSTING	ADHERENCE
WRENCHES	ABOUNDING	ACCOUNTED	ADHERENTS
WRESTLER	ABRASIONS	ACCRETION	ADHESIONS
WRESTLES	ABRIDGING	ACCUSTOMS	ADHESIVES
WRETCHED	ABROGATED	ACETYLENE	ADIABATIC
WRETCHES	ABROGATES	ACHIEVERS	ADJACENCY
WRIGGLED	ABSCESSED	ACHIEVING	ADJECTIVE
WRIGGLER	ABSCESSES	ACIDITIES	ADJOINING
WRIGGLES	ABSCISSAS	ACIDULOUS	ADJOURNED
WRINKLED	ABSCONDED	ACOUSTICS	ADJUDGING
WRINKLES	ABSENTEES	ACQUAINTS	ADJUSTERS
WRITABLE	ABSENTING	ACQUIESCE	ADJUSTING
WRITHING	ABSOLUTES	ACQUIRING	ADJUSTORS
WRITINGS	ABSOLVING	ACQUITTAL	ADJUTANTS
WRONGING	ABSORBENT	ACQUITTED	ADMIRABLE
YEARNING	ABSORBING	ACQUITTER	ADMIRABLY
YELLOWED	ABSTAINED	ACROBATIC	ADMIRALTY
YELLOWER	ABSTAINER	ACROPOLIS	ADMISSION
YIELDING	ABSTRACTS	ACTIVATED	ADMITTERS

ADMITTING	AFTERLIFE	ALLOCATES	AMPLITUDE
ADMIXTURE	AFTERMATH	ALLOCATOR	AMPUTATED
ADOPTIONS	AFTERMOST	ALLOPHONE	AMPUTATES
ADORATION	AFTERNOON	ALLOTMENT	AMUSEMENT
ADORNMENT	AFTERWARD	ALLOTTING	AMUSINGLY
ADSORBING	AGGRAVATE	ALLOWABLE	ANACONDAS
ADULATING	AGGREGATE	ALLOWABLY	ANAEROBIC
ADULATION	AGGRESSOR	ALLOWANCE	ANALOGIES
ADULTERER	AGGRIEVED	ALLUSIONS	ANALOGOUS
ADULTHOOD	AGGRIEVES	ALONENESS	ANALOGUES
ADUMBRATE	AGITATING	ALONGSIDE	ANALYZERS
ADVANCING	AGITATION	ALOOFNESS	ANALYZING
ADVANTAGE	AGITATORS	ALPHABETS	ANAPHORIC
ADVENTIST	AGNOSTICS	ALSATIANS	ANARCHISM
ADVENTURE	AGONIZING	ALTERABLE	ANARCHIST
ADVERBIAL	AGREEABLE	ALTERNATE	ANCESTORS
ADVERSARY	AGREEABLY	ALTITUDES	ANCESTRAL
ADVERSELY	AGREEMENT	AMAZEMENT	ANCHORAGE
ADVERSITY	AIMLESSLY	AMAZINGLY	ANCHORING
ADVERTISE	AIRFIELDS	AMBIGUITY	ANCHORITE
ADVISABLE	AIRFRAMES	AMBIGUOUS	ANCHOVIES
ADVISABLY	AIRPLANES	AMBITIONS	ANCIENTLY
ADVISEDLY	AIRSTRIPS	AMBITIOUS	ANCILLARY
ADVOCATED	ALABASTER	AMBROSIAL	ANECDOTAL
ADVOCATES	ALBATROSS	AMBULANCE	ANECDOTES
AEROSPACE	ALERTEDLY	AMBUSCADE	ANGLICANS
AESTHETIC	ALERTNESS	AMENDMENT	ANGUISHED
AFFECTING	ALGAECIDE	AMENITIES	ANGULARLY
AFFECTION	ALGEBRAIC	AMERICANA	ANHYDROUS
AFFECTIVE	ALGORITHM	AMERICANS	ANIMATELY
AFFIANCED	ALIENATED	AMORALITY	ANIMATING
AFFIDAVIT	ALIENATES	AMORPHOUS	ANIMATION
AFFILIATE	ALIGNMENT	AMORTIZED	ANIMATORS
AFFIRMING	ALKALOIDS	AMORTIZES	ANIMOSITY
AFFLICTED	ALLEGEDLY	AMOUNTERS	ANNOTATED
AFFLUENCE	ALLEGORIC	AMOUNTING	ANNOTATES
AFFORDING	ALLERGIES	AMPERSAND	ANNOUNCED
AFFRICATE	ALLEYWAYS	AMPHIBIAN	ANNOUNCER
AFFRONTED	ALLIANCES	AMPLIFIED	ANNOUNCES
AFORESAID	ALLIGATOR	AMPLIFIER	ANNOYANCE
AFTERGLOW	ALLOCATED	AMPLIFIES	ANNULLING

ANNULMENT	APPELLATE	ARGONAUTS	ASSASSINS
ANOINTING	APPENDAGE	ARGUMENTS	ASSAULTED
ANOMALIES	APPENDERS	ARMADILLO	ASSEMBLED
ANOMALOUS	APPENDING	ARMAMENTS	ASSEMBLER
ANONYMITY	APPERTAIN	ARMCHAIRS	ASSEMBLES
ANONYMOUS	APPETITES	ARMISTICE	ASSENTING
ANSWERERS	APPETIZER	ARPEGGIOS	ASSERTERS
ANSWERING	APPLAUDED	ARRAIGNED	ASSERTING
ANTARCTIC	APPLEJACK	ARRANGERS	ASSERTION
ANTEATERS	APPLIANCE	ARRANGING	ASSERTIVE
ANTELOPES	APPLICANT	ARRESTERS	ASSESSING
ANTHOLOGY	APPOINTED	ARRESTING	ASSESSORS
ANTIDOTES	APPOINTEE	ARRESTORS	ASSIDUITY
ANTIPATHY	APPOINTER	ARROGANCE	ASSIDUOUS
ANTIPODES	APPORTION	ARROGATED	ASSIGNEES
ANTIQUATE	APPRAISAL	ARROGATES	ASSIGNERS
ANTIQUITY	APPRAISED	ARROWHEAD	ASSIGNING
ANTISERUM	APPRAISER	ARTERIOLE	ASSISTANT
ANTITOXIN	APPRAISES	ARTHRITIS	ASSISTING
ANTITRUST	APPREHEND	ARTHROPOD	ASSOCIATE
ANXIETIES	APPRISING	ARTICHOKE	ASSONANCE
ANXIOUSLY	APPROBATE	ARTIFACTS	ASSURANCE
APARTMENT	APPROVALS	ARTIFICER	ASSUREDLY
APATHETIC	APPROVERS	ARTIFICES	ASTERISKS
APERIODIC	APPROVING	ARTILLERY	ASTEROIDS
APETALOUS	APTITUDES	ASCENDANT	ASTOUNDED
APHORISMS	AQUEDUCTS	ASCENDENT	ASTROLOGY
APHRODITE	ARABESQUE	ASCENDERS	ASTRONAUT
APOCRYPHA	ARABICIZE	ASCENDING	ASTRONOMY
APOLOGIES	ARACHNIDS	ASCENSION	ASYMMETRY
APOLOGIST	ARBITRARY	ASCERTAIN	ASYMPTOTE
APOLOGIZE	ARBITRATE	ASCRIBING	ATAVISTIC
APOSTOLIC	ARCHANGEL	ASHAMEDLY	ATEMPORAL
APPALLING	ARCHENEMY	ASPARAGUS	ATHEISTIC
APPARATUS	ARCHETYPE	ASPERSION	ATHLETICS
APPEALERS	ARCHIBALD	ASPIRANTS	ATOMIZING
APPEALING	ARCHITECT	ASPIRATED	ATONEMENT
APPEARERS	ARCHIVERS	ASPIRATES	ATROCIOUS
APPEARING	ARCHIVING	ASPIRATOR	ATROPHIED
APPEASING	ARCHIVIST	ASSAILANT	ATROPHIES
APPELLANT	ARDUOUSLY	ASSAILING	ATTACHERS

ATTACHING	AUTONOMIC	BALANCERS	BATHROBES
ATTACKERS	AUTOPILOT	BALANCING	BATHROOMS
ATTACKING	AUTOPSIED	BALCONIES	BATTALION
ATTAINERS	AUTOPSIES	BALKINESS	BATTERIES
ATTAINING	AUXILIARY	BALLERINA	BATTERING
ATTEMPTED	AVAILABLE	BALLISTIC	BEACHHEAD
ATTEMPTER	AVAILABLY	BALLOONED	BEARDLESS
ATTENDANT	AVALANCHE	BALLOONER	BEATITUDE
ATTENDEES	AVERAGING	BALLPARKS	BEAUTEOUS
ATTENDERS	AVERSIONS	BALLROOMS	BEAUTIFUL
ATTENDING	AVOCATION	BANDAGING	BECALMING
ATTENTION	AVOIDABLE	BANDSTAND	BECKONING
ATTENTIVE	AVOIDABLY	BANISHING	BEDAZZLED
ATTENUATE	AVOIDANCE	BANISTERS	BEDAZZLES
ATTESTING	AWAKENING	BANKRUPTS	BEDEVILED
ATTITUDES	AWARENESS	BANTERING	BEDRAGGLE
ATTORNEYS	AWFULNESS	BAPTISMAL	BEDRIDDEN
ATTRACTED	AWKWARDLY	BAPTISTRY	BEDSPREAD
ATTRACTOR	AXIOMATIC	BAPTIZING	BEDSPRING
ATTRIBUTE	BACHELORS	BARBARIAN	BEDSTEADS
ATTRITION	BACKBENDS	BARBARISM	BEEFSTEAK
AUDACIOUS	BACKBOARD	BARBARITY	BEFALLING
AUDIENCES	BACKBONES	BARBAROUS	BEFITTING
AUDIOGRAM	BACKDROPS	BARBECUED	BEFOGGING
AUDIOLOGY	BACKORDER	BARBECUES	BEFOULING
AUDITIONS	BACKPACKS	BAREFACED	BEFRIENDS
AUGMENTED	BACKPLANE	BARGAINED	BEFUDDLED
AUSTERELY	BACKPLATE	BARITONES	BEFUDDLES
AUSTERITY	BACKSLASH	BARNSTORM	BEGETTING
AUTHENTIC	BACKSPACE	BARNYARDS	BEGINNERS
AUTHORING	BACKSTAGE	BAROMETER	BEGINNING
AUTHORITY	BACKTRACK	BARRELLED	BEGRUDGED
AUTHORIZE	BACKWARDS	BARRICADE	BEGRUDGES
AUTOCRACY	BACKWATER	BARTENDER	BEGUILING
AUTOCRATS	BACKYARDS	BARTERING	BEHEADING
AUTOGRAPH	BACTERIAL	BASEBALLS	BEHEMOTHS
AUTOINDEX	BACTERIUM	BASEBOARD	BEHOLDERS
AUTOMATED	BADGERING	BASELINES	BEHOLDING
AUTOMATES	BADMINTON	BASEMENTS	BELATEDLY
AUTOMATIC	BAGATELLE	BASICALLY	BELIEVERS
AUTOMATON	BALALAIKA	BASSINETS	BELIEVING

BELITTLED	BINOCULAR	BLOCKADED	BOULEVARD
BELITTLES	BINUCLEAR	BLOCKADES	BOUNDLESS
BELLICOSE	BIOGRAPHY	BLOCKAGES	BOUNTEOUS
BELLOWING	BIOLOGIST	BLOODBATH	BOUNTIFUL
BELLYACHE	BIOSPHERE	BLOODIEST	BOURGEOIS
BELLYFULL	BIPARTITE	BLOODLESS	BOWSTRING
BELONGING	BIRDBATHS	BLOODSHED	BOYCOTTED
BEMOANING	BIRTHDAYS	BLOODSHOT	BOYFRIEND
BENCHMARK	BISECTING	BLOSSOMED	BRACELETS
BENIGHTED	BISECTION	BLUDGEONS	BRACKETED
BEQUEATHS	BISECTORS	BLUEBERRY	BRAINSTEM
BEREAVING	BITTEREST	BLUEBIRDS	BRAINWASH
BERYLLIUM	BITTERNUT	BLUEPRINT	BRANCHING
BESEECHES	BIVARIATE	BLUNDERED	BRASHNESS
BESETTING	BLACKBIRD	BLUNTNESS	BRASSIERE
BESIEGERS	BLACKENED	BLUSTERED	BRAVENESS
BESIEGING	BLACKFOOT	BOASTINGS	BREACHERS
BESOTTING	BLACKJACK	BOATHOUSE	BREACHING
BETRAYING	BLACKLIST	BOATLOADS	BREAKABLE
BETROTHAL	BLACKMAIL	BOATSWAIN	BREAKAWAY
BETROTHED	BLACKNESS	BOATYARDS	BREAKDOWN
BETTERING	BLACKOUTS	BOBOLINKS	BREAKFAST
BEVERAGES	BLAMELESS	BODYGUARD	BREATHERS
BEWAILING	BLANCHING	BOLSTERED	BREATHING
BEWILDERS	BLANDNESS	BOMBARDED	BREWERIES
BEWITCHED	BLANKETED	BOMBASTIC	BRIEFCASE
BEWITCHES	BLANKETER	BOMBPROOF	BRIEFINGS
BICKERING	BLANKNESS	BOOKCASES	BRIEFNESS
BICONCAVE	BLASPHEME	BOOKSHELF	BRIGADIER
BICYCLERS	BLASPHEMY	BOOKSTORE	BRIGADOON
BICYCLING	BLATANTLY	BOOMERANG	BRIGHTENS
BIFURCATE	BLEACHERS	BOOTSTRAP	BRIGHTEST
BIJECTION	BLEACHING	BORDELLOS	BRILLIANT
BIJECTIVE	BLEAKNESS	BORDERING	BRIMSTONE
BILATERAL	BLEEDINGS	BORROWERS	BRISKNESS
BILINGUAL	BLEMISHES	BORROWING	BRISTLING
BILLBOARD	BLESSINGS	BOTANICAL	BROACHING
BILLETING	BLINDFOLD	BOTANISTS	BROADCAST
BILLIARDS	BLINDNESS	BOTHERING	BROADENED
BILLIONTH	BLISTERED	BOTTOMING	BROADENER
BIMONTHLY	BLIZZARDS	BOTULINUS	BROADNESS

BROADSIDE	BUTTERCUP	CAPITALLY	CAUSALITY
BROCHURES	BUTTERERS	CAPRICORN	CAUSATION
BROKERAGE	BUTTERFAT	CAPTAINED	CAUSEWAYS
BRONCHIAL	BUTTERFLY	CAPTIVATE	CAUSTICLY
BROTHERLY	BUTTERING	CAPTIVITY	CAUTIONED
BROWBEATS	BUTTERNUT	CAPTURERS	CAUTIONER
BROWNNESS	BUTTONING	CAPTURING	CAVERNOUS
BRUSHFIRE	BYPASSING	CARBONATE	CEASELESS
BRUSHLIKE	BYPRODUCT	CARBONIZE	CELEBRATE
BRUSQUELY	BYSTANDER	CARBUNCLE	CELEBRITY
BRUTALITY	BYZANTINE	CARCASSES	CELESTIAL
BRUTALIZE	BYZANTIUM	CARCINOMA	CELLULOSE
BUCKSKINS	CABDRIVER	CARDBOARD	CEMENTING
BUCKWHEAT	CADILLACS	CARDINALS	CENSORING
BUDDHISTS	CAESARIAN	CAREFULLY	CENTENARY
BUDGETARY	CAESARIZE	CARESSING	CENTIPEDE
BUDGETERS	CAFETERIA	CARETAKER	CENTRALLY
BUDGETING	CALCULATE	CARIBBEAN	CENTURIES
BUFFALOES	CALENDARS	CARNATION	CERTAINLY
BUFFERING	CALIBRATE	CARNIVALS	CERTAINTY
BUFFETING	CALLOUSED	CARPENTER	CERTIFIED
BUILDINGS	CALLOUSLY	CARPENTRY	CERTIFIER
BULKHEADS	CALMINGLY	CARPETING	CERTIFIES
BULLDOZED	CALVINIST	CARRIAGES	CESSATION
BULLDOZER	CALVINIZE	CARRYOVER	CHABLISES
BULLDOZES	CAMEMBERT	CARTILAGE	CHAIRLADY
BULLETINS	CAMERAMAN	CARTRIDGE	CHALLENGE
BUMBLEBEE	CAMPAIGNS	CARTWHEEL	CHAMBERED
BUMPTIOUS	CANCEROUS	CASCADING	CHAMELEON
BUNGALOWS	CANDIDACY	CASEMENTS	CHAMPAGNE
BUNKMATES	CANDIDATE	CASSEROLE	CHAMPIONS
BURDENING	CANNIBALS	CASTIGATE	CHANNELED
BURGEONED	CANNISTER	CATALYSTS	CHANTILLY
BURLESQUE	CANONICAL	CATALYTIC	CHAPERONE
BURNINGLY	CANTONESE	CATCHABLE	CHAPLAINS
BURNISHED	CANVASSED	CATHEDRAL	CHARACTER
BURNISHES	CANVASSER	CATHETERS	CHARITIES
BURNSIDES	CANVASSES	CATHOLICS	CHARTABLE
BURNTNESS	CAPACIOUS	CATTLEMAN	CHARTERED
BURROWING	CAPACITOR	CAUCASIAN	CHARTINGS
BUTCHERED	CAPILLARY	CAULDRONS	CHASTISED

CHASTISER	CLAIMABLE	COARSENED	COMFORTER
CHASTISES	CLAIMANTS	COASTLINE	COMICALLY
CHATTERED	CLAMBERED	COCKROACH	COMMANDED
CHATTERER	CLAMOROUS	COCKTAILS	COMMANDER
CHAUFFEUR	CLAPBOARD	CODEWORDS	COMMENCED
CHEAPENED	CLARIFIED	CODIFIERS	COMMENCES
CHEAPNESS	CLARIFIES	CODIFYING	COMMENDED
CHECKABLE	CLASSICAL	COERCIBLE	COMMENTED
CHECKLIST	CLASSMATE	COEXISTED	COMMITTED
CHEEKBONE	CLASSROOM	COFFEECUP	COMMITTEE
CHEERLESS	CLATTERED	COFFEEPOT	COMMODITY
CHEMICALS	CLEANNESS	COGITATED	COMMODORE
CHEMISTRY	CLEANSERS	COGITATES	COMMONERS
CHERISHED	CLEANSING	COGNITION	COMMONEST
CHERISHES	CLEARANCE	COGNITIVE	COMMOTION
CHEROKEES	CLEARINGS	COGNIZANT	COMMUNION
CHESTNUTS	CLEARNESS	COHERENCE	COMMUNIST
CHEYENNES	CLERGYMAN	COINCIDED	COMMUNITY
CHICANERY	CLERGYMEN	COINCIDES	COMMUTERS
CHICKADEE	CLEVEREST	COLLAPSED	COMMUTING
CHIEFTAIN	CLIENTELE	COLLAPSES	COMPACTED
CHILDHOOD	CLINICIAN	COLLARING	COMPACTER
CHILDLIKE	CLIPBOARD	COLLEAGUE	COMPACTLY
CHIPMUNKS	CLIPPINGS	COLLECTED	COMPACTOR
CHOCOLATE	CLOAKROOM	COLLECTOR	COMPANIES
CHRISTENS	CLOBBERED	COLLEGIAN	COMPANION
CHRISTIAN	CLOCKINGS	COLLIDING	COMPARING
CHRISTMAS	CLOCKWISE	COLLISION	COMPELLED
CHRONICLE	CLOCKWORK	COLLOIDAL	COMPETENT
CHUBBIEST	CLOISTERS	COLLUSION	COMPETING
CHURCHMAN	CLOSENESS	COLONIALS	COMPILERS
CIGARETTE	CLOUDIEST	COLONISTS	COMPILING
CINEMATIC	CLOUDLESS	COLONIZED	COMPLAINS
CIRCUITRY	CLUBHOUSE	COLONIZER	COMPLAINT
CIRCULANT	CLUSTERED	COLONIZES	COMPLETED
CIRCULATE	CLUTCHING	COLUMNIZE	COMPLETES
CITATIONS	CLUTTERED	COMBATANT	COMPLEXES
CITYSCAPE	COAGULATE	COMBATIVE	COMPLEXLY
CIVILIANS	COALESCED	COMBINING	COMPLIANT
CIVILIZED	COALESCES	COMEDIANS	COMPLYING
CIVILIZES	COALITION	COMFORTED	COMPONENT

COMPOSERS	CONFIDANT	CONSONANT	CONVERSED
COMPOSING	CONFIDENT	CONSORTED	CONVERSES
COMPOSITE	CONFIDING	CONSPIRED	CONVERTED
COMPOSURE	CONFIGURE	CONSPIRES	CONVERTER
COMPOUNDS	CONFINING	CONSTABLE	CONVEYERS
COMPRISED	CONFIRMED	CONSTANCY	CONVEYING
COMPRISES	CONFLICTS	CONSTANTS	CONVICTED
COMPUTERS	CONFLUENT	CONSTRAIN	CONVINCED
COMPUTING	CONFORMAL	CONSTRICT	CONVINCER
COMRADELY	CONFORMED	CONSTRUCT	CONVINCES
CONCEALED	CONFOUNDS	CONSTRUED	CONVIVIAL
CONCEALER	CONFRONTS	CONSULATE	CONVOYING
CONCEDING	CONFUSERS	CONSULTED	COOPERATE
CONCEITED	CONFUSING	CONSUMERS	COPIOUSLY
CONCEIVED	CONFUSION	CONSUMING	COPYRIGHT
CONCEIVES	CONGENIAL	CONTACTED	CORDIALLY
CONCENSUS	CONGESTED	CONTAGION	CORIANDER
CONCERNED	CONGRUENT	CONTAINED	CORKSCREW
CONCERTED	CONJOINED	CONTAINER	CORMORANT
CONCISELY	CONJUGATE	CONTENDED	CORNFIELD
CONCLUDED	CONJUNCTS	CONTENDER	COROLLARY
CONCLUDES	CONJURING	CONTENTED	CORPORALS
CONCOURSE	CONNECTED	CONTENTLY	CORPORATE
CONCRETES	CONNECTOR	CONTESTED	CORPULENT
CONCUBINE	CONNOTING	CONTESTER	CORRECTED
CONCURRED	CONNUBIAL	CONTINENT	CORRECTLY
CONDEMNED	CONQUERED	CONTINUAL	CORRECTOR
CONDEMNER	CONQUERER	CONTINUED	CORRELATE
CONDENSED	CONQUEROR	CONTINUES	CORRIDORS
CONDENSER	CONQUESTS	CONTINUUM	CORROSION
CONDENSES	CONSCIOUS	CONTOURED	CORROSIVE
CONDITION	CONSCRIPT	CONTRACTS	CORRUGATE
CONDONING	CONSENTED	CONTRASTS	CORRUPTED
CONDUCIVE	CONSENTER	CONTRIVED	CORRUPTER
CONDUCTED	CONSERVED	CONTRIVER	COSMETICS
CONDUCTOR	CONSERVES	CONTRIVES	COSMOLOGY
CONFERRED	CONSIDERS	CONTUMACY	COSPONSOR
CONFERRER	CONSIGNED	CONUNDRUM	COSTUMING
CONFESSED	CONSISTED	CONVENING	COTANGENT
CONFESSES	CONSOLERS	CONVERGED	COTILLION
CONFESSOR	CONSOLING	CONVERGES	COTYLEDON

COUNTABLE	CROCODILE	CUSTOMARY	DECIDABLE
COUNTABLY	CROSSABLE	CUSTOMERS	DECIDEDLY
COUNTERED	CROSSBARS	CUSTOMIZE	DECIDUOUS
COUNTLESS	CROSSINGS	CUTANEOUS	DECIMATED
COUNTRIES	CROSSOVER	CUTTHROAT	DECIMATES
COUPLINGS	CROSSROAD	CUTTINGLY	DECIPHERS
COURTEOUS	CROSSTALK	CYCLOIDAL	DECISIONS
COURTESAN	CROSSWALK	CYCLOTRON	DECLARERS
COURTIERS	CROSSWORD	CYLINDERS	DECLARING
COURTROOM	CROTCHETY	CYNICALLY	DECLINERS
COURTSHIP	CROUCHING	CYTOPLASM	DECLINING
COURTYARD	CRUCIALLY	DADAISTIC	DECODINGS
COVARIANT	CRUCIFIED	DAFFODILS	DECOMPILE
COVENANTS	CRUCIFIES	DAMNATION	DECOMPOSE
COVERABLE	CRUDENESS	DANDELION	DECORATED
COVERINGS	CRUMBLING	DANGEROUS	DECORATES
COVERLETS	CRUMPLING	DASHBOARD	DECOUPLED
COWARDICE	CRUNCHIER	DASHINGLY	DECOUPLES
CRABAPPLE	CRUNCHING	DATABASES	DECREASED
CRACKLING	CRUSADERS	DATAGRAMS	DECREASES
CRAFTSMAN	CRUSADING	DATAMEDIA	DECREEING
CRANBERRY	CRUSHABLE	DAUGHTERS	DECREMENT
CRANKIEST	CRYOGENIC	DAUNTLESS	DECRYPTED
CRAZINESS	CUBBYHOLE	DAYDREAMS	DECSYSTEM
CREATIONS	CUCUMBERS	DAYLIGHTS	DEDICATED
CREATURES	CULMINATE	DEADLINES	DEDICATES
CREDITING	CULTIVATE	DEADLOCKS	DEDUCIBLE
CREDITORS	CULTURING	DEBATABLE	DEDUCTING
CREDULITY	CUNNINGLY	DEBUGGERS	DEDUCTION
CREDULOUS	CUPBOARDS	DEBUGGING	DEDUCTIVE
CREMATING	CURIOSITY	DEBUTANTE	DEEPENING
CREMATION	CURIOUSER	DECATHLON	DEFAULTED
CREMATORY	CURIOUSLY	DECEASING	DEFAULTER
CRESCENTS	CURRENTLY	DECEITFUL	DEFEATING
CRIMINALS	CURSORILY	DECEIVERS	DEFECTING
CRIMINATE	CURTAILED	DECEIVING	DEFECTION
CRIPPLING	CURTAINED	DECENCIES	DEFECTIVE
CRISPNESS	CURVATURE	DECENNIAL	DEFENDANT
CRITERION	CUSHIONED	DECEPTION	DEFENDERS
CRITICIZE	CUSTODIAL	DECEPTIVE	DEFENDING
CRITIQUES	CUSTODIAN	DECERTIFY	DEFENSIVE

DEFERENCE	DEPLETING	DETAILING	DIFFICULT
DEFERMENT	DEPLETION	DETAINING	DIFFUSELY
DEFERRERS	DEPLORING	DETECTING	DIFFUSERS
DEFERRING	DEPLOYING	DETECTION	(DIFFUSING
DEFIANTLY	DEPOSITED	DETECTIVE	DIFFUSION
DEFICIENT	DEPOSITOR	DETECTORS	DIFFUSIVE
DEFINABLE	DEPRAVITY	DETENTION	DIGESTING
DEFORMITY	DEPRECATE	DETERGENT	DIGESTION
DEGRADING	DEPRESSED	DETERMINE	DIGESTIVE
DEHYDRATE	DEPRESSES	DETERRENT	DIGITALIS
DELEGATED	DEPRIVING	DETERRING	DIGITALLY
DELEGATES	DEQUEUING	DETRACTOR	DIGITIZED
DELETIONS	DERAILING	DETRIMENT	DIGITIZED
DELICIOUS	DERIVABLE	DEVASTATE	DIGITIZES
DELIGHTED	DESCENDED	DEVELOPED	DIGNIFIED
DELIMITED	DESCENDER	DEVELOPER	DIGNITIES
DELIMITER	DESCRIBED	DEVIATING	DIGRESSED
DELINEATE	DESCRIBER	DEVIATION	DIGRESSES
DELIRIOUS	DESCRIBES	DEVISINGS	DILIGENCE
DELIVERED	DESECRATE	DEVOTEDLY	DIMENSION
DELIVERER	DESERTERS	DEVOTIONS	DINGINESS
DELUSIONS	DESERTING	DEXTERITY	DIPHTHONG
DEMAGNIFY	DESERTION	DIAGNOSED	DIPLOMACY
DEMAGOGUE	DESERVING	DIAGNOSES	DIPLOMATS
DEMANDING	DESIGNATE	DIAGNOSIS	DIRECTING
DEMARCATE	DESIGNERS	DIAGONALS	DIRECTION
DEMOCRACY	DESIGNING	DIALECTIC	DIRECTIVE
DEMOCRATS	DESIRABLE	DIALOGUES	DIRECTORS
DENIGRATE	DESIRABLY	DIAMETERS	DIRECTORY
DENOTABLE	DESPAIRED	DIAMETRIC	DIRTINESS
DENOUNCED	DESPERADO	DIAPHRAGM	DISABLERS
DENOUNCES	DESPERATE	DIATRIBES	DISABLING
DENSENESS	DESPISING	DICHOTOMY	DISAGREED
DENSITIES	DESPOTISM	DICTATING	DISAGREES
DENTISTRY	DESSICATE	DICTATION	DISALLOWS
DEODORANT	DESTINIES	DICTATORS	DISAPPEAR
DEPARTING	DESTITUTE	DIETICIAN	DISARMING
DEPARTURE	DESTROYED	DIETITIAN	DISASTERS
DEPENDENT	DESTROYER	DIFFERENT	DISBANDED
DEPENDING	DESULTORY	DIFFERERS	DISBURSED
DEPICTING	DETACHING	DIFFERING	DISBURSES

DISCARDED	DISPENSED	DIVERSION	DRENCHING
DISCERNED	DISPENSER	DIVERSION	DRESSINGS
DISCHARGE	DISPENSES	DIVERSITY	DRINKABLE
DISCIPLES	DISPERSAL	DIVERTING	DRIVEWAYS
DISCLAIMS	DISPERSED	DIVESTING	DROMEDARY
DISCLOSED	DISPERSES	DIVIDENDS	DROPPINGS
DISCLOSES	DISPLACED	DIVISIBLE	DROWNINGS
DISCOUNTS	DISPLACES	DIVISIONS	DRUGGISTS
DISCOURSE	DISPLAYED	DIVULGING	DRUGSTORE
DISCOVERS	DISPLAYER	DIZZINESS	DRUNKARDS
DISCOVERY	DISPLEASE	DOCTORATE	DUALITIES
DISCREDIT	DISPOSALS	DOCTRINAL	DUBIOUSLY
DISCUSSED	DISPOSING	DOCTRINES	DUCHESSES
DISCUSSES	DISPROVED	DOCUMENTS	DUMBBELLS
DISENGAGE	DISPROVES	DOGMATISM	DUPLICATE
DISFIGURE	DISPUTERS	DOLEFULLY	DUPLICITY
DISGRACED	DISPUTING	DOMINANCE	DURATIONS
DISGRACES	DISREGARD	DOMINATED	DUSKINESS
DISGUISED	DISRUPTED	DOMINATES	DUTIFULLY
DISGUISES	DISSEMBLE	DOORSTEPS	DWELLINGS
DISGUSTED	DISSENTED	DORMITORY	DWINDLING
DISHONEST	DISSENTER	DOUBTABLE	DYNAMITED
DISHWATER	DISSIDENT	DOUBTLESS	DYNAMITES
DISJUNCTS	DISSOLVED	DOUGHNUTS	DYNASTIES
DISKETTES	DISSOLVES	DOWNGRADE	DYSENTERY
DISLIKING	DISSONANT	DOWNLINKS	DYSPEPTIC
DISLOCATE	DISTANCES	DOWNLOADS	DYSTROPHY
DISLODGED	DISTANTLY	DOWNPLAYS	EAGERNESS
DISMAYING	DISTASTES	DOWNRIGHT	EARLINESS
DISMEMBER	DISTEMPER	DOWNTOWN	EARMARKED
DISMISSAL	DISTILLED	DOWNWARD	EARNESTLY
DISMISSED	DISTILLER	DRAFTSMAN	EARTHLING
DISMISSER	DISTORTED	DRAGONFLY	EARTHWORM
DISMISSES	DISTRACTS	DRAGOONED	EASEMENTS
DISMOUNTS	DISTRICTS	DRAMATICS	EASTBOUND
DISOBEYED	DISTURBED	DRAMATIST	EASTERNER
DISORDERS	DISTURBER	DRAPERIES	EASTWARDS
DISOWNING	DIVERGENT	DRAWBACKS	EASYGOING
DISPARATE	DIVERGING	DRAWNNESS	EAVESDROP
DISPARITY	DIVERSELY	DREAMBOAT	ECCENTRIC
DISPELLED	DIVERSIFY	DREAMLIKE	ECLIPSING

ECONOMICS	EMBARRASS	ENDEARING	ENVELOPES
ECONOMIES	EMBASSIES	ENDLESSLY	ENVIOUSLY
ECONOMIST	EMBEDDING	ENDORSING	ENVISAGED
ECONOMIZE	EMBELLISH	ENDOWMENT	ENVISAGES
ECOSYSTEM	EMBODYING	ENDURABLE	ENVISIONS
EDITORIAL	EMBRACING	ENDURABLY	EPHEMERAL
EDUCATING	EMBROIDER	ENDURANCE	EPICENTRE
EDUCATION	EMERGENCE	ENERGETIC	EPICURIZE
EDUCATORS	EMERGENCY	ENFORCERS	EPIDEMICS
EDWARDIAN	EMIGRANTS	ENFORCING	EPIDERMIS
EDWARDINE	EMIGRATED	ENGENDERS	EPILEPTIC
EFFECTING	EMIGRATES	ENGINEERS	EPISCOPAL
EFFECTIVE	EMINENTLY	ENGRAVING	EPITAXIAL
EFFECTORS	EMOTIONAL	ENGROSSED	EPITOMIZE
EFFICIENT	EMPHASIZE	ENHANCING	EQUALIZED
EGYPTIANS	EMPIRICAL	ENIGMATIC	EQUALIZER
EIGHTEENS	EMPLOYEES	ENJOINING	EQUALIZES
EIGHTFOLD	EMPLOYERS	ENJOYABLE	EQUATIONS
EIGHTIETH	EMPLOYING	ENJOYABLY	EQUIPMENT
EJACULATE	EMPOWERED	ENJOYMENT	EQUIPPING
ELABORATE	EMPTINESS	ENLARGERS	EQUITABLE
ELECTIONS	EMULATING	ENLARGING	EQUITABLY
ELECTIVES	EMULATION	ENLIGHTEN	EQUIVOCAL
ELECTORAL	EMULATORS	ENLIVENED	ERADICATE
ELECTRIFY	ENACTMENT	ENNOBLING	ERECTIONS
ELECTRODE	ENAMELING	ENRAPTURE	ERRONEOUS
ELECTRONS	ENCAMPING	ENRICHING	ESCALATED
ELEGANTLY	ENCHANTED	ENROLLING	ESCALATES
ELEMENTAL	ENCHANTER	ENSEMBLES	ESCAPABLE
ELEPHANTS	ENCIPHERS	ENSLAVING	ESCAPADES
ELEVATION	ENCIRCLED	ENSNARING	ESCHEWING
ELEVATORS	ENCIRCLES	ENTAILING	ESCORTING
ELICITING	ENCLOSING	ENTERTAIN	ESPIONAGE
ELIMINATE	ENCLOSURE	ENTITLING	ESPOUSING
ELOQUENCE	ENCODINGS	ENTRANCED	ESSENIZES
ELSEWHERE	ENCOMPASS	ENTRANCES	ESSENTIAL
ELUCIDATE	ENCOUNTER	ENTREATED	ESTABLISH
ELUSIVELY	ENCOURAGE	ENTRUSTED	ESTEEMING
EMACIATED	ENCRYPTED	ENUMERATE	ESTIMATED
EMANATING	ENCUMBERS	ENVELOPED	ESTIMATES
EMBARGOES	ENDANGERS	ENVELOPER	ETERNALLY

ETHERNETS	EXCRETING	EXPLORERS	FAITHLESS
ETHICALLY	EXCRETION	EXPLORING	FALLACIES
ETIQUETTE	EXCRETORY	EXPLOSION	FALLOPIAN
ETYMOLOGY	EXCURSION	EXPLOSIVE	FALSEHOOD
EUPHEMISM	EXCUSABLE	EXPONENTS	FALSENESS
EUROPEANS	EXCUSABLY	EXPORTERS	FALSIFIED
EVACUATED	EXECUTING	EXPORTING	FALSIFIES
EVALUATED	EXECUTION	EXPOSURES	FANCINESS
EVALUATES	EXECUTIVE	EXPOUNDED	FANTASIES
EVALUATOR	EXECUTORS	EXPOUNDER	FANTASIZE
EVAPORATE	EXEMPLARY	EXPRESSED	FANTASTIC
EVERGREEN	EXEMPLIFY	EXPRESSES	FAREWELLS
EVERYBODY	EXEMPTING	EXPRESSLY	FARMHOUSE
EVICTIONS	EXEMPTION	EXPULSION	FARMYARDS
EVIDENCED	EXERCISED	EXPUNGING	FASCINATE
EVIDENCES	EXERCISER	EXPURGATE	FASHIONED
EVIDENTLY	EXERCISES	EXQUISITE	FASTENERS
EVOLUTION	EXERTIONS	EXTENDING	FASTENING
EXACTIONS	EXHAUSTED	EXTENSION	FATHOMING
EXACTNESS	EXHIBITED	EXTENSIVE	FATIGUING
EXAMINERS	EXHIBITOR	EXTENUATE	FATTENERS
EXAMINING	EXISTENCE	EXTERIORS	FATTENING
EXCAVATED	EXPANDERS	EXTIRPATE	FAULTLESS
EXCAVATES	EXPANDING	EXTORTION	FEARFULLY
EXCEEDING	EXPANSION	EXTRACTED	FEATHERED
EXCELLENT	EXPANSIVE	EXTRACTOR	FEATURING
EXCELLING	EXPECTANT	EXTREMELY	FEDERALLY
EXCEPTING	EXPECTING	EXTREMIST	FEELINGLY
EXCEPTION	EXPEDIENT	EXTREMITY	FELONIOUS
EXCERPTED	EXPEDITED	EXTRICATE	FERMENTED
EXCESSIVE	EXPEDITES	EXTRINSIC	FEROCIOUS
EXCHANGED	EXPELLING	EXTROVERT	FERTILELY
EXCHANGES	EXPENDING	EYEPIECES	FERTILITY
EXCHEQUER	EXPENSIVE	FABRICATE	FERTILIZE
EXCITABLE	EXPERTISE	FACSIMILE	FERVENTLY
EXCITEDLY	EXPLAINED	FACTORIAL	FESTIVALS
EXCLAIMED	EXPLAINER	FACTORIES	FESTIVELY
EXCLAIMER	EXPLETIVE	FACTORING	FESTIVITY
EXCLUDING	EXPLODING	FACTUALLY	FEUDALISM
EXCLUSION	EXPLOITED	FACULTIES	FIBROSITY
EXCLUSIVE	EXPLOITER	FAINTNESS	FIBROUSLY

FICTIONAL	FLEDGLING	FORMALISM	FREQUENCY
FIELDWORK	FLEETNESS	FORMALITY	FREQUENTS
FIFTEENTH	FLEMISHED	FORMALIZE	FRESHENED
FIGURINGS	FLEMISHES	FORMATION	FRESHENER
FILAMENTS	FLINCHING	FORMATIVE	FRESHNESS
FILENAMES	FLOORINGS	FORMATTED	FRETFULLY
FILTERING	FLOTATION	FORMATTER	FRICATIVE
FILTHIEST	FLOUNDERS	FORMULATE	FRICTIONS
FINALIZED	FLOWCHART	FORSAKING	FRIGHTENS
FINALIZES	FLOWERING	FORTHWITH	FRIGHTFUL
FINANCIAL	FLOWERPOT	FORTIFIED	FRIVOLITY
FINANCIER	FLUCTUATE	FORTIFIES	FRIVOLOUS
FINANCING	FLUFFIEST	FORTITUDE	FRONTIERS
FINESSING	FLUORESCE	FORTNIGHT	FROSTBITE
FINGERING	FLUTTERED	FORTUNATE	FRUITLESS
FINGERTIP	FOLLOWERS	FORWARDED	FRUSTRATE
FINISHERS	FOLLOWING	FORWARDER	FUGITIVES
FINISHING	FOODSTUFF	FOSTERING	FULFILLED
FIREBREAK	FOOLHARDY	FOULMOUTH	FULMINATE
FIREFLIES	FOOLISHLY	FOUNDERED	FUNCTIONS
FIRELIGHT	FOOLPROOF	FOUNDLING	FUNGICIDE
FIREPLACE	FOOTBALLS	FOUNDRIES	FUNNELING
FIREPOWER	FOOTNOTES	FOUNTAINS	FUNNINESS
FIREPROOF	FOOTPRINT	FOURSCORE	FURIOUSER
FIRESTONE	FOOTSTEPS	FOURTEENS	FURIOUSLY
FIREWORKS	FORBIDDEN	FRACTIONS	FURNISHED
FIRMAMENT	FORECASTS	FRACTURED	FURNISHES
FIRSTHAND	FOREGOING	FRACTURES	FURNITURE
FISHERMAN	FOREHEADS	FRAGMENTS	FURTHERED
FISHERMEN	FOREIGNER	FRAGRANCE	FURTIVELY
FISTICUFF	FORESIGHT	FRAMEWORK	FUZZINESS
FITTINGLY	FORESTALL	FRANCAISE	GABARDINE
FIXATIONS	FORESTERS	FRANCHISE	GALLANTLY
FIXEDNESS	FORETELLS	FRANKNESS	GALLANTRY
FLAMMABLE	FOREWARNS	FRATERNAL	GALLERIED
FLASHBACK	FORFEITED	FREEMASON	GALLERIES
FLATTENED	FORGERIES	FREESTYLE	GALLOPING
FLATTERED	FORGETFUL	FREEWHEEL	GALLSTONE
FLATTERER	FORGIVING	FREIGHTED	GANGPLANK
FLATULENT	FORGOTTEN	FREIGHTER	GANGSTERS
FLAUNTING	FORLORNLY	FRENCHMAN	GARDENERS

GARDENING	GODFATHER	GROCERIES	HAPPENING
GARLANDED	GODMOTHER	GROSSNESS	HAPPINESS
GASEOUSLY	GODPARENT	GROSVENOR	HARASSING
GATHERERS	GOLDENROD	GROTESQUE	HARBINGER
GATHERING	GOLDSMITH	GROUNDERS	HARDINESS
GAUDINESS	GOSSIPING	GROUNDING	HARDSHIPS
GAUNTNESS	GOTHICISM	GROUPINGS	HARDWIRED
GENEALOGY	GOTHICIZE	GRUMBLING	HARMFULLY
GENERALLY	GOVERNESS	GUARANTEE	HARMONICS
GENERATED	GOVERNING	GUARDEDLY	HARMONIES
GENERATES	GOVERNORS	GUARDIANS	HARMONIST
GENERATOR	GRABBINGS	GUERRILLA	HARMONIZE
GENTLEMAN	GRADATION	GUESSWORK	HARNESSED
GENTLEMEN	GRADIENTS	GUIDEBOOK	HARROWING
GENUINELY	GRADUALLY	GUIDELINE	HARSHNESS
GEOGRAPHY	GRADUATED	GUILTIEST	HARVESTED
GEOLOGIST	GRADUATES	GUILTLESS	HARVESTER
GEOMETRIC	GRAMMATIC	GUNPOWDER	HASTENING
GEORGIANS	GRANARIES	GYMNASIUM	HASTINESS
GERIATRIC	GRANDIOSE	GYMNASTIC	HATEFULLY
GERMICIDE	GRANDNESS	GYROSCOPE	HAUGHTILY
GERMINATE	GRANDSONS	HACKNEYED	HAZARDOUS
GESTURING	GRANULATE	HAGGARDLY	HEADACHES
GIBBERISH	GRAPEVINE	HAILSTONE	HEADLANDS
GIDDINESS	GRAPHICAL	HAILSTORM	HEADLIGHT
GIGABYTES	GRAPPLING	HAIRINESS	HEADLINED
GIGACYCLE	GRASPABLE	HALLMARKS	HEADLINES
GIGAHERTZ	GRASSIEST	HALLOWEEN	HEADPHONE
GLADIATOR	GRASSLAND	HALTINGLY	HEALTHFUL
GLAMOROUS	GRATIFIED	HAMBURGER	HEALTHIER
GLANDULAR	GRATITUDE	HAMMERING	HEALTHILY
GLARINGLY	GRAVENESS	HANDBOOKS	HEARTBEAT
GLEANINGS	GRAVEYARD	HANDCUFFS	HEARTIEST
GLEEFULLY	GRAVITATE	HANDICAPS	HEARTLESS
GLIMMERED	GREATNESS	HANDINESS	HEAVINESS
GLISTENED	GREENBELT	HANDIWORK	HEDGEHOGS
GLITTERED	GREENNESS	HANDSHAKE	HEIGHTENS
GLORIFIED	GREETINGS	HANDSOMER	HEINOUSLY
GLORIFIES	GREYHOUND	HANGOVERS	HEIRESSES
GLOWINGLY	GRIEVANCE	HAPHAZARD	HELLENIZE
GODDESSES	GRINDINGS	HAPLESSLY	HELPFULLY

HELVETICA	HOODWINKS	ILLOGICAL	IMPOTENCY
HEPATITIS	HOPEFULLY	ILLUSIONS	IMPRECISE
HERALDING	HORRIFIED	IMAGINARY	IMPRESSED
HERBIVORE	HORRIFIES	IMAGINING	IMPRESSER
HERCULEAN	HORSEBACK	IMBALANCE	IMPRESSES
HEREABOUT	HORSEPLAY	IMITATING	IMPRINTED
HEREAFTER	HORSESHOE	IMITATION	IMPRISONS
HEREUNDER	HOSPITALS	IMITATIVE	IMPROMPTU
HERITAGES	HOSTESSES	IMMEDIACY	IMPROVING
HESITATED	HOSTILELY	IMMEDIATE	IMPROVISE
HESITATES	HOSTILITY	IMMENSELY	IMPRUDENT
HEURISTIC	HOURGLASS	IMMERSION	IMPULSION
HEXAGONAL	HOUSEBOAT	IMMIGRANT	IMPULSIVE
HIBERNATE	HOUSEHOLD	IMMIGRATE	INABILITY
HIDEOUSLY	HOUSETOPS	IMMOVABLE	INANIMATE
HIERARCHY	HOUSEWIFE	IMMOVABLY	INAUDIBLE
HIGHLANDS	HOUSEWORK	IMMUTABLE	INAUGURAL
HIGHLIGHT	HUMANNESS	IMPACTING	INCAPABLE
HILARIOUS	HUMILIATE	IMPACTION	INCENTIVE
HILLBILLY	HUNDREDTH	IMPACTORS	INCEPTION
HILLSIDES	HUNGARIAN	IMPAIRING	INCESSANT
HINDERING	HUNGERING	IMPARTIAL	INCIDENCE
HINDRANCE	HUNGRIEST	IMPASSIVE	INCIDENTS
HINDSIGHT	HURRICANE	IMPATIENT	INCIPIENT
HISTOGRAM	HURRIEDLY	IMPEACHED	INCLEMENT
HISTORIAN	HUSBANDRY	IMPEDANCE	INCLINING
HISTORIES	HUSKINESS	IMPELLING	INCLOSING
HITCHHIKE	HYDRAULIC	IMPENDING	INCLUDING
HOARINESS	HYPERTEXT	IMPERFECT	INCLUSION
HOBBYISTS	HYPHENATE	IMPERILED	INCLUSIVE
HOLLOWING	HYPOCRISY	IMPERIOUS	INCORRECT
HOLOCAUST	HYPOCRITE	IMPINGING	INCREASED
HOMEBREW	ICELANDIC	IMPLANTED	INCREASES
HOMEMAKER	IDEALIZED	IMPLEMENT	INCREMENT
HOMEOPATH	IDEALIZES	IMPLICANT	INCUBATED
HOMEOWNER	IDENTICAL	IMPLICATE	INCUBATES
HOMESTEAD	IGNORAMUS	IMPLORING	INCUBATOR
HOMEWARDS	IGNORANCE	IMPORTANT	INCULCATE
HOMICIDAL	ILLEGALLY	IMPORTERS	INCUMBENT
HONEYCOMB	ILLICITLY	IMPOSTORS	INCURABLE
HONEYMOON	ILLNESSES	IMPOTENCE	INCURRING

INCURSION	INFRINGES	INSOLVENT	INTERLINK
INDELIBLE	INFURIATE	INSOMNIAC	INTERNALS
INDEMNIFY	INFUSIONS	INSPECTED	INTERNING
INDENTING	INGENIOUS	INSPECTOR	INTERPLAY
INDENTURE	INGENUITY	INSPIRING	INTERPOSE
INDEXABLE	INGENUOUS	INSTALLED	INTERPRET
INDICATED	INGESTION	INSTALLER	INTERRUPT
INDICATES	INHABITED	INSTANCES	INTERSECT
INDICATOR	INHERITED	INSTANTER	INTERVALS
INDIGNANT	INHERITOR	INSTANTLY	INTERVENE
INDIGNITY	INHIBITED	INSTIGATE	INTERVIEW
INDIRECTS	INHIBITOR	INSTINCTS	INTESTATE
INDUCTING	INITIALLY	INSTITUTE	INTESTINE
INDUCTION	INITIATED	INSTRUCTS	INTIMATED
INDUCTIVE	INITIATES	INSULATED	INTRALINE
INDUCTORS	INITIATOR	INSULATES	INTRICACY
INDULGENT	INJECTING	INSULATOR	INTRICATE
INDULGING	INJECTION	INSULTING	INTRIGUED
INELEGANT	INJECTIVE	INSURANCE	INTRIGUES
INERTNESS	INJURIOUS	INSURGENT	INTRINSIC
INFANTILE	INJUSTICE	INTEGRALS	INTRODUCE
INFATUATE	INNERMOST	INTEGRATE	INTROVERT
INFECTING	INNOCENCE	INTEGRITY	INTRUDERS
INFECTION	INNOCENTS	INTELLECT	INTRUDING
INFECTIVE	INNOCUOUS	INTENDING	INTRUSION
INFERENCE	INOCULATE	INTENSELY	INTUBATED
INFERIORS	INORGANIC	INTENSIFY	INTUBATES
INFERRING	INQUIRERS	INTENSITY	INTUITION
INFERTILE	INQUIRIES	INTENSIVE	INTERNET
INFESTING	INQUIRING	INTENTION	INTUITIVE
INFINITUM	INSCRIBED	INTERACTS	INVALIDLY
INFIRMARY	INSCRIBES	INTERCEPT	INVARIANT
INFIRMITY	INSERTING	INTERCITY	INVASIONS
INFLATING	INSERTION	INTERDATA	INVECTIVE
INFLATION	INSIDIOUS	INTERDICT	INVENTING
INFLICTED	INSINCERE	INTERESTS	INVENTION
INFLUENCE	INSINUATE	INTERFACE	INVENTIVE
INFLUENZA	INSISTENT	INTERFERE	INVENTORS
INFORMERS	INSISTING	INTERIORS	INVENTORY
INFORMING	INSOLENCE	INTERJECT	INVERSELY
INFRINGED	INSOLUBLE	INTERLACE	INVERSION

INVERTERS	JUDDERING	LANGUAGES	LIBRARIAN
INVERTING	JUDICIARY	LANGUIDLY	LIBRARIES
INVESTING	JUDICIOUS	LARGENESS	LICENSING
INVESTORS	JUNCTIONS	LATERALLY	LIFEBLOOD
INVISIBLE	JUNCTURES	LATINIZED	LIFEGUARD
INVISIBLY	JUSTIFIED	LATINIZER	LIFESTYLE
INVOCABLE	JUSTIFIER	LATINIZES	LIFETIMES
INVOICING	JUSTIFIES	LATITUDES	LIGHTNESS
INVOLVING	JUVENILES	LAUGHABLE	LIGHTNING
IONICIZES	JUXTAPOSE	LAUGHABLY	LIKELIEST
IRATENESS	KAMIKAZES	LAUNCHING	LIMELIGHT
IRISHIZES	KERCHIEFS	LAUNDERED	LIMESTONE
IRRADIATE	KEYBOARDS	LAUNDERER	LIMITABLY
IRREGULAR	KEYSTROKE	LAVISHING	LIMITLESS
IRRIGATED	KILLINGLY	LAVOISIER	LIMOUSINE
IRRIGATES	KILOBLOCK	LAZYBONES	LINEARITY
IRRITABLE	KILOBYTES	LEATHERED	LINEARIZE
IRRITATED	KILOGRAMS	LEAVENING	LINGERING
IRRITATES	KILOHERTZ	LECTURERS	LINGUISTS
ISLANDERS	KILOJOULE	LECTURING	LIONESSES
ISOLATING	KILOMETRE	LEFTOVERS	LIQUIDATE
ISOLATION	KITTENISH	LEGALIZED	LIQUIDITY
ISOMETRIC	KNAPSACKS	LEGALIZES	LISTENERS
ISRAELITE	KNIGHTING	LEGENDARY	LISTENING
ITALICIZE	KNOWINGLY	LEGISLATE	LITERALLY
ITEMIZING	KNOWLEDGE	LEISURELY	LITIGIOUS
ITERATING	LABELLERS	LENGTHENS	LITTERBUG
ITERATION	LABELLING	LENIENTLY	LITTERING
ITERATIVE	LABORIOUS	LESSENING	LIVESTOCK
ITERATORS	LABYRINTH	LETTERING	LOATHSOME
ITINERARY	LACERATED	LEVELLEST	LOCALIZED
JACKKNIFE	LACERATES	LEVELLING	LOCALIZES
JAPANIZED	LACQUERED	LEVELNESS	LOCATIONS
JAPANIZES	LAFAYETTE	LEXICALLY	LOCATIVES
JARRINGLY	LAMENTING	LEXINGTON	LOCKSMITH
JEALOUSLY	LAMPLIGHT	LIABILITY	LOFTINESS
JELLYFISH	LANDLORDS	LIBERALLY	LOGARITHM
JERKINESS	LANDMARKS	LIBERATED	LOGICALLY
JITTERBUG	LANDOWNER	LIBERATES	LOGICIANS
JOCKSTRAP	LANDSCAPE	LIBERATOR	LOGISTICS
JOURNEYED	LANDSLIDE	LIBERTIES	LOINCLOTH

LOITERING	MAMMALIAN	MEDICALLY	MIDDLEMAN
LONELIEST	MANDATING	MEDICINAL	MIDDLEMEN
LONGEVITY	MANDATORY	MEDICINES	MIDNIGHTS
LONGITUDE	MANICURED	MEDITATED	MIDPOINTS
LOOKAHEAD	MANICURES	MEDITATES	MIDSTREAM
LOOPHOLES	MANIFESTS	MEGABYTES	MIDSUMMER
LOOSELEAF	MANIFOLDS	MEGAHERTZ	MIDWINTER
LOOSENESS	MANOMETER	MEGAWORDS	MIGHTIEST
LOOSENING	MARGARINE	MELLOWING	MIGRATING
LOVELIEST	MARIJUANA	MELODIOUS	MIGRATION
LOYALTIES	MARKETING	MELODRAMA	MIGRATORY
LUBRICANT	MARMALADE	MELTINGLY	MILESTONE
LUBRICATE	MARRIAGES	MEMORABLE	MILKINESS
LUCRATIVE	MARVELLED	MEMORANDA	MILKMAIDS
LUDICROUS	MASCULINE	MEMORIALS	MILLINERY
LUMBERING	MASOCHIST	MEMORIZED	MILLIONTH
LUNCHEONS	MASSACRED	MEMORIZER	MILLIPEDE
LUSTINESS	MASSACRES	MEMORIZES	MILLIVOLT
LUXURIOUS	MASSAGING	MENAGERIE	MILLIWATT
MACADAMIA	MASTERFUL	MENDACITY	MILLSTONE
MACHINERY	MASTERING	MENTALITY	MIMICKING
MACHINING	MATCHABLE	MENTIONED	MINCEMEAT
MADDENING	MATCHINGS	MENTIONER	MINDFULLY
MAGAZINES	MATCHLESS	MERCENARY	MINEFIELD
MAGICALLY	MATERIALS	MERCHANTS	MINIATURE
MAGICIANS	MATERNITY	MERCILESS	MINIMALLY
MAGNESIUM	MATRIARCH	MERCURIAL	MINIMIZED
MAGNETISM	MATRIMONY	MERRIMENT	MINIMIZER
MAGNIFIED	MAUSOLEUM	MESSENGER	MINIMIZES
MAGNIFIER	MAXIMALLY	MESSINESS	MINISTERS
MAGNIFIES	MAXIMIZED	METABOLIC	MINSTRELS
MAGNITUDE	MAXIMIZER	METAPHORS	MINUSCULE
MAILBOXES	MAXIMIZES	METEORITE	MINUTEMAN
MAINFRAME	MEANDERED	METRONOME	MIRRORING
MAINTAINS	MEANWHILE	MICROBIAL	MISERABLE
MAJESTIES	MEASURING	MICROCODE	MISERABLY
MAKESHIFT	MECHANISM	MICROCOSM	MISGIVING
MALAYSIAN	MECHANIZE	MICROFILM	MISGUIDED
MALFORMED	MEDALLION	MICROJUMP	MISJUDGED
MALICIOUS	MEDIATING	MICROWAVE	MISPLACED
MALIGNANT	MEDIATION	MICROWORD	MISPLACES

MISSHAPEN	MORTICIAN	MYSTERIES	NOBLENESS
MISSIONER	MORTIFIED	MYTHOLOGY	NOCTURNAL
MISSPELLS	MORTIFIES	NAIVENESS	NOISELESS
MISTAKING	MOTHBALLS	NAKEDNESS	NOISINESS
MISTINESS	MOTHERING	NAMESAKES	NOMINALLY
MISTLETOE	MOTIONING	NARCOTICS	NOMINATED
MISTYPING	MOTIVATED	NARRATION	NORMALITY
MITIGATED	MOTIVATES	NARRATIVE	NORMALIZE
MITIGATES	MOTORCARS	NARROWEST	NORMATIVE
MNEMONICS	MOTORISTS	NARROWING	NORTHEAST
MOCCASINS	MOTORIZED	NASTINESS	NORTHERLY
MODERATED	MOTORIZES	NATIONALS	NORTHWARD
MODERATES	MOUNTABLE	NATURALLY	NORTHWEST
MODERNITY	MOUNTAINS	NAUGHTIER	NORWEGIAN
MODERNIZE	MOUNTINGS	NAVIGABLE	NOSTALGIA
MODIFIERS	MOUSETRAP	NAVIGATED	NOSTALGIC
MODIFYING	MOVEMENTS	NAVIGATES	NOTARIZED
MODULARLY	MUDDINESS	NAVIGATOR	NOTARIZES
MODULATED	MULTIBYTE	NECESSARY	NOTATIONS
MODULATES	MULTICAST	NECESSITY	NOTEBOOKS
MODULATOR	MULTIPLES	NECKLACES	NOTIFIERS
MOISTNESS	MULTITUDE	NEGATIONS	NOTIFYING
MOLECULAR	MUMBLINGS	NEGATIVES	NOTORIETY
MOLECULES	MUNDANELY	NEGLECTED	NOTORIOUS
MOLESTING	MUNICIPAL	NEGLIGENT	NOURISHED
MOMENTARY	MUNITIONS	NEGOTIATE	NOURISHES
MOMENTOUS	MURDERERS	NERVOUSLY	NOVELISTS
MONASTERY	MURDERING	NETWORKED	NOVELTIES
MONITORED	MURDEROUS	NEUTRALLY	NUISANCES
MONKEYING	MURMURING	NEWCOMERS	NULLIFIED
MONOCULAR	MUSHROOMS	NEWSPAPER	NULLIFIES
MONOGRAM	MUSICALLY	NEWSSTAND	NUMBERING
MONSTROUS	MUSICIANS	NICKNAMED	NUMERABLE
MONUMENTS	MUSTACHED	NICKNAMES	NUMERATOR
MOODINESS	MUSTACHES	NIGHTCLUB	NUMERICAL
MOONLIGHT	MUSTINESS	NIGHTFALL	NURSERIES
MOONSHINE	MUTATIONS	NIGHTGOWN	NURTURING
MORPHISMS	MUTILATED	NIGHTMARE	NUTRITION
MORTALITY	MUTILATES	NIGHTTIME	NUTSHELLS
MORTARING	MUTTERERS	NINETEENS	OBEDIENCE
MORTGAGES	MUTTERING	NINETIETH	OBFUSCATE

OBJECTING	OFFICIOUS	ORNAMENTS	OVERRULED
OBJECTION	OFFSPRING	ORPHANAGE	OVERRULES
OBJECTIVE	OLIGARCHY	ORTHODOXY	OVERSEERS
OBJECTORS	OMINOUSLY	OSCILLATE	OVERSHOOT
OBLIGATED	OMISSIONS	OSTEOPATH	OVERSIGHT
OBLIQUELY	ONSLAUGHT	OSTRICHES	OVERSIZED
OBLIVIOUS	OPERATING	OTHERWISE	OVERSTATE
OBNOXIOUS	OPERATION	OURSELVES	OVERTAKEN
OBSCURELY	OPERATIVE	OUTBREAKS	OVERTAKER
OBSCURING	OPPONENTS	OUTBURSTS	OVERTAKES
OBSCURITY	OPPORTUNE	OUTERMOST	OVERTHREW
OBSERVANT	OPPOSABLE	OUTFITTED	OVERTHROW
OBSERVERS	OPPOSITES	OUTGROWTH	OVERTONES
OBSERVING	OPPRESSED	OUTLAWING	OVERTURES
OBSESSION	OPPRESSES	OUTLINING	OVERTURNS
OBSESSIVE	OPPRESSOR	OUTLIVING	OVERVIEWS
OBSOLETED	OPTHALMIC	OUTSIDERS	OVERWHELM
OBSOLETES	OPTICALLY	OUTSKIRTS	OVERWORKS
OBSTACLES	OPTIMALLY	OUTSTRIPS	OVERWRITE
OBSTINACY	OPTIMIZED	OUTVOTING	OWNERSHIP
OBSTINATE	OPTIMIZER	OUTWARDLY	PACEMAKER
OBTAINING	OPTIMIZES	OUTWEIGHS	PACKAGERS
OBVIATING	OPTOMETRY	OUTWITTED	PACKAGING
OBVIATION	ORANGUTAN	OVERBOARD	PAGEANTRY
OBVIOUSLY	ORATORIES	OVERCOATS	PAGINATED
OCCASIONS	ORBITALLY	OVERCOMES	PAGINATES
OCCIPITAL	ORCHESTRA	OVERCROWD	PAINFULLY
OCCLUSION	ORDAINING	OVERDRAFT	PAINTINGS
OCCUPANCY	ORDERINGS	OVERFLOWS	PAMPHLETS
OCCUPANTS	ORDERLIES	OVERGROWN	PANELISTS
OCCUPYING	ORDINANCE	OVERHANGS	PANICKING
OCCURRING	ORDINATES	OVERHEADS	PANORAMIC
OCTAGONAL	ORGANISTS	OVERHEARD	PANTOMIME
OCTAHEDRA	ORGANIZED	OVERHEARS	PANTYHOSE
ODOROUSLY	ORGANIZER	OVERJOYED	PAPERBACK
OFFENDERS	ORGANIZES	OVERLOADS	PAPERINGS
OFFENDING	ORGIASTIC	OVERLOOKS	PAPERWORK
OFFENSIVE	ORIENTALS	OVERNIGHT	PARABOLIC
OFFERINGS	ORIENTING	OVERPOWER	PARACHUTE
OFFICIALS	ORIGINALS	OVERPRINT	PARADIGMS
OFFICIATE	ORIGINATE	OVERRIDES	PARADOXES

PARAGRAPH	PATROLLED	PERMEABLE	PICKETING
PARALLELS	PATROLMAN	PERMEATED	PICNICKED
PARALYSIS	PATRONAGE	PERMEATES	PICTORIAL
PARALYZED	PATRONIZE	PERMITTED	PICTURING
PARALYZES	PATTERING	PERMUTING	PIECEMEAL
PARAMETER	PATTERNED	PERPETUAL	PIECEWISE
PARAMOUNT	PAVEMENTS	PERPLEXED	PIGGYBACK
PARANOIAC	PAVILIONS	PERSECUTE	PIGMENTED
PARASITES	PEACEABLE	PERSEVERE	PILFERAGE
PARASITIC	PEACETIME	PERSISTED	PINEAPPLE
PARCHMENT	PEASANTRY	PERSONAGE	PINNACLES
PARDONERS	PECUNIARY	PERSONIFY	PINPOINTS
PARDONING	PEDAGOGIC	PERSONNEL	PIONEERED
PAREGORIC	PENALIZED	PERSUADED	PIPELINED
PARENTAGE	PENALIZES	PERSUADER	PIPELINES
PAROCHIAL	PENALTIES	PERSUADES	PISTACHIO
PARROTING	PENDULUMS	PERTAINED	PITCHFORK
PARSIMONY	PENETRATE	PERTINENT	PITEOUSLY
PARTAKING	PENINSULA	PERTURBED	PITHINESS
PARTIALLY	PENNILESS	PERVADING	PITIFULLY
PARTICLES	PENSIONER	PERVASIVE	PITUITARY
PARTISANS	PENTECOST	PERVERTED	PITYINGLY
PARTITION	PENTHOUSE	PESSIMISM	PLACEMENT
PARTNERED	PEPPERING	PESSIMIST	PLACENTAL
PARTRIDGE	PEPPERONI	PESTICIDE	PLAINNESS
PASSENGER	PERCEIVED	PESTILENT	PLAINTIFF
PASSIVATE	PERCEIVER	PETITIONS	PLAINTIVE
PASSIVELY	PERCEIVES	PETROLEUM	PLAINVIEW
PASSIVITY	PERCHANCE	PETTICOAT	PLANARITY
PASSPORTS	PERENNIAL	PETTINESS	PLANELOAD
PASSWORDS	PERFECTED	PETULANCE	PLANETARY
PATCHWORK	PERFECTLY	PHEASANTS	PLANETOID
PATENTERS	PERFORMED	PHENOMENA	PLANTINGS
PATENTING	PERFORMER	PHONETICS	PLASTERED
PATHNAMES	PERFUMING	PHOSPHATE	PLASTERER
PATHOLOGY	PERIMETER	PHOTOCOPY	PLATELETS
PATIENTLY	PERIPHERY	PHRASINGS	PLATFORMS
PATRIARCH	PERISCOPE	PHYSICALS	PLATITUDE
PATRICIAN	PERISHERS	PHYSICIAN	PLATONISM
PATRIMONY	PERISHING	PHYSICIST	PLATONIST
PATRIOTIC	PERMANENT	PICKETERS	PLAUSIBLE

PLAYFULLY	PORCUPINE	PREDATORY	PRIMARIES
PLAYHOUSE	PORTENDED	PREDEFINE	PRIMARILY
PLAYMATES	PORTFOLIO	PREDICATE	PRIMENESS
PLAYTHING	PORTRAITS	PREDICTED	PRIMITIVE
PLEASURES	PORTRAYAL	PREDICTOR	PRINCIPAL
PLENTEOUS	PORTRAYED	PREEMPTED	PRINCIPLE
PLENTIFUL	POSITIONS	PREEMPTOR	PRINTABLE
PLUGGABLE	POSITIVES	PREFACING	PRINTABLY
PLUMPNESS	POSSESSED	PREFERRED	PRISONERS
PLUNDERED	POSSESSES	PREFERRED	PRIVACIES
PLUNDERER	POSSESSOR	PREFIXING	PRIVATELY
PLURALITY	POSTERIOR	PREGNANCY	PRIVATION
PLUTONIUM	POSTERITY	PREJUDGED	PRIVILEGE
PNEUMATIC	POSTPONED	PREJUDICE	PROBATING
PNEUMONIA	POSTULATE	PREMATURE	PROBATION
POCKETFUL	POTASSIUM	PRENTICED	PROBATIVE
POCKETING	POTENTATE	PREOCCUPY	PROCEDURE
POIGNANCY	POTENTIAL	PREPARING	PROCEEDED
POINTEDLY	POTPOURRI	PREPENDED	PROCESSED
POINTLESS	PENDULUM	PRESELECT	PROCESSES
POISONING	POWDERING	PRESENCES	PROCESSOR
POISONOUS	POWERLESS	PRESENTED	PROCLAIMS
POKERFACE	PRACTICAL	PRESENTER	PROCOTOLS
POLICEMAN	PRACTICED	PRESENTLY	PROCREATE
POLICEMEN	PRACTICES	PRESERVED	PROCURERS
POLISHERS	PRAGMATIC	PRESERVER	PROCURING
POLISHING	PREACHERS	PRESERVES	PRODUCERS
POLITICAL	PREACHING	PRESIDENT	PRODUCING
POLLUTANT	PREAMBLES	PRESIDING	PROFANELY
POLLUTING	PREASSIGN	PRESSINGS	PROFESSED
POLLUTION	PRECEDENT	PRESSURED	PROFESSES
POMPADOUR	PRECEDING	PRESUMING	PROFESSOR
POMPOSITY	PRECINCTS	PRETENDED	PROFFERED
POMPOUSLY	PRECIPICE	PRETENDER	PROFILING
PONDERING	PRECISELY	PRETENSES	PROFITEER
PONDEROUS	PRECISION	PRETTIEST	PROFITING
POPSICLES	PRECLUDED	PREVAILED	PROFITTED
POPULARLY	PRECLUDES	PREVALENT	PROFUSION
POPULATED	PRECOCITY	PREVENTED	PROGNOSIS
POPULATES	PRECURSOR	PREVIEWED	PROHIBITS
PORCELAIN	PREDATING	PRICELESS	PROJECTED

PROJECTOR	PROXIMATE	QUANTIZES
PROLONGED	PROXIMITY	QUARTERED
PROMENADE	PRUDENTLY	QUARTERLY
PROMINENT	PSEUDONYM	QUARTZITE
PROMISING	PSYCHOSES	QUAVERING
PROMOTERS	PSYCHOSIS	QUEERNESS
PROMOTING	PSYCHOTIC	QUENCHING
PROMOTION	PUBLICITY	QUESTIONS
PROMPTEST	PUBLICIZE	QUICKENED
PROMPTING	PUBLISHED	QUICKLIME
PRONENESS	PUBLISHER	QUICKNESS
PRONOUNCE	PUBLISHES	QUICKSAND
PROOFREAD	PUCKERING	QUIESCENT
PROPAGATE	PULMONARY	QUIETNESS
PROPELLED	PULSATION	QUIVERING
PROPELLER	PUNCTURED	QUIXOTISM
PROPHETIC	PUNCTURES	QUIZZICAL
PROPONENT	PUNISHING	QUOTATION
PROPOSALS	PUPPETEER	QUOTIENTS
PROPOSING	PURCHASED	RACETRACK
PROPOUNDS	PURCHASER	RACKETEER
PROPRIETY	PURCHASES	RADIANTLY
PROSCRIBE	PURGATORY	RADIATING
PROSECUTE	PURIFIERS	RADIATION
PROSPECTS	PURIFYING	RADIATORS
PROSPERED	PURITANIC	RADICALLY
PROSTRATE	PURPORTED	RADIOLOGY
PROTECTED	PURPORTER	RAILROADS
PROTECTOR	PURPOSELY	RAINCOATS
PROTESTED	PURPOSIVE	RAINDROPS
PROTESTOR	PUTTERING	RAINSTORM
PROTOCOLS	PUZZLINGS	RAMBLINGS
PROTOTYPE	QUADRANTS	RANDOMIZE
PROTOZOAN	QUADRATIC	RANGELAND
PROTRUDED	QUADRUPLE	RANSACKED
PROTRUDES	QUAGMIRES	RANSOMING
PROVIDENT	QUALIFIED	RAPACIOUS
PROVIDERS	QUALIFIER	RAPTUROUS
PROVIDING	QUALIFIES	RASPBERRY
PROVINCES	QUALITIES	RATIFYING
PROVISION	QUANTIZED	RATIONALE

RATIONALS	RECOMBINE	REFERENCE
RATIONING	RECOMMEND	REFERENDA
REACHABLE	RECOMPILE	REFERENTS
REACHABLY	RECOMPUTE	REFERRALS
REACTIONS	RECONCILE	REFERRING
READINESS	RECONNECT	REFILLING
REALIGNED	RECORDERS	REFLECTED
REALISTIC	RECORDING	REFLECTOR
REALITIES	RECOUNTED	REFLEXIVE
REALIZING	RECOVERED	REFORMATS
REANALYZE	RECREATED	REFORMERS
REAPPEARS	RECREATES	REFORMING
REARRANGE	RECRUITED	REFRACTED
REASONING	RECRUITER	REFRAINED
REASSIGNS	RECTANGLE	REFRESHED
REASSURED	RECURRENT	REFRESHER
REASSURES	RECURRING	REFRESHES
REAWAKENS	RECURSING	REFUTABLE
REBELLING	RECURSION	REGAINING
REBELLION	RECURSIVE	REGARDING
REBINDING	RECYCLING	REGIMENTS
REBOOTING	REDBREAST	REGISTERS
REBOUNDED	REDECLARE	REGISTRAR
REBUTTING	REDEEMERS	REGRESSED
RECALLING	REDEEMING	REGRESSES
RECAPTURE	REDEFINED	REGRETFUL
RECASTING	REDEFINES	REGRETTED
RECEIVERS	REDESIGNS	REGROUPED
RECEIVING	REDISPLAY	REGULARLY
RECEPTION	REDOUBLED	REGULATED
RECEPTIVE	REDRESSED	REGULATES
RECESSION	REDRESSES	REGULATOR
RECESSIVE	REDUCIBLE	REHEARSAL
RECIPIENT	REDUCIBLY	REHEARSED
RECKONING	REDUCTION	REHEARSER
RECLAIMED	REDUNDANT	REHEARSES
RECLAIMER	REELECTED	REIMBURSE
RECLINING	REENABLED	REINFORCE
RECOGNIZE	REENTERED	REINSERTS
RECOILING	REENTRANT	REINSTATE
RECOLLECT	REEXAMINE	REINVENTS

REITERATE	REPACKAGE	REQUIRING
REJECTING	REPAIRING	REQUISITE
REJECTION	REPAIRMAN	REROUTING
REJECTORS	REPAIRMEN	RESELECTS
REJOICING	REPEALING	RESELLING
REJOINDER	REPEATERS	RESEMBLED
REJOINING	REPEATING	RESEMBLES
RELABELED	REPELLENT	RESENTFUL
RELATIONS	REPENTING	RESENTING
RELATIVES	REPERTORY	RESERPINE
RELEASING	REPHRASED	RESERVING
RELEGATED	REPHRASES	RESERVOIR
RELEGATES	REPLACING	RESETTING
RELENTING	REPLAYING	RESIDENCE
RELEVANCE	REPLENISH	RESIDENTS
RELIEVERS	REPLETION	RESIGNING
RELIEVING	REPLICATE	RESILIENT
RELIGIONS	REPORTERS	RESISTANT
RELIGIOUS	REPORTING	RESISTING
RELISHING	REPRESENT	RESISTIVE
RELOADING	REPRESSED	RESISTORS
RELOCATED	REPRESSES	RESOLVERS
RELOCATES	REPRIEVED	RESOLVING
RELUCTANT	REPRIEVES	RESONANCE
REMAINDER	REPRIMAND	RESORTING
REMAINING	REPRINTED	RESOURCES
REMARKING	REPRISALS	RESPECTED
REMEDYING	REPROBATE	RESPECTER
REMEMBERS	REPRODUCE	RESPONDED
REMINDERS	REPTILIAN	RESPONDER
REMINDING	REPUBLICS	RESPONSES
REMISSION	REPUDIATE	RESTARTED
REMOVABLE	REPUGNANT	RESTATING
RENDERING	REPULSING	RESTFULLY
RENDITION	REPULSION	RESTORERS
RENEWABLE	REPULSIVE	RESTORING
RENOUNCES	REPUTABLE	RESTRAINS
RENOVATED	REPUTABLY	RESTRAINT
RENUMBERS	REPUTEDLY	RESTRICTS
REOPENING	REQUESTED	RESULTANT
REORDERED	REQUESTER	RESULTING

RESUMABLE
RESURGENT
RESURRECT
RETAILERS
RETAILING
RETAINERS
RETAINING
RETALIATE
RETARDING
RETENTION
RETENTIVE
RETICULAR
RETRACING
RETRACTED
RETRAINED
RETREATED
RETRIEVAL
RETRIEVED
RETRIEVER
RETRIEVES
RETURNING
REUNITING
REVAMPING
REVEALING
REVENUERS
REVERENCE
REVERENDS
REVERSALS
REVERSELY
REVERSING
REVERSION
REVERTING
REVIEWERS
REVIEWING
REVISIONS
REVISITED
REVOCABLE
REVOLTING
REVOLVERS
REVOLVING
REVULSION

REWARDING
REWINDING
REWORKING
REWRITING
REWRITTEN
RHEUMATIC
RICKSHAWS
RIDICULED
RIDICULES
RIGHTEOUS
RIGHTMOST
RIGHTNESS
RIGHTWARD
RINGINGLY
RIVALLING
RIVALRIES
RIVERBANK
RIVERSIDE
RIVERVIEW
ROADBLOCK
ROADSTERS
ROBBERIES
ROCKETING
ROMANCERS
ROMANCING
ROMANIZER
ROMANIZES
ROMANTICS
ROTARIANS
ROTATIONS
ROUGHNECK
ROUGHNESS
ROUNDHEAD
ROUNDNESS
ROUNDWORM
ROUTINELY
ROYALISTS
ROYALTIES
RUDDINESS
RUDIMENTS
RUFFIANLY

RUINATION
RUINOUSLY
RUPTURING
RUSTICATE
SACRAMENT
SACRIFICE
SACRILEGE
SADDLEBAG
SAFEGUARD
SAGACIOUS
SAGEBRUSH
SAINTHOOD
SALESGIRL
SALESLADY
SALTINESS
SALVAGING
SALVATION
SAMARITAN
SAMPLINGS
SANCTIONS
SANCTUARY
SANDPAPER
SANDSTONE
SARCASTIC
SATISFIED
SATISFIES
SATURATED
SATURATES
SATURDAYS
SATURNISM
SAUCEPANS
SAXONIZES
SAXOPHONE
SCABBARDS
SCAFFOLDS
SCALLOPED
SCANTIEST
SCAPEGOAT
SCARECROW
SCATTERED
SCENARIOS

SCHEDULED	SEARCHING	SENTENCES
SCHEDULER	SEARINGLY	SENTIMENT
SCHEDULES	SEASHORES	SENTINELS
SCHEMATIC	SEASONERS	SEPARABLE
SCHOLARLY	SEASONING	SEPARATED
SCHOOLERS	SECESSION	SEPARATES
SCHOOLING	SECLUSION	SEPARATOR
SCIENTIST	SECONDARY	SEPTEMBER
SCISSORED	SECONDERS	SEPULCHER
SCLEROSIS	SECONDING	SEQUENCED
SCLEROTIC	SECRETARY	SEQUENCER
SCORCHING	SECRETING	SEQUENCES
SCORECARD	SECRETION	SEQUESTER
SCORPIONS	SECRETIVE	SERGEANTS
SCOUNDREL	SECTARIAN	SERIALIZE
SCRAMBLED	SECTIONAL	SERIOUSLY
SCRAMBLER	SECTIONED	SERVICING
SCRAMBLES	SECURINGS	SERVITUDE
SCRAPINGS	SEDIMENTS	SEVENFOLD
SCRATCHED	SEDITIOUS	SEVENTEEN
SCRATCHER	SEDUCTION	SEVENTIES
SCRATCHES	SEDUCTIVE	SEVERALLY
SCRAWLING	SEEDLINGS	SEVERANCE
SCREAMERS	SEEMINGLY	SEXTUPLET
SCREAMING	SEGMENTED	SEXUALITY
SCREECHED	SEGREGATE	SHACKLING
SCREECHES	SELECTING	SHADINESS
SCREENING	SELECTION	SHADOWING
SCREWBALL	SELECTIVE	SHAKEDOWN
SCRIBBLED	SELECTORS	SHAKINESS
SCRIBBLER	SELFISHLY	SHALLOWER
SCRIBBLES	SEMANTICS	SHALLOWLY
SCRIMMAGE	SEMAPHORE	SHAMELESS
SCRIPTURE	SEMBLANCE	SHAPELESS
SCROLLING	SEMESTERS	SHAREABLE
SCUFFLING	SEMICOLON	SHARPENED
SCULPTORS	SENIORITY	SHARPNESS
SCULPTURE	SENSATION	SHATTERED
SCUTTLING	SENSELESS	SHEATHING
SEACOASTS	SENSITIVE	SHEEPSKIN
SEARCHERS	SENTENCED	SHELTERED

SHEPHERDS	SIGNALLED	SLUMBERED
SHIELDING	SIGNATURE	SMALLNESS
SHIFTIEST	SIGNIFIED	SMALLTIME
SHILLINGS	SIGNIFIES	SMARTNESS
SHININGLY	SILENCERS	SMILINGLY
SHIPBOARD	SILENCING	SMOOTHEST
SHIPMENTS	SILLINESS	SMOOTHING
SHIPSHAPE	SILVERING	SMOTHERED
SHIPWRECK	SIMILARLY	SMUGGLERS
SHIVERING	SIMMERING	SMUGGLING
SHOEMAKER	SIMPLETON	SNAKELIKE
SHOOTINGS	SIMULATED	SNAPSHOTS
SHORELINE	SIMULATES	SNATCHING
SHORTAGES	SIMULATOR	SNEAKIEST
SHORTCUTS	SINCERELY	SNOWFLAKE
SHORTENED	SINCEREST	SNOWSHOES
SHORTFALL	SINCERITY	SNOWSTORM
SHORTHAND	SINGINGLY	SNUGGLING
SHORTNESS	SINGLETON	SOBERNESS
SHORTSTOP	SINUSOIDS	SOCIALISM
SHOULDERS	SIPHONING	SOCIALIST
SHOWERING	SITUATING	SOCIALIZE
SHOWPIECE	SITUATION	SOCIETIES
SHREDDING	SIXTEENTH	SOCIOLOGY
SHREWDEST	SKELETONS	SOFTENING
SHRIEKING	SKEPTICAL	SOFTWARES
SHRILLING	SKETCHILY	SOJOURNER
SHRINKAGE	SKETCHING	SOLDIERLY
SHRINKING	SKETCHPAD	SOLEMNITY
SHRUBBERY	SKYLIGHTS	SOLICITED
SHUDDERED	SLACKNESS	SOLICITOR
SHUFFLING	SLANDERER	SOLIDNESS
SHUTDOWNS	SLAPSTICK	SOLILOQUY
SHUTTERED	SLAUGHTER	SOLITAIRE
SHUTTLING	SLEEPLESS	SOLITUDES
SIDEBOARD	SLEEPWALK	SOLUTIONS
SIDEBURNS	SLENDERER	SOMEPLACE
SIDELIGHT	SLIGHTEST	SOMETHING
SIDETRACK	SLIGHTING	SOMETIMES
SIDEWALKS	SLINGSHOT	SOMEWHERE
SIGHTINGS	SLOUCHING	SOMNOLENT

SOPHOMORE	SPLENETIC	STAIRCASE
SORCERERS	SPLICINGS	STAIRWAYS
SORROWFUL	SPLINTERS	STAIRWELL
SOUNDINGS	SPLINTERY	STALEMATE
SOUNDNESS	SPLITTERS	STALLINGS
SOURDOUGH	SPLITTING	STAMMERED
SOUTHEAST	SPOKESMAN	STAMMERER
SOUTHLAND	SPOKESMEN	STAMPEDED
SOUTHWARD	SPONSORED	STAMPEDES
SOUTHWEST	SPORTSMAN	STANCHEST
SOVEREIGN	SPOTLIGHT	STANCHION
SPACESHIP	SPRAWLING	STANDARDS
SPACESUIT	SPREADERS	STANDINGS
SPARENESS	SPREADING	STARBOARD
SPARINGLY	SPRIGHTLY	STARLIGHT
SPARKLING	SPRINGERS	STARTLING
SPATIALLY	SPRINGIER	STATEMENT
SPATTERED	SPRINGING	STATESMAN
SPEAKABLE	SPRINKLED	STATESMEN
SPEAKEASY	SPRINKLER	STATEWIDE
SPEARMINT	SPRINKLES	STATIONED
SPECIALLY	SPRINTERS	STATIONER
SPECIALTY	SPRINTING	STATISTIC
SPECIFICS	SPROUTING	STATUETTE
SPECIFIED	SPUTTERED	STATUTORY
SPECIFIER	SQUABBLED	STAUNCHLY
SPECIFIES	SQUABBLES	STEADFAST
SPECIMENS	SQUADRONS	STEADIEST
SPECTACLE	SQUASHING	STEADYING
SPECTATOR	SQUATTING	STEAMBOAT
SPECULATE	SQUAWKING	STEAMSHIP
SPEEDBOAT	SQUEAKING	STEEPNESS
SPELLINGS	SQUEALING	STEERABLE
SPHERICAL	SQUEAMISH	STENOTYPE
SPICINESS	SQUEEZING	STEPCHILD
SPINDLING	SQUINTING	STERILIZE
SPINNAKER	SQUIRRELS	STERNNESS
SPIRALING	STABILITY	STEVEDORE
SPIRITING	STABILIZE	STICKIEST
SPIRITUAL	STAGGERED	STIFFNESS
SPLASHING	STAINLESS	STILLBORN

STILLNESS	STRETCHER	SUBSTANCE
STIMULANT	STRETCHES	SUBSTRATE
STIMULATE	STRICTEST	SUBSUMING
STIPULATE	STRICTURE	SUBSYSTEM
STIRRINGS	STRINGENT	SUBTITLED
STITCHING	STRINGERS	SUBTITLES
STOCKADES	STRINGIER	SUBTRACTS
STOCKINGS	STRINGING	SUBVERTED
STOCKPILE	STRIPPERS	SUBVERTER
STOCKROOM	STRIPPING	SUCCEEDED
STOMACHED	STRIVINGS	SUCCESSES
STOMACHER	STROLLING	SUCCESSOR
STOMACHES	STRONGEST	SUCCUMBED
STOPCOCKS	STRONTIUM	SUFFERERS
STOPPABLE	STRUCTURE	SUFFERING
STOPWATCH	STRUGGLED	SUFFICING
STOREROOM	STRUGGLES	SUFFIXING
STORMIEST	STRUTTING	SUFFOCATE
STOUTNESS	STUFFIEST	SUGARINGS
STRAGGLED	STUMBLING	SUGGESTED
STRAGGLER	STUPIDEST	SUITCASES
STRAGGLES	STUPIDITY	SULKINESS
STRAINERS	STYLISHLY	SULPHURED
STRAINING	STYLISTIC	SULPHURIC
STRANDING	SUBATOMIC	SUMMARIES
STRANGELY	SUBDIVIDE	SUMMARILY
STRANGERS	SUBGROUPS	SUMMARIZE
STRANGEST	SUBJECTED	SUMMATION
STRANGLED	SUBLAYERS	SUMMONERS
STRANGLER	SUBMARINE	SUMMONING
STRANGLES	SUBMERGED	SUMMONSES
STRATAGEM	SUBMERGES	SUMPTUOUS
STRATEGIC	SUBMITTAL	SUNBONNET
STREAMERS	SUBMITTED	SUNFLOWER
STREAMING	SUBSCRIBE	SUNTANNED
STREETCAR	SUBSCRIPT	SUPERIORS
STRENGTHS	SUBSIDIES	SUPERPOSE
STRENUOUS	SUBSIDING	SUPERSEDE
STRESSFUL	SUBSIDIZE	SUPERVISE
STRESSING	SUBSISTED	SUPPLANTS
STRETCHED	SUBSPACES	SUPPLIERS

SUPPLYING	SYLLABLES	TELEPATHY
SUPPORTED	SYLLOGISM	TELEPHONE
SUPPORTER	SYMBIOSIS	TELEPHONY
SUPPOSING	SYMBIOTIC	TELESCOPE
SUPREMACY	SYMBOLICS	TELETYPES
SUPREMELY	SYMBOLISM	TELEVISED
SURCHARGE	SYMBOLIZE	TELEVISES
SURFACING	SYMMETRIC	TELEVISOR
SURLINESS	SYMPHONIC	TEMPERATE
SURMOUNTS	SYMPOSIUM	TEMPERING
SURPASSED	SYNAGOGUE	TEMPLATES
SURPLUSES	SYNCHRONY	TEMPORARY
SURPRISED	SYNCOPATE	TENACIOUS
SURPRISES	SYNDICATE	TENEMENTS
SURRENDER	SYNDROMES	TENSENESS
SURROGATE	SYNERGISM	TENTACLED
SURROUNDS	SYNTACTIC	TENTACLES
SURVEYING	SYNTHESIS	TENTATIVE
SURVEYORS	SYNTHETIC	TERMINALS
SURVIVALS	TABULATED	TERMINATE
SURVIVING	TABULATES	TERRIFIED
SURVIVORS	TABULATOR	TERRIFIES
SUSPECTED	TAILORING	TERRITORY
SUSPENDED	TALKATIVE	TERRORISM
SUSPENDER	TAMPERING	TERRORIST
SUSPENSES	TARDINESS	TERRORIZE
SUSPICION	TARGETING	TESTAMENT
SUSTAINED	TASTELESS	TESTICLES
SWAGGERED	TAXONOMIC	TESTIFIED
SWALLOWED	TAXPAYERS	TESTIFIER
SWEEPINGS	TEACHABLE	TESTIFIES
SWEETENED	TEARFULLY	TESTIMONY
SWEETENER	TEASPOONS	TEXTBOOKS
SWEETNESS	TECHNICAL	TEXTUALLY
SWELLINGS	TECHNIQUE	THANKLESS
SWIFTNESS	TEDIOUSLY	THEORETIC
SWITCHERS	TEENAGERS	THEORISTS
SWITCHING	TELEGRAMS	THEORIZED
SWITCHMAN	TELEGRAPH	THEORIZER
SWORDFISH	TELEMETRY	THEORIZES
SYCOPHANT	TELEOLOGY	THERAPIES

THERAPIST	TOMORROWS	TRAVERSES
THEREFORE	TOOTHPICK	TREACHERY
THEREUPON	TOPICALLY	TREASURED
THEREWITH	TORMENTED	TREASURER
THICKNESS	TORMENTER	TREASURES
THINKABLE	TORNADOES	TREATISES
THINKABLY	TORPEDOES	TREATMENT
THIRTEENS	TORTOISES	TREMBLING
THIRTIETH	TORTURERS	TRIANGLES
THOUSANDS	TORTURING	TRIBUNALS
THRASHING	TOTALLERS	TRIBUTARY
THREADERS	TOTALLING	TRICKIEST
THREADING	TOTTERING	TRICKLING
THREATENS	TOUCHABLE	TRIGGERED
THREEFOLD	TOUCHIEST	TRIHEDRAL
THRESHOLD	TOUGHNESS	TRILLIONS
THRILLERS	TOWELLING	TRIMMINGS
THRILLING	TOWNSHIPS	TRIUMPHAL
THROBBING	TRACEABLE	TRIUMPHED
THROTTLED	TRACTABLE	TRIVIALLY
THROTTLES	TRADEMARK	TROUBLING
THRUSTERS	TRADEOFFS	TRUMPETER
THRUSTING	TRADESMAN	TRUNCATED
THUNDERED	TRADITION	TRUNCATES
THUNDERER	TRAGEDIES	TURBULENT
THURSDAYS	TRAILINGS	TURQUOISE
THWARTING	TRAMPLING	TUTORIALS
TIGHTENED	TRANSCEND	TWENTIETH
TIGHTENER	TRANSFERS	TWILIGHTS
TIGHTNESS	TRANSFORM	TWINKLING
TIMBERING	TRANSIENT	TWITCHING
TIMESHARE	TRANSLATE	TWITTERED
TIMETABLE	TRANSMITS	TYPICALLY
TINKERING	TRANSPIRE	TYPIFYING
TINNINESS	TRANSPORT	UMBRELLAS
TOLERABLE	TRANSPOSE	UNALTERED
TOLERABLY	TRAPEZOID	UNANIMITY
TOLERANCE	TRAPPINGS	UNANIMOUS
TOLERATED	TRAUMATIC	UNBLOCKED
TOLERATES	TRAVERSAL	UNBOUNDED
TOMAHAWKS	TRAVERSED	UNBRIDLED

UNCERTAIN	UNIONIZER	UPGRADING
UNCHANGED	UNIONIZES	UPHOLDERS
UNCLAIMED	UNITARIAN	UPHOLDING
UNCLEANLY	UNIVALVES	UPHOLSTER
UNCLEARED	UNIVERSAL	UPPERMOST
UNCOVERED	UNIVERSES	UPRIGHTLY
UNDAMAGED	UNKNOWING	UPRISINGS
UNDAUNTED	UNLEASHED	UPROOTING
UNDECIDED	UNLEASHES	UPTURNING
UNDEFINED	UNLIMITED	URINATING
UNDELETED	UNLINKING	URINATION
UNDERDONE	UNLOADING	USABILITY
UNDERFLOW	UNMARRIED	USELESSLY
UNDERFOOT	UNMATCHED	UTILITIES
UNDERGOES	UNNATURAL	UTILIZING
UNDERGONE	UNNERVING	UTTERANCE
UNDERLIES	UNNOTICED	UTTERMOST
UNDERLINE	UNORDERED	VACANCIES
UNDERLING	UNPACKING	VACATIONS
UNDERMINE	UNPLANNED	VACUOUSLY
UNDERPLAY	UNPOPULAR	VACUUMING
UNDERTAKE	UNRELATED	VAGABONDS
UNDERTOOK	UNROLLING	VAGRANTLY
UNDERWEAR	UNSELFISH	VAGUENESS
UNDERWENT	UNSETTLED	VALENTINE
UNDIVIDED	UNSKILLED	VALIANTLY
UNDRESSED	UNSLOTTED	VALIDATED
UNDRESSES	UNTENABLE	VALIDATES
UNEQUALLY	UNTOUCHED	VALIDNESS
UNEXCUSED	UNTRAINED	VALUABLES
UNFITNESS	UNTREATED	VALUATION
UNFOLDING	UNUSUALLY	VANDALIZE
UNFOUNDED	UNVARYING	VANISHING
UNGUARDED	UNVEILING	VARIABLES
UNHAPPIER	UNWELCOME	VARIANCES
UNHAPPILY	UNWILLING	VARIANTLY
UNHEALTHY	UNWINDERS	VARIATION
UNIFORMED	UNWINDING	VARIETIES
UNIFORMLY	UNWITTING	VARIOUSLY
UNIMPEDED	UNWRAPPED	VARNISHES
UNIONIZED	UNWRITTEN	VEGETABLE

VEGETATED	VISCOUNTS	WHISTLERS
VEGETATES	VISIGOTHS	WHISTLING
VEHEMENCE	VISIONARY	WHITENERS
VEHICULAR	VISUALIZE	WHITENESS
VENERABLE	VIVIDNESS	WHITENING
VENGEANCE	VOCATIONS	WHITEWASH
VENTILATE	VOLUNTARY	WHITTLING
VENTRICLE	VOLUNTEER	WHOLENESS
VENTURERS	VOYAGINGS	WHOLESALE
VENTURING	VULCANISM	WHOLESOME
VERBALIZE	WAISTCOAT	WILLFULLY
VERIFIERS	WALLOWING	WILLINGLY
VERIFYING	WANDERERS	WINDMILLS
VERITABLE	WANDERING	WINNINGLY
VERSATILE	WARDROBES	WINTERING
VESTIGIAL	WAREHOUSE	WISTFULLY
VIABILITY	WARNINGLY	WITHDRAWN
VIBRATING	WARRANTED	WITHDRAWS
VIBRATION	WATCHINGS	WITHHOLDS
VICIOUSLY	WATERFALL	WITHSTAND
VICTIMIZE	WATERINGS	WITHSTOOD
VICTORIAN	WATERWAYS	WITNESSED
VICTORIES	WEAKENING	WITNESSES
VICTUALER	WEARINESS	WOMANHOOD
VIDEOTAPE	WEARISOME	WONDERFUL
VIEWPOINT	WEATHERED	WONDERING
VIGILANCE	WEDNESDAY	WOODCHUCK
VIGILANTE	WEIGHINGS	WOODCOCKS
VIGNETTES	WEIGHTING	WORDINESS
VILIFYING	WELCOMING	WORKBENCH
VILLAGERS	WESTBOUND	WORKBOOKS
VINDICATE	WESTERNER	WORKHORSE
VINEYARDS	WESTWARDS	WORKSHOPS
VIOLATING	WHEREUPON	WORKSPACE
VIOLATION	WHICHEVER	WORLDWIDE
VIOLATORS	WHIMPERED	WORRISOME
VIOLENTLY	WHIMSICAL	WORTHIEST
VIOLINIST	WHIPPINGS	WORTHLESS
VIRGINITY	WHIRLPOOL	WRAPPINGS
VIRTUALLY	WHIRLWIND	WRENCHING
VIRTUOSOS	WHISPERED	WRESTLING

WRIGGLING
XYLOPHONE
YARDSTICK
YEARNINGS
YELLOWEST
YELLOWING
YELLOWISH
YESTERDAY
YOUNGSTER
ZEALOUSLY

10

AARDWOLVES
ABANDONERS
ABANDONING
ABASEMENTS
ABASHMENTS
ABATEMENTS
ABBREVIATE
ABDICATING
ABDICATION
ABDICATORS
ABDUCENTES
ABDUCTIONS
ABDUCTORES
ABERRANCES
ABERRANTLY
ABERRATION
ABEYANCIES
ABHORRENCE
ABJECTIONS
ABJECTNESS
ABJURATION
ABLATIVELY
ABNORMALLY
ABOLISHERS
ABOLISHING
ABOLITIONS
ABOMINABLE
ABOMINABLY

ABOMINATED
ABOMINATES
ABOMINATOR
ABORIGINAL
ABORIGINES
ABORTIVELY
ABRASIVELY
ABROGATING
ABROGATION
ABRUPTIONS
ABRUPTNESS
ABSCESSING
ABSCONDERS
ABSCONDING
ABSOLUTELY
ABSOLUTION
ABSOLUTISM
ABSOLUTIST
ABSOLUTIVE
ABSORBABLE
ABSORBANCE
ABSORBANCY
ABSORBANTS
ABSORBENCY
ABSORBENTS
ABSORPTION
ABSORPTIVE
ABSTAINERS
ABSTAINING
ABSTEMIOUS
ABSTENTION
ABSTINENCE
ABSTRACTED
ABSTRACTER
ABSTRACTLY
ABSTRACTOR
ABSTRICTED
ABSTRUSELY
ABSTRUSEST
ABSTRUSITY
ABSURDISMS

ABSURDISTS
ABSURDNESS
ABUNDANCES
ABUNDANTLY
ACADEMICAL
ACADEMISMS
ACCELERANT
ACCELERATE
ACCENTLESS
ACCENTUATE
ACCEPTABLE
ACCEPTABLY
ACCEPTANCE
ACCEPTEDLY
ACCESSIBLE
ACCESSIBLY
ACCESSIONS
ACCIDENCES
ACCIDENTAL
ACCIDENTLY
ACCLAIMERS
ACCLAIMING
ACCLIMATED
ACCLIMATES
ACCOMPLICE
ACCOMPLISH
ACCORDANCE
ACCORDIONS
ACCOUNTANT
ACCOUNTING
ACCREDITED
ACCRETIONS
ACCRUEMENT
ACCUMULATE
ACCURACIES
ACCURATELY
ACCURSEDLY
ACCUSATION
ACCUSATIVE
ACCUSATORY
ACCUSINGLY

ACCUSTOMED	ACTIVITIES	ADMIRATION
ACERBATING	ACTIVIZING	ADMIRINGLY
ACERBITIES	ACTUALIZED	ADMISSIBLE
ACETAMIDES	ACTUALIZES	ADMISSIONS
ACETIFYING	ACTUATIONS	ADMITTANCE
ACETYLATED	ACYLATIONS	ADMITTEDLY
ACETYLATES	ADAPTATION	ADMIXTURES
ACETYLENES	ADAPTIVELY	ADMONISHED
ACHIEVABLE	ADAPTIVITY	ADMONISHER
ACHINESSES	ADDICTIONS	ADMONISHES
ACIDIFIERS	ADDITIONAL	ADMONITION
ACIDIFYING	ADDITIVELY	ADMONITORY
ACIDIMETER	ADDITIVITY	ADOLESCENT
ACIDIMETRY	ADDRESSEES	ADOPTIVELY
ACIDNESSES	ADDRESSERS	ADORATIONS
ACIDULATED	ADDRESSING	ADORNMENTS
ACIDULATES	ADDUCTIONS	ADRENALINE
ACOUSTICAL	ADENOSINES	ADROITNESS
ACQUAINTED	ADENOVIRAL	ADSORBABLE
ACQUIESCED	ADENOVIRUS	ADSORBATES
ACQUIESCES	ADEQUACIES	ADSORBENTS
ACQUIRABLE	ADEQUATELY	ADSORPTION
ACQUISITOR	ADHERENCES	ADSORPTIVE
ACQUITTALS	ADHERENTLY	ADULATIONS
ACQUITTERS	ADHESIONAL	ADULTERANT
ACQUITTING	ADHESIVELY	ADULTERATE
ACRIDITIES	ADHIBITING	ADULTERERS
ACRIMONIES	ADJACENTLY	ADULTERESS
ACROBATICS	ADJECTIVAL	ADULTERIES
ACROPHOBES	ADJECTIVES	ADULTERINE
ACROPHOBIA	ADJOURNING	ADULTEROUS
ACROSTICAL	ADJUDICATE	ADULTHOODS
ACTABILITY	ADJUNCTION	ADVANTAGED
ACTIONABLE	ADJUNCTIVE	ADVANTAGES
ACTIONABLY	ADJURATION	ADVENTIVES
ACTIONLESS	ADJURATORY	ADVENTURED
ACTIVATING	ADJUSTABLE	ADVENTURER
ACTIVATION	ADJUSTMENT	ADVENTURES
ACTIVATORS	ADMEASURED	ADVERBIALS
ACTIVENESS	ADMEASURES	ADVERTENCE
ACTIVISTIC	ADMINISTER	ADVERTENCY

ADVERTISED	AFFORDABLE	AIRSTREAMS
ADVERTISER	AFFORDABLY	AITCHBONES
ADVERTISES	AFFRIGHTED	ALABASTERS
ADVERTIZED	AFFRONTING	ALACRITIES
ADVERTIZES	AFICIONADA	ALACRITOUS
ADVISEMENT	AFICIONADO	ALARMINGLY
ADVISORIES	AFTERBIRTH	ALBINISTIC
ADVOCACIES	AFTERGLOWS	ALBUMINOUS
ADVOCATING	AFTERMATHS	ALCHEMICAL
ADVOCATION	AFTERNOONS	ALCHEMISTS
ADVOCATIVE	AFTERSHAVE	ALCHEMIZED
ADVOCATORS	AFTERSHOCK	ALCHEMIZES
AERIALISTS	AFTERTASTE	ALCOHOLICS
AEROBATICS	AFTERWARDS	ALCOHOLISM
AERODROMES	AFTERWORLD	ALDERWOMAN
AEROGRAMME	AGAPANTHUS	ALDERWOMEN
AEROMETERS	AGEDNESSES	ALGEBRAIST
AERONAUTIC	AGGRANDIZE	ALGORITHMS
AEROPLANES	AGGRAVATED	ALIENATING
AEROSPACES	AGGRAVATES	ALIENATION
AESTHETICS	AGGREGATED	ALIENATORS
AFFABILITY	AGGREGATES	ALIGHTMENT
AFFECTABLE	AGGRESSING	ALIGNMENTS
AFFECTEDLY	AGGRESSION	ALIMENTARY
AFFECTIONS	AGGRESSIVE	ALIMENTING
AFFECTLESS	AGGRESSORS	ALINEMENTS
AFFERENTLY	AGGRIEVING	ALITERATES
AFFIANCING	AGITATEDLY	ALKALINITY
AFFIDAVITS	AGITATIONS	ALKALINIZE
AFFILIATED	AGORAPHOBE	ALKALIZING
AFFILIATES	AGREEMENTS	ALLEGATION
AFFINITIES	AIRBRUSHED	ALLEGIANCE
AFFIRMABLE	AIRBRUSHES	ALLEGORIES
AFFIRMANCE	AIRCOACHES	ALLEGORIST
AFFIXATION	AIRDROPPED	ALLEGORIZE
AFFIXMENTS	AIRFREIGHT	ALLEGRETTO
AFFLICTING	AIRINESSES	ALLERGENIC
AFFLICTION	AIRLIFTING	ALLERGISTS
AFFLICTIVE	AIRMAILING	ALLEVIATED
AFFLUENCES	AIRMANSHIP	ALLEVIATES
AFFLUENTLY	AIRPROOFED	ALLEVIATOR

ALLIGATORS	AMBULATORY	ANARCHISMS
ALLOCATING	AMBUSHMENT	ANARCHISTS
ALLOCATION	AMELIORATE	ANASTOMOSE
ALLOCATORS	AMENDATORY	ANASTROPHE
ALLOTMENTS	AMENDMENTS	ANATHEMATA
ALLOTROPIC	AMERCEMENT	ANATOMICAL
ALLOWANCED	AMERCIABLE	ANATOMISED
ALLOWANCES	AMIABILITY	ANATOMISTS
ALLUREMENT	AMMONIACAL	ANATOMIZED
ALLURINGLY	AMMONIATED	ANATOMIZES
ALLUSIVELY	AMMONIATES	ANCESTORED
ALMSGIVERS	AMMUNITION	ANCESTRESS
ALMSGIVING	AMNESTYING	ANCESTRIES
ALMSHOUSES	AMORALISMS	ANCHORAGES
ALPHABETED	AMORTIZING	ANCHORITES
ALPHABETIC	AMPERSANDS	ANCHORITIC
ALPHAMERIC	AMPHIBIANS	ANCHORLESS
ALTERATION	AMPHIBIOUS	ANDROMEDAS
ALTERCATED	AMPICILLIN	ANECDOTAGE
ALTERCATES	AMPLIFIERS	ANECDOTIST
ALTERNATED	AMPLIFYING	ANEMOMETER
ALTERNATES	AMPLITUDES	ANEMOMETRY
ALTERNATOR	AMPUTATING	ANGELOLOGY
ALTIMETERS	AMPUTATION	ANGIOGENIC
ALTOGETHER	AMUSEMENTS	ANGIOGRAMS
ALTRUISTIC	ANABOLISMS	ANGIOSPERM
ALUMINATES	ANACHRONIC	ANGLERFISH
ALUMINIUMS	ANADROMOUS	ANGLEWORMS
ALUMINIZED	ANAGLYPHIC	ANGLICISMS
ALUMINIZES	ANAGRAMMED	ANGLICIZED
AMALGAMATE	ANALGESICS	ANGLICIZES
AMASSMENTS	ANALOGICAL	ANGLOPHONE
AMATEURISH	ANALOGISTS	ANGUISHING
AMATEURISM	ANALOGIZED	ANGULARITY
AMAZEMENTS	ANALOGIZES	ANGULATING
AMBASSADOR	ANALYTICAL	ANGULATION
AMBITIONED	ANALYZABLE	ANIMALISMS
AMBIVALENT	ANAMORPHIC	ANIMALIZED
AMBULANCES	ANAPLASIAS	ANIMALIZES
AMBULATING	ANAPLASTIC	ANIMATEDLY
AMBULATION	ANARCHICAL	ANIMATIONS

ANKLEBONES	ANTIDOTING	APOTHECARY
ANKYLOSAUR	ANTIFREEZE	APPARELLED
ANNALISTIC	ANTIFUNGAL	APPARENTLY
ANNEXATION	ANTIGROWTH	APPARITION
ANNIHILATE	ANTIMONIES	APPARITORS
ANNOTATING	ANTINOMIES	APPEALABLE
ANNOTATION	ANTIPODEAN	APPEARANCE
ANNOTATIVE	ANTIQUATED	APPEASABLE
ANNOTATORS	ANTIQUATES	APPELLANTS
ANNOUNCERS	ANTISEPTIC	APPENDAGES
ANNOUNCING	ANTISERUMS	APPENDANTS
ANNOYANCES	ANTISEXIST	APPENDICES
ANNOYINGLY	ANTISEXUAL	APPENDIXES
ANNUALIZED	ANTISOCIAL	APPERTAINS
ANNUALIZES	ANTITHESES	APPETISERS
ANNULATION	ANTITHESIS	APPETISING
ANNULMENTS	ANTITHETIC	APPETIZERS
ANNUNCIATE	APARTHEIDS	APPETIZING
ANODICALLY	APARTMENTS	APPLAUDERS
ANOINTMENT	APHORISING	APPLAUDING
ANSWERABLE	APHORISTIC	APPLECARTS
ANTAGONISM	APHORIZING	APPLEJACKS
ANTAGONIST	APOCALYPSE	APPLIANCES
ANTAGONIZE	APOCRYPHAL	APPLICABLE
ANTEBELLUM	APOLITICAL	APPLICANTS
ANTECEDENT	APOLOGETIC	APPLICATOR
ANTECEDING	APOLOGISED	APPOINTEES
ANTECESSOR	APOLOGISES	APPOINTING
ANTERIORLY	APOLOGISTS	APPOINTIVE
ANTEVERTED	APOLOGIZED	APPORTIONS
ANTHELIXES	APOLOGIZER	APPOSITELY
ANTHRACITE	APOLOGIZES	APPOSITION
ANTHROPOID	APOPLECTIC	APPOSITIVE
ANTHURIUMS	APOPLEXIES	APPRAISALS
ANTIBIOTIC	APOSPOROUS	APPRAISEES
ANTIBODIES	APOSTACIES	APPRAISERS
ANTICAKING	APOSTASIES	APPRAISING
ANTICANCER	APOSTATISE	APPRAISIVE
ANTICIPANT	APOSTATIZE	APPRECIATE
ANTICIPATE	APOSTOLATE	APPREHENDS
ANTICLIMAX	APOSTROPHE	APPRENTICE

APPROACHED	ARITHMETIC	ASCENDIBLE
APPROACHES	ARMADILLOS	ASCENSIONS
APPROBATED	ARMISTICES	ASCERTAINS
APPROBATES	ARMORIALLY	ASCETICISM
APPROVABLE	AROMATIZED	ASCORBATES
APPROVABLY	AROMATIZES	ASCRIBABLE
AQUAMARINE	ARPEGGIATE	ASCRIPTION
AQUAPLANED	ARRAIGNING	ASCRIPTIVE
AQUAPLANER	ARRESTANTS	ASEXUALITY
AQUAPLANES	ARRESTMENT	ASPARTAMES
AQUIFEROUS	ARRHYTHMIA	ASPARTATES
AQUILEGIAS	ARRHYTHMIC	ASPERATING
AQUILINITY	ARROGANCES	ASPERSIONS
ARABESQUES	ARROGANTLY	ASPHALTING
ARABICIZED	ARROGATING	ASPHALTITE
ARABICIZES	ARROGATION	ASPHERICAL
ARACHNOIDS	ARROWHEADS	ASPHYXIATE
ARBITRABLE	ARROWROOTS	ASPIDISTRA
ARBITRAGED	ARTEMISIAS	ASPIRATING
ARBITRAGER	ARTERIALLY	ASPIRATION
ARBITRAGES	ARTERIOLES	ASPIRATORS
ARBITRATED	ARTFULNESS	ASSAILABLE
ARBITRATES	ARTHRITICS	ASSAILANTS
ARBITRATOR	ARTHROPODS	ASSAULTERS
ARBOREALLY	ARTICHOKES	ASSAULTING
ARBORETUMS	ARTICULACY	ASSAULTIVE
ARBORIZING	ARTICULATE	ASSEMBLAGE
ARBORVITAE	ARTIFICERS	ASSEMBLERS
ARCHANGELS	ARTIFICIAL	ASSEMBLIES
ARCHBISHOP	ARTINESSES	ASSEMBLING
ARCHDEACON	ARTISTRIES	ASSERTEDLY
ARCHEOLOGY	ASAFOETIDA	ASSERTIONS
ARCHETYPAL	ASBESTOSES	ASSESSABLE
ARCHETYPES	ASBESTOSIS	ASSESSMENT
ARCHFIENDS	ASCENDABLE	ASSIGNABLE
ARCHITECTS	ASCENDANCE	ASSIGNMENT
ARCHITRAVE	ASCENDANCY	ASSIMILATE
ARCHIVISTS	ASCENDANTS	ASSISTANCE
ARCHIVOLTS	ASCENDENCE	ASSISTANTS
ARCTICALLY	ASCENDENCY	ASSOCIATED
ARISTOCRAT	ASCENDENTS	ASSOCIATES

ASSORTMENT	ATTENUATES	AUTOMATION
ASSUMPTION	ATTENUATOR	AUTOMATISM
ASSUMPTIVE	ATTORNMENT	AUTOMATIST
ASSURANCES	ATTRACTANT	AUTOMATIZE
ASTARBOARD	ATTRACTING	AUTOMATONS
ASTERISKED	ATTRACTION	AUTOMOBILE
ASTEROIDAL	ATTRACTIVE	AUTOMOTIVE
ASTHMATICS	ATTRACTORS	AUTONOMIES
ASTIGMATIC	ATTRIBUTED	AUTONOMIST
ASTONISHED	ATTRIBUTES	AUTONOMOUS
ASTONISHES	ATTRITIONS	AUTOPILOTS
ASTOUNDING	ATTUNEMENT	AUTOPSYING
ASTRICTING	ATYPICALLY	AUTUMNALLY
ASTRINGENT	AUBERGINES	AVALANCHED
ASTRINGING	AUCTIONEER	AVALANCHES
ASTROLOGER	AUCTIONING	AVARICIOUS
ASTROMETRY	AUDACITIES	AVENTURINE
ASTRONAUTS	AUDIBILITY	AVERSENESS
ASTRONOMER	AUDIOTAPES	AVERSIVELY
ASTRONOMIC	AUDITIONED	AVIATRICES
ASTUTENESS	AUDITORIES	AVIDNESSES
ASYMMETRIC	AUDITORILY	AVOCATIONS
ATMOSPHERE	AUDITORIUM	AVOIDANCES
ATOMICALLY	AUGMENTERS	AVOUCHMENT
ATONALISMS	AUGMENTING	AWAYNESSES
ATONALISTS	AUGMENTORS	AWKWARDEST
ATONEMENTS	AUGUSTNESS	AXILLARIES
ATROCITIES	AUSPICIOUS	AZEOTROPES
ATROPHYING	AUTHORISED	BABBLEMENT
ATTACHABLE	AUTHORISES	BABYSITTER
ATTACHMENT	AUTHORIZED	BACKBITERS
ATTAINABLE	AUTHORIZER	BACKBITING
ATTAINDERS	AUTHORIZES	BACKBITTEN
ATTAINMENT	AUTHORSHIP	BACKBOARDS
ATTAINTING	AUTOCLAVED	BACKCLOTHS
ATTEMPERED	AUTOCLAVES	BACKCOURTS
ATTEMPTING	AUTOCRATIC	BACKDATING
ATTENDANCE	AUTOGRAPHS	BACKFILLED
ATTENDANTS	AUTOGRAPHY	BACKFIRING
ATTENTIONS	AUTOMATICS	BACKFITTED
ATTENUATED	AUTOMATING	BACKGAMMON

BACKGROUND
BACKHANDED
BACKHANDER
BACKHAULED
BACKHOUSES
BACKLASHED
BACKLASHER
BACKLASHES
BACKLIGHTS
BACKLISTED
BACKLOGGED
BACKPACKED
BACKPACKER
BACKPEDALS
BACKRUSHES
BACKSLIDER
BACKSLIDES
BACKSPACED
BACKSPACES
BACKSPLASH
BACKSTAIRS
BACKSTITCH
BACKSTREET
BACKSTROKE
BACKTRACKS
BACKWARDLY
BACKWASHED
BACKWASHES
BACKWATERS
BACTERIZED
BACTERIZES
BADMOUTHED
BAFFLEMENT
BAFFLINGLY
BAGATELLES
BALACLAVAS
BALALAIKAS
BALDERDASH
BALDHEADED
BALDNESSES
BALLASTING

BALLERINAS
BALLISTICS
BALLOONING
BALLOONIST
BALLPLAYER
BALLPOINTS
BALLYHOOED
BALUSTRADE
BAMBOOZLED
BAMBOOZLES
BANALITIES
BANALIZING
BANDICOOTS
BANDLEADER
BANDMASTER
BANDSTANDS
BANISHMENT
BANISTERED
BANKROLLED
BANKROLLER
BANKRUPTCY
BANKRUPTED
BANNISTERS
BANQUETERS
BANQUETING
BANQUETTES
BAPTISTERY
BARBARIANS
BARBECUERS
BARBECUING
BARBEQUING
BARBERSHOP
BARBITONES
BAREBACKED
BAREFOOTED
BAREHEADED
BARENESSES
BARGAINERS
BARGAINING
BARKEEPERS
BAROMETERS

BAROMETRIC
BARONESSES
BARONETAGE
BARQUETTES
BARRACKERS
BARRACKING
BARRACUDAS
BARRELFULS
BARRELHEAD
BARRELLING
BARRENNESS
BARRICADED
BARRICADES
BARRISTERS
BARTENDERS
BARTENDING
BASEBOARDS
BASELINERS
BASENESSES
BASICITIES
BASKETBALL
BASKETLIKE
BASKETRIES
BASKETSFUL
BASKETWORK
BASSOONIST
BASTARDISE
BASTARDIZE
BATTALIONS
BATTLEMENT
BATTLESHIP
BAYONETING
BAYONETTED
BEACHCOMBS
BEACHFRONT
BEACHGOERS
BEACHHEADS
BEANSTALKS
BEASTLIEST
BEATITUDES
BEAUTICIAN

BEAUTIFIED	BELEAGUERS	BETROTHEDS
BEAUTIFIER	BELIEVABLE	BETROTHING
BEAUTIFIES	BELIEVABLY	BETTERMENT
BECOMINGLY	BELITTLERS	BEWILDERED
BEDAZZLING	BELITTLING	BEWITCHERY
BEDCHAMBER	BELLFLOWER	BEWITCHING
BEDCLOTHES	BELONGINGS	BIANNUALLY
BEDEAFENED	BELVEDERES	BIASNESSES
BEDEVILING	BEMUDDLING	BIBLICALLY
BEDEVILLED	BEMUSEMENT	BIBLICISMS
BEDFELLOWS	BEMUZZLING	BIBLICISTS
BEDRAGGLED	BENCHMARKS	BIBLIOLOGY
BEDRAGGLES	BENEFACTOR	BICULTURAL
BEDRENCHED	BENEFICENT	BICYCLISTS
BEDRENCHES	BENEFICIAL	BIENNIALLY
BEDSPREADS	BENEFICING	BIFURCATED
BEDSPRINGS	BENEFITERS	BIFURCATES
BEDWARFING	BENEFITING	BIGAMOUSLY
BEEFEATERS	BENEFITTED	BIGHEARTED
BEEFSTEAKS	BENEVOLENT	BIGMOUTHED
BEEKEEPERS	BENIGNANCY	BILHARZIAL
BEEKEEPING	BEQUEATHED	BILHARZIAS
BEFINGERED	BESCORCHED	BILINGUALS
BEFLAGGING	BESCORCHES	BILLABONGS
BEFLOWERED	BESCOURING	BILLBOARDS
BEFOREHAND	BESEECHING	BILLIONTHS
BEFORETIME	BESHADOWED	BINOCULARS
BEFRIENDED	BESMIRCHED	BIOCHEMIST
BEFRINGING	BESMIRCHES	BIODEGRADE
BEFUDDLING	BESPOUSING	BIODYNAMIC
BEGINNINGS	BESTIALITY	BIOGENETIC
BEGIRDLING	BESTIALIZE	BIOGRAPHER
BEGLADDING	BESTIARIES	BIOGRAPHIC
BEGLAMOURS	BESTIRRING	BIOHAZARDS
BEGRUDGING	BESTREWING	BIOLOGICAL
BEHAVIOURS	BESTRIDDEN	BIOLOGISMS
BEHEADINGS	BESTRIDING	BIOLOGISTS
BEJEWELLED	BESTROWING	BIOMEDICAL
BEKNIGHTED	BESTSELLER	BIOMETRICS
BEKNOTTING	BETOKENING	BIOMETRIES
BELABOURED	BETROTHALS	BIOMORPHIC

BIOPHYSICS
BIPOLARITY
BIPOLARIZE
BIRDHOUSES
BIRTHDATES
BIRTHMARKS
BIRTHPLACE
BIRTHRATES
BIRTHRIGHT
BIRTHROOTS
BIRTHSTONE
BISECTIONS
BISEXUALLY
BISHOPRICS
BISULFATES
BISULFIDES
BISULFITES
BITCHINESS
BITTERNESS
BITTERROOT
BITTERWEED
BITUMINOUS
BIVOUACKED
BIWEEKLIES
BLABBERING
BLACKBALLS
BLACKBERRY
BLACKBIRDS
BLACKBOARD
BLACKENERS
BLACKENING
BLACKFLIES
BLACKGUARD
BLACKHEADS
BLACKJACKS
BLACKLISTS
BLACKMAILS
BLACKSMITH
BLACKTHORN
BLAMEFULLY
BLANCMANGE

BLANDISHED
BLANDISHER
BLANDISHES
BLANKETING
BLANQUETTE
BLARNEYING
BLASPHEMED
BLASPHEMER
BLASPHEMES
BLATHERERS
BLATHERING
BLEACHABLE
BLEARINESS
BLEMISHING
BLETHERING
BLINDFOLDS
BLINDINGLY
BLINDSIDED
BLINDSIDES
BLINKERING
BLISSFULLY
BLISTERING
BLITHERING
BLITHESOME
BLIZZARDLY
BLOCKADING
BLOCKHEADS
BLOODBATHS
BLOODHOUND
BLOODINESS
BLOODLINES
BLOODROOTS
BLOODSHEDS
BLOODSTAIN
BLOODSTOCK
BLOODSTONE
BLOODWORMS
BLOSSOMING
BLOTCHIEST
BLOWFISHES
BLUBBERING

BLUDGEONED
BLUEBEARDS
BLUEBOTTLE
BLUEPRINTS
BLUNDERERS
BLUNDERING
BLURRINESS
BLURRINGLY
BLUSHINGLY
BLUSTFRERS
BLUSTERING
BLUSTEROUS
BOARDROOMS
BOARDWALKS
BOASTFULLY
BOATHOUSES
BOATSWAINS
BOBSLEDDED
BOBSLEDDER
BOBTAILING
BODYGUARDS
BODYSURFER
BOILERSUIT
BOISTEROUS
BOLDNESSES
BOLSTERING
BOMBARDIER
BOMBARDING
BOMBARDONS
BOMBINATED
BOMBINATES
BOMBSHELLS
BOMBSIGHTS
BONEHEADED
BONESETTER
BOOKBINDER
BOOKKEEPER
BOOKMAKERS
BOOKMAKING
BOOKMARKER
BOOKSELLER

BOOKSTALLS
BOOKSTORES
BOOMERANGS
BOOTLEGGED
BOOTLEGGER
BOOTLICKED
BOOTLICKER
BORDERLINE
BORROWINGS
BOTANICALS
BOTANIZING
BOTHERSOME
BOTTLENECK
BOTTOMLESS
BOTTOMMOST
BOULEVARDS
BOUNCINGLY
BOUNDARIES
BOUNDERISH
BOURGEOISE
BOURGEONED
BOYCOTTERS
BOYCOTTING
BOYFRIENDS
BOYISHNESS
BRACKETING
BRAINCHILD
BRAINPOWER
BRAINSTORM
BRANCHLESS
BRANCHLETS
BRANDISHED
BRANDISHES
BRASSERIES
BRASSIERES
BRASSINESS
BREADBOARD
BREADBOXES
BREADFRUIT
BREADLINES
BREAKABLES

BREAKAWAYS
BREAKDOWNS
BREAKFASTS
BREAKWATER
BREASTBONE
BREATHABLE
BREATHIEST
BREATHINGS
BREATHLESS
BREEZELESS
BREEZEWAYS
BREEZINESS
BRICKLAYER
BRICKWORKS
BRICKYARDS
BRIDEGROOM
BRIDESMAID
BRIDGEHEAD
BRIDGEWORK
BRIEFCASES
BRIGADIERS
BRIGANTINE
BRIGHTENED
BRIGHTENER
BRIGHTNESS
BRILLIANCE
BRILLIANCY
BRILLIANTS
BRIMSTONES
BROADCASTS
BROADENING
BROADSHEET
BROADSIDES
BROADSWORD
BROCHETTES
BROIDERIES
BROIDERING
BROKENNESS
BROKERAGES
BROKERINGS
BROMELIADS

BRONCHIOLE
BRONCHITES
BRONCHITIC
BRONCHITIS
BROODINESS
BROODINGLY
BROODMARES
BROOMSTICK
BROTHERING
BROWBEATEN
BRUSHLANDS
BRUTALISED
BRUTALISES
BRUTALIZED
BRUTALIZES
BRUTIFYING
BUBBLEGUMS
BUCCANEERS
BUCKBOARDS
BUCKETFULS
BUCKETSFUL
BUCKTHORNS
BUCKWHEATS
BUDGERIGAR
BUDGETEERS
BUFFOONERY
BUFFOONISH
BULLDOGGED
BULLDOZERS
BULLDOZING
BULLETINED
BULLFIGHTS
BULLHEADED
BULLNECKED
BULLRUSHES
BULWARKING
BUMBLEBEES
BUMBLINGLY
BUOYANCIES
BURDENSOME
BUREAUCRAT

BURGEONING	CAKEWALKER	CANDIDATES
BURGLARIES	CALABASHES	CANDIDNESS
BURGUNDIES	CALABOOSES	CANDYFLOSS
BURLESQUES	CALAMANDER	CANDYTUFTS
BURNISHERS	CALAMITIES	CANNELLONI
BURNISHING	CALAMITOUS	CANNISTERS
BURSITISES	CALCAREOUS	CANNONBALL
BUSHELLING	CALCIFYING	CANNONEERS
BUSHMASTER	CALCULABLE	CANONIZING
BUSHRANGER	CALCULATED	CANOODLING
BUSHWHACKS	CALCULATES	CANTALOUPE
BUSINESSES	CALCULATOR	CANTILEVER
BUSYBODIES	CALENDARED	CANVASLIKE
BUSYNESSES	CALENDERED	CANVASSERS
BUTCHERIES	CALENDERER	CANVASSING
BUTCHERING	CALENDULAS	CAPABILITY
BUTTERBALL	CALIBRATED	CAPACITATE
BUTTERCUPS	CALIBRATES	CAPACITIES
BUTTERMILK	CALIBRATOR	CAPACITIVE
BUTTERNUTS	CALIPERING	CAPACITORS
BUTTERWEED	CALLIPERED	CAPITALISM
BUTTERWORT	CALLOUSING	CAPITALIST
BUTTONHOLE	CALLOWNESS	CAPITALIZE
BUTTONLESS	CALMATIVES	CAPITATION
BUTTRESSED	CALMNESSES	CAPITULARY
BUTTRESSES	CALORIZING	CAPITULATE
BYPRODUCTS	CALUMNIATE	CAPONIZING
BYSTANDERS	CALUMNIOUS	CAPPUCCINO
CABALLEROS	CAMCORDERS	CAPRICIOUS
CABLEGRAMS	CAMOUFLAGE	CAPSULATED
CABRIOLETS	CAMPAIGNED	CAPSULIZED
CACCIATORE	CAMPAIGNER	CAPSULIZES
CACOGRAPHY	CAMPANILES	CAPTAINING
CADAVEROUS	CAMPANULAS	CAPTIONING
CADETSHIPS	CAMPGROUND	CAPTIOUSLY
CAESAREANS	CAMPHORAT	CAPTIVATED
CAESARIANS	CANCELLERS	CAPTIVATES
CAFETERIAS	CANCELLING	CAPTIVATOR
CAJOLEMENT	CANCELLOUS	CARAMELIZE
CAJOLERIES	CANDELABRA	CARAVANERS
CAKEWALKED	CANDESCENT	CARAVANING

CARAVANNED
CARAVANNER
CARBONADES
CARBONATED
CARBONATES
CARBONIZED
CARBONIZES
CARBONLESS
CARBUNCLED
CARBUNCLES
CARCINOGEN
CARCINOIDS
CARCINOMAS
CARDBOARDS
CARDHOLDER
CARDINALLY
CARDIOGRAM
CARDIOLOGY
CARDPLAYER
CARDSHARPS
CAREGIVERS
CAREGIVING
CARELESSLY
CARETAKERS
CARETAKING
CARICATURE
CARJACKERS
CARJACKING
CARNATIONS
CARNIVORES
CAROTENOID
CARPELLARY
CARPELLATE
CARPENTERS
CARPETINGS
CARROUSELS
CARTILAGES
CARTOONING
CARTOONISH
CARTOONIST
CARTOUCHES

CARTRIDGES
CARTWHEELS
CARYATIDES
CASEINATES
CASEWORKER
CASHIERING
CASSEROLES
CASSOULETS
CASTELLANS
CASTIGATED
CASTIGATES
CASTIGATOR
CASTRATING
CASTRATION
CASTRATORS
CASTRATORY
CASUALNESS
CASUALTIES
CATACLYSMS
CATALECTIC
CATALEPTIC
CATALOGUED
CATALOGUER
CATALOGUES
CATALYZERS
CATALYZING
CATAMARANS
CATAPULTED
CATATONICS
CATCALLING
CATCHMENTS
CATCHPENNY
CATCHPOLES
CATCHWORDS
CATECHISMS
CATECHIZED
CATECHIZER
CATECHIZES
CATEGORIES
CATEGORIZE
CATERWAULS

CATHEDRALS
CATNAPPERS
CATNAPPING
CAUSATIONS
CAUSATIVES
CAUSTICITY
CAUTERIZED
CAUTERIZES
CAUTIONARY
CAUTIONING
CAUTIOUSLY
CAVALCADES
CAVALIERED
CAVALLETTI
CAVALRYMAN
CAVALRYMEN
CEDARWOODS
CELANDINES
CELEBRANTS
CELEBRATED
CELEBRATES
CELEBRATOR
CELERITIES
CELESTIALS
CELESTITES
CELIBACIES
CELLBLOCKS
CELLOPHANE
CELLULITES
CELLULITIS
CELLULOIDS
CELLULOSES
CELLULOSIC
CEMETERIES
CENSORIOUS
CENSORSHIP
CENSURABLE
CENTENNIAL
CENTESIMAL
CENTIGRADE
CENTIGRAMS

CENTIPEDES	CHANCELLOR	CHATTERERS
CENTRALISE	CHANCERIES	CHATTERING
CENTRALISM	CHANCINESS	CHATTINESS
CENTRALIST	CHANDELIER	CHAUFFEURS
CENTRALITY	CHANGEABLE	CHAUSSURES
CENTRALIZE	CHANGEABLY	CHAUVINISM
CENTRICITY	CHANGELESS	CHAUVINIST
CENTRIFUGE	CHANGELING	CHEAPENING
CENTURIONS	CHANGEOVER	CHEAPISHLY
CERAMICIST	CHANNELERS	CHEAPJACKS
CEREBELLUM	CHANNELING	CHEAPSKATE
CEREBRALLY	CHANNELIZE	CHECKLISTS
CEREBRATED	CHANNELLED	CHECKMARKS
CEREBRATES	CHAPERONED	CHECKMATED
CEREMONIAL	CHAPERONES	CHECKMATES
CEREMONIES	CHAPLAINCY	CHECKPOINT
CERTIFIERS	CHAPTERING	CHECKREINS
CERTIFYING	CHARABANCS	CHEEKBONES
CERTITUDES	CHARACTERS	CHEEKINESS
CESSATIONS	CHARCOALED	CHEERFULLY
CHAFFERING	CHARDONNAY	CHEERINESS
CHAGRINNED	CHARGEABLE	CHEERLEADS
CHAINSAWED	CHARGEHAND	CHEESECAKE
CHAINWHEEL	CHARIOTEER	CHEESINESS
CHAIRLIFTS	CHARIOTING	CHEMICALLY
CHAIRWOMAN	CHARISMATA	CHEQUERING
CHAIRWOMEN	CHARITABLE	CHERISHERS
CHALCEDONY	CHARITABLY	CHERISHING
CHALKBOARD	CHARLADIES	CHERRYLIKE
CHALLENGED	CHARLATANS	CHERUBLIKE
CHALLENGER	CHARMINGLY	CHESSBOARD
CHALLENGES	CHARTERERS	CHEVALIERS
CHAMBERING	CHARTERING	CHICKADEES
CHAMELEONS	CHARTREUSE	CHICKENING
CHAMFERING	CHASTENERS	CHICKENPOX
CHAMOISING	CHASTENESS	CHICKORIES
CHAMOMILES	CHASTENING	CHICKWEEDS
CHAMPAGNES	CHASTISERS	CHIEFTAINS
CHAMPAIGNS	CHASTISING	CHIFFCHAFF
CHAMPIGNON	CHASTITIES	CHIFFONIER
CHAMPIONED	CHATTERBOX	CHIHUAHUAS

CHILBLAINS
CHILDBIRTH
CHILDHOODS
CHILDISHLY
CHILDLIEST
CHILDPROOF
CHILLINESS
CHILLINGLY
CHIMPANZEE
CHINCHILLA
CHIROMANCY
CHISELLERS
CHISELLING
CHITTERING
CHIVALRIES
CHIVALROUS
CHLAMYDIAL
CHLOROFORM
CHOCOHOLIC
CHOCOLATES
CHOCOLATEY
CHOICENESS
CHONDRITES
CHONDRITIC
CHOPPINESS
CHOPSTICKS
CHORISTERS
CHORUSSING
CHOWDERING
CHRISTENED
CHROMATICS
CHROMOSOME
CHRONICITY
CHRONICLED
CHRONICLER
CHRONICLES
CHRONOLOGY
CHRYSALIDS
CHUBBINESS
CHUCKHOLES
CHUCKWALLA

CHUMMINESS
CHUNTERING
CHURCHGOER
CHURCHIEST
CHURCHINGS
CHURCHLESS
CHURCHLIER
CHURCHYARD
CHURLISHLY
CICATRICES
CIGARETTES
CIGARILLOS
CINEMAGOER
CINEMATIZE
CINERARIUM
CINQUEFOIL
CIPHERTEXT
CIRCUITIES
CIRCUITING
CIRCUITOUS
CIRCULARLY
CIRCULATED
CIRCULATES
CIRCULATOR
CIRCUMCISE
CIRCUMFLEX
CIRCUMFUSE
CIRCUMVENT
CITRONELLA
CITYSCAPES
CIVILISING
CIVILITIES
CIVILIZERS
CIVILIZING
CLABBERING
CLAMBERERS
CLAMBERING
CLAMMINESS
CLAMOURING
CLAMSHELLS
CLANKINGLY

CLANNISHLY
CLAPBOARDS
CLARIFIERS
CLARIFYING
CLASSICISM
CLASSICIST
CLASSICIZE
CLASSIFIED
CLASSIFIER
CLASSIFIES
CLASSINESS
CLASSMATES
CLASSROOMS
CLATTERERS
CLATTERING
CLAVICHORD
CLAVICULAR
CLEARANCES
CLEMENCIES
CLERICALLY
CLERKSHIPS
CLEVERNESS
CLIENTELES
CLIENTLESS
CLIMAXLESS
CLINICALLY
CLINICIANS
CLINKERING
CLIPBOARDS
CLIPSHEETS
CLOAKROOMS
CLOBBERING
CLOCKWORKS
CLODHOPPER
CLOISTERED
CLOUDBURST
CLOUDINESS
CLOWNISHLY
CLUBFOOTED
CLUBHOUSES
CLUMSINESS

CLUSTERING
CLUTTERING
COACHWORKS
COAGULABLE
COAGULANTS
COAGULATED
COAGULATES
COALESCENT
COALESCING
COALFIELDS
COALITIONS
COARSENESS
COARSENING
COASSISTED
COASSUMING
COASTGUARD
COASTLANDS
COASTLINES
COASTWARDS
COATIMUNDI
COATTENDED
COATTESTED
COAUTHORED
COBWEBBING
COCHINEALS
COCKATIELS
COCKATRICE
COCKCHAFER
COCKFIGHTS
COCKNEYISM
COCKSCOMBS
COCKSFOOTS
COCREATING
COCREATORS
COCULTURED
COCULTURES
COCURATORS
CODERIVING
CODESIGNED
CODEVELOPS
CODICOLOGY

CODIRECTED
CODIRECTOR
CODISCOVER
CODSWALLOP
COERCIVELY
COERCIVITY
COEXISTENT
COEXISTING
COFFEEPOTS
COGITATING
COGITATION
COGITATIVE
COGNATIONS
COGNITIONS
COGNIZABLE
COGNIZABLY
COGNIZANCE
COHABITANT
COHABITING
COHERENCES
COHERENTLY
COHESIVELY
COIFFURING
COINCIDENT
COINCIDING
COLLAPSING
COLLARBONE
COLLARLESS
COLLATERAL
COLLATIONS
COLLEAGUES
COLLECTING
COLLECTION
COLLECTIVE
COLLECTORS
COLLEGIANS
COLLEGIATE
COLLEGIUMS
COLLIERIES
COLLIGATED
COLLIGATES

COLLIMATED
COLLIMATES
COLLIMATOR
COLLISIONS
COLLOQUIAL
COLLOQUIES
COLLOQUIST
COLLOQUIUM
COLLUSIONS
COLONIALLY
COLONISING
COLONIZERS
COLONIZING
COLONNADED
COLONNADES
COLOSSALLY
COLOSSEUMS
COLOSSUSES
COLOSTRUMS
COLUMBINES
COLUMNISTS
COMBATANTS
COMBATTING
COMBINABLE
COMBUSTING
COMBUSTION
COMBUSTIVE
COMBUSTORS
COMEDIENNE
COMELINESS
COMESTIBLE
COMFORTERS
COMFORTING
COMICALITY
COMINGLING
COMMANDANT
COMMANDEER
COMMANDERS
COMMANDERY
COMMANDING
COMMANDOES

COMMENCERS
COMMENCING
COMMENDERS
COMMENDING
COMMENSALS
COMMENTARY
COMMENTATE
COMMENTING
COMMERCIAL
COMMERCING
COMMINGLED
COMMINGLES
COMMISSARS
COMMISSARY
COMMISSION
COMMISSURE
COMMITMENT
COMMITTALS
COMMITTEES
COMMITTING
COMMIXTURE
COMMODIOUS
COMMODORES
COMMONALTY
COMMONNESS
COMMOTIONS
COMMUNALLY
COMMUNIONS
COMMUNISED
COMMUNISES
COMMUNISMS
COMMUNISTS
COMMUNIZED
COMMUNIZES
COMMUTABLE
COMMUTATED
COMMUTATES
COMMUTATOR
COMPACTING
COMPACTION
COMPACTORS

COMPANIONS
COMPANYING
COMPARABLE
COMPARABLY
COMPARATOR
COMPARISON
COMPARTING
COMPASSING
COMPASSION
COMPATIBLE
COMPATIBLY
COMPATRIOT
COMPEERING
COMPELLING
COMPENDIUM
COMPENSATE
COMPETENCE
COMPETENCY
COMPETITOR
COMPLACENT
COMPLAINED
COMPLAINER
COMPLAINTS
COMPLECTED
COMPLEMENT
COMPLETELY
COMPLETING
COMPLETION
COMPLETIST
COMPLETIVE
COMPLEXIFY
COMPLEXING
COMPLEXION
COMPLEXITY
COMPLIANCE
COMPLIANCY
COMPLICACY
COMPLICATE
COMPLICITY
COMPLIMENT
COMPONENTS

COMPORTING
COMPOSEDLY
COMPOSITED
COMPOSITES
COMPOSITOR
COMPOSTING
COMPOSURES
COMPOUNDED
COMPOUNDER
COMPREHEND
COMPRESSED
COMPRESSES
COMPRESSOR
COMPRISING
COMPRIZING
COMPROMISE
COMPULSION
COMPULSIVE
COMPULSORY
COMPUTABLE
CONCEALERS
CONCEALING
CONCEDEDLY
CONCEITING
CONCEIVERS
CONCEIVING
CONCENTERS
CONCENTRIC
CONCEPTION
CONCEPTIVE
CONCEPTUAL
CONCERNING
CONCERTINA
CONCERTING
CONCERTINO
CONCERTIZE
CONCESSION
CONCESSIVE
CONCHOLOGY
CONCIERGES
CONCILIATE

CONCLUDING
CONCLUSION
CONCLUSIVE
CONCLUSORY
CONCOCTERS
CONCOCTING
CONCOCTION
CONCOCTIVE
CONCORDANT
CONCORDATS
CONCOURSES
CONCRETELY
CONCRETING
CONCRETION
CONCRETISM
CONCRETIST
CONCRETIZE
CONCUBINES
CONCURRENT
CONCURRING
CONCUSSING
CONCUSSION
CONCUSSIVE
CONDEMNERS
CONDEMNING
CONDEMNORS
CONDENSATE
CONDENSERS
CONDENSING
CONDESCEND
CONDIMENTS
CONDITIONS
CONDOLENCE
CONDONABLE
CONDUCTING
CONDUCTION
CONDUCTIVE
CONDUCTORS
CONEFLOWER
CONFECTING
CONFECTION

CONFEDERAL
CONFERENCE
CONFERMENT
CONFERRALS
CONFERRERS
CONFERRING
CONFESSING
CONFESSION
CONFESSORS
CONFIDANTE
CONFIDANTS
CONFIDENCE
CONFIGURED
CONFIGURES
CONFIRMING
CONFISCATE
CONFITURES
CONFLATING
CONFLATION
CONFLICTED
CONFLUENCE
CONFLUENTS
CONFORMERS
CONFORMING
CONFORMISM
CONFORMIST
CONFORMITY
CONFOUNDED
CONFOUNDER
CONFRONTAL
CONFRONTED
CONFRONTER
CONFUSEDLY
CONFUSIONS
CONGEALING
CONGENERIC
CONGENITAL
CONGESTING
CONGESTION
CONGESTIVE
CONGLOBATE

CONGLOBING
CONGREGANT
CONGREGATE
CONGRESSED
CONGRESSES
CONGRUENCE
CONGRUENCY
CONIFEROUS
CONJECTURE
CONJOINING
CONJOINTLY
CONJUGALLY
CONJUGANTS
CONJUGATED
CONJUGATES
CONNECTERS
CONNECTING
CONNECTION
CONNECTIVE
CONNECTORS
CONNEXIONS
CONNIVANCE
CONQUERING
CONQUERORS
CONSCIENCE
CONSCRIBED
CONSCRIBES
CONSCRIPTS
CONSECRATE
CONSENSUAL
CONSENTERS
CONSENTING
CONSEQUENT
CONSERVERS
CONSERVING
CONSIDERED
CONSIGNEES
CONSIGNING
CONSIGNORS
CONSISTENT
CONSISTING

CONSISTORY
CONSOCIATE
CONSONANCE
CONSONANCY
CONSONANTS
CONSORTING
CONSORTIUM
CONSPIRACY
CONSPIRING
CONSTABLES
CONSTANTLY
CONSTIPATE
CONSTITUTE
CONSTRAINS
CONSTRAINT
CONSTRICTS
CONSTRUCTS
CONSTRUING
CONSULATES
CONSULSHIP
CONSULTANT
CONSULTERS
CONSULTING
CONSULTIVE
CONSULTORS
CONSUMABLE
CONSUMEDLY
CONSUMMATE
CONTACTING
CONTAGIONS
CONTAGIOUS
CONTAINERS
CONTAINING
CONTENDERS
CONTENDING
CONTENTING
CONTENTION
CONTESTANT
CONTESTERS
CONTESTING
CONTEXTUAL

CONTEXTURE
CONTIGUITY
CONTIGUOUS
CONTINENCE
CONTINENTS
CONTINGENT
CONTINUANT
CONTINUATE
CONTINUERS
CONTINUING
CONTINUITY
CONTINUOUS
CONTORTING
CONTORTION
CONTORTIVE
CONTOURING
CONTRABAND
CONTRACTED
CONTRACTOR
CONTRADICT
CONTRALTOS
CONTRARIES
CONTRARILY
CONTRASTED
CONTRAVENE
CONTRIBUTE
CONTRITELY
CONTRITION
CONTRIVERS
CONTRIVING
CONTROLLED
CONTROLLER
CONTROVERT
CONTUSIONS
CONUNDRUMS
CONVALESCE
CONVECTING
CONVECTION
CONVECTIVE
CONVECTORS
CONVENIENT

CONVENTING
CONVENTION
CONVENTUAL
CONVERGENT
CONVERGING
CONVERSANT
CONVERSELY
CONVERSERS
CONVERSING
CONVERSION
CONVERTERS
CONVERTING
CONVERTORS
CONVEYANCE
CONVICTING
CONVICTION
CONVINCERS
CONVINCING
CONVOLUTED
CONVOLUTES
CONVOLVING
CONVULSANT
CONVULSING
CONVULSION
CONVULSIVE
COOLHEADED
COOLNESSES
COOPERATED
COOPERATES
COOPERATOR
COORDINATE
COPPERHEAD
COPRESENTS
COPRODUCED
COPRODUCER
COPRODUCES
COPRODUCTS
COPULATING
COPULATION
COPULATIVE
COPULATORY

COPURIFIED
COPURIFIES
COPYCATTED
COPYEDITED
COPYHOLDER
COPYREADER
COPYRIGHTS
COPYWRITER
COQUETRIES
COQUETTING
COQUETTISH
CORDIALITY
CORDUROYED
CORDWAINER
CORELATING
CORESIDENT
CORIANDERS
CORKSCREWS
CORMORANTS
CORNBREADS
CORNCRAKES
CORNERBACK
CORNERWAYS
CORNERWISE
CORNETISTS
CORNETTIST
CORNFIELDS
CORNFLAKES
CORNFLOWER
CORNSTALKS
CORNSTARCH
CORNUCOPIA
CORONARIES
CORONATING
CORONATION
COROTATING
COROTATION
CORPORALLY
CORPORATOR
CORPULENCE
CORPULENCY

CORPUSCLES
CORRALLING
CORRECTING
CORRECTION
CORRECTIVE
CORRECTORS
CORRELATED
CORRELATES
CORRELATOR
CORRESPOND
CORRIGIBLE
CORRODIBLE
CORROSIONS
CORROSIVES
CORRUGATED
CORRUGATES
CORRUPTERS
CORRUPTEST
CORRUPTING
CORRUPTION
CORRUPTIVE
CORRUPTORS
CORSELETTE
CORSETIERE
CORSETRIES
CORTISONES
COSCRIPTED
COSINESSES
COSMICALLY
COSMONAUTS
COSTARRING
COSTLESSLY
COSTLINESS
COSTUMIERS
COTYLEDONS
COUNCILLOR
COUNCILMAN
COUNCILMEN
COUNSELLED
COUNSELLOR
COUNTDOWNS

COUNTERACT
COUNTERBID
COUNTERCRY
COUNTERING
COUNTERSPY
COUNTERTOP
COUNTESSES
COUNTRYMAN
COUNTRYMEN
COURAGEOUS
COURGETTES
COURSEWARE
COURTESANS
COURTESIED
COURTESIES
COURTHOUSE
COURTLIEST
COURTROOMS
COURTSHIPS
COURTSIDES
COURTYARDS
COUSCOUSES
COUSINHOOD
COUSINSHIP
COUTURIERS
COVALENCES
COVALENTLY
COVENANTED
COVENANTEE
COVENANTER
COVENANTOR
COVERTNESS
COVERTURES
COVETINGLY
COVETOUSLY
COWARDICES
COXSWAINED
COZINESSES
CRACKAJACK
CRACKDOWNS
CRACKLINGS

CRAFTINESS
CRAGGINESS
CRANESBILL
CRANIOLOGY
CRANKINESS
CRANKSHAFT
CRASHINGLY
CRASSITUDE
CRATERLIKE
CREAMERIES
CREAMINESS
CREASELESS
CREATIVELY
CREATIVITY
CREDENTIAL
CREDITABLE
CREDITABLY
CREEPINESS
CREMATIONS
CREMATORIA
CRENATIONS
CRENELATED
CRENELLING
CRENULATED
CREOSOTING
CREPITATED
CREPITATES
CREPUSCLES
CREPUSCULE
CRESCENDOS
CRESCENTIC
CREVASSING
CREWELWORK
CRICKETERS
CRICKETING
CRIMINALLY
CRIMINATED
CRIMINATES
CRINKLIEST
CRINOLINED
CRINOLINES

CRISPBREAD
CRISPENING
CRISPINESS
CRISSCROSS
CRITERIONS
CRITERIUMS
CRITICALLY
CRITICISED
CRITICISES
CRITICISMS
CRITICIZED
CRITICIZER
CRITICIZES
CROCHETERS
CROCHETING
CROCKERIES
CROCODILES
CROISSANTS
CROQUETTES
CROSSBEAMS
CROSSBILLS
CROSSBREDS
CROSSBREED
CROSSFIRES
CROSSHATCH
CROSSHEADS
CROSSOVERS
CROSSPATCH
CROSSPIECE
CROSSROADS
CROSSWORDS
CROWBARRED
CRUCIFIXES
CRUCIFORMS
CRUCIFYING
CRUMBLIEST
CRUMBLINGS
CRUMMINESS
CRUMPLIEST
CRUNCHABLE
CRUNCHIEST

CRUSHINGLY
CRUSHPROOF
CRUSTACEAN
CRUSTINESS
CRYOGENICS
CRYOSCOPES
CRYOSCOPIC
CRYPTOGRAM
CRYPTOLOGY
CRYSTALIZE
CUBBYHOLES
CUCKOLDING
CUCKOOPINT
CUDDLESOME
CUDGELLING
CULINARILY
CULMINATED
CULMINATES
CULTIVABLE
CULTIVATED
CULTIVATES
CULTIVATOR
CULTURALLY
CUMBERSOME
CUMMERBUND
CUMULATING
CUMULATION
CUMULATIVE
CUNEIFORMS
CURABILITY
CURATIVELY
CURBSTONES
CURRENCIES
CURRICULAR
CURRICULUM
CURRYCOMBS
CURSEDNESS
CURTAILERS
CURTAILING
CURTAINING
CURTSEYING

CURVACEOUS	DAYDREAMED	DECENNIUMS
CURVATURES	DAYDREAMER	DECEPTIONS
CUSHIONING	DAZZLINGLY	DECIMALIZE
CUSSEDNESS	DEACONRIES	DECIMATING
CUSTODIANS	DEACTIVATE	DECIMATION
CUSTOMISED	DEADENINGS	DECIPHERED
CUSTOMISES	DEADHEADED	DECIPHERER
CUSTOMIZED	DEADLIFTED	DECISIONAL
CUSTOMIZER	DEADLIGHTS	DECISIONED
CUSTOMIZES	DEADLINESS	DECISIVELY
CUTABILITY	DEADLOCKED	DECLAIMERS
CUTTHROATS	DEADNESSES	DECLAIMING
CUTTLEBONE	DEADPANNED	DECLARABLE
CUTTLEFISH	DEADPANNER	DECLARANTS
CYBERNETIC	DEADWEIGHT	DECLASSIFY
CYBERSPACE	DEAFNESSES	DECLASSING
CYCLOTRONS	DEALERSHIP	DECLENSION
CYLINDERED	DEATHTRAPS	DECLINABLE
CYMBALISTS	DEATHWATCH	DECOCTIONS
DACHSHUNDS	DEBARMENTS	DECOLLATED
DAGGERLIKE	DEBASEMENT	DECOLLATES
DAINTINESS	DEBATEMENT	DECOLONIZE
DAIRYMAIDS	DEBAUCHERY	DECOLOURED
DALLIANCES	DEBAUCHING	DECOMPOSED
DALMATIANS	DEBILITATE	DECOMPOSER
DAMAGINGLY	DEBILITIES	DECOMPOSES
DAMNATIONS	DEBONAIRLY	DECOMPOUND
DAMNIFYING	DEBRIEFING	DECOMPRESS
DAMPNESSES	DEBRUISING	DECONGESTS
DAMSELFISH	DEBUTANTES	DECONTROLS
DANDELIONS	DECADENCES	DECORATING
DANDIFYING	DECADENTLY	DECORATION
DANDYISHLY	DECAHEDRON	DECORATIVE
DANKNESSES	DECAMPMENT	DECORATORS
DAPPERNESS	DECAPITATE	DECOROUSLY
DAREDEVILS	DECATHLETE	DECOUPAGED
DARINGNESS	DECATHLONS	DECOUPAGES
DARKNESSES	DECEIVABLE	DECOUPLING
DARTBOARDS	DECELERATE	DECREASING
DASHBOARDS	DECENARIES	DECREMENTS
DAUNTINGLY	DECENNIALS	DECREPITLY

DECROWNING
DECRYPTING
DECRYPTION
DEDICATEES
DEDICATING
DEDICATION
DEDICATORS
DEDICATORY
DEDUCTIBLE
DEDUCTIONS
DEEPNESSES
DEERHOUNDS
DEFACEMENT
DEFAMATION
DEFAMATORY
DEFEATISTS
DEFECTIONS
DEFECTIVES
DEFEMINIZE
DEFENDABLE
DEFENDANTS
DEFENSIVES
DEFERENCES
DEFERMENTS
DEFERRABLE
DEFICIENCY
DEFICIENTS
DEFILEMENT
DEFINITELY
DEFINITION
DEFINITIVE
DEFINITIZE
DEFINITUDE
DEFLAGRATE
DEFLATIONS
DEFLECTING
DEFLECTION
DEFLECTIVE
DEFLECTORS
DEFLOWERED
DEFOCUSING

DEFOCUSSED
DEFOCUSSES
DEFOLIATED
DEFOLIATES
DEFOLIATOR
DEFORESTED
DEFORMABLE
DEFRAUDERS
DEFRAUDING
DEFROCKING
DEFROSTERS
DEFROSTING
DEFTNESSES
DEGENERACY
DEGENERATE
DEGRADABLE
DEGRADEDLY
DEGREASERS
DEGREASING
DEHUMANIZE
DEHUMIDIFY
DEHYDRATED
DEHYDRATES
DEHYDRATOR
DEJECTEDLY
DEJECTIONS
DELECTABLE
DELECTABLY
DELEGACIES
DELEGATING
DELEGATION
DELEGATORS
DELIBERATE
DELICACIES
DELICATELY
DELIGHTERS
DELIGHTFUL
DELIGHTING
DELIMITERS
DELIMITING
DELINEATED

DELINEATES
DELINEATOR
DELINQUENT
DELIVERERS
DELIVERIES
DELIVERING
DELPHINIUM
DELUSIONAL
DELUSIVELY
DEMANDABLE
DEMANDANTS
DEMARCATED
DEMARCATES
DEMEANOURS
DEMENTEDLY
DEMOBILIZE
DEMOCRATIC
DEMODULATE
DEMOGRAPHY
DEMOISELLE
DEMOLISHED
DEMOLISHER
DEMOLISHES
DEMOLITION
DEMONIACAL
DEMONIZING
DEMONOLOGY
DEMORALIZE
DEMOUNTING
DEMURENESS
DENIGRATED
DENIGRATES
DENIGRATOR
DENOTATION
DENOTATIVE
DENOTEMENT
DENOUEMENT
DENOUNCERS
DENOUNCING
DENSIFYING
DENTITIONS

DENTURISTS
DENUDATING
DENUDATION
DENUDEMENT
DEODORANTS
DEODORIZED
DEODORIZER
DEODORIZES
DEONTOLOGY
DEPARTMENT
DEPARTURES
DEPENDABLE
DEPENDABLY
DEPENDANCE
DEPENDANTS
DEPENDENCE
DEPENDENCY
DEPENDENTS
DEPICTIONS
DEPILATING
DEPILATION
DEPILATORY
DEPLETABLE
DEPLETIONS
DEPLORABLE
DEPLORABLY
DEPLOYABLE
DEPLOYMENT
DEPOLARIZE
DEPOLISHED
DEPOLISHES
DEPOPULATE
DEPORTABLE
DEPORTMENT
DEPOSITARY
DEPOSITING
DEPOSITION
DEPOSITORS
DEPOSITORY
DEPRAVEDLY
DEPRECATED

DEPRECATES
DEPRECIATE
DEPREDATED
DEPREDATES
DEPREDATOR
DEPRESSANT
DEPRESSING
DEPRESSION
DEPRESSIVE
DEPRESSORS
DEPUTIZING
DERAIGNING
DERAILMENT
DEREGULATE
DERISIVELY
DERIVATION
DERIVATIVE
DERIVATIZE
DERMATITIS
DEROGATIVE
DEROGATORY
DESALINATE
DESALINIZE
DESCANTING
DESCENDANT
DESCENDENT
DESCENDERS
DESCENDING
DESCENSION
DESCRIBERS
DESCRIBING
DESCRIPTOR
DESECRATED
DESECRATER
DESECRATES
DESECRATOR
DESELECTED
DESERTIONS
DESERVEDLY
DESERVINGS
DESICCANTS

DESICCATED
DESICCATES
DESICCATOR
DESIGNATED
DESIGNATES
DESIGNATOR
DESIGNEDLY
DESIGNMENT
DESIRABLES
DESIROUSLY
DESOLATELY
DESOLATERS
DESOLATING
DESOLATION
DESOLATORS
DESORPTION
DESPAIRERS
DESPAIRING
DESPATCHED
DESPATCHES
DESPERADOS
DESPICABLE
DESPICABLY
DESPOILERS
DESPOILING
DESPONDENT
DESPONDING
DESPOTISMS
DESTAINING
DESTROYERS
DESTROYING
DESTRUCTED
DETACHABLE
DETACHABLY
DETACHEDLY
DETACHMENT
DETAILEDLY
DETAINMENT
DETECTABLE
DETECTIONS
DETECTIVES

DETENTIONS
DETERGENCY
DETERGENTS
DETERMENTS
DETERMINED
DETERMINER
DETERMINES
DETERRABLE
DETERRENCE
DETERRENTS
DETESTABLE
DETESTABLY
DETHRONING
DETONATING
DETONATION
DETONATIVE
DETONATORS
DETOXICANT
DETOXICATE
DETOXIFIED
DETOXIFIES
DETRACTING
DETRACTION
DETRACTIVE
DETRACTORS
DETRAINING
DETRIMENTS
DEVALUATED
DEVALUATES
DEVASTATED
DEVASTATES
DEVASTATOR
DEVELOPERS
DEVELOPING
DEVIANCIES
DEVIATIONS
DEVILISHLY
DEVILMENTS
DEVOLUTION
DEVOTEMENT
DEVOTIONAL

DEVOUTNESS
DIABOLICAL
DIABOLISMS
DIABOLISTS
DIABOLIZED
DIABOLIZES
DIAGNOSING
DIAGNOSTIC
DIAGONALLY
DIAGRAMMED
DIALOGUING
DIAPHRAGMS
DIARRHOEAS
DICTATIONS
DICTIONARY
DIDACTICAL
DIDGERIDOO
DIETICIANS
DIETITIANS
DIFFERENCE
DIFFICULTY
DIFFIDENCE
DIFFRACTED
DIFFUSIBLE
DIFFUSIONS
DIGESTIBLE
DIGESTIONS
DIGESTIVES
DIGITALIZE
DIGITIZING
DIGNIFYING
DIGRESSING
DIGRESSION
DIGRESSIVE
DILAPIDATE
DILATATION
DILATORILY
DILEMMATIC
DILETTANTE
DILETTANTI
DILIGENCES

DILIGENTLY
DILLYDALLY
DILUTENESS
DIMENSIONS
DIMINISHED
DIMINISHES
DIMINUTIVE
DIMORPHISM
DIMORPHOUS
DINNERTIME
DIPHTHERIA
DIPHTHONGS
DIPHYLETIC
DIPLOMATIC
DIRECTIONS
DIRECTIVES
DIRECTNESS
DIRIGIBLES
DISABILITY
DISAFFECTS
DISAFFIRMS
DISALLOWED
DISAPPEARS
DISAPPOINT
DISAPPROVE
DISARRANGE
DISARRAYED
DISASTROUS
DISBANDING
DISBARMENT
DISBARRING
DISBELIEFS
DISBELIEVE
DISBURSERS
DISBURSING
DISCANTING
DISCARDERS
DISCARDING
DISCERNERS
DISCERNING
DISCHARGED

DISCHARGEE
DISCHARGER
DISCHARGES
DISCIPLINE
DISCIPLING
DISCLAIMED
DISCLAIMER
DISCLOSERS
DISCLOSING
DISCLOSURE
DISCOMFORT
DISCONCERT
DISCONFIRM
DISCONNECT
DISCONTENT
DISCORDANT
DISCORDING
DISCOUNTED
DISCOUNTER
DISCOURAGE
DISCOURSED
DISCOURSER
DISCOURSES
DISCOVERED
DISCOVERER
DISCREDITS
DISCREETER
DISCREETLY
DISCRETELY
DISCRETION
DISCUSSERS
DISCUSSING
DISCUSSION
DISDAINFUL
DISDAINING
DISEMBARKS
DISEMBOWEL
DISENCHANT
DISENDOWED
DISENGAGED
DISENGAGES

DISENTAILS
DISENTHRAL
DISENTITLE
DISESTEEMS
DISFIGURED
DISFIGURES
DISFROCKED
DISFURNISH
DISGORGING
DISGRACERS
DISGRACING
DISGRUNTLE
DISGUISERS
DISGUISING
DISGUSTFUL
DISGUSTING
DISHARMONY
DISHCLOTHS
DISHEARTEN
DISHERITED
DISHONESTY
DISHONORED
DISHTOWELS
DISHWASHER
DISINCLINE
DISINFECTS
DISINFESTS
DISINHERIT
DISINHIBIT
DISINVESTS
DISINVITED
DISINVITES
DISJOINTED
DISLIKABLE
DISLOCATED
DISLOCATES
DISLODGING
DISLOYALLY
DISLOYALTY
DISMANTLED
DISMANTLES

DISMEMBERS
DISMISSALS
DISMISSING
DISMISSION
DISMISSIVE
DISMOUNTED
DISOBEYERS
DISOBEYING
DISOBLIGED
DISOBLIGES
DISORDERED
DISORDERLY
DISORIENTS
DISPARAGED
DISPARAGER
DISPARAGES
DISPARTING
DISPASSION
DISPATCHED
DISPATCHER
DISPATCHES
DISPELLING
DISPENDING
DISPENSARY
DISPENSERS
DISPENSING
DISPERSALS
DISPERSANT
DISPERSERS
DISPERSING
DISPERSION
DISPERSIVE
DISPIRITED
DISPITEOUS
DISPLACING
DISPLANTED
DISPLAYING
DISPLEASED
DISPLEASES
DISPLODING
DISPLOSION

DISPOSABLE	DISSOLUBLE	DIVESTMENT
DISPOSSESS	DISSOLVENT	DIVINATION
DISPOSURES	DISSOLVERS	DIVINATORY
DISPROVING	DISSOLVING	DIVINISING
DISPUTABLE	DISSONANCE	DIVINITIES
DISPUTABLY	DISSUADERS	DIVINIZING
DISPUTANTS	DISSUADING	DIVISIONAL
DISQUALIFY	DISSUASION	DIVISIVELY
DISQUIETED	DISSUASIVE	DIVULGENCE
DISQUIETLY	DISTAINING	DIZZYINGLY
DISREGARDS	DISTANCING	DOCILITIES
DISRELATED	DISTASTING	DOCKWORKER
DISREPAIRS	DISTEMPERS	DOCTORATES
DISREPUTES	DISTENDING	DOCTORSHIP
DISRESPECT	DISTENSION	DOCUMENTAL
DISRUPTERS	DISTENTION	DOCUMENTED
DISRUPTING	DISTILLATE	DOCUMENTER
DISRUPTION	DISTILLERS	DOGGEDNESS
DISRUPTIVE	DISTILLERY	DOGLEGGING
DISSATISFY	DISTILLING	DOGMATICAL
DISSECTING	DISTINCTER	DOGMATISMS
DISSECTION	DISTINCTLY	DOGMATISTS
DISSECTORS	DISTORTERS	DOGMATIZED
DISSEMBLED	DISTORTING	DOGMATIZER
DISSEMBLER	DISTORTION	DOGMATIZES
DISSEMBLES	DISTRACTED	DOGNAPPERS
DISSENSION	DISTRAINED	DOGNAPPING
DISSENTERS	DISTRAINER	DOGSBODIES
DISSENTING	DISTRAINTS	DOGSLEDDED
DISSENTION	DISTRAUGHT	DOGSLEDDER
DISSERTATE	DISTRESSED	DOGWATCHES
DISSERTING	DISTRESSES	DOLLHOUSES
DISSERVICE	DISTRIBUTE	DOMICILING
DISSERVING	DISTRICTED	DOMINANCES
DISSIDENCE	DISTRUSTED	DOMINANTLY
DISSIDENTS	DISTURBERS	DOMINATING
DISSIMILAR	DISTURBING	DOMINATION
DISSIPATED	DIVEBOMBED	DOMINATIVE
DISSIPATER	DIVERGENCE	DOMINATORS
DISSIPATES	DIVERGENCY	DOMINATRIX
DISSOCIATE	DIVERSIONS	DOMINEERED

674

DONKEYWORK
DOODLEBUGS
DOORKEEPER
DOORPLATES
DOPINESSES
DORMANCIES
DOUBTFULLY
DOUBTINGLY
DOVETAILED
DOVISHNESS
DOWNBURSTS
DOWNFALLEN
DOWNGRADED
DOWNGRADES
DOWNLOADED
DOWNSCALED
DOWNSCALES
DOWNSHIFTS
DOWNSIZING
DOWNSLIDES
DOWNSTAIRS
DOWNSTREAM
DRAFTINESS
DRAGGINGLY
DRAINPIPES
DRAMATISED
DRAMATISES
DRAMATISTS
DRAMATIZED
DRAMATIZES
DRAUGHTIER
DRAUGHTING
DRAWBRIDGE
DRAWERFULS
DRAWSTRING
DREADFULLY
DREADLOCKS
DREAMFULLY
DREAMINESS
DREAMLANDS
DREAMTIMES

DREAMWORLD
DREARINESS
DRESSINESS
DRESSMAKER
DRIFTINGLY
DRIFTWOODS
DRINKABLES
DRIPSTONES
DRIVELLING
DRIVENNESS
DRIVERLESS
DRIVESHAFT
DROOPINGLY
DROWSINESS
DRUDGERIES
DRUDGINGLY
DRUGSTORES
DRUMSTICKS
DUCKBOARDS
DULCIFYING
DUMBSTRUCK
DUMFOUNDED
DUNDERHEAD
DUNGEONING
DUPLICATED
DUPLICATES
DUPLICATOR
DURABILITY
DWARFISHLY
DYNAMITERS
DYNAMITING
DYSENTERIC
DYSPEPSIAS
DYSPEPSIES
DYSPEPTICS
DYSPHAGIAS
DYSPHASIAS
DYSPHASICS
DYSPLASIAS
DYSPLASTIC
EARMARKING

EARTHBOUND
EARTHINESS
EARTHLINGS
EARTHQUAKE
EARTHWORMS
EARWIGGING
EASTERLIES
EASTERNERS
EAVESDROPS
EBULLIENCE
EBULLIENCY
EBULLITION
ECCENTRICS
ECHINODERM
ECLAMPSIAS
ECLIPSISES
ECOLOGICAL
ECOLOGISTS
ECONOMICAL
ECONOMISED
ECONOMISES
ECONOMISTS
ECONOMIZED
ECONOMIZER
ECONOMIZES
ECOSPECIES
ECOSPHERES
ECOSYSTEMS
ECTODERMAL
ECTOMORPHS
ECTOPLASMS
ECTOTHERMS
ECUMENICAL
ECUMENISMS
ECUMENISTS
EDIBLENESS
EDITORIALS
EDITORSHIP
EDUCATIONS
EFFACEABLE
EFFACEMENT

EFFECTIVES	ELIMINATOR	EMBROIDERS
EFFECTUATE	ELLIPSOIDS	EMBROIDERY
EFFEMINACY	ELLIPTICAL	EMENDATION
EFFEMINATE	ELOCUTIONS	EMERGENCES
EFFERENTLY	ELONGATING	EMETICALLY
EFFERVESCE	ELONGATION	EMIGRATING
EFFICACIES	ELOPEMENTS	EMIGRATION
EFFICACITY	ELOQUENCES	EMINENCIES
EFFICIENCY	ELOQUENTLY	EMISSARIES
EFFORTLESS	ELUCIDATED	EMITTANCES
EFFRONTERY	ELUCIDATES	EMOLLIENTS
EFFULGENCE	ELUCIDATOR	EMOLUMENTS
EFFUSIVELY	ELUVIATING	EMPATHETIC
EGOCENTRIC	ELUVIATION	EMPATHISED
EGOISTICAL	EMACIATING	EMPATHISES
EGOMANIACS	EMACIATION	EMPATHIZED
EIDERDOWNS	EMANATIONS	EMPATHIZES
EIGHTEENTH	EMANCIPATE	EMPHASISED
EIGHTIETHS	EMASCULATE	EMPHASISES
EJACULATED	EMBALMMENT	EMPHASIZED
EJACULATES	EMBANKMENT	EMPHASIZES
EJACULATOR	EMBARGOING	EMPLOYABLE
EJECTMENTS	EMBARKMENT	EMPLOYMENT
ELABORATED	EMBASSAGES	EMPOISONED
ELABORATES	EMBATTLING	EMPOWERING
ELASTICITY	EMBEDDINGS	EMULATIONS
ELASTOMERS	EMBEDMENTS	EMULSIFIED
ELATEDNESS	EMBEZZLERS	EMULSIFIER
ELDERBERRY	EMBEZZLING	EMULSIFIES
ELDERSHIPS	EMBITTERED	ENACTMENTS
ELECTIVELY	EMBLAZONED	ENAMELISTS
ELECTORATE	EMBLAZONER	ENAMELLING
ELECTRICAL	EMBLAZONRY	ENAMOURING
ELECTRODES	EMBLEMATIC	ENCAMPMENT
ELECTRONIC	EMBLEMENTS	ENCAPSULED
ELEGANCIES	EMBODIMENT	ENCAPSULES
ELEMENTALS	EMBOLDENED	ENCASEMENT
ELEMENTARY	EMBOLISMIC	ENCASHABLE
ELEVATIONS	EMBOSOMING	ENCASHMENT
ELIMINATED	EMBOSSMENT	ENCAUSTICS
ELIMINATES	EMBOWELLED	ENCEPHALON

ENCHANTERS	ENERGIZING	ENTICEMENT
ENCHANTING	ENERVATING	ENTICINGLY
ENCHILADAS	ENERVATION	ENTIRENESS
ENCIPHERED	ENFEEBLING	ENTIRETIES
ENCIPHERER	ENGAGEMENT	ENTOMBMENT
ENCIRCLING	ENGAGINGLY	ENTOMOLOGY
ENCLASPING	ENGARLANDS	ENTRANCING
ENCLOSURES	ENGENDERED	ENTRAPMENT
ENCOUNTERS	ENGINEERED	ENTRAPPING
ENCOURAGED	ENGIRDLING	ENTREATIES
ENCOURAGER	ENGRAFTING	ENTREATING
ENCOURAGES	ENGRAINING	ENTRECOTES
ENCROACHED	ENGRAVINGS	ENTRENCHED
ENCROACHER	ENGROSSERS	ENTRENCHES
ENCROACHES	ENGROSSING	ENTRUSTING
ENCRUSTING	ENGULFMENT	ENUMERABLE
ENCRYPTING	ENHARMONIC	ENUMERATED
ENCRYPTION	ENJOYMENTS	ENUMERATES
FNCUMBERED	ENLIGHTENS	ENUMERATOR
ENDANGERED	ENLISTMENT	ENUNCIABLE
ENDEARMENT	ENLIVENING	ENUNCIATED
ENDEAVOURS	ENMESHMENT	ENUNCIATES
ENDEMICITY	ENORMITIES	ENUNCIATOR
ENDOMORPHS	ENORMOUSLY	ENVELOPING
ENDOMORPHY	ENRAPTURED	ENVIRONING
ENDOPLASMS	ENRAPTURES	ENVISAGING
ENDORPHINS	ENRAVISHED	ENVISIONED
ENDORSABLE	ENRAVISHES	EPAULETTES
ENDOSCOPES	ENREGISTER	EPICENTRAL
ENDOSCOPIC	ENRICHMENT	EPICENTRES
ENDOSPERMS	ENROLLMENT	EPICUREANS
ENDOSPORES	ENSCROLLED	EPICURISMS
ENDOTHERMS	ENSHRINING	EPIGLOTTAL
ENDOTHERMY	ENSHROUDED	EPIGLOTTIC
ENDOTOXINS	ENTAILMENT	EPIGLOTTIS
ENDOWMENTS	ENTANGLING	EPILEPTICS
ENDURANCES	ENTERPRISE	EPISCOPACY
ENDURINGLY	ENTERTAINS	EPISCOPATE
ENERGETICS	ENTHRALLED	EPITOMICAL
ENERGISING	ENTHUSIASM	EPITOMISED
ENERGIZERS	ENTHUSIAST	EPITOMISES

EPITOMIZED	ESOPHAGEAL	EVANESCENT
EPITOMIZES	ESPADRILLE	EVANESCING
EQUABILITY	ESPECIALLY	EVANGELISM
EQUALISERS	ESPLANADES	EVANGELIST
EQUALISING	ESSENTIALS	EVANGELIZE
EQUALITIES	ESTIMATING	EVAPORATED
EQUALIZERS	ESTIMATION	EVAPORATES
EQUALIZING	ESTIMATIVE	EVAPORATOR
EQUANIMITY	ESTIMATORS	EVENTFULLY
EQUATIONAL	ETERNALIZE	EVENTUALLY
EQUATORIAL	ETERNISING	EVENTUATED
EQUESTRIAN	ETERNITIES	EVENTUATES
EQUILIBRIA	ETERNIZING	EVERGLADES
EQUIPMENTS	ETHICALITY	EVERGREENS
EQUIPOISED	ETHNICALLY	EVERYPLACE
EQUITATION	ETIQUETTES	EVERYTHING
EQUIVALENT	EUCALYPTUS	EVERYWHERE
EQUIVOCATE	EULOGISING	EVIDENCING
ERADIATING	EULOGISTIC	EVIDENTIAL
ERADICABLE	EULOGIZERS	EVILDOINGS
ERADICATED	EULOGIZING	EVISCERATE
ERADICATES	EUPHEMISMS	EVOCATIONS
ERADICATOR	EUPHEMISTS	EVOLUTIONS
ERICACEOUS	EUPHEMIZED	EVOLVEMENT
EROTICISMS	EUPHEMIZER	EXACERBATE
EROTICISTS	EUPHEMIZES	EXACTINGLY
EROTICIZED	EUPHONIOUS	EXACTITUDE
EROTICIZES	EUPHONIUMS	EXAGGERATE
ERRATICISM	EUPHORBIAS	EXALTATION
ERUDITIONS	EUPHORIANT	EXAMINABLE
ERUPTIVELY	EUPHRASIES	EXAMINANTS
ESCALATING	EUTHANIZED	EXASPERATE
ESCALATION	EUTHANIZES	EXCAVATING
ESCALATORS	EUTHENISTS	EXCAVATION
ESCALATORY	EVACUATING	EXCAVATORS
ESCALLOPED	EVACUATION	EXCELLENCE
ESCALOPING	EVACUATIVE	EXCELLENCY
ESCAPEMENT	EVALUATING	EXCELSIORS
ESCAPOLOGY	EVALUATION	EXCEPTIONS
ESCARPMENT	EVALUATIVE	EXCERPTERS
ESCUTCHEON	EVALUATORS	EXCERPTING

EXCHANGERS
EXCHANGING
EXCHEQUERS
EXCITATION
EXCITATIVE
EXCITEMENT
EXCITINGLY
EXCLAIMERS
EXCLAIMING
EXCLUDABLE
EXCLUSIONS
EXCLUSIVES
EXCREMENTS
EXCRETIONS
EXCRUCIATE
EXCULPATED
EXCULPATES
EXCURSIONS
EXCURSUSES
EXCUSATORY
EXECRATING
EXECRATION
EXECRATIVE
EXECRATORS
EXECUTABLE
EXECUTANTS
EXECUTIONS
EXECUTIVES
EXEMPTIONS
EXERCISERS
EXERCISING
EXFOLIATED
EXFOLIATES
EXHALATION
EXHAUSTERS
EXHAUSTING
EXHAUSTION
EXHAUSTIVE
EXHIBITING
EXHIBITION
EXHIBITIVE

EXHIBITORS
EXHIBITORY
EXHILARATE
EXHUMATION
EXIGENCIES
EXISTENCES
EXONERATED
EXONERATES
EXORBITANT
EXORCISERS
EXORCISING
EXORCISTIC
EXORCIZING
EXOSPHERES
EXOSPHERIC
EXOTHERMAL
EXOTHERMIC
EXOTICALLY
EXOTICISMS
EXPANDABLE
EXPANSIBLE
EXPANSIONS
EXPATIATED
EXPATIATES
EXPATRIATE
EXPECTABLE
EXPECTABLY
EXPECTANCE
EXPECTANCY
EXPECTANTS
EXPECTEDLY
EXPEDIENCE
EXPEDIENCY
EXPEDIENTS
EXPEDITERS
EXPEDITING
EXPEDITION
EXPEDITORS
EXPELLABLE
EXPENDABLE
EXPERIENCE

EXPERIMENT
EXPERTISES
EXPERTISMS
EXPERTIZED
EXPERTIZES
EXPERTNESS
EXPIATIONS
EXPIRATION
EXPIRATORY
EXPLAINERS
EXPLAINING
EXPLANTING
EXPLETIVES
EXPLICABLE
EXPLICABLY
EXPLICATED
EXPLICATES
EXPLICATOR
EXPLICITLY
EXPLOITERS
EXPLOITING
EXPLOITIVE
EXPLOSIONS
EXPLOSIVES
EXPORTABLE
EXPOSITING
EXPOSITION
EXPOSITIVE
EXPOSITORS
EXPOSITORY
EXPOUNDERS
EXPOUNDING
EXPRESSAGE
EXPRESSERS
EXPRESSING
EXPRESSION
EXPRESSIVE
EXPRESSWAY
EXPULSIONS
EXPUNCTION
EXPURGATED

EXPURGATES	EXTRUDABLE	FAIRLEADER
EXPURGATOR	EXTRUSIONS	FAIRNESSES
EXQUISITES	EXTUBATING	FAIRYLANDS
EXSERTIONS	EXUBERANCE	FAITHFULLY
EXTEMPORAL	EXUBERATED	FALCONRIES
EXTENDABLE	EXUBERATES	FALLACIOUS
EXTENDEDLY	EXUDATIONS	FALLOWNESS
EXTENDIBLE	EXULTANCES	FALSEHOODS
EXTENSIBLE	EXULTANTLY	FALSEWORKS
EXTENSIONS	EXULTATION	FALSIFIERS
EXTENUATED	EXULTINGLY	FALSIFYING
EXTENUATES	EYEBALLING	FAMILIARLY
EXTENUATOR	EYEDROPPER	FAMILISTIC
EXTERIORLY	EYEGLASSES	FAMISHMENT
EXTERMINED	EYELETTING	FAMOUSNESS
EXTERMINES	EYEPOPPERS	FANATICISM
EXTERNALLY	EYESTRAINS	FANATICIZE
EXTERNSHIP	EYEWITNESS	FANCIFULLY
EXTINCTING	FABRICANTS	FANCIFYING
EXTINCTION	FABRICATED	FANCYWORKS
EXTINCTIVE	FABRICATES	FANTASISED
EXTINGUISH	FABRICATOR	FANTASIZED
EXTIRPATED	FABULISTIC	FANTASIZER
EXTIRPATES	FABULOUSLY	FANTASIZES
EXTIRPATOR	FACECLOTHS	FANTASTICS
EXTOLMENTS	FACEPLATES	FANTASYING
EXTORTIONS	FACILENESS	FARCICALLY
EXTRACTING	FACILITATE	FAREWELLED
EXTRACTION	FACILITIES	FARMHOUSES
EXTRACTIVE	FACSIMILES	FARMSTEADS
EXTRACTORS	FACTIOUSLY	FARMWORKER
EXTRADITED	FACTITIOUS	FARRIERIES
EXTRADITES	FACTORABLE	FARSIGHTED
EXTRANEOUS	FACTORIALS	FASCINATED
EXTRAVERTS	FACTORIZED	FASCINATES
EXTREMISMS	FACTORIZES	FASCINATOR
EXTREMISTS	FACTORSHIP	FASHIONERS
EXTRICABLE	FACTUALISM	FASHIONING
EXTRICATED	FACTUALIST	FASTENINGS
EXTRICATES	FACTUALITY	FASTIDIOUS
EXTROVERTS	FAIRGROUND	FASTIGIATE

FASTNESSES
FATALISTIC
FATALITIES
FATHERHOOD
FATHERLAND
FATHERLESS
FATHERLIKE
FATHOMABLE
FATHOMLESS
FAULTINESS
FAVORITISM
FEARFULLER
FEARLESSLY
FEARSOMELY
FEATHERING
FECKLESSLY
FECUNDATED
FECUNDATES
FEDERACIES
FEDERALISM
FEDERALIST
FEDERALIZE
FEDERATING
FEDERATION
FEDERATIVE
FEEBLENESS
FEEDSTOCKS
FEEDSTUFFS
FEISTINESS
FELICITATE
FELICITIES
FELICITOUS
FELINITIES
FELLOWSHIP
FEMINACIES
FEMININELY
FEMININITY
FEMINISING
FEMINISTIC
FEMINITIES
FEMINIZING

FENESTRATE
FERMENTERS
FERMENTING
FERMENTORS
FEROCITIES
FERRYBOATS
FERTILIZED
FERTILIZER
FERTILIZES
FERVIDNESS
FESTOONING
FETCHINGLY
FETISHISMS
FETISHISTS
FETTUCCINE
FETTUCCINI
FEUDALISMS
FEUDALISTS
FEUDALIZED
FEUDALIZES
FEVERISHLY
FIBREBOARD
FIBREGLASS
FIBRILLATE
FIBROSITIS
FICKLENESS
FICTIONEER
FICTIONIST
FICTIONIZE
FICTITIOUS
FIDELITIES
FIENDISHLY
FIERCENESS
FIFTEENTHS
FIGURATION
FIGURATIVE
FIGUREHEAD
FILIATIONS
FILMMAKERS
FILMMAKING
FILMSETTER

FILMSTRIPS
FILTERABLE
FILTHINESS
FILTRATING
FILTRATION
FINALISING
FINALITIES
FINALIZING
FINANCIERS
FINANCINGS
FINGERHOLD
FINGERINGS
FINGERLIKE
FINGERNAIL
FINGERPOST
FINGERTIPS
FINITENESS
FINNICKIER
FIREBREAKS
FIREBRICKS
FIREFIGHTS
FIREGUARDS
FIREHOUSES
FIRELIGHTS
FIREPLACES
FIRESTONES
FIRESTORMS
FIRMAMENTS
FIRMNESSES
FIRSTBORNS
FIRSTLINGS
FISHMONGER
FISHTAILED
FISTFIGHTS
FISTICUFFS
FITFULNESS
FLABBINESS
FLACCIDITY
FLAGELLANT
FLAGELLATE
FLAGEOLETS

FLAGGINGLY	FLITTERING	FOCALIZING
FLAGRANCES	FLOATATION	FOLLICULAR
FLAGRANTLY	FLOCCULANT	FOLLOWINGS
FLAGSTAFFS	FLOCCULATE	FONDNESSES
FLAGSTAVES	FLOCCULENT	FOODSTUFFS
FLAGSTICKS	FLOODGATES	FOOTBALLER
FLAGSTONES	FLOODLIGHT	FOOTBRIDGE
FLAMBOYANT	FLOODPLAIN	FOOTLIGHTS
FLAMEPROOF	FLOODWATER	FOOTLOCKER
FLAMINGOES	FLOORBOARD	FOOTPRINTS
FLAMMABLES	FLOORCLOTH	FOOTSTOOLS
FLANNELLED	FLOPPINESS	FORBEARERS
FLASHBACKS	FLORIBUNDA	FORBEARING
FLASHBULBS	FLORIDNESS	FORBIDDERS
FLASHCARDS	FLOTATIONS	FORBIDDING
FLASHINESS	FLOUNCIEST	FORCEFULLY
FLASHLAMPS	FLOUNCINGS	FORCEMEATS
FLASHLIGHT	FLOUNDERED	FOREARMING
FLATFISHES	FLOURISHED	FOREBODERS
FLATFOOTED	FLOURISHER	FOREBODIES
FLATLANDER	FLOURISHES	FOREBODING
FLATTENERS	FLOWERETTE	FORECASTED
FLATTENING	FLOWERIEST	FORECASTER
FLATTERERS	FLOWERLESS	FORECLOSED
FLATTERIES	FLOWERLIKE	FORECLOSES
FLATTERING	FLOWERPOTS	FORECOURTS
FLATULENCE	FLUCTUATED	FOREDATING
FLATULENCY	FLUCTUATES	FOREDOOMED
FLAUNTIEST	FLUFFINESS	FOREFATHER
FLAVOURING	FLUGELHORN	FOREFINGER
FLAWLESSLY	FLUIDIZERS	FOREFRONTS
FLEDGLINGS	FLUIDIZING	FOREGATHER
FLEETINGLY	FLUMMOXING	FOREGROUND
FLESHINESS	FLUORESCED	FOREHANDED
FLICKERING	FLUORESCES	FOREHOOVES
FLIGHTIEST	FLUORIDATE	FOREIGNERS
FLIGHTLESS	FLUORINATE	FOREJUDGED
FLIMSINESS	FLUSTERING	FOREJUDGES
FLINTLOCKS	FLUTTERERS	FORERUNNER
FLIPPANTLY	FLUTTERING	FORESEEING
FLIRTATION	FLYCATCHER	FORESHADOW

FORESHORES	FORTIFYING	FRATERNIZE
FORESIGHTS	FORTISSIMO	FRATRICIDE
FORESPEAKS	FORTITUDES	FRAUDULENT
FORESPOKEN	FORTNIGHTS	FREAKINESS
FORESTRIES	FORTRESSED	FREAKISHLY
FORESWEARS	FORTRESSES	FREEHOLDER
FORETELLER	FORTUITIES	FREELANCED
FOREWARNED	FORTUITOUS	FREELANCER
FORFEITERS	FORWARDERS	FREELANCES
FORFEITING	FORWARDEST	FREELOADED
FORFEITURE	FORWARDING	FREELOADER
FORGETTERS	FOSSILIZED	FREESTYLER
FORGETTING	FOSSILIZES	FREESTYLES
FORGIVABLE	FOSTERLING	FREEWHEELS
FORGIVABLY	FOUNDATION	FREEZINGLY
FORJUDGING	FOUNDERING	FREIGHTAGE
FORKLIFTED	FOUNDLINGS	FREIGHTERS
FORMALISMS	FOUNTAINED	FREIGHTING
FORMALISTS	FOURSQUARE	FRENZIEDLY
FORMALIZED	FOURTEENTH	FREQUENCES
FORMALIZER	FOXHUNTERS	FREQUENTED
FORMALIZES	FOXHUNTING	FREQUENTER
FORMALNESS	FOXINESSES	FREQUENTLY
FORMATIONS	FOXTROTTED	FRESHENERS
FORMATIVES	FRACTIONAL	FRESHENING
FORMATTERS	FRACTIONED	FRESHWATER
FORMATTING	FRACTURING	FRICASSEED
FORMIDABLE	FRAGMENTAL	FRICASSEES
FORMIDABLY	FRAGMENTED	FRICTIONAL
FORMLESSLY	FRAGRANCES	FRIENDLESS
FORMULATED	FRAGRANTLY	FRIENDLIER
FORMULATES	FRAMBOISES	FRIENDLIES
FORMULATOR	FRAMEWORKS	FRIENDSHIP
FORMULIZED	FRANCHISED	FRIEZELIKE
FORMULIZES	FRANCHISEE	FRIGHTENED
FORNICATED	FRANCHISER	FRIGIDNESS
FORNICATES	FRANCHISES	FRIPPERIES
FORNICATOR	FRANCHISOR	FRISKINESS
FORSYTHIAS	FRANGIPANE	FRITILLARY
FORTHRIGHT	FRANGIPANI	FRITTERERS
FORTIFIERS	FRATERNITY	FRITTERING

FRIVOLLERS	FUSIBILITY	GAUCHENESS
FRIVOLLING	FUSILLADES	GAUNTLETED
FRIZZINESS	FUSIONISTS	GAZETTEERS
FROLICKING	FUTILENESS	GEARSHIFTS
FROLICSOME	FUTILITIES	GELATINIZE
FRONTALITY	FUTURELESS	GELATINOUS
FRONTWARDS	FUTURISTIC	GENERALIST
FROSTINESS	FUTURITIES	GENERALITY
FROTHINESS	FUTUROLOGY	GENERALIZE
FROWNINGLY	GABARDINES	GENERATING
FRUITERERS	GABERDINES	GENERATION
FRUITFULLY	GADGETRIES	GENERATIVE
FRUITINESS	GAINSAYERS	GENERATORS
FRUSTRATED	GAINSAYING	GENEROSITY
FRUSTRATES	GALAVANTED	GENEROUSLY
FUGITIVELY	GALLANTING	GENTEELISM
FULFILLERS	GALLERYING	GENTLEFOLK
FULFILLING	GALLIVANTS	GENTLENESS
FULMINATED	GALLSTONES	GENUFLECTS
FULMINATES	GALUMPHING	GEOCHEMIST
FUMATORIES	GALVANISMS	GEOGRAPHER
FUMBLINGLY	GALVANIZED	GEOGRAPHIC
FUMIGATING	GALVANIZER	GEOLOGICAL
FUMIGATION	GALVANIZES	GEOLOGISTS
FUMIGATORS	GAMBOLLING	GEOLOGIZED
FUMITORIES	GAMEKEEPER	GEOLOGIZES
FUNCTIONAL	GANGPLANKS	GEOMANCIES
FUNCTIONED	GANGRENOUS	GEOMETRICS
FUNDAMENTS	GARGANTUAN	GEOMETRIDS
FUNDRAISER	GARIBALDIS	GEOMETRIES
FUNEREALLY	GARISHNESS	GEOMETRIZE
FUNGICIDAL	GARNISHING	GEOMORPHIC
FUNGICIDES	GARNITURES	GEOPHYSICS
FUNNELLING	GARRISONED	GEOTHERMAL
FURBISHERS	GARROTTING	GERIATRICS
FURBISHING	GASOMETERS	GERMICIDAL
FURLOUGHED	GASTRONOMY	GERMICIDES
FURNISHERS	GASTROPODS	GERMINALLY
FURNISHING	GATEHOUSES	GERMINATED
FURNITURES	GATEKEEPER	GERMINATES
FURTHERING	GATHERINGS	GESTATIONS

GESTURALLY
GHASTLIEST
GHOSTLIEST
GHOSTWRITE
GHOULISHLY
GIGGLINGLY
GIMMICKING
GINGERROOT
GINGERSNAP
GINGIVITIS
GIRLFRIEND
GLACIATING
GLACIATION
GLACIOLOGY
GLADDENING
GLADIATORS
GLADNESSES
GLADSOMELY
GLAMOURING
GLAMOURIZE
GLAMOUROUS
GLANCINGLY
GLASSHOUSE
GLASSMAKER
GLASSPAPER
GLASSWARES
GLASSWORKS
GLIMMERING
GLISTENING
GLISTERING
GLITTERING
GLOATINGLY
GLOBALISMS
GLOBALISTS
GLOBALIZED
GLOBALIZES
GLOOMINESS
GLORIFIERS
GLORIFYING
GLORIOUSLY
GLOSSARIES

GLOSSINESS
GLUCOSIDES
GLUTAMINES
GLUTTONIES
GLUTTONOUS
GLYCERINES
GOALKEEPER
GOALMOUTHS
GODFATHERS
GODMOTHERS
GODPARENTS
GOLDENSEAL
GOLDFISHES
GOLDSMITHS
GONDOLIERS
GONORRHEAL
GONORRHEAS
GOODNESSES
GOODWILLED
GOOSEBERRY
GOOSEFLESH
GOOSEGRASS
GOOSENECKS
GORGEOUSLY
GOSPELLERS
GOSSIPPING
GOTHICALLY
GOTHICIZED
GOTHICIZES
GOVERNABLE
GOVERNANCE
GOVERNMENT
GRACEFULLY
GRACIOUSLY
GRADATIONS
GRADUALISM
GRADUALIST
GRADUATING
GRADUATION
GRADUATORS
GRAININESS

GRAMOPHONE
GRANDCHILD
GRANDDADDY
GRANDNIECE
GRANDSIRES
GRANDSTAND
GRANDUNCLE
GRANULATED
GRANULATES
GRANULATOR
GRANULITES
GRAPEFRUIT
GRAPEVINES
GRAPHOLOGY
GRAPPLINGS
GRASPINGLY
GRASSLANDS
GRASSROOTS
GRATEFULLY
GRATIFYING
GRATITUDES
GRATUITIES
GRATUITOUS
GRAVELLING
GRAVESTONE
GRAVEYARDS
GRAVITATED
GRAVITATES
GREASELESS
GREASINESS
GREATCOATS
GREEDINESS
GREENERIES
GREENFINCH
GREENFLIES
GREENGAGES
GREENHOUSE
GREENLINGS
GREENSTUFF
GREENSWARD
GREGARIOUS

GRENADIERS	GUARDRAILS	HAMBURGERS
GREYHOUNDS	GUARDROOMS	HAMMERHEAD
GREYNESSES	GUDGEONING	HAMMERLESS
GRIDLOCKED	GUERRILLAS	HAMSTRINGS
GRIEVANCES	GUESTHOUSE	HANDCRAFTS
GRIEVOUSLY	GUIDEBOOKS	HANDCUFFED
GRINDINGLY	GUIDELINES	HANDEDNESS
GRINDSTONE	GUIDEPOSTS	HANDFASTED
GRINNINGLY	GUILEFULLY	HANDICRAFT
GRIPPINGLY	GUILLEMETS	HANDIWORKS
GRISLINESS	GUILLEMOTS	HANDLEBARS
GRITTINESS	GUILLOTINE	HANDLELESS
GRIZZLIEST	GUITARISTS	HANDMAIDEN
GROGGINESS	GUNFIGHTER	HANDPICKED
GROSGRAINS	GUNPOWDERS	HANDPRINTS
GROTESQUES	GUNRUNNERS	HANDSHAKES
GROUCHIEST	GUNRUNNING	HANDSOMELY
GROUNDHOGS	GUNSLINGER	HANDSOMEST
GROUNDINGS	GUTTERINGS	HANDSTANDS
GROUNDLESS	GYMNASIUMS	HAPHAZARDS
GROUNDLING	GYMNASTICS	HAPPENINGS
GROUNDMASS	GYPSOPHILA	HARANGUERS
GROUNDNUTS	GYRATIONAL	HARANGUING
GROUNDSELS	GYROPLANES	HARASSMENT
GROUNDSMAN	GYROSCOPES	HARBINGERS
GROUNDSMEN	GYROSCOPIC	HARBOURING
GROUNDWORK	HABILITATE	HARDBOARDS
GROVELLING	HABITATION	HARDCOVERS
GROWLINGLY	HABITUALLY	HARDENINGS
GRUBBINESS	HABITUATED	HARDFISTED
GRUBSTAKES	HABITUATES	HARDHANDED
GRUDGINGLY	HACKNEYING	HARDHEADED
GRUESOMELY	HAILSTONES	HARLEQUINS
GRUMPINESS	HAILSTORMS	HARLOTRIES
GUACAMOLES	HAIRPIECES	HARMLESSLY
GUARANTEED	HAIRSPRING	HARMONICAS
GUARANTEES	HAIRSTREAK	HARMONIOUS
GUARANTIED	HAIRSTYLES	HARMONIUMS
GUARANTIES	HALLELUJAH	HARMONIZED
GUARANTORS	HALLMARKED	HARMONIZER
GUARDHOUSE	HALOGENOUS	HARMONIZES

HARNESSING
HARPOONERS
HARPOONING
HARRUMPHED
HARSHENING
HARTEBEEST
HARUMPHING
HARVESTERS
HARVESTING
HARVESTMAN
HARVESTMEN
HATCHBACKS
HATCHERIES
HATCHLINGS
HATCHMENTS
HAUGHTIEST
HAUNTINGLY
HAVERSACKS
HAWFINCHES
HAWKSBILLS
HAZINESSES
HEADBOARDS
HEADHUNTED
HEADHUNTER
HEADLIGHTS
HEADLINERS
HEADLINING
HEADMASTER
HEADPHONES
HEADPIECES
HEADSTANDS
HEADSTRONG
HEALTHIEST
HEARKENING
HEARTACHES
HEARTBEATS
HEARTBREAK
HEARTBURNS
HEARTENING
HEARTINESS
HEARTTHROB

HEARTWORMS
HEATHENISM
HEATHLANDS
HEATSTROKE
HEAVENWARD
HECTOGRAPH
HEDONISTIC
HEEDLESSLY
HEIGHTENED
HELICOPTER
HELIOGRAPH
HELIOTROPE
HELLEBORES
HELPLESSLY
HEMISPHERE
HENCEFORTH
HENPECKING
HEPTAGONAL
HERALDRIES
HERBACEOUS
HERBALISTS
HERBICIDAL
HERBICIDES
HERBIVORES
HEREABOUTS
HEREAFTERS
HEREDITARY
HEREDITIES
HERETOFORE
HERMITAGES
HERNIATION
HEROICALLY
HESITANCES
HESITANTLY
HESITATERS
HESITATING
HESITATION
HETEROGONY
HETERONOMY
HIBERNATED
HIBERNATES

HIBERNATOR
HIBISCUSES
HICCOUGHED
HICCUPPING
HIERARCHAL
HIERARCHIC
HIEROGLYPH
HIGHBALLED
HIGHBROWED
HIGHCHAIRS
HIGHFLYERS
HIGHJACKED
HIGHLANDER
HIGHLIGHTS
HIGHNESSES
HIGHTAILED
HIGHWAYMAN
HIGHWAYMEN
HIJACKINGS
HILARITIES
HINDRANCES
HINDSIGHTS
HIPPODROME
HIRSUTISMS
HISTOGRAMS
HISTOLOGIC
HISTORIANS
HISTORICAL
HISTRIONIC
HITCHHIKED
HITCHHIKER
HITCHHIKES
HITHERMOST
HITHERWARD
HOARFROSTS
HOARSENESS
HOARSENING
HOBBYHORSE
HOBGOBLINS
HOBNAILING
HOBNOBBERS

HOBNOBBING	HOROSCOPES	HUMANISING
HOKEYPOKEY	HORRENDOUS	HUMANISTIC
HOLIDAYERS	HORRIDNESS	HUMANITIES
HOLIDAYING	HORRIFYING	HUMANIZERS
HOLINESSES	HORSEBACKS	HUMANIZING
HOLLOWNESS	HORSEFLIES	HUMBLENESS
HOLLYHOCKS	HORSEHAIRS	HUMBUGGING
HOLOCAUSTS	HORSEHIDES	HUMDINGERS
HOLOGRAPHS	HORSEPOWER	HUMIDIFIED
HOLOGRAPHY	HORSESHOES	HUMIDIFIER
HOLSTERING	HORSETAILS	HUMIDIFIES
HOMECOMING	HORSEWHIPS	HUMIDITIES
HOMELINESS	HORSEWOMAN	HUMILIATED
HOMEMAKERS	HORSEWOMEN	HUMILIATES
HOMEMAKING	HOSPITABLE	HUMILITIES
HOMEOPATHS	HOSPITABLY	HUMOROUSLY
HOMEOPATHY	HOSTELLERS	HUMPBACKED
HOMEOWNERS	HOSTELLING	HUNCHBACKS
HOMESTEADS	HOSTELRIES	HUNDREDTHS
HOMOGENIZE	HOSTESSING	HUNGRINESS
HOMOGENOUS	HOTCHPOTCH	HURRICANES
HOMOGONIES	HOTFOOTING	HUSBANDING
HOMOPHOBES	HOTPRESSED	HUSBANDMAN
HOMOPHOBIA	HOTPRESSES	HUSBANDMEN
HOMOPHOBIC	HOUSEBOATS	HYDRANGEAS
HOMOPHONES	HOUSEBOUND	HYDRATIONS
HOMOPHONIC	HOUSEBREAK	HYDRAULICS
HOMOSEXUAL	HOUSECLEAN	HYDROFOILS
HONEYCOMBS	HOUSECOATS	HYDROLYSES
HONEYMOONS	HOUSEFLIES	HYDROLYSIS
HONORARIES	HOUSEHOLDS	HYDROLYTIC
HONORARILY	HOUSEKEEPS	HYDROLYZED
HONOURABLE	HOUSEMAIDS	HYDROLYZES
HOODWINKED	HOUSEMATES	HYDROMANCY
HOODWINKER	HOUSEPLANT	HYDROMETER
HOOFPRINTS	HOUSEWARES	HYDROPATHY
HOPELESSLY	HOUSEWIVES	HYDROPHONE
HORIZONTAL	HOUSEWORKS	HYDROPLANE
HORNEDNESS	HOVERCRAFT	HYDROPOWER
HOROLOGIES	HULLABALOO	HYGIENISTS
HOROLOGIST	HUMANENESS	HYPERBOLAE

HYPERBOLAS
HYPERBOLES
HYPERBOLIC
HYPERMANIA
HYPERMANIC
HYPERMEDIA
HYPERMETER
HYPERPLANE
HYPERSONIC
HYPERSPACE
HYPERTENSE
HYPERTEXTS
HYPHENATED
HYPHENATES
HYPNOTISMS
HYPNOTISTS
HYPNOTIZED
HYPNOTIZES
HYPOCAUSTS
HYPOCRITES
HYPODERMAL
HYPODERMIC
HYPODERMIS
HYPOPLASIA
HYPOPLOIDS
HYPOSTASES
HYPOSTASIS
HYPOSTATIC
HYPOTENUSE
HYPOTHESES
HYPOTHESIS
HYSTERICAL
ICEBREAKER
ICONOSCOPE
IDEALISING
IDEALISTIC
IDEALITIES
IDEALIZERS
IDEALIZING
IDEALOGIES
IDENTIFIED

IDENTIFIER
IDENTIFIES
IDENTITIES
IDEOGRAMIC
IDEOGRAPHS
IDEOGRAPHY
IDEOLOGIES
IDEOLOGIST
IDEOLOGIZE
IDEOLOGUES
IDIOBLASTS
IDLENESSES
IDOLATRIES
IDOLATROUS
IGNOBILITY
IGNOMINIES
IGNORANCES
IGNORANTLY
ILLAUDABLE
ILLAUDABLY
ILLEGALITY
ILLEGALIZE
ILLITERACY
ILLITERATE
ILLUMINANT
ILLUMINATE
ILLUSIONAL
ILLUSIVELY
ILLUSORILY
ILLUSTRATE
IMAGINABLE
IMAGINABLY
IMBALANCED
IMBALANCES
IMBECILITY
IMBRICATED
IMBRICATES
IMITATIONS
IMMACULACY
IMMACULATE
IMMANENCES

IMMANENTLY
IMMATERIAL
IMMATURELY
IMMATURITY
IMMEMORIAL
IMMERSIBLE
IMMERSIONS
IMMIGRANTS
IMMIGRATED
IMMIGRATES
IMMINENCES
IMMINENTLY
IMMISCIBLE
IMMOBILISM
IMMOBILITY
IMMOBILIZE
IMMODERACY
IMMODERATE
IMMODESTLY
IMMORALISM
IMMORALIST
IMMORALITY
IMMORTALLY
IMMOVABLES
IMMUNISING
IMMUNITIES
IMMUNIZING
IMMUNOLOGY
IMPACTIONS
IMPAIRMENT
IMPALEMENT
IMPALPABLE
IMPALPABLY
IMPANELLED
IMPARITIES
IMPARTIBLE
IMPARTIBLY
IMPARTMENT
IMPASSABLE
IMPASSABLY
IMPASSIBLE

IMPASSIBLY	IMPOSITION	INACTIVATE
IMPASSIONS	IMPOSSIBLE	INACTIVELY
IMPATIENCE	IMPOSSIBLY	INACTIVITY
IMPEACHING	IMPOSTHUME	INADEQUACY
IMPEARLING	IMPOSTUMES	INADEQUATE
IMPECCABLE	IMPOSTURES	INAPPARENT
IMPECCABLY	IMPOTENCES	INAPTITUDE
IMPEDANCES	IMPOTENTLY	INARGUABLE
IMPEDIMENT	IMPOUNDING	INARGUABLY
IMPENITENT	IMPOVERISH	INARTISTIC
IMPERATIVE	IMPOWERING	INAUGURALS
IMPERATORS	IMPRECATED	INAUGURATE
IMPERFECTS	IMPREGNATE	INBOUNDING
IMPERIALLY	IMPRESARIO	INBREATHED
IMPERILLED	IMPRESSING	INBREATHES
IMPERSONAL	IMPRESSION	INBREEDING
IMPERVIOUS	IMPRESSIVE	INCANDESCE
IMPETRATED	IMPRESSURE	INCAPACITY
IMPETRATES	IMPRINTERS	INCARNATED
IMPISHNESS	IMPRINTING	INCARNATES
IMPLACABLE	IMPRISONED	INCAUTIONS
IMPLACABLY	IMPROBABLE	INCAUTIOUS
IMPLANTERS	IMPROBABLY	INCENDIARY
IMPLANTING	IMPROMPTUS	INCENTIVES
IMPLEADING	IMPROPERLY	INCEPTIONS
IMPLEDGING	IMPROVABLE	INCEPTIVES
IMPLEMENTS	IMPROVISED	INCESSANCY
IMPLICATED	IMPROVISER	INCESTUOUS
IMPLICATES	IMPROVISES	INCIDENCES
IMPLICITLY	IMPROVISOR	INCIDENTAL
IMPLOSIONS	IMPRUDENCE	INCINERATE
IMPLOSIVES	IMPUDENCES	INCIPIENCE
IMPOLICIES	IMPUDENTLY	INCIPIENCY
IMPOLITELY	IMPUDICITY	INCISIVELY
IMPORTABLE	IMPUGNABLE	INCITATION
IMPORTANCE	IMPULSIONS	INCITEMENT
IMPORTANCY	IMPUNITIES	INCIVILITY
IMPORTUNED	IMPURENESS	INCLEMENCY
IMPORTUNER	IMPURITIES	INCLINABLE
IMPORTUNES	INACCURACY	INCLININGS
IMPOSINGLY	INACCURATE	INCLIPPING

690

INCLOSURES
INCLUDABLE
INCLUDIBLE
INCLUSIONS
INCOGITANT
INCOGNITOS
INCOHERENT
INCOMPLETE
INCONSTANT
INCREASING
INCREDIBLE
INCREDIBLY
INCREMENTS
INCRESCENT
INCROSSING
INCRUSTING
INCUBATING
INCUBATION
INCUBATIVE
INCUBATORS
INCUBATORY
INCULCATED
INCULCATES
INCULCATOR
INCULPABLE
INCULPATED
INCULPATES
INCUMBENCY
INCUMBENTS
INCUMBERED
INCUNABLES
INCURABLES
INCURRENCE
INCURSIONS
INCURVATED
INCURVATES
INDECENTLY
INDECISION
INDECISIVE
INDECOROUS
INDECORUMS

INDEFINITE
INDELICACY
INDELICATE
INDENTIONS
INDENTURED
INDENTURES
INDEXATION
INDICATING
INDICATION
INDICATIVE
INDICATORS
INDICATORY
INDICTABLE
INDICTIONS
INDICTMENT
INDIGENCES
INDIGENIZE
INDIGENOUS
INDIGESTED
INDIRECTLY
INDISCREET
INDISPOSED
INDISPOSES
INDISTINCT
INDIVIDUAL
INDOLENCES
INDOLENTLY
INDUCEMENT
INDUCTIONS
INDULGENCE
INDURATING
INDURATION
INDURATIVE
INDUSTRIAL
INDUSTRIES
INDWELLERS
INDWELLING
INEARTHING
INEBRIANTS
INEBRIATED
INEBRIATES

INEDUCABLE
INEFFICACY
INELEGANCE
INELIGIBLE
INELOQUENT
INEPTITUDE
INEQUALITY
INEQUITIES
INERTIALLY
INEVITABLE
INEVITABLY
INEXISTENT
INEXORABLE
INEXORABLY
INEXPERTLY
INEXPIABLE
INEXPIABLY
INEXPLICIT
INFALLIBLE
INFALLIBLY
INFAMOUSLY
INFANTRIES
INFARCTION
INFATUATED
INFATUATES
INFEASIBLE
INFECTIONS
INFECTIOUS
INFERENCES
INFERIORLY
INFERNALLY
INFESTANTS
INFIDELITY
INFIGHTERS
INFIGHTING
INFILTRATE
INFINITELY
INFINITIES
INFINITIVE
INFINITUDE
INFIXATION

INFLATABLE	INHALATION	INNOVATIVE	INSOLVABLE
INFLATIONS	INHALATORS	INNOVATORS	INSOLVABLY
INFLECTING	INHARMONIC	INNOVATORY	INSOLVENCY
INFLECTION	INHERENCES	INNUENDOES	INSOLVENTS
INFLECTIVE	INHERENTLY	INNUMERACY	INSOMNIACS
INFLEXIBLE	INHERITING	INNUMERATE	INSPECTING
INFLEXIBLY	INHERITORS	INNUMEROUS	INSPECTION
INFLEXIONS	INHIBITING	INOCULATED	INSPECTIVE
INFLICTERS	INHIBITION	INOCULATES	INSPECTORS
INFLICTING	INHIBITIVE	INOPERABLE	INSPIRATOR
INFLICTION	INHIBITORS	INORDINATE	INSPIRITED
INFLICTIVE	INHIBITORY	INPATIENTS	INSTALLERS
INFLICTORS	INHUMANELY	INQUIETUDE	INSTALLING
INFLUENCED	INHUMANITY	INQUISITOR	INSTALMENT
INFLUENCES	INIMITABLE	INSANITARY	INSTIGATED
INFLUENZAL	INIMITABLY	INSANITIES	INSTIGATES
INFLUENZAS	INIQUITIES	INSATIABLE	INSTIGATOR
INFORMALLY	INIQUITOUS	INSATIABLY	INSTILLERS
INFORMANTS	INITIALISM	INSCRIBERS	INSTILLING
INFORMEDLY	INITIALIZE	INSCRIBING	INSTITUTED
INFRACTING	INITIALLED	INSCROLLED	INSTITUTER
INFRACTION	INITIATING	INSECURELY	INSTITUTES
INFRASONIC	INITIATION	INSECURITY	INSTITUTOR
INFREQUENT	INITIATIVE	INSEMINATE	INSTRUCTED
INFRINGERS	INITIATORS	INSENSIBLE	INSTRUCTOR
INFRINGING	INITIATORY	INSENSIBLY	INSTRUMENT
INFURIATED	INJECTABLE	INSENTIENT	INSULARISM
INFURIATES	INJECTANTS	INSERTIONS	INSULARITY
INGESTIBLE	INJECTIONS	INSINUATED	INSULATING
INGESTIONS	INJUNCTION	INSINUATES	INSULATION
INGLENOOKS	INJUNCTIVE	INSIPIDITY	INSULATORS
INGLORIOUS	INJUSTICES	INSISTENCE	INSURANCES
INGRAFTING	INNATENESS	INSISTENCY	INSURGENCE
INGRAINING	INNERSOLES	INSOBRIETY	INSURGENCY
INGRATIATE	INNERVATED	INSOCIABLE	INSURGENTS
INGREDIENT	INNERVATES	INSOCIABLY	INTACTNESS
INGRESSION	INNKEEPERS	INSOLATING	INTANGIBLE
INGRESSIVE	INNOCENCES	INSOLATION	INTANGIBLY
INHABITANT	INNOCENTLY	INSOLENCES	INTEGRALLY
INHABITERS	INNOVATING	INSOLENTLY	INTEGRATED
INHABITING	INNOVATION	INSOLUBLES	INTEGRATES

INTEGRATOR	INTERNODAL	INTROJECTS	INVOCATING
INTELLECTS	INTERNODES	INTROSPECT	INVOCATION
INTENDANCE	INTERNSHIP	INTROVERTS	INVOCATORY
INTENDANTS	INTERPOSED	INTRUSIONS	INVOLUTING
INTENDEDLY	INTERPOSER	INTRUSIVES	INVOLUTION
INTENSIONS	INTERPOSES	INTRUSTING	INVOLVEDLY
INTENSIVES	INTERPRETS	INTUBATING	INWARDNESS
INTENTIONS	INTERRUPTS	INTUBATION	IONIZATION
INTENTNESS	INTERSECTS	INTUITABLE	IONOSPHERE
INTERACTED	INTERSPACE	INTUITIONS	IRIDESCENT
INTERBREED	INTERSTATE	INTWISTING	IRONFISTED
INTERCEDED	INTERTWINE	INUNDATING	IRONHANDED
INTERCEDER	INTERTWIST	INUNDATION	IRONICALLY
INTERCEDES	INTERVENED	INUNDATORS	IRONMONGER
INTERCEPTS	INTERVENER	INUNDATORY	IRONWORKER
INTERDICTS	INTERVENES	INUREMENTS	IRRADIANCE
INTERESTED	INTERVIEWS	INVALIDATE	IRRADIATED
INTERFACED	INTERWEAVE	INVALIDING	IRRADIATES
INTERFACES	INTERWOVEN	INVALIDISM	IRRADIATOR
INTERFERED	INTESTINAL	INVALIDITY	IRRATIONAL
INTERFERER	INTESTINES	INVALUABLE	IRREDENTAS
INTERFERES	INTHRALLED	INVALUABLY	IRREGULARS
INTERIORLY	INTIMACIES	INVARIABLE	IRRELATIVE
INTERJECTS	INTIMATELY	INVARIABLY	IRRELEVANT
INTERLACED	INTIMATING	INVARIANCE	IRRESOLUTE
INTERLACES	INTIMATION	INVARIANTS	IRREVERENT
INTERLEAVE	INTIMIDATE	INVASIVELY	IRRIGATING
INTERLINED	INTOLERANT	INVECTIVES	IRRIGATION
INTERLINES	INTONATING	INVENTIONS	IRRIGATORS
INTERLINKS	INTONATION	INVERSIONS	IRRITATING
INTERLOCKS	INTOXICANT	INVESTMENT	IRRITATION
INTERLOPED	INTOXICATE	INVETERACY	IRRITATIVE
INTERLOPER	INTREATING	INVETERATE	IRRUPTIONS
INTERLOPES	INTRENCHED	INVIGORATE	ISOLATIONS
INTERLUDES	INTRENCHES	INVINCIBLE	ISOMETRICS
INTERMENTS	INTREPIDLY	INVINCIBLY	ISOTHERMAL
INTERMIXED	INTRIGUERS	INVIOLABLE	ITALICISED
INTERMIXES	INTRIGUING	INVIOLABLY	ITALICISES
INTERNALLY	INTRODUCED	INVISIBLES	ITALICIZED
INTERNISTS	INTRODUCER	INVITATION	ITALICIZES
INTERNMENT	INTRODUCES	INVITINGLY	ITERATIONS

ITINERANCY	JOYFULNESS	KIDNAPPEES
ITINERANTS	JOYOUSNESS	KIDNAPPERS
ITINERATED	JOYRIDINGS	KIDNAPPING
ITINERATES	JUBILANCES	KILOCYCLES
JACKKNIFED	JUBILANTLY	KILOJOULES
JACKKNIVES	JUBILATING	KILOLITRES
JACKRABBIT	JUBILATION	KILOMETRES
JAGGEDNESS	JUDGEMENTS	KILOPARSEC
JAILBREAKS	JUDGMENTAL	KINDLESSLY
JAILHOUSES	JUDICATORY	KINDLINESS
JANITORIAL	JUDICATURE	KINDNESSES
JAPANIZING	JUDICIALLY	KINEMATICS
JARDINIERE	JUGGERNAUT	KINESCOPED
JARGONIZED	JULIENNING	KINESCOPES
JARGONIZES	JUNCTIONAL	KINETICIST
JAUNDICING	JUNGLELIKE	KINGFISHER
JAUNTINESS	JUSTIFIERS	KINGLINESS
JAVELINING	JUSTIFYING	KITTIWAKES
JAWBREAKER	JUSTNESSES	KIWIFRUITS
JAYWALKERS	JUVENILITY	KLUTZINESS
JAYWALKING	JUXTAPOSED	KNAPSACKED
JEALOUSIES	JUXTAPOSES	KNEECAPPED
JELLYBEANS	KEENNESSES	KNICKKNACK
JEOPARDIES	KENNELLING	KNIFEPOINT
JEOPARDING	KERCHIEVES	KNIGHTHOOD
JEOPARDISE	KERFUFFLES	KNOBBLIEST
JEOPARDIZE	KERNELLING	KNOCKABOUT
JETTISONED	KERPLUNKED	KNOCKDOWNS
JITTERBUGS	KETTLEDRUM	KNOWLEDGES
JOCKSTRAPS	KEYBOARDED	KOOKABURRA
JOCULARITY	KEYBOARDER	LABIALIZED
JOKINESSES	KEYBUTTONS	LABIALIZES
JOLLIFYING	KEYPUNCHED	LABILITIES
JOURNALISM	KEYPUNCHER	LABIOVELAR
JOURNALIST	KEYPUNCHES	LABORATORY
JOURNALIZE	KEYSTROKED	LABYRINTHS
JOURNEYERS	KEYSTROKES	LACERATING
JOURNEYING	KICKBOARDS	LACERATION
JOURNEYMAN	KICKBOXERS	LACERATIVE
JOURNEYMEN	KICKBOXING	LACINESSES
JOVIALTIES	KICKSTANDS	LACKLUSTRE

LACQUERERS
LACQUERING
LACQUEYING
LACRIMATOR
LACTATIONS
LACTOGENIC
LADDERLIKE
LAMBASTING
LAMENTABLE
LAMENTABLY
LAMENTEDLY
LAMINATING
LAMINATION
LAMINATORS
LAMPLIGHTS
LAMPOONERS
LAMPOONERY
LAMPOONING
LANDHOLDER
LANDLADIES
LANDLOCKED
LANDLUBBER
LANDMASSES
LANDOWNERS
LANDOWNING
LANDSCAPED
LANDSCAPER
LANDSCAPES
LANDSLIDES
LANGUISHED
LANGUISHER
LANGUISHES
LANKNESSES
LAPAROTOMY
LAPIDARIAN
LAPIDARIES
LAPIDATING
LAPIDIFIED
LAPIDIFIES
LARCENISTS
LARVICIDAL

LARVICIDES
LARYNGITES
LARYNGITIC
LARYNGITIS
LASCIVIOUS
LASSITUDES
LATECOMERS
LATENESSES
LATERALING
LATERALIZE
LATERIZING
LAUDATIONS
LAUGHINGLY
LAUNCHPADS
LAUNDERERS
LAUNDERING
LAUNDRETTE
LAUNDRYMAN
LAUREATING
LAUREATION
LAURELLING
LAVATORIES
LAVENDERED
LAVISHNESS
LAWBREAKER
LAWFULNESS
LAWMAKINGS
LAWNMOWERS
LAWYERLIKE
LAYPERSONS
LAZINESSES
LEADENNESS
LEADERLESS
LEADERSHIP
LEAFLETTED
LEAFSTALKS
LEAGUERING
LEANNESSES
LEASEHOLDS
LEATHERING
LEAVENINGS

LECTIONARY
LEGALISTIC
LEGALITIES
LEGALIZERS
LEGALIZING
LEGATESHIP
LEGENDRIES
LEGIBILITY
LEGISLATED
LEGISLATES
LEGISLATOR
LEGITIMACY
LEGITIMATE
LEGITIMISE
LEGITIMISM
LEGITIMIST
LEGITIMIZE
LEGUMINOUS
LEMONGRASS
LENGTHENED
LENGTHENER
LENGTHIEST
LENGTHWAYS
LENGTHWISE
LENIENCIES
LENTICULAR
LEOPARDESS
LEPRECHAUN
LESBIANISM
LETHARGIES
LETTERHEAD
LETTERINGS
LEUKAEMIAS
LEUKOCYTES
LEVERAGING
LEVITATING
LEVITATION
LEXICOLOGY
LIBERALISM
LIBERALIST
LIBERALITY

LIBERALIZE	LIONFISHES	LOADSTONES
LIBERATING	LIPOTROPIC	LOBOTOMIES
LIBERATION	LIPOTROPIN	LOBOTOMIZE
LIBERATORS	LIPREADING	LOBSTERING
LIBERTINES	LIPSTICKED	LOBSTERMAN
LIBRARIANS	LIQUEFIERS	LOBSTERMEN
LIBRATIONS	LIQUEFYING	LOCALISING
LICENSABLE	LIQUIDATED	LOCALITIES
LICENSURES	LIQUIDATES	LOCALIZING
LICENTIATE	LIQUIDATOR	LOCATIONAL
LICENTIOUS	LIQUIDIZED	LOCKKEEPER
LIEUTENANT	LIQUIDIZES	LOCKSMITHS
LIFEBLOODS	LIQUIDNESS	LOCOMOTING
LIFEGUARDS	LIQUIFYING	LOCOMOTION
LIFELESSLY	LIQUORICES	LOCOMOTIVE
LIFESAVERS	LISTENABLE	LOCOMOTORY
LIFESAVING	LISTLESSLY	LODESTONES
LIFESTYLES	LITERACIES	LODGEMENTS
LIGATURING	LITERALISM	LOGANBERRY
LIGHTBULBS	LITERALIST	LOGARITHMS
LIGHTENERS	LITERALITY	LOGGERHEAD
LIGHTENING	LITERALIZE	LOGICALITY
LIGHTHOUSE	LITERARILY	LOGISTICAL
LIGHTNINGS	LITERATELY	LOINCLOTHS
LIGHTPROOF	LITERATION	LONELINESS
LIGHTSHIPS	LITERATORS	LONESOMELY
LIKABILITY	LITERATURE	LONGBOWMAN
LIKELIHOOD	LITHOGRAPH	LONGHAIRED
LIKENESSES	LITIGATING	LONGITUDES
LIMELIGHTS	LITIGATION	LOOKALIKES
LIMESTONES	LITIGATORS	LOOPHOLING
LIMITATION	LITTERBUGS	LOPSIDEDLY
LIMITATIVE	LITURGICAL	LOQUACIOUS
LIMITINGLY	LITURGISTS	LORDLINESS
LIMOUSINES	LIVELIHOOD	LOUDMOUTHS
LIMPIDNESS	LIVELINESS	LOUDNESSES
LIMPNESSES	LIVERWORTS	LOUNGEWEAR
LINEARIZED	LIVESTOCKS	LOVELESSLY
LINEARIZES	LIVIDITIES	LOVELINESS
LINEATIONS	LIXIVIATED	LOVEMAKING
LINGUISTIC	LIXIVIATES	LOWERCASED

LOWERCASES	MACHINATES	MALIGNANCY
LOWLANDERS	MACHINATOR	MALINGERED
LUBRICANTS	MACHINISTS	MALINGERER
LUBRICATED	MACKINTOSH	MALODOROUS
LUBRICATES	MACULATING	MALTREATED
LUBRICATOR	MACULATION	MALTREATER
LUCIDITIES	MADELEINES	MAMMALIANS
LUCIFEROUS	MAELSTROMS	MAMMILLARY
LUGUBRIOUS	MAGISTRACY	MAMMOGRAMS
LULLABYING	MAGISTRATE	MANAGEABLE
LUMBERJACK	MAGNESIUMS	MANAGEABLY
LUMBERYARD	MAGNETISED	MANAGEMENT
LUMINAIRES	MAGNETISMS	MANAGERESS
LUMINANCES	MAGNETITES	MANAGERIAL
LUMINARIES	MAGNETIZED	MANDIBULAR
LUMINESCED	MAGNETIZER	MANDOLINES
LUMINESCES	MAGNETIZES	MANFULNESS
LUMINOSITY	MAGNETRONS	MANHANDLED
LUMPECTOMY	MAGNIFIERS	MANHANDLES
LUMPFISHES	MAGNIFYING	MANIACALLY
LUNCHMEATS	MAGNITUDES	MANICURING
LUNCHROOMS	MAHARAJAHS	MANICURIST
LUNCHTIMES	MAHOGANIES	MANIFESTED
LUSCIOUSLY	MAIDENHOOD	MANIFESTER
LUSHNESSES	MAINFRAMES	MANIFESTLY
LUSTRELESS	MAINLANDER	MANIFESTOS
LUSTROUSLY	MAINLINING	MANIFOLDED
LUXURIANCE	MAINSTREAM	MANIFOLDLY
LUXURIATED	MAINTAINED	MANIPULATE
LUXURIATES	MAINTAINER	MANNEQUINS
LYMPHATICS	MAISONETTE	MANNERISMS
LYMPHOCYTE	MAJORETTES	MANNERISTS
LYRICIZING	MAJORITIES	MANNERLESS
MACADAMIAS	MAKESHIFTS	MANOEUVRED
MACADAMIZE	MALAPROPOS	MANOEUVRES
MACARONIES	MALATHIONS	MANOMETERS
MACERATING	MALCONTENT	MANOMETRIC
MACERATION	MALEFACTOR	MANSERVANT
MACERATORS	MALEFICENT	MANUSCRIPT
MACHINABLE	MALEVOLENT	MARASCHINO
MACHINATED	MALIGNANCE	MARBLEIZED

MARBLEIZES	MASTICATES	MECHANISTS
MARGARINES	MASTICATOR	MECHANIZED
MARGARITAS	MASTURBATE	MECHANIZER
MARGINALLY	MATCHBOOKS	MECHANIZES
MARGINATED	MATCHBOXES	MEDAILLONS
MARGINATES	MATCHMAKER	MEDALLIONS
MARIJUANAS	MATCHSTICK	MEDALLISTS
MARINADING	MATCHWOODS	MEDDLESOME
MARINATING	MATERIALLY	MEDIATIONS
MARINATION	MATERNALLY	MEDICAMENT
MARIONETTE	MATHEMATIC	MEDICATING
MARKEDNESS	MATRIARCHS	MEDICATION
MARKETABLE	MATRIARCHY	MEDICINALS
MARKETEERS	MATRICIDAL	MEDICINING
MARKETINGS	MATRICIDES	MEDIEVALLY
MARKSWOMAN	MATTRESSES	MEDIOCRITY
MARMALADES	MATURATING	MEDITATING
MARQUESSES	MATURATION	MEDITATION
MARROWBONE	MATURITIES	MEDITATIVE
MARROWFATS	MAUNDERERS	MEDITATORS
MARSHALLED	MAUNDERING	MEGACYCLES
MARSHINESS	MAUSOLEUMS	MEGALITHIC
MARSHLANDS	MAXIMALIST	MEGAPHONED
MARSUPIALS	MAXIMISING	MEGAPHONES
MARTINGALE	MAXIMIZERS	MEGAPHONIC
MARTYRDOMS	MAXIMIZING	MELANCHOLY
MARTYRIZED	MAYONNAISE	MELATONINS
MARTYRIZES	MAYORESSES	MELIORATED
MARVELLING	MEADOWLAND	MELIORATES
MARVELLOUS	MEADOWLARK	MELIORATOR
MASCARPONE	MEAGRENESS	MELIORISMS
MASCULINES	MEANDERING	MELIORISTS
MASOCHISMS	MEANINGFUL	MELLOWNESS
MASOCHISTS	MEANNESSES	MELODIZERS
MASQUERADE	MEANWHILES	MELODIZING
MASSACRERS	MEASURABLE	MELODRAMAS
MASSACRING	MEASURABLY	MEMBERSHIP
MASTECTOMY	MEASUREDLY	MEMBRANOUS
MASTERMIND	MEATLOAVES	MEMORANDUM
MASTERWORK	MECHANICAL	MEMORIALLY
MASTICATED	MECHANISMS	MEMORIZERS

MEMORIZING	METATARSUS	MIDNIGHTLY
MENACINGLY	METEORITES	MIDSECTION
MENAGERIES	METEORITIC	MIDSHIPMAN
MENDACIOUS	METEOROIDS	MIDSHIPMEN
MENDICANCY	METHODICAL	MIDSTREAMS
MENDICANTS	METHODISMS	MIDSUMMERS
MENINGITIS	METHODISTS	MIDWINTERS
MENOPAUSAL	METHODIZED	MIGHTINESS
MENOPAUSES	METHODIZES	MIGNONETTE
MENSTRUATE	METHYLATED	MIGRAINOUS
MENTALISTS	METHYLATES	MIGRATIONS
MENTATIONS	METHYLATOR	MILESTONES
MENTIONERS	METICULOUS	MILITANTLY
MENTIONING	METRICALLY	MILITARIES
MENTORSHIP	METRICIZED	MILITARILY
MERCANTILE	METRICIZES	MILITARISM
MERCERIZED	METRIFYING	MILITARIST
MERCERIZES	METRONOMES	MILITARIZE
MERCHANTED	METRONOMIC	MILITATING
MERCIFULLY	METROPOLIS	MILITIAMAN
MERCURATED	METTLESOME	MILITIAMEN
MERCURATES	MEZZANINES	MILLENNIAL
MERCURIALS	MEZZOTINTS	MILLENNIUM
MERGANSERS	MICRIFYING	MILLIGRAMS
MERRIMENTS	MICROCHIPS	MILLILITRE
MERRYMAKER	MICROFILMS	MILLIMETER
MESMERISMS	MICROGRAMS	MILLIPEDES
MESMERISTS	MICROGRAPH	MILLIVOLTS
MESMERIZED	MICROMETER	MILLIWATTS
MESMERIZER	MICROPHONE	MILLSTONES
MESMERIZES	MICROPORES	MILLWRIGHT
MESSENGERS	MICROSCOPE	MINCEMEATS
METABOLISM	MICROSCOPY	MINDEDNESS
METACARPAL	MICROSPORE	MINDLESSLY
METACARPUS	MICROVOLTS	MINEFIELDS
METALIZING	MICROWATTS	MINERALIZE
METALLIZED	MICROWAVED	MINERALOGY
METALLOIDS	MICROWAVES	MINESTRONE
METALLURGY	MICTURATED	MINIATURES
METAPHYSIC	MICTURATES	MINIBUSSES
METATARSAL	MIDFIELDER	MINIMALISM

MINIMALIST	MISDIALLED	MISOGAMIST
MINIMIZERS	MISDIRECTS	MISOGYNIES
MINIMIZING	MISDOUBTED	MISOGYNIST
MINISCULES	MISEMPLOYS	MISORDERED
MINISKIRTS	MISENROLLS	MISPLACING
MINISTERED	MISERABLES	MISPLANNED
MINISTRANT	MISFIELDED	MISPLANTED
MINISTRIES	MISFITTING	MISPLAYING
MINORITIES	MISFOCUSED	MISPOINTED
MINUSCULES	MISFOCUSES	MISPOISING
MINUTENESS	MISFORMING	MISPRICING
MIRACULOUS	MISFORTUNE	MISPRINTED
MIRRORLIKE	MISGAUGING	MISPRISION
MIRTHFULLY	MISGIVINGS	MISQUOTING
MISADAPTED	MISGOVERNS	MISRAISING
MISADDRESS	MISGRADING	MISREADING
MISADJUSTS	MISGRAFTED	MISRECKONS
MISADVISED	MISGROWING	MISRECORDS
MISADVISES	MISGUESSED	MISRELATED
MISALIGNED	MISGUESSES	MISRELATES
MISAPPLIED	MISGUIDERS	MISRELYING
MISAPPLIES	MISGUIDING	MISRENDERS
MISBALANCE	MISHANDLED	MISREPORTS
MISBEHAVED	MISHANDLES	MISROUTING
MISBEHAVER	MISHANTERS	MISSHAPING
MISBEHAVES	MISHEARING	MISSIONARY
MISBELIEFS	MISHITTING	MISSIONING
MISBELIEVE	MISINFORMS	MISSIONIZE
MISCARRIED	MISJUDGING	MISSORTING
MISCARRIES	MISLEADING	MISSOUNDED
MISCELLANY	MISLOCATED	MISSPACING
MISCHARGED	MISLOCATES	MISSPELLED
MISCHARGES	MISLODGING	MISSTARTED
MISCONDUCT	MISMANAGED	MISSTATING
MISCREANTS	MISMANAGES	MISTAKABLE
MISCREATED	MISMARKING	MISTAKENLY
MISCREATES	MISMATCHED	MISTHOUGHT
MISDEFINED	MISMATCHES	MISTLETOES
MISDEFINES	MISMEETING	MISTOUCHED
MISDEVELOP	MISNOMERED	MISTOUCHES
MISDIALING	MISOGAMIES	MISTRACING

MISTRAINED	MONETARILY	MOROSITIES
MISTREATED	MONEYMAKER	MORPHOLOGY
MISTRESSES	MONGOLISMS	MORTGAGEES
MISTRUSTED	MONGOLOIDS	MORTGAGERS
MISWRITING	MONGRELIZE	MORTGAGING
MISWRITTEN	MONITORIAL	MORTGAGORS
MITIGATING	MONITORIES	MORTICIANS
MITIGATION	MONITORING	MORTIFYING
MITIGATIVE	MONOCHROME	MORTUARIES
MITIGATORS	MONOGAMIES	MOSAICALLY
MITIGATORY	MONOGAMIST	MOSAICISMS
MOBILITIES	MONOGAMOUS	MOSAICISTS
MOBILIZING	MONOGRAMED	MOSAICKING
MODALITIES	MONOGRAPHS	MOSQUITOES
MODERATELY	MONOLITHIC	MOTHBALLED
MODERATING	MONOLOGIES	MOTHERHOOD
MODERATION	MONOLOGIST	MOTHERLAND
MODERATORS	MONOLOGUES	MOTHERLESS
MODERNISED	MONOMETERS	MOTILITIES
MODERNISES	MONOPHONIC	MOTIONLESS
MODERNISMS	MONOPLANES	MOTIVATING
MODERNISTS	MONOPOLIES	MOTIVATION
MODERNIZED	MONOPOLIST	MOTIVATIVE
MODERNIZER	MONOPOLIZE	MOTIVATORS
MODERNIZES	MONOTONIES	MOTIVELESS
MODERNNESS	MONOTONOUS	MOTIVITIES
MODIFIABLE	MONUMENTAL	MOTORBIKES
MODULARITY	MOONFLOWER	MOTORBOATS
MODULATING	MOONLIGHTS	MOTORBUSES
MODULATION	MOONQUAKES	MOTORCADES
MODULATORS	MOONSCAPES	MOTORCYCLE
MODULATORY	MOONSHINES	MOTORIZING
MOISTENERS	MOONSTONES	MOULDERING
MOISTENING	MOONSTRUCK	MOURNFULLY
MOISTURIZE	MORALISTIC	MOURNINGLY
MOLLIFYING	MORALITIES	MOUSETRAPS
MOLYBDENUM	MORALIZERS	MOUSTACHES
MONARCHIAL	MORALIZING	MOUTHPIECE
MONARCHIES	MORATORIUM	MOVABILITY
MONARCHISM	MORBIDNESS	MOVELESSLY
MONARCHIST	MOROSENESS	MOVIEGOERS

MOVIEGOING
MOVIEMAKER
MOZZARELLA
MUDSKIPPER
MUDSLINGER
MULISHNESS
MULTIPLIED
MULTIPLIER
MULTIPLIES
MULTITUDES
MUMMIFYING
MUNICIPALS
MUNIFICENT
MUNITIONED
MUSCULARLY
MUSHROOMED
MUSICALITY
MUSICALIZE
MUSICOLOGY
MUSKETEERS
MUSQUASHES
MUTABILITY
MUTATIONAL
MUTILATING
MUTILATION
MUTILATORS
MUTINEERED
MUTINOUSLY
MUTUALISMS
MUTUALISTS
MUTUALIZED
MUTUALIZES
MYELOPATHY
MYOCARDIAL
MYOCARDIUM
MYOFIBRILS
MYOGLOBINS
MYOPATHIES
MYSTERIOUS
MYSTICALLY
MYSTICISMS

MYSTIFIERS
MYSTIFYING
MYTHICALLY
MYTHICIZED
MYTHICIZER
MYTHICIZES
MYTHMAKERS
MYTHMAKING
NAMELESSLY
NAMEPLATES
NANOMETERS
NANOSECOND
NARCISSISM
NARCISSIST
NARCOLEPSY
NARCOTIZED
NARCOTIZES
NARRATIONS
NARRATIVES
NARROWNESS
NASTURTIUM
NATALITIES
NATIONALLY
NATIONWIDE
NATIVENESS
NATIVITIES
NATURALISM
NATURALIST
NATURALIZE
NAUGHTIEST
NAUSEATING
NAUSEOUSLY
NAUTICALLY
NAUTILOIDS
NAUTILUSES
NAVICULARS
NAVIGATING
NAVIGATION
NAVIGATORS
NEBULIZERS
NEBULIZING

NEBULOSITY
NEBULOUSLY
NECROMANCY
NECROPOLES
NECROPOLIS
NECROPSIED
NECROPSIES
NECTARINES
NEEDLELIKE
NEEDLESSLY
NEEDLEWORK
NEGATIONAL
NEGATIVELY
NEGATIVING
NEGATIVISM
NEGATIVIST
NEGATIVITY
NEGLECTERS
NEGLECTFUL
NEGLECTING
NEGLIGENCE
NEGLIGIBLE
NEGLIGIBLY
NEGOTIABLE
NEGOTIANTS
NEGOTIATED
NEGOTIATES
NEGOTIATOR
NEIGHBOURS
NEMATOLOGY
NEOCLASSIC
NEONATALLY
NEOPHILIAC
NEOPLASIAS
NEOPLASTIC
NEOTROPICS
NETWORKING
NEURALGIAS
NEUROLOGIC
NEUROPATHY
NEUROTOXIC

NEUROTOXIN
NEUTRALISM
NEUTRALIST
NEUTRALITY
NEUTRALIZE
NEWFANGLED
NEWSAGENTS
NEWSCASTER
NEWSLETTER
NEWSMONGER
NEWSPAPERS
NEWSPEOPLE
NEWSPERSON
NEWSPRINTS
NEWSREADER
NEWSSTANDS
NEWSWEEKLY
NEWSWORTHY
NICKELLING
NICKNAMERS
NICKNAMING
NICTITATED
NICTITATES
NIGGLINGLY
NIGHNESSES
NIGHTCLUBS
NIGHTDRESS
NIGHTFALLS
NIGHTGOWNS
NIGHTHAWKS
NIGHTLIFES
NIGHTMARES
NIGHTSHADE
NIGHTSHIRT
NIGHTSPOTS
NIGHTTIMES
NIMBLENESS
NINCOMPOOP
NINETEENTH
NINETIETHS
NITPICKERS

NITPICKIER
NITPICKING
NITRATIONS
NITRIFIERS
NITRIFYING
NOBILITIES
NOBLEWOMAN
NOBLEWOMEN
NODULATION
NOMINALISM
NOMINALIST
NOMINATING
NOMINATION
NOMINATIVE
NOMINATORS
NONALIGNED
NONBELIEFS
NONCHALANT
NONFICTION
NONPLUSSED
NONPLUSSES
NONSMOKERS
NONSMOKING
NONSTARTER
NORMALCIES
NORMALIZED
NORMALIZER
NORMALIZES
NORTHBOUND
NORTHERNER
NORTHLANDS
NORTHWARDS
NOSEBLEEDS
NOSEPIECES
NOSINESSES
NOSTALGIAS
NOSTALGICS
NOSTALGIST
NOTABILITY
NOTATIONAL
NOTEPAPERS

NOTEWORTHY
NOTICEABLE
NOTICEABLY
NOTIFIABLE
NOTIONALLY
NOURISHERS
NOURISHING
NOVITIATES
NULLIFIERS
NULLIFYING
NUMBERLESS
NUMBSKULLS
NUMERACIES
NUMERATING
NUMERATION
NUMERATORS
NUMEROLOGY
NUMEROUSLY
NUMISMATIC
NUPTIALITY
NURSEMAIDS
NURSERYMAN
NUTCRACKER
NUTHATCHES
NUTRIMENTS
NUTRITIONS
NUTRITIOUS
OAFISHNESS
OASTHOUSES
OBDURACIES
OBDURATELY
OBEDIENCES
OBEDIENTLY
OBEISANCES
OBEISANTLY
OBITUARIES
OBITUARIST
OBJECTIONS
OBJECTIVES
OBJECTLESS
OBJURGATED

OBJURGATES	OFFICERING	OPTOMETRIC
OBLIGATING	OFFICIALLY	ORANGERIES
OBLIGATION	OFFICIANTS	ORANGUTANS
OBLIGATORY	OFFICIATED	ORATORICAL
OBLIGINGLY	OFFICIATES	ORCHESTRAL
OBLITERATE	OFFISHNESS	ORCHESTRAS
OBSEQUIOUS	OFFLOADING	ORCHIDLIKE
OBSERVABLE	OFFSETTING	ORDAINMENT
OBSERVABLY	OFFSPRINGS	ORDINANCES
OBSERVANCE	OILINESSES	ORDINARIES
OBSERVANTS	OLFACTIONS	ORDINARILY
OBSESSIONS	OLIGARCHIC	ORDINATION
OBSESSIVES	OMNIFICENT	ORGANICISM
OBSOLETELY	OMNIPOTENT	ORGANICIST
OBSOLETING	OMNIVOROUS	ORGANICITY
OBSTETRICS	ONCOLOGIES	ORGANISERS
OBSTRUCTED	ONCOLOGIST	ORGANISING
OBSTRUCTOR	ONTOLOGIES	ORGANIZERS
OBTAINABLE	ONTOLOGIST	ORGANIZING
OBTAINMENT	OPALESCENT	ORIENTATED
OBTRUSIONS	OPALESCING	ORIENTATES
OBTURATING	OPAQUENESS	ORIENTEERS
OBTURATION	OPENHANDED	ORIGINALLY
OBTURATORS	OPENNESSES	ORIGINATED
OBTUSENESS	OPERATIONS	ORIGINATES
OCCASIONAL	OPERATIVES	ORIGINATOR
OCCASIONED	OPERCULARS	ORNAMENTAL
OCCIDENTAL	OPERCULATE	ORNAMENTED
OCCIPITALS	OPERCULUMS	ORNATENESS
OCCLUSIONS	OPHTHALMIC	ORPHANAGES
OCCULTISMS	OPPOSITELY	ORTHODOXES
OCCULTISTS	OPPOSITION	ORTHODOXLY
OCCUPATION	OPPRESSING	OSCILLATED
OCCURRENCE	OPPRESSION	OSCILLATES
OCCURRENTS	OPPRESSIVE	OSCILLATOR
OCTAHEDRAL	OPPRESSORS	OSCULATING
OCTAHEDRON	OPTIMALITY	OSCULATION
OCULARISTS	OPTIMISTIC	OSCULATORY
ODIOUSNESS	OPTIMIZERS	OSTENSIBLE
OESOPHAGUS	OPTIMIZING	OSTENSIBLY
OFFENSIVES	OPTIONALLY	OSTEOPATHS

OSTEOPATHY
OSTRACISMS
OSTRACIZED
OSTRACIZES
OUTBIDDING
OUTRUNNING
OVERACTING
OVERACTION
OVERACTIVE
OVERBAKING
OVERBEATEN
OVERBOOKED
OVERBURDEN
OVERCOMING
OVERCOMMIT
OVERCOOKED
OVEREATING
OVERFILLED
OVERFISHED
OVERFLOWED
OVERHAULED
OVERKILLED
OVERLAYING
OVERLOADED
OVERLOOKED
OVERLORDED
OVERNIGHTS
OVERPASSED
OVERPASSES
OVERPAYING
OVERPLAYED
OVERPOWERS
OVERREACTS
OVERRIDDEN
OVERRIDING
OVERSEEING
OVERSHADOW
OVERSHOOTS
OVERSOAKED
OVERSPENDS
OVERSPILLS

OVERTAKING
OVERTALKED
OVERTASKED
OVERTAXING
OVERTHINKS
OVERTHROWN
OVERTHROWS
OVERTIRING
OVERTURING
OVERTURNED
OVERVALUED
OVERVALUES
OVERWEIGHT
OVERWHELMS
OVERWINTER
OVERWORKED
OVIPOSITED
OVIPOSITOR
OVULATIONS
OWLISHNESS
OWNERSHIPS
OXIDATIONS
OXYGENATED
OXYGENATES
OXYGENATOR
PACEMAKERS
PACEMAKING
PACESETTER
PACIFIABLE
PACIFICISM
PACIFICIST
PACIFISTIC
PACKHORSES
PADDOCKING
PADLOCKING
PAEDIATRIC
PAGINATING
PAGINATION
PAINKILLER
PAINLESSLY
PAINTBRUSH

PAINTWORKS
PALATALIZE
PALATIALLY
PALATINATE
PALAVERING
PALENESSES
PALINDROME
PALISADING
PALLADIUMS
PALLBEARER
PALLETIZED
PALLETIZER
PALLETIZES
PALPATIONS
PALPITATED
PALPITATES
PANCREASES
PANCREATIC
PANCREATIN
PANELLINGS
PANETTONES
PANTALONES
PANTALOONS
PANTOGRAPH
PANTOMIMES
PAPERBACKS
PAPERBOUND
PAPERMAKER
PAPERWORKS
PAPILLOTES
PARABIOSIS
PARABIOTIC
PARACHUTED
PARACHUTES
PARAFFINED
PARAGRAPHS
PARALLAXES
PARALLELED
PARALOGISM
PARALYSING
PARALYTICS

PARALYZERS	PASTEURIZE	PECULATING
PARALYZING	PASTORALLY	PECULATION
PARAMEDICS	PASTORATES	PECULATORS
PARAMETERS	PASTORSHIP	PECULIARLY
PARANORMAL	PATCHINESS	PEDAGOGICS
PARAPHRASE	PATCHOULIS	PEDAGOGIES
PARAPLEGIA	PATCHWORKS	PEDAGOGUES
PARAPLEGIC	PATENTABLE	PEDANTRIES
PARATROOPS	PATERNALLY	PEDDLERIES
PARBOILING	PATHFINDER	PEDESTRIAN
PARCELLING	PATHOGENIC	PEDIATRICS
PARCHMENTS	PATHOLOGIC	PEDIATRIST
PARDONABLE	PATINATING	PEDICULATE
PARDONABLY	PATINATION	PEDICULOUS
PARENTAGES	PATINIZING	PEDICURING
PARENTALLY	PATISSERIE	PEDICURIST
PARENTERAL	PATRIARCHS	PEDIMENTAL
PARENTHOOD	PATRIARCHY	PEDIMENTED
PARENTINGS	PATRICIANS	PEDOLOGIES
PARENTLESS	PATRICIATE	PEDOLOGIST
PARLIAMENT	PATRICIDAL	PEDOMETERS
PARRAKEETS	PATRICIDES	PEDUNCULAR
PARRICIDAL	PATRIOTISM	PENALITIES
PARRICIDES	PATRISTICS	PENALIZING
PARSONAGES	PATROLLERS	PENCILLING
PARTIALITY	PATROLLING	PENETRABLE
PARTICIPLE	PATRONAGES	PENETRATED
PARTICULAR	PATRONIZED	PENETRATES
PARTITIONS	PATRONIZES	PENHOLDERS
PARTNERING	PATTERNING	PENICILLIN
PARTRIDGES	PAUPERISMS	PENINSULAR
PARVOVIRUS	PAUPERIZED	PENINSULAS
PASSAGEWAY	PAUPERIZES	PENITENCES
PASSENGERS	PAUPIETTES	PENITENTLY
PASSIONATE	PAWNBROKER	PENMANSHIP
PASSIVATED	PEACEFULLY	PENSIONARY
PASSIVATES	PEACEMAKER	PENSIONERS
PASSIVISMS	PEACETIMES	PENSIONING
PASSIVISTS	PEAKEDNESS	PENSTEMONS
PASTEBOARD	PEASHOOTER	PENTAGONAL
PASTELLIST	PECCADILLO	PENTAGRAMS

PENTAHEDRA
PENTAMETER
PENTATHLON
PENTATONIC
PENTHOUSES
PENTSTEMON
PENULTIMAS
PEPPERCORN
PEPPERMINT
PERCEIVERS
PERCEIVING
PERCENTAGE
PERCENTILE
PERCEPTION
PERCEPTIVE
PERCEPTUAL
PERCIPIENT
PERCOLATED
PERCOLATES
PERCOLATOR
PERCUSSING
PERCUSSION
PERCUSSIVE
PERDITIONS
PERDURABLE
PERDURABLY
PEREGRINES
PEREMPTORY
PERENNIALS
PERFECTERS
PERFECTING
PERFECTION
PERFECTIVE
PERFIDIOUS
PERFOLIATE
PERFORATED
PERFORATES
PERFORATOR
PERFORMERS
PERFORMING
PERIHELION

PERILOUSLY
PERIMETERS
PERIODICAL
PERIPHERAL
PERISCOPES
PERISCOPIC
PERISHABLE
PERJURIOUS
PERMAFROST
PERMANENCE
PERMANENCY
PERMANENTS
PERMEATING
PERMEATION
PERMEATIVE
PERMISSION
PERMISSIVE
PERMITTERS
PERMITTING
PERMUTABLE
PERNICIOUS
PERNICKETY
PERPENDING
PERPETRATE
PERPETUATE
PERPETUITY
PERPLEXING
PERPLEXITY
PERQUISITE
PERSECUTED
PERSECUTES
PERSECUTOR
PERSEVERED
PERSEVERES
PERSIMMONS
PERSISTENT
PERSISTERS
PERSISTING
PERSONABLE
PERSONAGES
PERSONALLY

PERSONALTY
PERSONATED
PERSONATES
PERSONATOR
PERSONHOOD
PERSONNELS
PERSPIRING
PERSUADERS
PERSUADING
PERSUASION
PERSUASIVE
PERTAINING
PERTINENCE
PERTINENCY
PERTNESSES
PERTURBING
PERVASIONS
PERVERSELY
PERVERSION
PERVERSITY
PERVERSIVE
PERVERTERS
PERVERTING
PESSIMISMS
PESSIMISTS
PESTHOUSES
PESTICIDES
PESTILENCE
PETITENESS
PETITIONED
PETITIONER
PETNAPPING
PETRIFYING
PETROLEUMS
PETTICOATS
PETULANCES
PETULANTLY
PHALANGEAL
PHALANGERS
PHANTASIED
PHANTASIES

PHANTASMIC	PICNICKERS	PIXINESSES
PHARMACIES	PICNICKING	PLACARDING
PHARMACIST	PICTOGRAMS	PLACATIONS
PHARYNGEAL	PICTOGRAPH	PLACEMENTS
PHENOMENAL	PICTORIALS	PLACENTALS
PHENOMENAS	PICTURIZED	PLACIDNESS
PHENOMENON	PICTURIZES	PLAGIARIES
PHEROMONES	PIECEWORKS	PLAGIARISM
PHILANDERS	PIERCINGLY	PLAGIARIST
PHILATELIC	PIGEONHOLE	PLAGIARIZE
PHILOSOPHY	PIGGYBACKS	PLAINTIFFS
PHLEBOTOMY	PIGMENTING	PLANCHETTE
PHLEGMATIC	PIKESTAFFS	PLANETARIA
PHLOGISTIC	PILFERABLE	PLANETLIKE
PHONOGRAMS	PILFERAGES	PLANETOIDS
PHONOGRAPH	PILGRIMAGE	PLANTATION
PHOSPHATES	PILLOWCASE	PLASTERERS
PHOSPHIDES	PIMPERNELS	PLASTERING
PHOSPHINES	PINCERLIKE	PLASTICENE
PHOSPHITES	PINCUSHION	PLASTICINE
PHOSPHORES	PINEAPPLES	PLASTICITY
PHOSPHORIC	PINNACLING	PLASTICIZE
PHOSPHORUS	PINPOINTED	PLATEAUING
PHOSPHORYL	PINPRICKED	PLATEGLASS
PHOTOCELLS	PINSTRIPED	PLATEMAKER
PHOTODIODE	PINSTRIPES	PLATINIZED
PHOTOFLASH	PINWHEELED	PLATINIZES
PHOTOGENIC	PIONEERING	PLATITUDES
PHOTOGRAPH	PIPELINING	PLATOONING
PHOTOMETER	PIPERIDINE	PLATTERFUL
PHOTOMETRY	PIPSQUEAKS	PLATYPUSES
PHOTOSTATS	PIQUANCIES	PLAYACTING
PHYSICALLY	PIROUETTED	PLAYFELLOW
PHYSICIANS	PIROUETTES	PLAYFIELDS
PHYSICISTS	PISTACHIOS	PLAYGROUND
PHYSIOLOGY	PISTILLATE	PLAYHOUSES
PIANISSIMO	PISTOLLING	PLAYMAKERS
PIANOFORTE	PITCHFORKS	PLAYMAKING
PICCALILLI	PITILESSLY	PLAYTHINGS
PICKANINNY	PIXILATION	PLAYWRIGHT
PICKPOCKET	PIXILLATED	PLEADINGLY

PLEASANCES
PLEASANTER
PLEASANTLY
PLEASANTRY
PLEASINGLY
PLEASURING
PLENISHING
PLENITUDES
PLENTITUDE
PLEURISIES
PLIABILITY
PLICATIONS
PLODDINGLY
PLUCKINESS
PLUMMETING
PLUMPENING
PLUNDERERS
PLUNDERING
PLUNDEROUS
PLURALISMS
PLURALISTS
PLURALIZED
PLURALIZES
PLUSHINESS
PLUTOCRACY
PLUTOCRATS
PLUTONIUMS
PNEUMONIAS
POCKETABLE
POCKETBOOK
POCKETFULS
POCKETSFUL
POCKMARKED
PODIATRIES
PODIATRIST
POETICALLY
POETICISMS
POETICIZED
POETICIZES
POIGNANCES
POIGNANTLY

POINSETTIA
POISONINGS
POKINESSES
POLARITIES
POLARIZERS
POLARIZING
POLEMICIST
POLEMICIZE
POLEMIZING
POLITENESS
POLITESSES
POLITICIAN
POLITICIZE
POLLINATED
POLLINATES
POLLINATOR
POLLINIZER
POLLINOSES
POLLINOSIS
POLLUTANTS
POLLUTIONS
POLYAMIDES
POLYAMINES
POLYANTHAS
POLYANTHUS
POLYESTERS
POLYGAMIES
POLYGAMIST
POLYGAMIZE
POLYGAMOUS
POLYGONIES
POLYGRAPHS
POLYHEDRAL
POLYHEDRON
POLYMORPHS
POMMELLING
POMPADOURS
PONDERABLE
PONDEROSAS
PONTIFICAL
PONTIFICES

PONYTAILED
POORHOUSES
POPPYCOCKS
POPPYHEADS
POPULARITY
POPULARIZE
POPULATING
POPULATION
POPULISTIC
PORCELAINS
PORCUPINES
POROSITIES
POROUSNESS
PORTAMENTO
PORTCULLIS
PORTENDING
PORTENTOUS
PORTERAGES
PORTFOLIOS
PORTIONING
PORTLINESS
PORTRAYALS
PORTRAYERS
PORTRAYING
PORTRESSES
POSITIONAL
POSITIONED
POSITIVELY
POSITIVITY
POSSESSING
POSSESSION
POSSESSIVE
POSSESSORS
POSSESSORY
POSSIBLEST
POSTDATING
POSTERIORS
POSTHUMOUS
POSTILLION
POSTMASTER
POSTMORTEM

POSTPARTUM	PRECARIOUS	PREFERMENT
POSTPONERS	PRECAUTION	PREFERRERS
POSTPONING	PRECEDENCE	PREFERRING
POSTSCRIPT	PRECEDENCY	PREFIGURED
POSTULANCY	PRECEDENTS	PREFIGURES
POSTULANTS	PRECENSORS	PREHENSILE
POSTULATED	PRECEPTIVE	PREHENSION
POSTULATES	PRECEPTORS	PREHISTORY
POSTULATOR	PRECEPTORY	PREJUDICED
POTABILITY	PRECHECKED	PREJUDICES
POTASSIUMS	PRECHILLED	PRELATURES
POTBELLIED	PRECIOUSLY	PREMARITAL
POTBELLIES	PRECIPICES	PREMATURES
POTENTATES	PRECISIONS	PRENATALLY
POTENTIALS	PRECLEANED	PRENUPTIAL
POTENTIATE	PRECLEARED	PREORDAINS
POTENTILLA	PRECLUDING	PREORDERED
POTHUNTERS	PRECLUSION	PREPACKAGE
POTHUNTING	PRECLUSIVE	PREPACKING
POTPOURRIS	PRECOCIOUS	PREPARATOR
POULTICING	PRECURSORS	PREPAREDLY
POULTRYMAN	PRECURSORY	PREPAYMENT
POWDERLESS	PREDATIONS	PREPENSELY
POWDERLIKE	PREDEFINED	PREPLACING
POWERBOATS	PREDEFINES	PREPLANNED
POWERFULLY	PREDESTINE	PREPORTION
POWERHOUSE	PREDICTING	PREPOSSESS
PRACTICALS	PREDICTION	PREPOTENCY
PRACTICERS	PREDICTIVE	PRESBYTERY
PRACTICING	PREDICTORS	PRESCHOOLS
PRACTISING	PREDISPOSE	PRESCINDED
PRAGMATICS	PREEMPTING	PRESCRIBED
PRAGMATISM	PREEMPTION	PRESCRIBER
PRAGMATIST	PREEMPTIVE	PRESCRIBES
PRANKISHLY	PREEMPTORS	PRESCRIPTS
PRANKSTERS	PREEMPTORY	PRESELECTS
PREACHMENT	PREFABBING	PRESELLING
PREARRANGE	PREFECTURE	PRESENTERS
PREASSIGNS	PREFERABLE	PRESENTING
PREBOILING	PREFERABLY	PRESENTISM
PREBOOKING	PREFERENCE	PRESERVERS

PRESERVICE	PRIMITIVES	PRODUCTIVE
PRESERVING	PRIMORDIAL	PROFESSING
PRESETTING	PRINCEDOMS	PROFESSION
PRESHAPING	PRINCESHIP	PROFESSORS
PRESIDENCY	PRINCESSES	PROFFERING
PRESIDENTS	PRINCIPALS	PROFICIENT
PRESOAKING	PRINCIPIUM	PROFITABLE
PRESORTING	PRINCIPLED	PROFITABLY
PRESSINGLY	PRINCIPLES	PROFITEERS
PRESSROOMS	PRINTHEADS	PROFITLESS
PRESSURING	PRINTMAKER	PROFLIGACY
PRESSURIZE	PRIORITIES	PROFLIGATE
PRESUMABLE	PRIORITIZE	PROFOUNDLY
PRESUMABLY	PRISTINELY	PROFUNDITY
PRESUMEDLY	PRIVATIONS	PROFUSIONS
PRESUPPOSE	PRIVATISMS	PROGENITOR
PRESURGERY	PRIVATIVES	PROGNOSING
PRESWEETEN	PRIVATIZED	PROGNOSTIC
PRETASTING	PRIVATIZES	PROGRAMMED
PRETENDERS	PRIVILEGED	PROGRAMMER
PRETENDING	PRIVILEGES	PROGRAMMES
PRETENSION	PROBATIONS	PROGRESSED
PRETEXTING	PROCEDURAL	PROGRESSES
PRETTINESS	PROCEDURES	PROHIBITED
PREVAILING	PROCEEDING	PROJECTILE
PREVALENCE	PROCESSING	PROJECTING
PREVALENTS	PROCESSION	PROJECTION
PREVENTERS	PROCESSORS	PROJECTIVE
PREVENTING	PROCLAIMED	PROJECTORS
PREVENTION	PROCLAIMER	PROLAPSING
PREVENTIVE	PROCLIVITY	PROLOGUING
PREVIEWERS	PROCREATED	PROMENADED
PREVIEWING	PROCREATES	PROMENADES
PREVIOUSLY	PROCREATOR	PROMINENCE
PREVISIONS	PROCUMBENT	PROMISSORY
PREWARMING	PROCURABLE	PROMONTORY
PREWARNING	PROCURATOR	PROMOTABLE
PREWASHING	PRODIGALLY	PROMOTIONS
PRIESTHOOD	PRODIGIOUS	PROMPTNESS
PRIGGISHLY	PRODUCIBLE	PROMULGATE
PRIMEVALLY	PRODUCTION	PROMULGING

PRONOUNCED
PRONOUNCER
PRONOUNCES
PROOFREADS
PROPAGANDA
PROPAGATED
PROPAGATES
PROPAGATOR
PROPELLANT
PROPELLENT
PROPELLERS
PROPELLING
PROPELLORS
PROPENSITY
PROPERNESS
PROPERTIED
PROPERTIES
PROPHECIES
PROPHESIED
PROPHESIER
PROPHESIES
PROPHETESS
PROPITIATE
PROPITIOUS
PROPONENTS
PROPORTION
PROPOUNDED
PROPOUNDER
PROPRIETOR
PROPULSION
PROPULSIVE
PROROGATED
PROROGATES
PROROGUING
PROSCIUTTO
PROSCRIBED
PROSCRIBER
PROSCRIBES
PROSECTING
PROSECTORS
PROSECUTED

PROSECUTES
PROSECUTOR
PROSPECTED
PROSPECTOR
PROSPECTUS
PROSPERING
PROSPERITY
PROSPEROUS
PROSTHESES
PROSTHESIS
PROSTHETIC
PROSTITUTE
PROSTRATED
PROSTRATES
PROTECTANT
PROTECTING
PROTECTION
PROTECTIVE
PROTECTORS
PROTECTORY
PROTENDING
PROTENSIVE
PROTESTANT
PROTESTERS
PROTESTING
PROTESTORS
PROTOPLASM
PROTOPLAST
PROTOTYPAL
PROTOTYPED
PROTOTYPES
PROTOTYPIC
PROTOZOANS
PROTRACTED
PROTRACTOR
PROTRUDING
PROTRUSION
PROTRUSIVE
PROVENANCE
PROVENDERS
PROVERBIAL

PROVERBING
PROVIDENCE
PROVINCIAL
PROVISIONS
PROVITAMIN
PRUDENTIAL
PSALTERIES
PSEUDONYMS
PSYCHIATRY
PSYCHOLOGY
PSYCHOPATH
PSYCHOTICS
PTARMIGANS
PTEROSAURS
PUBESCENCE
PUBLICALLY
PUBLICISTS
PUBLICIZED
PUBLICIZES
PUBLICNESS
PUBLISHERS
PUBLISHING
PUERILISMS
PUGILISTIC
PUGNACIOUS
PULMONATES
PULSATIONS
PULVERABLE
PULVERIZED
PULVERIZER
PULVERIZES
PUMMELLING
PUNCHBALLS
PUNCTATION
PUNCTUALLY
PUNCTUATED
PUNCTUATES
PUNCTUATOR
PUNCTURING
PUNISHABLE
PUNISHMENT

PUNITIVELY	QUALIFYING	RACEHORSES
PUPPETEERS	QUALMISHLY	RACETRACKS
PUPPETLIKE	QUANDARIES	RACIALISMS
PUPPETRIES	QUANTIFIED	RACIALISTS
PURCHASERS	QUANTIFIER	RACINESSES
PURCHASING	QUANTIFIES	RACKETEERS
PUREBLOODS	QUANTITATE	RACONTEURS
PURENESSES	QUANTITIES	RADIANCIES
PURGATIVES	QUANTIZERS	RADIATIONS
PURITANISM	QUANTIZING	RADICALISM
PURLOINERS	QUARANTINE	RADICALIZE
PURLOINING	QUARRELLED	RADICATING
PURPORTING	QUARRELLER	RADICCHIOS
PURPOSEFUL	QUARRYINGS	RADIOGRAMS
PURSUANCES	QUARTERAGE	RADIOGRAPH
PURVEYANCE	QUARTERING	RADIOMETER
PUSHCHAIRS	QUARTETTES	RADIOMETRY
PUSSYFOOTS	QUATERNARY	RAGAMUFFIN
PUSTULANTS	QUATREFOIL	RAGGEDNESS
PUSTULATED	QUEASINESS	RAILROADED
PUTREFYING	QUENCHABLE	RAILROADER
PUTRESCENT	QUENCHLESS	RAINMAKERS
PUTRESCINE	QUESTIONED	RAINMAKING
PUZZLEMENT	QUESTIONER	RAINSTORMS
PUZZLINGLY	QUICKENERS	RAINWASHED
PYRACANTHA	QUICKENING	RAINWASHES
PYRAMIDING	QUICKSANDS	RAINWATERS
PYRETHRINS	QUICKSTEPS	RAKISHNESS
PYRETHRUMS	QUIESCENCE	RAMBLINGLY
PYROMANIAC	QUIETENING	RAMPAGEOUS
PYROMANIAS	QUINIDINES	RAMPANCIES
PYROMETERS	QUINOLINES	RAMPARTING
PYROMETRIC	QUINTETTES	RAMRODDING
QUADRANGLE	QUINTUPLED	RAMSHACKLE
QUADRILLES	QUINTUPLES	RANCIDNESS
QUADRUPEDS	QUINTUPLET	RANDOMIZED
QUADRUPLED	QUIRKINESS	RANDOMIZER
QUADRUPLES	QUITTANCES	RANDOMIZES
QUADRUPLET	QUIZMASTER	RANDOMNESS
QUAINTNESS	QUOTATIONS	RANSACKERS
QUALIFIERS	RACECOURSE	RANSACKING

RANUNCULUS	REASCENDED	RECHECKING
RAPACITIES	REASONABLE	RECHOOSING
RAPIDITIES	REASONABLY	RECHRISTEN
RATCHETING	REASONINGS	RECIPIENTS
RATIONALLY	REASSEMBLE	RECIPROCAL
RAUNCHIEST	REASSEMBLY	RECIRCLING
RAVISHMENT	REASSERTED	RECITALIST
RAZORBILLS	REASSESSED	RECITATION
RAZZMATAZZ	REASSESSES	RECITATIVE
REABSORBED	REASSIGNED	RECKLESSLY
REACQUAINT	REASSORTED	RECKONINGS
REACQUIRED	REASSUMING	RECLAIMING
REACQUIRES	REASSURING	RECLASPING
REACTIVATE	REATTACHED	RECLASSIFY
REACTIVELY	REATTACHES	RECLEANING
REACTIVITY	REATTACKED	RECLOSABLE
READAPTING	REATTAINED	RECLUSIONS
READDICTED	REATTEMPTS	RECOGNISED
READERSHIP	REAWAKENED	RECOGNISES
READJUSTED	REBALANCED	RECOGNIZED
READMITTED	REBALANCES	RECOGNIZER
REAFFIRMED	REBELLIONS	RECOGNIZES
REAFFIXING	REBELLIOUS	RECOLLECTS
REALIGNING	REBOUNDING	RECOLONIZE
REALLOCATE	REBUILDING	RECOMBINED
REALLOTTED	RECAPTURED	RECOMBINES
REANALYSES	RECAPTURES	RECOMMENCE
REANALYSIS	RECARRYING	RECOMMENDS
REANALYZED	RECEIPTING	RECOMPENSE
REANALYZES	RECEIVABLE	RECOMPILED
REANIMATED	RECENTNESS	RECOMPILES
REANIMATES	RECEPTACLE	RECOMPOSED
REAPPEARED	RECEPTIONS	RECOMPOSES
REAPPLYING	RECESSIONS	RECONCILED
REAPPOINTS	RECESSIVES	RECONCILER
REAPPRAISE	RECHANGING	RECONCILES
REAPPROVED	RECHANNELS	RECONFIRMS
REAPPROVES	RECHARGERS	RECONNECTS
REARRANGED	RECHARGING	RECONQUERS
REARRANGES	RECHARTERS	RECONQUEST
REARRESTED	RECHARTING	RECONSIDER

RECONVENED
RECONVENES
RECONVERTS
RECONVEYED
RECONVICTS
RECONVINCE
RECORDABLE
RECORDINGS
RECORDISTS
RECOUNTERS
RECOUNTING
RECOUPABLE
RECOUPLING
RECOUPMENT
RECOVERERS
RECOVERIES
RECOVERING
RECREATING
RECREATION
RECREATIVE
RECROSSING
RECRUITERS
RECRUITING
RECTANGLES
RECTIFIERS
RECTIFYING
RECTITUDES
RECUMBENCY
RECUPERATE
RECURRENCE
RECURSIONS
RECYCLABLE
REDAMAGING
REDECIDING
REDECORATE
REDEDICATE
REDEEMABLE
REDEFEATED
REDEFECTED
REDEFINING
REDELIVERS

REDELIVERY
REDEMANDED
REDEMPTION
REDEMPTIVE
REDEMPTORY
REDEPLOYED
REDEPOSITS
REDESCRIBE
REDESIGNED
REDEVELOPS
REDIALLING
REDIGESTED
REDIRECTED
REDISCOUNT
REDISCOVER
REDISPLAYS
REDISPOSED
REDISPOSES
REDISSOLVE
REDISTILLS
REDISTRICT
REDIVIDING
REDIVISION
REDOLENCES
REDOLENTLY
REDOUBLING
REDOUNDING
REDRESSING
REDRILLING
REDUCTIONS
REDUNDANCY
REEDUCATED
REEDUCATES
REEJECTING
REELECTING
REELECTION
REEMBARKED
REEMBODIED
REEMBODIES
REEMERGING
REEMISSION

REEMITTING
REEMPLOYED
REENACTING
REENERGIZE
REENFORCED
REENFORCES
REENLISTED
REENROLLED
REENTERING
REEQUIPPED
REESTIMATE
REEVALUATE
REEXAMINED
REEXAMINES
REEXPELLED
REEXPLORED
REEXPLORES
REEXPORTED
REEXPOSING
REEXPOSURE
REFASTENED
REFECTIONS
REFEREEING
REFERENCED
REFERENCES
REFERENDUM
REFIGHTING
REFIGURING
REFILLABLE
REFILTERED
REFINANCED
REFINANCES
REFINEMENT
REFINERIES
REFINISHED
REFINISHER
REFINISHES
REFLECTING
REFLECTION
REFLECTIVE
REFLECTORS

REFLEXIONS
REFLEXIVES
REFLOATING
REFLOODING
REFLOWERED
REFOCUSING
REFOCUSSED
REFOCUSSES
REFORMABLE
REFORMISMS
REFORMISTS
REFRACTING
REFRACTION
REFRACTIVE
REFRACTORS
REFRACTORY
REFRAINING
REFREEZING
REFRESHENS
REFRESHERS
REFRESHING
REFRONTING
REFUELLING
REFUGEEISM
REFUNDABLE
REFUTATION
REGALITIES
REGARDLESS
REGATHERED
REGENERACY
REGENERATE
REGIMENTAL
REGIMENTED
REGIONALLY
REGISTERED
REGISTRANT
REGISTRARS
REGISTRIES
REGRAFTING
REGRANTING
REGRESSING

REGRESSION
REGRESSIVE
REGRESSORS
REGRETTERS
REGRETTING
REGRINDING
REGULARITY
REGULARIZE
REGULATING
REGULATION
REGULATIVE
REGULATORS
REGULATORY
REHANDLING
REHEARSALS
REHEARSERS
REHEARSING
REHYDRATED
REHYDRATES
REIMBURSED
REIMBURSES
REIMMERSED
REIMMERSES
REIMPOSING
REINFECTED
REINFORCED
REINFORCER
REINFORCES
REINFORMED
REINSERTED
REINSTALLS
REINSTATED
REINSTATES
REINVENTED
REINVESTED
REINVITING
REINVOKING
REITERATED
REITERATES
REJECTIONS
REJOICINGS

REJOINDERS
REJUGGLING
REJUVENATE
REKINDLING
RELABELLED
RELATIONAL
RELATIVELY
RELATIVISM
RELATIVIST
RELATIVITY
RELATIVIZE
RELAUNCHED
RELAUNCHES
RELAXATION
RELEARNING
RELEASABLE
RELEGATING
RELEGATION
RELENTLESS
RELETTERED
RELEVANCES
RELEVANTLY
RELICENSED
RELICENSES
RELIEVABLE
RELIEVEDLY
RELIGHTING
RELINQUISH
RELISHABLE
RELOCATEES
RELOCATING
RELOCATION
RELUCTANCE
RELUCTANCY
REMAINDERS
REMARKABLE
REMARKABLY
REMARKETED
REMARRIAGE
REMARRYING
REMASTERED

REMEDIABLE
REMEDIALLY
REMEDIATED
REMEDIATES
REMEDILESS
REMEMBERED
REMEMBERER
REMINISCED
REMINISCES
REMISSIBLE
REMISSIBLY
REMISSIONS
REMITTABLE
REMITTANCE
REMODELLED
REMODIFIED
REMODIFIES
REMOISTENS
REMORSEFUL
REMORTGAGE
REMOTENESS
REMOTIVATE
REMOUNTING
REMOVEABLE
REMUNERATE
RENDEZVOUS
RENDITIONS
RENEGADING
RENOTIFIED
RENOTIFIES
RENOUNCING
RENOVATING
RENOVATION
RENOVATORS
RENUMBERED
RENUNCIATE
REOBJECTED
REOBSERVED
REOBSERVES
REOBTAINED
REOCCUPIED

REOCCUPIES
REOCCURRED
REOFFERING
REOPENINGS
REOPERATED
REOPERATES
REOPPOSING
REORDAINED
REORDERING
REORGANIZE
REORIENTED
REPACKAGED
REPACKAGER
REPACKAGES
REPAINTING
REPAIRABLE
REPANELLED
REPAPERING
REPARATION
REPARATIVE
REPATRIATE
REPAYMENTS
REPEATABLE
REPEATEDLY
REPELLANTS
REPELLENCY
REPELLENTS
REPENTANCE
REPERTOIRE
REPETITION
REPETITIVE
REPHRASING
REPLANNING
REPLANTING
REPLASTERS
REPLETIONS
REPLICABLE
REPLICATED
REPLICATES
REPLOTTING
REPLUMBING

REPLUNGING
REPOLISHED
REPOLISHES
REPOPULATE
REPORTABLE
REPORTEDLY
REPOSITING
REPOSITION
REPOSITORY
REPOWERING
REPREHENDS
REPRESENTS
REPRESSING
REPRESSION
REPRESSIVE
REPRESSORS
REPRIEVALS
REPRIEVING
REPRIMANDS
REPRINTERS
REPRINTING
REPROACHED
REPROACHER
REPROACHES
REPROBANCE
REPROBATED
REPROBATES
REPRODUCED
REPRODUCER
REPRODUCES S
REPTILIANS
REPUBLICAN
REPUDIATED
REPUDIATES
REPUDIATOR
REPUGNANCE
REPUGNANCY
REPULSIONS
REPURCHASE
REPURIFIED
REPURIFIES

REPURSUING
REPUTATION
REQUESTERS
REQUESTING
REQUESTORS
REQUISITES
RERECORDED
REREGISTER
REREGULATE
RERELEASED
RERELEASES
REREMINDED
REREPEATED
REREVIEWED
RESADDLING
RESALUTING
RESAMPLING
RESCHEDULE
RESCHOOLED
RESCINDING
RESCISSION
RESCISSORY
RESCREENED
RESCULPTED
RESEALABLE
RESEARCHED
RESEARCHER
RESEARCHES
RESEASONED
RESEMBLING
RESENTMENT
RESERVABLE
RESERVEDLY
RESERVICED
RESERVICES
RESERVISTS
RESERVOIRS
RESETTABLE
RESETTLING
RESHUFFLED
RESHUFFLES

RESIDENCES
RESIDUALLY
RESIGHTING
RESIGNEDLY
RESILIENCE
RESILIENCY
RESINATING
RESISTANCE
RESISTANTS
RESISTIBLE
RESISTLESS
RESITTINGS
RESKETCHED
RESKETCHES
RESMOOTHED
RESOLDERED
RESOLIDIFY
RESOLUTELY
RESOLUTEST
RESOLUTION
RESOLVABLE
RESOLVENTS
RESONANCES
RESONANTLY
RESONATING
RESONATORS
RESORPTION
RESORPTIVE
RESOUNDING
RESPEAKING
RESPECTFUL
RESPECTING
RESPECTIVE
RESPIRATOR
RESPONDENT
RESPONDING
RESPONSIVE
RESPONSORY
RESPOTTING
RESPRAYING
RESPROUTED

RESTACKING
RESTAFFING
RESTAMPING
RESTARTING
RESTAURANT
RESTFULLER
RESTITCHED
RESTITCHES
RESTITUTED
RESTITUTES
RESTLESSLY
RESTOCKING
RESTORABLE
RESTRAINED
RESTRAINER
RESTRAINTS
RESTRICTED
RESTUDYING
RESTUFFING
RESULTANTS
RESUMPTION
RESUPPLIED
RESUPPLIES
RESURFACED
RESURGENCE
RESURRECTS
RESURVEYED
RETACKLING
RETAILINGS
RETAILORED
RETALIATED
RETALIATES
RETARDANTS
RETARGETED
RETEACHING
RETELLINGS
RETEMPERED
RETENTIONS
RETEXTURED
RETEXTURES
RETHINKERS

RETHINKING
RETHREADED
RETICENCES
RETICENTLY
RETICULATE
RETIGHTENS
RETIREMENT
RETIRINGLY
RETOUCHING
RETRACKING
RETRACTING
RETRACTION
RETRANSMIT
RETREADING
RETRIEVALS
RETRIEVERS
RETRIEVING
RETRIMMING
RETROGRADE
RETROSPECT
RETURNABLE
RETWISTING
REUNIFYING
REUNIONIST
REUTILIZED
REUTILIZES
REUTTERING
REVALIDATE
REVALUATED
REVALUATES
REVEALMENT
REVELATION
REVELATORY
REVENGEFUL
REVERENCED
REVERENCER
REVERENCES
REVERENTLY
REVERIFIED
REVERIFIES
REVERSIBLE

REVERSIBLY
REVERSIONS
REVERTANTS
REVERTIBLE
REVIEWABLE
REVILEMENT
REVISITING
REVITALIZE
REVIVALISM
REVIVALIST
REVIVIFIED
REVIVIFIES
REVOLUTION
REVOLVABLE
REVULSIONS
REWAKENING
REWARDABLE
REWEIGHING
REWIDENING
REWRAPPING
RHAPSODIES
RHEOLOGIES
RHEOLOGIST
RHEOMETERS
RHETORICAL
RHEUMATICS
RHEUMATISM
RHEUMATOID
RHINESTONE
RHINOCEROS
RHOMBOIDAL
RHYTHMICAL
RHYTHMISTS
RHYTHMIZED
RHYTHMIZES
RIBALDRIES
RIBBONLIKE
RIBOFLAVIN
RICHNESSES
RICOCHETED
RIDICULING

RIDICULOUS
RIGAMAROLE
RIGHTFULLY
RIGIDITIES
RIGOROUSLY
RINGLEADER
RINGMASTER
RITUALISMS
RITUALISTS
RITUALIZED
RITUALIZES
RIVERBANKS
RIVERBOATS
RIVERFRONT
RIVERSIDES
RIVETINGLY
ROADBLOCKS
ROADRUNNER
ROADWORTHY
ROBUSTNESS
ROCKABILLY
ROCKETEERS
ROISTERING
ROISTEROUS
ROLLICKING
ROTATIONAL
ROTATIVELY
ROTISSERIE
ROTTWEILER
ROTUNDNESS
ROUGHNECKS
ROUNDABOUT
ROUNDHOUSE
ROUNDTABLE
ROUNDWORMS
RUBBERNECK
RUDBECKIAS
RUDIMENTAL
RUEFULNESS
RUFFIANISM
RUINATIONS

RULERSHIPS
RUMINANTLY
RUMINATING
RUMINATION
RUMINATIVE
RUNAROUNDS
RURALITIES
RURALIZING
RUSTICALLY
RUSTICATED
RUSTICATES
RUTHLESSLY
SABBATICAL
SABOTAGING
SACCHARINE
SACRAMENTS
SACREDNESS
SACRIFICED
SACRIFICER
SACRIFICES
SACRILEGES
SACROSANCT
SADDLEBAGS
SADDLERIES
SAFEGUARDS
SAGACITIES
SAILBOARDS
SAILCLOTHS
SAINTHOODS
SAINTLIEST
SAINTSHIPS
SALAMANDER
SALESGIRLS
SALESROOMS
SALESWOMAN
SALIVATING
SALIVATION
SALLOWNESS
SALMONELLA
SALUBRIOUS
SALUTARILY

SALUTATION
SALUTATORY
SALVATIONS
SAMARITANS
SANATORIUM
SANCTIFIED
SANCTIFIES
SANCTIMONY
SANCTIONED
SANDALWOOD
SANDBAGGED
SANDBLASTS
SANDPAPERS
SANDSTORMS
SANDWICHED
SANDWICHES
SANGUINELY
SANGUINITY
SANITARIAN
SANITARIES
SANITARILY
SANITATING
SANITATION
SANITIZING
SANITORIUM
SARCOPLASM
SATELLITES
SATIRIZING
SATISFYING
SATURATING
SATURATION
SAUCEBOATS
SAUCERLIKE
SAUERKRAUT
SAUNTERERS
SAUNTERING
SAVAGENESS
SAVAGERIES
SAXIFRAGES
SAXOPHONES
SCAFFOLDED

SCALLOPING
SCALLYWAGS
SCAMPERING
SCANDALIZE
SCANDALLED
SCANDALOUS
SCANTINESS
SCAPEGOATS
SCARCITIES
SCARECROWS
SCARPERING
SCATHINGLY
SCATTERING
SCAVENGERS
SCAVENGING
SCENARISTS
SCENICALLY
SCEPTICISM
SCHEDULING
SCHEMATIZE
SCHILLINGS
SCHNAUZERS
SCHNITZELS
SCHNORKELS
SCHOLASTIC
SCHOOLBAGS
SCHOOLBOOK
SCHOOLBOYS
SCHOOLGIRL
SCHOOLKIDS
SCHOOLROOM
SCHOOLTIME
SCHOOLWORK
SCIENTIFIC
SCIENTISMS
SCIENTISTS
SCIENTIZED
SCIENTIZES
SCINTILLAE
SCINTILLAS
SCISSORING

SCOREBOARD
SCORECARDS
SCORNFULLY
SCOUNDRELS
SCRABBLING
SCRAGGIEST
SCRAMBLERS
SCRAMBLING
SCRAPBOOKS
SCRAPHEAPS
SCRATCHERS
SCRATCHILY
SCRATCHING
SCRAWNIEST
SCREECHERS
SCREECHING
SCREENABLE
SCREENINGS
SCREENPLAY
SCRIBBLERS
SCRIBBLING
SCRIMMAGED
SCRIMMAGES
SCRIMSHAWS
SCRIPTURAL
SCRIPTURES
SCROLLWORK
SCROUNGERS
SCROUNGING
SCRUBBABLE
SCRUBLANDS
SCRUFFIEST
SCRUMMAGED
SCRUMMAGES
SCRUNCHING
SCRUPULOUS
SCRUTINEER
SCRUTINIES
SCRUTINIZE
SCULLERIES
SCULPTRESS

SCULPTURAL
SCULPTURED
SCULPTURES
SCUPPERING
SCURRILOUS
SCURVINESS
SCUTCHEONS
SEAMANLIKE
SEAMANSHIP
SEAMLESSLY
SEAMSTRESS
SEARCHABLE
SEARCHLESS
SEASONABLE
SEASONABLY
SEASONALLY
SEASONINGS
SEASONLESS
SECESSIONS
SECLUDEDLY
SECLUSIONS
SECONDHAND
SECRETIONS
SECTARIANS
SECTIONALS
SECTIONING
SECULARISM
SECULARIST
SECULARITY
SECULARIZE
SECUREMENT
SECURENESS
SECURITIES
SECURITIZE
SEDATENESS
SEDIMENTED
SEDUCEMENT
SEDUCTIONS
SEDUCTRESS
SEERSUCKER
SEGMENTARY

SEGMENTING
SEGREGATED
SEGREGATES
SELECTABLE
SELECTIONS
SELECTNESS
SELFLESSLY
SELFNESSES
SEMAPHORED
SEMAPHORES
SEMBLANCES
SEMIBREVES
SEMICIRCLE
SEMICOLONS
SEMINARIES
SEMINARIST
SEMIQUAVER
SENATORIAL
SENILITIES
SENSATIONS
SENSITIVES
SENSITIZED
SENSITIZER
SENSITIZES
SENSUALISM
SENSUALIST
SENSUALITY
SENSUALIZE
SENSUOSITY
SENSUOUSLY
SENTENCING
SENTIMENTS
SEPARATELY
SEPARATING
SEPARATION
SEPARATISM
SEPARATIST
SEPARATIVE
SEPARATORS
SEPTENNIAL
SEPULCHRAL

SEPULCHRED	SHAMEFACED	SHOWCASING
SEPULCHRES	SHAMEFULLY	SHOWERHEAD
SEQUACIOUS	SHAMPOOERS	SHOWPIECES
SEQUENCIES	SHAMPOOING	SHOWPLACES
SEQUENCING	SHANTYTOWN	SHREWDNESS
SEQUENTIAL	SHAPELIEST	SHREWISHLY
SEQUESTERS	SHARPENERS	SHRILLNESS
SEQUESTRUM	SHARPENING	SHRIMPLIKE
SERENADING	SHATTERING	SHRINKABLE
SERENITIES	SHEARWATER	SHRINKAGES
SERIALISMS	SHEEPISHLY	SHRIVELLED
SERIALISTS	SHEEPSHANK	SHUDDERING
SERIALIZED	SHEEPSKINS	SHUTTERING
SERIALIZES	SHEIKHDOMS	SIBILANTLY
SERMONIZED	SHELLPROOF	SIBILATION
SERMONIZES	SHELTERING	SICKLINESS
SEROLOGIES	SHEPHERDED	SICKNESSES
SEROLOGIST	SHIMMERING	SIDEBOARDS
SEROTONINS	SHIPWRECKS	SIDEBURNED
SERPENTINE	SHIPWRIGHT	SIDELIGHTS
SERRATIONS	SHIRTMAKER	SIDELINERS
SERVICEMAN	SHIRTTAILS	SIDELINING
SERVIETTES	SHOCKINGLY	SIDESTROKE
SERVITUDES	SHOCKPROOF	SIDEWINDER
SETTLEMENT	SHODDINESS	SIGHTSEERS
SEVENTEENS	SHOEMAKERS	SIGNALIZED
SEVENTIETH	SHOESHINES	SIGNALIZES
SEVERANCES	SHOESTRING	SIGNALLERS
SEVERENESS	SHOPKEEPER	SIGNALLING
SEVERITIES	SHOPLIFTED	SIGNATURES
SEWABILITY	SHOPLIFTER	SIGNIFYING
SEXINESSES	SHORELINES	SIGNPOSTED
SEXOLOGIST	SHORTBREAD	SILENTNESS
SEXTUPLETS	SHORTCAKES	SILHOUETTE
SEXUALIZED	SHORTENING	SILVERFISH
SEXUALIZES	SHORTFALLS	SILVERSIDE
SHADOWLIKE	SHORTLISTS	SILVERWARE
SHAGGINESS	SHOULDERED	SIMILARITY
SHAKEDOWNS	SHOVELFULS	SIMPLENESS
SHALLOWEST	SHOVELLERS	SIMPLETONS
SHALLOWING	SHOVELLING	SIMPLICITY

722

SIMPLIFIED	SLEEPWALKS	SNOWMOBILE
SIMPLIFIES	SLEEPYHEAD	SNOWSLIDES
SIMPLISTIC	SLEEVELESS	SNOWSTORMS
SIMULATING	SLIGHTNESS	SOAPSTONES
SIMULATION	SLINGSHOTS	SOBRIETIES
SIMULATORS	SLINKINESS	SOCIALISMS
SINGLETONS	SLIPSTREAM	SOCIALISTS
SINGULARLY	SLITHERING	SOCIALITES
SINISTERLY	SLOBBERING	SOCIALIZED
SINOLOGIES	SLOPPINESS	SOCIALIZER
SINOLOGIST	SLOTHFULLY	SOCIALIZES
SINUSOIDAL	SLUGGARDLY	SOJOURNERS
SISTERHOOD	SLUGGISHLY	SOJOURNING
SITUATIONS	SLUMBERING	SOLACEMENT
SIXTEENTHS	SLUTTISHLY	SOLARIZING
SKATEBOARD	SMARTENING	SOLDIERIES
SKEDADDLED	SMATTERING	SOLDIERING
SKELETALLY	SMOOTHENED	SOLEMNIZED
SKEPTICISM	SMOOTHNESS	SOLEMNIZES
SKETCHBOOK	SMOTHERING	SOLEMNNESS
SKILLFULLY	SMOULDERED	SOLENOIDAL
SKINFLINTS	SMUDGINESS	SOLICITING
SKIPPERING	SMUTTINESS	SOLICITORS
SKIRMISHED	SNAKEBITES	SOLICITOUS
SKIRMISHES	SNAKESKINS	SOLICITUDE
SKITTERING	SNAPDRAGON	SOLIDARISM
SKITTISHLY	SNAPPISHLY	SOLIDARIST
SKYJACKERS	SNEAKINESS	SOLIDARITY
SKYJACKING	SNEAKINGLY	SOLIDIFIED
SKYLIGHTED	SNICKERING	SOLIDIFIES
SKYROCKETS	SNIFFISHLY	SOLITAIRES
SKYSCRAPER	SNIGGERING	SOLITARILY
SLACKENING	SNIVELLING	SOLUBILITY
SLANDERING	SNOBBISHLY	SOMERSAULT
SLANDEROUS	SNOOKERING	SOMNOLENCE
SLANTINGLY	SNOOTINESS	SONGSTRESS
SLAPSTICKS	SNOWBALLED	SONGWRITER
SLAUGHTERS	SNOWBOARDS	SONOROUSLY
SLEAZINESS	SNOWCAPPED	SOOTHINGLY
SLEEPINESS	SNOWDRIFTS	SOOTHSAYER
SLEEPOVERS	SNOWFLAKES	SOPHOMORES

SOPORIFICS	SPHINCTERS	SPYGLASSES
SORDIDNESS	SPHINXLIKE	SPYMASTERS
SOUBRIQUET	SPIDERLIKE	SQUABBLERS
SOUNDPROOF	SPIDERWEBS	SQUABBLING
SOUNDTRACK	SPINDRIFTS	SQUADRONED
SOUTHERNER	SPINNAKERS	SQUANDERED
SOUTHWARDS	SPINNERETS	SQUANDERER
SOVEREIGNS	SPIRALLING	SQUARENESS
SPACECRAFT	SPIRITEDLY	SQUARISHLY
SPACESHIPS	SPIRITISMS	SQUEEZABLE
SPACESUITS	SPIRITLESS	SQUELCHING
SPACEWALKS	SPIRITUALS	STABILIZED
SPACIOUSLY	SPITEFULLY	STABILIZER
SPAGHETTIS	SPLATTERED	STABILIZES
SPARKLIEST	SPLENDIDLY	STABLEMATE
SPARKPLUGS	SPLENDOURS	STABLENESS
SPARSENESS	SPLENDROUS	STAGECOACH
SPARSITIES	SPLINTERED	STAGEHANDS
SPATIALITY	SPLUTTERED	STAGGERING
SPATTERING	SPOILSPORT	STAGHOUNDS
SPEARHEADS	SPOKESHAVE	STAGNANTLY
SPEARMINTS	SPONSORING	STAGNATING
SPEARWORTS	SPOONBILLS	STAGNATION
SPECIALIST	SPOONERISM	STAINPROOF
SPECIALITY	SPORTINGLY	STAIRCASES
SPECIALIZE	SPORTIVELY	STAIRWELLS
SPECIFIERS	SPORTSWEAR	STALACTITE
SPECIFYING	SPOTLESSLY	STALAGMITE
SPECTACLED	SPOTLIGHTS	STALEMATES
SPECTACLES	SPOTTINESS	STALWARTLY
SPECTATING	SPRADDLING	STAMMERERS
SPECTATORS	SPREADABLE	STAMMERING
SPECTRALLY	SPRINGBOKS	STAMPEDING
SPECULATED	SPRINGIEST	STANCHIONS
SPECULATES	SPRINGLIKE	STANDARDLY
SPEECHLESS	SPRINGTIME	STANDPIPES
SPEEDBOATS	SPRINKLERS	STANDPOINT
SPEEDINESS	SPRINKLING	STANDSTILL
SPELLBOUND	SPRUCENESS	STARFISHES
SPERMICIDE	SPURIOUSLY	STARGAZERS
SPHEROIDAL	SPUTTERING	STARGAZING

STARSTRUCK
STARVATION
STATEMENTS
STATEROOMS
STATICALLY
STATIONARY
STATIONERS
STATIONERY
STATIONING
STATISTICS
STATUESQUE
STATUETTES
STAUNCHEST
STAUNCHING
STEADINESS
STEALTHIER
STEALTHILY
STEAMBOATS
STEAMSHIPS
STEELWORKS
STEELYARDS
STEEPENING
STENCILLED
STENCILLER
STENOTYPED
STENOTYPES
STEPFATHER
STEPLADDER
STEPMOTHER
STEPPARENT
STEPSISTER
STEREOGRAM
STEREOTYPE
STERILIZED
STERILIZER
STERILIZES
STERNWARDS
STEVEDORES
STEWARDESS
STEWARDING
STICKINESS

STIFFENERS
STIFFENING
STIFLINGLY
STIGMATIST
STIGMATIZE
STILETTOED
STILETTOES
STILLBIRTH
STILLBORNS
STIMULANTS
STIMULATED
STIMULATES
STIMULATOR
STINGINESS
STINKINGLY
STINKWEEDS
STIPULATED
STIPULATES
STIPULATOR
STIRRINGLY
STITCHWORT
STOCKADING
STOCKPILED
STOCKPILER
STOCKPILES
STOMACHING
STONECHATS
STONEMASON
STONEWARES
STONEWORKS
STOREROOMS
STORKSBILL
STORYBOOKS
STRADDLERS
STRADDLING
STRAGGLERS
STRAGGLING
STRAIGHTEN
STRAIGHTER
STRAITENED
STRAITNESS

STRANGLING
STRAPPINGS
STRATAGEMS
STRATEGIES
STRATEGIST
STRATEGIZE
STRATIFIED
STRATIFIES
STRATIFORM
STRAWBERRY
STREAMLINE
STREETCARS
STREETLAMP
STREETWISE
STRENGTHEN
STRESSLESS
STRETCHERS
STRETCHING
STRIATIONS
STRICTNESS
STRICTURES
STRIDENTLY
STRIKINGLY
STRINGENCY
STRINGINGS
STRINGLESS
STRIPELESS
STRIPPABLE
STRIPTEASE
STROGANOFF
STRONGHOLD
STRUCTURAL
STRUCTURED
STRUCTURES
STRUGGLING
STRYCHNINE
STUBBORNLY
STUCCOWORK
STUDIOUSLY
STUFFINESS
STULTIFIED

STULTIFIES	SUBTERFUGE	SUMMERLIKE
STUNNINGLY	SUBTITLING	SUMMERLONG
STUNTWOMAN	SUBTLENESS	SUMMERTIME
STUPEFYING	SUBTLETIES	SUMMONSING
STUPENDOUS	SUBTRACTED	SUNBATHERS
STUPIDNESS	SUBVERSION	SUNBATHING
STURDINESS	SUBVERSIVE	SUNBONNETS
STUTTERING	SUCCEEDING	SUNBURNING
STYLISTICS	SUCCESSFUL	SUNDRESSES
SUBALTERNS	SUCCESSION	SUNFLOWERS
SUBDIVIDED	SUCCESSIVE	SUNGLASSES
SUBDIVIDES	SUCCESSORS	SUNSCREENS
SUBHEADING	SUCCINCTLY	SUNSEEKERS
SUBJECTING	SUCCOURING	SUNSTROKES
SUBJECTION	SUCCULENCE	SUPERCEDED
SUBJECTIVE	SUCCULENTS	SUPERCEDES
SUBJUGATED	SUCCUMBING	SUPERHUMAN
SUBJUGATES	SUCTIONING	SUPERIORLY
SUBLETTING	SUDDENNESS	SUPERMINDS
SUBLIMATED	SUFFERABLE	SUPERSEDED
SUBLIMINAL	SUFFERABLY	SUPERSEDES
SUBMERGING	SUFFERANCE	SUPERSONIC
SUBMERSING	SUFFERINGS	SUPERSTARS
SUBMERSION	SUFFICIENT	SUPERSTORE
SUBMISSION	SUFFOCATED	SUPERVENED
SUBMISSIVE	SUFFOCATES	SUPERVENES
SUBMITTALS	SUFFRAGIST	SUPERVISED
SUBMITTING	SUFFUSIONS	SUPERVISES
SUBSCRIBED	SUGGESTING	SUPERVISOR
SUBSCRIBES	SUGGESTION	SUPPERTIME
SUBSCRIPTS	SUGGESTIVE	SUPPLANTED
SUBSECTION	SUICIDALLY	SUPPLEMENT
SUBSEQUENT	SULLENNESS	SUPPLENESS
SUBSIDIARY	SULPHATING	SUPPLIANCE
SUBSIDIZED	SULPHURING	SUPPLIANTS
SUBSIDIZES	SULPHUROUS	SUPPLICANT
SUBSISTENT	SULTANATES	SUPPLICATE
SUBSISTING	SULTRINESS	SUPPORTERS
SUBSPECIES	SUMMARIZED	SUPPORTING
SUBSTITUTE	SUMMARIZES	SUPPORTIVE
SUBSTRATES	SUMMATIONS	SUPPOSABLE

SUPPOSABLY	SUSPENSORY	SYMPATHIES
SUPPOSEDLY	SUSPICIONS	SYMPATHIZE
SUPPRESSED	SUSPICIOUS	SYMPHONIES
SUPPRESSES	SUSTAINERS	SYMPHONIST
SUPPRESSOR	SUSTAINING	SYMPOSIUMS
SUPPURATED	SUSTENANCE	SYNAGOGUES
SUPPURATES	SWAGGERING	SYNCOPATED
SURCHARGED	SWALLOWING	SYNCOPATES
SURCHARGES	SWAMPLANDS	SYNCOPATOR
SURCINGLES	SWEATBANDS	SYNDICATED
SUREFOOTED	SWEATPANTS	SYNDICATES
SURENESSES	SWEATSHIRT	SYNDICATOR
SURFACINGS	SWEATSHOPS	SYNERGETIC
SURFACTANT	SWEEPINGLY	SYNERGISMS
SURFBOARDS	SWEETBREAD	SYNERGISTS
SURFEITERS	SWEETENERS	SYNONYMIES
SURFEITING	SWEETENING	SYNONYMIST
SURGICALLY	SWEETHEART	SYNONYMITY
SURMOUNTED	SWEETMEATS	SYNONYMIZE
SURPASSING	SWEETSHOPS	SYNONYMOUS
SURPRISALS	SWELTERING	SYNOPSIZED
SURPRISERS	SWIMMINGLY	SYNOPSIZES
SURPRISING	SWINEHERDS	SYNOPTICAL
SURREALISM	SWIRLINGLY	SYNTHETICS
SURREALIST	SWITCHABLE	SYSTEMATIC
SURRENDERS	SWITCHBACK	SYSTEMIZED
SURROGATED	SWIVELLING	TABERNACLE
SURROGATES	SYCOPHANCY	TABLECLOTH
SURROUNDED	SYCOPHANTS	TABLESPOON
SURVEILLED	SYLLABUSES	TABULATING
SURVEYINGS	SYLLOGISMS	TABULATION
SURVIVABLE	SYLLOGISTS	TABULATORS
SURVIVANCE	SYLLOGIZED	TACTICALLY
SUSCEPTIVE	SYLLOGIZES	TACTICIANS
SUSPECTING	SYMBOLICAL	TACTLESSLY
SUSPENDERS	SYMBOLISMS	TAILPIECES
SUSPENDING	SYMBOLISTS	TAILPLANES
SUSPENSERS	SYMBOLIZED	TALENTLESS
SUSPENSION	SYMBOLIZER	TAMBOURINE
SUSPENSIVE	SYMBOLIZES	TANGERINES
SUSPENSORS	SYMMETRIES	TANGLEMENT

TANTALATES	TELEVISION	TERTIARIES
TANTALIZED	TEMPERABLE	TESSELLATE
TANTALIZER	TEMPERANCE	TESTAMENTS
TANTALIZES	TEMPESTING	TESTICULAR
TANTAMOUNT	TEMPORALLY	TESTIFIERS
TAPESTRIES	TEMPORIZED	TESTIFYING
TARANTELLA	TEMPORIZER	TETCHINESS
TARANTULAE	TEMPORIZES	TEXTURALLY
TARANTULAS	TEMPTATION	TEXTURIZED
TARGETABLE	TEMPTINGLY	TEXTURIZES
TARMACADAM	TENABILITY	THANKFULLY
TARNISHING	TENACITIES	THEATRICAL
TARPAULINS	TENDENCIES	THEMSELVES
TASKMASTER	TENDERFOOT	THEOLOGIAN
TASTEFULLY	TENDERIZED	THEOLOGIES
TATTOOISTS	TENDERIZER	THEOLOGISE
TAUNTINGLY	TENDERIZES	THEOLOGIZE
TAUTNESSES	TENDERLOIN	THEORIZERS
TAWDRINESS	TENDERNESS	THEORIZING
TAXIDERMIC	TENDINITIS	THERAPISTS
TAXONOMIES	TENDRILLED	THEREABOUT
TAXONOMIST	TENEBRIOUS	THEREAFTER
TEARJERKER	TENEBRISMS	THEREUNDER
TEARSTAINS	TENSIONING	THERMOSTAT
TECHNICALS	TENTACULAR	THICKENERS
TECHNICIAN	TENTATIVES	THICKENING
TECHNIQUES	TENTERHOOK	THIEVISHLY
TECHNOLOGY	TERMINABLE	THIGHBONES
TEETOTALLY	TERMINABLY	THIMBLEFUL
TELECASTER	TERMINALLY	THINKINGLY
TELEGRAPHS	TERMINATED	THINNESSES
TELEGRAPHY	TERMINATES	THIRTEENTH
TELEPATHIC	TERMINATOR	THOROUGHLY
TELEPHONED	TERMINUSES	THOUGHTFUL
TELEPHONES	TERRARIUMS	THOUSANDTH
TELEPHONIC	TERRIFYING	THRASHINGS
TELEPHOTOS	TERRORISMS	THREADBARE
TELESCOPED	TERRORISTS	THREADLIKE
TELESCOPES	TERRORIZED	THREADWORM
TELESCOPIC	TERRORIZES	THREATENED
TELEVISING	TERRORLESS	THREEPENCE

THREEPENNY
THREESCORE
THREESOMES
THRESHOLDS
THRIFTIEST
THRIFTLESS
THRIVINGLY
THROATIEST
THROMBOSES
THROMBOSIS
THROMBOTIC
THROTTLING
THROUGHOUT
THROUGHPUT
THUMBNAILS
THUMBPRINT
THUMBSCREW
THUNDERING
THUNDEROUS
TICKTACKED
TICKTOCKED
TICTACKING
TICTOCKING
TIDINESSES
TIEBREAKER
TIGHTENERS
TIGHTENING
TIGHTROPES
TIMBERWORK
TIMBRELLED
TIMEKEEPER
TIMELESSLY
TIMELINESS
TIMEPIECES
TIMESAVERS
TIMESAVING
TIMESCALES
TIMETABLES
TIMOROUSLY
TIMPANISTS
TINCTURING

TINGLINGLY
TINSELLING
TIRELESSLY
TIRESOMELY
TITILLATED
TITILLATES
TITIVATING
TITIVATION
TITTIVATED
TITTIVATES
TOADSTOOLS
TOBOGGANED
TOBOGGANER
TOILETRIES
TOLERANCES
TOLERANTLY
TOLERATING
TOLERATION
TOLERATIVE
TOLERATORS
TOLLBOOTHS
TOMATILLOS
TOMBSTONES
TOMFOOLERY
TOMOGRAPHY
TONALITIES
TONELESSLY
TONGUELESS
TONGUELIKE
TOOTHACHES
TOOTHBRUSH
TOOTHPASTE
TOOTHPICKS
TOPOGRAPHY
TOPOLOGIES
TOPOLOGIST
TORCHLIGHT
TORMENTERS
TORMENTING
TORMENTORS
TORPEDOING

TORRENTIAL
TORRIDNESS
TORTELLINI
TORTUOSITY
TORTUOUSLY
TOTALISTIC
TOTALITIES
TOTALIZERS
TOTALIZING
TOUCHDOWNS
TOUCHINESS
TOUCHINGLY
TOUCHLINES
TOUGHENING
TOURMALINE
TOURNAMENT
TOURNIQUET
TOWELETTES
TOWELLINGS
TOWNHOUSES
TOWNSCAPES
TOXICOLOGY
TRACKSUITS
TRADEMARKS
TRADITIONS
TRAFFICKED
TRAGICALLY
TRAINLOADS
TRAJECTORY
TRANQUILLY
TRANSACTED
TRANSACTOR
TRANSCENDS
TRANSCRIBE
TRANSCRIPT
TRANSDUCED
TRANSDUCES
TRANSFERAL
TRANSFEREE
TRANSFEROR
TRANSFIXED

TRANSFIXES	TREATMENTS	TRUCULENCE
TRANSFORMS	TRELLISING	TRUCULENCY
TRANSFUSED	TREMENDOUS	TRUMPETERS
TRANSFUSES	TRESPASSED	TRUMPETING
TRANSGRESS	TRESPASSER	TRUNCATING
TRANSIENCE	TRESPASSES	TRUNCATION
TRANSIENTS	TRIANGULAR	TRUNCHEONS
TRANSISTOR	TRIATHLETE	TRUSTFULLY
TRANSITION	TRIATHLONS	TRUSTINGLY
TRANSITIVE	TRIBALISMS	TRUTHFULLY
TRANSITORY	TRIBULATED	TUBERCULAR
TRANSLATED	TRIBULATES	TUBERCULIN
TRANSLATES	TRIBUNATES	TUMBLEWEED
TRANSLATOR	TRICKERIES	TUMIDITIES
TRANSMUTED	TRICKINESS	TUMULTUARY
TRANSMUTES	TRICKSTERS	TUMULTUOUS
TRANSPIRED	TRICOLORED	TUNNELLIKE
TRANSPIRES	TRIFOLIATE	TUNNELLING
TRANSPLANT	TRIFURCATE	TURBULENCE
TRANSPORTS	TRIGGERING	TURGIDNESS
TRANSPOSED	TRILATERAL	TURMOILING
TRANSPOSES	TRILINGUAL	TURNABOUTS
TRANSVERSE	TRILITERAL	TURNAROUND
TRAPEZOIDS	TRIMESTERS	TURNSTILES
TRASHINESS	TRINKETING	TURNTABLES
TRAUMATISM	TRIPARTITE	TURPENTINE
TRAUMATIZE	TRIPLICATE	TURQUOISES
TRAVAILING	TRISECTION	TURTLEDOVE
TRAVELLERS	TRISECTORS	TURTLENECK
TRAVELLING	TRIUMPHANT	TUTORSHIPS
TRAVELOGUE	TRIUMPHING	TUTOYERING
TRAVERSALS	TRIVIALIST	TWENTIETHS
TRAVERSERS	TRIVIALITY	TWINKLINGS
TRAVERSING	TRIVIALIZE	TWITTERING
TRAVESTIED	TROLLEYING	TYMPANISTS
TRAVESTIES	TROMBONIST	TYMPANITIC
TRAWLERMAN	TROOPSHIPS	TYPESCRIPT
TREADMILLS	TROPICALLY	TYPESETTER
TREASURERS	TROUSSEAUX	TYPESTYLES
TREASURIES	TROWELLING	TYPEWRITER
TREASURING	TRUCKLOADS	TYPEWRITES

TYPICALITY
TYPOGRAPHY
TYRANNIZED
TYRANNIZER
TYRANNIZES
UBIQUITOUS
ULCERATING
ULCERATION
ULCERATIVE
ULTERIORLY
ULTIMACIES
ULTIMATELY
ULTIMATING
ULTIMATUMS
ULTRACLEAN
ULTRASONIC
ULTRASOUND
UMBILICALS
UMBILICATE
UNABATEDLY
UNABRIDGED
UNABSORBED
UNADJUSTED
UNADMITTED
UNAFFECTED
UNALLURING
UNAMENABLE
UNAPPARENT
UNAPPEASED
UNAPPROVED
UNARGUABLE
UNARGUABLY
UNASSUAGED
UNASSUMING
UNATTACHED
UNATTENDED
UNATTESTED
UNAVAILING
UNAWAKENED
UNBALANCED
UNBALANCES

UNBANDAGED
UNBANDAGES
UNBAPTIZED
UNBEARABLE
UNBEARABLY
UNBEATABLE
UNBEATABLY
UNBECOMING
UNBELIEVER
UNBLEACHED
UNBLINKING
UNBURDENED
UNBUTTONED
UNCENSORED
UNCLENCHED
UNCLENCHES
UNCLINCHED
UNCLINCHES
UNCOMMONLY
UNCOVERING
UNCROSSING
UNCRUMPLED
UNCRUMPLES
UNCTUOUSLY
UNCULTURED
UNDECADENT
UNDECEIVED
UNDECEIVES
UNDECLARED
UNDEFEATED
UNDEFENDED
UNDENIABLE
UNDENIABLY
UNDERACTED
UNDERBELLY
UNDERCOVER
UNDERLINED
UNDERLINES
UNDERLINGS
UNDERLYING
UNDERMINED

UNDERMINES
UNDERNEATH
UNDERPANTS
UNDERPARTS
UNDERSCORE
UNDERSIZED
UNDERSKIRT
UNDERSTAND
UNDERSTATE
UNDERSTOOD
UNDERSTUDY
UNDERTAKEN
UNDERTAKER
UNDERTAKES
UNDERTAXED
UNDERTAXES
UNDERTONES
UNDERVALUE
UNDERWATER
UNDERWHELM
UNDERWORLD
UNDERWRITE
UNDETECTED
UNDETERRED
UNDIGESTED
UNDIRECTED
UNDISMAYED
UNDISPUTED
UNDRESSING
UNDULATING
UNDULATION
UNDULATORY
UNEARTHING
UNEASINESS
UNECONOMIC
UNEDUCATED
UNEMPLOYED
UNENCLOSED
UNENDINGLY
UNENFORCED
UNENLARGED

UNENRICHED
UNENVIABLE
UNEQUALLED
UNEQUIPPED
UNERRINGLY
UNEVENNESS
UNEVENTFUL
UNEXAMINED
UNEXAMPLED
UNEXCITING
UNEXPECTED
UNEXPENDED
UNEXPLODED
UNEXPLORED
UNFAIRNESS
UNFAITHFUL
UNFAMILIAR
UNFASTENED
UNFATHERED
UNFEASIBLE
UNFETTERED
UNFILTERED
UNFINISHED
UNFOCUSSED
UNFORESEEN
UNFRIENDLY
UNGRACEFUL
UNGRACIOUS
UNGRATEFUL
UNHAMPERED
UNHAPPIEST
UNHERALDED
UNHINDERED
UNHITCHING
UNHOLINESS
UNHYGIENIC
UNICYCLIST
UNIFORMING
UNIFORMITY
UNILATERAL
UNIMPAIRED

UNIMPOSING
UNIMPROVED
UNINFECTED
UNINFLATED
UNINFORMED
UNINSPIRED
UNINVITING
UNIQUENESS
UNIVERSALS
UNIVERSITY
UNJUSTNESS
UNKINDNESS
UNLADYLIKE
UNLAWFULLY
UNLEASHING
UNLEAVENED
UNLEVELLED
UNLICENSED
UNLIKELIER
UNLIKENESS
UNLOOSENED
UNLUCKIEST
UNMEASURED
UNMERCIFUL
UNMODIFIED
UNMOLESTED
UNOBSERVED
UNOCCUPIED
UNOFFICIAL
UNOPENABLE
UNORIGINAL
UNORTHODOX
UNPLEASANT
UNPLUGGING
UNPOLISHED
UNPOLLUTED
UNPREPARED
UNPROVOKED
UNRAVELLED
UNREADABLE
UNREASONED

UNRECORDED
UNREDEEMED
UNREFORMED
UNRELIABLE
UNRELIEVED
UNREQUITED
UNRESERVED
UNRESOLVED
UNRESTORED
UNREVEALED
UNREVIEWED
UNREWARDED
UNRHYTHMIC
UNRIVALLED
UNSADDLING
UNSANITARY
UNSATURATE
UNSCRAMBLE
UNSELECTED
UNSELLABLE
UNSETTLING
UNSOCIABLE
UNSOCIABLY
UNSOCIALLY
UNSOLVABLE
UNSPECIFIC
UNSTEADIED
UNSTEADIES
UNSTEADILY
UNSTITCHED
UNSTITCHES
UNSUITABLE
UNSUITABLY
UNSWERVING
UNTHINKING
UNTIDINESS
UNTIRINGLY
UNTOGETHER
UNTOWARDLY
UNTROUBLED
UNTRUSTING

UNTRUTHFUL
UNWAVERING
UNWEARABLE
UNWONTEDLY
UNWORKABLE
UNWRAPPING
UNWREATHED
UNYIELDING
UPBRINGING
UPGRADABLE
UPHOLSTERS
UPHOLSTERY
UPLIGHTING
UPMANSHIPS
UPPERCASED
UPPERCASES
UPPERPARTS
UPPISHNESS
UPPITYNESS
UPREACHING
UPRIGHTING
UPROARIOUS
UPSHIFTING
UPSHOOTING
UPSTANDING
UPSTARTING
UPSTEPPING
UPSWEEPING
UPSWELLING
URBANISTIC
URBANITIES
URBANIZING
URETHRITIS
URINALYSIS
URINATIONS
URTICARIAL
URTICATING
URTICATION
USEFULNESS
USHERETTES
USURPATION

UTILIZABLE
UTTERANCES
UTTERMOSTS
VACATIONED
VACCINATED
VACCINATES
VACILLATED
VACILLATES
VAGABONDED
VAGRANCIES
VALENTINES
VALIDATING
VALIDATION
VALIDITIES
VALORIZING
VALOROUSLY
VALUATIONS
VANDALISMS
VANDALIZED
VANDALIZES
VANQUISHED
VANQUISHER
VANQUISHES
VAPORIZERS
VAPORIZING
VAPOROUSLY
VARIATIONS
VARICOSITY
VARIEGATED
VARIEGATES
VARIEGATOR
VARIOMETER
VARNISHERS
VARNISHING
VEGETABLES
VEGETARIAN
VEGETATING
VEGETATION
VEGETATIVE
VEHEMENCES
VEHEMENTLY

VELVETLIKE
VENALITIES
VENERATING
VENERATION
VENERATORS
VENGEANCES
VENGEFULLY
VENOMOUSLY
VENTILATED
VENTILATES
VENTILATOR
VENTRICLES
VENTRICOSE
VENTRICULI
VERBALISMS
VERBALISTS
VERBALIZED
VERBALIZES
VERBICIDES
VERIFIABLE
VERMICELLI
VERMICIDES
VERMILIONS
VERMILLION
VERNACULAR
VERSIFYING
VERTEBRATE
VERTICALLY
VESTIBULAR
VESTIBULED
VESTIBULES
VETERINARY
VIBRANCIES
VIBRAPHONE
VIBRATIONS
VICINITIES
VICTIMIZED
VICTIMIZER
VICTIMIZES
VICTORIOUS
VICTUALERS

VICTUALING	VISUALIZED	VULCANISMS
VICTUALLED	VISUALIZER	VULCANIZED
VICTUALLER	VISUALIZES	VULCANIZER
VIDEOPHONE	VITALISTIC	VULCANIZES
VIDEOTAPED	VITALITIES	VULGARIANS
VIDEOTAPES	VITALIZING	VULGARISMS
VIEWFINDER	VITRIFYING	VULGARIZED
VIEWPOINTS	VITRIOLLED	VULGARIZER
VIGILANCES	VITUPERATE	VULGARIZES
VIGILANTES	VIVACITIES	VULNERABLE
VIGILANTLY	VIVISECTED	VULNERABLY
VIGNETTERS	VIVISECTOR	WAINWRIGHT
VIGNETTING	VOCABULARY	WAISTBANDS
VIGNETTIST	VOCALITIES	WAISTCOATS
VIGOROUSLY	VOCALIZERS	WAISTLINES
VILLAINESS	VOCALIZING	WAITRESSED
VILLAINIES	VOCATIONAL	WAITRESSES
VILLAINOUS	VOCATIVELY	WALKABOUTS
VINDICATED	VOCIFERANT	WALKATHONS
VINDICATES	VOCIFERATE	WALLFLOWER
VINDICATOR	VOCIFEROUS	WALLPAPERS
VINDICTIVE	VOICEPRINT	WANDERINGS
VIOLATIONS	VOIDNESSES	WANDERLUST
VIOLINISTS	VOLATILITY	WANTONNESS
VIRGINALLY	VOLATILIZE	WAREHOUSED
VIRIDITIES	VOLLEYBALL	WAREHOUSES
VIRILITIES	VOLUMETRIC	WARINESSES
VIROLOGIES	VOLUMINOUS	WARMONGERS
VIROLOGIST	VOLUNTEERS	WARRANTEES
VIRTUALITY	VOLUPTUARY	WARRANTIES
VIRTUELESS	VOLUPTUOUS	WARRANTING
VIRTUOSITY	VOODOOISTS	WARRANTORS
VIRTUOUSLY	VORACITIES	WASHBASINS
VIRULENCES	VORTICALLY	WASHBOARDS
VIRULENTLY	VORTICISMS	WASHCLOTHS
VISCERALLY	VORTICISTS	WASHETERIA
VISCOUNTCY	VOTIVENESS	WASHSTANDS
VISIBILITY	VOUCHSAFED	WASSAILERS
VISIONALLY	VOUCHSAFES	WASSAILING
VISIONLESS	VOWELIZING	WASTEFULLY
VISITATION	VOYEURISMS	WASTELANDS

WASTEPAPER
WASTEWATER
WATCHABLES
WATCHBANDS
WATCHFULLY
WATCHTOWER
WATERCRESS
WATERFALLS
WATERFOWLS
WATERFRONT
WATERMARKS
WATERMELON
WATERPOWER
WATERPROOF
WATERSCAPE
WATERSHEDS
WATERTIGHT
WATERWHEEL
WATERWORKS
WAVELENGTH
WAVELESSLY
WAVERINGLY
WAVESHAPES
WAVINESSES
WAXINESSES
WEAKNESSES
WEALTHIEST
WEAPONRIES
WEASELLING
WEATHERING
WEATHERIZE
WEATHERMAN
WEATHERMEN
WEAVERBIRD
WEEKENDERS
WEEKENDING
WEEKNIGHTS
WEIGHTIEST
WEIGHTLESS
WEREWOLVES
WESTERLIES

WESTERNERS
WESTERNIZE
WHALEBOATS
WHALEBONES
WHATSOEVER
WHEELBASES
WHEELCHAIR
WHEEZINESS
WHENSOEVER
WHEREABOUT
WHEREFORES
WHETSTONES
WHICKERING
WHIMPERING
WHIRLIGIGS
WHIRLPOOLS
WHIRLWINDS
WHISPERERS
WHISPERING
WHISTLINGS
WHITEBAITS
WHITENINGS
WHODUNNITS
WHOLESALED
WHOLESALER
WHOLESALES
WHOMSOEVER
WHOREHOUSE
WICKEDNESS
WICKERWORK
WIDESPREAD
WILDEBEEST
WILDERMENT
WILDERNESS
WILDFLOWER
WILLOWLIKE
WINDBLASTS
WINDBREAKS
WINDBURNED
WINDJAMMER
WINDLASSED

WINDLASSES
WINDLESSLY
WINDMILLED
WINDOWLESS
WINDOWPANE
WINDOWSILL
WINDSCREEN
WINDSHIELD
WINDSURFED
WINEMAKERS
WINEMAKING
WINTERIZED
WINTERIZES
WINTERTIME
WINTRINESS
WIREHAIRED
WIRELESSED
WIRELESSES
WIRETAPPED
WIRETAPPER
WISECRACKS
WITCHCRAFT
WITCHERIES
WITHDRAWAL
WITHHOLDER
WITHSTANDS
WITNESSING
WITTICISMS
WIZARDRIES
WOBBLINESS
WOEFULNESS
WOLFHOUNDS
WOLVERINES
WOMANIZERS
WOMANIZING
WONDERLAND
WONDERMENT
WONDROUSLY
WOODBLOCKS
WOODCARVER
WOODCHUCKS

WOODCRAFTS
WOODCUTTER
WOODENNESS
WOODENWARE
WOODLANDER
WOODPECKER
WOODSTOVES
WOODWORKER
WOOLLINESS
WORDLESSLY
WORDMONGER
WORDSMITHS
WORKAHOLIC
WORKBASKET
WORKFORCES
WORKHORSES
WORKHOUSES
WORKPEOPLE
WORKPIECES
WORKPLACES
WORKSHEETS
WORKTABLES
WORLDLIEST
WORLDLINGS
WORRIMENTS
WORRYWARTS
WORSHIPPED
WORSHIPPER
WORTHINESS
WORTHWHILE
WRAITHLIKE
WRAPAROUND
WRATHFULLY
WRESTLINGS
WRETCHEDLY
WRIGGLIEST
WRINKLIEST
WRISTBANDS
WRISTLOCKS
WRISTWATCH
WRONGDOERS

WRONGDOING
WRONGFULLY
XENOGENEIC
XENOGENIES
XENOLITHIC
XENOPHILES
XENOPHOBES
XENOPHOBIA
XENOPHOBIC
XENOTROPIC
XEROGRAPHY
XEROPHYTES
XEROPHYTIC
XYLOGRAPHS
XYLOGRAPHY
XYLOPHONES
XYLOTOMIES
YARDMASTER
YARDSTICKS
YEARNINGLY
YEOMANRIES
YESTERDAYS
YESTERYEAR
YOUNGSTERS
YOURSELVES
YOUTHENING
YOUTHFULLY
ZABAGLIONE
ZANINESSES
ZEALOTRIES
ZIGZAGGING
ZOMBIELIKE
ZOMBIFYING
ZOOKEEPERS
ZOOLATRIES
ZOOLOGICAL
ZOOLOGISTS
ZOOMETRIES
ZOOMORPHIC
ZOOPHILIES
ZOOPHILOUS

ZOOSTEROLS
ZYGOMORPHY
ZYGOSITIES
ZYGOSPORES
ZYMOLOGIES